Political participation and democracy in Britain

Why do some people involve themselves in politics and others not? Which issues are they most concerned with? What do they get out of it? Answering such questions is fundamental to understanding political life and, more generally, the workings of liberal democracies. And this book presents the results of one of the most extensive surveys of the political activities and interests of British citizens ever undertaken – the British Political Participation Study directed by Professors Geraint Parry and George Moyser and funded by the Economic and Social Research Council.

Political participation and democracy in Britain is based on the findings of a sample survey of nearly 1,600 people across England, Scotland and Wales as well as a further 1,600 men and women and nearly 300 leaders in six specially selected and contrasting local communities. In 1984 and 1985, these people were asked about the extent to which they had taken action such as writing to their Member of Parliament, working in a group to raise a local problem, going on a protest march or canvassing for a political party. They were also asked about their experiences in taking action and the impressions they had formed of political institutions and processes.

By focusing on the more regular day-to-day patterns of citizen political activity, the authors found wider levels of participation than previous research has revealed. They analyse these findings in terms of age, gender, social class and education and look at the reactions of local leaders to the efforts people make to influence them. The authors also draw comparisons with political participation in other countries and, in their concluding section, highlight trends in citizen activity which might lead to new patterns of political life in late twentieth century Britain and possibly beyond.

Political participation and democracy in Britain

GERAINT PARRY
University of Manchester

GEORGE MOYSER
University of Vermont

and NEIL DAY
University of Melbourne

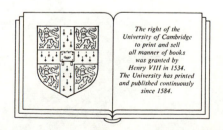

The right of the University of Cambridge to print and sell all manner of books was granted by Henry VIII in 1534. The University has printed and published continuously since 1584.

CAMBRIDGE UNIVERSITY PRESS
CAMBRIDGE

NEW YORK   PORT CHESTER

MELBOURNE   SYDNEY

Published by the Press Syndicate of the University of Cambridge
The Pitt Building, Trumpington Street, Cambridge CB2 1RP
40 West 20th Street, New York, NY 10011–4211, USA
10 Stamford Road, Oakleigh, Melbourne 3166, Australia

First published 1992

Printed in Great Britain by The University Press, Cambridge

British Library cataloguing in publication data

Parry, Geraint 1936–
Political participation and democracy in Britain
1. Great Britain. Politics. Parliament of public
I. Title   II. Moyser, George 1945–   III. Day, Neil
306.20941

Library of Congress cataloguing in publication data

Parry, Geraint.
Political participation and democracy in Britain / Geraint Parry, George Moyser,
and Neil Day.
p.   cm.
Includes bibliographical references and index.
ISBN 0521332982   0521336023 (pbk)
1. Political participation–Great Britain.   I. Moyser, George.
II. Day, Neil.   III. Title.
JN1121.P377   1991
323′.042′0941–dc20   90-40492   CIP

ISBN 0 521 33298 2 hardback
ISBN 0 521 33602 3 paperback

Contents

Figures

Charts and map

Tables

Preface

This volume reports the main findings of a project, the British Political Participation Study, first conceived several years ago by the two principal investigators, Geraint Parry and George Moyser. The Study got underway officially in 1983 with funding from the British Economic and Social Research Council under Award No. E00220003. This grant made the research possible and our first debt is to the Council. We thank its staff for their helpful advice and assistance in preparing the grant application, and in subsequent phases of the research project itself. Financial assistance for travel was also provided to us by the British Academy, the American Political Science Association and our two universities. To them we also express our gratitude.

The text of the book, apart from chapter 13 and the appendix on Survey Methods, both drafted by Neil Day, was written jointly by the two co-directors of the Study, Geraint Parry and George Moyser. It is a testament to the marvels of modern transatlantic electronic mail that much of this writing and associated data analysis was accomplished while we were both separated by 4,000 miles of water!

Neil Day served most capably as the Senior Research Associate on the Study for three and a half years and we are very grateful to the College of Advanced Education in Melbourne, Australia, for releasing him on secondment to take up this important position.

The survey work itself was carried out in 1984–5 by a team from Social and Community Planning Research, led by Gillian Courtenay, who also advised on questionnaire design. Our thanks are due to SCPR and its interviewing staff throughout the country. We do not forget, of course, the time given by the thousands of British citizens around whose responses the book has been built.

At various stages in the course of the project we also had the services, as research associate, of Annis May Timpson and, as research assistant, of Kurshida Mirza and Alan Tice. We wish to express our great appreciation of their contributions, as well as that of David Cleaver who worked as a research student on aspects of the study. Kate Baker was secretary to the project and displayed remarkable versatility and fortitude in coping with the many and varied demands placed upon her. Stephanie Hamer maintained the Manchester end of the communications link with Vermont. John Smith, Stephen Cavrack and Alan Howard proved ever helpful in providing technical advice and assistance with computing. A particularly special acknowledgement is due to Jean Ashton who typed and re-typed later versions of the book speedily and impeccably.

It is also particularly gratifying to record our numerous colleagues in the community of political science on both sides of the Atlantic who have so readily offered help and advice throughout the project. They are so many that it is invidious to single out individuals. We hope that they will accept this general tribute. An exception must be made, however, for Ian Budge and Hugh Berrington who both kindly agreed to read the entire book in typescript and to whose comments we have striven to respond. Needless to say, all imperfections and shortcomings remain entirely our responsibility.

We also wish to express our gratitude to Michael Holdsworth and Cambridge University Press for their help, not to mention their patience. But the final remarks in this preface must express the deepest of all our debts which are to our families. These we cannot hope to repay in their entirety, although we suspect that completing this book may help!

Geraint Parry and George Moyser
Principal Investigators for the ESRC British Political Participation Study
Hale, Cheshire; Shelburne, Vermont

PART I

THEORIES AND METHODS

1

PARTICIPATION AND DEMOCRACY

'Government by the people' is the fundamental definition of democracy, and one which implies participation by the people. Any book about political participation is also a book about democracy. Hence, the present work looks at how Britain is functioning as a democracy in the late twentieth century. It is based on the findings of a sample survey of nearly 1,600 people across England, Scotland and Wales and of a further 1,600 people and nearly 300 leaders in six specially selected and contrasting local communities. In the survey, people were asked about the extent to which they had taken action such as writing to their Member of Parliament, working in a group to raise a local problem, going on a protest march or canvassing for a political party. They were also asked about their experiences in taking action and the impressions they had formed of political institutions and processes.

The study is very much concerned with the more regular, day-to-day patterns of citizen political activity rather than confined to voting in general and local elections when interest in politics is artificially heightened by the activity of the parties and of what can be called the 'political class'. Elections are, indeed, important moments in citizen political participation and their outcomes can change the contours of politics. As such, they have rightly been the subject of extensive investigation and they are included within the picture of participation to be presented here. However, by contrast, the less episodic forms of participation have received little attention in Britain. Yet the result of a complaint to the local town hall about the control of factory pollution or the findings of an inquiry into the reorganisation of local schools, may seem to be of at least as much immediate concern to the citizens affected as the outcome of a general election. Moreover, the patterns of political behaviour involved are ones which tend to alter only slowly and form part of the British political scene over long periods, regardless of which party gains national office. Since Britain, for all its problems – political, social and economic – remains one of the models for liberal democracy, light which may be shed on British political life should also help to illuminate our understanding of other comparable systems. This is not to claim that the study of citizen participation is the only key to understanding how a democracy like Britain operates. There are many other factors influencing the processes which lead to government policies and which affect the implementation of these policies. Political leaders, in particular, are not merely a part of a transmission belt turning the wishes of the citizens into a programme of action. They

3

possess an initiative of their own. Moreover, some policies appear to be the outcome of domestic and international forces over which neither citizens nor leaders have much control. When all those things are admitted, citizen participation remains, nevertheless, of the greatest importance. Without it there would be no democracy.

The extent to which the ordinary person is properly involved in the politics of a democracy such as Britain is, however, a matter of considerable debate. In later chapters we shall be reporting an array of findings from our study into the degree to which the average Briton does or does not take part in the political life of the country. How one estimates the health of democracy on the basis of these findings will depend to a high degree on one's hopes or expectations about the extent to which people will involve themselves in politics.

There are two very broad theories of democracy which have quite different implications for popular participation. The ancestry of the first theory can be traced back to ancient Greece. Amongst later proponents can be numbered Rousseau, John Stuart Mill and the Guild Socialist thinker, G. D. H. Cole (Pateman 1970; Lively 1975; Held 1987). For this tradition of thought, government by the people implies the maximum possible participation of the citizen in shaping laws and policies. The idea of the sovereignty of the people should be made as real as possible. In the ancient world, and still in the thought of Rousseau, this implied direct democracy – the people of a city-state assembled in one place to debate and to pass the basic laws. In the context of the large modern state with which we are familiar, participatory government has inevitably meant something different and more complex. The people of Britain clearly cannot literally be assembled in one place to hear the political debate, as Aristotle required of a genuine popular government (Aristotle 1948:343). However, the prospect of direct democracy may be about to be revived as a result of the possibilities opened up by new communications technology which would permit a 'voting machine' to be installed in every home. We shall refer again to this brave new democratic world in the final chapter.

Meanwhile, direct involvement of the ordinary citizen is largely limited to the local sphere. In Britain, a few full parish meetings take place, just as the American Town Meeting, celebrated in democratic mythology, survives, particularly in New England (Bryan 1974; Mansbridge 1980). But, for the greater part, the action that ordinary citizens can take has a more indirect effect on decisions. They seek to influence representatives whom they have elected for a term in office or officials who have, in general, permanent appointments. There are various methods of influence open to citizens – writing letters, meeting representatives, signing a petition, attending public inquiries, going on demonstrations. All are aimed at forming the opinions of others who are in some degree of authority and in a position to make or implement actual policies and decisions.

Hence, a modern participatory democracy will be one in which citizens avail themselves of these modes of activity to a high degree. An idealised picture of such a polity would portray a populace interested in politics, turning out in numbers to vote in national and local politics, attending electoral meetings, forming groups to campaign for shared objectives, contacting representatives and officials. The interest in politics could be expected to ensure that many issues and problems would take on a political dimension and that their solutions would be sought through political action. At the same time, the governmental institutions would be such as to facilitate participation by providing many points of access for citizens to communicate their views. Participation is, at least in part, a function of the opportunities provided for it, as J. S. Mill pointed out (1972).

This is very much the picture of democracy for which participatory democrats have yearned (Pateman 1970; Barber 1984). They have been well aware that the image fell short of reality. So far short of reality did it fall, that another theory of democracy developed which claimed, by contrast, to be securely grounded on the actual practice of those political systems commonly described as democracies. This 'realist' theory is primarily associated with its earliest, systematic protagonist, Joseph Schumpeter (1943) and has subsequently been elaborated, particularly by Giovanni Sartori (1962, 1987; see Bachrach 1967; Pateman 1970:1–21; Held 1987:17–24, 39–42, 164–85). In this view of democracy, citizen participation plays only a limited role. Democracy is distinguished by political competition between groups of leaders for the support of the population, which is expressed at periodic elections. The victorious group, a political party, receives authority to govern for a term of years. Between elections, citizens have little part to play. They may criticise, but they are not expected to seek to govern. They must respect a 'division of labour' between themselves and government and must, in Schumpeter's celebrated phrase, refrain from 'back-seat driving' (1943:295). The citizens place checks on leaders at elections. They are 'controllers' rather than 'participants' (Parry and Moyser 1984a).

Representative government thus places a limit on participation by the people. It is sometimes suggested that to encourage more widespread participation might, far from enhancing democracy, destabilise it. Schumpeter believed that most people were uninterested in politics and consequently took few steps to inform themselves about it. To encourage participation by such persons would be to introduce into government ignorance and indifference in place of the expertise, however cynically motivated, of the professional politician. Fears were also expressed that the mass of the population was less committed to the values of democracy than was the political elite (McClosky 1964) and that greater involvement by the wider population could result in authoritarianism and illiberalism (see Kavanagh 1972a for a succinct discussion). It could, in certain circumstances, also be socially disruptive where, for example, a deeply divided community encouraged antagonistic political activity.

By contrast to the participatory democrats, the so-called 'realists' do not, therefore, measure the health of a liberal democracy by the high levels of involvement by the citizenry but, rather, by the stability of the system and by its capacity to permit checks on the leaders. Therefore, the despondency of one study of political participation in a number of democracies, including Britain, in which the authors found low levels of participation and wondered despairingly 'how the business of representative democracy is ever carried out' (Barnes, Kaase *et al.*, 1979:84) would be regarded as entirely misplaced by a member of the 'realist' school.

What constitutes impressive or 'healthy' levels of participation will, hence, depend partly on which side of this great debate one takes a stand. It will also depend on the related issue as to what one believes that participation can achieve.

The importance of participation

A famous book about politics had the arresting sub-title: *Who Gets What, When, How* (Lasswell 1936). If political participation is the process of 'getting', then it is readily seen why it should be an activity of some significance. If it were established that the various activities of group pressure, the individual contacting of Members of Parliament or demonstrations in the street paid off by bringing the participants the returns at which they aimed, then the social and economic background of such participants would become politically significant. It might be that the activists were environmentalists who obtained the re-routing of a major road away from an area of natural beauty, or villagers who fought to keep the local primary school open, or members of a residents' association who were able to participate in the planning of a development area. Alternatively, they might be campaigners against nuclear weapons who laid continuous seige to an airbase or miners who sought unsuccessfully to keep their pit open. Why certain people are disposed to participate whilst others remain inactive, and what makes them succeed where others fail, is of some consequence to understanding the workings of liberal democracy and the extent of support for it. For similar reasons, the degree to which there is any 'bias' in the background of political participants can have a bearing on how far one believes participation is something to be encouraged and in what form and in which directions.

The Italian political scientist, Alessandro Pizzorno, has argued (1970) that political participation has served two contrasting functions. On the one side, it has enabled those classes of people who have been less successful in the economic market place to use political means to counter-balance their fortunes. This has been the fundamental purpose of socialist parties and of the political activities of trades unions. On the other side, those who are already advantaged socially and economically are also able to employ political means to reinforce their advantages. Indeed, those who are better-off would appear to possess many resources which they can utilise to good effect. They are able to mount costly, organised campaigns; they generally possess the educational and communicative skills which ease access to those in decision-making positions; in some societies and situations they may even be able to purchase influence by bribery. One not uncommon example of public participation in Britain occurs when middle class persons, often in professional occupations, form a group to preserve the amenities of the local area, where they live. This may possibly occur at the expense of a commercial or industrial development which would provide jobs for those less well-off. Thus, it can be important in a democracy to know how far the opportunities to participate are seized fairly evenly by people across the broad spectrum of society or whether the most intense political activists tend to be overwhelmingly drawn from one stratum of society or from those with some particular political leaning. Conversely, it may be a matter of concern if there exists an 'underclass' of people who are economically and socially disadvantaged and who also fail to make their own mark on the nation's agenda through political action.

It follows that a policy of increasing the amount of participation by citizens can have, in principle, a variety of outcomes. It may advantage the already advantaged or it may go some way towards counter-balancing social and economic inequality (Verba and Nie

1972: 12–6). One reason for studying the state of political participation is for the light it can shed on the 'bias' of participation and its likely consequences in a range of situations.

Most acts of public participation are directed towards persons who are in authority, and able to influence decisions, or those such as leaders of pressure groups who are intermediaries in the process of policy-making. The response of these leaders, collectively to be termed 'elites', is crucial to the success of participatory ventures and, presumably, to the citizens' satisfaction with the system. The study of elites is the other side of the coin to the study of participation by the mass of the citizens. The responsiveness of leaders is affected by a number of factors which are not necessarily easy to disentangle. In the first place, some political leaders may be totally unsympathetic to particular forms of political action, regardless of the actual aims of the actors involved. Thus, various forms of direct pressure, such as demonstrations or boycotts, might elicit adverse responses, while approaches conducted through established formal channels might receive a more ready hearing. When leaders do take up issues as a result of pressure placed on them by individuals or groups, it becomes relevant to ask whether their positions are being shaped in any degree by the citizenry as a whole, or by only the most active, and possibly socially 'biased', sections of the population. The extent to which the agendas of those in authority 'concur' with the priorities of the population in general or only those of certain social sectors is clearly important to understanding the nature of the processes of political communication in a democracy. In short, do participants get what they want?

It is essential to know whether there is bias in the ranks of the participants and of the leaders; it also matters whether participation is effective or not. 'Government by the people' would be a fraudulent slogan were citizen activity found, by and large, to be futile or merely symbolic. If, in the face of a cohesive political elite, or a closed bureaucracy or a dominant ruling class, the ordinary man or woman in the street could not get his or her voice heard, or had no prospect of a response from those in authority, there would be 'participation without power' (Alford and Friedland 1985: 260). It is not enough to assume the rights of participation carry with them the prospect of tangible benefits. It also needs to be established which modes of participation do, in fact, bring rewards and to whom.

At the same time, by their very status as leaders, elites can influence the attitudes of citizens. Indeed, it is a central claim of the 'elitist' approach in political science that leaders, rather than individual citizens or social groups, are the major determinants of what are to be regarded as political issues (Field and Higley 1980; Nordlinger 1981). Leaders are not, therefore, merely passive recipients of pressure from individuals and groups. They are often responsible for placing issues on the agenda. A good deal of public participation is reactive. People respond to decisions or to proposals by those in authority. In this way, matters assume an importance in the minds of individual citizens which they would not have possessed but for elite intervention. The acts of leaders make news and such publicity, sometimes fostered by elites themselves, can generate support. Trades union leaders may call out their members for a protest march against unemployment. The leaders of a pressure group may ask its members to bombard elected representatives with letters, possibly in a standard prepared format. In such ways can participation be 'mobilised'. At its extreme, some governments mobilise people into mass demonstrations in support of the regime, in which participation lacks any very real voluntary character and may, hence, on some views not deserve the name of participation. In a democratic society, however, the mobilising role of groups, whether organised or informal, is an essential feature of the process of setting agendas.

For all the importance attached to political participation in some democratic theory, it remains the case, as will become evident in this study, that it is only a minority of the population that is at all active over matters that in the broadest sense could be termed 'political'. In this respect, the realist school of democrats provides the more accurate description of contemporary practice. Given that participation is a minority pursuit, the attitudes of the non-participants become, paradoxically, all the more important. People may decide for a variety of reasons not to become involved. They may be broadly satisfied with the ways in which policy decisions are reached and consequently happy to leave activism to others. Occasionally a matter closely affecting them may prompt them to action, but these moments are few and far between. For the most part, politics touches people only in an indirect manner. Their interests are in their family, in their leisure, their work. All of these are, certainly, affected by political decisions, but these decisions are mediated by other forces and the way in which they affect daily life is often obscure. Hence, politics appears remote. As one prominent writer on democracy put it: 'Instead of seeking to explain why citizens are not interested, concerned and active, the task is to explain why a few citizens *are*' (Dahl 1961:279).

For some people, the decision not to take any action could be a matter of rational calculation of the costs and benefits. They may perceive that political decisions have a real impact on themselves but calculate that, as individuals, they are unable to exercise any significant influence on outcomes. This lack of political 'efficacy' may or may not be well-founded in reality, but it transforms non-participation into a calculated response to situations rather than being a manifestation of apathy. If their power to affect decisions were in some way increased, such persons are likely to become active (Goodin and Dryzek 1980). Individuals may increase their power by acting collectively in pressure groups instead of individually. This can be coupled with an enhanced consciousness of themselves as political actors, which in turn boosts a sense of confidence. To a considerable degree, this has occurred amongst women in recent decades.

Institutional changes can also increase open access to important stages of decision-making and make it more possible for ordinary people to exercise influence. Thus, in 1969, the Skeffington Committee Report into participation in planning processes in Britain recommended that greater opportunities should be created to allow the public to influence planning proposals whilst they were still at the formative stage, and before they had been finalised (Skeffington 1969). The ability of the public to participate in decisions on government services will also depend partly on the type of service and on the attitudes of those professionally employed in providing them (see Boaden *et al.* 1982). The medical professional tends to resist participatory pressures more effectively than do planners and, conversely, the public is probably more ready to defer to medical expertise and to acknowledge, rightly or wrongly, its own incapacity to influence decision-making over medical services. The 'political opportunity structure' is thus a significant factor shaping both the absolute level of participation and the specific directions it takes within a particular polity.

Thus, lack of interest, lack of power or lack of a sense of power may all be factors leading to the prevalent pattern of non-participation in politics. Each factor is important, in that it has different implications for the potential for increased participation, assuming this to be a proper democratic objective. Increasing opportunities for participation will mean little to the apathetic. The powerless will also not be tempted to act without some assurance that any new rights are backed by duties on the authorities to respond. Any tendency for the non-participants to be disproportionately drawn from certain sectors of the population rather than others is potentially as politically and socially significant as it is in the case of the participant minority. If the apathetic or the alienated are especially to be found amongst particular social classes or in specific minority groups, these groups may fail to benefit from the distribution of rewards and benefits in society which could, in turn, undermine support for the political system as a whole.

The impulse to participate

What leads some people to participate in politics whilst others – the majority – do not? Political theorists have identified a number of different accounts of what motivates, or might motivate, participation. Alternatively, these may be regarded as types of justification for participation (Parry 1972, 1974; Hardin 1982). The primary models of participation are 'instrumental', 'communitarian', 'educative' and 'expressive'.

Instrumental participation

The instrumentalist theory is, in essence, the most straightforward and all-embracing. It assumes that participation is intended to promote or defend the goals of the participants with the minimum of costs and the maximum of effect. Instrumentalism is here interpreted widely in that these goals may be altruistic (such as campaigning for famine relief for Ethiopia) or more narrowly self-interested (preventing a commercial development in a residential zone) or, more likely, as will be indicated later, a mixture of the two (very many local environmental campaigns). It is a view of politics shared by such thinkers and scholars as Jeremy Bentham, James Mill and, in recent times, Robert A. Dahl (Dahl 1963:60–2). As a result, the major studies of political participation in liberal democracies have all assumed an instrumentalist position. Thus, Verba and Nie say that 'participation is to us most importantly an instrumental activity through which citizens attempt to influence the government to act in ways the citizens prefer' (1972:102). Similarly, Barnes, Kaase *et al.* assert that their 'approach to the understanding of political participation is an instrumental and rationalistic one' (1979:39). It is assumed, therefore, that the fundamental reason why some people participate, whilst others do not, is that the participants consider that action is likely to bring them benefits in excess of any costs involved.

There are, however, important differences between scholars who share this broad instrumentalist perspective on participation. One school of thought explains the decision to participate as resulting from a number of social forces affecting the general outlook people have on political life, in particular affecting their confidence about any action they might undertake – a socio-psychological theory. A rival account regards participation and non-participation as a direct, rational, calculated response to a given situation. It stresses the context in which people act, the issues which confront them, the interests which are at stake and the opportunities available for political involvement. It is a rational, 'economic' theory of conduct.

The social-psychological approach suggests that certain people develop 'civic' attitudes which predispose them to participate. Their upbringing and personal environment encourage the development of skills and resources which are conducive to political interest and involvement. Civic attitudes include an interest in, and knowledge of, politics, a sense of political effectiveness and also a feeling that there is an obligation to participate. Such civic attitudes are, it is generally alleged, more likely to emerge amongst 'upper-status' individuals. These individuals are better-educated and, hence, it is claimed, more knowledgeable about politics. Knowing how to move around the political arena, they have a greater sense of efficacy. Their financial security permits them to invest time, energy and money on organisation which can gain political advantages. They are also surrounded by like-minded persons who reinforce this general civic orientation. For these reasons, the foremost exponents of the social-psychological approach, Verba and Nie, term it a 'socio-economic status model' (1972:19). They express it figuratively:

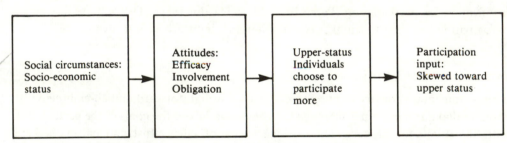

Chart 1.1 The standard socio-economic model of Verba and Nie

For Verba and Nie, therefore, civic attitudes explain why some people, usually of higher status, are active whilst others remain inactive. A major drawback of this socio-psychological approach is that it may pay less attention to the context in which political participation takes place. The issues which might typically prompt political action, such as unemployment, housing, planning, education or defence, play a subordinate role in the explanation. Nor is so much attention paid to the structure within which participants, or potential participants, operate. The relative power of individuals to influence outcomes and the extent of opportunities to participate receive less consideration.

The 'economic' model of participation, by contrast, suggests that people act in very strict instrumental terms and assess the value of public involvement in terms of the likelihood of achieving their objectives, compared with the time, energy and frustration which could be anticipated. The explanation of why some people are impelled to participate would commence with the issues, needs and problems which they face and with their economic and social interests. The broad civic orientation of people is considered of minor importance in explaining decisions to participate, compared with the direct interest that people have in solutions to their particular needs and problems.

Following this approach, the starting point for understanding participation is with issues and with the needs and interests of the individuals and groups which they affect. People's needs, interests and desires are, of course, many and various. They may be shaped by people's economic position, their education, their accommodation, their leisure pursuits or their religion. Thus, if one is unemployed, or has children in primary education, or is living in council housing, this will tend to push one's participatory activity in certain directions rather than others. The result is a diverse range of 'issue publics' – different groupings active over different issues.

The range of participating groupings is almost unlimited but most political studies are interested in some in particular. The relative participation of different social classes has been a theme of all investigations and, as was mentioned above, the socio-psychological theory has presented explanations for the higher political involvement, on average, of persons from upper-status occupations in terms of their orientation to public life. An economic theory of participation would offer a different explanation. The higher participation of upper-status persons reflects the investment such persons have in society and the economy, and which they wish to conserve, coupled with the availability to them of the resources of finance, organisation and contacts which give them relatively good prospects of a favourable outcome to their activity. Conversely, the less well-off lack the resources and power, relative to others, to achieve their objectives and, despite their great needs, the poor, homeless, or the unemployed may conclude that political participation is not worthwhile (Goodin and Dryzek 1980).

If one disregarded the element of costs one might anticipate on rational, economic grounds that, where they did participate at all, those in lower-status occupations would be relatively, and perhaps even absolutely, more active over a range of matters of immediate concern, such as unemployment or the availability of council housing. Their needs being greater, their participation might be more, at least over the issues in which they were most concerned. In analogous fashion, one could examine the participatory profiles of other groups in the population, such as those working in the public sector or those who consume services which are collectively rather than privately provided, such as public transport, state health services and state education (Dunleavy 1979; Saunders 1984). Different groups in society might on this view be active over different issues and, consequently, each of the various categories of issue – unemployment, housing, education – would be associated with its own distinctive set of participants or 'issue publics'. The impulse to participate might be illustrated schematically as in chart 1.2.

This pattern is, however, too simple. Not all the unemployed decide to act over unemployment and not all council tenants take up housing issues with their councillors. This may not, moreover, be simply a matter of the costs in terms of time and effort compared with the likely return. What constitutes a person's interests is complex and disputable (Barry 1965; Connolly 1974). Most people play several roles simultaneously and have a number of interests. These have to be placed in an order of priority and some may well conflict with one another. A woman teacher, for instance, who works in a state school and owns a private house, may be pulled in a number of different directions, supporting public sector policies in one area of her interests and private sector policies in another, whilst also pursuing wider feminist goals.

This is not merely a matter of an economic calculation of the likely costs and benefits of action. There is also a social and ideological context as well as a personal context to

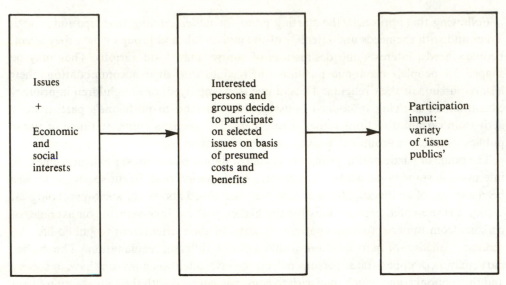

Chart 1.2 A cost-benefit model of participation

participation. Potential participants must, in addition, have conceived their situation in a way that they believe can be modified through action in the public sphere. The woman teacher of our earlier example might have to conceive of her situation as that of a female who is systematically and adversely affected by public policy before she is likely to seek to modify this situation through some kind of political participation. Similarly, persons regularly consuming public services are, one may presume, more likely to become involved politically about the quality of these services if they are conscious of their collective provision and of possible political threats to them. Such consciousness is normally a social rather than an individual experience, affected by interaction with persons in like situations and often developed by pressure groups and political parties which can raise a matter into an issue. They can mobilise people to act who would otherwise not do so. Collective action may be construed as a means of changing the balance of power, enabling those who are individually not so effective to gain influence. In this way, working-class parties have traditionally sought to rectify, through political action, the unfavourable effects of market forces. But collective action is also a means of changing people's awareness, not only of their efficacy but of the issues themselves. Thus, in explaining the decision to participate or not to participate, one must bear in mind not only the individual calculation of costs and benefits (Downs 1957; Olson 1971) but the ways in which the social milieu can come to affect people's perceptions of what their interests are.

Communitarian participation

The communitarian theory of participation suggests that one motive, or justification, for taking part in politics is not an instrumental calculation of benefit to oneself, but a concern for the community of which a person is a part. At the core of a great deal of participatory democratic theory, at least since the time of Rousseau's *Social Contract* (published in 1762), is the view that where people are highly integrated into the local community, and where they identify strongly with it, participation would be greater. In these circumstances, people have a more detailed understanding of local needs and problems and recognise that these needs are often shared with their neighbours. When people perceive their interdependence with others, they will seek to act to sustain their communal relationships. It is often thought that this sense of community identity is greater in smaller, more tightly-knit societies. For this reason, the advocates of participatory community politics are also very often advocates of decentralisation (Barber 1984). Accordingly, one explanation for the relatively low levels of participation in modern societies is that these societies are excessively centralised and remote from their citizens. 'Communities' have been in decline and, as a result, ordinary people have not been stimulated to engage in a form of public life which appears to affect them only in an indirect manner.

Despite the long history of this theory of democracy, there have been few attempts to establish whether there is, in fact, any such relationship between community and participation. The important study by Verba and Nie did, however, provide some evidence of the relationship in America (1972:229–47). Any such investigation faces some difficult and intriguing problems which arise largely from the concept of 'community' itself. The term is used descriptively and prescriptively at one and the same time. To describe somewhere as a 'community' is, in most instances, also to recommend it for possessing certain qualities and values. Raymond Williams has said of community that 'unlike all other terms of social organisation (*state*, *nation*, *society*, *etc.*) it seems never to be used unfavourably' (Williams 1976:66). Nevertheless, what gives a locality its 'communal' quality is not necessarily the same for everybody, but is closely related to other values that a person holds (Plant 1978). Thus, a tradition-minded conservative may call a hierarchical, deferential rural village a 'community' whereas a socialist may consider that community can only occur in an egalitarian society (McCulloch 1984). The extent and nature of participation to which such different conceptions of community can give rise are likely to vary markedly. Indeed, it may be the case that only certain notions of community are associated with the impulse to participate. Wider participation may, perhaps, be stimulated where people think of themselves as equals and where they believe their neighbours are mutually supportive, whereas the hierarchical 'community' may rely more on its local leaders for political direction. For this reason, it becomes important not only to establish whether people living in a particular area regard it as a community, but whether they share a belief in what makes for a community.

There are, however, those who are sceptical about the value of the communitarian view in the modern world. Modern, socially mobile societies have led, it is said, to the decline of the isolated, stable, well-bounded locality which fostered 'community' identity. Instead, a country like Britain is highly urbanised and characterised by complex patterns of social and economic interactions which can stimulate participation (Milbrath and Goel 1977:89–90). Such participation would be based more on interests which are shared by social and economic groupings than on any sense of community identification.

It has also been argued that nowadays people are as likely to feel a sense of communal identity with those who share their interests and life-style than with people who are simply their neighbours (Plant 1978). Thus, there is an 'academic community' of university teachers and researchers who would feel a sense of identity with colleagues across continents. People feel sympathy with other workers in the same industry in different parts of a country – and sometimes strike in their support. Others may feel attached to those who share their particular hobby or sport, such as chess-players who play matches by post. The notion of community has, of course, long been associated with communities of religious believers who transcend any particular locality. Increasingly, the term 'community' is applied to ethnic minorities who live in inner cities (and are in part territorially defined) but who are sometimes presumed to share common aspirations resulting from their ethnic or religious identity.

It would, however, be a mistake to dismiss the possible effect, even in modern circumstances, of local community. For all the greater mobility of population, it remains the case that most of people's lives are conducted within the confines of the locality in which they reside. They send their children to local schools, shop locally, attend their local church, follow a local football team. Most of the public services they consume are delivered by local government, however much they may be funded centrally. Inevitably there remains, as will be seen in later chapters, a considerable local dimension to any participation they undertake in order to influence delivery of services, planning proposals, or the availability of shopping facilities (Agnew 1987). Relatively few people go beyond the confines of their locality to take public action. It is almost the mark of the professional politician that he or she, unlike the ordinary citizen, acts beyond the local stage.

It is, therefore, likely that some appreciation of local issues and problems will shape the patterns of participation. There has been a growing recognition of the impact of 'place' upon politics, particularly in studies of voting (see Agnew 1987) and of economic policy-making (see Cooke 1989). It is all the more important, therefore, to consider to what degree citizen participation is driven by interests common to groups and classes across the nation or is moved by specifically local considerations – whether or not these are in turn inspired by an ideal of community which for some is merely a tempting myth in the modern world or, even worse, a rationalisation of what are, in reality, sectional local interests.

Educative theories

The third approach to participation sees it as an educative experience. It is a view of participation which has been associated with various forms of radical, participatory democratic theory (Pateman 1970; Parry 1972; S. Benn 1979). Taking part in the processes of public decision-making is said to be an education in political life which will develop the citizen's sense of competence and responsibility. The citizen's knowledge of politics increases through involvement in it. John Stuart Mill believed that this would have a moral influence as people came to appreciate more fully the interests and aspirations of their fellows (Mill 1972). A more participatory society would be one which was more likely to be integrated and trusting.

This conception of participation differs in one important respect from the previous ones. Although self-development is sometimes presented as a *reason* for participation, it is better understood as an *effect* of it. It is doubtful whether most people participate for the sake of self-development. Rather, they act for some instrumental or communitarian reason, with political education and moral development as a side-effect (Parry 1974:200; Elster 1983:97–100). Nevertheless, thinkers such as J. S. Mill and G. D. H. Cole believed that political institutions should be so devised as to give the maximum opportunities for participation and, hence, for self-development. Indeed, most developmental theorists would argue that one should not expect any investigation of participation in contemporary societies to provide evidence of strong developmental effects since such societies are precisely not designed to provide the necessary participatory opportunities but, rather, to keep citizens at arm's length (Barber 1984; Marquand 1988).

There is considerable force to this objection. Yet there remain good reasons for examining the educative effects of participation even in existing political processes. The experience of participation, not only of the results but of the process itself, is crucial to the vitality of democracy itself. Do those with a record of political involvement develop in political confidence or do they become disenchanted with the system and more inclined to withdraw from the political scene? How likely are they to pursue similar channels of action again, thus reinforcing existing structures, or are they more likely to break new ground, perhaps by radical, direct action? The development of political consciousness through participation becomes, hence, a factor influencing the potential for future political participation.

Expressive participation

In some instances, people may not participate in the expectation of directly achieving a goal or out of a concern for their community. Rather, they act in order to express their feelings or display their stance about a matter. Their activity is an expression of their political identity. At its broadest, this may be a form of symbolic participation. American examples of such symbolic activity might include singing the national anthem, saluting the flag and the pledge of allegiance (Conway 1985:8–11). Flag-burning might also be added. Equivalents in Britain could include going to an annual Remembrance Day ceremony or attending a state occasion.

Less purely symbolic would be joining a demonstration or rally in order to display solidarity with other persons or ideas. At its grandest, expressive action may reflect what Russell Hardin has called 'the desire to be there' (1982:108). People wish to be part of great events such as the civil rights marches in the USA or the opening of the Berlin Wall in 1989. In these cases, however, the expressive and the instrumental elements become more difficult to distinguish. If one takes part in a civil rights march or in a demonstration over political prisoners outside the embassy of a country notoriously impervious to outside pressure, one may merely be registering one's presence, or identity. But there is usually some hope of adding one's tiny voice in order to create a clamour, however unrealistic this is seen from some instrumental perspectives (Downs 1957; Barry 1970; Olson 1971; but see Benn 1979; Dunleavy 1988). The same action may thus have, at the same time, both expressive and instrumental aspects. Voting, the most frequent of all political activities, expresses one's sense of citizenship and is, therefore, widely regarded as a duty. But, when aggregated, votes bring down governments and make some difference.

For these and other reasons, the extent of such expressive activity is difficult to determine. With the measures used in the present study, it was not possible to examine this dimension. A conscious decision was taken to exclude the most symbolic of activities as broadening the definition too widely. However important they may be to system-maintenance and nation-building (in non-democratic, mobilised societies as well as in democratic polities), they are less relevant to policy formation. In other less symbolic instances we were, unfortunately, unable to operationalise the concept satisfactorily.[1] Accordingly, it plays little further role in the study, apart from some comments on the expressive quality of voting. It may be that such expressive conduct is confined to events where great issues are at stake. In Britain, however, such occasions appear rare. It will be seen that most participation is more mundane in its concerns but, as we shall argue, it is not necessarily the less important for that.

Defining participation

The point has been reached where some attempt must be made to define political participation. In one sense, the entire study is an attempt at definition. To a very great extent, the survey of citizens and leaders on which the study is based sought to allow those whom we interviewed to define the subject-matter themselves. Nevertheless, it is incumbent on us to indicate the scope of the work.

The study adopts a very broad definition of political participation as 'taking part in the processes of formulation, passage and implementation of public policies'. It is concerned with action by citizens which is aimed at influencing decisions which are, in most cases, ultimately taken by public representatives and officials. This may be action which seeks to shape the attitudes of decision-makers to matters yet to be decided, or it may be action in protest against the outcome of some decision. Broad as this definition is, it nevertheless excludes some activities which might, on some views, be regarded as participation.

We have excluded behaviour which, although having a governmental aspect, is not directly aimed at influencing public representatives and officials, such as deciding to participate in a government youth training scheme or going to an office of a government department to receive a routine welfare benefit. Nor have we included participation in the workplace, even though theorists have, with good reason, often regarded this as a training for political participation in a narrower sense. We have sought to define participation as a form of action. For this reason, to show an interest in politics or to talk about it to members of the family is not regarded as sufficient. Nor is it enough simply to display attitudes of support or hostility to certain forms of political action. Such more passive behaviour is clearly important to the functioning of a democracy and we have collected some evidence on its extent as part of the background to the more active involvement on which the study focuses. Nor have we considered evidence about people's readiness or willingness to take action to be evidence about participation itself (but see Barnes, Kaase *et al.* 1979). Nevertheless, we have also paid some attention to such 'potential participation' in the course of summing up the prospects for political action in the final chapter.

Even with these restrictions, there is a very considerable range of activity which falls within the compass of the study. Participation is a word which is probably more in use amongst practitioners and students of politics than it is amongst members of the public. It is a portmanteau term and, as such, requires unpacking. When unpacked, it is seen to comprise a large number of activities. Amongst them are voting, writing to a Member of Parliament or contacting a local councillor, going to the town hall or a government department office to discuss a problem, canvassing support for a political party, attending a public meeting to protest about an issue, signing a petition, joining a pressure group, going on a demonstration march.

From this list it will be seen that participation is composed of a variety of activities which differ greatly in the time and effort they require, the skill and knowledge needed to perform them and the conflict they are likely to engender. At one time, participation was seen as a much more uni-dimensional activity. People were thought to do more or less of it across the board. In the first edition of his path-breaking survey of the subject (which he has subsequently modified), Lester Milbrath suggested that participants could be categorised into the 'apathetic' (about one-third of the American population), the 'spectators' (around 60%) leaving only 2% or so who were the 'gladiators' who performed a wide range of political actions (Milbrath 1965:16–22). Participants could, therefore, be ranged in a hierarchy and participation was seen as cumulative, with persons who engaged in one political action being engaged in others as well.

However, the very variety of participatory activities suggests another hypothesis which is equally plausible. It might be the case that different actions attract different types of people. Some are prepared to engage in conflictual activities whilst others are psychologically unprepared for them. It is a common experience in political parties that some supporters refuse to canvass support for the party on the door step but are happy to work behind the scenes by addressing envelopes in which to send out party publicity. In less psychological, and more instrumental terms, certain activities may hold out better prospects of short-term results than others and attract participants for whom a longer campaign, with a more uncertain outcome, would not seem worthwhile.

Participation thus takes on a multi-dimensional appearance. This was first examined in an empirical manner in the seminal study, *Participation in America* by Sidney Verba and Norman H. Nie, followed by a similar comparative study of seven countries (Verba, Nie and Kim 1978). These studies demonstrated that participatory activities had a structure which was common to different societies and cultures. They distinguished several 'modes' of participation – voting, campaigning for parties, communal activity (which consisted of cooperative activity and citizen contacting on social issues), and particularised contacting which occurred when people contacted a representative or official on matters concerned with the individual and his or her family. Verba and Nie then discovered that, on the whole, people tended (if they were not totally inactive) to specialise in one or other mode of participation. Participants could not be arranged in a single hierarchy.

It is this approach which has guided the present study, and one task will be to show how far the same structure of participation is replicated in Britain. However, the present work extends the range of participatory activities to incorporate acts of political protest, including some which are contrary to the law, which Verba and Nie did not consider in their treatment. There has been much discussion of the prevalence of various forms of political protest action which are to some degree outside the confines of conventional politics – demonstrations, political strikes, boycotts, acts of interference with traffic, and instances of physical violence and even of riot. Whilst it is uncertain how far these have increased, one cross-national study of such forms of protest, which included Britain, suggested that certain forms of direct action might have entered into the political 'repertoire' of ordinary citizens (Barnes, Kaase *et al.* 1979:137–63). The variety of persons and groups who are regularly reported as going on protest marches or engaged in boycotts and sit-ins adds apparent force to this claim. Clearly, it is of some significance to understanding the prospects of democratic institutions to establish how far such 'unconventional' forms of participation constitute another distinct mode of action performed by a category of protesters – the 'rent-a-crowd' of some political rhetoric – or whether it is indeed the case that some forms of protest are really part of the 'conventional' political world.

Terms such as 'conventional' and 'unconventional' are inevitably controversial, depending for their meaning on notions of what is proper to democratic politics. Schumpeter, in his insistence that citizens must respect the division of labour between themselves and the professional politicians they elect, believed many forms of mass action to be improper. He deplored, for example, the practice of some groups of 'bombarding' Members of Parliament with letters and telegrams in order to place them under pressure (Schumpeter 1943:295). Mass petitioning of parliaments has, however, a long history and rules – and 'conventions' – have developed for handling demonstrations and marches. For these reasons, there is no simple, objective way of distinguishing the conventional and the unconventional. The limits of what is considered tolerable change over time. The line between the 'conventional' and the 'unconventional' may also vary from locality to locality, reflecting community norms and values about what is, or is not, legitimate conduct and about the intensity of the issue. If we are to establish how far protest activity is simply one weapon in the political armoury of the typical citizen, it is necessary to examine protest not, first of all, as an entirely distinct phenomenon but in its relation to all the other modes of action which people undertake.

A good deal of participation is concerned with influencing the formulation of alternative policies. In some respects this is the more important stage of decision-making. Complaints and protests after the event have often less prospect of success other than, perhaps, in avoiding a repetition of the alleged mistake. There is, in addition, another area of participation, but one which has been little noted by studies of the subject. A variety of opportunities exists for people to participate in the process of implementation of policies – in the 'output' of government. In the courts there are lay magistrates. There are part-time policemen. There is a range of bodies which have advisory and sometimes executive roles in the administration of government, such as in the health service. Voluntary organisations provide services which, in principle, could just as readily be formally part of national or local government, such as 'meals on wheels' for the housebound. Such activities do not necessarily involve entirely routine, administrative tasks. They may not draw in vast numbers of people, yet this 'output' participation is part of a long tradition of voluntary service in Britain and its significance should not be forgotten.

If there are, as we have earlier hinted, grounds for thinking that participation is both rooted in social circumstances and prompted by a specific context of issues and problems, it is necessary to examine it from both viewpoints before seeking to bring the two perspectives into relation with one another. For these reasons, we shall be approaching participation from two directions. First, we shall adopt the traditional sociological perspective by examining the social, economic and political backgrounds of participants. Thus, we shall examine whether those who are active in various ways are drawn disproportionately from any particular social class, or possess certain levels of education or are members of specific organisations. In this way we shall explore the social and political patterns of participation. Secondly, we shall look at the more immediate context of participation by examining the kinds of issues which people said concerned them most and which, in some cases, actually triggered their action. Taken together, the two lines of investigation are intended to provide a picture of the British population's involvement in day-to-day politics in its broadest sense and of the kinds of issues, needs and problems which most concerned people and which stimulated at least some of them to positive action.

'Politics' and participation

It has been assumed so far that all forms of participation 'in the process of formulation, passage or implementation of public policies' are properly described as *political* participation. This is, in fact, a controversial assumption. The definition of 'the political' is a matter which raises notoriously difficult philosophical problems. Sheldon Wolin has argued that 'the political' is the creation of political thinkers (1961:5). We might add that it is also created by the politicians and by the usage of those who take part in public life. Wolin himself argues that the distinctive feature of politics is that it is concerned with the regulations which are general to a state. His view echoes a famous definition by Michael Oakeshott of politics as the activity of 'attending to the general arrangements' of a group of people (Oakeshott 1962:112). Following this conception, the study of political participation would be confined to those activities directed at affecting the general rules and arrangements of a state or a local community. It would be concerned with the formulation of laws and policies at a relatively high level. However, a great deal of the behaviour we shall be studying is not of this character. It consists of groups complaining to their representatives about the way in which a particular policy, such as closing a village school, is being applied. More narrowly, individuals take up with a town hall official failings in the refuse collection service or problems with repairs to their council house. In the sense that such actions are directed at persons in some governmental position, they can also be described as 'political' participation though they lack the more general dimension that writers such as Wolin regard as essential to 'the political' (Parry and Moyser 1988).

As a starting point, the present study regards action directed at governmental authorities as 'political'. This has the advantage of sweeping in a range of activities 'pertaining to the state or body of citizens, its government and policy' (*Oxford English Dictionary*). But its implications must also be recognised. As Verba and Nie point out, much individual contacting of representatives and officials is solely for personal benefit and 'involves none of the broader issues involved in most political activity' (1972:71). The resident complaining about repairs to her own council house is acting more like a consumer of a product than as a politically-motivated citizen. If she were renting from a private landlord, her action would be identical, but for the fact that she did not contact a (local) government official. Yet her situation has a political significance, as the debate over the 'privatisation' of council houses indicates. The sum of complaints about council house repairs can amount to a local political issue, even when no individual complainant regards his or her complaint in these terms. The individual may not describe an action or an issue as 'political' because it is particular and personal. However, if individuals come to regard government as responsible for creating, solving or even helping them to cope with problems they face (such as unemployment), these personal difficulties can be transformed into political problems (Brody and Sniderman 1977). The line between the political and the non-political can shift. 'Politics' has also another connotation. For some people it carries with it the sense of involvement with political parties and, more pejoratively, of being partisan and factious. Such persons may well disclaim any attribution to them of 'political' conduct.

Any definition of 'political participation' is inevitably tendentious and contestable. Neither a restrictive nor an all-embracing conception is without its difficulties. Yet, whatever definitional problems there may be, these do not affect the importance of our subject matter. What we are seeking to describe is the people of Britain in their efforts to affect what the government of Britain does in their name, and what they think of the effects of their efforts.

A model of participation and the plan of the book

We have sought to pull these elements of participation into a model around which the present book is constructed. The model is illustrated in chart 1.3. Like that of Verba and Nie, it is, at bottom, a resource-based model. What conditions whether a person will participate or not is, aside from an interest which is at stake, the extent to which he or she possesses the resources to act. These resources are individual (wealth and education) and organisational (ties to groups). Lying behind these resources are certain other economic, social, cultural and ideological factors which partly enhance or diminish the chances to obtain resources and partly shape one's readiness to employ them for political action. These factors include social class, gender, age, place of residence and personal and collective values. Resources, coupled with advantageous social background, place some people in a better position to take up action. Nevertheless, not all such persons will do so and there will be others, perhaps relatively fewer, who despite the lack of resources do participate. In addition to resources and background there must also be some circumstance which 'triggers' involvement. Although, as we shall see, it is possible to say something about the kinds of circumstance, and especially the sorts of issue, which are more likely to prompt action, there is, inevitably, an element of contingency involved. One may happen to live in a particular rural area threatened by a new road development; the local authority may propose to close the neighbourhood school; the government may plan to remove financial support from a project on which one is engaged. These are matters not initiated by the participant and could, in principle, affect any person within the country.

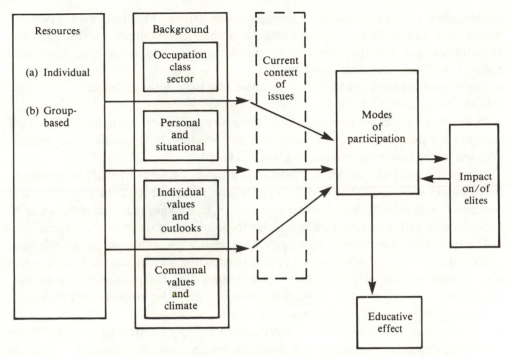

Chart 1.3 A model of political participation

What prompts action, then, are issues which affect people's perceived interests. Thus, although issues appear as the next block in chart 1.3, it may be appropriate to picture the context of issues as surrounding the entire model. For not only do issues prompt action, the kind of issue can determine what sort of action is appropriate. The action taken may be one of several modes of participation – voting, contacting, collective action, party campaigning or direct action. Each, as we shall see, has its distinctive characteristics.

The final element of the model is constituted by the impact of participation. From an instrumentalist standpoint, the impact is measured by the benefits perceived by the active citizens and, especially, by the extent to which elites (in the present study, local leaders) respond to the participatory input of individuals and groups – the concurrence between the agendas of leaders and citizens. One side-product is the political education of the participant. The experience of getting involved in an issue and of the responsiveness of elites to one's efforts can teach a person things about the political system – about its openness or its rigidities – which can in turn affect one's readiness for future participation.

This is one element of what in terms of 'systems analysis' (Easton 1965) would be described as 'feedback'. To analyse such a longer-run political process would require a different methodological approach. A survey taken at one political time can only hint at the dynamics of political participation. For this reason, the 'feedback loop' is omitted from chart 1.3 but it is latent in the model. It must be recognised that, in reality, each element in the model interacts with and modifies the rest. Social scientists can only hope to grasp at part of what could be considered 'political ecology'. In this case, the actions of elites both respond to and affect the agendas of citizens. Elite responses may affect positively or negatively the resources with which the model commenced. The successes or failures of the several modes of participation teach people, in an open democratic polity, how to conduct their future politics.

The plan of the book is based upon the model we have outlined, but does not follow it in its precise order.

In the next chapter we conclude the introductory section by discussing the political context for a study of participation in Britain and provide a brief outline of the methods adopted in the survey upon which the work is based.

The second section is entitled 'Patterns and Pathways'. It seeks to establish how much participation exists in Britain and who participate most and least. In particular, it is concerned with what kinds of social and economic backgrounds and what sorts of outlooks and values appear most conducive to becoming active in public affairs.

The third part then turns to investigate what sorts of issues British people are most interested in raising and which ones they take most action upon. It also seeks to discover what people get out of participation. Is it worthwhile? Do participants think they achieve what they wanted? In a broader sense, do they also consider that they have learned anything from the experience?

The fourth part is based upon surveys carried out in six contrasting localities. After describing the characteristics of the localities, we examine the extent to which the national patterns of participation are replicated in each community. How far do local circumstances produce variations in political activity or is Britain, in this respect, a highly homogeneous polity? The local studies also provide the opportunity to examine the effectiveness of participation. As well as portraying the patterns of citizen activity, we also look at the reaction of local leaders to the efforts people make to influence them. How far do the priorities of the leaders agree with those of the citizens and to what extent does participation succeed in shaping the agenda of politics?

In the concluding section, we single out some of the most striking features on the map of participation and seek to highlight the trends in citizen activity which might lead to new patterns of political life in late twentieth century Britain and possibly beyond.

2

THE STUDY OF PARTICIPATION AND ITS POLITICAL CONTEXT

The context

Participation is, we have argued, one major theme in democratic theory. But it is not a paramount concern of all versions of democracy. Some theories of democracy place greater emphasis on accountability to the electorate than on the political involvement of the citizens. Accordingly, it is not surprising that the importance of participation in political debate can vary from period to period as different views of democracy rise and fall in favour. It is, therefore, necessary to say something about the salience of participation in the 1980s when our survey was undertaken.

The term 'participation' came rapidly to the fore in the politics of many Western democracies, including Britain, in the 1960s. The circumstances in which participation became a political slogan are relatively easy to describe. It is less easy to explain the reasons why there occurred such a convergence of conditions in which the call for greater citizen involvement seemed appropriate. By the middle 1960s the West had, since the end of the Second World War, experienced twenty years of the greatest general increase in material standards of living ever recorded. In Europe, at least, this had been led by a bureaucratically organised state in association with corporate capitalism (Shonfield 1965). Some reflective politicians, such as Anthony Crosland, whilst acknowledging the need for consultative institutions at the neighbourhood level, concluded that material contentment would permit ordinary persons to devote greater attention to their growing leisure interests and be, quite properly, less concerned with interfering with the lives of others through political participation (Crosland 1975:89). Yet the 1960s saw an apparent upsurge of direct political action by ordinary men and, perhaps ultimately most significant, women. In the USA, there were protest marches over the civil rights of blacks, rapidly followed by massive protests against the Vietnam War. Violent unrest in the cities, almost totally unpredicted by social science, revealed previously unremarked levels of deprivation and alienation. In Europe, student protests disrupted educational institutions. In 1968, French students, supported by some sectors of the workers, seemed about to topple the government and the constitution. In Britain, the Campaign for Nuclear Disarmament had mobilised large numbers of people in mass demonstrations (Parkin 1968).

One of the most perceptive commentators on Britain, the American political scientist

Samuel Beer, was led to conclude that these developments since the 1960s had been sufficient to transform British political culture (Beer 1982). Beer argued that the established civic culture, which had rested on a balance between deference to authority and participation, had given way to one in which the ideal of participation had obtained exaggerated prominence. The suggestion was not that Britain was more participatory than other countries, especially the USA, but that its traditional stability had arisen from political practices which were governed by strong elements of citizen self-restraint. In the manner of Schumpeter, whom he cites with approval, Beer considered that a division of labour between a political class which is generally trusted and respected, and a people which adopts a restrained and pragmatic attitude to political involvement, constituted the key to the stability of British democracy. This subtle mix was, however, under attack as a result of an upsurge of participatory ideals which were critical of the traditional authority system (Beer 1982:107–14).

Beer labelled the general movement of ideas critical of the old culture 'the romantic revolt' and its political aspect 'the new populism'. He confessed that he could not entirely explain why this romantic resurgence should appear when it did. Its manifestations were to be seen in a number of linked forms which affected a wide range of social, cultural and political institutions. It spread through popular culture until it became 'absorbed into the fabric of everyday life' represented, in Beer's mind, by the acceptance of

cohabitation, abortion, homosexuality, pornography, protesters blocking traffic, squatters occupying buildings, tenants going on strikes, school-teachers going on strike, undergraduates sitting on university committees, women doing jobs traditionally considered men's work, blacks in jobs formerly performed by whites... (Beer 1982:149)

In politics, the new populism was marked by programmes with an emphasis on the 'quality of life' rather than materialist values. Populism was critical of bureaucracy and of hierarchy in general and was, instead, radically decentralising. At the core was the idea of participation.

Some of Beer's evidence for this romantic and populistic movement is, frankly, impressionistic. A severe critic goes further and states that the 'kindest comment that can be made about this thesis is that it is vague' (Norton 1984:356). However, Beer did adduce evidence which is highly relevant to our present concerns. In particular, he cited survey-based evidence from the work of Alan Marsh (1977) which suggested that there had been a decline in trust and deference and a rise in demands for more participatory opportunities. This conclusion was supported by the publication of the comparative study of, mainly, protest participation conducted by a team led by Samuel Barnes and Max Kaase to which Marsh also contributed, and which included Britain within its coverage (Barnes, Kaase *et al.* 1979). Based on surveys conducted in the mid-1970s, it concluded that in Western democracies people were now much more ready to undertake political action beyond the conventional electoral arena. Citizens had widened their political 'repertory' to include a range of more direct participatory actions such as protest marches or boycotts. It should be noted that this was primarily a study of attitudes to participation – of readiness of take action – and not of actual levels of protest activity. Nevertheless, it seemed to suggest a potential for greater and more radical participation of considerable significance.

One reason for expecting that resort to new forms of participation would continue to increase was the growth in 'post-materialist values'. In a highly influential analysis of modern society Ronald Inglehart has argued that, as the material well-being of the inhabitants of advanced societies has grown, more people have turned their attention to new types of political issue. They are less concerned with policies designed for economic advancement and more with problems which have resulted from material progress – such as damage to the environment – or with issues which have little to do with materialism – such as open government and participation itself (Inglehart 1977). These values are most likely to be found amongst the affluent and the young. The issues themselves fall outside those around which old party alignments have been built. Hence, orthodox political participation, through electoral action, may be less likely to put the issues on the agenda. The use of various forms of direct political action can then appear appropriate to the post-materialist. Moreover, participation itself may seem a value. Beer incorporated Inglehart's post-materialist analysis into his account of the changing British culture and, indeed, regarded such a tendency as part of the 'romantic mainstream' (Beer 1982:146).

Overall, however, Britain was, along with Austria, the least participatory of the five countries studied by the Barnes and Kaase team. Nor, moreover, did Inglehart, in his contribution to the same project, report that the British were particularly prone to adopt a post-materialist stance (Barnes, Kaase *et al.* 1979:548). The extent of the participatory transformation of British political culture has, therefore, remained uncertain. This is a question made all the more difficult to resolve, as Norton points out, because of the paucity of survey evidence from earlier periods as to social and political attitudes (Norton 1984:351–3), as well, we would add, as the lack of data as to levels of actual participatory activity. Moreover, even allowing for the force of the argument about the rise of post-materialist values, it would follow from the terms of the hypothesis that with the downturn of the economy in the middle 1970s, material concerns would once more rise and, hence, the priority of participation could again decline.

There are, however, other reasons to think that, whatever the impact on citizen behaviour, ideas of participation have formed part of the *Zeitgeist* since the 1960s. The major political parties have paid varying degrees of attention to the participatory impulse. The British Labour Party has always contained within its 'broad church' centralising and decentralising socialist tendencies. In many respects, these reflect a tension between two visions of socialism – one stressing power to the people and the other emphasising the need for a form of state authority to redistribute benefits according to a principle of need. This has been the case in the period from the sixties to the eighties. Beer argues that a significant influence on new populist politics was the group surrounding the journal *The New Left Review* which, particularly in its early years, placed participation high on its agenda of humanist socialism. The impact of this view went well beyond its original restricted circle. In the mid-1970s, the left of the party, with Tony Benn at the forefront, put forward a manifesto for the party which laid considerable stress on broadening participation. Although adopting a broadly participatory stance, Benn had relatively little to say in his published writings and speeches about citizen and group action. His concern was with 'open government', the internal democratisation of the Labour Party itself and industrial democracy (T. Benn 1979). In this respect, the most successful of the participatory programmes was the internal reform of the party including widening the selectorate for the leadership and increasing the influence of activist members over the selection and deselection of candidates.

Despite this significant participatory strand, the countervailing centralising tendency in the Labour Party was rather more effective in shaping policy. The Wilson Governments of 1964 and 1966 had come to power on a programme of technological revolution which, however critical of establishment values, had little obvious place for individual participation. The forms of planning espoused by these governments and the successor Wilson-Callaghan Governments of 1974–9 were essentially corporatist. The years of Mrs Thatcher's Conservative Party hegemony after 1979 produced, however, a new participatory thrust in the Labour Party, emerging particularly in those local bases of urban power which the party still retained (Gyford 1985). Local socialism aimed to develop political involvement by tenants' groups and other social movements. Certain Labour local authorities sought, with varying success, to set up neighbourhood offices to run social services and thus, it was hoped, improve public access. Still more radically, there were efforts to institute neighbourhood representative bodies which would permit individuals and groups an input into decisions on how such services were to be provided for the particular area (Fudge 1984; see also Smith 1985). Amongst the prominent advocates of a local approach to socialism was David Blunkett, who was the Leader of Sheffield City Council from 1980 to 1987. Local policies on health, social services, transport and the economy should, in his view, be accompanied by greater administrative decentralisation and citizen participation. The standpoint of participatory socialism is exemplified in the suggestion from Blunkett and his co-author that

We may be seeing a more active dialogue in local politics, but unless the structure of local politics is altered, people will still have very little say over what is done. There is much evidence that ordinary people are not happy to leave decisions to the politicians alone, even if they support their policies.
(Blunkett and Jackson 1987:94)

The Liberal Party has consistently supported extended participation. Under the leadership of Jo Grimond the idea of participation was put in the forefront of the Liberal programme. The party has advocated industrial democracy, usually in the form of power-sharing, decentralisation and devolution. In the 1970s, the party adopted a strategy of 'community politics' which sought to involve it in dealing with the problems of the local community, however specific and even apparently small the issues might appear as seen from the perspective of 'high politics' – the 'politics of the cracked paving stone' to the critics. The Liberals also supported community councils and neighbourhood groups. Participation would enhance the influence of the citizen and increase political accountability (Holme 1985). The strategy was, moreover, associated with some striking electoral successes in local politics, even if it was less clearly appropriate as a basis for a national programme (Mole 1983; Steed 1983:88–92). The most radical wing of the Liberals at that period included within the idea of community politics various forms of direct action – sit-ins, boycotts, demonstrations involving, in some circumstances, law-breaking. In the words of one of the leading activists:

In the course of this process, a participatory spirit will be injected into the community and people will realize that it is they who possess the real power: the power to confront, to challenge, to agitate, the power to create a participatory democracy.
(Hain 1975:160)

From 1981, the Liberals were allied with the Social Democratic Party. Having broken away from Labour, the SDP brought an ambiguous inheritance which is reflected in the first edition of *Face the Future* by David Owen, who was later to lead the party but who at the time of writing this book was still happy to describe his position as 'socialist' (Owen 1981). Owen placed much emphasis on participatory policies involving such measures as decentralisation, industrial democracy and cooperatives, and locally managed health authorities. On the other hand, Owen was still tempted by more corporatist arrangements in other areas such as energy policy and industrial strategy. Although this possibly reflects a recognition that different levels of government require quite different decision-making arrangements, the programme of early 1981 also shows the extent to which reflective opposition politicians were pulled in both participatory and centralist directions. Nevertheless, in 1985, all of Owen's original participatory proposals were still incorporated in the SDP's handbook *The Only Way to a Fairer Britain*. A similar participatory line was taken by a second member of the 'Gang of Four' who created the SDP. The title of Shirley Williams's book *Politics is for People* is itself indicative and the final chapter proposed strengthened local government, a legal requirement for industrial democracy, citizen participation in school governing bodies, hospital administration, management of housing estates and the running of social services (Williams 1981:204–5).

Clearly, therefore, participation was on the agenda. But in 1984, when our survey commenced, Britain was in the fifth year of what was to be a long period of Conservative rule under Mrs Thatcher. None of the many varieties of Conservatism has found much place for citizen participation. Conservatives tend to view citizens as subjects of the Crown possessing political and civil rights and who elect governments with authority to exercise political judgement on their behalf. Governments are called to account for the exercise of this judgement. Traditionally-minded Conservatives such as Sir Ian Gilmour or William Waldegrave or Lord Hailsham will discuss constitutional reform and they may differ in their views of its appropriateness (Hailsham 1959; Gilmour 1977; Waldegrave 1978) but in no case is individual participation in political decision-making a major concern. The conservatism of Mrs Thatcher, difficult as it is to define (Kavanagh 1987), is different from these earlier forms. Although generally traditionalist and authoritarian in the moral sphere, it espouses individual freedom in the economic realm and in certain areas of social services. Unlike traditional Toryism, it shows little sympathy with local government which is a major arena for citizen participation. The 'New Right' doctrines, to which Mrs Thatcher's governments have leant, look to market mechanisms as the means for expanding individual choice (King 1987). To employ the language of Hirschman (1970), the individual within a market system exercises control not as a citizen who uses 'voice' but as a consumer who 'exits' by shifting to an alternative supplier.

Although the New Right is critical of the power of the centralised state and of bureaucracy, its response is not instinctively participatory. It seeks, instead, to turn state responsibilities over to private suppliers who, to very varying degrees, will compete in the market for consumers. One effect is to reduce the scope of the 'political' sphere. Alternatively, internal market arrangements are to be created within such bodies as the health service but with the object of improving efficiency rather than maximising choice.

Occasionally, participatory remedies have emerged partly, one suspects, where full market solutions have not succeeded or been attempted. Thus the Conservative Government, as well as expanding the role of school governors, also legislated to allow parents to vote to take their schools out of the control of local education authorities – a true market solution would have been the much-discussed system of education vouchers which would permit parents to purchase education from competing suppliers. Similarly, council tenants (those who had not already bought their homes as a result of the privatisation programme) have had, in certain cases, a vote under 1988 legislation as to whether they wished to retain the local authority as a landlord rather than become tenants of a private landlord or a housing association.

From a New Right perspective, these must, however, be second-best solutions. Moreover, some are 'one-off' occasions and not part of a continuing process of citizen involvement. The appropriate objective would be, where possible, a market arrangement whether of a standard variety or an 'internal market' within a public provision such as the National Health Service. Nevertheless, despite the dominance of a market-oriented Conservative Government in the 1980s, the issue of political participation was not forced off the agenda. In 1983, such an 'establishment' figure as Sir Douglas Wass, the recently retired Permanent Secretary to the Treasury and Joint Head of the Home Civil Service, concluded his BBC Reith Lectures on the state of British Government with a lecture entitled 'Participation – the Sole Bond' (Wass 1984:101–20). He found participation in present-day democracy minimal and even called for the re-establishment of 'the Greek idea in concept if not in precise form'. As has been argued, the opposition parties who together had the support of a majority of voters, ensured that the idea of a more participatory society was at least presented as a potential alternative to the type of individualism associated with the market philosophy. It is true that, compared with the big issues of social services or foreign affairs, the values of democracy and participation play a modest role in party manifestos (Budge, Robertson and Hearl 1987:54). Nevertheless, they are present and are, relatively, more prominent in the Liberal programme.[1]

By the late 1980s, indeed, participatory ideas were appearing to make a renewed impact. A mounting opposition critique of the approach of Mrs Thatcher's government had concentrated on its alleged cultivation of profit-oriented and uncaring individualism. The critique was sufficient to produce a response from Mrs Thatcher in her speech to the Conservative Party Conference in October 1988 in which she implicitly enjoined individuals to choose also to be active citizens in a caring community. The message was also that to be 'post-materialist' in this way implied being already sufficiently well-off materially. *The Economist* chose to remind her of a prior commitment to individual responsibility and material progress, dismissing such terms as 'citizenship' and 'community' as woolly and carrying little meaning in the modern world (*The Economist* 8.10.1988:13–14).

Although these latter political developments took place after the participation survey was concluded, they are cited as an indication of the continuity of the topic as an element in political debate. As important has been the effect of a number of legislative and administrative changes since the 1960s which have propelled participation and protest onto the stage. It was also a period in which a number of ideas concerning participation achieved sufficient status to prompt major commissions of inquiry. The Bullock Report made proposals in 1977 for introducing restricted forms of industrial democracy which have, however, never been adopted (Bullock 1977; see also Guest and Knight 1979). In 1973, the Kilbrandon Report examined changes in the constitution, concentrating especially on devolution to Scotland and Wales (Royal Commission 1973). In doing so, it generated some research on attitudes to government and democratic rights (for a discussion, see Hart 1978:59–69). In 1978, a measure of devolution to Scotland and Wales was passed by Parliament which would have granted a new participatory right to vote for an Assembly. It was, however, contingent upon a special majority in a referendum which, in 1979, the measure failed to achieve and, hence, it lapsed.

The most lasting legislative measure affecting participation was the 1968 Town and Country Planning Act which codified and extended the rights of individual citizens to make representations to local authorities about their outline planning proposals and required the authorities to take account of them. The relevant processes of participation itself were described in the Report of the Committee on Public Participation in Planning under the chairmanship of Arthur Skeffington, published as *People and Planning* in 1969. The Skeffington Report opened its proposals by saying that

Participation involves doing as well as talking and there will be full participation only when the public are able to take an active part throughout the plan-making process.(Skeffington 1969:1)

This required that the public receive information about planning proposals in advance and that they be allowed opportunities to put forward views both about broad structure plans and detailed local proposals. The Report described a range of consultative and participatory techniques including social surveys, exhibitions, community forums and advisory panels. Many such techniques, it acknowledged, would be most suited to the involvement of organisations. But, it added,

These contain the active minority, the yeast of the community, but it is also important to seek out the views of those who do not join societies or attend meetings.   (Skeffington 1969:16)

It suggested the appointment of officers whose responsibility would be to stimulate personal involvement.

The results have not been dramatic in the broader structure planning processes (Boaden *et al.* 1982:62–9). More detailed local planning is subject to a system of quasi-judicial public inquiries. These have covered, amongst many other matters, housing proposals, commercial developments, disposal of nuclear waste and public highways. Some of these inquiries, especially into road schemes, have been highly publicised but there have been thousands of such inquiries a year. As well as individual participants, around such inquiries have arisen a host of single-issue lobbies. This is the arena, *par excellence*, of reactive participation. Not surprisingly, those involved are commonly described as local 'objectors'. Their motivation has led to the journalistic label 'Nimby' – 'Not in My Back Yard', implying that their sense of community is, at best, parochial. Their frequency is such as to permit television comedies to be written around them. The overall extent of participation concerned with environment and planning will be much discussed in later chapters. Meanwhile, the importance of statutory provision in this sphere is that the amount of participation must be related to the 'windows of opportunity' available, which is greater in planning matters than most others.

The major contrast is with health services. The nature of medical provision is such that it is readily regarded as the archetypal sphere in which individual lay participation is inappropriate. And certainly the various bodies which have been set up to monitor the National Health Service, such as the Community Health Councils, are appointed and not participatory. At best, there has been indirect participation through persons nominated by local authorities (usually councillors) and by voluntary organisations. Individual action cannot therefore find very open channels. Nevertheless, these are sensitive areas and there have been few matters more likely to lead to campaigns of protest than a threat to close a local hospital or a specialist ward.

Throughout the period since the 1960s, the term 'community' has been so widely employed as to become part of symbolic politics. It has been particularly, though not necessarily, associated with forms of local participation within inner cities designed to regenerate neighbourhoods or assist their generally deprived populations. Large numbers of such action groups have arisen claiming, with varying degrees of accuracy and of rivalry, to represent their local 'community' which may be described in terms of a residential area or of a partially non-spatial entity such as an ethnic grouping. Others, such as tenants' associations, are based on a particular type of residential arrangement. Some provide voluntary services. Others campaign over specific issues. They vary in their relationships with local authorities, ranging from antagonism to forms of quasi-cooption where they are funded, in whole or in part, by the authority, are regularly consulted or perform surrogate local social services such as care for youth or the disabled.

These action groups are the scene of intensive participation which may give rise to a misleading impression as to the actual numbers of persons involved. Nevertheless, their impact is disproportionate to the numbers. Amongst their effects has been to sustain an image of participation, sometimes in a radical form. A controversial instance was the limited experiment instituted in 1969 by the Home Office of Community Development Projects which were designed to encourage local initiatives which would promote new voluntarily-run social services. Each scheme had a local action team and research backing. In the event, certain of these teams developed radical approaches to the analysis of local needs and demanded solutions unacceptable to government, and some were closed prematurely (Smith, Lees and Topping 1977; Loney 1983). The competing logics of central control and local autonomy came into conflict. The purpose and the success of participation are viewed very differently by those for whom it is a means to achieve reform from above and those who regard it as an avenue for challenge from below (Arblaster 1972; Cochrane 1986).

Other participatory or quasi-participatory ventures have ranged from community councils to arrangements to decentralise town hall services to neighbourhoods in order to improve access (Hoggett and Hambleton 1987). The scale of these participatory experiments may not have been large. Their success in stimulating sustained citizen involvement has often been limited. So much so that in the view of one group of well-informed critics:

public participation … has performed an important symbolic function in British local and national politics but with a few small-scale exceptions it has failed to achieve all that its proponents wished.   (Boaden *et al.* 1982:179)

Sympathisers similarly concluded that, whilst decentralisation had become 'a trend rather than a fad', any associated growth in democratisation had been 'faltering' (Hoggett and Hambleton 1987:3).

Participation has, therefore, remained one part of the political language of Britain. The actual extent to which it is practised across the country as a whole has, however, never previously been fully examined. Nor, consequently, has it been possible to appreciate how far those citizens who have become involved in public action have been satisfied or dissatisfied with their experiences. It is this which our survey has sought to uncover.

The research design

Overview

Every method of research into political action and behaviour has its weaknesses and limitations. To opt, therefore, for a survey approach is not intended to deny the value of other ways of collecting evidence. Other research strategies may be as, or more, appropriate in given situations. Nor is survey evidence 'cost-free'. There are undoubted problems in face-to-face encounters between professional interviewers and ordinary citizens. Furthermore, the same could also be said, in general, about interviews with local leaders which also formed part of our overall strategy.

Nevertheless, the survey is probably the most appropriate instrument to uncover the extent of political participation amongst the people of Britain and to understand why some are more active than others. This requires some exploration of what social, economic, and political traits are associated with activism. It also leads to an assessment of what immediate circumstances, in particular the issues, needs or problems of individuals, led to their personal involvement in the public arena. What is needed, in short, is systematic information about ordinary individuals from all walks of life. This is where the tried and tested means of a sample survey come into their own.

Perhaps its central virtue is that a relatively small number of carefully selected respondents (about 1,500) can provide relatively accurate and representative information about a very large population – here the approximately 43 million individuals of voting age living in Britain.[2] Within certain limits, the results presented in succeeding chapters derived from our sample can be taken as applying to that much larger body: the picture of participation is, more or less, a fair version of the picture that would be obtained were all 43 million to cooperate in our study – hardly a likely prospect! Surveys, in short, allow a range of inferences to be made about very large populations that could not otherwise readily be made.

This is not, however, to deny the importance, at times, of just such whole-population information. Election results, for example, are indeed counts of everyone who voted. In the case of the 1987 General Election, such results derive from more than 32 million individual votes cast in 650 separate contests. There, one can be absolutely sure that the picture is an accurate one. As a result, a lot of sophisticated analysis has gone into their study and much has been revealed (see, for example, the standard 'Analysis' appendices incorporated into the Nuffield election series). But the problems in using such evidence for the present purposes are two-fold. First, we are concerned about far more than voting. As will be seen, voting looms large in the participatory map, but it is far from being the only element. Indeed, in some crucial respects, it is a very misleading guide to the nature of participation in Britain simply because so many individuals bother to do it. So while election results can tell us a lot about voting, it turns out that they provide virtually no guide about the other forms of political activity that are so important to the functioning of a democracy like that in Britain.

A second, and equally important, limitation is that the information is only published in an aggregate form. Nothing is known about individual choices other than the overall result.[3] Certain hints can be gleaned about what must have happened at the individual level from observing the varied outcomes across so many different constituencies. But to infer individual level relationships from those aggregate patterns is not a straightforward one-to-one matter. For that would be to commit the so-called 'ecological fallacy' (see, for example, Alker 1965).

On the other hand, aggregate voting statistics do provide the basis for establishing trends – in turnout, net volatility and the like. Here, surveys are, in practice, much weaker. It is possible to undertake surveys through time, either in the form of panels or by repeating similar questions for freshly drawn samples. In Britain, both have been used, but again mainly in the area of electoral behaviour (see, for example, Butler and Stokes 1969; Alt 1984). For other forms of participation, the present study is in many respects the *first* baseline to be established. However, we have tried, where possible, to relate the measures of participatory acts to those of earlier studies. But differences of time frame and, not least, conceptualisation of what participation is all about unfortunately make attempts at establishing a cumulative set of findings very difficult indeed (but see chapter 19). The present research, therefore, aims to establish a new and relatively comprehensive baseline so that future studies can then make better inferences about possible participatory trends.

Part of the usefulness of such a survey baseline is its relative precision – its capacity to be expressed in numerical form. This, of course, raises (apart from any technical questions about margins of error etc.) the long-debated question of quantitative versus qualitative research. This is not the place to debate the matter. But it is worth making one or two relevant points. First, the language of numbers can sift information and provide substantive insights of considerable subtlety and power. One of the major benefits of the survey approach is that it yields systematic information that is generally amenable to statistical treatment. At the same time, quantification has its limitations, and even its distortions. The remedy, however, lies in better and more careful use of statistical techniques rather than their abandonment (see, for example, Tufte 1970).

It also lies in an appreciation for the complementarity and, at times, greater appropriateness of other, more qualitative, approaches. Verba, Nie and Kim (1978), for example, rightly praise the work on political participation of Zukin (1975) whose research design entailed intensive discussions with, and personal observation of, *ten* Yugoslav families. This is a typical example of what they call a 'close configurative case study' (1978:30) (see also Parry, Moyser and Wagstaffe 1987). As these authors note, this approach yields

observations that can be richer and more varied. The scholar can know the place and people he is studying firsthand; he can take into account the complexities of the particular situation. Studies of this kind are not superficial...The individuals or communities one studies are treated as fully rounded entities, not as ciphers in a statistical analysis.   (Verba, Nie and Kim 1978:30)

Individuals in such surveys as the present one can, indeed, appear to be statistical ciphers. That is one of the costs of trying to establish a broad and general picture. Equally, the particular milieux from which they come do not feature as prominently as if we had only ten individuals or a small group of activists to deal with rather than over 3,000 citizens. However, context has not been ignored. On the contrary, the study breaks new ground in trying to build into the general national picture a greater sense of the local context by a more detailed study of six specially selected localities. The latter half of the book sets out our findings on this front.

At the same time, even these are not qualitative studies. Qualitative, in-depth treatments of participation tend, by their nature, to be particularistic. Their virtue lies in the detail, the nuance, the sense of being very close to those being observed. But the question must then arise as to the extent to which understandings derived from them also apply to the other millions of citizens that composed the nation? These are critical questions. It is, therefore, necessary that the baseline be established through broad-scale surveys. Against such a baseline, qualitative studies of particular localities, individuals and, especially, intensively participatory groups and activities, come into their own. Research could push down into the specific roots of the human political experience but, most importantly, within an empirical framework of national, and indeed cross-national, understandings.

Details

The research programme reported in this book can be divided into two halves, national and local. At the national level, we undertook a representative sample survey, between late 1984 and early 1985, of all those aged over 18 in England, Scotland and Wales (for technical details, see appendix A and Courtenay 1984). This entailed face-to-face interviews by professional interviewers from our contracted survey agency, Social and Community Planning Research (SCPR). They used a fully-structured questionnaire incorporating both open- and closed-ended questions that took about an hour on average to work through.

While this time limit (intended to sustain the overall response rate) imposed limitations on the coverage, it still allowed a wide range of participatory acts to be examined. Some, moreover, could be pursued in considerable detail. To achieve this, we employed two approaches. One consisted of a set of standardised questions about a large number (over 30) of participatory acts. These were broken up into a number of smaller sets or 'batteries' of questions and hence might be called the 'battery approach'. As such, it is a familiar one within those other studies of participation that have used sample surveys (for example, Verba and Nie 1972; Barnes, Kaase *et al.* 1979). These earlier inventories of questions were borne in mind when constructing the present study in order to enable, in principle, one national study to add to, and be set in the context of, a range of other studies from different time-points and countries. It was from this battery information that the basic set of participatory scales was derived. These scales were used in turn to construct a national map (see chapter 3) and then extensively analysed in subsequent chapters (4 through 10).

We also made provision to solicit extensive additional information to provide some depth and meaning to the basic acts themselves. These were generally selected on the basis of the two actions individual respondents had done most of in each of the different batteries. In principle, therefore, all respondents could have been involved in this exercise. In fact, however, as we shall see in chapter 3, participation is, generally speaking, a minority affair. Thus, only that minority who had in fact undertaken one or more actions in the given battery then 'told their story'. Nevertheless, this meant that, in all but a few actions, we had many hundreds of respondents who did tell us about the subject matter of the action, the target to which it was addressed, and their perceptions of its success or failure. This substantial set of materials has been analysed and written up in chapters 11, 12 and 13. Together, they serve to emphasise that, whilst we hold strictly to a behaviour-based measurement of participation, we have sought to set that behaviour in a framework that allows the individual respondent to speak more fully as to its meaning, context and political import (see also, for example, Parry and Moyser 1988). An incidental, but very important, advantage is that it provides internal corroboration of the accuracy of more quantitative materials. Respondents were enabled to tell their own stories about their experiences.

Perhaps the richest set of materials from that viewpoint is that drawn from our second approach. In this instance, rather than seeking responses to a standardised inventory of participatory items devised by ourselves, the subject was introduced through a deliberately broad-set question about the individual's issues, needs and problems. Further discussion of this is provided in chapter 11, where the results are extensively examined. When individuals mentioned such problems, one such 'prime issue' was selected and a number of questions were asked about actions that the respondent had taken in connection with raising or attempting to resolve that issue in the public domain. In this way, information about acts of participation was derived that may have been perhaps less systematic, and perhaps more idiosyncratic. But it did provide a means whereby we could look further into the crucial question as to how citizen political action is triggered off, in particular which kinds of issue stimulate participation and which fail to do so. This approach provided a rich, more qualitative understanding of the subject based squarely on the respondents' concerns. In this way, therefore, a primarily 'quantitative' survey can, in fact, also combine more 'qualitative' elements, to the material benefit of both.

The second part of the study is devoted to participation at the local level. It seeks to investigate the interaction between locality and politics. How far does participation display a single national pattern or a number of different local profiles? For these purposes, we selected six localities, four in England, one in Scotland and one in Wales. The detailed process by which they were selected, and their particular contextual characteristics are set out in chapter 14. Perhaps the main design point to highlight here is the choice of what elsewhere we have called the 'limited numbers strategy' (Parry and Moyser 1983). That is, we opted for a design that included only a few research sites so that, in each, it was possible to undertake extensive surveys of both ordinary citizens and local leaders. In this way, some of the 'flavour' of each locality can be captured as part of the attempt to understand the nuances of the local participatory patterns (see chapter 15). The strategy thus differed from that adopted by Verba and Nie (1972) in which a large number of localities were included, but at the expense of only having relatively few interviews (of citizens and elites) in each. Their alternative may allow for the quantitative analysis of localities as macro units, but loses something when the aim is to get inside each area and seek to understand the local participatory processes and mass-elite linkages at work. As always, it is a trade-off entailed by finite resources. Our solution perhaps tips towards detail and 'quality' at the expense of generality and 'quantity'.

Within these research areas, a citizen survey was undertaken, although each was on a more modest scale compared with the national study. When all six mass surveys are added together, however, the number of interviews completed slightly exceeded the national set. In this sense, the local component represents fully half of the total research effort in terms both of resources deployed and amount of information produced. The format of these local mass surveys intentionally followed the general structure and detailed wording of the national questionnaire. In this way, the national findings provide a strictly comparable framework within which the local results have been set. In addition, there were, of course, a number of questions to do with local politics, and a few unique to each area. To make room, it was necessary, in turn, to delete some questions that therefore only appeared in the national study. But the emphasis was upon a close coordination between the two levels.

The other half of the local studies involved studying local leaders. For what is the point, from a political and democratic point of view, of looking at citizen participation if one has no idea as to its impact, its effectiveness, its reception and perception by those at the top? This is why elite studies are needed to complement mass studies of participation. The manner whereby these elites were selected is set out in chapter 16. Over 50 interviews were conducted on average in each locality. Once more, to ensure standardisation and comparability, these were of a face-to-face structured variety, again by professional SCPR interviewers. The topics covered embraced questions about the leaders' perceptions of participation, their personal involvement in local politics and the issues which concerned them. Where necessary, the wording of the questions was designed to ensure maximum comparability with that employed in the citizens' surveys. This made it possible, for example, to undertake examinations of the extent to which the priorities of leaders matched those of citizens – an essential part of understanding 'mass-elite linkages' (see chapters 16 and 17). On the other hand, the questions in these elite interviews were generally more open than in the citizen questionnaire, as would befit the character and sophistication of the respondents, many of whom were political 'professionals'. By and large, however, the more structured technique, needed to generate the necessary standardised and comparable information, worked very well.

We have, therefore, sought to construct a research design that is appropriate to the wide range of objectives involved in a study of participation. This has involved balancing sometimes conflicting imperatives, and within a context of inevitable resource constraints. The proof, of course, lies in the eating – the use we have made of the very large amount of information the study generated. Of this the reader must be the judge.

PART II

PATTERNS AND PATHWAYS

3

PATTERNS OF POLITICAL PARTICIPATION

In order to understand the role of political participation in a liberal democracy, one must first describe it. For it is in specifying the particular building blocks, the various activities making up what we term political participation, that answers begin to emerge about the complex ways in which it fits into the wider democratic order (see Parry 1972:3–17). In other words, the initial task to be tackled is to identify and lay out the basic 'cartography' of political action in Britain. How many continents and how far apart are they? Where are the mountains and how high? Where are the valleys and how deep? These are the central tasks of this chapter.

The indicators of political participation

As we have seen in chapter 1, our understanding of political participation is set deliberately broad to try to capture a fair representation of the numerous ways in which ordinary citizens seek to influence the policy-making process, be it local, national or even international. If the concept is to retain its sharpness and concreteness, it must refer to forms of action. That is, participation, as we conceive the term, is about citizens doing things (compare in a very different political environment, Burns 1988:9–11). Thus, it should not encompass elements pertaining to political interest or civic duty or the citizen's sense of his or her potential effectiveness in influencing policy-making. These factors certainly help one to understand why some participate whilst others do not, but they must not be confused with the action itself – as has sometimes been the case (see, for example, Inglehart 1981). Equally, we are not concerned here with a citizen's willingness to participate or whether, under certain circumstances, he or she might get involved. Again, this may throw interesting light on what leads people to act – and will be discussed in the course of this study – but should not be considered part of the act itself (but see Barnes, Kaase *et al.*, 1979: ch. 3).

There are even certain actions relating to politics which we have excluded on the grounds of conceptual clarity. These are activities in which the instrumental quality of seeking to influence policy-making in some substantive way, even if indirectly, seems to be absent. Watching party political broadcasts on television would fail this test. It is an activity, but is passive. It may put the individual, through the information it conveys, in a better position to participate and it may stimulate political interest. But, in our view, it lacks that clear stamp of active instrumentality that we are seeking.

More difficult, however, is the question of political discussion which some might regard as a genuine political action. Our judgement is that whether it is political participation or not depends upon the nature of the discussion. Thus, if the discussion is one in which a citizen is engaged in seeking to mobilise a friend or colleague for a cause or issue or to persuade that person to vote in a particular way, then the instrumentality would seem to be there and it would, in principle, 'count'. On the other hand, the discussion might take the form of a classroom seminar about politics, or a private conversation between neighbours, in which there was no intention at all to influence the broader political process. For these reasons, 'political discussion' is a dangerous and potentially flawed measure to use. For it certainly cannot be presumed that all responses, or even the majority of responses, would have met the instrumental test. We, have, therefore, sought to ensure that the measurement of political participation clearly retains its sharpness and consistency by not including political discussion as such. We do incorporate certain items that entail discussion, but they are such that appear to entail some clear intention to influence action.

Traditionally, studies of political participation understood strictly as action were mainly concerned with electoral activities, particularly voting. Important though this may be, however, there is much more to participation than that. Indeed, elections in Britain are relatively transient events in the political calendar, representing for the citizen an important but restricted opportunity to influence events. Most of the time, the business of raising issues, identifying alternative solutions and making policy decisions is carried out at some remove from elections and their associated campaigns. It is, therefore, necessary to take account of participation outside the electoral arena – as has been increasingly recognised (see Verba and Nie 1972).

In particular, we must give due recognition to citizen involvement in a wide array of groups that seek to influence policy-making. These groups may be formal or informal, local or national, overtly political or only intermittently engaged in such affairs. But, collectively, they represent a most important mechanism through which citizen preferences are made known to those who make the decisions. Indeed, some argue that issue-oriented 'preference groups' (Moran 1985:144; see also Dalton *et al.* 1984:471) are becoming an ever more important part of the whole process, challenging and possibly even partially supplanting the more traditional party-based mechanisms of representation. In the present era of fast-changing collectivist politics citizen participation through such groups plays a prominent part.

At the same time, collective action, be it group-based or party-based, is not the whole story. Verba and Nie drew attention to a set of activities that had been overlooked possibly because these activities are individualistic and more often concerned with personal and family problems or needs. We refer here to the range of 'contacting' actions, whether by letter, by telephone or face-to-face, by which citizens may choose to try to raise matters directly with those authorities whom they see as being in a position to respond. These may include Members of Parliament, or local town hall officials or even the mass media, who arguably are playing a more important intermediary role in getting citizen grievances attended to by governmental agencies.

Finally, there is the whole array of 'protest' activities which form a further and essential part of the potential repertoire available to the citizen. Given the backdrop against which our surveys were conducted – the Miners' Strike of 1984–85 and the 'Brighton Bomb' planted at the Conservative Party Conference, also in 1984, and the continued protests focused on the Cruise missile base at Greenham Common (Foote 1988) – it would have been very difficult to ignore the role that protest plays in contemporary public life. Indeed, protest has become firmly established as part of the array of actions citizens and groups might consider using to make themselves heard. It cannot be ignored as part of any present-day study of political participation.

Standing slightly apart from these other activities which aim to influence the making of policy is another kind of citizen involvement in its implementation. This may consist in voluntary work in some aspect of state welfare. It may be service as a magistrate or as a special constable in the police force. People may be members of government advisory bodies or tribunals. These activities have a long tradition in British public life. Some might be taken to represent the peak of positive citizenship. For these reasons, they were included within the survey. In the event, the numbers involved being low, and the scatter of such roles fairly wide, it was not feasible to incorporate such 'output' participation within the general analysis. Certain features of these activities are intriguing and would reward a more focused treatment. It is, for example, the case that such forms of involvement are generally perceived by the respondents as more 'political' than the range of actions directed at influencing authorities (see note 2). They are, therefore, in the eyes of the public, a highly political form of participation performed by a very select band of persons.

The variety of forms of protest, contacting, or party campaign activity is such that it would not be possible to try to cover every conceivable type of participation in the survey. Nevertheless, in an effort to cover the most significant and numerous across the nation, we gathered information from our interviewees about 33 different actions, using a standardised set of response categories to facilitate the kind of numerical analysis that is required. These were supplemented by more open questions which could elicit qualitative information about a variety of further actions taken by people in connection with issues which were of prime concern to them. Setting aside the 'output participation', the core set of actions which were examined amounted to 23.[1] The investigation by the Verba and Nie teams (1972:31; Nie *et al.* 1988:4–5) included initially twelve separate items and the Barnes, Kaase team (1979:541–4) seventeen. In the light of this research experience, it seems reasonable to hope that the present range of questions should prove sufficient to achieve a comprehensive map of citizen involvement in the British political system.

The precise wording of these various indicators is set out in chart 3.1, together with the shorthand labels and numbering system whereby they will be referred to in subsequent tables. They are grouped, for convenience, into five broad families corresponding to the major forms of participation (excluding 'output' participation) outlined above. Thus, amongst the 23 we have three concerned with voting in, respectively, local, national and European elections. The first of these asks respondents to estimate the general frequency with which they tend to participate in local elections. In this particular instance, it was not possible to be more concrete because, in Britain, the number and timing of such contests varies widely according to the type of locality. In face of such diversity, therefore, we opted for this general format in order to gather comparable information. For the other two voting items, however, we did have specific and common frames of reference – the General Election of June, 1983 and the European Election of June, 1984. Here we simply asked whether they had voted or not – a decision which, presumably, was still relatively fresh in the minds of most respondents.

For the other four 'families', we adopted a standard time perspective (the past five years) and set of alternative responses (never; only once; now and then; often). Within this framework, we asked four questions concerning involvement in party campaigns, three about activity within groups and five relating to individual contacting. We also asked about eight different forms of political protest which, set against the previous fifteen that were more clearly within the 'conventional' arena of participation, seemed to provide an appropriate balance between these two notionally distinct styles.

The levels of political participation

The first task in constructing our map is to look at the overall levels of reported activity for each indicator of participation. This gives a basic idea of what the terrain looks like – whether, for example, there is a lot or only a little citizen participation in Britain. But it also points in the direction of the ultimate task, which is to examine the contribution of participation to democracy. For, as Verba and Nie have also argued, in some basic sense, 'the more participation there is in decisions, the more democracy there is' (Verba and Nie 1972:1). To assist in evaluating the results, we also provide some similar findings from other countries – so that the map of Britain can be set in the context of other national maps.

The percentages of the total national sample reporting having done each political action[2] at least once (i.e. combining 'often', 'now and then' and 'only once') are set out in table 3.1. The results show that voting, as a general category, is the one activity in which most citizens say that they have taken part.[3] Indeed, it is the one area that typically involves a very substantial proportion of the mass population. In this respect, Britain is not that much different from other Western democracies. In West Germany, Austria and Japan, for example, the same general pattern holds true (Verba, Nie and Kim 1971:36; Barnes, Kaase *et al.* 1979:542; Dalton 1988:47). In the United States, surveys indicate that there has been a decline in voting turnout at both the national and local levels, starting some time after 1960 (Campbell 1979:233; Abramson and Aldrich 1982; Nie *et al.* 1988:4; see also Bennett and Resnick 1988:35). Nevertheless, it is still the case that voting remains the most all-embracing form of political action. All in all, Britain fits into a well-established cross-national pattern. In this sense, the close attention paid to voting turnout by students of participation is not at all misplaced. Clearly, if the citizenry engage in any political activity in abundance, it is voting in elections.

And yet it is apparent in table 3.1 that there is far more to participation than that. Substantial minorities report having contacted political institutions and political figures of various sorts. This activity, it might be said, is generally relatively remote from (though not unconnected to) the electoral arena. As many as a fifth, for example, have

Chart 3.1 *Measures of political participation – labels and definitions*

Label	Definition
A: Voting	
1. Vote Local	'I vote in every/most local election(s)'
2. Vote General	'...thinking back to the General Election in June 1983...which Party did you vote for in that election or perhaps you didn't vote...'
3. Vote European	'Could you think first of the election to the European Parliament which was held this June. Talking to people...we have found that a lot of them did not vote. How about you? Did you vote...?
B: Party campaigning	'In the past (5 years) have you...'
4. Fund raising	'...been involved in fund-raising for a political party or candidate?'
5. Canvassed	'...canvassed or knocked on doors for a political party or candidate?'
6. Clerical work	'...done clerical, or office work for a political party or candidate?'
7. Attended rally	'...attended a campaign meeting or rally for a party or candidate?'
C: Group activity	'In the past (5 years) have you...'
8. Informal group	'...got together with other people to raise an issue?'
9. Organised group	'...supported, or worked in, an organised group to raise an issue?'
10. Issue in group	'...how often over the past five years or so (have) you personally...used the club/group (as member/regular attender) to raise a political need or issue?'
D: Contacting	'In the past (5 years) have you yourself ever contacted a...'
11. Member of Parliament	'...Member of Parliament?'
12. Civil servant	'...Department of Central Government, or a Civil Servant?'
13. Councillor	'...Local Councillor?'
14. Town hall	'...Town Hall or County Hall official?' (excluding routine contacts)
15. Media	'...radio or television programme, or a newspaper, about a political issue?'
E: Protesting	'In the past (5 years) have you yourself...'
16. Attended protest meeting	'...attended a public meeting to protest about an issue?'
17. Organised petition	'...taken a petition round asking people to sign it?'
18. Signed petition	'...how often over the past 5 years have you signed a petition?'
19. Blocked traffic	'...blocked traffic with a street demonstration?'
20. Protest march	'...taken part in a protest march which had not been banned by the police?'
21. Political strike	'...taken part in a strike about an issue which you feel is political?'
22. Political boycott	'...taken part in a boycott about a political issue?'
23. Physical force	'...used physical force against political opponents?'

Table 3.1 *How much participation is there in Britain?* (*N = c. 1,570*)

	% yes/ At least once
Voting	
1 Vote Local	68·8
2 Vote General	82·5
3 Vote European	47·3
Party campaigning	
4 Fund raising	5·2
5 Canvassed	3·5
6 Clerical work	3·5
7 Attended rally	8·6
Group activity	
8 Informal group	13.8
9 Organised group	11·2
10 Issue in group	4·7
Contacting	
11 Member of Parliament	9·7
12 Civil servant	7·3
13 Councillor	20·7
14 Town hall	17·4
15 Media	3·8
Protesting	
16 Attended protest meeting	14·6
17 Organised petition	8·0
18 Signed petition	63·3
19 Blocked traffic	1·1
20 Protest march	5·2
21 Political strike	6·5
22 Political boycott	4·3
23 Physical force	0·2

got in touch with a local councillor, over half of these on more than one occasion. Here, differences of wording and response categories make comparisons with other countries somewhat more hazardous. But the proportions involved do not seem greatly out of line with those found elsewhere in Western Europe (Barnes, Kaase *et al.* 1979: 542–3; see also Mabileau, Moyser *et al.* 1989).

On the other hand, in the US, there does seem to have been more contacting. Thus, a fifth were reported by Verba and Nie (1972:31) as having ever contacted a local government official in 1967, which is not out of line with the British figure of 17·4 % for those who had had dealings with their town hall – specifically excluding routine matters such as paying rent and rates. However, the American rate increased to a third by 1987 (Nie *et al.* 1988:4–5) which does seem to be significantly higher. It would seem very unlikely that the difference of time-frame is enough to account for the gap. Similarly, when Americans were asked whether they had ever contacted a state or national government official, the 1987 rate was 29 %, which is again much higher than the 1967 figure of 17% (Nie *et al.* 1988:4–5). But both these are above the rate we find for Britons, only 7·3% of whom had contacted a civil servant. In this instance, if comparisons are to be made, it must be recalled that, in Britain, civil servants are officials of national government, many (but by no means all) of whom are employed in head offices, whereas in the American case, such officials may be either state or national employees.

Even taking this into account, however, it seems there remains more participation of this type in America than in Britain. Another study, for example, found that 22% of Americans had contacted their Member of the House of Representatives in the last four years (Bennett and Resnick 1988:35). This is more than twice as great as our figure of 9·7% for Britons contacting their Member of the House of Commons over a somewhat longer time span. Despite the difficulties of making cross-national comparisons (see Verba, Nie and Kim 1978: ch. 2; Przeworski and Teune 1970: chs. 5, 6), it does seem overall that even if Britons participate roughly at the same level as their fellow Europeans, they do much less contacting than citizens across the Atlantic. However, it is important to note that in both countries there is more contacting at the local level than at the national level, although the gap between the two would appear to be larger in Britain than in America.

Table 3.1 shows that groups also provide the context for modest levels of citizen activity. Amongst the three items under this heading, getting together with others in a relatively informal manner drew a 13·8% response, and working through more institutionalised group channels was reported by 11·2%. Here again, it seems that the rates may be somewhat lower than in the US where 34% were reported by Nie *et al.* (1988:4–5) as having worked with others, and 17% had on some previous occasion taken part in forming a group or organization. On the other hand, figures reported by Barnes, Kaase *et al.* (1979:541–2) suggest that America is atypical in this area too and that, by West European standards, Britain's rate of group activity is not particularly out of line (see also Dalton 1988:47).

With campaigning, we move even further down the ladder of British political involvement into single figures. The highest participation was in the relatively undemanding task of attending an election rally, but even this was only undertaken by about one citizen in twelve. Otherwise, the more demanding and time-consuming ventures, such as canvassing, attracted no more than 3·5% and 5·2% respectively. In part, of course, the opportunity for these actions tends to be restricted to election periods (national and local) which must depress the figures somewhat. The rate of participation is seemingly no higher elsewhere in Europe, where again roughly similar rates of campaigning are recorded (Barnes, Kaase *et al.* 1979:541–2; Dalton 1988:47).

Yet again, the exception amongst liberal democracies seems to be the USA where in 1987 over a quarter (27%) claimed to have 'ever actively worked for a party or candidate during an election' (Nie *et al.* 1988:4–5). On the other hand, another study in the same year (Bennett and Resnick 1988:35) found only 11% had done so. But either way, the rate exceeds that of the British. Yet, when one considers the nature and frequency of American elections, this is perhaps not surprising. A far wider range of offices is the subject of party-contested elections in the US. Furthermore, it is standard practice for many rival candidates to engage in intra-party primary contests (that involve citizens in voting) to select the one party candidate who goes forward to the actual election for the office itself. This means that for each party and each contested office, there may be a large number of candidate campaigns drawing upon citizen support. Clearly, therefore, these very different circumstances from Britain, where parties nominate candidates without the involvement of the public at large, must be taken into account in drawing conclusions about the import of what are obviously significant differences in citizen involvement between the two countries.

The arena of political protest produces the only other activity, besides voting, which involves a majority of the British population. Nearly two-thirds had signed a petition, 40% on more than one occasion. In most other countries for which roughly equivalent information exists, there is a correspondingly large involvement. In France and West Germany, for example, 44% and 46% respectively had signed a petition (Dalton 1988:65). In this (for once) America is not exceptional. The same study found 61% had put their names to a petition, another reported 55% (Bennett and Resnick 1988:35). Here, therefore, Britain fits into a broader and consistent pattern of substantial participation. Although its rate may possibly be at the top end, it is certainly not unusual. Petitioning is now up there with voting as a form of political action. One might surmise that this arises because, like voting, it is an act that requires little effort and is on a subject chosen by the petition organiser rather than the signer.

In all these countries, as in Britain, petitioning is highly atypical of the extent of involvement in other forms of political protest if, for the moment, we place petitioning under that umbrella. Of all the other seven measures in table 3.1, only one, attending a protest meeting, is in double figures (14·6%) and the rest are well down into single digits, a pattern generally shared by those other democracies. And, as a specific contrast to signing a petition, only 8% had bothered to take the more strenuous step of organising one.

Nevertheless, Barnes, Kaase *et al.* (1979:79–80) claim to have found significantly different national propensities to engage in political protest. According to their analysis, Holland has a distinctly more 'permissive' culture, in which significantly larger numbers would 'venture...into more extreme forms of protest' (1979:79) than in either West Germany or Britain. However, as we have previously hinted, much of their evidence rests on attitudes, on potential, rather than action itself. Thus, if one looks at reports of protest actually done, the differences are very small. On average, only 2·6% of Dutch citizens had undertaken one of the forms of protest other than petitioning, a figure little different from West Germany (2·0%) or Britain (2·3%). As our survey, across the five more comparable items, averages 3·5% – at a time of perhaps unusually high protest activity – it seems clear that, generally speaking, political protest in Britain is typical of most other Western democracies in involving only a very small proportion of the citizenry. For example, the British results indicate that 5·2% had taken part in a protest march, which is on a par with the 6% of Americans who had taken part in a public demonstration in the last four years (Bennett and Resnick 1988:35).

On the other hand, the numbers who have taken part in protesting are of roughly the same order as get involved in Britain's election campaigns and party rallies. From this perspective, therefore, the small numbers relative to the population as a whole may belie their significance in terms of the political process itself. In this sense, political protest remains a significant part of the participatory input. At the same time, and in crude quantitative terms, it is far from being a major feature of the map we are describing.

Overall, outside the realm of voting, the British citizenry are not highly active within the political system. They may be aware of politics and even have an interest in it, but they tend not to speak out all that much beyond the confines of a voting booth. In this, however, they are not perhaps atypical of ordinary people in other West European democracies. In the United States, by contrast, the low level of voting turnout is counter-balanced by substantially higher rates in other forms of conventional participation.[4] This somewhat paradoxical pattern of participation would be worthy of further investigation. Meanwhile, by this yardstick, Britain's citizenry is in aggregate not as participatory. For some, as chapter 1 pointed out, the general level of participation in modern democracies, including even in the USA, is seen as a cause for alarm. Others, however, might be more sanguine. For them it is sufficient that citizens get involved in holding the elites to account from time to time through voting. Beyond that, it is perhaps better to let the professionals get on with the job. Which view one takes in this great debate is ultimately a matter of preference and judgement. But, whatever one's stance, it is clear that Britain in the 1980s is not a democracy where widespread citizen participation is the norm. At the same time, there are significant minorities who actively sustain political life. Such interplay between passive and active citizenship is part of the essence of modern democracy and is, consequently, central to any understanding of political participation.

The concentration of political participation

In drawing the map of participation, it is not only important to ask how many participate in each particular area but also how participation is distributed through the British population. Is it the same people who say they participate when responding to our list of activities? This is crucial to a concern with democracy because there is a major difference between a situation in which different groups of citizens participate across each of the activities and one where it is generally the same few people saying that they are involved each time.

To provide evidence of the extent of such concentration, we simply counted the number of political actions undertaken by each respondent. This gives a clearer picture of how much political activity the average citizen in Britain undertakes within a five-year context. It also gives a better view about how many 'super-gladiators' there are – that peak of citizens that really do get involved in a wide range of political activities. Conversely, we can also begin to determine how many people are merely spectators. Or we may find that in Britain few citizens are to be found in these categories – that participation is spread, in a more egalitarian manner, relatively evenly across the population as a whole.

A first set of results for all twenty-three activities are set out in figure 3.1. It confirms what was seen in table 3.1, namely that relative to a notional maximum of 23 actions, the overall rate of participation is rather low. The average citizen has engaged in only a little over four of the activities (4.2) at least once over the five-year period. The most common profile (indicated by the mode) is three. By and large, the bulk of the

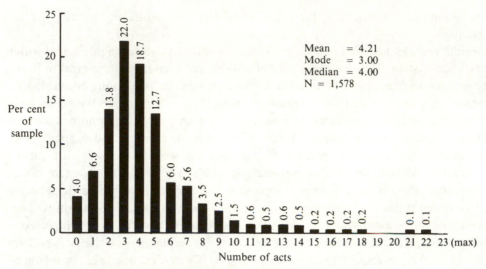

Figure 3.1 Number of acts of political participation (23 items)

population is to be found at or near that general level of activity. As many as two-thirds of the total are clustered in the two to five activity range. Only a very small minority, 4·0% on this basis, appear to be totally inert and register zero on our scale. On the other hand, there is a somewhat larger number that deviate from the profile of the majority by being relatively very active. Just over a fifth have a rate of six or higher. But perhaps it is necessary to set the standard for 'super-gladiator' rather higher. If we use ten as an arbitrary minimum qualification, only 4·4% could be classified that way – balancing the spectators. Amongst that number, there was one citizen who said 'yes' to 22 out of the 23 items, only 'missing', perhaps not surprisingly, on the use of physical force against political opponents. That person sets a standard of active citizenship which might be the envy of some radical democrats but is clearly not emulated by any but a tiny handful of others. Or, to put the matter another way, very high levels of activity are indeed concentrated amongst a rather small number of people. On the other hand, at least a minimum level of involvement is spread across nearly all.

Though figure 3.1 represents an important and very concrete baseline, it should be remembered that it does include voting and signing petitions. These actions require relatively little effort and, at least for the latter, may for some respondents imply the most casual and momentary of activities. We should, therefore, now look at the question of concentration and rates of mass participation through a more restricted lens and concentrate attention on those actions that do clearly require some time and effort.

For this purpose, therefore, we have excluded from our count four items – the three measures of voting and signing a petition. These were the four most frequently mentioned actions in table 3.1. Not surprisingly, the picture changes dramatically, as can be seen in figure 3.2. This shows that the average citizen has undertaken only about one and a half of the more demanding political activities over a five-year period. Indeed, the modal, or most common, response is none! Fully 45·8%, or nearly half, remained politically passive when more than a minimal amount of effort was required to raise their voices. In short, by this standard, the general tendency is not to participate – or at best

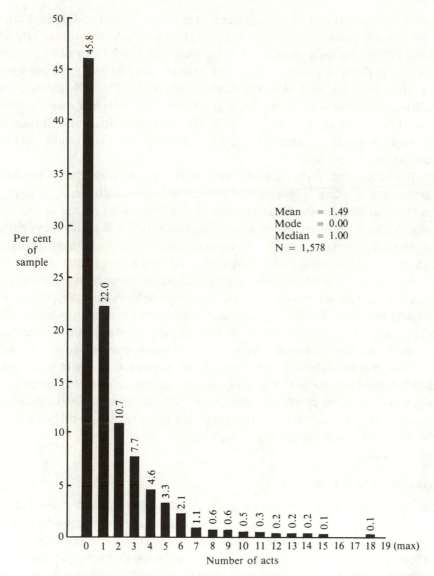

Figure 3.2 Number of acts of political participation, excluding voting and signing petitions (19 items)

very rarely indeed. Over three-quarters (78·5%) had ventured into the arena as gladiators only twice. For them, politics is largely a spectator sport.

Participation by citizens at a higher level is, conversely, very much a minority affair. In that respect, figures 3.1 and 3.2 deliver the same message. But whereas in figure 3.1 the spectators balanced the gladiators, in figure 3.2 (and using the same threshold but reduced by four items to six) those in the stands outnumber those in the arena by about eight to one. Mapped in this way, active participation is indeed concentrated in the hands of a very small proportion of the adult British population.

Some further sense of this can be gained if, as before, these results are set against the yardstick of another country – in this case the United States. We have already seen that, action by action, Americans do by and large seem to participate more and this is borne out by the 1987 survey reported by Nie *et al.* (1988:4–5) in which the average rate of activity beyond voting (signing a petition not being included) was 2·53, or not far short of double the British figure. Equally, at each activity level, many more Americans were to be found participating than in Britain. For example, whereas 13·7% of British citizens had undertaken at least four actions, the American figure (with a smaller total number to count) was 31% (Nie *et al.* 1988:4–5). Clearly, therefore, participation in Britain is substantially more concentrated than in America, whatever the uncertainties about question wording and time frames.

Whether a West European yardstick would show up the British citizenry in a different light is an interesting question. The evidence already discussed might imply that this would be so (see also Bennett and Resnick 1988:6). Unfortunately, we are not aware of any comparable analyses of concentration in those countries, and so this possibility must remain moot. However, what might change perceptions somewhat are the different compositions of the various populations being compared. The average adult American, for example, in 1987 had had around 13·4 years of schooling whereas the comparable figure in Britain was, from our survey, around 11.1, or roughly where the US was in 1967. Nie *et al.* (1988) show that this upward shift in education has had a considerable effect upon aggregate levels of participation. By this token, therefore, a true comparison of two (or more) populations would require complex adjustments of compositional differences, a task that would take us well beyond the scope of the present study (see Przeworski and Teune 1970:26–30).[5] We shall, however, make some further comments on these issues in subsequent chapters. Changes in levels of education will also have some relevance to any consideration of the long-term potential for participation – a matter to be discussed in our concluding thoughts.

The structure of participation

The evidence of the previous section begins to throw light upon the underlying nature of the participatory map. It shows that individual activism varies very considerably in Britain. Many, arguably almost half the population, can be characterised as spectators remaining effectively silent, at least outside of election contests. Conversely, a relatively small minority can truly be called gladiators, getting involved repeatedly in different forms of political action. This, in turn, suggests that political activity is a phenomenon with some pattern or structure to it. It is not, on the face of it, a random matter but one in which there are systematic individual differences in involvement in the political arena.

As a tool to look into the details of that structure, however, a simple count of individual actions is too limited an instrument. We must turn to more powerful statistical techniques specially devised for just this sort of task. In particular, factor analysis is a general method that can reveal patterns that may lie behind the detailed individual responses to our 23 questions about participation.[6] This procedure enables us to determine the extent to which we can re-express those responses in terms of a smaller number of more generalised forms of political activity. These would be, in a sense, equivalent to our count operation – which summarised individual action in one single score. The important difference is that here the number of these more general measures

Table 3.2 *The modes of political participation*

	Voting	Party campaigning	Collective action	Contacting	Direct action	Political violence
1 Vote local	0·82	—	—	—	—	—
2 Vote general	0·78	—	—	—	—	—
3 Vote European	0·72	—	—	—	—	—
4 Fund raising	—	0·85	—	—	—	—
5 Canvassed	—	0·85	—	—	—	—
6 Clerical work	—	0·78	—	—	—	—
7 Attended rally	—	0·59	0·23	—	—	—
8 Informal group	—	—	0·76	—	—	—
9 Organised group	—	—	0·72	—	—	—
10 Issue in group	—	0·21	0·58	—	—	—
11 Member of Parliament	—	—	—	0·73	—	—
12 Civil servant	—	—	—	0·69	—	0·22
13 Councillor	—	—	—	0·62	—	0·22
14 Town hall	—	—	—	0·54	—	0·23
15 Media	—	—	—	0·52	—	—
16 Attended prot. m/ing	—	—	0·60	—	0·22	—
17 Organised petition	—	—	0·51	—	—	—
18 Signed petition	—	—	0·49	—	—	—
19 Blocked traffic	—	—	—	—	0·76	0·23
20 Protest march	—	—	—	—	0·70	—
21 Political strike	—	—	—	—	0·58	0·35
22 Political boycott	—	—	—	—	0·45	—
23 Physical force	—	—	—	—	0·24	0·84

Scores represent the factor loadings, greater than ±0·20, derived from a rotated oblique factor pattern matrix (delta = 0). Total item variance explained by the six factors = 53·7%.[7]

(or 'factors'), and their specific make-up, would be determined essentially by the responses of those interviewed rather than being imposed by the researchers.

The results of the factor analysis of the 23 items of participation are set out in table 3.2. This indicates that there are six more general scales which, taken together, capture and express the underlying structure of the relationships between the 23 specific items of participation. It is very striking that these turn out to correspond closely to the distinct 'modes' of political participation which Verba and Nie detected in America (1972: ch. 3; see also Nie *et al*. 1988:6–7) and in other countries (Verba, Nie and Kim 1971:33–44) with, however, the addition of protest dimensions which were not part of the investigation by the Verba and Nie teams. The clear conclusion is that, in Britain as elsewhere, participation is a phenomenon with several facets. In other words, when describing a map of political action, it is necessary first of all to distinguish between several different forms of political action. One cannot simply speak of citizen involvement solely as though it were all of one piece – as in effect was assumed in our summary count operation. Six counts or scales are needed to do the job accurately.

The content of each of these specialised scales of participation is also set out in table

3.2 where, for clarity, only the stronger relationships (or 'factor loadings') between individual items and particular scales larger than 0·20 have been recorded.

Voting

The first of these scales, clearly, is a scale that measures participation through voting, because the only items that are counted in it are the three individual voting items – in the General Election, local elections and the European election. All three contribute roughly to the same degree to the voting scale, although casting a ballot in the European Election was slightly less important than the other two in distinguishing statistically between those who participate a lot in this way and those who participate very little.

Party campaigning

The second scale is almost equally sharply defined by four other specific activities, all relating to party campaigning (i.e. fund-raising, canvassing, clerical work and attending a rally). Fund-raising and canvassing, have a particularly central role in defining the scale because of their high loadings (0·85). Conversely, while clearly part of this campaigning mode, attending a party rally is more peripheral, possibly because it is more passive or less overtly gladiatorial than the first two. Finally, we have here, in responses to the question about raising an issue in an organised group, one of the very few instances where an item registers to a small extent on one scale while simultaneously featuring more prominently on another (in this instance, the third scale). This hints at the fact that whereas six very discrete modes of participation have been identified, they are not wholly disconnected one from the other. Thus, although this second scale is almost entirely about partisan-based collective action, there is some very small spill-over into other group-based forms of participation.

Collective action

The reason for such an outcome is perhaps made clearer if we look at the third scale itself. This is more complicated in that, uniquely amongst the six scales, it comprises items drawn from more than one of the notional 'family' of activities as they were initially set out in chart 3.1. Indeed, more important than that, the items also bridge the divide, often used, between 'conventional' and 'unconventional' spheres of political action, i.e. between voting, electoral, group and contacting activities on the one side and more direct forms of citizen protest on the other. This third scale is proof, in short, that such a distinction is, in practice, not easy to sustain. For here we have a mode of participation combining three 'conventional' group activities with three items of 'unconventional' political protest.

The product is a brand of political action that can perhaps best be described as 'collective action'. It consists principally of working through organised or through informal groups and to a less extent of using the group to raise an issue – the 'group activity' items in chart 3.1. But these are then combined with three relatively mild forms of protest activity – signing a petition, taking a petition round and attending a protest meeting. All of these forms of protest imply a degree of collective organisation and are techniques to which campaigning groups can readily resort. Indeed, this scale would also seem to capture an important phenomenon in contemporary British, and West European, politics – the 'pure pressure group' or 'political movement' (Moran 1985:141–2). These are, in essence, single-issue cause groups whose purpose is to challenge the traditional assumptions of policy-makers about such issues as defence and environmental protection and mobilise public opinion through dramatic gestures of political protest duly recorded and broadcast by the mass media (see also Dalton 1988:61; Byrne and Lovenduski 1983).

Contacting

The fourth 'mode' is, like the first two and unlike the third, again a relatively simple composite of the five items in chart 3.1 to do with contacting. In this instance, the most central to the scale are the two relating to contacts with the national level – the Member of Parliament and the civil service. These, more than the others, isolate and discriminate between citizens who contact a lot and those who contact only a little. What they contact about, of course, is an important matter which will be considered in later chapters. Here we need only note that in contacting we have yet another discrete mode of political participation which must be included in the overall map.

Direct action

Those 'protest' items left after the inclusion of three (i.e. signing and circulating petitions and attending a meeting) in the collective action scale form the fifth and sixth modes identified by the factor analysis. Their presence is perhaps some vindication of the distinction between conventional participation and protest, even though, as we have seen, important caveats have to be made about it. The fifth mode comprises the four major demonstrative forms of political protest included in our battery of questions. Amongst these, the most important in the formation of the scale are blocking traffic and protest marches, followed by joining political strikes and, lastly, engaging in a boycott. All in all, this would seem to identify what might be called a 'mainstream', yet distinct, form of 'direct action' in the British political context. On the one hand they constitute a set of actions clearly more conflictual and confrontational than the petitioning items. Indeed petitioning cannot, on this reading, be considered as part of political protest but as part of the collective action mode. On the other hand, these forms of direct action are considerably less extreme, and more frequent, than the one item which forms the sixth scale – the use of physical force against political opponents.

Political violence

The measure of physical force, in fact, only generated four positive responses, including an animal rights activist and a respondent who had done a tour of duty with the British army in Northern Ireland. The use of force is, therefore, so rare and so distinct from any other mode of action, including protest, as to constitute a very special case of participation. This is confirmed by responses to further questions about whether those interviewed would ever consider taking the various forms of action in the future. Only

37 individuals, or 0·3%, even thought that they might resort to physical force. By contrast, 178 persons, or 11·6%, said that they at least 'might' contemplate the next most infrequent protest activity, which was blocking traffic. It is clear that, in Britain at least, a sharp line is drawn both in people's minds and in their behaviour between political protest and political violence. The distinction corresponds very much with that made by Muller (1979) between 'civil disobedience' and 'political violence'. It may also reflect differential 'parameters of licence' (Barnes, Kaase *et al.* 1979:60–5). Certainly, it is striking that the three forms of 'protest' action most frequently undertaken are those which are so closely related to 'conventional' types of group action as to form part of a single 'collective action' mode of participation.

The picture of 'political protest' drawn from the findings reported in table 3.2 is just as 'multi-dimensional' as is conventional participation. There are those protest actions which 'belong' with collective action, i.e. petitioning and attending a meeting. There are what might be called 'mainstream' forms of protest like going on a protest march or being involved in a political strike. Finally, there is political violence, which is entirely set apart. In this conclusion, we diverge sharply from the analysis offered by the Barnes, Kaase team which represents the major earlier study of protest in Britain and other countries. This perceived protest as constituting a single scale from mild to extreme forms, the most extreme being personal violence which no one in that survey reported having employed. Admittedly, our conclusion could be said to reflect the fact that there were not more types of political violence mentioned in our battery of questions with correspondingly larger numbers of responses by interviewers referring to acts of violence. As it is, neither in the numbers of positive responses to our direct questions nor on the basis of the answers to more open-ended questions about activities are there sufficient data for us to construct a scale placing people on a continuum from mild protest to violence. Whatever the impression given by media reporting of occasional violent incidents, political violence is something so set apart from the 'mainstream' of political protest in mainland Britain that it barely registers in a national survey. There is, consequently, very little that we can say, with the materials presently to hand, beyond reporting its infrequency.

We have seen from table 3.2 how the original 23 items of political participation group themselves into six (or, eliminating political violence, five) discrete 'factors' or scales, each representing a particular form or mode of involvement. But what do these mean in concrete terms? What do they look like when we examine how active or inert our citizens are on each of them? To provide some answers, each scale could be considered as a specific 'ladder' of political activity, each ladder being composed on the basis of the factor analysis results set out in table 3.2. Thus, for example, the voting ladder combines responses on the original three questions about voting turnout so that those towards the top of the ladder would have relatively active and regular voting records, and those towards the bottom would be citizens who tended to stay at home and not vote. Similar ladders can be constructed for all the other scales, and the position of a respondent on them reflects how much action that particular citizen reports doing on the items that form each one.

Individuals have been given a score according to the amount of participation they have done on each mode. Those who are very active on the particular mode of participation receive a very high score and those very passive obtain a very low score. Furthermore, because individuals are spread out across each ladder differently, the ladders have to be very different in length. In some cases, the most active person is so 'extreme' that there has to be a very high ladder to accommodate him or her on the topmost rung. Meanwhile, the bulk of the population can be on the bottom few rungs. In other cases, the ladder is shorter because the most and the least participatory persons do not differ very much in their amounts of activity. In order to be able to make comparisons between the ladders, some statistical adjustments have been made so that they all have certain characteristics in common. The participation scores for the individuals, from highest to lowest, have been so arranged that the arithmetic average score (the *mean* score) is set at zero. Hence, all those individuals who participate less than the mean are given negative scores, whilst those who participate more have positive scores. But it should be noted that this does not necessarily imply that there will be 50% of individuals above and 50% below the mean of zero. This would only happen in the unlikely event of there being a perfectly symmetrical distribution of participants. As we shall see, this is not the case. Participants are not spread evenly or in any other symmetrical way up the rungs of the ladder. Thus, for example, in those cases where most people are bunched near the bottom of the ladder matched by a few very 'high scoring' persons further up, the middle person (the *median* individual) will be a low scorer; he or she may not obtain the *mean* of zero but have a negative score.

The other adjustment made, besides standardising the mean, is to equalise the amount of variation on each ladder. This is measured by the standard deviation and has been set at 100.[8] What we have done, in other words, is to make sure that each ladder has the same average amount of difference between individuals on each ladder. This is necessary because each ladder is composed of responses to a different number of items. On the voting ladder, for example, there are three – voting in European, general and local elections. For the contacting ladder, on the other hand, there are five items. As we do not want the ladder scores to reflect these somewhat arbitrary differences, the simplest solution is to standardise the variation across them all. Once they are put on the same basis, they can be more straightforwardly compared. This does not, of course, mean that the distributions end up looking the same. As we shall see, they certainly do not. What it does mean is that the differences in the way individuals are distributed on each of the ladders can be interpreted in a substantive way without having constantly to refer to technical factors in the way they were constructed.

The results for the five main scales are set out in figure 3.3. The voting ladder is exceptional in two main ways. First, it is much shorter than any of the others. Despite the average variation across all respondents being exactly the same as for the other scales, the difference between the most and least active is only 367, or five times less than the longest ladder – for political protest. The reason for this is that voting is an unusually widespread form of participation, but also one which is necessarily limited by the number of elections held during the five-year period. Hence, whether one votes a lot or a little, it is impossible to be markedly more or less active as a voter than the average person.[9] Or, to put it another way, those at the top and bottom of the voting ladder cannot be that far away from the mean.

The second difference is that the amount of the ladder below the mean is larger than

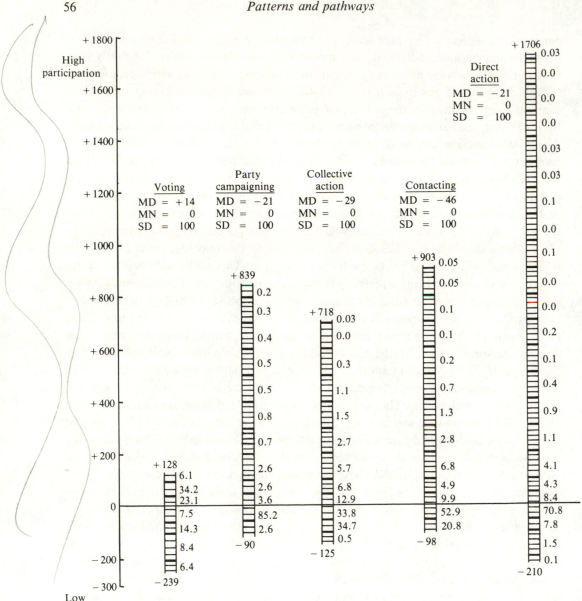

Figure 3.3 The five ladders of political participation. The figures along the ladders indicate the percentage of respondents with the relevant ranges of scores on the scales. MD = median; MN = mean; SD = standard deviation; N = 1,574.

that above. Again, this reflects the nature of voting in Britain, where large numbers of citizens do turn out and vote fairly regularly. In this situation, the person who does not bother ever to cast a ballot is more different from the norm than the individual who never misses an opportunity to vote.[10] We can, in fact, see the result of this in the score in figure 3.3 for the 'median' citizen – the one who has 50% of all the respondents below him or her and 50% above. This median score is +14 which means that more than half the total must also have positive scores, and a minority negative scores. Or, to put it another way, being a very infrequent voter is much more atypical than being a regular voter. Indeed, the citizen at the bottom of the ladder (-239) is nearly twice as far away from the average citizen as the most regular voter ($+129$).

It might, finally, be noted that these exceptional characteristics are not found only in Britain. In the United States exactly the same outcome is to be found. There, Verba and Nie (1972:129–30, fn. 5) found the voting ladder to be 296 units long, or half the length of the longest other ladder ('communal' participation). The median individual had a positive score of $+36$, and the highest and lowest scores were $+71$ and -225 respectively. It seems, therefore, that the British voting ladder is likely to be very typical of similar ladders in other liberal democracies – reflecting the similar underlying characteristics of voting.

The other four scales share an opposite set of tendencies to voting, although the extent to which this is the case is in some respects much greater in the case of direct action. Thus, three ladders – for campaigning, collective action and contacting – are very similar. They are all of roughly the same length – about two and a half times the length of the voting scale – and they are all much longer above the mean score of zero than below. They all, finally, have median scores that are negative, -21 for campaigning, for example, and -29 for collective action.

The reasons for these characteristics are also precisely the opposite of those for voting. Here we have forms of participation that are not widespread, and yet where, in principle, the opportunities for doing them are less restricted than for voting. One can, for example, raise funds or do clerical work for a party more or less any time. Equally, contacting and forming a group does not have to wait for election day either. But, despite this openness, relatively few avail themselves of the opportunity to do so.[11] The result is a ladder on which those that do so (at the top) are much further away from the mean than those right at the bottom. In the case of campaigning, for example, the hyper-activist who scored $+839$ is nearly ten times further away from the mean than the citizen at the very bottom of the ladder, who scored -90.

If, alternatively, one were to visualise, for a moment, these three ladders as having 100 rungs, there would be 50% of the respondents clustered tightly together on about the bottom ten rungs and the other 50% spread out increasingly thinly up the remaining 90 rungs. By the same comparison, the direct action ladder would have 200 rungs with 50% again down on around the bottom ten steps and the other 50% along, this time, the remaining 190. The most active protester looks down from a dizzy height onto both the average and the least active individual.

These ladders, and their associated characteristics, provide us with the main tools for the study of political participation in Britain. But we can delve even deeper into the structure of action by examining the relationships between the ladders themselves. As we have seen, the factor analysis showed that participation is structured into distinct modes. Nevertheless, the fact that these modes are distinct does not necessarily imply that they are totally unrelated. In fact, in allowing for scales to emerge which could be related to one another rather than constraining them to be independent (see table 3.3), we explicitly left this question open for the response patterns themselves to resolve. This was done in part because we had noted that all or most of the 23 individual items of participation had some positive association with one another. This might, in turn, suggest that the scales themselves would be related in some way.

In order to test this possibility, we started by looking at the correlations between the five ladders to see if any of the association amongst the original items could still be detected. The results, set out in part A of table 3.3, indicate that there are, indeed, at least some linkages amongst the scales. It is true that, on average, they are not very strong, which merely reinforces the extent to which each is a distinct mode of participation. But some correlations are large enough to be worthy of comment and further exploration. The biggest correlation, for example, is between collective action and contacting ($r = 0.37$). Not far behind is the association between collective action and campaigning (0.32). In so far as the third largest correlation ties together contacting and campaigning, we can begin to see something of an empirical bond amongst these three forms of participation analogous, at a deeper structural level, to the bonds that tied bundles of items together in the factor analysis of table 3.2.

That this triad of ladders shares a linkage that does not extend to the other two can be seen initially in the other correlations. Only one of them, that between collective action and direct action, is of the same general strength. This particular association is quite understandable, if we remember that collective action contains in its composition three items (attending a protest meeting, signing and circulating a petition) which were originally listed under the protest umbrella. However, the correlations between the direct action scale and the other two ladders are very weak. The voting ladder has uniformly low associations, and that with direct action is effectively zero. Those two scales are totally independent of each other.

What this means is that whether a citizen votes a lot or a little has absolutely nothing to do with how active a protestor that person is. This finding is particularly significant for understanding political participation in Britain. Clearly, as a general rule, there is no systematic trade-off between voting and protest. In Britain, whether one votes or takes part in protest are entirely unrelated matters.

What is going on here can best be summarised and re-expressed in more technical terms through the magnitude of the average correlations between the five scales at the bottom of part A of table 3.3, or the loadings of a 'second-order' factor analysis which are set out in part B. They tell the same story, which is that there is a modest extent to which the individual ladders come together to form a single overall 'super-ladder'. Or, at least three of them do – the three already noted as having uniformly moderate correlations between themselves: collective action, contacting and campaigning. These three, in other words, form the core of a general across-the-board scale of political participation with collective action at the top of the list. One could say, in other words, that if one wanted to measure political participation in Britain in a general way, or to distinguish best between gladiators and spectators, one would use, above all, a measure of collective action such as we have operationalised. Bearing in mind that this measure contains items of political protest, albeit such 'moderate' activities as going to a protest meeting and petitioning, we see here evidence of one way that certain types of protest do enter the centre-stage of the political arena.

Contacting and campaigning, as forms of political action, also do almost as well as collective action in defining the empirical core of participation, and all three together are, of course, the best guide of all. On the other hand, the least relevant would be a measure of voting which, judging by the factor loadings, clearly has the smallest

Table 3.3 *Relationships amongst the five scales of participation*

	Voting	Party campaigning	Collective action	Contacting	Direct action
A: Correlations					
Voting	1·00	—	—	—	—
Party campaigning	0·13	1·00	—	—	—
Collective action	0·13	0·32	1·00	—	—
Contacting	0·11	0·25	0·37	1·00	—
Direct action	0·02	0·12	0·24	0·13	1·00
Average correlation	0·08	0·17	0·22	0·18	0·10
B: Factor analysis					
Factor loadings*	0·26	0·64	0·77	0·68	0·46

* Oblique factor pattern (delta = 0).

association with the overall super-ladder. This is, perhaps, ironical bearing in mind the extent to which it has been taken in the past as the primary indicator of participation.

It is important to be clear, however, as to what is, and is not, being asserted. We are not claiming, as some participatory democrats have done, that voting is an 'unimportant' form of political participation. We have already pointed out that for many people it is their only form of political action. For some democratic theorists, it is also the only type of citizen action that matters. Rather, our intention is to affirm a paradox about voting. The very fact that so many people vote means that one cannot predict whether a person who votes will take part in any other forms of action. This makes voting a very poor instrument either for showing the extent of participation more generally or helping to pick out those citizens who are high on the overall ladder as against those who are low.

The 'super-ladder' of participation will be called the 'overall participation scale' and will be used throughout the chapters that make up part II of this study. We justify its use on three grounds. First, there is some empirical support without which, obviously, we would not proceed. It is the case, as has been seen, that participation in Britain is above all multi-dimensional in character. Nevertheless, those different dimensions are related to one another, albeit relatively weakly and more in some instances than others. The use of the single scale is also justifiable on expository grounds – as a summary of patterns of participation as a whole, even if that summary tends to be rather rough and ready. It allows us, in other words, to try to present pictures of the shape of the wood, even if at some cost to the representation of individual trees within it. But where there are important particular deviations from those general patterns, we say so. Thirdly, there is a sense in which the import of participation lies in its aggregate volume as much as in its component parts. To that extent, using a scale which combines all forms of participation into one measure has a certain substantive merit. This argument also applies to the use of the simple additive scores set out in figures 3.1 and 3.2.

Hence, the centrepiece of the general analysis is undoubtedly the 'overall participation scale' and so it is appropriate to conclude the discussion of the structure of political

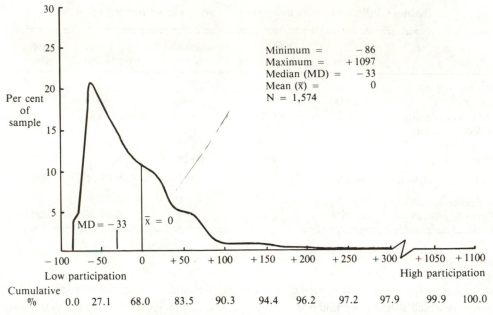

Figure 3.4 The overall political participation scale

action by describing it in some detail. This is done in figure 3.4 in the form of a graph displaying a ladder exactly 1,183 units long. This makes it much shorter than the protesting ladder, but slightly longer than those for collective action, contacting or campaigning. There are 4·0% of the total who are tied at the bottom with a score of −86. These are the 'hard-core' spectators whom we have already met in figure 3.1. Just above them, there is a very large number of individuals all with negative scores. In fact, 68% are in this position, a measure of the 'bulk' necessary to counter-balance the small numbers of 'super-gladiators' strung out across the top part of the ladder. We can see, indeed, that the top 80% of the ladder (scores of +150 or more) is occupied by no more than 5·6% of the total sample. At the very highest levels of activity, exactly half of the ladder contains a mere 0·6% of citizens. Or, to put the matter another, and by now familiar, way, being a gladiator, especially a 'super-gladiator', is comparatively a very rare phenomenon indeed. The 'prize' of *victor ludorum* goes to one person who scored 1,097, just ahead of another at 1,044. These are the two who said that they had performed 21 and 22 out of the 23 types of action referred to in our questions. To give just one measure of how remarkable they are, the size of the distance between them and the next persons on the ladder (250 units down to 795) would contain, at the bottom of the ladder, 95% of the remaining citizens. Such is the extent of the maldistribution of political participation in the British populace today, a maldistribution that seems more pronounced than in the United States (see Verba and Nie 1972:129). Political activity in Britain is sustained by a small segment of the population.

We can now draw together the main features of our map of political participation in Britain. The course of the analysis has moved successively, from 23 individual indicators to six broader modes and thence to a single overall summary scale. As these various scales (or ladders) will form the basis of the remaining chapters in this part of the volume, it is worthwhile re-presenting them in diagrammatic form as set out in chart 3.2.

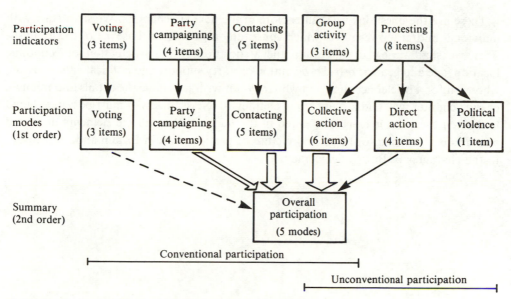

* Thickness of arrows between individual modes and summary scale
  indicates strength of contribution in composing that scale.

Chart 3.2 Structure and nomenclature of political participation

The chart shows how the underlying structure of the map reveals itself. The fine detail, as it were, are the 23 individual indicators, listed in chart 3.1, ranging from voting in a general election to the use of physical force against political opponents. This represents a very broad range of citizen participation. This very detailed map is then resolved into six broader modes of action. In one instance, however, that of political violence, there were too few responses to provide a stable and reliable measure and so it was dropped. We can then compose the remaining five modes into one summary scale. The advantage of this single scale is that it allows us to present participation in terms of one ladder. But, whereas this ladder is very useful for certain purposes of presentation, it must be stressed, once again, that it entails a considerable loss of detail. Political participation is very strongly multi-dimensional in character. Nevertheless, to the much lesser extent that one single dimension can stand in its stead as a summary statement of participation, the overall scale can serve a useful purpose.

This super-scale, as is indicated by the strength of the arrows in the chart, derives principally from collective action but also receives major inputs from party campaigning and contacting. As such, it encompasses or transcends the distinction often drawn between electoral and non-electoral and between conventional and unconventional. In late-twentieth-century Britain, citizen participation means far more than taking part in the electoral arena. It involves a range of other specialised engagements in groups, in protesting and in contacting representatives and officials. It is here that we find the activists who sustain democratic politics, often on behalf of their fellow citizens.

But who are these activists and where do they come from? Or, to put it another way, why are some individuals high on some, or even all, of the ladders of participation whilst others seem anchored firmly at the bottom? What is it that facilitates, or enables, participation?

These are the questions we shall explore in the next six chapters. We shall start with individual and group resources which constitute, together, the baseline of the analysis. Then we shall review in succession the association with participation of economic location, age and gender, broad civic outlooks, party support and political values. Those who wish for a briefer account, and who may not wish to pursue the details and nuances of each chapter, will find a summary in chapter 10. Nevertheless, it must be remembered that often the truth is to be discovered in the nuances. And all the elements discussed contribute something to the general picture of participation in Britain and, as a result, to the character of British democracy.

4

INDIVIDUAL RESOURCES

We have seen in the previous chapter that individuals in Britain vary quite considerably both in their propensities to enter the political arena and in the styles of participation they espouse. There are those for whom political action is a major preoccupation even though they still clearly remain 'ordinary citizens' rather than becoming professional politicians. Conversely, there are others, far more typical of the generality of British adults, who remain relatively passive. They may be aware of the political world, especially at election times, but find no real place in it for themselves. Some citizens, in other words, exercise their rights to be heard fully and repeatedly while others remain more or less silent.

Why is this so? What leads some people to participate and others not? This is a key question which lies at the heart of how mass involvement in the political system comes about. Views about the prospects for something more than the modest levels of participation currently found in Britain may be affected by any understanding that can be gained of what in fact drives people to action.

As was suggested in chapter 1, there are two very broad possibilities to be considered. One is that participation is promoted by issues. Individuals may differ significantly in the extent to which they perceive issues about which they feel sufficiently moved to take some form of public action. Some individuals, indeed, may feel unable to identify any problems or needs that might suggest a need for personal intervention in the public domain. Others, by contrast, may have a number of burning questions about which they feel impelled to take action. In some cases, intervention is in reaction to an issue created by the authorities. In others, the individual may formulate the issue himself or herself or with others and put it on the agenda. This kind of explicit issue-based model has not, however, been given so much attention in studies of participation, especially at the national level, even though it focuses on the immediate context of events that triggered action off. It is, however, a critical part of the theme of chapter 11.

The second way of looking at what drives participation is more common. It moves back from considering these immediate triggering factors to look at longer term conditions which distinguish the active from the inert. The aim is to establish whether there are more enduring conditions or forces which lead some categories of people to have a greater propensity to act than others. A consideration of these forces may then throw light upon how the issues themselves, which form the content of the participatory input, are treated within the political system. It is these more 'background' or structural elements that are the subject of the present chapter and the remainder of part II.

An analytical framework

In looking at the factors which constrain or promote participation, we start with the notion of 'resources'. By 'resources' we mean material wealth, education and skills, and membership of organised groups. These are all 'resources' in the sense that they can be employed to advantage by those who possess them in any attempts to promote their own interests by some form of political action. Wealth may be used to fund more successful campaigns of protest against a threat to one's immediate environment; education can improve one's capacity to communicate one's views; membership of groups can provide access to positions of influence in society or further collective backing for one's objectives. Thus, resources can put one in a better position to participate with a possibly greater prospect of success. A lack of resources might be expected to make successful participation appear much more of an uphill struggle.

But the possession of resources could be said not merely to facilitate participation but also be an incentive to it. If, as seems to be the case, participation is largely an instrumental activity in which people act to promote or defend their interests, then those in advantageous positions may well use such positions to further their interests through political participation as much as through any other social or economic means. That, at least, is the proposition we wish to explore in this chapter. Is it the case that those who are well endowed with resources show a markedly greater propensity to become participants?

In choosing this as the starting point we are making no claim to novelty. Instead, we are seeking to build upon a body of empirical theory that takes a generally similar view and upon empirical research of other countries that has adduced considerable evidence in its support. In their classic study of America, Verba and Nie (1972) termed this the 'standard model'.[1] However, we should enter three important caveats before proceeding. First, in adopting this starting point, we are not ruling out of consideration the possibility that some people may engage in political action for other than instrumental reasons. It may be that, for such people, resources are of less consequence, at least as an incentive to participate, even though participation may also be made easier and more effective.

Secondly, there is no assumption that resources are equally relevant to all the various modes of participation in which people engage. Certainly, their role is generally significant, but the extent and shape of the part they play may well vary in important respects according to the particular type of activity. Different resources may, in short, turn out to be more relevant in one sphere than in another.

Thirdly, in proposing the resource hypothesis as a point of departure, it is not implied that other individual circumstances may not be relevant. Later chapters will, indeed, go on to look at a wide array of social, economic and attitudinal factors to see what contribution they can make to our overall understanding of participation. But, in doing so, that contribution will be treated as something over and above the impact made by resources. In that sense, therefore, resources are taken to be the baseline to which other elements are added. However, this does not mean that those other factors are prevented from being recognised as powerful influences in their own right, possibly eclipsing resources in particular situations. The method of analysis enables these factors to be considered as distinct elements. But it does entail that these other factors must be empirically and theoretically distinct from resources. The additional background characteristics must contribute something separate from resources themselves. Sometimes this distinction is reasonably clear. In principle, one can suppose that age and gender might represent influences on patterns of participation, aside from questions of resources. In other cases, the division is more arguable, especially perhaps in the case of occupational class with which the possession of resources is so intimately connected.

The position can be made clearer if we consider what is meant concretely by 'resources'. The approach we have adopted is broadly in line with that developed by Verba and his fellow researchers (Verba, Nie and Kim 1978; Schlozman and Verba 1979). Like them, we make a basic, if somewhat heuristic, distinction between individual resources and those based on groups. Under the heading of individual resources, Verba's teams include a wide variety of ingredients – 'money or other material resources, time, prestige and political skill' (Verba, Nie and Kim 1978:11). They then argue that the possession of a number of attitudes highly relevant to political participation is resource-related. Attitudes such as 'a sense of political efficacy, intense political interest, or adherence to civic norms supportive of political activity' (Schlozman and Verba 1979:225; also Verba and Nie 1972:13) are likely to be generated by wealth and the exposure to education. Resources, combined with these resource-created attitudes, can then be converted into political activity.

But whilst this is a very persuasive argument, we wish for the moment to keep entirely separate the question of how resources relate to political outlooks and action (see chapters 8 and 9). In particular, we do not wish to make any prior assumption that the link between material, educational and organisational resources and action is provided by the possession of what might be regarded as resources of a more socio-psychological nature in the form of a number of civic attitudes or orientations. Furthermore, experience in the USA shows that there is not necessarily a constant or simple linkage between resources and attitudes (Conway 1985:44–5). The nature of this linkage, and the consequences for participation, deserve separate and detailed consideration.

Our own analysis is, at this first stage, equally, if not more, compatible with the 'rational choice' view that there is a direct link between resources and participation provided by a person's 'rational' assessment of the chances of successful action given his or her resources relative to others (Goodin and Dryzek 1980). In other words, if the poor can realistically size up the situation as one in which they are individually virtually powerless whilst the rich are powerful, it would hardly be worthwhile their participating, and their civic orientations would not need to come into the argument.

Our focus is on two central aspects of individual resources. The first taps a material component and is based on several indicators of individual (or family) wealth. The second measures an essentially non-material resource in the form of personal skills. This is operationalised by an assessment of the level of formal educational qualifications attained by individuals.

Group-based resources, by contrast, derive in essence from an individual's membership of formally organised collectivities. In the British political system, as in most other modern democratic polities, such groups can play an important role both in setting the agenda and in influencing governmental decisions. Most central to this are the parties which, of course, specialise in political affairs and compete for control of the decision-making process. Membership in the governing party, for example, be it at local or national level, therefore provides a channel of influence not available to others. Here it is necessary to draw a distinction which is important to much of the subsequent analysis. The definition of participation we have employed is based on actions, on doing things which are intended to have some effect on political outcomes. We do not, accordingly, include mere membership of a group, even of a political party, as constituting an act of participation in itself. It is perfectly possible to join a group or a party or a trade union and to play an entirely passive role. This is something those running such organisations will readily admit. Even the action of joining a group, union or party does not always imply a commitment to its purposes but may be done as a result of peer pressure, economic necessity or social aspiration. For these reasons, we have, throughout, sought to retain this distinction between membership as such and the actions, which membership may well encourage, which make someone into a participant.

Thus memberships of political parties, formal groups such as trades unions and even social clubs are counted as resources which place someone in a position to participate politically. Membership of social clubs may not necessarily be directly relevant to political participation, although the extent to which social and political issues are discussed, even in such organisations, is something we take into account. Moreover, such clubs and organisations, as well as developing their own collective interests and action, can, in certain circumstances, provide backing for action by individual members through contacts, information and moral support.

Resources such as these are, of course, not unrelated to other social factors; people do not possess them entirely as some form of natural endowment, even in the case of skills. If resources are behind participation, there are other social forces which in turn provide the background for resources. In particular, occupational class is likely to be closely related to the possession of most of these resources. A person's location in the labour market is a major element determining what resources he or she will have to employ for a variety of purposes. However, there are good theoretical and practical reasons for distinguishing between resources and class rather than incorporating both in a more inclusive notion of class. The point will be made more fully in chapter 6 but, briefly, there is some variation between class location and the possession of certain resources, and this variation is potentially of political significance. Only by separating these elements can one try to detect what effects are to be attributed to resources and what to class in a restricted sense of the term.

Generally speaking, one would anticipate that those in subordinate and usually less well-paid occupational classes will have fewer individual resources. However, the traditional political response of such classes has been to mobilise for collective action, especially in trades unions and parties based on the working class. In this way, they may acquire group resources. The creation of the British Labour Party is a classic instance. For these reasons, individual and group resources need to be looked at both separately and together. It may be true, as Verba, Nie and Kim put it, that 'organisation...is the weapon of the weak' (1978:15) – that, by acting collectively, individuals who lack personal resources can compensate for their disadvantages. However, as noted in chapter 1, this can cut two ways. Participation, and especially collective action exploiting group-based resources, can be used by the worse-off to correct by political means the imbalances which have been produced by economic forces or by social history. But participation and organisation can also be the weapon of those already well-endowed as individuals. Indeed, the very resources they possess as individuals can stand them in good stead in enabling them to set up, or at least to join, powerful and effective organisations (see Pizzorno 1970).

Finally, organisations may offer support to some groups of people for reasons other than individual resources. For example, religious organisations, including in some countries religious parties, may seek to activate co-religionists as a group rather than only the better-off amongst them. In other words, organisations can mobilise some and filter out others. The relationship between the various individual or group resources and participation can, therefore, differ from one society to another. What we now have to turn to examine is the question whether, in Britain, it is the case that resources are closely linked to political participation and, if so, which particular resource or combination of resources is the prime moving force.[2]

Measures of individual resources

As mentioned in the previous section, the analysis of the effect of individual resources is based upon two measures, representing material and non-material dimensions of the concept. The material dimension takes in a number of specific indicators – income, home ownership, car ownership and ownership of stocks and shares. Taken together they would appear sufficient to discriminate those with substantial personal or household resources – 'the wealthy' – from those with relatively few – 'the poor'.

The evidence shows that, at the time of our study in 1984–5, as many as 72% of households in our survey either owned, or had regular use of, a car. A relatively similar proportion, some 68·4%, also claimed to own their accommodation – either outright or with the aid of a loan or a mortgage. The third ingredient, however, stocks and shares ownership, extended only to some 12·9%, although in this instance particularly, there is reason to think that subsequent Government privatisation schemes may have enlarged the proportion significantly.[3] The fourth element also suggests important disparities between different sections of society. Respondents were asked to place themselves in one of twelve income bands. Just under a tenth (9·5%) selected the lowest band and a further 12·1% the next lowest. By contrast, 6·8% of respondents placed themselves in the second highest stratum and there were a further 5·6% who were in the topmost band of all. The income of the top band was approximately 13 times that of the lowest band.

A factor analysis of these four elements was then undertaken to produce a single overall wealth index. As it turned out, income was the most central item, although the results also indicated that home ownership and household access to a car were almost as important ingredients. The one item distinctly less statistically relevant to the wealth scale was share ownership, although even its contribution was far from negligible. But the most important conclusion was that the four items did, indeed, form a single scale. By this means, we are able to make refined distinctions between wealthy and poor.

The non-material side of individual resources was measured through formal educational qualifications. This we took to be a better and more explicit operationalisation of skills than a mere count of the number of years of schooling irrespective of whether any formal skills were acquired. It does, of course, put something of a premium upon those skills measurable by formal educational means, such as literacy and numeracy, rather than more informal social skills like leadership or the ability to mix well with others. The latter may well be relevant to political participation, but appropriate and, above all, reliable evidence on these elements is unfortunately not available.

Responses as to formal educational qualifications showed that nearly half (46·5%) had none at all. Equally, a further 11·8% had certificates representing achievements below GCE 'Ordinary' Level, the traditional first rung on the scholastic ladder. At the top end, 6·6% indicated that they held a university or polytechnic degree, or its equivalent, and 9·8% said that they held a college-level diploma ranking just below graduate status.

One final, but important, preliminary question concerns the relationship between these two sets of individual resources. Do they operate relatively independently of each other, or is it the case that they seem to form one relatively integrated syndrome in which the well-resourced are advantaged across the board? The evidence, as can be seen in table 4.1, seems clearly to favour the second alternative. Whether we look at the relationship in terms of the relative wealth of different educational strata, or the educational achievements of various wealth groupings, there is quite a strong association between the two. For example, just 10·4% of those with no educational qualifications came from the wealthiest quarter of the population compared with 63·4% of college graduates. On the other hand, the relationship is not so strong that lacking formal educational skills entails exclusion from the wealthiest stratum, or that holding a degree is a guarantee of relative affluence. The only instance of this sort is that not a single graduate in our survey was found amongst the very poorest 5% of the population – which may provide some incentive to undergraduate studies! But, by and large, the wealthy do have relatively high levels of educational skills, while the poor do not. In that sense, Britain is a society in which material and non-material resources consistently favour some individuals, whilst simultaneously disadvantaging others.

Education

Our concern, however, is whether these individual resource differences are reflected at all in patterns of political participation. To take educational skills first, are university and polytechnic graduates significantly more likely to be politically active than those lacking these kinds of skills, or does it make little difference? The evidence, not surprisingly perhaps, is that generally there is such an effect, the extent of which can be seen in figure 4.1.[4] The evidence is couched in terms of the average score of any given category of persons on the ladder of overall political participation. Positive scores indicate that the group in question tended to participate more than the general average (zero), while negative ones suggest the opposite. The larger the differences across the groups, the more significant is the specific attribute (in this case, education) for explaining variations in the given form of participation. (A measure of this, eta, is provided in the figure. The eta

Table 4.1 *Wealth and education*

	% in poorest 25%	% in richest 25%	N
Educational qualifications			
None	37·6	10·4	595
Less than 'O' level	21·2	23·7	156
'O' level and equivalent	9·6	30·0	240
'A' level and equivalent	20·2	35·1	94
College/Further Education Diploma	5·7	49·3	140
Degree	11·8	63·4	93
Total	24·0	25·2	1318
Wealth stratum	% no qualifications	% degree	
Poorest 5%	67·7	0·0	65
Next poorest 19%	71·4	4·4	252
Next poorest 18%	58·1	2·9	241
Above average 33%	39·7	4·0	428
Second richest 20%	21·5	16·9	261
Richest 5%	8·5	21·1	71
Total	46·5	6·6	1318

value ranges between zero (no association at all) and $+1·0$ (a perfect association). As a rule of thumb, we suggest that any value under 0·10 is very weak and 0·20 might be called weak to moderate in strength, whereas 0·20 to 0·30 might suggest a moderate to quite strong association. Any over 0·30 (and they are relatively scarce in survey research) we would consider strong, with those over 0·40 very strong.)[5]

Looking at the relationship between education and participation in detail, we can see a relatively strong linear progression in levels of participation from the bottom of the educational ladder to the top. (This is reflected in the linear correlation, r, which has a value of $+0·27$, being similar to the eta of 0·29.) What this represents in concrete terms can be appreciated by relating the scores to the graph in figure 3.4. The 46·4% of the population without any formal educational skills are located right in the midst of the low participants below the mean, towards the very bottom of the ladder. By contrast, the degree-holders are not only an educational elite, but they are also a participatory 'elite'. Their score of $+80$ puts them almost at the point where the long thin stratum of hyper-participants begins. Indeed, they are amongst the top 12% of participants in the entire sample.

The connection between education and participation can be put in more concrete terms by looking at the average number of actions, beyond voting and signing petitions, undertaken by each stratum. These are displayed in figure 4.2. Thus, the formally uneducated undertake about one action, on average, beyond voting and signing petitions. This is almost exactly on the median for the population as a whole (see figure 3.2). Conversely, the degree-holders engage in nearly $3\frac{1}{2}$ actions on average which, in the context of the overall British profile, puts them in a very politicised position.

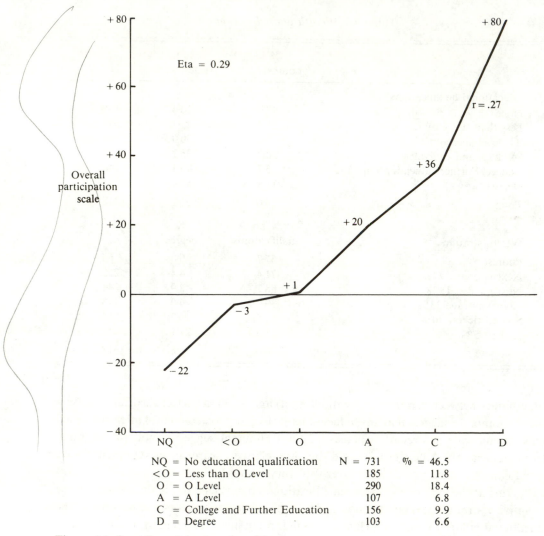

Figure 4.1 Overall participation, by education

So far the analysis has only looked at the apparent effect of educational resources on political participation by itself. It is necessary, however, to consider the possibility that at least part of these variations may be spurious – the result of wealth differentials, or even group-based factors, rather than education *per se*. Such a task is readily accomplished with the use of multiple classification analysis (see below, note 4). This makes it possible to highlight the relationship between education and participation whilst simultaneously controlling for a number (up to a computational limit of 20) of other possibly confounding 'independent' variables.[6] In the event, the relationship with education, though substantially reduced, does remain intact, as can be seen in figure 4.3. Thus, the least educated remain also the least participatory, and the degree-holders remain markedly more active than any of the other groups ($r = 0.15$). However, the strength of the educational effect is nearly halved – as can be seen in the difference between the basic correlation measures (eta $= 0.29$) and the adjusted correlation (beta $= 0.15$). (The beta statistic summarises the strength of the relationship, linear or

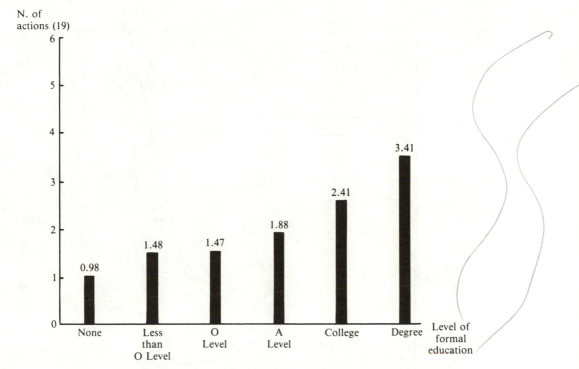

N. of
actions (19)

Figure 4.2 Number of actions, beyond voting and signing petitions by education

non-linear, between, in this instance education and participation, after making allowance for other factors, in this case for other resources.[7]) This reduction in the explanatory power of education, through its partial overlap or association with other resource factors, is also reflected in the reduction in the range of participation scores between the least and best educated from 102 points to 52.

The net effect of these resource adjustments can also be seen in the count of political actions (beyond voting and petitioning). Here, the rate of action of the least educated rises (from 0·98 in figure 4.2 to 1.20) and that of the degree-holder declines (from 3·41 to 2·44). But there is still a pronounced effect: the graduates, on this revised basis, remain twice as participatory as those lacking educational qualifications. In short, education is an important resource for individual participation, and continues to be so even when other resource factors are taken into account.

Perhaps the best way of exploring the substantive meaning of this educational effect is to look at the relationship it forms with each particular mode of political participation. These are set out in figure 4.4, using the same format as in figure 4.3. As can be seen, there are some significant variations in some of the patterns. Nevertheless, in general, what holds for the overall measure also holds for the specific modes. That is, educational resources are relevant to most forms of participation and although that relevance is reduced, it is not eliminated when resource factors are drawn into the analysis.

Collective action is the clearest in this regard. There is a moderate basic relationship (eta = 0·30; simple r = 0·27) which is considerably reduced but remains significant when other controls are applied (beta = 0·19; partial r = 0·16). For this mode, therefore, individual educational resources remain relevant and 'convertible'. This may in part

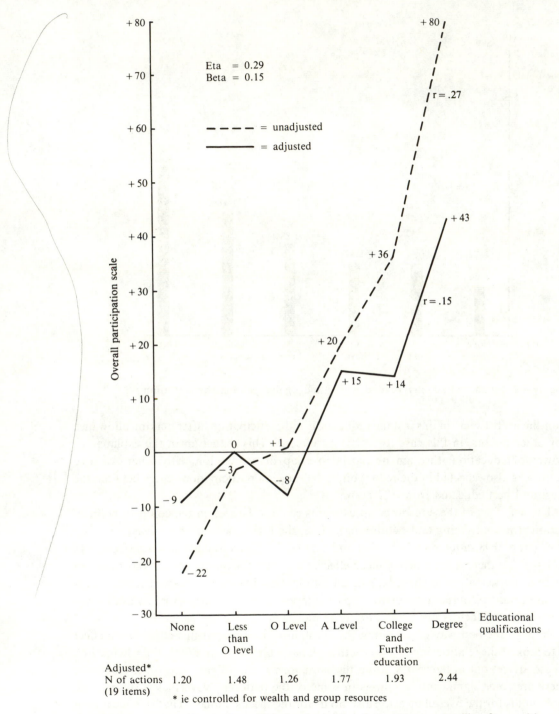

Figure 4.3 Amount of overall participation by levels of education, controlling for wealth and group resources

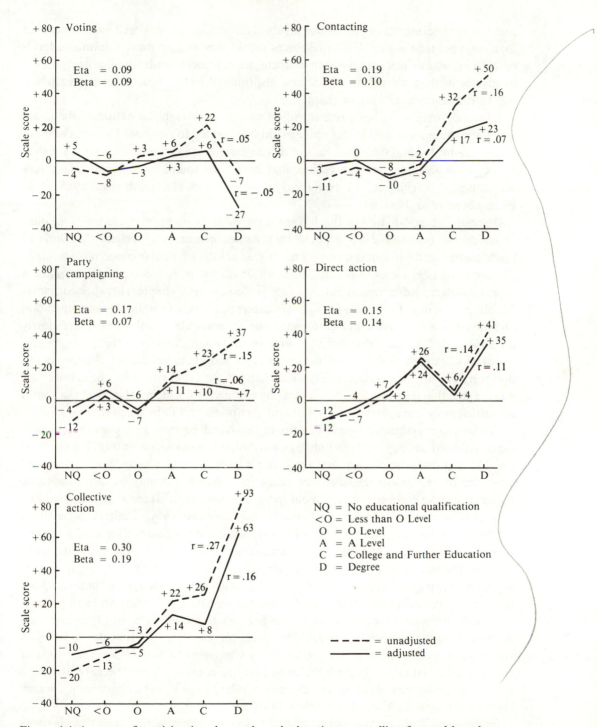

Figure 4.4 Amount of participation, by mode and education, controlling for wealth and group-based resources

come about because the organisations involved are less hierarchical and elite-dominated than, say, political parties. These resources would then remain more relevant to levels of activity within the groups than if there were leaders controlling organisational involvement 'from above'. But quite how institutional factors bear on collective action will be discussed more fully in chapter 5.

Education may also play a role in collective action through the nature of the issues which the groups involved in this mode might be expected to espouse. These, as we have noted, are probably the kind of radical or progressive causes, such as women's rights, environmentalism and animal welfare, that have been found strongly to attract very well-educated people (see, for example, Parkin 1968:166–81; Heath *et al.* 1985:64–6; Himmelweit *et al.* 1981:60).

One possible explanation of this linkage is provided by the 'post-materialist' account in which the better-educated espouse such causes because they reflect the kinds of fundamental aesthetic and intellectual needs that are the particular concern of that type of individual (see, for example, Inglehart 1977:42).[8] It is, however, better to make a more considered judgement about this when we look in later chapters at other correlates of collective action. For, as we indicate in chapter 9, the relationship between education and values is not always a straightforward one. In particular, feminism is more clearly an emphasis of the well-educated than environmentalism. A concern for 'green/peace' issues now extends well beyond the confines of university graduates. At this point, however, we can state unequivocally that whatever the explanation for the connection, it is the case that the educated, degree-holding elite are by far the most active in this form of participation even after their wealth and group-resources are taken into account.

Contacting also shows a basic similarity to the overall pattern. For, even though both the unadjusted and adjusted relationships are distinctly weaker (eta = 0·19, beta = 0·10; r = 0·16 and 0·06), we can see that the better educated contact more, both before and after wealth and group resources are taken into account. It may be that graduates, noticeably, have more to contact about, especially over such issues as property-related and other local 'environmental' matters as well as about education itself. As we shall see in a later chapter, they do have longer issue agendas. But the controls for wealth suggest that it is more than that. It seems that educational skills, in a strict sense of the term, may in this instance be an important part of the explanation. For it might well be expected that formal educational skills would provide exactly the kind of individualised resources that would make this type of participation easier. After all, contacting puts a particular premium on individuals working out how to put forward their 'demand' and identifying an appropriate 'target'. In practice, however, it is only those with educational qualifications at the tertiary level who seem to benefit from this type of educational advantage. They are the most likely to contact, in part because of wealth and group affiliations. But they are also more willing or able to be active in this sphere through the skills that higher education imparts.

Educational skills are also clearly related to levels of direct action such that, perhaps surprisingly, those with the highest qualifications, the degree-holders, are again the most active (eta = 0·15, beta = 0·14, r = 0·14 and 0·11). Protest, in other words, is not located where some might expect to find it, at the bottom of the educational hierarchy, but amongst those at the top – those who have, to this extent at least, been successes in life.

But, given that collective action and direct action are related phenomena (see table 3.3), perhaps this is not difficult to explain. Indeed, we suspect that, in part, a similar imperative may be at work – namely the use of direct action techniques to address those issues espoused by the 'progressive' intelligentsia. This has been offered as a major explanation of protest in other research (Marsh 1977; Inglehart 1977; Barnes, Kaase *et al.* 1978; Dalton 1988). Moran, on the other hand, takes a rather different view. He grants the importance of the well-educated as a source of political protest, but argues that 'the most serious challenges to authority come not from the most privileged but from the most deprived' (Moran 1985:40). This claim is, obviously, best examined in terms of wealth resources. But, solely in terms of education, it is those who are formally the most advantaged who are the primary base of protest whereas those who have no educational qualifications are the most quiescent.

It is also apparent from figure 4.4, however, that in this instance, an important distinction must be made between those having a university or polytechnic (and A-level) educational experience, and those who gained a qualification by attending a teacher training college (or other similar non-university/polytechnic professional qualification). Those from the latter category are, in fact, no more prone to protest than the population at large (nor are they noticeably involved in collective action). Thus, if it is a matter of radical values being at work here, these would seem to be much more associated with the degree-granting bodies of the higher educational sector than with the institutions of further education. Finally, it can be seen that the association between education and protest is largely unaffected by wealth or group resources. This might well be the case if, as we have suggested, the roots of the connection lie more in the realm of values imparted by a specific experience of higher education.

Party campaigning also has a modest positive association with education, taken on its own (eta = 0·17, r = 0·15). However, much of this evaporates once wealth and group-based factors are taken into account (beta = 0·07, r = 0·06). Indeed, unlike contacting, where the linear correlation was very similar, not one educational group deviates much from the overall mean – the largest being the 'A level' group at +11. The result, therefore, is a relationship that departs more from the pattern for overall participation. We are tempted to suggest that party campaigning may be a form of participation where there is, to use Verba, Nie and Kim's terminology, 'institutional interference' (1978:80), i.e. where the parties mobilise people across different backgrounds. This, too, we will examine later. For the present, however, we can say that campaign activity is not something that seems to depend in any important way on individual educational skills.

The fifth mode, voting, is without doubt the most deviant of all. First, even the unadjusted relationship is a very weak one, with an eta of 0·09 (and r = 0·05). Furthermore, only one group, those with college-type qualifications, have an initial score that deviates to any extent from the overall average. However, its unusual character only becomes clear when we adjust the turnout rates for differences in wealth and group-based resources. This shows that, although voting turnout rates still do not vary much, we now find a slightly negative linear relationship (beta = 0·09, partial r = −0·05) in which the best-educated, the degree-holding elite, are, relative to their resource base, the least likely to vote.

The extent of this under-participation by graduates can best be highlighted by comparing them with their nearest educational peers – the college group. Thus, in table 4.2, we set out turnout rates for both, together with their scores on a voting scale that adds all three voting items together. We also include these scores adjusted for resource differences. The table shows that university and polytechnic educated individuals vote at a distinctly lower rate regardless of resource factors. In the European elections, the turnout differential was nearly 11 points, and in the General Election, nearly 8 %. At the local level, the difference was smallest, with 2·3 % fewer amongst the graduates claiming that they voted in 'every' or 'some' local elections.

This pattern is summarised in the voting scale. The college group achieved a very high relative score, as one might perhaps expect, bearing in mind their educational background. In fact, their score was much the highest of any. The graduates, on the other hand, achieved a voting rate no better than those with no educational qualifications at all! And when resource factors were brought into account, whereas the latter group went to the top (with a score of 2·21), the graduates dropped to the bottom (1·82), far behind any other category.

All in all, therefore, it seems from our sample that voting defies the general rule about participation. In this instance, the best educated are the least active. Why this is so is less clear. We might say, as have others (Verba and Nie 1972) that voting is such an easy act that resources are largely irrelevant. Clearly, that is generally true here. The voting relationship is the weakest and the least significant (p = 0·043). But, there must be a bit more to it than that because the relationship is, after all, negative – mainly or possibly entirely because of the graduates. So why are they so different? It would be easy to say that the highly educated have other, more efficacious, channels to use. Or that they are the post-materialists with issue agendas ignored by the parties and which in turn leads them to abstain. But this is speculative, not least because other studies in Britain have typically reported only positive associations between education and turnout (see, for example, Himmelweit *et al.* 1981:23; Dalton 1988:51; Sarlvik and Crewe 1983:101). Part, but only part, of the explanation is age. As will be seen in chapter 7, age and turnout have a substantial association. In this case, adjustments for age differences do reduce, but they do not eliminate, the graduate voting deficit.

On the other hand, it is fair to say that the particular relationship of graduates to voting turnout has not received much close attention in the British context. Furthermore, in summarising findings in other countries, Milbrath and Goel also report that voting is an exception to the common finding that the better educated are the more participatory (1977:100–1). And Verba, Nie and Kim (1971:57) report a correlation between education and voting across five countries that is also negative (−0·06). In this context, therefore, perhaps the relationship that we have uncovered is not out of line with those in some other countries (except the USA).[9] But insofar as Milbrath and Goel are also very speculative about why this relationship is a deviant one, perhaps it deserves closer scrutiny than it has so far received.

Wealth

We now turn to wealth, our measure of the material resource base of individuals. The relationship it has with overall participation is set out in figure 4.5. As can be seen, on

Table 4.2 *Voting turnout amongst those with higher education*

	College	University/ polytechnic	Gap (U/P-C)
% voted in 1984 European	59·4	48·5	−10·9
% voted in 1983 General	84·2	76·5	−7·7
% voted in every/most/some Local	89·0	86·7	−2·3
Voting scale score*	2·29	2·09	−0·20
Adjusted voting score**	2·14	1·82	−0·32

* Scale constructed as first two items 1 = voted, 0 = not voted; third item 1 = every/most/some, 0 = never.
** Controlling for wealth and group resources.

the unadjusted figures, the relationship looks very similar to that for educational skills, if somewhat weaker. The bivariate association between the categories of wealth and levels of participation produced by the multiple classification analysis is 0·22 – a moderate relationship by our rule of thumb. Insofar as the simple r is nearly the same size (+0·20), it can also be deduced that the effect is primarily a linear one. The wealthiest quarter, and especially those in the top 5%, participate at relatively high levels, whereas the poorest quarter are well below average. On this basis, indeed, the division of the sample in chapter 3 into 68% who were below the mean and 32% who were above, is reflected in a similar split between the more and less wealthy. The 'haves' seem to participate more, and the 'have-nots' less.

However, when the influence of wealth is adjusted for other resources, it would appear that by itself wealth is not a resource of great moment. The statistics that summarise this effect are very weak indeed (beta = 0·06, r = 0·02). If anything, there are hints of a mild curvilinear pattern (as is hinted at in the discrepancy between the non-linear beta being somewhat larger than the linear r) such that above average activism can be found at both ends of the wealth spectrum. The stronger impulse to participate remains at the top – the richest 5% having the highest adjusted score of +18. But the next highest, fractionally, are the poorest 5% (+7). We might, perhaps, speculate that the latter phenomenon is a product of collective solidarity amongst the poor. But, in its organisational aspects at least, such a possibility has been removed by our adjustments. This does not, however, necessarily rule out some more ideologically rooted mobilisation effect, such as was found amongst American blacks in the 1960s (Verba and Nie 1972); a kind of group consciousness for the poor.

In the British political climate, with a strong socialist tradition that focuses on this social constituency, together with groups that constitute a vocal 'poverty lobby' such as the Child Poverty Action Group (see Field 1982; Alcock 1987), this is entirely plausible. But again one must be cautious because it is only a very slight effect. Furthermore, if we look at the results using the 19-item count of participatory acts, whilst there is an upward shift amongst the very poor (from 1·36 for the 'next poorest 19%' to 1·42, on the adjusted figures) this is still slightly below the overall average of 1·45. On this measure, the only important effect of wealth is to boost significantly the activity rate of the wealthiest quarter. This results in the richest 5% being 44% more participatory than the

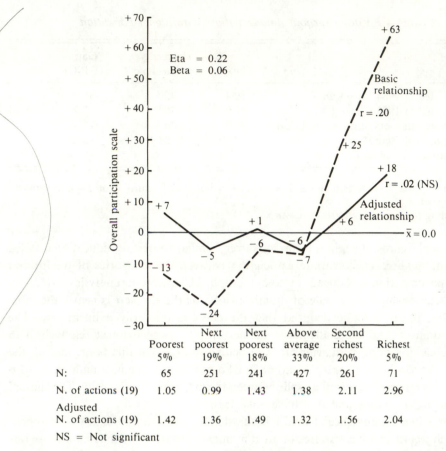

Figure 4.5 Overall participation by wealth, controlling for education and group-based resources

bottom 5%. Generally, therefore, the net impact of wealth on overall participation levels is not as impressive as educational resources. To the extent that individual resources are relevant to political activity in Britain, it is the non-material educational skills that make the bigger difference.

It is still appropriate, nevertheless, to explore the impact that wealth resources have on individual participatory modes. It is possible, as we saw with education, for significantly different patterns to exist. In this instance, focusing on specialised modes might throw further light on the character of the boost we observed at both the top and bottom end of the wealth spectrum.

The evidence, displayed in figure 4.6, suggests that there is again a considerable variation across the various modes. Certainly, one cannot merely apply the overall conclusion, that wealth is not very important, to all of the specialised modes. In fact, the presence of opposite relationships (negative and positive) may have led to the association between wealth and political action being somewhat understated when they were put together in the overall participation pattern. This is a good illustration of the dangers of considering participation solely as a unitary phenomenon. As with education, the process of activation varies from arena to arena. But this is also true of the two types

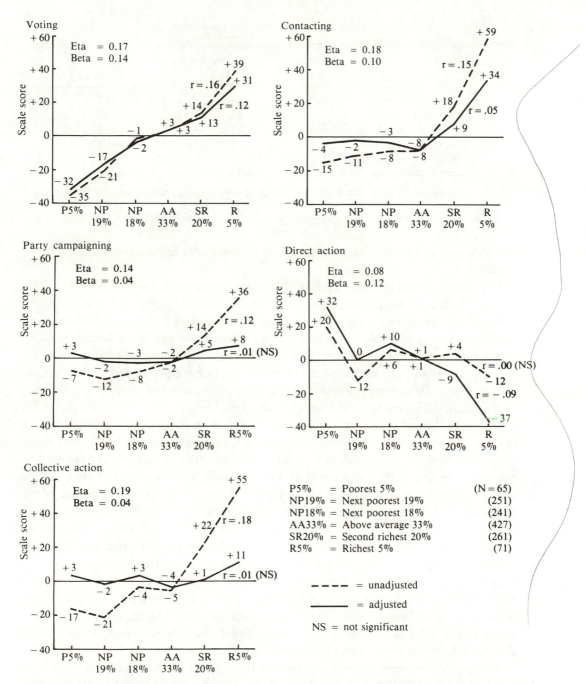

Figure 4.6 Participation, by mode and wealth, controlling for education and group-based resources

Table 4.3 *Voter turnout, by wealth*

	Poorest 5%	Richest 5%	Gap (R-P)
% voted European	34·2	63·4	+29·2
% voted General	68·5	90·2	+21·7
% voted in every/most/some Local	83·3	95·5	+12·2
Voting scale score*	1·71	2·48	+0·77
Adjusted voting score**	1·73	2·44	+0·71

* Scale constructed as first two items 1 = voted, 0 = not voted; third item 1 = every/most/some, 0 = never.
** Controlling for education and group resources.

of individual resources. Their impact on participation is not necessarily additive or reinforcing.

The clearest instance of this is voting. We saw that educational resources had a mildly negative effect on the propensity to vote. In the case of wealth, the relationship is positive, corresponding to the more standard expectation as to how resources relate to participation. As is shown in figure 4.6, wealth remains a significant factor in voting turnout, enhancing the voting rates of the wealthy and depressing the rates of the poor. We can see what this means more concretely by looking at the individual turnout measures and the summary 3-item index. Insofar as the controls make little difference to the relationship, the turnout rates are a fair representation of how wealth skews the character of the active electorate. The extent of this is set out in table 4.3 where, for the sake of simplicity, only the turnout rates for two most extreme wealth strata are presented. Here we can see, plainly enough, that the effect of being in the richest 5% boosts turnout in all three types of elections compared with those at the bottom of the wealth hierarchy. It is greatest of all in the European contest, possibly because of the cognitive and other resources needed to stimulate participation – resources most obviously held by the wealthiest (see Inglehart 1977). However, even in the general election contest there is a substantial gap of nearly 22 points. Given that the two strata no doubt have very different partisan complexions, the difference here could, in principle, have an important effect upon the overall outcome. It is, of course, true that, across all three measures taken together, many amongst the very poor vote, and vote frequently. Nevertheless, the very poor do not vote anywhere near as frequently as those at the top of the tree. The wealthy, in short, punch their electoral weight much more decisively (but see Crewe, Fox and Alt 1977).

The question remains, however, as to how this pattern is reconciled with the impact of educational resources. For, as we saw, although the types of resources are mutually reinforcing in the sense that the people who have more of the one tend also to have more of the other, the effects on participation are not of this order. Or at least they are not in the case of the graduates. Can we throw further light on their voting turnout by taking the wealth factor into account?

The answer seems to be that we can. If we compare the scores of graduates with their nearest educational peers, those from college, on our 3-item voting scale, we find an interesting difference. For those above the average in wealth, the graduates score 2·23 and the college group 2·58. This is still the converse of what a simple resource-additive model would suggest, but both groups are above the overall average of 2·10. Amongst those below the wealth mean, the story is rather different. The poorer college-educated have a turnout rate of 2·15 – a drop of 43 points, although still above average. The poorer graduates, on the other hand (albeit that there are only 18 of them), drop dramatically to 1·33 which is 90 points below their wealthier fellow graduates, and, moreover, 50 points below those who are the least well resourced of all – the group in the poorest 5% and who lack any educational qualifications.

We can put it more concretely still by reporting the relevant turnout figures in the 1983 General Election. The wealthier individuals within both the college and the graduate categories voted at about the same rate – 87·6% and 86·5% respectively. For their poorer counterparts, however, the rates were 82·6% for the college group and only 33·3% for the graduates. It is clear, therefore, that it is something to do with the dissonance between, or combination of, high achievement in terms of non-material (educational) resources with low material (wealth) achievement that accounts in major part for the deviance of the graduates as a whole. Whether this implies a degree of alienation from the political system as a whole, or specifically negative attitudes towards parties and the party system, or some other factor such as certain occupational norms associated with high education and low pay, would require further investigation. But the analysis here has at least refined the principal target group to be examined.

Turning, now, to the relationship between wealth and the other modes of participation also set out in figure 4.6, we can look next, and somewhat briefly, at party campaigning and collective action. The pattern in both instances is basically the same as that for overall participation: a roughly linear and positive basic relationship that is largely nullified when the other resource factors are taken into account. However, it is possible that a slight curvilinear tendency exists (albeit even weaker than with overall participation) whereby the best resourced participate most, but the least resourced are not all that far behind. In the case of party campaigning, this may represent some form of ideological mobilisation such as was previously discussed – although there is no sign of it in the voting sphere, which is where one might also expect to find it if it were real. Between education and wealth, therefore, we have a very poor purchase on differences in this sphere. As we mentioned before, if resources can explain anything about party campaigning, then it seems that we must turn to institutionally-based group resources for the answer. Clearly, individual factors of this sort play very little part.

So far as collective action is concerned, the pattern does nothing to undermine the view that higher rates amongst the better resourced are connected more with education than with wealth as such. In other words, being wealthy is obviously no handicap (the richest 5% score +11, higher than any other wealth category) but the main contribution to the higher rates of collective action amongst better individually-resourced people comes from those with higher education.

The relationship between wealth and contacting falls somewhere between the positive linear influence exerted on voting and the more or less negligible impact on campaigning and collective action. The graph in figure 4.6 shows that it is a relationship of two parts, one for the 'haves' (those in the wealthiest quarter) and one for those who have less or have little (all the rest). Amongst the less well-off, all contacting rates are initially below average but differences of wealth are converted into higher activity. After adjustments for other resources, they still remain slightly below the mean (with scores ranging between -2 and -8) but there is no longer any linear pattern. It is entirely flattened out.

For the wealthier quarter of the sample, however, not only is contacting well above the mean (with the wealthiest 5% at the very top), but they remain significantly more active even when the figures are adjusted. The rates are $+34$ for the top 5% and $+9$ for the next 20%. As the same pattern can be discerned in the educational sphere, it does indeed seem as though this type of participation is very much undertaken by individuals who possess substantial personal resources. Both high educational skills, and high levels of wealth, appear roughly equal advantages when contacting representatives and officials.

We turn, finally, to direct action which forms an association with wealth that is the exact opposite in form from that for voting. In short, it is negative (beta $= 0.12$, partial $r = -0.09$). On the adjusted figures particularly, protest is the one form of participation in which the poor are more active than the rich. All of which might seem quite comprehensible. For it is the wealthiest who, on the surface, would appear to have the most to lose and the poorest the most to gain by direct action.

On the other hand, we have again an instance where the impact of one type of individual resource is clearly at odds with that of the other. The locus of protest in educational terms was amongst the graduates, the most resourced. Here, the opposite is the case. It is worthwhile, therefore, focusing more closely upon the location of political protest in terms of individual resources. To this end, we constructed a 4-item scale of direct action comprising those items that make up the protesting form of participation analogous to the count of voting turnout discussed previously. Mean scale scores were then computed for each combination of wealth and education. From these we have presented, in table 4.4, results for the key combinations – the lowest and two highest educational categories combined with all the wealth grades.

Although the very poor do not stand out on this scale to the same extent as in figure 4.6 (here they were exactly on the overall mean of 0.17 rather than above it), it is clear that the uneducated poor are not a bastion of direct action. Their score (0.08) is less than half that for the group as a whole. The implication is that, for the very poor, some measure of formal education is needed to trigger off personal involvement in direct action. For example, although numbers are very small, sixteen out of the sixty-five did possess at least some 'O' levels. Their score on the direct action scale was 0.48, or 0.57 if just the 'A' level group is considered – six or seven times the rate for those without any education at all. This, then, is clearly one location of political protest – the materially very disadvantaged who, through at least some education, have made a connection between their position in society and personal political action. The educational resources are the necessary ingredients to release materially-rooted discontent.

The other locus of protest in table 4.4 is to be found in a very different part of the resource spectrum – among those who have had very exceptional levels of education but who have not been highly rewarded in strictly material terms. Thus, although numbers are small (because the standard pattern in Britain, as elsewhere, is for high educational attainment to lead to high levels of material wealth), we can see in table 4.4 that for the

Table 4.4 *Levels of direct action, by formal education and wealth*

	No qualifications	College	University/ polytechnic	Overall*
Poorest 5%	0·08	—	—	0·17
N	44	1	0	65
Next poorest 19%	0·09	(0·00)	(0·18)	0·11
N	180	7	11	252
Next poorest 18%	0·08	0·39	(0·69)	0·20
N	140	15	7	241
Above average 33%	0·14	0·21	0·90	0·19
N	170	47	17	478
Second richest 20%	0·07	0·31	0·44	0·21
N	56	29	44	261
Richest 5%	(0·11)	0·24	0·21	0·18
N	6	20	15	71
Overall	0·09	0·24	0·49	0·17
N	734	156	105	1,578

* All 6 educational categories. Brackets indicate low case counts

university and polytechnic group, levels of direct action are much higher in the intermediate wealth bands than amongst those in the richest 5%. The score for those in the 'above average 33%' group, for example (0·90), is four times higher than for the wealthiest stratum (0·21) as well as being the highest score for any combination of our material and non-material resource categories.

There are hints, however, that at the most extreme disjuncture of the two – those graduates in the 'next poorest 19%' – direct action falls off again. Equally, the association with the college group is distinctly more ambiguous. There are some fairly high scores recorded in table 4.4, and the suggestion of a curvilinear pattern. But it is not as clear or as sharp as for the university and polytechnic group. In other words, it is the combination of graduate educational status and neither very high nor very low material position that seems to define, in individual resource terms, the principal locus of direct action in our sample.

Protest does not, therefore, appear to be related to resources in any straightforward way. It has two roots. The first and more minor one is to be found amongst those who are materially very disadvantaged but whose education may have encouraged them to make the connection between their disadvantages and political action. Amongst this category are a number of the unemployed.[10] The second and more important root is amongst those with very substantial educational assets but who lack the material status that typically goes with such a background. It is not easy to characterise this group. But, insofar as we have narrowed the linkage between higher education and direct action to those of modest material resources, the image of the modern protester created by Inglehart (1977) seems to be ever more apt. For it is precisely those socialised in university and polytechnic milieux to espouse post-materialist values but also, crucially, lacking high levels of material endowments that might be expected to embrace direct action most fully. They are not restrained to anything like the same extent as those fellow graduates from the materially richest 5% from adopting political tactics that might put such possessions and life-styles in danger.

Summary

All in all we can see that individual resources are indeed relevant to the forms and levels of political participation. Whilst it is not easy to make generalisations, we can say that education is the more consistent factor, both in the strength and the nature of its impact. More education tends to mean more participation, and that pattern holds up even when other resource factors are drawn into the analysis. Only voting (albeit an important exception) shows a different pattern. There, the graduates are much less likely to vote, or rather those towards the bottom of the wealth hierarchy.

For wealth, the results are generally weaker and less consistent. Once other resources are taken into account, the overall relationship largely fades away, although a residual boost, especially amongst the most wealthy, is still apparent. The same is also true of party campaigning and collective action, where wealth resources generally seem to be of little account. Voting is the only form of participation where the basic hypothesis, that the better resourced do more, survives, which is perhaps ironical given the opposite result for education and voting. The only other significant influence of wealth is for protest, but there its role was more to act in combination with educational experiences than to be a powerful ingredient in its own right.

Overall, therefore, it is not consistently the case that individual resources advantage the already advantaged. The pattern is more complex and contradictory than that. However, it is true that no one form of participation, even protest, is the preserve of the disadvantaged. And it is equally true that there are several instances where the highly resourced do indeed participate more. But only contacting comes close to supporting the idea that both material and non-material individual resources can be readily converted into higher rates of political activity. From that point of view, contacting is indeed the most 'individualised' form of participation, the one most consistently dependent upon individual resource endowments. Thus, insofar as Britain's patterns of participation might be thought to reproduce the inequalities of the economic and social sphere, with that one exception, this is not the case. Individual resources are certainly important in shaping participation, but the way they become important varies too much to support this kind of generalisation. The question remains, however, as to whether the same also applied to group-based resources and it is to those that we now turn.

5

GROUP RESOURCES

Groups are fundamental to liberal democratic politics. A political scientist who once claimed that 'when the groups are stated, everything is stated' was certainly exaggerating, but it was a pardonable exaggeration. Every reader will be able to think in an instant of a myriad of groups whose activities touch regularly or intermittently on politics, both national and local. They may be nationally well-known groups such as major trades unions or the Royal Society for the Protection of Animals, or they may be relatively obscure local groups concerned to support a hospital or preserve the green belt. As we shall see, around two-thirds of the adult British population belong to at least one group, aside from trades unions, whilst over half either are or have been members of a union or staff association.

There are at least two ways in which groups can be important to participation. First, membership of groups can provide the individual with information about policies and actions which may affect his or her life. Through interacting with others who have like interests, persons become more aware of their social and political environment. Still more should this be so if a person is a member of a multiplicity of groups. In a sense, one has then an upward relationship with the group, using it as a resource. Secondly, where persons are members of a group, they are available to be mobilised in a downward relationship, by the group and its leaders. The group invites them to act in its own interests. It asks the member to take part in a protest march or to write a letter to a Member of Parliament.

Either approach to the relationship of groups and participation may be seen as part of a 'social interaction' theory of political behaviour (Putnam 1966) according to which the more that people interact socially with other individuals and groups, the more they will be prone to take political action. Social interaction may be cooperative or conflictual, it may be instrumentally motivated or community-minded, but a product of the exchanges between those involved is to increase awareness of issues, attitudes and opportunities for action. Interaction ensures that people receive certain participatory 'cues' and may also be positively mobilised to enter the political arena.

We shall begin by looking at the extent of mobilisation and in the remainder of the chapter examine the general relationship between formal membership of groups and participation in general and in its various modes.

Mobilisation

We may begin to appreciate the importance of group-based resources for political participation by looking at the circumstances in which people were led to take action. Some activities are primarily self-initiated but there are others which are taken largely after prompting, encouragement or pressure from others, including both other individuals and groups. This constitutes a broad distinction between mobilised actions, in the sense of actions the idea for which came first from other persons or groups, and non-mobilised or self-initiated actions, where the individual thought of acting by himself or herself.

Non-mobilised actions, depending on personal initiative, are perhaps those where the possession of individual resources is most relevant and the existence of groups of lesser immediate significance. By contrast, mobilised action locates groups, almost by definition, at the centre of the participatory process. Groups provide the stimulus without which action may not even have been contemplated, let alone taken. Additionally, groups can provide the extra encouragement and strength to sustain the actions which they have prompted.

This distinction between mobilised and non-mobilised actions is perhaps easier to draw in theory than in practice. Hardly any action can be entirely uninfluenced by forces in a person's general environment. Equally, in a free society, no action is simply an automatic response to that environment. Most action, in other words, is a blend of self-motivation and external suggestion. Nevertheless, it is possible that the balance varies greatly in particular instances and we can tap this by asking individuals how they 'first got the idea of taking action'. This question was asked in relation to a variety of activities which were taken by people over the one 'prime' issue – which is the term we shall give to the matter in which they were most involved – and also in connection with any other contacting, group and protest activities in which they might have been engaged.

The 1,415 responses to these questions were then grouped under relevant headings as set out in table 5.1. What we have called mobilised action turns out to constitute 56·8% of the total range of actions examined. However, there are clearly shades of mobilisation involved and some may question whether, for example, the promptings of family and friends or even informal groups should be included. Clearly there is room for argument about this. But although such cases are perhaps on the margin of mobilised and self-initiated action, they deserve to be distinguished from those replies which unequivocally claimed the action as the product of the person's own ideas.

We have also included actions generated by officials and representatives within the category of group-based action on the grounds that the force of their stimulus arises from their role in an organisational structure. A number of actions were also reported as having been suggested by the media either as a result of news coverage or of some more specific and individual contact. There may, again, be debate about including these within the realm of group-instigated actions. What remains are the clear and direct references to formal or informal group promptings. Formal groups such as trades unions or interest groups which give an impetus to action imply the existence of some institutionalised channels of communication. But at other times action is a matter of

Table 5.1 *Mobilised and non-mobilised political action*

	Action on prime issue %	Contacting %	Group action %	Protesting %	All actions %
Non-mobilised	48·8	67·5	20·0	19·1	43·2
Mobilised					
Formal group	12·7	5·1	24·8	46·6	20·4
Informal group	4·5	1·4	19·0	0·6	4·0
Unspecified group	4·1	0·7	5·7	8·3	4·5
Media	5·8	4·5	5·7	6·3	5·7
Officials and representatives	10·0	6·8	5·7	4·0	7·6
Family and friends	14·1	64·0	19·1	15·1	14·7
Total mobilised	51·2	32·5	80·0	80·9	56·8
Total non-mobilised and mobilised	100·0	100·0	100·0	100·0	100·0
N	668	292	105	350	1,415

becoming involved at the instigation of an informal or *ad hoc* group of neighbours concerned over a local development or parents worried at some proposed change in local schooling.

When we look at the figures we find that just over a third of mobilised activities are in some way suggested by formal, organised groups, or a fifth of the total range of citizen action. However, we could add to this the party campaign activists, comprising about 5% of our sample, whose action is, almost by definition, instigated by a formal group (and who for this reason were not asked this particular question about their party actions). This would boost further the importance of formal groups. A little way behind the formal groups appears the stimulus provided by family and friends (14·7%) with whom one might be inclined to associate the informal groups of neighbours and local activists (4·0%).

If we turn to the various modes of action we find that there are significant differences, as can be seen in the table. Some types of action are much more strongly group-based than others. The actions taken over the prime issue were very diverse. People chose a variety of ways of acting in order to express their concern over the matter which was most central to them. But in aggregate, as table 5.1 shows, just over half such actions were prompted rather than self-generated. The remaining columns report the responses to the questions concerning the 23 items of participation and can, therefore, be grouped according to types of action. We can clearly see the importance of mobilisation, particularly in regard to protest activities, just over 80% of which receive their cue from external agencies. This very high figure may, in part, be the result of including items like 'political strikes' that necessarily entail a degree of formal organisation and prompting by leaders. But it may also arise through the need for relatively large numbers of individuals to be involved in order for the protest to have a reasonable chance of success.

There have been instances of one-man demonstrations in Britain, as elsewhere. Occasionally, these simple acts have very profound consequences; one thinks, for example, of Jan Palach's self-immolation in Prague. But these are obviously exceptions. Too often, the one-person boycott sinks without trace, the one-member march becomes a lonely vigil and the petition with a mere handful of signatures is thrown away. For protest to make a difference numbers count, and numbers need organisation, as well as leaders to mobilise participants. There is, on top of this, a certain risk element that also has to be considered. Because, by its nature, protest sometimes tends to border on the illegal, and may indeed cross over into illegality, there is safety in numbers. The person who tries to block traffic by himself or herself, for example, runs a far higher risk of ending up in jail (or in hospital!) than if traffic is blocked by tens or, even better, hundreds. For that reason it is understandable that the bulk of protest action in Britain is initiated by others getting the individual to join in rather than by the individual thinking of that course of action on his or her own. It is also clear, moreover, that the majority of those promptings derive from formal organisations, and almost none from neighbourhood and similar more informal groups.

The same is not quite so true of group action. Here, action is mobilised to the same extent as protest (80%), but the prominence of formal groups is less marked. They are still the principal instigatory source but, at 24·8% of the total, are not dominant. Furthermore, informal groups (19%) and family and friends (19·1%) are almost as important in providing the individual with that crucial triggering impulse to do something.

Contacting, on the other hand, is clearly not of a piece with either protest or group action. Over two-thirds of this type of action are 'non-mobilised' – over three times the rate for the others. Conversely, the mobilised elements of contacting amount to only 32·5%, or less than half the protest and group action rate. However, given that contacting has been described previously as very much an individualistic form of participation, these large differences are not surprising. Indeed, they are further evidence that both confirms that description and adds to its meaning. What may be more surprising, therefore, is that as many as one-third of contacts are 'mobilised'. Yet, if we look at table 5.1 more closely, we can see that the principal source of that 'mobilisation' is family and friends – a category we have noted as possibly falling outside of any strict definition of the term. If, in fact, we do exclude that category, a mere 18·5% are mobilised. Put another way, the role played by 'formal groups' which are, surely, the core of what mobilisation entails here, is about one-fifth of what it is for group action and only one-ninth for protest. Clearly, therefore, the various forms of participation differ widely in how they get initiated amongst the citizenry. For contacting, it is an essentially private affair; for protest quite the opposite.

And yet, despite these wide differences, it remains true that a large body of action is not mobilised but self-initiated (43·2%). A vast amount of participation in Britain is, therefore, voluntaristic. Nevertheless, there is also a great deal of participation which is situated in a network of informal and formal group support. Without this backing, participation, and especially protest, would presumably be at a lower level than it is. Hence, the importance of ties to organisations as a resource for participation. What, therefore, is the connection between individual linkages with groups and the propensity to participate?

Measures of group resources

Our measurement of group-based resources is founded upon memberships of a number of different types of formal groups. These memberships, or 'ties', between citizen and organisation represent a boundary defining the set of groups the individual can work through to achieve his or her ends. Equally, they demarcate those whom leaders can seek directly to mobilise from those that are beyond their immediate reach. Group membership, in other words, is the building block of group resources, as educational diplomas and material assets are a primary basis of individual resources. We shall, of course, look beyond the simple effect of membership *per se*, and we also recognise that this may underestimate the role of informal groupings. But, as we have seen in terms of overall mobilisation, the latter have only one-fifth of the 'weight' of formal groups. This suggests that while informal networks may be a minor part of the equation, an analysis of group resources is most appropriately based upon those groups that have an on-going organisation. Through such groups, the citizenry exert greater leverage within the national political game.

It seemed appropriate to single out for separate treatment party and trades union (and staff association) memberships. Both these types of organisation play a very significant and distinctive role in public policy-making in Britain. Otherwise, we have grouped together under the heading of 'voluntary groups' all the other types of formal organisation, such as social clubs, hobby or sports clubs, religious associations, feminist groups and charitable bodies. This may entail, in some instances, a loss of nuance, but the gain is that the overall role of formal groups in stimulating or facilitating participation can be more readily appreciated.

The extent of such memberships within the British adult population is indicated by the proportions of our national sample claiming a membership under the three headings as set out in table 5.2. Amongst these, membership of a political party is clearly the group resource which is most directly relevant to political participation. However, it is restricted to a very small portion of the population – a problem which has concerned all the major political parties. A mere 6·8 % of the sample say that they are party members, although a handful also regard themselves as indirectly members of the Labour Party through payment of a political levy. As we shall see, these party affiliates have a somewhat greater significance than their numbers suggest. Trades union involvement in politics scarcely requires emphasising, not only at the level of national debate and negotiations or through the association with the Labour Party, but also at the local level in dealings with local governmental authorities and local employers. Unions are also frequently the instigators of protests in the form of demonstrations over pay, pensions and services or strikes which may for some participants have a 'political' content. But membership of trades unions has also been in decline in Britain, as well as changing in character as traditional industry declines and attempts are made to extend union penetration of services and the professions (Marsh and King, 1987). In our sample, self-proclaimed trades unionists are a minority, albeit a substantial one (27 %). But a sign of the times is that there are slightly more 'past' members than current ones.

'Voluntary groups' obviously vary greatly in their immediate political significance. Some 'cause' groups concerned with housing, political prisoners or animal welfare may be highly active in the political arena. Others may have only an intermittent involvement.

Table 5.2 *The extent of ties, by type of group*

	% members	N
Political party		
Non-member	92·6	1,453
Labour Party via trade union only	0·6	10
Individual member	6·8	107
Total	100·0	1,570
Trade union/staff association		
Non-member	43·0	678
Past member	30·0	474
Current member	27.0	425
Total	100·0	1,577
Other voluntary groups/organisations		
None	36·0	567
One	27·6	435
Two	15·3	242
Three	9·8	154
Four	5·5	87
Five	3·0	47
Six or More	2·8	45
Total	100·0	1,577

Still others may never touch upon the political realm even in its broadest definition. Yet almost any activity may become politicised. In recent years, sports bodies in Britain have been involved in political disputes over sporting links with South Africa and over crowd violence. Voltaire told us to 'cultivate our gardens' in the private sphere. Yet rose-growers in Britain have pressured government for licensing of fungicides and allotment growers have been locked in disputes with developers seeking their land for building. We shall take this matter up later when we examine the degree to which the groups and their members are politically active. Meanwhile, the importance of these voluntary groups lies in the fact that some two-thirds of the population belong to at least one such formal association. Whilst those involved in more than one group are much smaller in number (36%), almost 6% nevertheless claim to belong to five or more and thus appear to be highly integrated into social life in a way which may potentially have implications for political participation.

The overall picture, across all three types of group memberships, can perhaps be made clearer if we momentarily combine them into one simple scale. The results are set out in figure 5.1. They show that very few citizens are deeply embedded in formal organisational networks. Two people have as many as twelve groups, and a further 33 (2·2% of the total) are members of seven or more. But these are clearly very atypical. A majority of citizens are down at the bottom end of the scale either with no ties (26·7%) or only one 28·2%). In fact, the overall average is less than two. The picture, therefore, is closer to that of a mass society, privatised and atomised, than an organic society with a multiplicity of formalised interconnections. However, it remains the case that most

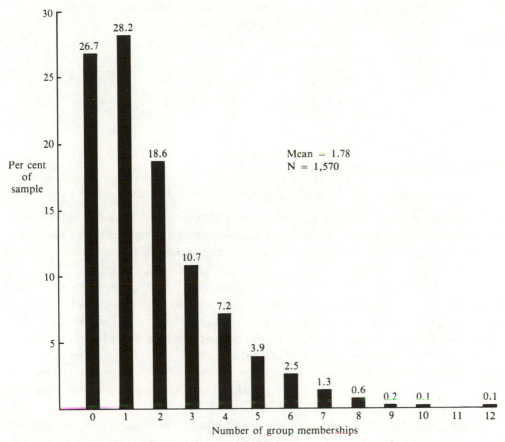

Figure 5.1 Overall rate of group memberships (all voluntary group memberships, current trade union memberships, and party memberships)

citizens have at least some connections to groups through which political leverage may be exerted, even if one is perhaps more impressed by the inequality in the way those resources are distributed.

To understand more fully the implications of these differences, it is worth examining two further questions. First, we have to ask whether the various kinds of organisational ties are entirely independent of one another or whether they are cumulative in nature. Secondly, are those with substantial *individual* resources in the form of education or wealth also those who enjoy the backing of extensive group-based resources, thus placing them in an apparently even stronger participatory position?

The extent to which organisational ties are cumulative is potentially important in resource terms. Individuals who belong to a multiplicity of groups have, in principle, a number of options open to them. They may be able to call on more than one organisation, or at least supporters in these organisations, to back up their action. Someone concerned with local schooling who belongs to an educational pressure group and a trade union may be able to employ both in support of action or, alternatively, may be prompted into action by both. Or they may act with the support of an organisation on any of a number of fronts. Such a person is open to mobilisation from several sources

Table 5.3 *Average number of voluntary group ties amongst trades unions and party members*

	Average	N
Party:		
Non-member	1·32	1,453
Member	2·15	117
Trades unions:		
Non-member	1·26	675
Past member	1·32	472
Current member	1·68	423

and, in terms of our last example, may be led to act on either a basically union matter or in the educational arena. In certain situations, multiple allegiances may admittedly pull in opposing directions causing conflict or indecision and inaction, but these are probably rare.

Our evidence, reported in table 5.3, suggests that organisational ties do indeed reinforce one another. Thus, party members have, on average, nearly twice as many voluntary group ties as non-members. Even so, this only amounts to, on average, slightly more than two memberships each. Similarly, current members of trades unions or staff associations also have a significantly greater number of links to other voluntary organisations than do either past members or non-members. We might note in passing, however, that non-trades unionists are somewhat more likely than trades unionists to be individual party members (8·6% as against 5·6%).

Overall, therefore, those who have party or trades union resources to call upon are better endowed in terms of other group ties as well. In principle, they do have a variety of sources of support for actions which they may contemplate. Alternatively, they may be more capable of being mobilised as a result of being accessible to the leaders of the groups by dint of their attendance at group meetings or merely of appearing on a membership list. Even when not actually participating, they may be potential participants who can be most readily activated by groups. In this respect, there is something in Inglehart's argument that such participation could be 'elite-directed' (Inglehart 1977:229).

The second aspect of the structure of resources is the extent of association between group and individual resources. We have already noted earlier the potential importance of this association. Organisational backing may be able to compensate for any disadvantages which a person may experience in participation as a consequence of lacking the kinds of educationally acquired skills necessary for successful advocacy or the wealth which is commonly supposed to improve access to positions of influence. The support of an organisation could change the balance of costs and benefits so as to make action worthwhile which it would not be if contemplated on one's own. On the other hand, the skills that education provides are very much those that can be useful in establishing and running organisations. The extent to which pressure groups are set up and administered by well-educated, professional, middle-class personnel is well-attested (Potter 1961). Similarly, the better-off have certain advantages when it comes to

Table 5.4 *Levels of education and wealth, by type of voluntary group*

Type of group	Wealth**		Education*		N. of members
	Member	Non-member	Member	Non-member	
Social club	−0·09	+0·02	2·22	2·49	426
Hobby club	+0·40	−0·14	2·97	2·25	382
Armed Forces Association	+0·17	−0·02	2·29	2·43	66
Evening class	+0·45	−0·06	3·69	2·27	170
Cultural group	+0·64	−0·04	4·07	2·35	71
Religious group	+0·13	−0·06	2·91	2·31	305
Professional society	+0·85	−0·09	4·72	2·21	132
Voluntary service group	+0·56	−0·04	3·26	2·38	75
Community group	+0·53	−0·04	3·49	2·36	96
Self-help group	+0·81	−0·01	3·81	2·41	16
Feminist group	+0·29	−0·01	3·63	2·41	11
All groups	+0·15	−0·31	2·72	1·87	1,011***

* 0 = no qualifications, 6 = degree.
** Average scores on the composite wealth scale (see chapter 4).
*** N of members for all groups is less than the sum of members of each type of group (1,750) because of multiple group memberships.

providing themselves with collective resources. The most effective and influential groups are normally those with an established organisational structure (Newton 1976). This involves the provision of administrative and secretarial services, membership lists, offices. All of this costs money, and the better-off can afford to pay for these support services through high membership subscriptions, which are in any case often tax deductible expenses. We saw earlier that, in themselves, education and wealth were only moderately associated with participation. However, it remains possible that there is an indirect association, mediated by organisations. Resources could be cumulative rather than fragmented in their participatory effects.

In order to establish whether there is any relationship between group and individual resources, we looked first at the educational and wealth profiles of each type of group to which our respondents belonged. The two sets of relationships are set out in table 5.4.

There is a clear and generally consistent difference in wealth between members and non-members of these groups. By and large, group members tend to be more wealthy than average (i.e. have positive scores on our wealth scale) and non-members are less wealthy (negative scores). This is true, for example, of members of voluntary service groups (+0·56), cultural groups (+0·53) and the small number who belonged to feminist groups (+0·29). In each instance, the members were generally better resourced, in material terms, than non-members. For all these groups, therefore, membership, a group resource, would serve to reinforce those who were already relatively well resourced in individual material terms. Put another way, if group memberships do stimulate participation, they consistently boost the participation of the better off. This is particularly true of professional societies (+0·85) and self-help groups (+0·81), which have the highest wealth profiles. It is also true of hobby clubs and religious groups which claim relatively large memberships (382 and 305 respectively). Insofar as the net effect is a product of both the size of the wealth differential and the membership level, the general tendency is quite clear: group resources reinforce material resources.

Notable exceptions are the members of social clubs such as working mens' and senior citizens' organisations. Here we find, perhaps not surprisingly, the one case where group resources work to the advantage of the less well-off. The effect is not large (−0·09), and is, in fact, the smallest of any. But it serves to indicate that group resources need not necessarily advantage the better-off sections of society. In this instance, indeed, a large number (426) of social club members who are somewhat disadvantaged, can potentially use their memberships to redress the balance.

The pattern for educational resources is a similar one. Overall, group members are considerably better educated than non-members. Cultural group members and, above all, those attached to professional societies, are at the top with average ratings of 4·07 and 4·72 respectively – way above non-members. This time, however, there are two exceptions – social clubs once again, and, in addition, members of armed forces associations. In both cases, members are somewhat less well-educated than non-members. Social clubs, therefore, are a clear case of how group and individual resources need not work in synchronisation. But, the dominant tendency in Britain is that they do.

A further way of looking at this relationship is to examine the resource profiles of those with multiple group memberships, rather than memberships of a particular type. The results are set out in table 5.5, and show a generally consistent pattern: those with more group ties are also those with higher individual resources. In the case of wealth, there is a simple progression – more ties, more wealth – although the big jump is from four social group ties to five. For education, the relationship is nearly the same but, for reasons that are not entirely clear, the very highest category of ties (six or more) has an average educational profile somewhat below those citizens with four and five group memberships. Once more, this hints at the possibility that high education and multiple group ties need not go hand in hand. In fact, neither of the two respondents with the highest number of group affiliations had any formal qualifications – they were the classic 'self-made men'. But these are clearly extreme exceptions. They point the way to how group ties might function as an alternative basis on which the less well-endowed, in individual terms, might participate. But, in general, this is far from the case. In Britain, almost without exception, group resources tend to be at the disposal of the wealthy and well-educated, not the poor and ill-educated.

The second type of group resources we have to consider are memberships of trades unions and their white collar equivalents, staff associations. They are of particular interest in this context because their historic purpose has been to provide the means whereby workers could redress their disadvantages in the market through collective action. They were created, in other words, to promote the economic interests of those less well-off. Very quickly, however, the trades unions turned to political as well as economic action, helping to establish the Labour Representation Committee in 1900. This rapidly led to a fully-fledged Labour Party through which unions continue to exercise political influence to this day (see Ingle 1987).

Against this historical background, we might expect that trades unions would function like social clubs, only more so. They would, that is, continue to mobilise and be a

Table 5.5 *Wealth and education, by number of voluntary group memberships*

	Wealth**	Education*	N
0	−0·31	1·87	567
1	−0·08	2·26	435
2	+0·18	2·61	242
3	+0·25	3·20	154
4	+0·33	3·59	87
5	+0·75	3·67	47
6+	+0·80	3·53	45
Total	0·00	2·42	1,577

* 0 = no qualifications, 6 = degree.
** Average scores on the composite wealth scale (see chapter 4).

Table 5.6 *Wealth and education by trades union and staff association memberships*

	Wealth**	Education*	N
Current members			
Trades union	+0·10	2·52	371
Staff Association	+0·68	3·84	54
Past members			
Trades union	−0·14	2·11	427
Staff Association	+0·58	3·23	47
Non-members			
Current	−0·08	2·32	1,151
Ever	−0·09	2·39	678
Total	0·00	2·42	1,578

* 0 = no qualifications, 6 = degree.
** Average scores on the composite wealth scale (see chapter 4).

resource base for the less advantaged in the political arena. On the other hand, in recent times trades unions have undergone profound changes. Members have been shed from amongst blue collar and unskilled workers, while white collar and professional occupations have been unionised at a rapid pace. This has caused visible tensions within the Trades Union Congress.

Are these changes reflected in the relationship between union and staff association membership and individual resources? Or do they still recruit principally from the ranks of the less-advantaged? The answer, from our evidence, is that indeed this is no longer so. Unions and staff associations, like most forms of groups, are now on balance linked rather more to the better-educated and wealthier sections of society.

To see in detail what has happened to the wealth and educational profiles of union and staff association members, we present separate results for past and current members in table 5.6. In making comparisons, we have to be aware that past members are typically older people who would, on that account, be less well-educated and, possibly, less

wealthy. How much this affects the figures is hard to say, but there is a clear difference
between current and past members of both staff associations and trades unions. Present-
day affiliates are wealthier and better educated than those who have dropped their
memberships. What is particularly interesting, however, is that whereas staff association
members, both past and present, are well above the national averages in wealth and
education, this is only true of current trades unionists. In other words, there are strong
hints here that trades unions have indeed shifted their base and now organise workers
and others who are more affluent and better educated than the average adult. They
remain still a considerable distance behind their staff association counterparts, but they
are now to be counted more amongst the mobilisers of the 'haves' than the 'have-nots'.
Some measure of this can be gained from looking at the non-members – particularly
those who have never been affiliated to a union or staff association. Past union members
are less wealthy and less well-educated than this group (-0.14 and 2.11 compared with
-0.09 and 2.39). For current members, on the other hand, the opposite is the case.

It is, therefore, reasonable to combine current trades union and staff association
members into a single set of those who can draw upon this type of group connection for
political participation. Detailed figures show that they are slightly under-represented
amongst the very wealthiest 5%, but otherwise they generally fall in line with the vast
majority of other groups we have considered.

We turn now to the third and last set of groups – party memberships. Here, too, we
might expect to find some diversity in the members' resources. After all, the Conservative
Party solicits the support of the relatively prosperous and the Labour Party the votes of
the materially disadvantaged. But is this reflected amongst those citizens who actually
join – those who can directly exploit their associations with a party for political
purposes? We know that the leadership of the Labour Party, for example, has
experienced embourgeoisement (Burch and Moran 1985) and now has a preponderantly
university-educated and professional composition. Equally, others have found Labour
activists also to be more middle-class (Whiteley 1981) than the population at large, if less
so than other party activists (see also Berry 1970; Barton and Döring 1986; but also
Moran 1985:105–13). It has also been suggested that the type of Labour affiliation –
automatically through a trade union or through individual membership – has a
considerable bearing on the matter.

Our evidence generally confirms all these previous findings – as can be seen in table
5.7. Our small number of party members are both much wealthier and distinctly better
educated than non-members. Overall, therefore, party ties can be added to almost all
those already discussed in promoting the capacity of the better resourced sections of
society to participate. Breaking this general effect into the three main party groupings
for which we have enough cases (and, even then, only seven for the Liberals), we do find,
however, some interesting variations. The Conservative members are the wealthiest
($+0.89$) followed by the Liberals ($+0.58$). Individual Labour members, too, are above
average ($+0.33$). These individual Labour affiliates are, moreover, very highly educated.
So, perhaps, what they fall short on in material terms, they make up on in non-material
resources. The members of other parties also possess formal educational achievements
well above those of non-members.

All in all, therefore, party ties do nothing to diminish the resource advantage of those

Table 5.7 *Wealth and education by party membership*

	Wealth**	Education*	N
Conservative	+0·89	3·01	69
Labour	+0·06	3·03	31
Branch	+0·33	3·77	21
Trades Unions	−0·41	1·54	10
Liberal	+0·58	2·98	7
All members	+0·56	3·04	117
Non-members	−0·05	2·37	1,453
Total	0·00	2·42	1,570

* 0 = no qualifications, 6 = degree.
** Average scores on the composite wealth scale (see chapter 4).

already well-endowed as individuals. In short, group ties reinforce, and are reinforced by, individual resources. In this way, the structure of group-based resources does not, with the exception of social clubs, serve to compensate for any political disadvantages which accrue to those less wealthy and formally less well-educated. Rather, those who are personally well-placed to promote their own interests are also more likely to be able to bring into play a network of groups in support. Looked at in another way, the wealthier and the better-educated are, as a consequence of their greater number of organisational linkages, open to be mobilised or activated by these groups in the pursuit of their campaigns. The question remains, however, as to whether these group resources do indeed boost participation – or is participation in Britain largely individualistic in nature? It is to this crucial question that we now turn.

Voluntary groups

We look first at the relationship between memberships of voluntary groups and participation. Because of the very distinct wealth and educational profiles of social clubs, these have been kept in a separate category. The composite effect of all other voluntary groups on the overall participation scale is set out in figure 5.2. As before, we present the results, in graphical form, of a multiple classification analysis. The eta, or simple non-linear measure of association is a substantial 0·39. By the rule of thumb set out in chapter 4 (p. 69), this would rate as a strong, almost a very strong, association. Furthermore, the fact that the correlation coefficient r is nearly as large (+0·37) confirms what the figure clearly shows graphically, that the relationship is essentially a positive and linear one. The 'adjusted relationship', representing the linkage between voluntary group ties and overall participation after removing the possibly confounding effects of other resource effects, tells a generally similar story. The beta (0·28) and partial r (+0·25) indicate a somewhat reduced association, but one that is still 'moderate to strong' in nature. In short, this shows that such ties do indeed impart a substantial effect. Despite their activities being often remote from the political arena, these groups are a very relevant resource for participation. The strength of the association with participation is nearly twice that of education and many times stronger than that of wealth (see figures 4.3 and 4.5). Those with no ties at all are well below the average level of participation, with an adjusted score (−20) much lower even than those lacking any formal education (−9). Those with just one voluntary group membership, on the other hand, participate almost at that average level (−4), which is a testament to the effect of crossing even the first threshold. However, to participate significantly above average is associated with possessing at least three ties. This, of course, only applies to a small minority (10%). But, for that minority participation scores exceed those achieved either by the graduates or by the very wealthy. At the same time, it is important to remember that there is an overlap involved. Those with several group ties tend to be those who also possess higher individual resources of education and wealth. Group and individual resources provide a double boost to participation but it is the group ties much more than the individual factors that give them such a politically active profile.

It has to be noted, of course, that the discussion of figure 5.2 is predicated upon the assumption that individuals acquire resources which then enable them to participate. This is the basic causal model behind much of the research into resource-based explanations of political activism. At the same time, it has to be recognised that the true association between voluntary group memberships and action might be more subtle and complex. Political participation might stimulate individuals to join more voluntary groups, for example, as their commitments to pursuing issues and causes in the public arena grows. The research materials available in the present study do not enable us to trace whether participation stimulates the acquisition of yet more group ties. It is therefore worth keeping in mind that, whilst the general tenor of the account is to treat participation as the *explanandum* and group ties (as well as political values to be considered later) as the *explanans*, these more complex associations are likely to form part of the full story.

One very concrete way of looking at the association between voluntary group ties and participation is to consider the simple additive scale of 19 actions. The scores on this scale associated with each level of ties, and adjusted for the effects of other resource factors, are also set out in figure 5.2 at the bottom. Those with no such ties average just slightly more than one act of participation beyond voting and signing a petition (1·17). This is somewhat less than the activity rate of the uneducated (1·20) and the very poorest 5% (1·42). Not to have such ties, therefore, has a more depressive effect on participation than lacking individual resources. The potency of voluntary group ties is also manifested at the other end of the scale. Here, we may recall, the wealthiest 5% registered just over two acts (2·04) and the graduates nearly two and a half (2·44). But those with four or more ties to voluntary groups (excluding social clubs) perform over four and a half political actions on average (4·54) – again nearly twice as much as either of the other factors. In short, group ties provide a major boost to participation, and their absence is an important explanation of inactivity.

As we have noted, the boost of these kinds of ties is delivered, in varying degrees, to the wealthy and well-educated – further reinforcing their advantages. But we found that, by contrast, social clubs provided an organisational base for at least some of those on

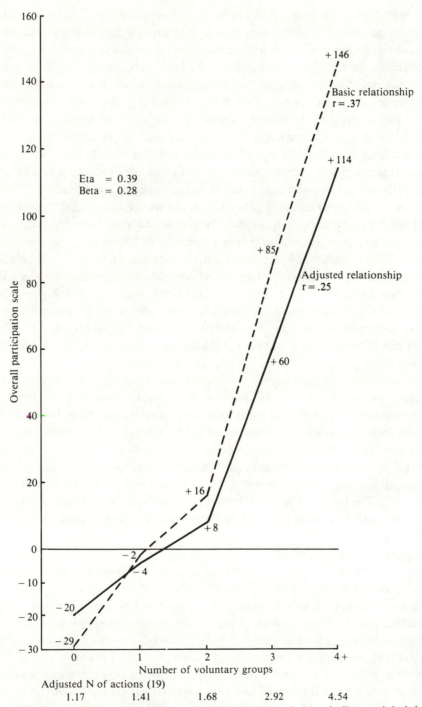

Figure 5.2 Overall participation by number of voluntary group ties (excluding social clubs), controlling for other ties and individual resources

the other side of the fence. The crucial question is whether social clubs do for the disadvantaged what all other types of voluntary groups tend to do for the advantaged.

The short answer is no. If we look at the effect on overall participation of membership in such clubs for the 27% of our sample who held such affiliations (the largest category of all), the net effect is negligible and totally insignificant. The beta is a mere 0·01 and the score for the members is −2, implying, if anything, that such ties depress activity. This is also reflected in the adjusted scores on the 19-item scale which are 1·55 for non-members and 1·47 for members. In so far as this seems to be the primary social organisational base for the less-advantaged, the fact that it does not generate any enhanced participation merely emphasises still more the extent to which inequalities in the distribution of resources get reflected in the participatory arena.

So far we have looked at the general pattern, but we can extend the analysis in two directions, first by unpacking participation into the particular modes, and then by refining membership ties into more subtle measures of voluntary group linkages. Results for the different modes of participation are set out in figure 5.3. It should be noted, however, that here we have amalgamated all voluntary groups together. The figure shows that there are indeed important variations in the boost that these group ties provide. The least impact seems to be upon direct action. Here, those with multiple ties protest slightly more, but the beta is only 0·06 and the correlation is a statistically insignificant +0·01. For this type of participation, these kinds of ties are, effectively, irrelevant.

The same can almost be said of campaigning. Here the relationship is somewhat stronger (beta = 0·08; r = +0·06) but also more erratic. Generally, multiple voluntary group ties are associated with higher campaign activity but those with 6 or more ties actually register a slightly negative score (−3). Unfortunately, there are too few (37 cases) to allow for a detailed investigation of this anomaly. Voting also shares some of these patterns. It has a marginally stronger relationship (beta = 0·12; r = +0·08) but there is, again, a negative score registered at the top end – this time amongst those with 5 ties (−7). The net result is that electoral participation, be it voting or campaigning, is only influenced to a modest degree by the extent of citizen memberships in voluntary groups.

However, the picture is different with the last two modes, contacting and collective action. In the case of contacting, increasing levels of voluntary group ties up to four generate only moderate gains. Thereafter, the boost is very strong: those with five affiliations score +59 and those with 6 or more +104 (on an adjusted basis). That contacting is so sensitive to such group memberships is perhaps surprising in view of previous comments about its individualistic character. Nevertheless, it is not hard to see why individuals who maintain extensive formal social networks should thereby be enabled to engage in political contacting so readily – a point to which we shall return.

It is also not difficult to appreciate why collective action should be the most sensitive of all to membership of voluntary groups. Here the beta is 0·30 and the correlation +0·27, both substantially higher than those linking this type of participation to education and wealth. The relationship itself is not quite a simple linear one but, unlike campaigning and voting, those with three or more voluntary group memberships all consistently register positive scores, and those with two or less are all negative. So a

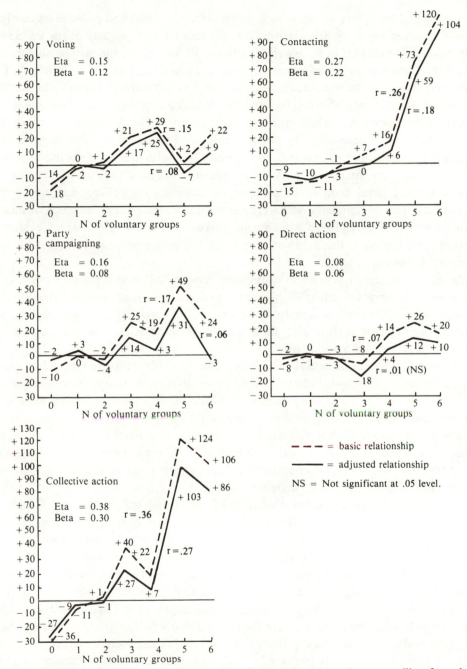

Figure 5.3 Participation by mode and number of voluntary group ties, controlling for other ties and individual resources

person who is well-established in a network of voluntary organisations is clearly well set-up to participate in forms of collective action.

To explore further why these groups might provide such important resources for political involvement, we need to examine more closely the nature of the ties. To do so, we have focused upon two major elements, the level of a person's activity within his or

her groups and the extent to which each group discusses social and political issues. The
level of a person's activity helps to establish the saliency and potency of the tie. Some
individuals may take part in no group activities at all. For them, the membership might
be at best a latent or potential resource, better than nothing but not by much. At the
other end, there may be individuals who take part in virtually all the activities of the
group. For them, membership can be a very immediate and potent asset. They know the
leaders, they know the other members, they know how to use or exploit the
organisations, when necessary, for political ends. Equally, discussion of political and
social issues establishes how immediately relevant the particular group is to the public
sphere.[1] As we have noted, voluntary groups are not always on the face of it 'political'
groups. By and large, their focus on sports or hobbies or welfare lies outside the
traditional realms of political and governmental affairs. But groups in which members
discuss public issues regularly will, by that token, provide a more direct basis for
political participation to the members than those organisations in which broader issues
are never discussed.

We should, therefore, be able to distinguish between different types of groups. One
type would be characterised by high activity levels and frequent political discussions.
Another set would have low activity levels and would rarely, if ever, discuss broader
concerns. Two questions then arise. First, do these differences exist in practice, and are
they of any import for participation?

Evidence on the first question is provided in table 5.8. This shows that there are indeed
very considerable variations in both dimensions of group ties. Using the scale noted at
the bottom of the table, we find that the overall amount of activity (1·59) lies about half
way between members taking part in 'a few' and 'most' activities. But some groups
deviate sharply and in both directions. At the bottom of the activity ladder are armed
forces associations and professional societies where the typical member is involved in
only a 'few' activities. Conversely, participation in evening classes and self-help groups
register scores above the 'most' activities level.

There are similar variations in discussion of social and political affairs. Generally
speaking, ratings are low – as might be expected given that most of the groups are not
specifically political in nature. On the scale we have devised, the overall score is just
under half way between discussions taking place 'never' and 'sometimes'. The most
apolitical of all, according to their members, were the armed forces associations. Despite
their military character, they serve a primarily social rather than political function.
Evening classes and hobby clubs are also, unsurprisingly, at this end of the spectrum.
The most politicised, by contrast, were the feminist and self-help groups, both of which
categories registered scores nearly three times as high as the overall average.

Clearly, therefore, there is plenty of scope in both dimensions for memberships to
mean a lot more in some cases than in others. The armed forces associations, for
example, manifest both low membership participation and low politicisation. We might
suspect, therefore, that a membership in that type of group would do very little for
activity in the political domain. Indeed, evidence we have already discussed suggests that
this may be so. Social clubs, while not as pure a case as the armed forces associations,
rank ninth out of eleven in membership activity and seventh in political and social issue
discussion. In both instances, their scores are well below the overall means. Here,

Table 5.8 *Levels of activity and political discussion by type of voluntary group*

Type of group	Activity level*		Political level**		
	Score	(Rank)	Score	(Rank)	N
Social club	1·18	(9)	0·38	(7)	419
Hobby club	1·83	(7)	0·35	(8 =)	377
Armed Forces Association	1·10	(11)	0·23	(11)	64
Evening class	2·47	(1)	0·26	(10)	162
Cultural group	1·85	(6)	0·35	(8 =)	70
Religious group	1·45	(8)	0·48	(5)	290
Professional society	1·12	(10)	0·72	(3)	131
Voluntary service group	1·88	(4 =)	0·47	(6)	73
Community group	1·88	(4 =)	0·68	(4)	93
Self-Help group	2·07	(2)	1·18	(2)	16
Feminist group	1·96	(3)	1·27	(1)	11
Total groups	1·59	—	0·43	—	1,706

* Members take part in activities: None = 0; A few = 1; Most = 2; All = 3.
** Members discuss political and social issues: Never = 0; Sometimes = 1; Often = 2.

therefore, we have evidence as to why social clubs fail to act as a basis for political participation. They fail because the ties lack any relevant political substance. By contrast, ties to self-help and feminist groups score well on both dimensions. These are clearly important, politically relevant resources. But, if this is the case, they are resources that, in the case of the self-help groups at least, mobilise a relatively wealthy and well-educated, if very small, set of adherents.

The central question, however, is whether activity and political discussion levels do indeed make a difference for political participation. As we can see in figure 5.4, the answer is yes on both counts. In the figure, we set out adjusted rates of overall participation, first for all voluntary group ties, then for those ties which involve some minimal activity and, finally, for those ties that entail both activity and political discussion. We further distinguish, in each instance, between those citizens with just a single tie, those with two, and those with three or more. We can see from this that the number of ties does make a difference. Moreover, this difference increases both as the level of active involvement in the group grows and as the amount of political discussion rises.

The picture is one of a number of quantitative and qualitative leaps. The first distinction between one or two ties counts for very little – although both count for more than no ties at all (see figure 5.2). It is only those with multiple links that really stand out above the participatory norm. When we look at those who are active within groups, we find that possessing two active linkages does raise a person in the participatory scale but not by much (+ 3). Being active in three or more, on the other hand, is a big step up since it doubles the participation score from + 33 to + 68. However, only half the number of individuals are now involved (21·9 % to 11·9 %). This means that the gap between those with multiple active ties and just one or two expands.

But the really big leap is made when we move from active ties to those that are both

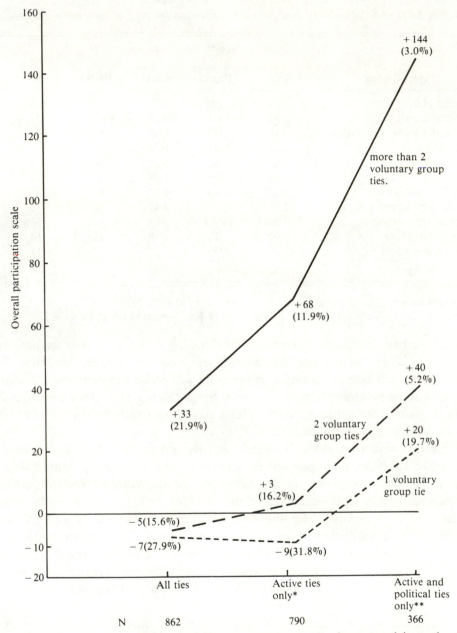

Figure 5.4 Overall participation by voluntary group ties, levels of group activity and political discussion, controlling for group and individual resources. (%) = % of total sample in category; * = only members taking part in at least 'a few' activities; ** = only members who are active and discuss social and political issues at least 'sometimes'.

active and entail group political discussion. Even those who are active within one or two such politicised groups participate at rates well above the mean. Only a small number (3%) have a larger number of memberships of this sort but their participation is boosted to a dramatic +144. This is the highest figure seen so far in the analysis of the overall participation scale.

Here we have, therefore, a major ingredient in understanding the process that leads to political activity in Britain. Those people who are well-entrenched and active in voluntary groups where political and social issues get discussed are very participatory individuals. And, as we have seen, they are also personally well-resourced individuals.

Trades unions and staff associations

In the light of the analysis so far it is clear why trades unions and staff associations should be considered carefully and separately for their effect on political participation. First, as in other countries such as Japan (Verba, Nie and Kim 1978:103), they are very numerous. As many as 27% of our respondents are current members of either a trade union (24%) or its white collar equivalent, a staff association (3%). Beyond that, a further 30% claimed to have been a member in the past. This category, therefore, represents a resource that has been available, at one time or another, to a majority of our interviewees. Secondly, the concerns of unions are generally more politically relevant than those of most of the voluntary groups we have so far considered. Indeed, in our questionnaire, we took for granted that in Britain at the time of our survey, most or all of those active in trades unions and staff associations would report that these organisations were involved at some stage in 'discussion of social and political issues'. For example, throughout the interview period, one major union, the National Union of Mineworkers, was engaged in a massive confrontation with the Conservative Government that also brought into the fray the leaders of the Trades Union Congress and the Labour movement more generally.

This instance of union action serves as a reminder of the role trades unions have played as a political resource for the economically and socially disadvantaged. They have, in the past, represented the classic example of collective action, within the political as well as the economic realms, to compensate for the effect of the market. However, as we have seen, present-day trades unionism generally draws into its membership those who are, on average, in the wealthier and more educated half of the populace. Clearly this is not true of every union, but it is true of trades union members in our sample taken together.

The question we must now explore is how relevant these ties are to political participation. From all that we have seen, we should expect them to be so. But we must let the data, once again, speak for themselves.

The boost to overall political participation associated with trades union and staff association membership is set out in figure 5.5. What is perhaps surprising is not that there is a significant effect but that it is not larger than it is. Thus, we can see that current membership of either type of group enhances participation by 13 points for a trades union and 16 for the staff association. The sizeable unadjusted effect in the latter case ($+37$) is much more a reflection of individual and other advantages of staff association members than the product of the membership itself. Past membership of either type of group, however, apparently leaves little imprint upon current participatory behaviour. This reinforces an assumption that underlies this chapter – that group resources are most relevant when they are current rather than when they have lapsed. Nevertheless, it is once more those who have never been a member of a trades union or staff association (43% of our sample) who are the least participatory. Even a lapsed membership, it seems, especially a staff association membership, is better than nothing.

The extent to which participation is enhanced or diminished can, as before, also be judged by the number of actions (out of 19) associated with each category of membership. By this measure, those who have never been members are at the bottom whereas those with lapsed membership are in the middle and current members at the top. The spread suggests that staff association adherents are almost twice as active as life-long non-members (2·16 to 1·26). Comparing this to the effect of voluntary groups where there was a difference of nearly four times between top and bottom may suggest that, contrary to their appearance of great relevance, trades unions and staff associations are not as important as we originally supposed.

However, it is important that we compare like with like. Here we are focusing on one tie, one group membership. If we then compare the effect of this with the effect of belonging to one voluntary group (as set out in figure 5.4), it would seem that trades unions and staff associations carry a far bigger punch than the average voluntary group tie. The score for one voluntary tie was −7, which is better than no such ties (−20), but plainly not as potent as a trade union tie (+13) or a staff association membership (+16). By this yardstick, therefore, what might have been seen as a modest impact looks a bit more substantial. But, at the same time, it is plainly much better to have multiple voluntary group ties than just one trade union or staff association membership as a resource to call upon.

When the relationship between union membership and particular modes of participation is examined, as in figure 5.6, we can see that its character varies considerably. In the case of the two electoral modes, for example (voting and campaigning), trades union membership, perhaps surprisingly, counts for nothing. Staff association links, on the other hand, make a greater difference but in contradictory directions. Indeed, for this type of participation, the strongest boost comes from past rather than current staff association ties, for reasons that are not immediately apparent.

In the field of contacting, likewise, it appears that this type of resource makes relatively little difference. Once other factors are taken into account, neither trades union nor staff association ties provide a major stimulus. If these are conduits for taking up the grievances of individual members within the political and governmental realm, they do not stand out in our data.

The largest effects appear in the areas of direct action and collective action. In the former case, the beta (0·15) suggests that it is the most important so far considered, although its influence can only be rated as moderate. It is also apparent that the particular kinds of impact made by trades union and staff association memberships are strikingly different. A current trade union affiliation gave a significant boost to protest, while a staff association link did precisely the opposite. To put this in better perspective, however, the impulse to protest provided by the trade union tie was, in fact, somewhat less than if an individual had a university degree or been in the poorest 5% of the population (see figures 4.4 and 4.6). Equally, the de-mobilisation induced by a staff association attachment was no more than being in the richest 5%.

Given the broader political context of the times, and the specific inclusion within our list of protest activities of 'political strikes', it is perhaps surprising that this trades union

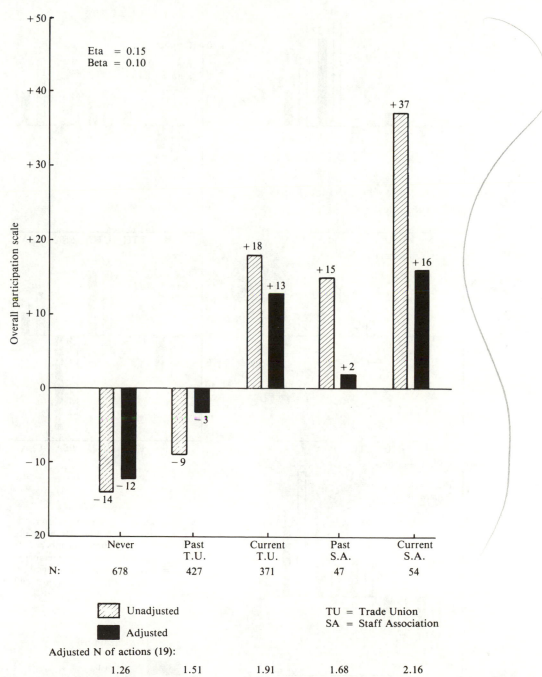

Figure 5.5 Overall participation by trade union and staff association ties, controlling for other ties and individual resources

effect was not even larger. But it is worth pointing out that the Barnes, Kaase *et al.* study also made a similar finding in connection with their examination of the potential for protest (1979:128). They, too, were surprised to find only weak support for the influence of trades union membership. The highest correlation (0·15) in the five nations they

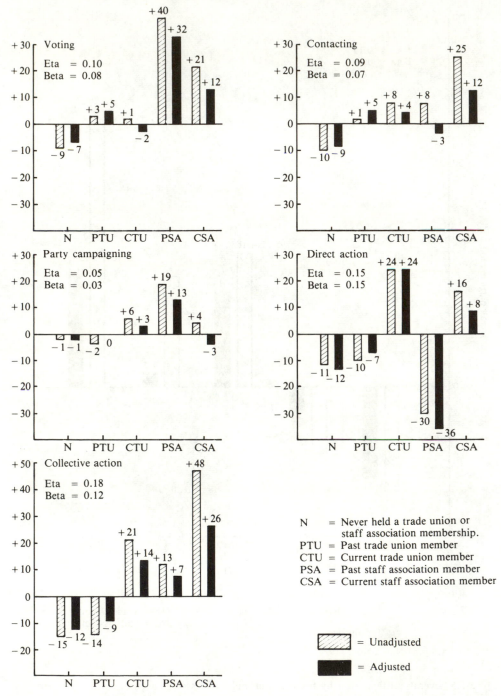

Figure 5.6 Participation by mode and trade union/staff association ties, controlling for other ties and individual resources

looked at was, indeed, in Britain (1979:100). Despite differences of wording and technique, this is exactly the same strength as we report. Thus the evidence fits the comment that:

Table 5.9 *Levels of activity amongst trades union and staff association members* (%)

| | Past | | Current | | |
Level	Trades unions	Staff Associations	Trades unions	Staff Associations	All
Very active	4·5	6·5	3·2	9·3	4·4
Fairly active	12·2	10·9	19·7	20·4	15·7
Not very active	29·6	30·4	36·9	44·4	33·6
Not at all active	53·7	52·2	40·2	25·9	46·3
Total	100·0	100·0	100·0	100·0	100·0
N	425	47	371	54	896
Activity score*	0·68	0·72	0·86	1·13	0·78

* Very = 3; Fairly = 2; Not Very = 1; Not at all = 0.

This result does not necessarily imply that a popular image of union militancy is a false one. It implies merely that … protest among even unionized workers is matched in strength by … protest in other sectors of the community …   (1979:128)

In our own study, we have already seen that those other sectors are to be found within the wealthier and more educated echelons of the population.

The other mode of participation, collective action, also produces surprisingly weak effects, although here both union and staff association ties pull in the same direction. It is surprising because this type of political involvement is of the essence of British trades unionism over the decades. Yet it seems that neither unions nor staff associations are major resources that stimulate members to collective action, although both types of membership are of some value (+14 for unions and +26 for staff associations).

One possible explanation may be that collective action, as we have tapped it, is more associated with promotional than functional pressure groups. But a more concrete and important clue can perhaps be gleaned from considering the nature of these union and staff associations ties. If we presume that they were generally politicised, in our sense of being involved in social and political discussions, then we must focus on the extent of a person's activity within the union for a possible explanation.

In the course of our interviews, we asked all trades union and staff association members, both past and present, whether they were 'very active', 'fairly active', 'not very active', or 'not at all active'. Overall, as can be seen in table 5.9, only 4.4% considered themselves 'very active' either in the past or currently. Conversely, nearly half (46·3 %) saw themselves as 'not at all active'. Interestingly enough, we can also see a difference in activity levels between the past, lapsed (or retired) members and those with a current affiliation. But even amongst the present members, only 3·2% of the trades unionists saw themselves as very active, and 9·3% of those in staff associations. Indeed, if we compute an activity score for these ties on an equivalent basis to voluntary group ties (see table 5.8), we can see that they come out bottom. The least active voluntary group category comprised armed forces associations with a score of 1·10. This is about the same as the current staff association rate (1·13) and considerably higher than the trades union figure of 0·86.

All this suggests that, on a wider comparative basis, trades union and staff association ties generally entail very little activity for the typical member. Given the significance of such activity in turning group ties into an important participatory resource, this provides solid evidence as to why such an apparently relevant link should count for relatively little. The fact is that for the majority, such ties do count for very little. They go with the job and are there in the background to be activated only when necessary. Voluntary group memberships, on the other hand, are less likely to be held in such a passive way. From the point of view of political participation, this tends to override their greater remoteness from the political arena – at least when there are several of them.

When we factor levels of union activity (both past and current) in, the result is as set out in figure 5.7. As can be seen, they make a very big difference, at least for the 'very active'. That tiny group (4·4%) has an overall participation score of +96 (on an adjusted basis), which is not far off that recorded by that somewhat larger group who had four or more voluntary group ties. This suggests, once more, the potential of trades union and staff association memberships for political action. They are indeed greater than for voluntary group ties, but the levels of union activity associated with them means that the potential is only fully realised for a very small minority.

How are the individual modes affected? In brief, the results show, with one exception, a uniform pattern whereby the more active unionists participate more and the very active participate very much more. This is true, above all, of political protest where the (adjusted) scores for the very active and fairly active are +92 and +30 respectively. The same might also be said of collective action. Here, those who are very active in the union achieve the highest score of +52, and the fairly active +26. As union activity goes down, so does the level of involvement in collective forms of participation. Other than that, in the case of party campaigning and contacting, major boosts from union and staff association memberships are restricted just to those very active in the union, who have scores, respectively, of +73 and +59. In general, therefore, very high levels of activity in union life are needed before union or staff association membership turns into an important resource for participation. But for that highly active few, it is plainly a major stimulus.

The exception in all of this is voting. Here, the net effect is very modest and the relationship not entirely consistent. Thus, the 'very active' achieve a score on this ladder of only +5, which is no more than that of the not very active. The political activity of the trades union and staff association activists is far more marked in the areas of protest, campaigning, and the like, than it is in the basic act of voting itself.

The question then arises as to how far trades union membership in itself boosts participation or how far it is only those who are active in the union who appear to be led to participate more than the general norm. If we control for the level of activity, we find indeed that membership alone has little impact on participation. The only noteworthy effect of current membership is on collective action (+18). Thus, it would seem that it is not the 'ethos' of unionism which stimulates participation. Rather, it is a case of a relatively small and active minority within the membership itself also being active in the wider political arena outside the union. Moreover, this minority is, rather surprisingly at first glance, relatively wealthy and well-educated. As with voluntary groups, therefore, it is more the nature of the ties than their mere presence that governs what groups can do for citizen participation.

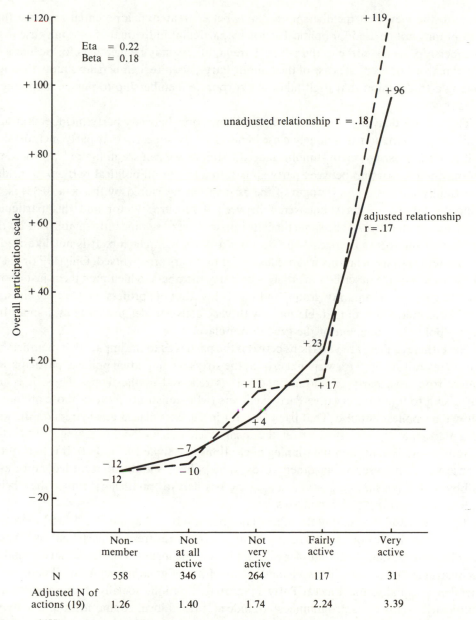

Figure 5.7 Overall participation by level of trade union/staff association activity, controlling for other groups ties and individual resources

Party

We turn now to the third and last of our group-based resources – membership of a political party. Here we are dealing with a linkage that, unlike those considered so far, is clearly within the political arena. In that sense, its relevance as a resource for participation is clear, its potential unambiguous. Indeed, so close is it to political action that some authors have treated it as a form of participation (see, for example, Verba and Nie 1972). We have already addressed the merits of this conceptual issue in chapter 4 and come to the view that membership *per se* is better treated as a potential resource that may or may not be used for political action by particular individuals. Some may use their memberships as an entrée to the political arena, others may be members for business or social reasons or, as in the case of the Labour Party, acquire membership simply through joining a trade union that itself takes out corporate membership to pursue its political aims.

There is no denying, however, that the connection between party membership and political participation is uniquely close. This strongly suggests that party membership will prove a most powerful stimulus indeed. And, as we can see in figure 5.8, where we set out the relationship between party affiliation and overall political participation, this is certainly the case. The strength of the association measured by the beta (0·33) is, in fact, the largest we have uncovered between a resource factor and this particular participatory ladder. At the same time, its impact is very significantly diminished by the very small numbers of citizens who do hold a party membership. It is not like trades unions and staff associations where substantial numbers are involved. Only 117 or 7·4% of the total sample described themselves as party members, which puts them just above the category of 'community group' and just below that of 'professional society' in size. They are, therefore, comparable more with very active trades unionists as a small but highly politicised segment of the general populace.

Nevertheless, there are variations between the parties as to the impact that membership has on overall activity. As we might expect, the stress on individual political participation differs from one party to another and this is reflected in the figure. Thus, it is not surprising to find Conservative Party members (who constitute 59% of those affiliated) show the smallest impulse. That party has not in the past placed great stress on the idea of a participatory society. Nor, at the local level, is it noted for taking politics too seriously – at least beyond the winning of elections (see Ingle 1987:61–2). It is part of the Conservative philosophy, in other words, that politics should be regarded more as a hobby than a consuming passion, something best left to 'politicians' rather than being indulged in by rank-and-file citizens.

The same cannot be said of the other major parties. Both Labour Party and Liberal (as it was at the time of our survey) Party have placed more stress on participation, even if for different reasons. In the former case, politics is the means whereby society would be reconstructed on socialist lines – a matter, therefore, of great moment for all committed members. Equally, the Liberal Party made participation, socially, economically and politically, a part of its programme and, indeed, turned local commitment and activism into an electoral strategy (see chapter 2). The fruits, in both instances, are participation rates approximately three times that of Conservative members, or double if the 19 actions scale is used. Party members in general, and non-Conservatives in particular, are indeed a small but highly participatory section of society.

It might, of course, be said that we are restating the obvious: that party members are politically active. What is perhaps less obvious was the extent to which this was so for particular parties, and the strength of these links when compared with the other group ties we have been examining. Similarly, it is obvious that party membership is highly relevant to some modes of participation. But this is not necessarily true of all, as may be seen from figure 5.9. Thus it will come as no surprise that party campaigning is the area in which the biggest boost is recorded. The beta is six times the magnitude for any

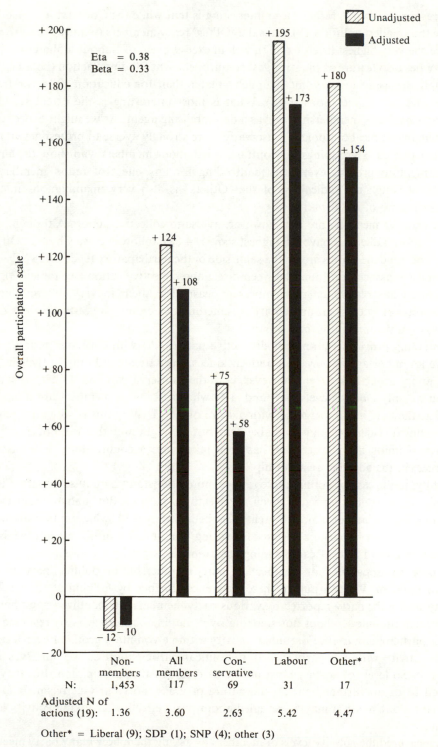

Other* = Liberal (9); SDP (1); SNP (4); other (3)

Figure 5.8 Overall participation by party membership, controlling for other group and individual resources

other resource. What is rather more interesting is that while the Conservative members receive the smallest uplift (+131), it is the 'Other' party members (mainly Liberals) who achieve the very highest levels (+242), well in excess, even, of Labour affiliates (+146).

Party ties also feature as the strongest resource element for direct action (beta = 0·23), although the association is not so much greater than for education (0·14) or trades unions and staff associations (0·15). What is most interesting is the extent to which Conservative Party membership acts as a de-mobilising agent. As we might expect from their general political outlooks, Conservatives are strongly averse to protest activity. Of the other two party groupings, by contrast, it is Labour members who show the largest commitment to protest, even after controlling for any effect of union membership (+138), although the radicalism of the 'Others' is also very unambiguous in their (adjusted) score of +86.

Conservative members are not, however, averse to collective action. Although, once again, Labour adherents have the highest scores (+88), followed closely by the 'Others' (+70), this time the Tories are on the same side of the participatory fence (+28). Despite the empirical association found between direct and collective action (see table 3.3), it is clear that Conservative Party members at least view them in very different lights. Promotional or interest group activity is something which may involve members of all parties, even if some more than others.

Contacting provides yet another distinctive pattern. As with collective action, party ties are an important resource. In both instances, they are second only in their impact to voluntary group links. Here, however, both the Conservatives and 'Other' adherents contact at only modest levels (+8 and +7) whereas Labour members are almost as active as they are in campaigning with a score of +131. Why this is so would require more detailed evidence than is available here, but we might note that it is not simply the product of union ties whose effect has been taken into account, along with all other resources, in the adjusted relationship.

Finally, in the case of voting, there is once more a substantial impulse imparted to all parties – as is to be expected given its electoral nature. But unlike the case of campaigning, its impact is not so great. The beta is only 0·14, which puts it alongside wealth as the most important resource for voting. But an effect of this magnitude, being less than one-third that of campaigning for example, is hardly a major one.

By now it is apparent that the effects of party membership on political participation are not uniform. We can pursue these differences further by looking at the levels of activity within the party reported by various party members. Here, however, we have to be very careful indeed about not stepping over the line between what is resource and what is participation itself. For, unlike activity within a voluntary group or even a trades union, activity within a party clearly is political participation as we ourselves have defined it. So levels of activity must not be used to explain participation. But they can be used to throw further light on the nature of grass-roots party activism. It is also possible to look at what may be revealed about party effects after taking activity levels into account.

We measured the activity levels of members by asking them how many party meetings they attended in a year. The results are set out in table 5.10 and show some interesting but also consistent patterns. As we surmised, it is the case that not all party members are,

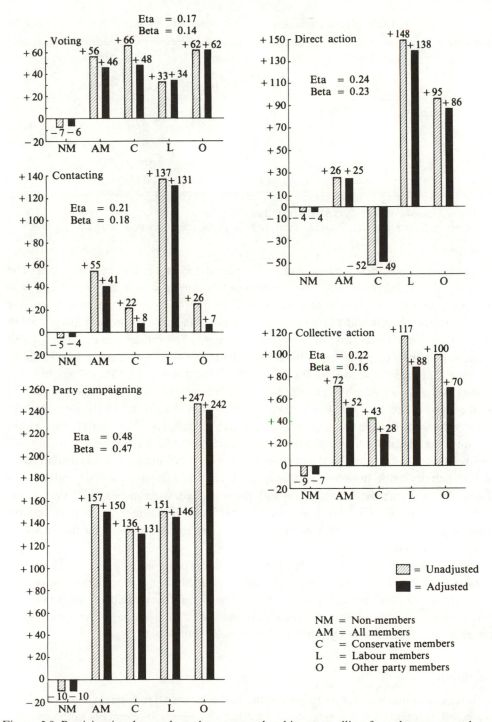

Figure 5.9 Participation by mode and party membership, controlling for other group and individual resources

Table 5.10 *Attendance at party meetings, by party*

| | | Labour | | | |
	Conservative	Union	Branch	Other*	All
Never	58·2	[90·0]**	38·1	35·3	53·5
1–5	26·9	[10·0]	19·0	23·5	24·1
6 or more	14·9	[0·0]	42·9	41·2	22·4
Total	100·0	100·0	100·0	100·0	100·0
N	67	10	21	17	115

* Other = Liberal (9); SDP (1); SNP (4); Other (3).
** Figures in square brackets indicate that the base N for the given percentage is less than or equal to 15.

ipso facto, active members. In fact, over half never attend any party meetings at all! The remainder divide roughly equally between those who attend one to five meetings a year and those who go to six or more. We can, therefore, distinguish between a passive resource (membership) and participation (activity). The former does not always entail the latter, as many a political party will ruefully avow. The differences in activity levels between the parties turn out to be quite marked and consistent with the earlier findings. It is clear that the least active are the Conservative members, only 15% of whom could be described as very active, thus confirming in this respect an image of 'largely a sleeping membership' (Gamble 1979:40) but, as has been seen, like other party members the Conservatives on average participate to a very high degree. The other parties have about the same overall distributions: just over 40% very active and just over one-third totally inactive. The consequences for the party-participation relationship of these disparities in levels of activity is not, however, all that great. Were we to use party activity rather than membership as a predictor, we would find (as with trades union ties, etc.) that it was activity more than membership that was the more powerful ingredient. But, as we have noted, this is merely to predict participation measured in one way by participation measured in another.[2]

It remains the case that being a member of a political party is strongly associated with political participation. This, as we have acknowledged, is no more than one would expect. However, the nature of this relationship is far from uniform. In general, it stimulates participation, but in one important instance it discourages it. And the impact of membership varies both by party and by mode of activity.

Conclusion

Resources are important for participation but by no means all resources in all situations. As a result, it is not an easy task to draw together all the various elements in the analysis of both this and the previous chapter. There are too many factors to be taken into account and too many variations between one resource and another, and between one participatory arena and another, to admit of a summing up that does not risk misleading the reader. Nevertheless, one possible way of trying to encapsulate our findings is by combining individual resources into one simple scale, doing the same for group resources and then looking at how they relate to participation. This entails a considerable loss of nuance, but it can throw into better relief some of the broader patterns that lie behind the detail. To that extent, it is a worthwhile exercise, even if one that must be treated with some caution. We have, therefore, combined education and income levels into one basic index of individual-based resources. We have also added together all group ties, whether with voluntary groups, trades unions or political parties, to provide a very simplified but convenient measure of group-based resources. We have then used them to account for our scales of participation.

These summary results are set out in figure 5.10 which does indeed succeed in highlighting some of the broader points that emerge from the chapter. First, individual and group resources are positively related. The correlation between the two indices is 0·30, which is not huge but is certainly also not insignificant. By and large, disparities in resources at one level tend to complement and reinforce disparities at the other level. This is not in any exclusive way, but nevertheless in a manner that has persistent and important consequences for participation.

Secondly, resources taken together account for just over one-third (37·1%) of the variation up and down the ladder of overall participation. This gives a clearer idea of how effective the resource model is as a baseline explanation. The answer is that it is a very solid basic explanation, although one that leaves plenty of variation in citizen behaviour left over to be accounted for in other ways.

Thirdly, it is important to recognise that participation is not all of one piece. This was part of the message of chapter 3. But it is true in the present context as well. For, as can be seen in the figure, there is a considerable variation in the capacity of the resource model to explain the different modes of participation. As it turns out, none does as well as the summary scale which, in this respect at least, does not, in fact, summarise all that well.[3] But among the five modes, campaigning is the most susceptible to a resource interpretation with 30·2% of its variation accounted for by these two simple indices. After that come collective action (22·5%) and contacting (14·8%). Below these three we fall into a zone where less than 10% of the variation is explained by resources, which could be regarded as the qualitative threshold between an explanation that does reasonably well and one that does not do very well.

This means that direct action (9·3%) and, above all, voting (5·0%) are not, as a general rule, strongly influenced by resource factors. For these forms of activity we must look elsewhere for effective explanations as to why some citizens do a lot and others do a little. This does not mean that particular sub-groups of the population, as defined in resource terms, are not strongly associated, positively or negatively, with these types of activity. We have shown several instances of this. But it does suggest that across the population taken as a whole, the impact made by resources on protesting and voting is not all that great.

The fourth broad observation we can make from figure 5.10 concerns the relative importance for participation of individual and group resources. Here again, there is a consistent pattern, but one that is more pronounced in some types of activity than others. Group resources are generally much more consequential than individual resources. For overall participation, the group resources index has a beta nearly three

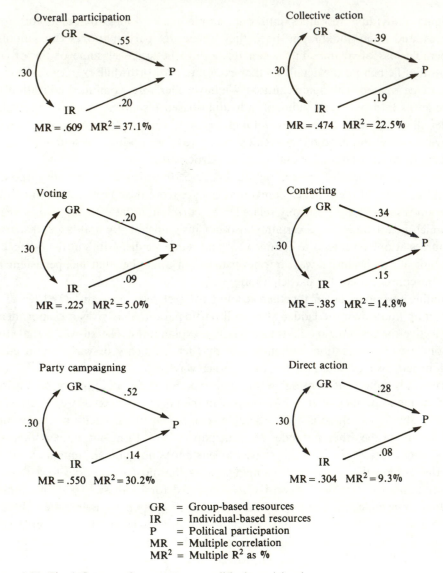

Figure 5.10 The influence of resources on political participation

times as strong as the individual scale (0·55 to 0·20). In this instance, the result is quite representative. There are activities where the two types of resource are more in balance, such as contacting, but even here group factors are more than twice as strong as individual ones. Thus, even in contacting, which has been described as primarily individualist, group resources appear more important than the personal resources of wealth and education. Indeed, the balance between the two sets of resources appears little different from that for collective action where one would naturally expect group factors to dominate. However, this may be one of those instances where the summary measure conceals as much as it reveals.

At the outset of the chapter, it was suggested that contacting was, by and large, something undertaken on the initiative of the individual rather than mobilised by groups. By contrast, collective action was overwhelmingly mobilised action, as was protest. This suggests that the relationship between individual resources and action is different in the two cases. In collective action, a person's membership of a group permits the group itself and its leaders to reach out and, in a descending fashion, mobilise the individual to action. Still more is this true of direct action, whilst the link between campaigning and party organisation is self-evident. This is reflected in figure 5.10 where the group resource betas are between three and a half and four times as strong as those at the individual level. In the case of contacting, the person may act alone but membership of a group and, still more, being part of a network of groups, is important in a different way. The group is used by the individual, in an ascending fashion, as a source of information and of orientation towards issues, action and the responsible authorities. In general, the social interactionist approach to political behaviour gains a strong measure of support from the analysis. Those who are well-integrated into group life are, on the whole, more participatory. And, as the theory would predict, still more involved are those who are most active within their group. Action generates action.

It is tempting to adapt two aphorisms of political science to describe the conclusions of our argument so far concerning resources. The first is that 'resources are the basis of political participation; all else is embellishment and detail'. The second adaptation is that 'who says organisation, says participation'. But, as ever with aphorisms, they need elaboration and qualification. We have seen that resources take us only so far. It is now necessary to consider the other elements in our model of participation – starting with those economic factors associated with unemployment and class.

6

ECONOMIC LOCATION

One of the major tenets underlying the analysis of capitalist societies is that political outlooks and behaviour are fundamentally shaped by the pursuit of individual and group economic self-interest. We need, therefore, to consider how these economic factors impinge on political participation. This is especially the case if participation is, as it is widely conceived by theorists and respondents alike, principally an instrumental activity undertaken to realise goals or protect interests through political means.

However, to move from such an abstract conception to concrete indicators and tests is to move from near consensus amongst social analysts to confusion, conflict and even acrimonious debate (see, for example, Cotgrove 1982:93–4; Crewe 1986; Heath, Jowell and Curtice 1987). There is general agreement in other words that economic circumstances influence political action, but much less concurrence over the measures to be used to demonstrate the linkage, and therefore over the interpretations to be made and the conclusions to be drawn.

As the discussion in this chapter unfolds, some of the terms of the debate, and the detailed choices we have made will become plain. But our initial and most fundamental decision was to determine the set of measures of economic location to be deployed. In the event, we settled on four. These were, respectively, the politically sensitive distinction between those in employment, those unemployed and those economically inactive; secondly, class itself; thirdly, employment sector, distinguishing here between public and private; and finally a measure of consumption cleavages – the relative dependency of individuals on goods and services supplied by the public as against the private sector. These four do not, of course, exhaust what might be studied under the general economic heading, but they seem to provide at least the major ingredients. Certainly they should offer an adequate test of how position in the economic marketplace gets translated, if at all, into the type and level of activity in the political marketplace.

Finally, it is necessary to outline the broad form of the analysis. As we have seen, generally speaking, resources and institutional ties provide a relatively powerful account of how individuals come to participate in British politics. This is, therefore, an important circumstance to take into account when looking at the effects of economic location. For much of the thrust of class-based analyses of political behaviour has been to do with the greater resources of middle class, as against working class, individuals. Equally the presence of trades unions and a political party based traditionally upon a working-class constituency provide alternative ways in which resource disadvantages might be overcome by membership ties which unlock the collective resources of the labour movement. These are possibilities which must be explored and, in doing so, the particular impact of class and other economic factors on political participation can be clarified.

Employed–unemployed

It is a common-place amongst critics of current trends in Britain that one of the most significant political divides is between the 'haves' and 'have-nots'. One key element that perhaps distinguishes the two better than any other is being employed or unemployed. Those with a job have, at worst, been given some substantial protection against the difficulties that particular regions and sectors of the economy have experienced. At best, they have benefited from a very considerable degree of prosperity buttressed by tax cuts and salary increases that have generally exceeded price inflation. Those without a job, on the other hand, have experienced a social security and benefits system that has become more strict as well as seeing the gap between their own standard of living and that of the employed widen considerably. Furthermore, unemployment is often merely one part of a broader syndrome of individual, family and areal deprivation that also encompasses problems of health, housing, education, and crime.

How do these two disparate groups,[1] often separated by a gulf of economic, social and environmental conditions, react to their circumstances? Are there any signs of the unemployed taking to the streets in acts of political protest? Or are they motivated by their circumstances to become active in groups and party campaigns, or to contact governmental and other targets to put unemployment even more firmly on the nation's agenda? Or is it that unemployment provides the time and opportunity for the individual to act on prior political commitments? On the other hand, it may be that such individuals typically find the struggle to cope with the day-to-day vicissitudes of life leaves little time left over for playing politics. Finally, for them, protracted disappointments may have turned into apathy.

To examine these various possibilities, the participation profiles of the unemployed, of those in work, and of those not 'economically active' (mainly the retired, spouses looking after the home, and students) are presented, using the overall scale, in figure 6.1. The 'raw' figures suggest that it is the 'withdrawal' hypothesis which is the more accurate. However, the evidence also shows very substantial disparities both in individual resources and in ties to organisations that must be taken into account. Thus, in educational terms for example, just over half the unemployed (50·5%) had no qualifications at all, whilst a mere two (2·1%) had a degree. By contrast, only a third of the employed were without any qualifications and as many as 10·4% were graduates. Similar differences show up on our wealth index: only a tiny handful (0·4%) of the employed were in the poorest stratum, compared with 18·8% of the unemployed. Conversely, 7·4% of those in jobs were amongst the wealthiest group where not one of the unemployed was to be found. Finally, a substantial gap also exists in the extent of membership ties. Using our combined index of union, party and voluntary group linkages, less than a third (32·1%) of employed individuals registered zero ties as against nearly half (47·7%) of the unemployed.

The effect of all this on political participation can be observed from figure 6.1 in the pattern of the 'adjusted deviations' derived from a multiple classification analysis (see notes 4–7 in chapter 4). From their very low resource base, the unemployed in fact show a modest tendency in the opposite direction – towards activism.[2] In other words, the unemployed are not particularly active citizens all in all, but, relative to their poor resources, they are somewhat more participatory than average. If anything, it would seem that unemployment does politicise individuals whereas those who remain in a job are mildly quiescent. It is possible to argue, however, that what is at work here is not so much political action being prompted by unemployment as unemployment providing the opportunity for prior politicisation to be activated. The unemployed may have more time for politics than their employed counterparts.[3] It is, therefore, not easy to interpret the relationship and, in fact, different interpretations may apply in different individual cases.

Finally, there is that rather disparate group of individuals who, for one reason or another, were outside the labour market. Their pattern, like that of the unemployed, shifts from relative inertia to relative activism when resource and similar factors are taken into account. Furthermore, an inspection of their educational background and organisational ties, shows them to be even more disadvantaged in these terms than the unemployed. Nearly two-thirds (63·4%) had no qualifications, and almost as many (59·6%) lacked any institutional links that they might exploit – all of which is part and parcel of why, in absolute terms, they are on the low side of the overall participatory divide. However, as with the unemployed, their relative propensity to be active (+15) is also open to different interpretations. In their case, there is not presumably the immediate stimulus of unemployment present because, by definition, they are economically inactive. This also means that they have even more time and opportunity to be politically active – to the extent their resources allow. All in all, therefore, the factor of opportunity would seem to be a potentially strong one. This does not necessarily mean that it is so for the unemployed as well, but it does clearly indicate that it is an element which cannot be ignored. Whatever the case, however, both the inactive and the unemployed are not quite as voiceless as their resource position might suggest.

Detailed analysis suggests that it is through campaigning for political parties and involvement in political protest that the unemployed most clearly display their relative activism. In party campaigning, as can be seen in figure 6.1, the effect is again only noticeable on the adjusted figures, but the linkage with direct action appears with or without such controls. On this basis, therefore, it does seem as though unemployment acts as a stimulus to, or opportunity for, action through both conventional and less conventional channels. To this extent, the 'withdrawal' hypothesis can be ruled out. On the other hand, party campaigning and protest are the only two forms of action that are above the average. Certainly, the figures for voting and group activity indicate that the unemployed are, if anything, a bit less participatory than the sample as a whole.

All in all, then, there is a distinctive connection between unemployment itself and political action – after due allowances for a lack of resources are made. To the extent that it is a matter of opportunity, then it is an opportunity for direct action that is

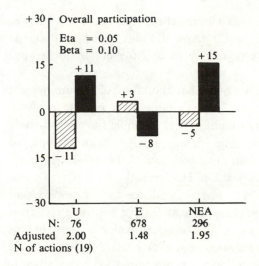

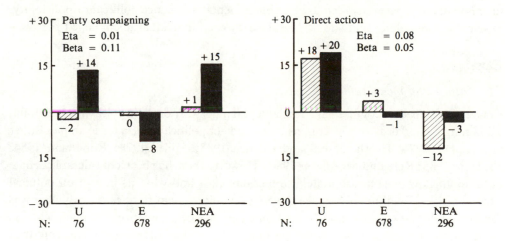

Figure 6.1 Employment, unemployment and participation

grasped. But it has to be said that, in comparison with the effect of resources themselves, the condition of unemployment is obviously not a major stimulus (or opportunity) in itself to join in the political battle, just as remaining in employment is not a huge disincentive.

Mild though it may be, it is interesting to note that the effect of unemployment appears to be somewhat stronger than in the United States. In a parallel analysis, Schlozman and Verba (1979) describe a set of findings that resemble the present study in several ways. Thus, like us, they found that, superficially, the American unemployed were less interested and involved in politics than those with jobs (1979:241–2). Controls for occupation, age and gender reversed this position. However, the unemployed's new advantage was statistically insignificant. There was no evidence that unemployment politicised those concerned – in terms of participation at least. Unfortunately, their measures of participation did not separate out political protest which is, perhaps, the one area in the British data where there is the clearest sign of an effect. Nevertheless, the impression persists that unemployment does politicise Britons somewhat more, albeit in limited ways, than seems to be the case in the United States. It may be that this is connected to the difference between the two countries in the extent to which unemployment is generally seen to be a governmental and hence political responsibility, rather than something that should be solved by each individual unemployed person.

Class

The nature and measurement of class

Class has long been recognised as a fundamental if possibly declining cleavage in Britain, explaining a good deal of how citizens think and act politically (see, for example, Butler and Stokes 1974; Heath, Jowell and Curtice 1985; Miller 1978; Robertson 1984; Franklin 1985; Rose and McAllister 1986). However there has been considerable debate both about how most appropriately to measure class and what its impact on political choices now is. Traditionally, analysts were generally content to operate with what was fundamentally a two-class model based on categories of occupation – manual workers as against non-manual workers, or working class as against middle class. This then allowed a fairly simple assessment of the key relationship with the then two major political parties – Labour and Conservative (see, for example, Bonham 1954; Butler and Stokes 1974). It also sustained much of the class-based rhetoric of British political commentary – of 'us against them' and 'workers against bosses' – as well as becoming deeply engrained as a broader social and cultural phenomenon.[4]

In fact, however, students of political behaviour have employed a six-fold scale of occupations developed by pollsters and market researchers which stretched from higher management to unskilled workers (see Kahan *et al.* 1966; Butler and Stokes 1974; Rose 1974:500–2). This was then divided into a 'working class' composed of unskilled workers and skilled and semi-skilled workers and a wide 'middle class' comprising the rest. For market researchers, concerned with identifying the purchasing powers, spending habits and consumer preferences of different social strata, this approach offered, and continues to offer, advantages in that it associates occupational groups with a hierarchy of income, social status and life-style (see Heath, Jowell and Curtice

1985:13–14). But whilst a division of this hierarchy into classes did serve fairly well in the past in predicting the propensity of people to vote Labour or Conservative, by the 1970s and 1980s the traditional linkages between class and voting patterns were disrupted. Accordingly, social scientists began to look again at the categorisation of occupational groupings in order to distinguish more clearly their distinctive economic interests and how these might translate into partisan preferences (Goldthorpe and Hope 1974; Goldthorpe 1980; Robertson 1984; Heath, Jowell and Curtice 1985; Dunleavy and Husbands 1985). These new approaches have sought to separate income and consumption from class itself as separate and distinct influences on political action.

It should be noted that this conceptual 'revisionism' is very much in line with Marx's position. As Cohen put it (1978:73), 'A person's class is established by nothing but his objective place in the network of ownership relations, however difficult it may be to define such places neatly.' The result, as we see it, is a concept that is sharper in meaning and therefore more useful as a tool of social and political explanation.

The general thinking behind this approach can be illustrated from the work of Heath, Jowell and Curtice (1985) in the case of wage labourers. They argue that this group has a distinctive economic interest based on its market position which gives substance to its formation as a 'class':

Broadly speaking, wage labourers have different interests from those of the self-employed or from those of salaried managers and professionals. Their incomes may overlap, but the conditions under which they earn that income differ quite markedly...For example, manual wage labourers have relatively little security of employment and relatively poor fringe benefits such as sick pay and pension schemes. They have little control over their own working conditions and little discretion, being subject to managerial authority, over what they do at work. They also have relatively poor chances (despite some social mobility) of gaining promotion to the better paid and secure managerial positions. As a result manual wage-earners cannot be sure to improve their lot through *individual* action. Instead they must look to *collective* action, either through trades unions or political parties. They have a shared interest, in other words, in collective bargaining over wages and working conditions and in government intervention to reduce the risks of unemployment and redundancy.

(Heath, Jowell and Curtice 1985:14–5)

Here, then, is a class, formed around a common set of economic interests which clearly indicate a particular set of political values and styles of action.

By the same token, other economic classes can also be distinguished which collectively provide a systematic and coherent framework through which economic location and political participation can be analysed. We have been very much persuaded by this general line of argument and have accordingly adopted it in our treatment of class. In particular, a differentiated classification has advantages when seeking to explain the patterns of participation and their relation to issues, which are more varied than the range of party preferences open to voters (see Robertson 1984:107). Without going into further details, the five-fold schema we have employed[5] can be set out as follows with the proportions of each class identified in our sample:

1. *The working class* (37·7%) includes both skilled, semi-skilled and unskilled manual employees,[6] but removes into a separate category those who are

2. *Foremen and technicians* (6·3%). These are 'a kind of blue-collar elite' (Heath, Jowell and Curtice 1985:16) in that they exercise a limited degree of shop-floor

authority, and a certain amount of personal discretion and autonomy. This puts them in a marginal position between the working class from which they have been recruited and the managerial class (see below).

3. *The petty bourgeoisie* (10·7%) stand outside the class structure of large-scale industry in that they are self-employed, and therefore not only are they 'directly exposed to market forces without the cushioning of bureaucratic employment or trade union membership' (Heath, Jowell and Curtice 1985:15), they also have an interest in private enterprise and individual initiatives. Besides skilled artisans working on their own account, small proprietors (possibly with a few employees) and shop-keepers, they also include the relatively small number of farmers within the British labour force.[7]

4. *The routine nonmanual* (20·6%) class includes clerks, typists and salesworkers, etc., who are subordinate to the managerial class, and marginal to it, even though providing one source of recruitment for more senior posts.

5. Finally, there is the '*salariat*' (24·8%), comprising 'managers, semi-professionals' (Heath, Jowell and Curtice 1985:16). Individuals in this class have the greatest autonomy and discretion and a relatively secure basis of employment. They include the leading echelons of industry, commerce and the professions.

These, then, are the five classes that form the basis of our analysis. They provide a fairly simple scheme through which economic interest, as dictated by market position, can be scrutinised for its effect in terms of political action. However, at appropriate points, more particular relationships within the salariat and the working class will be discussed in order to clarify and emphasise the patterns that emerge.

Class and participation

The basic linkage between class and the overall participation scale is laid out in figure 6.2. From this, two features are immediately apparent. First, the only two classes which are, initially at least, more active than average are the salariat and the foremen and technicians. It seems, therefore, that the greatest readiness to participate is to be found amongst the two leading economic echelons of the 'middle class' and 'working class' respectively. Secondly, we can see that, again on an unadjusted basis, the members of the salariat are much more participatory (even more so in the case of the higher salariat at +52) than their manual counterparts, the foremen and technicians.

The relationship between class and the specific modes of action is, as in figure 6.3, in most respects quite similar to that discovered for overall participation. Class appears to have a relatively strong influence on the propensity for collective action. The salariat out-participate all others (+30). The petty bourgeoisie display their individualistic character by markedly under-participating (−25). The working class do not appear to compensate very heavily by collective action for any weakness they may suffer as individual actors. The salariat also lead strongly in party campaigning (+23) with the working class well behind (−14). The petty bourgeoisie are slightly more ready to be involved in these activities.

In the case of contacting, the petty bourgeoisie, significantly, participate in this more personal mode slightly above the average as do foremen and technicians. Otherwise the pattern is roughly the same as for collective activity. A similar relationship holds for

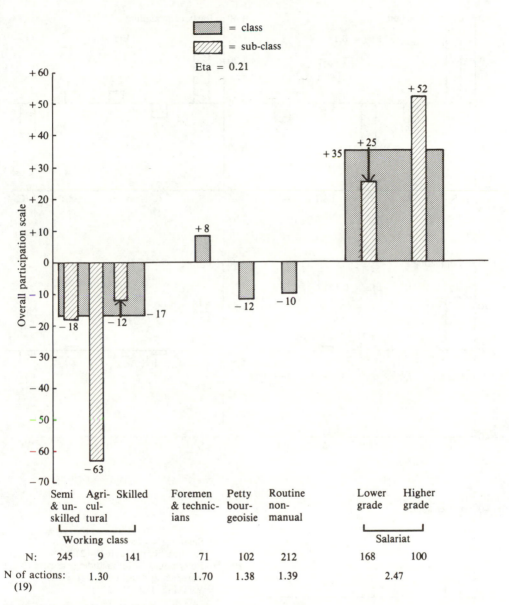

Figure 6.2 Overall participation by class

voting where, again, the salariat is most ready to turn out to vote (+18) and the working class the least (−12). The overall relationship with direct action is insignificant and the most notable difference is the negative attitude of the petty bourgeoisie.

A central question, however, is whether such patterns solely reflect differences of class. To answer this question we must be clear as to what we mean by class. Class could be defined very broadly, to include income, education and life-style for example – class as embodying a whole way of life. In this framework, the results set out in figure 6.2 could be taken as a guide to the predictive power of class with little modification. One would then conclude that for overall participation, at least, class is quite a substantial influence. Thus, at the most extreme, the gap between the admittedly very small number of

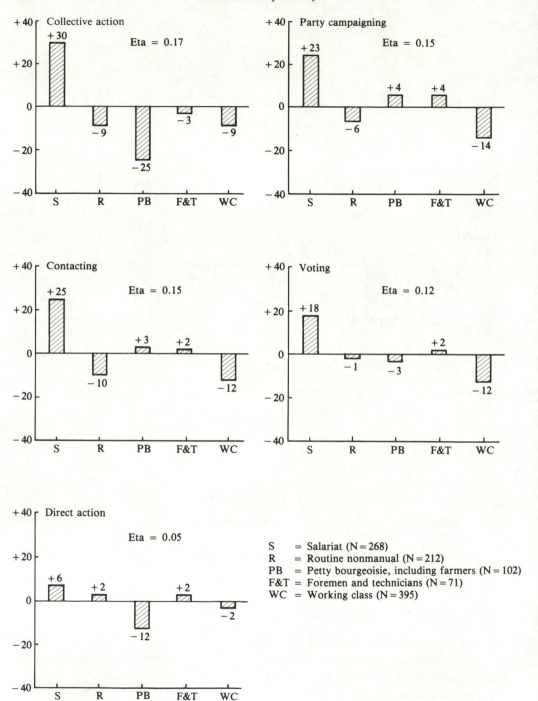

Figure 6.3 Participation by mode and class

agricultural workers and those in the higher grades of the salariat is a wide one (115 points). The contrast between working class (−17) and the salariat as a whole (+35) is also considerable.

We have argued, however, that class is better understood in a more restricted sense as a person's location in the economic structure. The major methodological advantage is that, within the framework of a class analysis, it allows one to distinguish *explanans* and *explanandum*. Writing from an explicitly Marxist perspective, Cohen argues that a person's

consciousness, culture, and politics do not enter the *definition* of his class position. Indeed, these exclusions are required to protect the substantive character of the Marxian thesis that class position strongly conditions consciousness, culture and politics. (Cohen 1978:73)

Hence, our own approach is, firstly, to examine how far a person's position in relation to production relations – that person's class – conditions the possession of those resources which make for participation. Is it the case that certain classes have a highly disproportionate share of individual and organisational resources? Or, in other words, does the hierarchy of classes match exactly the hierarchy of resources in society? Secondly, it is necessary to enquire whether, to the degree that there is a relationship between class and resources, certain resources are more concentrated in certain classes than in others. To what extent, for example, are the personal resources of the managerial classes counter-balanced by the organisational resources of the working class? If so, from the standpoint of political activism, this would suggest that an egalitarian should seek to reinforce the organisational base of the working class.

Our method will follow the lines of analysis we have already been employing. Having established above a positive connection between class and resources, we shall control for those resources in order to establish whether class, *strictu sensu*, leaves any imprint on participation – whether, that is, economic location itself constitutes an interest which translates into political action. But firstly, it is necessary to establish the precise match between resources and position in the economic structure.

As can be seen in table 6.1, the assumption that class and resources are empirically associated is certainly true. Only a tenth of the salariat as a whole lack any formal educational qualifications compared with nearly two thirds of the working class. If the focus is then narrowed to the higher salariat, and the semi- and unskilled within the working class, the gap widens even further – to 7·3 % and 73·1 % respectively. Equivalent patterns exist at the other end of the educational scale. One quarter of the salariat are graduates, an achievement shared by only four people (0·8 %) in working-class occupations. In terms of wealth, the class differentials in education are broadly repeated. Four times as many working-class individuals are in the nation's poorest 25 %, compared with those from the salariat. Equally, the gap widens enormously when the higher salariat and semi- and unskilled are set beside each other. Amongst the higher salariat a mere 1 % are 'poor', whereas fully one third (33·7 %) of the semi- and unskilled are in this position.

Here, however, it is also apparent that there is not a simple linear relationship between class and wealth. Unlike education, wealth varies significantly in a non-linear way. Thus, focusing on the wealth stratum in table 6.1, the salariat are clearly the wealthiest by a considerable margin (and, above all, the higher grades, three quarters of whom fall into this category). Thereafter, however, it is the petty bourgeoisie, followed closely by the foremen and technicians, who come next in line, with the routine nonmanuals only in fourth place. This, indeed, is of a piece with analysis by Heath, Jowell and Curtice of

Table 6.1 *Class by selected resource characteristics*

	Salariat	Routine nonmanual	Petty bourgeois	Foremen and technicians	Working class	Whole sample
Education						
No qualifications	11·5	28·6	42·0	54·3	64·9	41·1
Degree	24·9	3·8	2·2	0·0	0·8	7·5
Wealth						
Poorest 25%*	7·1	18·9	7·5	12·7	28·9	18·3
Richest 25%*	57·3	20·3	34·9	29·6	8·4	27·1
Ties						
None	28·1	45·3	52·6	21·0	41·2	38·7
Five+	8·8	3·0	0·7	3·7	1·6	3·6
Average	1·80	1·10	0·84	1·57	1·22	1·32
N	320	265	137	81	485	1,288

Entries are the percentages of each class that have the given resource characteristics.
* Because of missing data, the actual distribution for the 'whole' sample has shifted from the proportions indicated.

hourly earnings as between the five classes. They also found that foremen and technicians were relatively advantaged, and routine nonmanuals disadvantaged in these terms (1985:16). However, the wealth measure used here, which is based on other criteria in addition to merely income, suggests that the classes do not diverge so sharply. On the other hand, we share with Heath, Jowell and Curtice the view that class, in terms of individual resources at least, 'is not neatly hierarchical' (1985:16).

What they do not consider, but which is, of course, an essential part of the analysis of class and political behaviour, is whether the working class especially 'picks up' relatively speaking when the more collectivist resources implied by group ties are brought into play. The answer in table 6.1 seems to be that this is only partially true. If we simply look at the average number of ties, be they to a party, trade union (or staff association) or voluntary group, then the working class comes in third place at 1·22 ties per individual. This is higher than the routine nonmanuals (1·10) and much higher than the petty bourgeoisie (0·84). Indeed, the latter constitute perhaps the most discrepant case in that they possess relatively large personal resources but relatively limited collectivist support. This is, of course, of a piece with the general character of their occupations as self-employed persons. But perhaps of more immediate importance is the fact that the foremen and technicians have noticeably more organisational ties than the working class (at 1·57), and that the salariat has the highest number of all (1·80). So, across all three criteria, the salariat is consistently and strongly advantaged – above all the higher salariat. But, equally, the foremen and technicians show that their ties are relatively substantial, and their position in wealth terms is by no means weak compared with the population at large. Only in the educational sector do they follow a pattern much closer to the working-class norm.[8] All in all, therefore, they do exhibit distinct signs of being a manual elite, just as the higher salariat does within the ranks of the nonmanuals.

The empirical relationship between class and resources is, clearly, a relatively complex one overall. The salariat seems advantaged across the board, other classes do better in some ways than in others but no class consistently takes bottom place. There is, therefore, no one-to-one correspondence between class and resources. The two hierarchies do not match precisely, even though there is a strong relationship between them. This implies that a class analysis is not an exact substitute for a resource-based analysis. To examine this further, it is necessary to look at how the differences between the resources of the various classes feed into, and alter, the class-participation nexus. As earlier chapters have shown, the various sets of resources are not equally important overall. Moreover, their relevance for participation varies from one mode of activity to another.

The initial evidence, for the overall participation scale, is set out in figure 6.4. When differences of educational, wealth, and organisational resources are removed, the pattern is modified very considerably, although some imprint of the original unadjusted relationship from figure 6.2 can be detected. Thus, when resources are 'equalised' in this way, those in the salariat remain more participatory, but to a much reduced extent. The same is also true of the foremen and technicians. Thus, the apparent initial effect of class on participation is largely the result of resources. But this is not a tautology since, as we have just seen, those resources, whilst related to class, do not precisely correspond with the hierarchy of class. At the same time, the removal of the effect of those resources does not entirely eliminate the impact of class.

It is not, therefore, surprising that the working class move up to a position just below the overall average. Much of their relative inactivity is attributable to their disadvantageous resource position. All in all, the effect of adjusting for resource differentials is to reduce the explanatory power of class to about one-third of that in figure 6.2. This is reflected in the beta which is now a very modest 0·04. It is also reflected in the gap between agricultural workers and higher grade members of the salariat – down to 41 points. Class, in short, achieves a substantial resonance only when resources are counted in as part of a broader 'class effect'. If class is defined in a narrower way, then much of its relevance for participation in general evaporates. This is not to say, however, that class construed in this restricted sense is entirely irrelevant, for there is a residual weak class effect. Agricultural workers in particular, and the working class in general, under-participate to a modest degree, while the salariat and petty bourgeoisie over-participate, also to a modest extent. Why might this be so?

One possible answer is that, even when resources have been removed, there remain certain other factors, possibly arising from a person's economic location, which we have not so far identified but which affect the propensity to participate. For example, the autonomy which distinguishes the productive situation of many of the salariat may provide them with greater flexibility to allocate their time to political activity than could be possessed by the average member of the routine non-manual, foremen or working class. Aside from resources which facilitate action, there may be other reasons why the salariat appear more prone to act to conserve their economic standing than the working class is to improve it. Some of these reasons may, indeed, flow also from the differences

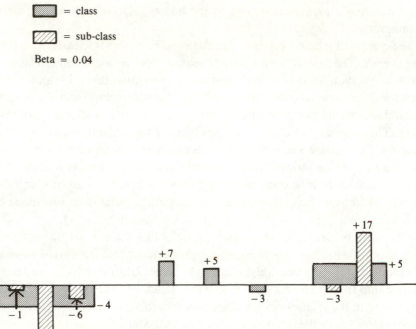

Figure 6.4 Overall participation by class, controlling for individual and group resources

in resources. A historical record of political and economic success may reinforce a propensity to act amongst the better-off classes and a relative lack of impact may diminish the political confidence of others. In chapter 8 we shall look at the effect in combination with resources of such values as a sense of political efficacy on participation. But, as we shall see, there are other outlooks, such as a positive evaluation of political action, which are not reducible in any obvious or direct way to economic class interest.

Meanwhile, one further way of trying to throw light on the nature of this 'adjusted' class relationship is to move from the overall scale, which is, after all, only a summary, to the individual modes. Here, however, it is not clear why the working class should

Table 6.2 *Collective action, party campaigning and direct action by class*

	Collective action	Party campaigning	Direct action
Salariat	−2	+6	−6
Higher grade	+19	+16	−19
Lower grade	−9	−2	+1
Routine non-manual	−5	−2	0
*Petty bourgeoisie**	−13	+18	−1
Foremen and technicians	0	+2	+6
Working class	+6	−7	+2
Skilled manual	+9	−13	+7
Semi and unskilled	+4	−4	0
Agricultural	−6	+9	−11
Beta	0·05	0·07	0·04

Adjusted for individual and group resources.
* Excluding farmers (N = 3).

always exhibit a disincentive to participate. On the contrary, it seems plausible to hypothesise some association between the working class and at least the collectivised forms of political action. The reasoning behind this was articulated previously: the working class has less security of employment, poor fringe benefits, little control over working conditions and poor promotion prospects. The remedy, therefore, arguably lies in organisation, in mutual aid, in solidarity and strength through weight of numbers.

These class effects may be tested by using three collectivised modes: collective action, party campaigning and direct action. If there is a discernible and consistent class influence deriving from economic interest, then these three taken together should pick it up. As can be seen from table 6.2, however, the results are somewhat disappointing. The working class has a slightly higher than average score on collective action (+6), but a negative one on party-campaigning (−7). Equally, the internal working class formations also show certain inconsistencies. The semi- and unskilled workers, who might be expected to show a stronger effect than unskilled workers, do not, although the differences are not great. The agricultural workers' profile is the opposite of that of the industrial workers', possibly reflecting the problems facing a dispersed class in operating collectively, quite aside from the obstacles which have traditionally faced farmworkers in attempts at unionisation which has here been discounted (Danziger 1988:80–93).

Direct action involves activities which are aimed at the defence of economic interest, such as 'political' strikes or marches in support of the retention of jobs, but also others, such as the boycott of goods, which are more clearly political. This mixture of elements might be reflected in the scores of the various classes. It might help to explain the very low, if positive, score of +2 for the working class. The skilled manual, however, are the most prone to direct action (+7), but agricultural workers are again uninvolved (−11). The working class are, therefore, generally disposed towards collectivised forms of action but not to any particularly significant degree.

It is, of course, possible that our measures of collective action are not picking up, or

Table 6.3 *Contacting by class*

Salariat	+9
Higher grade	+18
Lower grade	0
Routine non-manual	−3
Petty bourgeoisie	+9
Foremen and technicians	−1
Working class	−6
Skilled manual	−10
Semi and unskilled	−1
Agricultural	−20
Beta	0·07

Adjusted for individual and group resources.

are disguising in some way, a connection between the lower class formations and collectivised action. After all, we have noted previously that the collective action scale does seem to relate more to the 'new politics' than the 'old'. Similarly, a better explanation of the campaign pattern is, perhaps, the fact that the petty bourgeoisie and salariat are strongly committed to the Tory Party, while the skilled manuals espouse the Labour Party (Heath, Jowell and Curtice 1985:20–1). The campaign pattern, therefore, is more likely to be revealing the variable imprint of class-based economic interest on party commitments rather than on collectivised action as such. Thus, if economic interest does feed systematically into collective political action, it does so in varied ways.

A second hypothesis concerning the relationship between class and participation might be that members of the petty bourgeoisie and salariat would have a higher propensity to engage in more individualistic forms of participation. In testing this suggestion, there is only one scale, that of contacting. As table 6.3 suggests, the evidence here of a class effect is also not strong, but generally favourable to the hypothesis. The salariat in general (+9), and the higher grades in particular (+18), are more prone than average to contact. The same is true of the petty bourgeoisie (+9). Conversely, routine nonmanuals (−3), foremen and technicians (−3) and the working class (−6) are less active in this area.

The conclusion would seem to be that once the effect of resources, as we have identified them, is removed, the residual class effect on participation is not a strong one. It is patchy and not entirely consistent. This means that if class is construed in the restricted and conceptually sharper terms that we have used, it adds relatively little to the understanding of political participation. However, it is important to appreciate that we are far from dismissing the importance of class in a wider sense. We have shown that class and both individual and organisational resources are strongly linked in Britain. Behind resources, and powerfully conditioning them, is a person's location in the structure of relations of production. Nevertheless, class does not entirely *determine* resources. The hierarchies of class and resources do not match precisely. Consequently, we would contend that a more refined analysis of participation is attainable through the employment of a resource rather than a class analysis. Even so, when considering in the rest of this book the participatory profile of those well- or poorly-endowed with resources, the reader should recall the very considerable, though far from complete, degree to which these resources do, indeed, appear in Britain to stem from economic class.

Employment sector

One further, and potentially important, element in defining an individual's location in the economic marketplace is his or her sector of employment. The important distinction here is between those in the public as against the private sector (Dunleavy and Husbands 1985:132–3; Alt and Turner 1982). The growth of public sector employment in the post-war period would seem likely to create a new and increasingly important division of interests. Clearly enough, when the Conservative Party and Labour Party take very different policy stands on these two economic spheres, in terms of privatisation programmes, trade union issues and fiscal treatment, then the ways in which the respective interests of individuals employed in them get expressed in the political system become an important question.

What is not clear, however, is whether sectoral economic interests affect the actual level of electoral participation, in the form of turnout. Nor has it been established how such factors influence other avenues of participation outside the electoral domain where parties do less to highlight such cleavages. The basic relationship between employment sector and political participation turns out to be simple and consistent across every particular mode: those in public sector occupations are more active. This comes across clearly in the unadjusted figures in figure 6.5, although the relationship is not as strong as in the case of the unadjusted class relationship. On this basis, therefore, it is tempting to conclude that being employed by the state has the effect of raising political awareness.

The question, however, is whether this conclusion stands up once differential resources are taken into account. In fact, it appears from our evidence that an analogous effect also undermines the apparent association between the public sector and their heightened rates of participation. Three times as many public sector employees, for example, hold a degree (13% to 4.5%). Similarly, a somewhat higher proportion of them are to be found amongst the nation's wealthiest quarter (28.5% to 26.7%). But perhaps the greatest discrepancy occurs in the area of organisational linkages. Here, less than half as many public employees have no ties as private sector individuals (21.9% to 47.0%). All in all, therefore, the public sector employees are consistently better resourced for participation than the private.

The effect of this on patterns of political participation is also set out in the graphs of figure 6.5. So far as the overall scale is concerned, the relationship observed previously is eroded to the point where those in the public sector, relative to their resource base, actually participate at the same level as those in the private sphere – and precisely on the mean. The beta (0.03) confirms that effectively the association is washed out: the apparent sectoral impact at this level of generality is entirely accounted for by differential resources. A somewhat similar pattern also emerges in the areas of collective activity, party campaigning and of contacting (the latter two not displayed in the figure).

However, there are two areas, voting and direct action, where a residual sectoral influence can just be discerned – the figures for both of which are also set out in figure

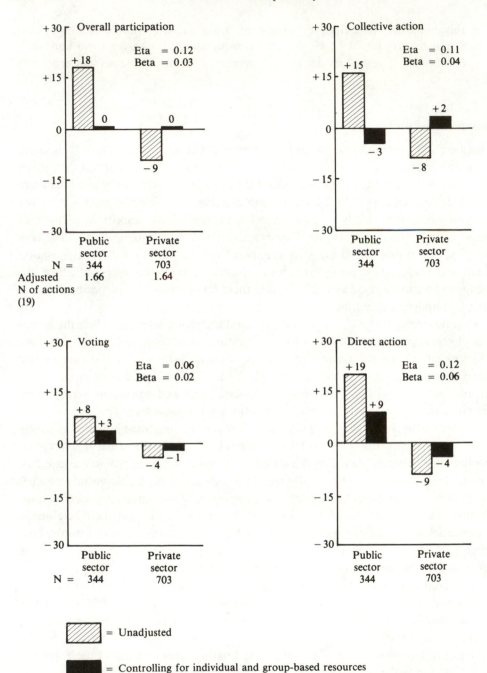

Figure 6.5 Participation by employment sector

6.5. Here, the initial positive impulse associated with the public sector (albeit very mild in the case of voting turnout) remains even on an adjusted basis. Though we would not wish to make much of either pattern, it is perhaps understandable that, in the key area of elections where more is immediately at stake for public sector employees and where the activities of parties have focused attention on the state and its limits, this should give

Table 6.4 *Direct action by class and employment sector*

	Sector			
Class	Private	(N)	Public	N
Lower salariat	−2 (−5)*	(84)	+12 (+38)*	84
Routine office workers	−4 (−7)*	(95)	+15 (+27)*	64
Foremen and technicians	−5 (−12)*	(35)	+18 (+15)*	36
Skilled working	−5 (−3)*	(111)	+38 (+39)*	30

* Unadjusted scores.

some impetus, even if very slight, to involvement. The association with protest, on the other hand, is best looked at from the point of view of both sector and class together.

We found previously that, relative to resources, the only above-average signs of direct action on a class basis involved the lower salariat and routine office-workers (a sub-group of routine nonmanuals) at the nonmanual level, and foremen and skilled workers in the manual strata. But none of their scores, except possibly for the last group (+6) were particularly noteworthy. When we look inside each of these four classes at their public and private sector components, however, the picture is sharpened somewhat, as Table 6.4 indicates.

Thus, when class and sector are examined in combination, we find that those in the private sector, regardless of class background, remain mildly on the non-protest side of the fence. But, within the public sector, not only are they on the positive side, but the degree to which this is the case increases as one moves from lower salariat to the skilled workers. In consequence, the clearest source of direct action in these joint terms is the public sector component of the skilled working class. By the same token, this class is also the most sharply divided of all – at least in the domain of political protest.

To put the matter in context, the deviation of +38 recorded by the public sector skilled workers is on the surface quite dramatic, putting them as a group within the top 13% on the political protest scale. Equally, it is a position which persists almost regardless of their resources and organisational affiliations – as is indicated by the lack of change as between the unadjusted and adjusted relationship. It would seem that this blue-collar stratum in the public services is a significant source of political protest in Britain. However, given that levels of direct action are generally low, it would be quite wrong to infer that even amongst this group of people there is intense and active unrest. Only a minority of blue-collar public sector workers do protest and thus their high rate of action is very much to be seen as relative to the overall pattern. Nevertheless, there are signs that they constitute a group which can be mobilised to demonstrate or take other forms of action, especially over such matters as threatened cuts in social services.

Interesting though these influences are, they are obviously relatively narrow when set against the whole range of participation with which we are concerned. Employment sector plays an occasional role, but it too is not a major determinant of political participation in Britain.

Consumption sector

The view that sectorally-based, rather than class-based, interests can exert an influence on individual political outlooks and behaviour need not be restricted to employment but can be extended to other aspects of life. In a mixed economy there is, by definition, a range of opportunities to obtain goods and services from either public or private sector suppliers. The balance of supply will to a great extent depend on the political and ideological positions of governments and parties, although a number of historical factors have a bearing. Thus the mix of public as against private housing is subject to change, as more people are in a financial position to purchase their own homes, but also as governments affect the supply – most radically by the Conservative Government's decision to allow the sale of council houses to sitting tenants. In a number of other areas of service provision, such as education, health and transport, the choice between consuming public or private services has also been subject to debate.

    The argument that this can lead to a 'consumption cleavage' in society rests on the view that society is divided between those who consume essential services from private suppliers and those who rely on supply by the state or local government (see Castells 1978; Dunleavy 1979; Saunders 1984; Dunleavy and Husbands 1985:136–44; Taylor-Gooby 1986).[9] The upshot of the theories is that those who are able to use private services (which means that they are able to pay, often highly, for them) will tend to support those party policies which favour their maintenance and extension and will have less interest in support for costly public provision. This leaves a large body of, usually poorer, persons who have to rely on public services and thus appear to have an interest in policies for the support of the national health service, or state education. Differences between theorists arise over the adoption of a 'cumulative sectors' or a 'fragmented sectors' approach (Dunleavy and Husbands 1985:139–42). The cumulative version, adopted by Dunleavy and Husbands, argues that one should look at the effects of the various policy areas together by establishing an overall consumption sector location (see also Duke and Edgell 1984). Saunders adopts the more plural fragmented approach which would anticipate that people's experiences of public or private provision would not entirely overlap but vary according to the policy area involved, which will have its own distinctive political pattern (Saunders 1981).

   The prime concern of these writers is with what consumption experiences tell us about party alignments. Our concern is different. It is with whether consumption factors also influence levels of participation. The first step is to establish whether there is a linkage. As with the treatment of the employment sector, by controlling for class, wealth, education and organisational ties, we shall seek to establish whether or not consumption effects largely disappear. This would support what Dunleavy and Husbands call the 'class-inclusive pattern' (1985:139; see also Harrop 1980). By looking at a set of consumption sector items both together and as separate components, it is also possible to make some judgements about the rival merits of the 'fragmented sectors' and the

Table 6.5 *Attitudes towards private business and industry by consumption sector*

	Mean rating	N
1. Strong private	6·28	142
2. Moderate private	5·57	99
3. Weak private	5·69	195
4. Weak public	5·55	366
5. Moderate public	5·48	240
6. Strong public	5·10	157
Overall	5·59	1,199

'cumulative sectors' approaches, at least so far as accounts of participation are concerned.

The survey included items relevant to four consumption sectors: transport (household access to a private car or van rather than reliance on public transport); educational background (having attended a state as against a 'fee-charging' secondary school); housing (council as against private sector); health (household private medical treatment rather than using the national health care system). A factor analysis was performed in order to ascertain whether these formed a coherent empirical measure (apart from any differences in political effects). This clearly showed that they did indeed generate a single dimension or scale.[10] The scale was then divided into six strata representing varying individual consumption mixes from those strongly oriented towards public sector services to those largely dependent on what the private sector provides. Finally, the validity of the scale was checked by examining its relationship with a key attitude item. This concerned evaluations of 'the way that big private businesses and industries are run' in Britain. Presumably, if interests are significantly shaped by sectoral service provision, this would be reflected in orientations towards private industry. Using a 'marks out of ten' format to indicate relative satisfaction or dissatisfaction, the results for each of the six consumption strata are as set out in table 6.5. Whilst only moderate in strength, it does suggest that the overall consumption index taps a meaningful array of interests and outlooks that plausibly might have an impact on political participation.

The initial relationship between the consumption index and the overall participation scale can be seen in figure 6.6. This indicates that there is a broadly linear pattern, of moderate strength, in which those in the private sector show the greatest propensity to participate. To this extent, the connection is the opposite of the unadjusted employment sector effect. But the analysis must also incorporate the possible changes that might arise from equalising resources between the consumption strata. Those who are orientated towards private service provision must have the resources that opting out of the state sector implies.[11]

In fact, the 'strong private' stratum not only is massively, and to an extent necessarily, distinguishable from the 'strong public' group in terms of wealth, it also differs markedly in educational resources and organisational ties. Thus, of those in the relevant private category, only 12·1 % had no formal qualifications, and a fifth (20·8 %) were graduates. Amongst their polar opposites in the public sector camp, however, the

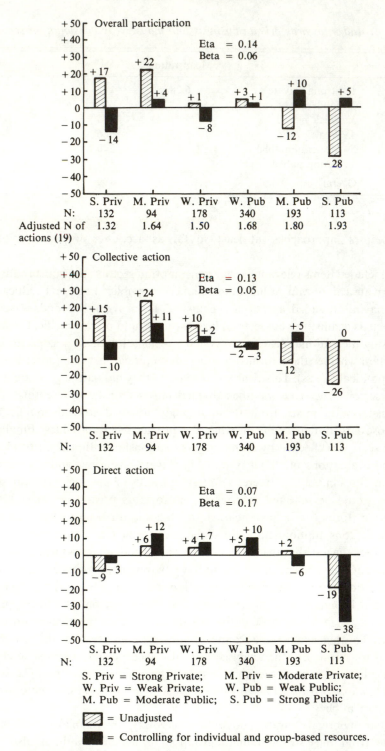

Figure 6.6 Participation by consumption sector

position was entirely the reverse: over three quarters (76·8 %) had no qualifications and not a single individual had obtained a degree. Similarly, the pattern of organisational linkages suggests that the 'strong private' consumption group have nearly twice as many ties as the 'strong public' – 1·56 on average compared with 0·83.

The effect of these differences on the overall participation scale can also be seen in figure 6.6. The result is, perhaps not unexpectedly, largely to wipe out the apparent propensity of private consumers to participate at higher rates. It is indeed a spurious product of their resource advantage rather than anything intrinsically to do with their consumption of services. The deviations that remain suggest a slightly higher propensity for action amongst public consumers.

To check if this was the end of the matter, we first looked at the adjusted relationships within each mode of participation and then examined the specific effects of each of the four ingredients in the consumption index. So far as links with specific modes of participation are concerned, the results broadly repeat those for the overall scale. What start out as interesting initial relationships are rendered much weaker, and the individual category effects generally become inconsistent and uninterpretable.

Each specific consumption factor was also examined in order to test the validity of the 'cumulative sectors' approach on which the analysis has so far been based. In fact, the results are generally bad news for the view that consumption effects are consistent from area to area. Whether on an unadjusted or adjusted basis, the sectoral effects are not always the same. Using the overall participation scale in three spheres, transport, health and housing, it is the public sector which has a positive score. But, as can be seen in figure 6.7, in every instance the tendency is so slight as to be totally insignificant. The major exception, in both respects, is in the educational sector. Here, there is a strong and statistically significant association between private educational provision and political activism. This is, it seems, the one area where a possible consumption effect on participation in general can be detected.

Conclusion

It is difficult to try to sum up briefly the relationship between economic and sectoral location and political participation. Clearly, there are connections but they vary in strength and shape both according to the economic criterion and the participatory arena being considered. Indeed, with some combinations there seems to be little or no connection at all that we can discern. In some others, however, the imprint of location on participation is very visible and striking. Perhaps what is surprising in a political context in which so much of the debate is about matters of material interest, is that the relevance of these economic factors seems on the whole so weak. The extent to which this is the case can, perhaps, be judged by using one set of summary statistics which indicate the proportion of variance in each participation scale that can be explained by the four economic variables taken together.[12]

On this basis, the predictive power of class (in a very strict sense), sector and consumption pales by comparison with individual resources and organisational ties. For the overall participation scale, for example, whereas individual and group resources can account by themselves for over 37 % of its variance, the economic interest characteristics

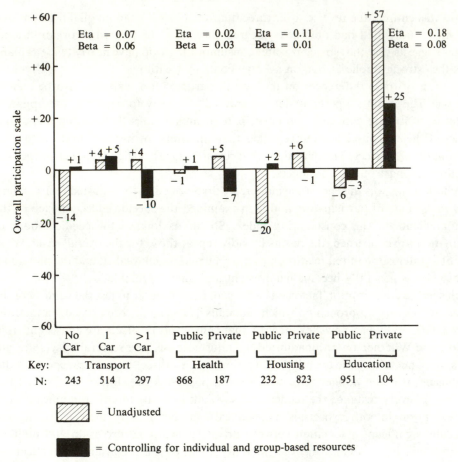

Figure 6.7 Specific consumption sector effects on overall participation

only add a little more than 2%. Within the more specific modes, the picture varies somewhat although economic location never challenges the preeminence of resources. In fact, whereas resources fluctuate sharply, class and so forth have a seemingly stable capacity to account for about 3% of every scale except collective action where it drops to a mere 1·25%. This does mean, however, that class, sector and consumption have nearly half the power of resources and ties to explain voting turnout (3% to 7·1%) and contacting is not dissimilar (3·1% to 8·2%). But for party campaigning (and to a lesser extent group activity), class relatively speaking counts for very little indeed – a mere 2·9% as against 30% for resource factors. If, therefore, these are even a rough approximation of the truth, they clearly suggest that neither class (*strictu sensu*), nor sector nor consumption patterns have a pervasive influence over the level and type of individual political participation in Britain. We must, therefore, turn to other personal and situational factors to see if we can add substantially to our resource-based explanation.

7

PERSONAL FACTORS

We saw in the previous chapter how class and other economic characteristics added only partially and in detail to our understanding of the process whereby individuals become politically activated. Here we turn to a consideration of some other factors which might add more substantially to the story. These we refer to as 'personal and situational', insofar as they relate directly to the individual and his or her immediate situation in life. The chapter itself is organised around two central factors of this type – gender and age – and the contribution they make to participation. In undertaking this analysis, however, we move into a number of other circumstances, such as marital status, family structure, employment status and geographical mobility that expand and amplify our findings well beyond those two elements. Taken together, the whole group of factors, whilst obviously not exhaustive, should help us further to understand the forces that shape what citizens do in the political arena. We turn first to the question of gender.

Gender

Studies of political participation in numerous countries have regularly discovered a 'gender gap' whereby men have been found to be more involved and active than women. Milbrath and Goel, for example, found this finding to be 'one of the most thoroughly substantiated in social science' (1977:116). Verba, Nie and Kim seemed merely to confirm this generalisation when they uncovered male activity rates that were substantially in excess of female rates (except possibly in the USA, where the gap was a relatively modest one), in all the countries included in their study (1978:235). Indeed, Lafferty, in summarising his research on political participation in Norway, suggested that 'sex is a more important determinant of political activity than either socio-economic position or organisational involvement' (1979; see also Lafferty 1978).

In the specific case of Britain, however, such limited work as exists is more cautious as to the presence of a participatory gender gap. Crewe, Fox and Alt, for example, suggested that in relatively recent elections, at least, 'the well known tendency throughout liberal democracies for women to vote in smaller proportions than men is not only statistically insignificant ... but attributable more to their greater longevity than to their sex' (1977:59; see also Lovenduski 1986:126). The gap they found was at best only 3%, and as little as 1% if adjusted for age effects.

Rather than set out the reasons advanced by those, like Lafferty or Verba, Nie and Kim, who found gender differences in other countries, it is perhaps more appropriate to find out if there is a significant effect in Britain in the first place. It is equally necessary to distinguish between different modes of participation, for the lack of any gap in turnout in British elections might well misrepresent the situation in other spheres of participation. Lovenduski (1986), for example, echoes Verba, Nie and Kim (1979) in suggesting that there may well be larger discrepancies in other non-electoral areas of conventional political activity. She notes the possibility that women might be particularly attracted to 'activity intended to influence public policy which is not formally integrated into normal political processes or which has not been institutionalized' (1986:126). She recalls that in Britain women have been closely involved in community action groups, claimants' activities, child-care projects, the peace movement and, not least, the Miners' Strike of 1984–5. If this kind of activity is sufficiently common amongst women, it is possible that the traditional gender gap may have vanished or even reversed itself in the areas of collective action and direct action – our two modes which seem to reflect most clearly the '*ad hoc* politics' Lovenduski has in mind (see also Randall 1982). Barnes, Kaase *et al.* (1979:184) give some credence to this possibility by finding their 'protestors' to be proportionately more female than male in all countries in their study except Austria. On the other hand, Dalton (1988:69–70), drawing upon the same data, finds that the general connection between propensity to protest and gender consistently favours males. All of which suggests that a more detailed scrutiny of the individual modes, including direct action, is required.

Evidence on the basic difference in activity rates between men and women in our survey, across our different participation scales, is set out in table 7.1. As can be seen, in terms of the overall pattern, there is a 'gender gap' in Britain: men are more politically active than women. However, the difference is a very modest one, both in its own terms and in a broader context. Thus, it is important to point out that the figures are only means – useful for establishing overall tendencies but not for conveying the amount of variation within each gender category, which is substantial. In fact, the variability in both is such that there are almost as many (or as few!) politically active women as men. Conversely, there are about as many politically inactive men as women.[1] To put it another way, the difference on our 19-item action scale is less than a fifth of just one action: the men on average undertake 1·6 actions and the women 1·41: a 'gender gap', but a distinctly small one.[2]

In the broader context of the analysis, the relationship between overall participation and gender is equally weak. The eta, 0·04, is, for example, five times less than the class eta (figure 6.2) or nearly ten times less than that for voluntary groups (figure 5.2). Indeed, no factor so far examined in this volume has had as small a basic relationship with overall participation as gender. It seems, on the face of it, that, for the general population, this really is a case of a minor nuance and a rather tiny detail.

Such a conclusion is reinforced by putting the figures in a cross-national context. Verba, Nie and Kim (1979:235), for example, report gender gaps in seven countries that average 56 points – more than six times as large as the British. Moreover, the smallest (in the USA) was 17, which is nearly twice as big. On this basis, at least, the gender gap is not only small but atypically so. It is as though democratic and egalitarian norms, or

Table 7.1 *Differences in political participation rates by gender*

Mode	Men	Women	Gap
Overall	+5	−4	+9
Voting	−6	+5	−11
Party campaigning	+1	−1	+2
Contacting	+5	−4	+9
Collective action	+5	−4	+9
Direct action	+5	−4	+9
N of actions (19)*	1·60	1·41	+0·19

* This is a simple count of the number of times a given individual has performed every item of participation (excluding the 'easy' acts of voting and signing a petition) at least once in the five-year period. For further discussions, see chapter 3.

relevant structural changes, that might erode the gender gap, have gone further in British mass society than elsewhere (see Lovenduski 1986; Christy 1987). Nevertheless, it is worth pressing this overall result a bit further to see how much it is also true both of particular participatory behaviours and of particular sub-categories of women.

The first step is to disaggregate the overall scale into the modes of participation which go to compose it. The results are also displayed in table 7.1. Here we find that, in the cases of contacting, collective action and direct action, the gap remains basically the same as before: men slightly out-participate women. On this evidence, therefore, there is no obvious *general* propensity for women to be more drawn than men to the world of '*ad hoc* politics' – of group-based issue politics or confrontational protest. Some are attracted to such activities (a matter to be further explored below) but, as a whole, we find women are somewhat less attracted to them than men (see also Dalton 1988:69).

A slight change in the story occurs in the electoral arena. In the case of party campaigning, the gap evaporates almost to vanishing point (and the associated eta to a total insignificant 0·01). Whatever the gender differences may be at the higher levels of Britain's party organisations – and they clearly are substantial (see, for example, Hills 1981:17–26) – there is, on the basis of our evidence, little or no gender difference in the recruitment of grass-roots volunteers to campaign for their favoured election candidate or political party. For example, 3·5% of women have canvassed and knocked on doors for their party, effectively the same as for men (3·4%). And in clerical work, possibly an area where, because of traditional attitudes, women might well have been found to be more active, again there was no significant discrepancy – 3·0% for males and 3·8% for females.

In the case of voting, however, there is a gender gap – but one that favours women rather than men. Here, exceptionally, women in Britain seem not only to have caught up with, but actually to have overtaken men in turnout levels. But closer inspection of the constituent items of the voting scale show that this is more true of local and European contests. In both cases, there was about a 5-point gap: 49·7% of women said they had voted in the 1984 European Election as against 44·6% of men. Similarly, 69·9% of females voted in 'every' local election, or 'most' local elections compared with 64·8% of males. Only in the General Election of 1983 was there a slight male edge –

83·3% of men claiming to have turned out in our survey compared with 82·2% of women. On this evidence, therefore, it is clear that the findings of Crewe, Fox and Alt (1977) are supported. There is now no significant gender gap at all in general elections – with or without age factors taken into account. At the same time, it also seems that evidence based solely on national elections may be somewhat misleading.

When we break the genders into sub-groups, it is possible to identify some further detailed departures from the general pattern. For example, we can look first at the extent of gender differences when age is taken into account. As has been seen, other scholars have suggested that the gap was at one time substantial. Are there echoes of this amongst older women? How different is the relationship amongst young men and women?

Using a very discriminating measure of age, dividing it mainly into five-year bands, we can plot the gender gap on our summary measure of overall participation to see if it does favour males more strongly in the oldest age brackets. The answer, as the results set out in figure 7.1 demonstrate, seems to be that it does not. This figure and the next show the extent to which male participation exceeds female participation. A positive score indicates that male activity is higher but a negative score shows female activity to be higher.

For those over 50, there is little to suggest any more than the average, relatively small, male advantage. In the case of those aged under 50, on the other hand, there are greater divergencies. Amongst the very youngest adults (under 23) women show the greater activism. But, in that wide age range between 23 and 49, the opposite is the case – and strongly so. Indeed, this is the period in which there is the strongest and most persistent gender gap. In short, age does highlight some important details, but they are not consistent with the supposed generational effects.

So what is it that accounts for that substantial gender gap within early to middle age? One strong and obvious possibility lies in life cycle effects which are gender-related. Specifically, these differences may be due to work and family position (Lafferty 1979:14–21). That period (23 to 49) is, after all, the peak period of child-bearing and rearing. It is equally a period during which gender differences in career patterns may emerge and be consolidated. Do such experiences affect political participation?

As can be seen in figure 7.2, there are clearly important differences between males and females in the consequential effects of marital status, family and work. To start, being married (or cohabiting) is, in itself, associated with a further heightening of the gender gap on the overall participation scale in favour of men (from +9 to +15). Conversely, among those who are single (never married, or divorced) or separated,[3] the balance of activism clearly favours women (−12). In other words, the formation of a basic family unit, through marriage or otherwise, seems to entail an accentuation of the basic tendency for the male partners to take a more active role in public affairs, and for the female partners to be somewhat less active.

The presence or absence of children within this unit makes a further important impact on the gender gap. Amongst those that are married or cohabiting, the addition of young children (under 15) further shifts the balance towards males (+21), whereas couples without children have a gender gap (+11) that is about the same as for all males and females. This again strongly suggests that the division of labour within a more complex household is such as further to de-activate women relative to men in public spheres.

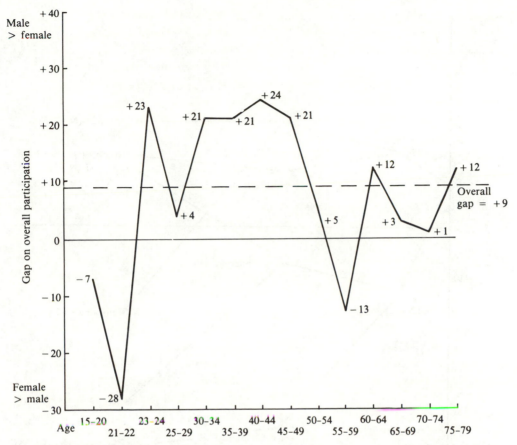

Figure 7.1 The gender gap in overall participation, by age (scores are the net difference between men and women within each age grouping on the overall participation scale)

Indeed, in Britain, married women with children in the home are the least participatory relative to men in the same circumstances.

Thus, there are, in these basic family experiences and apparent internal divisions of labour, strong hints as to why the gender gap favouring men is so relatively large within the 23 to 49 age group. Most people in the survey, 80·5% in fact in the 23 to 49 age range (excluding the small number of widowed), are married or cohabiting. Of these, 68·5% have at least one child under fifteen. Hence, this particular family arrangement is a dominant one for individuals within the relevant age bracket and so the effects associated with it on the balance of gender participation must be equivalently pronounced.

The addition of children to a one-adult household, on the other hand, has a very different and major impact on the gender gap. As can again be seen in figure 7.2, among single adults (those never married, and those divorced or separated) with no children, women are more participatory than men, although the difference is slight (a balance of −7). However, the presence of children in such households seems to be associated with a dramatically higher rate of activity by women relative to men, producing a gender gap of 40 points in favour of women. Indeed, it is single parent women who are most drawn

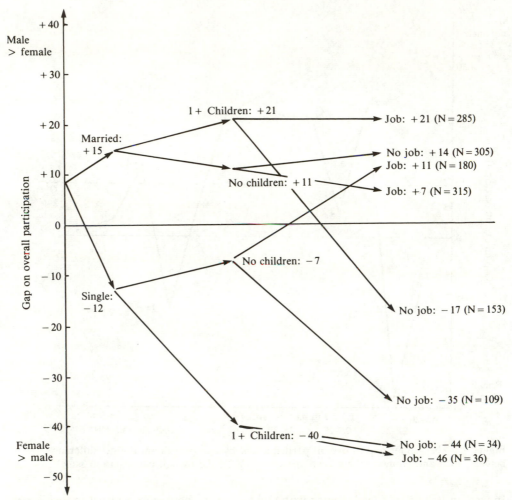

Figure 7.2 Gender gap on overall participation, by family and work position (scores are the net difference between men and women within each grouping on the overall participation scale)

into the political arena in absolute terms (a score of +21), whilst men who are in the corresponding position are deactivated (−19). This may appear somewhat surprising but the women in this category in the sample are relatively well-educated, which may affect their level of participation, even though they are not favourably endowed with other kinds of resources. The involvement of such single female parents may also say something about the activating effect of the feminine agenda. At the same time, its overall impact is muted by the relatively small numbers involved.[4] As few as 19·5% of those, male or female, age 23 to 49 are in one-adult households and, of these, only 21·7% had children under fifteen to care for.

But what about work position? How does this affect political participation generally? The answer, from figure 7.2, is that it makes a big difference for those who are married with children and those who are single with no children, but not much difference for the rest. The numerically more important case is obviously the former – those who are married or cohabiting with children. We have seen how, in general, women in such families are relatively less active. Men and women who are married with children and working, both participate more than those without jobs, but, as figure 7.2 shows, the gender balance in favour of men (+21) is no different from the situation where work situation is left out of account. Where, however, the married adult with children lacks a job, the balance tips sharply to favour women (balance score of −17). Insofar as most married adults who have children but no job are women (84·3% of those concerned), this represents an important qualification to the general negative effect on female participation of being married and having children. It would seem that women who have no job are more ready to seize the time available to participate than their male counterparts (or, rather, they are less inactive, since in absolute terms such jobless married persons with children are not very participatory).

Possession of a job also makes a difference to the participatory rate of single, childless men and women. They are not numerous in our sample (15·1% of those aged between 23 and 49) and thus do not make a big impact on the overall gender balance. Nevertheless, single males with a job tend to out-participate women in the same position but single women without a job greatly out-participate their male equivalents. Indeed, such women, in terms of gender balance, are not far short of women who are single parents. The total absence of personal ties – of marriage, children or job – seems to be a situation where female participation prospers, at least relative to male participation. Insofar as this is a condition particularly associated with very young adults, we have further evidence linking family and work position with the gender gap. For, as we saw in figure 7.1, up to the age of 23, females participate relatively more than males, although in absolute terms, only those women over 21 have a positive score (+13). But that is distinctly better than males over 21 (−15) which is the subject at issue here.

A second way in which the relationship between gender and participation can be explored in more detail is by drawing into the account the impact of resources. If it is the case that there are sizeable resource imbalances, as is true of other countries (see, for example, Verba, Nie and Kim 1978:244), how are the unadjusted participation rates reported in table 7.1 affected? Do they, in fact, hide a gender gap that, relative to resources, may even be the opposite of that previously described? We have seen that some women often seem to turn to political action more readily than men when circumstances allow – for example, those who remain single, or, if they get married, who do not have children, or, even if they have children, who do not have a job outside the home. Is it, therefore, the case that if women's resources are set equal to men's (assuming men are advantaged in this regard in Britain), then the general gender balance for all women moves in their favour?

An appropriate first step is to see whether or not there is a resource-based gender gap that might alter the picture in the way suggested. The figures reported in table 7.2 clearly show that there is. Thus, fewer men lack any formal qualifications than women (42·6% to 49·4%), whilst somewhat more possess a degree (7·4% to 6·1%). In the matter of wealth, there is also a gap that favours men, although the extent of it is more difficult to ascertain. This is because the income ingredient of our wealth scale incorporates the joint incomes of those who are married or are cohabiting. In the case of women, as we have seen, this affects a majority (66·6%) and therefore renders somewhat suspect their individual income and wealth rating. This is even more true of that 29·1% of women

Table 7.2 *Resources, by gender*

	Male	Female	Gender gap % M–% F
Education			
% No formal qualifications	42·6	49·4	−6·8
% Degree	7·4	6·1	+1·3
Wealth			
Poorest 5%	4·1	5·7	−1·6
Richest 5%	6·9	4·2	+2·7
Voluntary groups			
% No memberships	31·2	39·5	−8·3
% 5+ memberships	9·4	4·8	+4·6
Trades unions			
% Non-member	47·5	68·4	−20·9
% Active member	8·9	4·4	+4·5
Political parties			
% Non-member	92·4	92·9	−0·5
% Active member	3·3	3·6	−0·3

who are married (or co-habiting) and looking after the home. For over half of them (54%), the rent or mortgage is paid for exclusively by their spouse (or co-habitee).[5]

However, it should be noted that income is only one of four items forming the wealth scale. Another, stock and share ownership, does pertain to the individual rather than the household since the question was posed in that form. Here, men are slightly more likely to be owners of such assets than women – 13·5% to 12·4%. For those that are married, the gap is somewhat wider – 15·7% as against 12·6%. Amongst single adults, on the other hand, women are slightly more favoured (9% to 8·3%) as is also true of the widowed, 10% to 16·4%. In this area, therefore, there is not a major gender imbalance, or even one that consistently favours men over women. So while it is necessary to be sensitive to possibilities of distortions resulting from measurements of income, the overall moderate gender gap in the wealth scale is perhaps not a major misrepresentation of the truth.

When it comes to group-based resources, men are again generally favoured. More are active members of voluntary groups and trades unions, although this is true of only a small proportion of either gender. Only in the case of active party membership (which, however, is as much a measure of participation itself as a resource) women do have an advantage, although again it is a slim one. Thus, across all resources, men have the edge. There may be some uncertainty about the exact extent of that edge, but the impression is that it is relatively pervasive, if also relatively small.

But, to the extent that it does exist, how does it affect levels of participation? Do men still out-participate women relative to their higher resource base, or are women perhaps more active relative to their lower resource profile? As is shown in table 7.3, the answer is that when resources are equalised, women do generally participate slightly more than men. However, the gender gap here is even less than in table 7.2. It might be better to say that if resource differentials are taken into account, even that small gender gap in Britain is wiped out. The only possible exception to this is in voting, where equalising resources serves to heighten the already greater turnout rate of women, generating a beta of 0·09. But the fact that this is the largest specific gender effect of all once again affirms how generally modest the impact of gender is in Britain, whether or not resources are taken into account. Having said that, it can also be claimed that on an adjusted basis, it is only in contacting and direct action that the slight male 'lead' is preserved. So while age, family and work position make interesting and even dramatic differences in certain detailed respects, the broader gender gap, such as it is, is largely explained by resource differentials.

To that extent, Britain is again untypical of other countries. In Verba, Nie and Kim (1978:268), for example, resource controls reduced the male lead on the overall participation scale in every country – from an average of + 56 to + 33. But that means that there still was a gender gap to explain, albeit a small one in Holland (+7) and America (+9). But Britain's gap of −2 is obviously different even from these. In the special case of voting, however, the British results are in some respects less at odds with those countries. Here, resource controls turned three of the seven scores in the Verba, Nie and Kim study negative – meaning that women on an adjusted basis voted more than men. But even in those instances, Austria (−2), the Netherlands (−7) and Yugoslavia (−7), the reversed gender gap does not reach Britain's level (−16). It would seem, therefore, that the gender gap, so far as mass participation is concerned, has been closed more completely in Britain than in any of the other six liberal democracies Verba and his team studied. This is far from saying that it has closed to the same extent at the elite level, as some of our local findings will show (see chapter 16 below).

To conclude the discussion of gender and participation we might focus on one group of women who are, in a sense, at the leading edge of advancing female participation in British politics. These are the women who were members of a feminist group. As was seen in chapter 5, they are very few in number (only 1·3 % of our female sample) but they reported that they were active members of their groups and they were highly politicised in the sense of raising issues within their group (see table 5.8). These groups are, indeed, very often committed to new forms of internal democracy (Rowbotham 1986). But how active are these members outside of this group context, and in what ways?

As is shown in table 7.4, they are clearly very active indeed. An average score of + 144 on the overall participation scale puts them in the top 6% of the whole sample. What is equally interesting, however, is that they are particularly oriented towards collective and direct action (+ 143 and + 141 respectively). Here we see signs of that linkage between women and issue-oriented '*ad hoc* politics' referred to by Lovenduski (1986) and Randall (1982). There may not be a general association between women and such a style of politics, but there is so far as the members of feminist groups are concerned. That such a linkage surfaces so sharply is satisfying confirmation of the extent to which such modes of participation are concerned with these particular types of issue.

It may also be worth noting that these women were less oriented towards voting or contacting. Given the numbers involved, relatively little should be made of it, but their average ranking on the voting and, to some extent, the contacting ladders does at least

Table 7.3 *Differences in political participation rates by gender, controlling for other personal and resource factors*

Mode	Men	Women	Gap
Overall	−1	+1	−2
Voting	−9	+7	−16
Party campaigning	−3	+3	−6
Contacting	+2	−2	+4
Collective action	−1	+1	−2
Direct action	+3	−2	+5
N of actions (19)	1·51	1·55	−0·04

Table 7.4 *Political participation of members of feminist groups (N = 11)*

Mode	Score
Overall	+144
Voting	−2
Party campaigning	+72
Contacting	+13
Collective action	+143
Direct action	+141
N of actions (19)	3·85

suggest a certain preference for modes of action involving group solidarity and directed towards specific issues. Contacting tends to lack the sense of solidarity, whilst voting is an expression of a more generalised political position. Party campaigning, on the other hand, is an electoral activity where the individual can stress a given issue and work with like-minded others inside a given party. That feminist group members seem to be very active in such campaigns (+72) suggests that what is being rejected is not so much conventional politics as a certain political strategy or style that does not allow for an effective collective stress on a chosen issue. Party campaigning does allow for this, but, given the need for parties to stress a range of issues and to aggregate diverse views, not as well as collective and direct action.

Thus, feminist group members are, indeed, part of a novel participatory vanguard for that 56% of our sample who are female. As Sheila Rowbotham (1986:97) has put it,

Small groups in the women's liberation movement – originally called conscious-raising groups – have provided an organizational form which has enabled women to find a way of expressing their needs in political language.

Women in general may be slightly less active than men, but this is one demonstration of the extent to which women are transcending structural, cultural and other barriers to take a very active part in politics. At the same time, it must be recalled that, in our resource terms, such women in the sample are very much more advantaged than women as a whole. As a group, they are, for example, 50% better educated than women at large and have twice as many group memberships – even apart from their feminist associations. They are, in short, very well-resourced individuals, and to that extent do not necessarily represent a harbinger of how the general relationship between gender and participation is likely to change and develop in the near future.

Age

We turn now to the second personal attribute which has received as much, if not more, attention than gender in analysing political participation. And for good reasons. Age has been shown in numerous studies across many countries to exert a noticeable influence over levels of activity, although the nature and strength of that influence has varied considerably from country to country and from mode to mode.

The general character of that influence seems to be one in which 'participation rises in the early years, peaks in middle age, and falls in later years' (Nie, Verba and Kim 1974:326). At least this seems to be the pattern for conventional participation. However, important differences and even exceptions are not hard to discover. For example, Verba and Nie (1972:139, 141) report that voting had a slightly different pattern of rise and fall in the USA. They also found that 'particularized contacting' – a special form of contacting on issues immediately relating to the individual participant – was not related at all to age (1972:138). Similarly, a re-analysis of data from the Barnes, Kaase *et al.* Political Action Study by Dalton (1988:48–56) shows that the impact of age varies considerably. In predicting voting turnout in the US and Great Britain, for example, he found it to be a substantial influence (betas of 0·24 and 0·20 respectively). In West Germany, on the other hand, it was fairly marginal (beta of 0·06).

For campaign activity, the pattern was different again. In the American case, the impact was effectively zero (beta of 0·01), a result which, incidentally, does not support the evidence of Verba and Nie (1972) who reported that, in their survey, campaign participation followed what was, for them at least, a standard rise and fall trajectory. In the West German case, on the other hand, the relationship is reported by Dalton (1988:55) as negative – that young people in that country participate in campaigning more than older people. This was also true, exceptionally, of communal participation in West Germany (see also Barnes, Kaase *et al.* 1979:100). So, overall, although there is considerable evidence that age does make a difference, there are also instances where it does not, or where the pattern appears to be the opposite of the standard 'rise and fall'.

Not the least of these exceptions lies in the area of unconventional participation – of direct action and political violence. Here, such research findings as there are suggest that the 'standard pattern' is not the same as for conventional participation. Thus, both Dalton's (1988) re-analysis and that of Barnes, Kaase *et al.* (1979) agree that in all the countries studied, young people were more prone to this form of activity than older people. Across the board, the correlations were consistently negative. Dalton (1988:69–70), for example, found betas of −0·29 in the USA and Great Britain, −0·25 in West Germany and −0·28 in France.

For our purposes, therefore, it is important that, in looking at the overall relationship between age and participation, we also leave room for the examination of individual modes, and in particular of political protest. For if 'rise and fall' approximates a normal pattern in the conventional sphere, it does not appear to hold for the world of unconventional action.

It is appropriate, however, to begin the analysis at the most general level – looking at the basic relationship between age and the summary measures of political participation. These are set out in figure 7.3 – for both the overall scale and the simple 19-item additive measure. To obtain some fine detail, respondents have been grouped into relatively narrow five-year age bands, with the exception of those in their early twenties (two-year groups) and the very elderly (75 to 97). As can be seen in the figure, our data do indeed suggest quite strongly a 'rise and fall' relationship. Participation is very low for those under twenty, rises steeply until the mid-forties and then drops (somewhat erratically) until old age, when participation rates end up at the lowest ebb of all.

To put it in the more concrete terms of the simple 19-item count which, not surprisingly, tracks the participation scale very closely, those under twenty average 0·69, or something over half an action beyond those of voting and signing a petition.[6] The rate then climbs, with a minor down-turn in the late 20s, to peak at 2·32 for those aged 40–44. This is a score over three times that of the under-20s. Indeed, the 30s and 40s, early middle age, are clearly the peak years generally for political activity. Thereafter, the scores move basically downward, until they hit 0·45 for the over 75s. This is but two-thirds the rate of the under 20s and one-fifth that of people in their early forties.

What explains these swings of activity? To try to provide a definitive answer unfortunately poses some fundamental difficulties. Age groups can, in principle, reflect a number of different age-related processes, most particularly those of a life-cycle and generational nature. These cannot be readily disentangled with evidence from one point in time (see, for example, Converse 1976:10–11; Dalton 1977). In other words, what we observe is a static relationship between age and participation. But do the differences we observe arise from a generational process in which each age cohort would retain its participatory profile as it ages? Or do they derive from causes associated with the life-cycle, such that a cohort, as it ages, takes on the pattern of participation typically associated with each new stage of life? Or are there ingredients of both, ingredients that might moreover vary from mode to mode?

Debates about these possibilities have been inconclusive, not least because most other sources of information about participation, being static, are beset with the same difficulties. Verba and Nie (1972), for example, assume that the age relationships in their study derive largely from a process whereby problems of 'start-up' for those early in the life-cycle, and 'slow-down' for those towards the end of it, depress activity amongst the young and elderly. For them, the major imprint of age is the life-cycle. Further evidence in support of their position is presented in a later report (Nie, Verba and Kim 1974). There they recognise the dubiety of some of the assumptions involved (1974:321), but because there are cross-national uniformities in the apparent effects of ageing, they come to the conclusion that the life-cycle interpretation is the correct explanation of the 'main effects' (1974:323). Particular deviations, deriving from historical experiences specific to individual countries, are essentially secondary.

On the other hand, strong claims for generational effects on participation have been made by Inglehart (1971, 1977, 1981) and Barnes, Kaase *et al.* (1979) (see also Dalton 1988). They focused especially upon political protest, but suggested that the high levels

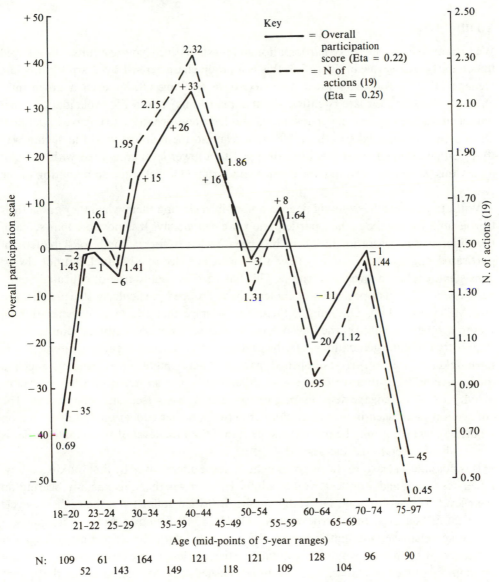

Figure 7.3 Overall participation, by age

of protest potential found amongst the young were largely the product of unprecedented levels of affluence experienced by the post-war generations of youth in Western democracies. Furthermore, an attempt to subject this thesis to a test that included the life-cycle explanation as a rival hypothesis came to the conclusion that, indeed, generational forces were mainly responsible, although some life-cycle effects could be detected (Dalton 1977).

All in all, therefore, it seems impossible to rule out either process. It seems entirely plausible that complex mixtures of the two may be at work, mixtures that cannot be definitively disentangled. What we can do, however, is explore some of the relationships associated with age which might in turn suggest the kind of processes that are at work.

Youth

We turn first to the pattern of participation amongst relatively young adults – those aged under thirty. As we saw in figure 7.3, this is a group characterised by sharply rising late teenage (18 to 20) activity rates, followed by a levelling off, or even a down-turn, amongst those in their late twenties. What explains this? Is it a life-cycle matter – that young adults are rootless, under-resourced and have few incentives to engage in politics? Or is it that young adults in the 1980s now relate to the political world in such a way that participation amongst them has dropped to a lower level compared with those of a previous generation now in their thirties and forties? Or is it some combination of the two?

Without tracking those young people, and re-interviewing them when they are in their thirties and forties about their participation, we cannot say. It is possible that some of the difference is generational. There has been evidence, for example, of a pattern of partisan dealignment in Britain (Crewe 1984) which has led to a gradual, but not always consistent, decline in levels of turnout. This has been especially true of educated young people whose levels of partisan attachments have dropped particularly sharply (Harrop and Miller 1987:143). One might, therefore, surmise that the present generation of young people has indeed turned away from participation in conventional politics more than is true of older generations. On the other hand, this detachment may, in fact, only have taken place *vis-à-vis* established parties. There might have been as much a qualitative as a quantitative change – in other words, not so much of a lower level of activity as of an engagement in politics on a new basis (see also chapter 9). The connection established in an earlier chapter between higher education and direct action might be recalled. It may be more the style rather than the level of participation that is the result of generational factors.

It is possible, at least, to throw some light on these alternatives by first looking at how under-resourced and 'rootless' young adults are, and whether this has any bearing on their levels of participation. Do young adults in Britain suffer from the early life-cycle problem of 'start-up' that Verba and Nie (1972:145–7) found in America?

The key characteristic that is supposedly associated with this syndrome is length of residence. If the reason why young adults participate less is because they are typically newcomers to their localities, without an established stake or commitment that might stimulate personal political action and lacking the local ties and knowledge that might facilitate it, then making an adjustment for this should raise their apparent rates – if the effect is there (see Conway 1985:18).

It is not surprising to find that young adults under 30 are indeed relative newcomers to the area of their current residence, although many have built up a substantial number of years there at the time of our interviews.[7] On average, the under-30s had lived for 11·3 years in their local area – half the overall rate. A fifth had only been residents for less than two years, and another 22·5% between two and five years – both proportions in excess of the populations as a whole (8·9% and 14·0%). They are, in short, not as well rooted in their localities as older people.

But does this depress participation in Britain? Surprisingly enough, the answer seems to be no. Despite the handicaps to registration, and other difficulties of newcomers, the

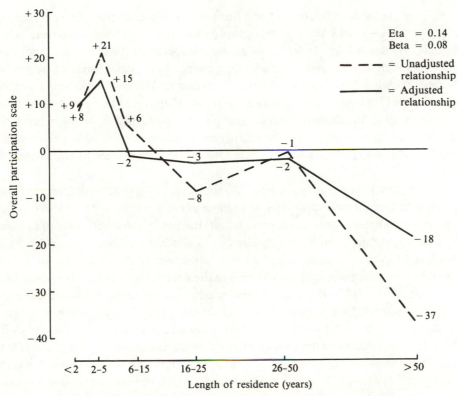

Figure 7.4 Overall participation, by length of residence, controlling for resources and personal factors

newly arrived are somewhat more likely to participate than the more established. The full relationship with overall participation, with and without taking resource factors into account, is set out in figure 7.4. There we can see that the most participatory are the newcomers, not the old-timers! What fillip length of residence imparts (and it is not great) benefits the young, not the elderly. This means, therefore, that if there are life-cycle reasons for the inactivity of the young, they can hardly be found, in Britain at least, in any 'start-up' costs associated with being recently arrived residents in their neighbourhoods. We must look elsewhere.

One other possibility is the effect of family position – marital status and the presence of dependent children. Almost by definition, young adults will tend to be single and have fewer children under fifteen to care for than those at somewhat later stages of their life-cycle. These, we have seen, have considerable effects on the gender balance of participation. But do they also have a bearing on the level of activity of young adults, be they men or women?

Here the evidence is hardly any more supportive of a life-cycle interpretation. Over half (55·5%) of young adults are indeed 'single' (i.e. never married) compared with a mere 6·4% of those in early middle age (30 to 49) and 3·1% of those in late middle age (50 to 64). Conversely, comparatively fewer are married (or cohabiting) at that stage – 42·5% as against 84·5% and 78·1% for the next two age cohorts. In this case, furthermore, single people are generally less participatory than those who are married.

However, even the basic difference is not a huge one: the overall participation score of single people is −7 and of married people +44 (eta = 0·10). Moreover, when adjustments are made for resources and relevant personal factors (like age), the difference between singles and marrieds disappears – both have adjusted scores of exactly zero. So, when Conway, for example, notes that in America single people are less politically active (1975:18), this is true in Britain only if age and other effects associated with marital status, but distinct from it, are ignored. In fact, it is only amongst the divorced (4·5% of the sample) that a consistent (and positive) imprint upon participation can be discerned (+13). Once again, therefore, life-cycle factors seem to have relatively little relevance.

Family structure is not greatly different. Again, there is a life-cycle difference: fewer young adults have children under fifteen than those of early middle age (35% to 65·4%), although more than those who are older than that. But again, the stimulation of political activity that might flow from having children in local schools or needing local nursery and medical support is a weak one. Without adjustments, the difference in overall participation is −5 for those without children in their care and +11 for those with such responsibilities (eta = 0·10). But adjustments for other factors reduces this to a mere −1 and +2 (beta = 0·05). Such a tiny life-cycle effect can hardly explain the gap between young and middle-aged adults in itself. In fact, if we add together all the factors so far discussed, length of residence, marital and family status, the effect on young adults is to widen their participatory disadvantage – from a basic score of −13 (summarising the effect in figure 7.3) to −23! In other words, the net impact of these factors is not to raise their apparent activity rates but to lower it.

Yet one other possibility, and closer perhaps to the central thrust of the analysis, might lie in the resource disadvantages associated with the early period of the life cycle. If, indeed, young adults participate less because they have fewer social and organisational ties and fewer political contacts (Conway 1985:18), then adjusting for the familiar measures of these group resources should raise their activity rates.

The resource base of young adults, set against figures for the adult population as a whole, are set out in table 7.5. What is perhaps interesting is that their resource disadvantage is so apparently slight, and in one instance (education) is not so much a disadvantage as a distinct advantage. Young adults have consistently fewer memberships of formal groups of various kinds. A third have no ties to voluntary groups, slightly less than for the adult population at large, and a majority belong to no union – although that is also true of all adults. Only possibly in the case of such 'political contacts' (Conway 1985:18) as membership of a party can one find any disadvantage that is at all substantial. This may possibly reflect a generationally-based turning away from parties, as much as a life-cycle question of 'start-up'. The end product, putting them all together, is at best a 2% gap in the proportion of those with no group resources – 23·6% for young adults compared with 25·4%. But, given the importance of group resources for participation, even this discrepancy might help explain the deficit.

At the individual level, the pattern is not consistent. Not surprisingly, proportionately more (27·8%) are in the bottom quarter of the wealth hierarchy, while only 16·7% are in the top quarter. In terms of education, however, young adults do quite well: far fewer lack any qualifications, and somewhat more hold degrees. Given that education is more

Table 7.5 *Group and individual resources of young adults* (%)

	Young adults (18–29)	All adults
Group		
No voluntary group memberships	33·4	35·7
No trades union memberships	58·6	59·0
No party memberships	97·1	92·6
No ties of any type	23·6	25·4
Individual		
No formal educational qualifications	18·7	46·7
Degree level qualification	8·3	6·5
Poorest 25 %	27·8	25·9
Richest 25 %	16·7	25·1
N	366	1,566

important for overall participation than wealth (see chapter 4), we might, in fact, find that the resource base of young adults produces countervailing effects and leaves the picture not greatly changed.

This is, indeed, how matters turn out. As has been seen, young adults start out with a score of −13 which drifts down to −23 when we take residential, marital and family factors into account. The addition of group resources does raise their relative activity rate by 6 points to −17, which shows that even a small discrepancy in this area can have consequences. It is not enough, however, fully to account for their low participation – young adults still under-participate even relative to their group resources. Finally, the addition of education and wealth moves them back down again (to −22), showing that relative to these advantages, young adults do rather badly. The net result, therefore, of all resources is more or less to leave the young as they were – less active than would be expected given their life-cycle circumstances.

It remains a possibility that generational experiences may have played some part in re-shaping both the level and the style of 'youth participation' in Britain. This can be examined briefly by looking at the patterns of each particular mode of action. These are set out in table 7.6, together with the overall participation scale scores already discussed. They show considerable variation and, in the important case of direct action, a pattern where young adults participate above the general average rather than below.

The 'worst' case is voting. Here, the basic under-participation of young adults is as low as −38, and even with personal and resource factors taken into account, the score is only raised 3 points. However, this must in part reflect the legal prohibition of those under 18 from voting in any election. In our survey, thirty-two claimed to have been too young to vote in the 1983 General Election two years previously, which is only 2·1 % of all adults, but 8·7 % of those in the 18 to 29 age bracket. The measure of participation in local elections was similarly affected. It is also worth noting that voting is the one form of participation in which short term residents do, indeed, participate less than their neighbours (see also Squire, Wolfinger and Glass 1985), possibly because of registration

Table 7.6 *Levels of participation among young adults (18–29), controlling for resources and personal factors (N = 321)*

Mode	Unadjusted score	(eta)	Adjusted score	(beta)
Overall	−13	(0·17)	−22	(0·13)
Voting	−38	(0·23)	−35	(0·22)
Party campaigning	−11	(0·08)	−14	(0·10)
Contacting	−20	(0·18)	−26	(0·10)
Collective action	−1	(0·17)	−9	(0·10)
Direct action	+22	(0·14)	+14	(0·10)

procedures – but this relationship is swamped by the opposite tendency in all other modes.

In the cases of party campaigning and contacting, which are the other two areas of conventional participation not directly affected by such institutional barriers, the lower activity levels of young adults are still visible, but the association is not quite so strong. For campaigning, being single is an asset, but not for contacting. Having children under fifteen provides a modest boost in both instances. However, whatever the details of personal and resource circumstances, the net result is to leave young adults looking even less participatory than if life-cycle factors of these sorts were left out of consideration. Young people appear averse to conventional political participation in a way which cannot be explained by the life-cycle variables we have looked at in this chapter.

Outside the conventional arena, we find a different pattern. Here, there is evidence perhaps of a generational imprint on participatory styles. The 'deficit' is still to be found in collective action, but of all the forms of under-participation, it is the smallest (−1 or −9 on an adjusted basis). In direct action, however, the reverse is true. Young adults over- rather than under-participate. This may, of course, also reflect in part the life-cycle. As Barnes, Kaase *et al.* note, 'Young people enjoy the physical vigor, the freedom from day-to-day responsibilities of career and family, and have the *time* to participate in the pursuit of the energetic kinds of political activity ... Protest behavior is therefore held to be primarily an outcome of the *joie de vivre* of youth itself' (1979:101). There is a degree of substance in this view. Low levels of residence, being single and having no children are all positive factors related to direct action in our study. But even when we try to discount them, along with resource explanations, young adults in Britain still have an abiding attachment to direct action.

Is this still some lingering life-cycle phenomenon? Perhaps. It is hard to measure '*joie de vivre*', and we did not include any questions about youthful vigour! But we can perhaps speculate as to whether or not the tendency of young people in the Britain of the 1980s has changed the style of their political engagement compared with previous generations, turning away from conventional politics towards those activities perhaps more in line with their issue concerns and their underlying values. Only time will tell. But at the very least, we cannot discount some generational effects being present here, just as we cannot find much tangible evidence so far that the life-cycle hypothesis carries a great deal of explanatory power (see also Dalton 1988:68–70). These issues are important, not least because they have very different implications for the shape of participatory politics in the future.

Early middle age

With the important exception of direct action, the period of young adulthood is marked by a fairly consistent lower level of participation, albeit one in which there is some upward movement from the late teens to the twenties (see figure 7.3). Middle age, encompassing as we have defined it a broader sweep from thirty through to the brink of retirement (for many) at 65, is not so uniform. In fact, the evidence strongly suggests that it breaks down into two – early middle age, which includes those between 30–49, and late middle age, from 50 to 65. These two eras in the life-cycle are markedly different and, as we shall see, the patterns of participation are different too.

As was seen in figure 7.3, those in early middle age exhibit relatively high levels of political participation. Whether this is a life-cycle or generational phenomenon is, of course, an open question, but whatever the cause, those in their thirties and forties were the most participatory of any age cohort. On an unadjusted basis, the peak on the overall participation ladder came in the late thirties ($+34$), with those in their early forties just behind ($+31$). These were the golden years of active citizenship, as reflected in the score for all people of early middle age, $+22$. This is nearly twice as participatory as the young adults were non-participatory, and gives some measure of the clear division between the two.[8] They are also the years in which the gender gap, favouring males, tends to be at its peak (see figure 7.1 above).

Bearing in mind the detailed study of various life-cycle characteristics in earlier pages, it is possible to home in more quickly on the possible causes of this strikingly different picture between young adults and their somewhat older fellow citizens. The thirties and forties are a period of major change from the twenties. Those who remain single drop from 55·5% to 6·4% and the proportion without under-age children in their care halves from 64·9% to 34·6%. But, as we have seen, these have little direct bearing on participation. Other circumstances also change. Those with a paid job[9] rise from 65·4% to 73·7% as do the numbers joining the ranks of the mortgaged classes – up from 47·7% to 67·1%. Here too, however, the possibility of a connection with heightened participation is at best indirect. In themselves, both these conditions are associated with greater than average activity levels, but the opposite is the case if adjustments are made for the age, gender and resource profiles of those concerned. Furthermore, the rise in employment coupled with buying a house (and thereby acquiring a mortgage) may be part of the reason why geographical mobility slows down. Compared with young adults, those resident at their current address less than two years drops to less than half – from 20·2% to 8·2% and the average length rises from 11·3 years to 17·0. And, from what has already been seen, this should reduce all participation except voting.

All in all, therefore, though there are changes in marital, family and other circumstances, it is difficult to discover in these quarters reasons why political activity should rise so sharply. Indeed, when adjustments are made for them, the overall rate remains almost unchanged at $+20$. But there are other life-cycle changes, affecting the control of resources, which may supply a more substantial explanation. At the individual level, wealth improves sharply. The rise in economic activity, the acquisition of a house (albeit not necessarily owned outright), and other associated trends, have a considerable effect. From 27·8 % of young adults being in the poorest quarter, the proportion declines to 9·7 %. Conversely, those in the richest 25 % triple from 4·0 % to 14·0 %. Here may be part of the reason why participation rises, although the effect is likely to be limited if one bears in mind the rather weak impulses associated with differences of wealth (see figure 4.4).

Educational profiles also change, but here the differences are more likely to reflect generational rather than life-cycle differences because, for most people, formal education is at an end. The younger adults in their twenties are, in fact, better educated with, for example, only 18·7 % having no formal qualifications at all compared with 37·2 % for those in early middle age. On the other hand, the numbers with a degree or a college diploma go up, from 18·9 % to 21·7 %. This probably is more a matter of the completion of advanced education in the early thirties than a generationally-based drop amongst those now in their twenties. All in all, however, it is hard to see how a small rise at the top end of the market could so out-weigh a drop in overall educational levels as to provide the key explanation.

Group resources may provide an answer. Here, non-membership of trades unions falls (possibly a further consequence of rising economic activity) – from 58·6 % to 52·8 % – and active participation within unions rises. A similar pattern, albeit on a much smaller scale, also occurs in political parties: non-membership drops 7 points to 91·1 % and for those that are members, activity levels triple. Finally, the same pattern also holds for voluntary groups. In short, by becoming more settled in work, in marriage and family, and residentially, those of early middle age become more enmeshed in politically relevant organisational networks. They become more available for mobilisation and they, in turn, can use those networks to become active politically.

That this is true at least in part can be seen by further adjusting the overall participation score for resources. Relative to these resources, their participation rate drops more than half to +9. Or, to put it another way, more than half of the above average activity of early middle age seems to be explained by group resource factors. This is further testament to the sensitivity in Britain of individual political activity to involvement in a network of organisations.

In table 7.7, we report the results discussed above as well as presenting the patterns for individual modes. If these figures are first compared with those of table 7.6, we can see that it is in voting and contacting that the biggest upward shift occurs from young adulthood to early middle age. Part of the explanation for the voting pattern is, of course, the fact that none of the older adults would be affected by being too young to vote in the relevant elections. At the same time, it is also likely that the change is a product of slowing rates of geographical mobility. This may equally be part of what lies behind the emphatic upward shift in contacting (from −20 to +23) where local knowledge and local commitments that go with longer residence may be relevant. Finally, it would appear that the commitment of young adults to direct action declines substantially, although collective action does rise. Once again, how much these particular changes are life-cycle or generational in nature is difficult to say.

What we can conclude is that, when we control for resource and other personal

Table 7.7 *Levels of participation in early middle age (30–39), controlling for resources and personal factors (N = 479)*

Mode	Unadjusted score	Adjusted score
Overall	+22	+9
Voting	+8	0
Party campaigning	+6	−3
Contacting	+23	+12
Collective action	+22	+10
Direct action	+3	+4

For etas and betas, see table 7.6.

factors, the propensity for early middle aged individuals to vote more frequently is totally accounted for (although the adjusted score of zero hides the fact that those aged 30 to 34 register −18, like those in their twenties, while at the other end those aged 45 to 49 are at +15, like those in later middle age, as we shall go on to see). Campaigning can be explained likewise, though this was barely above the mean to begin with. The same was true of direct action. Contacting and collective action, perhaps the core of the high participatory profile of the age group, is also very substantially explained within our model.

Overall, therefore, insofar as that model emphasises engagement in networks, and the consequences of a greater rootedness both in society and in the locality, it seems all the more reasonable to conclude that life-cycle factors play a substantial role in marking off those of early middle age than was the case with young adults. Rather than generally widening the gap to be explained, as was the case in table 7.6, the same factors largely close the gap. Quite possibly there remains a part for generational factors. But, from what we have seen, there does not seem to be the potential for as marked a generational effect as with those under 30. If there is, it is one of commitment to contacting, collective action and direct action (in that order). This may hint at a continuing youthful aversion to the world of conventional party politics.

Late middle age

Old age is supposed to be the time of a general political disengagement, of 'slow down' (Verba and Nie 1972:139). But, in fact, the evidence in figure 7.3 suggests that this starts rather earlier, and at different points for different modes of participation. Thus, as was seen in the case of direct action, the peak of activity came as early as 22. Thereafter the rate declined, although it was not until the late forties that the scores of given age cohorts dropped below the overall population average. Direct action is, however, very exceptional in its age trajectory and in the other modes the peak comes later. For contacting, this occurs in the 40 to 44 age group, and for collective action, 45 to 49. When all modes are put together, the crest is reached between 40 and 44. It is in this sense that we have described early middle age as generally the high point for participation as a whole.

The transition to late middle age appears to be the point at which a general slow-down in political activity starts – for many it occurs a decade at least before official retirement. Even for electoral participation – campaigning and voting – where the peaks occur later still, late middle age is a time in which signs of withdrawal first become visible.[10] Why does this come about?

As with the transition from young adulthood to early middle age, there are some very substantial life-cycle shifts entailed by moving into late middle age. For example, average lengths of residence increase 61% (from 17·0 years to 27·4 years), the largest change in this respect of any of the life-cycle periods we examine. This is a change that is generally associated with some withdrawal from active politics, except for voting, although the biggest depressive effect tends to come later – when over 50 years of residence have been accumulated (see figure 7.4). Only for direct action is there even a modest impact and even there it is but −8. All in all, then, this very substantial shift probably plays little role in the explanation of the overall pattern.

There are also some fairly dramatic changes in relation to the job market. Those in active employment fall from nearly three-quarters (73·7%) of those in early middle age to just under half (49·3%) in late middle age. Equally, the numbers 'looking after the home' rise from 19·6% to 28·9% and, for the first time, significant numbers withdraw into retirement – 12·0% as against none of those between 30 and 49. We can see, therefore, early signs of a withdrawal from economic and social involvement – women, particularly, but men too, leaving the job market. Ultimately, this can lead to political withdrawal but, as will be seen, the process, even where it occurs, can be long drawn out, indirect and much delayed. In this shorter term between 50 and 64 the net effect of all these changes, however, is not consistent with a lowering of overall participation. Thus, the impact of being in active employment is slightly to lessen political activity (an adjusted score of −6). Hence, the downward shift of those with jobs should, in itself, raise political involvement. Similarly, the effects of looking after the home and being retired are both associated with a weak participatory impulse (+4 and +4). This should produce, if anything, more rather than less activity. As we have seen, this is the case for campaigning and, above all, voting but not elsewhere.

Substantial changes occur also in the pattern of home ownership. The mortgaged classes become a minority (down from 67·1% to 25·5%) and those owning their own home outright become the largest group (up from 11·3% to 42·4%). Here, the linkages with participation are at least in the right direction, but the effects of both are small (−4 and −1). This too, therefore, yields little of great promise.

Marital status and family structure also offer signs of a certain withdrawal. Those who are married or cohabiting drop 7·5% but still remain by far the largest category (78·1%). They are more than matched by the numbers who become widowed – up from 0·8% to 11·7%. Given that being married carries a small participatory net uplift (as we have seen, for men more than for women) and becoming widowed entails a rather larger net diminution (−27 or −8 on an adjusted basis), both trends do provide some reason why a drop off should begin to occur in this age group. As would be expected, the decline in those with dependent children is enormous (down from 65·4% to 7·3%), leaving almost all (92·6%) with no young children to look after. But even though this may reduce involvement in and concern for such matters as educational facilities, there is not any immediately obvious or direct impact on participation itself.

Resource changes, though, once more may provide as good if not better an explanation. At the level of individual resources, both educational and wealth profiles are less favourable to participation. In the former case, those without any qualifications nearly double from 37·2% of those aged between 30 and 49 to 67·0% for the late middle aged. Equally, those with college and degree qualifications both fall – to 6·5% (from 12·1%) and 3·5% (from 9·6%). Unlike the shift to early middle age, therefore, we have a consistent decline in levels of education. Furthermore, it is clear that virtually all of this effect is generational because by this stage of the life-cycle very few are still actively acquiring qualifications of any sort. Career preparation and enhancement through education has largely ceased. Thus it is appropriate to set the explanatory power of education to one side whilst we pursue other resource changes that are more life-cycle in nature.

There is also a decline in material resources. Those in their thirties and forties are at the top in the scale of wealth and so the contrast with those of late middle age is of some importance. The numbers in the poorest quarter nearly triple, from 9·7% to 23·2%, while those in its richer equivalent drop from 14·0% to 5·0%. Insofar as wealth does have some impact on participation, this is indeed significant. But in what way? The downward shift in wealth is, in this respect, rather ambiguous. One important element in our measure of wealth is home ownership. There is, as we have seen, a big change in status from mortgage to outright ownership. But both count the same in our wealth scale. What does not count is rental accommodation which rises from 18·4% of those in early middle age to 30·5% in later middle age. We suspect that this change is generational – reflecting the historical rise of home ownership rather than a life-cycle switch from non-rental to rental housing.

Other elements in the distribution of wealth, however, are probably more affected by life-cycle circumstances. The downward trend in car ownership, for example, from 84·8% to 74·9% would seem to be the result of withdrawal from the job market and the rise in retirements and those looking after the home. This, in other words, is a life-cycle change in our measure of wealth. The same might also be true, at least in part, of income changes. Earnings, too, go down by 31%. To some extent this is again the product of job withdrawal, retirement and, for some, loss of earnings through widowhood. But it may also reflect generational differences in educational qualifications. All in all, therefore, the impact of wealth is complex and requires some unpacking. For this purpose, therefore, we will remove home-ownership from the wealth scale and treat it separately in order to make what remains at least less ambiguously life-cycle in nature (see also Verba and Nie 1972:143–45).

Finally, at the level of group resources, there are some modest but generally downward changes. As might be expected, active membership of a trade union declines, although only from 8·2% to 6·8%. The proportion of the few that are active party members, however, rises sharply from 4·1% to 4·4%. This may be tiny, but it may also be significant for party campaigning to which it is clearly related. Voluntary groups, on the other hand, display the dominant pattern of disengagement. The proportion who are members of five or more goes down from 8·6% to 4·4% and that of those totally unconnected rises from 29·8% to 37·2%.

The overall shift in relation to formal groups, we suspect, is essentially part of the life-cycle process we have described – a consequence of changes in the social and economic location of individuals as they move from early to late middle age. Why party commitments should be the exception, however, is hard to say – other than to suggest that it may relate to that gradual accumulation of partisan commitments which many researchers over the years have found to hold true (see, for example, Converse 1969, 1979; Butler and Stokes 1974:58; but see Asher 1980:73–5). The key question, however, is to what extent these changes in resources, and some of the other elements we have reviewed, like marital status, may explain the changes in participation. If we group together what would seem to be essentially life-cycle effects, and those, like education and home ownership, that are probably more generational in nature and then apply them both to the activity profile of the late middle aged, the results are as set out in table 7.8.

The overall pattern is quite simple. Just about the whole of the tendency of the late middle aged to under-participate is explained by the factors under review. Furthermore, about half seem to relate to events related to life-cycle changes and half to factors that seem more likely to be generational in nature. Both types of processes, that is, appear to lie behind their participatory profile. Amongst these, the evidence suggests that, once again, group resources and education are the most powerful ingredients. In other words, it is the decline in group ties as part of the onset of withdrawal, and low generationally-based educational backgrounds, that shape the outcome. After that, income plays some part, as well as residence patterns and marital status. Employment situation, however, is something that has a certain countervailing impact. Not all life-cycle changes entail a consistent negative impact on participation, but the net effect is certainly in that direction.

On the other hand, the results for the separate modes in table 7.8 indicate that there is considerable variation from one form of political activity to another. Collective action, direct action and contacting all show clear signs of de-activation amongst those of late middle age. On the other hand, the same life-cycle and generational factors that we have looked at, while providing a full explanation for contacting, leave much of the slow-down in the other two modes unexplained – about two-thirds in fact. So how the balance would change or the explanation improve by drawing in further age-related factors (such as a lack of *joie de vivre* or youthful vigour, or relevant political values of a more generational nature, for example) is difficult to say. But clearly in all three areas both age processes are important.

Electoral participation, as already noted, relates to late middle age in a very different way. Amongst those aged 50 to 64, party activity peaks and this is reflected in our measure of party campaigning. Indeed, taking life-cycle changes into account, that commitment to party work goes up even further. There is no sign of a slow-down here. The same is even more true of voting in which a substantial rise is recorded compared with early middle age. This is in many ways the golden age of voting turnout. Thus, within the terms of our survey, what this means is that 50·0% voted in 'every' local election (up from 40% for early middle age) and a further 27·4% said that they voted in 'most' (down from 33·6%). There were similarly high rates of turnout claimed in the 1983 General Election (88·0% compared with 85·8% early middle age) and in the 1984 European Election (56·2% to 47·4%).

Table 7.8 *Levels of participation in late middle age (50–64), controlling for resources and personal factors (N = 284)*

Mode	Unadjusted score	Adjusted for life-cycle related effects*	Adjusted for generationally related effects**
Overall	−8	−4	−1
Voting	+24	+23	+25
Party campaigning	+4	+9	+10
Contacting	−4	−3	−1
Collective action	−17	−15	−12
Direct action	−17	−14	−12

For etas and betas, see table 7.6.
* I.e. marital status; family structure; length of residence; group ties; income; car ownership.
** I.e. education; home ownership.

The evidence suggests that this is related to residence patterns, and even to retirement. But generally, neither the life-cycle nor the generational factors deployed seem to do much to help understand why this acceleration occurs. At the very least it shows that the participatory consequences associated with a transition into this phase of the life-cycle are not all of one piece. The more active and demanding activities do decline but not engagement in the electoral arena.

Old age

If we mark the start of 'old age' as 65, which is Britain's principal point of retirement, this phase of the life-cycle also contains a fairly wide age range. Roughly equal fractions are to be found in the 65–69, 70–74 and 75+ bands. The latter, furthermore, includes two nonagenarian interviewees, aged 96 and 91 respectively, and as many as forty-three octogenarians. It is also interesting to note that the 'senior citizens' constituted as many as 18·6% of all adults, only a few percentage points behind young adults (23·4%) and those in late middle age (22·8%). In short, the numerical expansion of those over 65 has reached a point where they are a very significant element in the political make-up of the British citizenry. This is also the case in most other Western democracies where mortality and birth rates are changing. Indeed, in West Germany, which now has the lowest birth rate in the world, and a falling population as a consequence, a political movement ('the Greys'!) was inaugurated in 1989 to mobilise the growing voting power of old people.

The question is, of course, to what extent do old people remain politically active? Do they bother to vote? Or has the process of withdrawal we saw beginning in late middle age so progressed that they are merely a very silent large minority?

As shown in figure 7.3, political participation in general is below average and declines for those over 75 to a point below any other age cohort (−45), including those under twenty (−35). As a group, therefore, there is political 'slow-down'. Nevertheless, old people, even those in the very oldest age brackets, are far from being politically inert. Indeed, those between 70 and 74 have an *unadjusted* score of a mere one point below the overall population average. So we need to examine more closely the patterns of withdrawal and their consequential participatory effects, fully recognising that passage over the 65 threshold does not entail an abrupt disengagement from the political world.

The personal and family situation of old people does, of course, continue the trends previously discussed. Those remaining married drop to just over half (56·4%), those becoming widowed rise to nearly one-third (30·3%). Equally, the presence of young dependants disappears and geographical mobility slows even more. On average, those over 65 have resided for 38·5 years at their current residence, 31% for over 50 years. Home ownership patterns also change: those having a mortgage drop to a tiny 2·6% while those owning their homes outright at this point form a majority (53·5%). But there is also a rise in those renting to 43·7% which is in part a life-cycle matter (moves into sheltered accommodation) but also a reflection of generational factors as, we suspect, it was for the relevant individuals in late middle age. Withdrawal from the active workforce also moves on. Only 3·7% claimed to be still in full-time (10+ hours) employment whilst exactly two-thirds gave their job status as 'retired'.

As a result, old people exhibit a further decline in the personal and group resources at their command. The numbers in the richest quarter shrink to a mere 4% whilst those in the poorest quarter rise to nearly half (48·6%). However, this again probably reflects to some extent a shift of generation as well as of life-cycle. On the one hand, car ownership and income both go down substantially in part because of retirement, widowhood and the like. But they are probably also lower because of a generationally-based drop in educational qualifications to which income and material well-being in general are related. Thus, for the over-65s, as many as three-quarters had no formal educational qualifications at all, and the elite of university degree holders was a mere 2·1%, a quarter of that amongst young adults.

Group resources also dwindle, but at different paces. Active trades unionists, for example, almost disappear (0·9%), but party commitments drop more gradually. Party members are hardly fewer in number (8·3%) than in late middle age (9%), but active members decline one-third to a tiny band of 2·8%. Finally, there is a visible disengagement from formal social networks. Nearly half (47·9%) have no active voluntary group ties at all (up from 37·2% for those aged 50 to 64) but the small minority with multiple memberships (5+) remains virtually unchanged at 4·6%. It seems, therefore, that withdrawal is the norm. At the same time, this is more true of some individuals than others. Active party members can still be found as well as those with a well-established network of organisational linkages. In consequence, we might expect to find some evidence of continued political activity. We might also expect to find that life-cycle changes are an important explanation of these behavioural changes and that, relative to their resource position, senior citizens are not quite so inactive as initial appearances might suggest.

The extent to which these expectations are true can be observed in table 7.9, which presents the mean levels of participation for those over 65 adjusted by what would seem to be mainly life-cycle and mainly generational factors. The unadjusted average on the overall ladder is the lowest (−18) for any of the broad age groups we have examined. But this still allows for some activity and some diversity. In fact, 23% of those over 65 register overall participation scores above the general population average. One

Table 7.9 *Levels of participation in old age (65–96), controlling for resources and personal factors (N = 291)*

Mode	Unadjusted score	Adjusted for life-cycle related effects*	Adjusted for generationally related effects**
Overall	−18	+1	0
Voting	+8	+14	+14
Party campaigning	−4	+8	+8
Contacting	−14	−3	−3
Collective action	−22	−6	−7
Direct action	−14	−2	−2

For etas and betas, see in table 7.6.
* I.e. marital status; family structure; length of residence; group ties; income; car ownership.
** I.e. education; home ownership.

individual had a score of +490 and was the sixteenth most politically active person in the entire survey![11] Clearly, old age and participation are not necessarily incompatible. Nevertheless, the general tendency is in the opposite direction and it must be noted that for the one elderly hyper-activist there were 23 who were at the absolute bottom of the ladder, with scores of −85. Indeed, they represented 39·7 % of all those in that situation.

When we look at why the elderly are so relatively inactive, table 7.9 suggests that, for overall participation, this is almost entirely the result of factors which appear to reflect life-cycle characteristics. Controlling for such elements as residence, marital status and social networks suggests that old people participate about as much or as little as these kinds of circumstances would suggest. The addition of more generationally influenced ingredients, such as education, adds next to nothing.[12]

At the same time, the overall relationship once again hides some significantly different patterns, although these do not affect the balance of life-cycle and generational explanations. As can be seen in the table, in every case, life-cycle factors have an effect on participation rates while those of a more generational nature do not. Outside that general tendency there is some variability. Collective action and direct action are both low, particularly the former. However, in contrast to the case with overall participation, the life-cycle factors do not entirely account for the degree of slow down, although what is left is very slight. Contacting is in a somewhat similar position, perhaps surprisingly so in view of the individual needs and problems the elderly face. In this instance, the slow down seems, in fact, to start more at 75 than at 65. Those in their early 70s register positive contacting scores, whether unadjusted (+2) or adjusted (+6). This indicates substantially more contacting than amongst the most elderly (75 to 91) whose scores are −42 and −24 respectively.[13]

Party campaigning and voting are different again. As with those of late middle age, rates of participation are in both cases above those recorded in other areas.[14] For campaigning, it is more those in their early seventies that are the most active, but all those over 65 are somewhat more active than their life-cycle circumstances would indicate (+8). Yet the greatest exception to the slow down rule comes in voting. Turnout is the one area where, without any adjustments at all, the elderly are more active than the population as a whole ($+8$). This continues the trend, at a more muted level, of late middle age. Slow-down in electoral participation clearly does lag throughout later life. Only when we look at those over 75 do voting rates drop below the average. And, when we make our standard adjustments, those in their late sixties turn out to be the most regular voters of any age group ($+30$) with the early seventies just behind ($+29$)!

In summary, old people can be politically active and some are very active indeed. The most active period, from our evidence, are the early seventies which seem to form an 'Indian Summer' for participation, where voting, campaigning, contacting and even collective action are plainly in evidence. It is really only after 75 that life-cycle forces seem finally to take their toll and rates plunge dramatically. But, even then, voting still holds up remarkably well with even our two nonagenarians claiming to have gone to the polls. It is the case that old people punch their voting weight, even if their record elsewhere is much weaker. Perhaps 'the Greys' will be recognised as such in the future in Britain more than they have in the past.

Conclusion

The survey of personal and situational factors, grouped around the twin elements of gender and age, has thrown up a considerable variety of additional influences that add to the picture of participation. In the case of gender, it is true that, across the board, its imprint was very weak. But for particular categories and combinations of individual circumstances, it revealed the ways in which gender shapes the amount and nature of participation. Age presented a generally more substantial impact, leaving a visible imprint across all forms of activity. The nature of its influence, however, is very difficult to determine from evidence collected at just one point in time. But our impression is that the effects of the life-cycle are greater than those caused by generational shifts. In particular, it is the changing pattern of resources, above all the rise and fall of resources deriving from formal affiliations, that seems to be the main process at work. In that sense, we see once more the abiding impact that resources in general have on political activity.

At the same time, there was also some support for a generationally-based influence on the behaviour of young adults, an influence seen in more muted form amongst those of early middle age. This process seemed to entail a certain shift from involvement in electoral politics towards more direct forms of action. This appeared to extend to collective action, although insofar as this mode straddles the divide between 'conventional' and 'unconventional' (see chapter 3), inevitably the evidence is going to be less pronounced.

If our interpretation is correct, then there may be a gradual change in the overall shape of the participatory input from ordinary citizens. The strong commitments to voting and party campaigning, so discernible amongst older citizens in our survey, may be eroded and slowly replaced by commitments to somewhat less eirenic and more directly issue-centred participation. As Inglehart suggested (1977), the elites in Britain may well be subject to sharper challenges and confrontations than in the past. Whether this is so will only be fully revealed after the tide of events has moved on. It may be that the sense of youthful disaffection from conventional politics was only a passing feature of the 1980s, or it may be a more lasting and therefore consequential change. For the present, however, we must at least raise the possibility that the role of the citizen is not going to be quite the same in the future as it has traditionally been in the past. Competing values and ideologies may play a more visible motivating role as citizens become ever more educated. Accordingly the next two chapters examine the part that outlooks and values play in stimulating citizens to stand up and try to have their say.

8

POLITICAL OUTLOOKS

What citizens do politically is not just a matter of their social and economic circumstances, it is also a matter of the particular outlooks they have about politics and the specific values they may seek to express. The importance of these personal perspectives is recognised in the idea of a national political culture which embodies, in principle, the totality of the citizenry's collective feelings about the political system and each individual's place within it (see, for example, Rosenbaum 1975; Kavanagh 1972c).[1] Almond and Verba's classic study (1963) was perhaps the first to give empirical grounding, on a cross-national basis at least, to the view that the individual civic outlooks which compose the political culture are an important influence.[2] In this chapter, we cannot hope to cover the whole remit of political culture. What we do propose is to focus principally on two major elements – political efficacy and cynicism – and their impact on the level and nature of participation.

Political efficacy

The potential relevance of political efficacy to participation can be seen in the way it was originally formulated – 'the feeling that individual political action does have, or can have, an impact upon the political process, i.e. that it is worthwhile to perform one's civic duties. It is the feeling that political and social change is possible, and that the individual citizen can play a part in bringing about this change' (Campbell, Gurin and Miller 1954). If, to put it another way, participation is instrumental, then a sense of political efficacy consists in the confidence of citizens that their actions can achieve the results which they desire. Some possess this confidence, and one might well expect that, as a consequence, they will be more ready to cross the threshold into the public realm. Others, however, lack a sense of personal efficacy, which may explain why they are relatively inactive. Almond and Verba, indeed, regarded being efficacious (or, as they put it, politically 'competent') as 'a key political attitude. The self-confident citizen appears to be the democratic citizen' (1963:257).

What we need to explore, therefore, is a series of questions about the relationship between efficacy and participation. How efficacious are the respondents in our survey and which citizens feel this way? Are those also the more active individuals? And are those who see themselves as less effective also less participatory? Or do they translate those feelings into more confrontational forms of engagement?

Table 8.1 *Sense of political efficacy*

	Low efficacy		High efficacy			
	Strongly agree %	Agree %	Disagree %	Strongly disagree %	Total*	N
1. Individual influence	11·7	53·6	31·2	3·5	100·0	1,523
2. Group influence	4·3	31·1	57·9	6·6	100·0	1,496
3. General Election vote	4·2	21·3	58·2	16·3	100·0	1,531
4. Local Election vote	3·3	17·0	64·2	15·5	100·0	1,532

* A small number of 'other' and 'don't know' responses have been excluded.

Our measure of political efficacy was composed of responses (from strongly agree to strongly disagree) to four items. The first two focused on whether or not the citizen would be able to affect Members of Parliament – as salient symbols of the national polity. The wording was as follows:

1. Individually, people like you [the respondent] can have no influence over Members of Parliament.
2. A group of people like you can have no influence over Members of Parliament.

The second pair of items were concerned with perceptions of the effectiveness of the vote – again as the most salient symbol of the means through which the citizen might exert influence. The wording used here was:

3. Your individual vote can make no difference in a General Election.
4. Your individual vote can make no difference in a Local Election.[3]

Our scale, therefore, taps what has been called 'subjective confidence' (Almond and Verba 1963:137).[4] Other equivalent terms are 'Ability to influence Government' (Muller 1970:794)[5] or 'internal political efficacy' (Balch 1974) – internal because it is about the belief the individual citizen has concerning his or her *own* abilities. This is contrasted with 'external political efficacy' which concerns the perceptions of the responsiveness of politicians to the interests of the mass public, something that is therefore more external to the individual citizen (see also Conway 1985:38).[6]

The distribution of outlooks revealed by the responses shows some interesting patterns which are set out in table 8.1. The question concerning individual citizen influence over MPs shows that a majority have generally inefficacious outlooks. Two-thirds agreed that people like themselves had no influence over what MPs might do or say, nearly 12% emphatically so. Conversely, only a minority thought they could exert some leverage, amongst whom a tiny 3·5% seemed particularly confident. Interestingly enough, however, when the question is posed about groups of citizens, rather than (as is traditionally the case) about citizens as individuals, the balance of opinion reverses itself. Now two-thirds think they are efficacious and only one-third do not. Clearly, therefore, the responses are not just abstract reflections or mere sentiments disconnected from reality, but genuine attempts to assess that reality as it affects each individual. People do seem to believe in the idea of 'strength in numbers', and that may well be a very rational assessment of the instrumentality of collective as against individual action (but cf. Kavanagh 1980:150).

Responses to the questions concerning the efficacy of the vote are more consistent, and more positive. In both instances, three-quarters or more thought that individual votes did make a difference. Here, however, the difference may well be something less than exerting ongoing or specific influence over those elected.[7] But at least there is broad support for some instrumentality attaching to elections. Interestingly enough, that support is marginally greater at the local than at the national level. Whether this might also accord with a rational assessment of the electoral process at the two levels is more dubious, given the extent to which local elections in Britain are affected by national consideration (cf. Kavanagh 1980:149–50).

On the whole, therefore, the table does suggest that feelings of political efficacy are fairly widely held in the population at large. This accords with the assessment made by Almond and Verba in their British survey of 30 years ago and not disavowed in a later summary of subsequent research (Kavanagh 1980; but see Topf 1989a:12). Indeed, if one looks at cross-national studies such as that by Barnes, Kaase *et al.* (1979), the British population is also seen to be relatively efficacious. For example, responses to a question about whether or not people have a say in government, showed that only one-third of the British surveyed thought they had – which is in line with our measure of individual influence. But rather more thought that way in Britain than in any of the other eight liberal democracies except America and Holland (see *Political Action*, 1979; results calculated by the present authors).

While the majority may feel generally effective, there are some citizens who display political confidence in all the circumstances represented by our four measures. Conversely, there are those who feel consistently the opposite – that neither themselves as individuals, nor as members of a group, nor their votes, add up to much. In light of this, two questions may be posed: who feels very effective, or very ineffective, and does it matter for participation?

To look at these more general patterns, the four measures were combined using factor analysis.[8] This produced a single scale or ladder of political efficacy with an average score of zero, a minimum of -349 and a maximum of $+287$. These scores reflect what has already been suggested, that to have a very positive outlook is somewhat more common (or less abnormal) than to have very negative feelings.[9]

In table 8.2, we present evidence as to the social and demographic bases of political efficacy. Clearly, such feelings are not randomly distributed. As the pattern of responses has already indicated, they do reflect a certain rational assessment of the citizen's political competence. And this is, in part, a product of the kinds of circumstances detailed in the table. It shows that the young feel considerably less effective than old people who, interestingly enough, have the highest scores of any age cohort when they are adjusted (cf. Milbrath and Goel 1977:60). Women also have somewhat less efficacious outlooks than men, although the general impact of gender is not as great as

Table 8.2 *Who feels politically effective?*

		Unadjusted score	Adjusted score*	Beta
1.	*Age*			0·17
	Young (15–29)	− 19	− 24	
	Old (65–91)	+ 6	+ 24	
2.	*Gender*			0·11
	Female	− 15	− 11	
	Male	+ 15	+ 11	
3.	*Class*			0·12
	Working class	− 19	− 8	
	Salariat	+ 41	+ 19	
4.	*Education*			0·21
	None	− 26	− 24	
	Degree	+ 22	0	
5.	*Wealth*			0·05
	Poorest 5%	− 28	− 4	
	Richest 5%	+ 53	+ 9	
6.	*Group ties*			0·18
	None	− 20	− 9	
	5+	+ 72	+ 50	

Multiple R = 0·421
* Controlling for the effects of all the other factors listed in the table.

age (cf. Milbrath and Goel 1977:60). Class, too, makes a difference, a considerable one if the unadjusted figures are used, distinctly less if resource elements are separated out. Education has the highest impact of all, a finding very much in line with Almond and Verba (1963:163–7). (See also Milbrath and Goel 1977:60, and the numerous studies cited there.)

Here, however, the relationship is not a straightforward one such that the more education one has received, the more politically effective one will feel. It is the case that the least formally qualified feel the least effective. The more efficacious, however, are not those with the highest qualifications (the degree holders) but those two rungs down the ladder who have obtained A levels or their equivalent. Thereafter, feelings of efficacy turn down for both those with college qualifications (+ 14) and, even more, with degrees (0). This is not because of age or the other factors included in table 8.2 which have been statistically set aside. But what we do see are some further important hints as to what exposure to higher educational entails for political outlooks. Despite the skills and other advantages university and polytechnic graduate status imparts, it also appears to impart a political outlook that is somewhat at odds with those skills and advantages. In those terms, graduates are not entirely the politically self-confident citizens of which Almond and Verba (1963:257) speak.

The two other resource factors are, on the other hand, more in line with general findings about efficacy and 'higher objective social positions' (Milbrath and Goel 1977:60). Although the weakest factor of all, the wealthy feel somewhat more confident and the poor less so. What is perhaps surprising is that the gap is as small as it is, most of the basic gap (of 81 points) being the product of other associated elements rather than poverty or wealth *per se*. Ties to parties, trades unions and social groups, however, do retain some considerable impact, and entirely in the expected direction.

Overall, therefore, the findings are not too surprising. Those who feel most competent, the salaried, older, male, richer and better connected perhaps have good reason for their confidence about their political potential. Nor is it surprising that a *sense* of powerlessness in the political realm goes with being young, female, working class, uneducated, poor and organisationally isolated. These would appear to be the circumstances of *actual* powerlessness. The only deviant case, but an important one, would seem to be the outlooks of the very well-educated.

But do such political outlooks count for anything in terms of participation or can it be largely explained by social and economic circumstance? The answer, as can be seen from the results of a multiple classification analysis set out in figure 8.1, is that outlooks do make a significant contribution and that this is not simply a matter of background factors. The unadjusted relationship is fairly straightforward – the more efficacious the citizen feels, the more he or she is likely to participate. But it is only amongst the most subjectively competent 15% that the boost is particularly apparent (+75). The plot of the overall scores adjusted for the resource differentials detailed in table 8.2 shows that about half that boost, and about half of the relationship in general, is not so much the product of outlook as of associated background characteristics. For example, the score for the more efficacious drops to +36, and the beta to 0·16 (from 0·33). Thus, there is a considerable gap of about 53 points between the 15% with the most positive outlooks and the 14% with the most negative self-images. This is about the magnitude of the effect of education (see figure 4.2) but much less than the impact made by group resources (see chapter 5). So very extreme political outlooks do make a difference but group resources remain important.

What is it, more precisely, about these outlooks that produces the effect on participation? For example, is having a sense of individual-based effectiveness more important than feeling effective within a group? And are these more or less important than thinking that one's vote makes a difference? If, for the moment, we unpack the scale into its constituent items, there is quite some variation in their influence over participation. The largest was that exerted by the first item – having confidence in one's *own* abilities to exert influence (beta = 0·12). Lacking this form of self-confidence was indeed a major depressant (−51) and the overall gap between strong agreers and strong disagreers (see table 8.1) was 61 points. Interestingly enough, item two, a sense of group-based efficacy, was of very little import. The beta was a tiny 0·02 and the spread a mere ten points. Clearly, for overall participation, it is the belief in individual competence (or, more strikingly, incompetence) that affects behaviour.

There is a similar discrepancy between the two vote items. Feeling that one's vote counts for something (or not) in local elections is seemingly more critical than for general elections. In the former case, a strong feeling that the individual's vote was of little effect was associated with a negative score of −18 whereas those with strong positive views

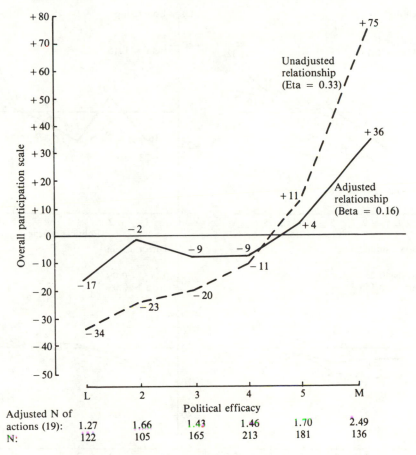

Figure 8.1 Overall participation by political efficacy, controlling for other cultural† and resource* factors

scored +7 (beta = 0·08). The General Election item, on the other hand, like group influence, made little difference (beta = 0·03). All in all, therefore, the key aspects of political efficacy, at least in regard to overall participation, are negative feelings about individual influence in the local arena. It is only when all are put together that the cumulative positive outlooks come more to the fore.

When we turn to consider the different modes of participation in figure 8.2, it is apparent, once again, that there is some diversity around the basic themes set out above. In the case of voting, there is an approximately step-by-step increase in participation as levels of political efficacy rise. The unadjusted relationship here is quite a strong one, with an eta of 0·24 and a spread of 74 points between top and bottom. However, much of this is attributable to other factors and the adjusted effect is about half the original (beta = 0·13). But the basic internal pattern remains intact, going from −26 for the least efficacious to +13 for those at the top end.[10]

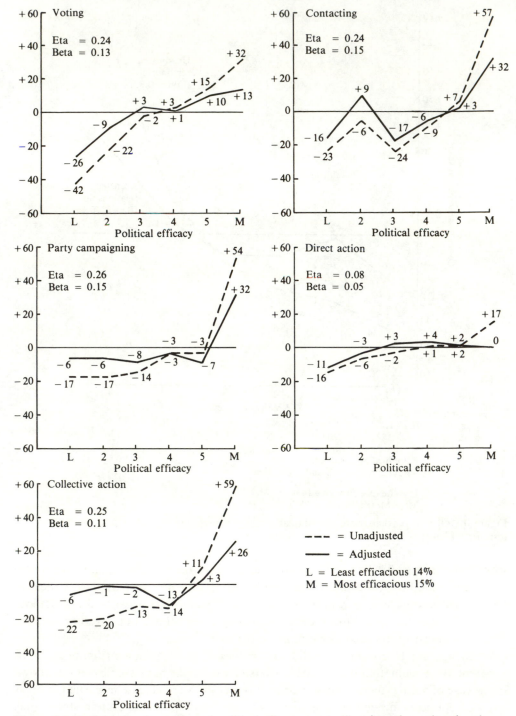

Figure 8.2 Participation by mode and political efficacy, controlling for other cultural and resource factors

The other electoral mode, campaign participation, also has a positive relationship with political efficacy, but one in which the only major effect is a boost to involvement at the top end (+32). Collective action and contacting, too, both basically follow the relationship displayed by overall participation. The linkages, however, are somewhat more erratic. In collective action, there is a clear positive boost to participation at the top end (+26) but little at the bottom (−6). Indeed, the lowest adjusted rate is recorded for the third highest efficacy band (−13)! In the case of contacting, the association between efficacy and activity exhibited, as before, a strong boost at the top (+32) and a more modest one at the bottom (−16). But in between the two, the second lowest efficacy category has an adjusted score of +9 and the third lowest −17. Here, a strong belief in individual influence was the single most powerful boost (+42 with a beta of 0·08).

Finally, we turn to direct action. In this instance, political efficacy diverges most strongly from the pattern displayed in figure 8.1 for overall participation, in that there is little impact at all (beta = 0·05). The one small effect of note is that very low efficacy is associated with reduced levels of activity (−11). This does mean, however, that direct action is not the *cri de coeur* of those who feel ineffective in the world of conventional politics. But nor is it the case that very high levels of political efficacy generally give a boost to such forms of protest. To that extent, therefore, our findings do not support those of Barnes, Kaase *et al.* (1979:438) who found consistently positive associations between internal political efficacy and protest potential both in their British data and in the other countries they studied.[11]

All in all, therefore, a sense of efficacy does contribute substantially to understanding patterns of political participation. There is a broad sense in which having positive feelings, particularly about one's own level of competence, do sustain higher levels of activity. But there are many nuances, and even exceptions, to this.

Political cynicism

Whereas a sense of political efficacy forms part of a citizen's view about his or her own role in the polity, political cynicism is one aspect of the individual's attitude to that polity. In particular, it is that element of the political culture which relates to how 'the authorities' are perceived – whether politicians are regarded as manipulating citizens, whether the leadership is thought to be corrupt and self-serving, whether public officials are seen as working for the welfare of all or just a few powerful interests (Milbrath and Goel 1977:63). It is, therefore, intimately related to the question of trust and distrust – of confidence in politicians, institutions and the whole business of politics (see Miller 1974:952).[12]

To measure such outlooks, we again focused on Members of Parliament as salient examples of national-level politicians. We posed two statements about them, one intended to gauge overtly cynical responses, the other to gauge trusting views. The wording of each was as follows:

1. Most Members of Parliament are out for themselves rather than the public good.
2. You can generally trust Members of Parliament to do what is right.

To these we added two further items, again both clearly cynical in orientation, but this time concerned with the polity at the local level to broaden the judgemental base. One focused on local councillors and the other local community activists.

3. Most local councillors are out for themselves rather than the public good.
4. Most people who are active in local community groups are out for themselves rather than the public good.

Taken together, citizens who felt that MPs were out for themselves and could not be trusted, and who also felt that local councillors and community activists were not working for the good of all, would appear to have a pervasively negative orientation towards politics. A plausible, initial hypothesis would be to expect that such an orientation would be associated with apathy if not outright withdrawal from political activity. Or rather, this might be true of conventional politics, the political game as played by MPs, local councillors and most community activists, but less true of direct action. Might not direct action in fact be predicated upon an assumption that conventional politics is indeed a dirty business and therefore requires strong tactics from without if goals are to be accomplished? These suppositions provide some guiding perspectives, but once more we had to look to the data to see whether or not they were borne out or whether alternative patterns and explanations might be forthcoming.

Exploration of the effect of cynical and distrustful political outlooks can begin with a look at the basic distribution of responses to our four statements. These are set out in table 8.3. The first two show relatively balanced sets of responses. In answer to the question whether or not MPs were out for themselves, 42·0% adopted a basically cynical outlook compared with 58·1% who had come to more positive judgements. But this was to some extent offset by there being twice as many who were strongly cynical (8·6%) as felt very positively (4·2%). The same pattern emerged in response to the question on trust. More were generally trustful (55·6% to 44·5%), but the small minority who were strongly distrustful were three times as numerous as the very trusting individuals (5·3% to 1·6%). Even so, opinion was slightly tipped towards the positive end of the spectrum.

In the case of local councillors and activists, this basically positive outlook was even more pronounced. Political actors at the local level appear to be held in rather higher regard than those operating nationally.[13] Thus, 67·2% of responses about local councillors were non-cynical and as many as 76·7% of views about community activists. Only a relatively small minority thought the latter to be 'do-gooders' doing good mainly for themselves. And, in both instances, the extremely cynical were outweighed by the strongly uncynical.

As with any set of statements where precise wording can influence the balance of responses, caution must be exercised about forming definitive judgments about the political culture. Responses can vary over time and even from year to year (Topf 1989a:table 7; see also Hart 1978). However, our impression of these results is that Britain's political culture is not a particularly cynical one. It is possible that cynicism may have increased in recent years, particularly in regard to national politics, although this is the subject of intensive academic debate (Marsh 1977; Hart 1978:79; Kavanagh 1980:153–5; Beer 1982:110–20; Norton 1984a:359–63). Our own evidence suggests that

Table 8.3 *Levels of political cynicism and distrust*

	High cynicism/distrust		Low cynicism/trust			
	Strongly agree	Agree	Disagree	Strongly disagree	Total	N
MPs out for themselves	8·6	33·4	53·9	4·2	100·0	1,434
MPs can(not) be trusted*	5·3	39·2	54·0	1·6	100·0	1,367
Local councillors out for themselves	4·5	28·4	61·9	5·3	100·0	1,440
Community activists out for themselves	3·2	20·1	68·3	8·4	100·0	1,446

* This item has been reflected in order to be consistent in direction with the other three items.

majority opinion still seems to be on the benign side of the fence. To that extent, these findings reaffirm the view of the British political culture as basically 'civic' (see Almond and Verba 1963:chs. 8 and 12; Kavanagh 1980:153). At the same time there are strong hints of a very disaffected minority with views in striking contradiction to these more widely held beliefs.[14]

Such a conclusion might be underscored if we briefly set Britain in a broader comparative context.[15] The study by Barnes, Kaase *et al.* (1979) contained two measures relating to cynicism and distrust. On these, Britain ranked fifth and sixth out of eight countries studied (*Political Action*, 1979:183–5, our calculations). Most trusting (and least cynical) were Austria, West Germany and Switzerland, with the USA and Italy at the bottom. The disparity between West Germany and Britain was repeated in a more recent survey (Topf 1989). Thus, although none of these countries could be described as very cynical in their general outlooks (except, possibly, Italy), Britain's levels of trust seem to be significantly below those in many other European democracies.

But what does it mean, in concrete terms, to say that one individual is very cynical in political outlook, and another not? Can one speak of a syndrome of cynicism? To answer these questions, we looked at the inter-relationships of the four items to see if they did indeed form a common scale. The results were very positive – there was a strong single dimension that incorporated all the items, although some were more central to it than others. Top of the list was the item relating to cynicism about MPs, followed closely by the same statement referring to local councillors. To that extent, the scale is very much centred on cynicism towards Britain's political authorities. The third item in centrality was that concerning the community activists, and the last, possibly because of its rather differing wording and orientation as much as its substance, was the question of trusting MPs to do what is right.[16] The maximum score (indicating the least cynical or most trusting outlook) was +274, the minimum −342. The fact that the most cynical score is further away from the mean (zero) than the most trusting, and that the median figure is +27, both reflect the slight anti-cynical orientation of the populace at large.

To flesh out what these two very different orientations indicate in political terms, we divided the scale into six categories or strata such that, using 'natural' breaks in it, we located the 12% most cynical (very negative scores) and the 10% least cynical (positive scores). The former would appear to encompass that disaffected minority detected in table 8.2. The latter, on the other hand, would represent those who shared the rather rosy sentiments of the majority, but to a very strong degree. We than looked at a number of political attitudes to highlight the differences between the two groups. These are set out in table 8.4 and suggest very strongly that the political cynicism scale does indeed tap divergent political outlooks.

First, there is, not unexpectedly, an empirical linkage between having a positive view of one's own competence and having a similar outlook about political authorities. The most cynical (12%) scored −60 on the political efficacy scale whereas the most trusting and uncynical 10% registered a figure of +44 – a spread of 140 points. This gives some support to those who argue that cynicism and efficacy are indeed separate but related components (normlessness and powerlessness) of a yet broader political outlook that Seeman (1959) labels as alienation (see also Miller 1974:952).[17] But table 8.4 also clearly indicates that the differences go well beyond assessments of the role of the individual citizen. The remaining items relate to judgements about Britain's regime as a parliamentary-style democracy, its incumbent government (at the time Mrs Thatcher's second Conservative administration), and the performance of the respondent's local government. In all instances, there was a considerable gulf between the most and least cynical. Those who were trusting and uncynical had very positive opinions about politics; those who had the opposite outlooks share very negative attitudes.

Nor do the differences end there. We also investigated possible differences of opinion regarding Britain's welfare system, the economic role of trades unions, and the way that private industry and nationalised industry are run. In all instances there was the same general disparity of outlook, the one negative, the other positive. In some instances the gap was small, but it was there. Politically cynical individuals, in other words, indeed have a generally negative world view, and those who trust politicians tend to see the rest of the polity and society through rose-tinted spectacles.

Who is it that views the political and social world in these contrasting ways? Or, to put it another way, to what extent are these outlooks rooted in particular social experiences? Table 8.5 suggests that, as with political efficacy, there is some linkage with socio-economic experiences although the strength of that linkage seems weaker in the present instance.[18] Amongst those experiences, age has an association, although perhaps more modest than might be expected. Even on an adjusted basis, the gap between young and old was only 21 points, and shrinks to 14 when adjustments are made for education, wealth and all the other factors in the table. Nevertheless, the young do remain slightly, if consistently, more cynical about politics than the population generally. Gender, on the other hand, appears to have no general relationship at all with cynicism. If, as feminists tend to argue, liberal democracy is male-dominated and therefore oriented to serve the interests of men rather than women, there is no obvious reflection of that here. This does not, of course, mean that all women are politically trusting. What it does mean is that women are neither more nor less trusting, on average, than men. Indeed, even those women who are members of feminist groups (see chapter 7) not only felt efficacious (+39), but were also on the uncynical side of the fence (+25).

Class reveals a more conventional portrait of the alienating effects of being a member

Table 8.4 *Political outlooks of the most (12%) and least (10%) cynical*

	Most cynical	Least cynical	All respondents
Political efficacy	−60	+44	0
Britain's parliamentary Government*	4·69	7·02	6·33
The present Conservative Government*	3·10	5·44	5·03
Your local council**	5·53	6·65	6·13
N	132	102	1,064

* Marks out of ten (10 = extremely favourable)
** Marks out of ten (10 = extremely favourable), referring to district or borough where respondent lives.

Table 8.5 *Who feels politically cynical?*

		Unadjusted score	Adjusted score*	Beta
1.	*Age*			
	Young (15–29)	−4	−11	0·07
	Old (65–91)	−17	+3	
2.	*Gender*			
	Female	0	0	0·00
	Male	0	0	
3.	*Class*			
	Working	−12	−2	0·06
	Salariat	+14	+1	
4.	*Education*			
	None	−21	−17	0·18
	Degree	+3	−6	
5.	*Wealth*			
	Poorest 5%	+4	+17	0·11
	Richest 5%	+12	−6	
6.	*Group ties*			
	None	−10	−6	0·12
	5+	+35	+30	

Negative scores = high cynicism; multiple R = 0·272.
* Controlling for the effects of all the other factors listed in the table.

of the working class (−12) whilst, not surprisingly, the salariat are of the opposite persuasion (+14). But, as so often in our class analysis, almost all of the difference evaporates if we separate from it wealth, education and group associations. If they are included, then class and cynicism are related to a very moderate extent (eta = 0·12). But if we strip these other elements out, then class *per se* adds little, the largest effect being amongst manual foremen (−11).

Education, however, retains a much stronger impact on cynicism. Even on an adjusted basis, the beta is quite substantial (0·18). And, not surprisingly, those at the bottom of the ladder were quite cynical in their outlooks (−17). The degree holders, on the other hand, were, like the young, perhaps less cynical than we might have expected (adjusted score of −6). Certainly, it is hard to see here any strong views that might help us to understand their commitment to direct action (figure 4.3). Just as they were neutral in terms of efficacy, so they are not far off being neutral in terms of cynicism. The seeds of their protest orientation must lie more in other directions.[19] Finally, the two measures of group resource also seem to make some impact on cynicism, although organisational affiliation is the more consistent. The more isolated, less organisationally connected individuals are the more cynical;[20] those who have multiple ties and are, hence, more socially integrated, are much less so. Wealth, however, seems to have no interpretable relationship.

The results in table 8.5, taken together, do not suggest that political cynicism is very sharply defined socially, economically or demographically. This type of political perspective, where the individual looks outwards towards the polity, seems to be only weakly shaped by social experiences. This is, perhaps, surprising. If political cynicism is supposed to reflect wider (and deeper) processes of alienation in society at large, then there is relatively little evidence of it here.

The crucial question, however, is whether this type of political outlook has any bearing on participation, and, if so, how activity is affected. Our original working hypothesis was that cynicism might depress participation, as low efficacy did. But we also pondered whether those who were cynical about the conventional political game might thereby be disposed towards forms of engagement that challenged that conventional arena, forms such as direct action.

In figure 8.3 we display the relationship between cynicism and the overall participation scale. An immediate impression is that it makes less impact on participation than political efficacy. The eta is only about one-third the size and the beta just under two-thirds. It can also be seen that the shape of the relationship appears to change: on an unadjusted basis, less cynicism suggests more participation but, when corrections are made, if anything the opposite is the case. Or, rather, the only major impact of cynicism left after necessary statistical adjustments comes among the most cynical whose negative outlook is associated with rather higher levels of participation (+24). This phenomenon is repeated in the simple 19-item count set out at the base of the figure. Those who are the most cynical do the most (beyond voting and signing petitions) with a score of 2·12. They are a considerable way ahead of the next two groups (at 1·77), although one of those is the least cynical category.[21] The contribution of cynicism to political activism is, therefore, somewhat contradictory and ill-defined, just as was its social roots. But, if anything does stand out so far, it is that strongly negative outlooks do not lead to apathy and disengagement. On the contrary, they seem to lead to a greater degree of activity than at any other point on our scale. The cynical individual who described himself as a 'middle of the road anarchist' and who did not vote because he 'dissociated himself from the whole apparatus of democracy' is not, therefore, typical of the distrustful elements in society.

Do the relationships with individual modes give us a better handle on the nature of this impulse? Is it the case that high levels of direct action lie behind the overall figures?

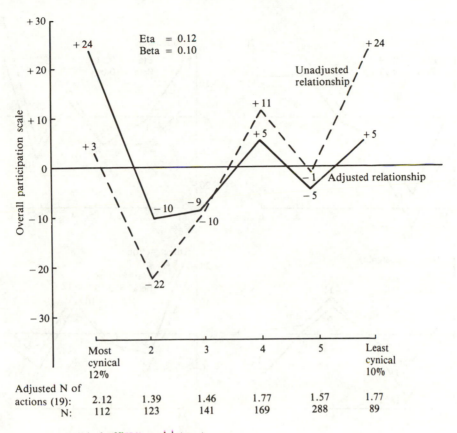

Eta = 0.12
Beta = 0.10

	Most cynical 12%	2	3	4	5	Least cynical 10%
Adjusted N of actions (19):	2.12	1.39	1.46	1.77	1.57	1.77
N:	112	123	141	169	288	89

† Political efficacy and interest.
* Education, wealth and group ties.

Figure 8.3 Overall participation by political cynicism, controlling for other cultural and resource factors

The evidence offered in figure 8.4 seems to confirm this possibility. As we can see, the direct action scale does peak amongst those with the most cynical outlooks (+23). Equally, the two lowest levels are registered amongst those with the most trusting orientations (−7 and −6). But there is also a peak in the middle, not as high as for the strongly cynical, but a peak nevertheless (+10). This can also be found in the overall scale pattern in figure 8.3. Further investigation shows that the rise in direct action amongst those who are neither strongly distrusting of political leaders nor trustful is perhaps more significant than figure 8.4 suggests. For if we look at the joint outlooks of efficacy and cynicism combined, we find that the highest level of direct action is to be found amongst those who are highly efficacious but only moderately cynical. Compared with those individuals, the highly efficacious and highly cynical are somewhat less active – as though too great a degree of cynicism, at least amongst people who feel very competent, does slightly stunt overt action.

If we return for a moment to the overall participation scale, we also find the same phenomenon, although the gap between the two groups (those with high efficacy plus medium cynicism versus those combining high efficacy and strong cynicism) is much

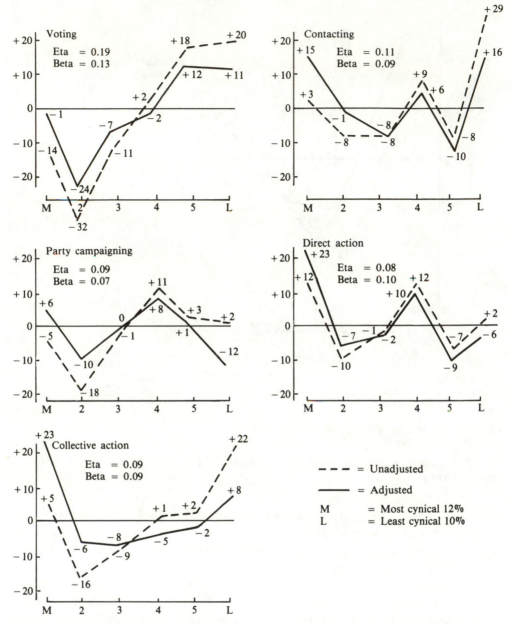

Figure 8.4 Participation by mode and political cynicism, controlling for other cultural and resource factors

smaller: it is the moderately cynical who also feel very efficacious that are the most active. All of which throws some important light on what is called the 'mistrustful-efficacious hypothesis' (Hart 1978:53; see also Fraser 1970; Hawkins, Marando and Taylor 1971). This suggests that participation will be maximised amongst those who feel highly competent but are also very mistrustful. The results, however, show this not to be so. In no mode of participation, in fact, did we find the 'mistrustful-efficacious' combination quite correct. Our results would offer better support for the hypothesis that it is the 'semi-mistrustful-efficacious' who are somewhat more prone to take political action.

This alternative hypothesis provides a further plausible challenge to the idea, with which the discussion opened, that cynicism would undermine participatory intentions. It can be argued instead that a certain amount of cynicism is healthy for democracy (Parry 1976). It is better not to be too trusting of politicians. The price of liberty is eternal vigilance and a readiness to back that vigilance by action to defend one's interests when threatened by authorities who cannot be entirely relied upon to protect them. There is good reason to think that the much-vaunted stability of the British system of government has long gone with a certain scepticism about the intentions and achievements of the political elite. If there has been a decline in trusting attitudes amongst the British population (which is far from certain), there is little evidence that it has seriously rocked the political boat (Budge 1971). The curvilinear pattern of the findings, then, becomes more explicable as both the cynical, wary of threats to their interests and values, and the more trusting, with a belief in the responsiveness of the system, find reasons to act. At the same time, it would appear that a sense of efficacy is also required, whether one is trusting or cynical. What the 'semi-mistrustful-efficacious' combination suggests is that beyond a certain (not readily definable) point, cynicism can go too far and begin to undermine one's faith in the point of acting.

It is, therefore, interesting to find hints that collective action, direct action's closest neighbour (see table 3.3), also shares some of the same general linkages between cynicism and activity. Taking cynicism by itself, the peak likewise comes amongst the most disillusioned (+23). However, there is one important difference. The relationship with collective action is more clearly curvilinear such that both the very untrusting and also (if to a lesser extent) the very trusting individuals are inclined to this form of participation. This is further highlighted when efficacy is drawn into the picture. Here, unlike the case with direct action, it is those who combine being highly efficacious with being very trusting that are the most active, just ahead this time of those who feel very competent but have medium and high cynicism.

The basic curvilinear pattern, whereby both extremes of the cynicism spectrum appear to participate more than those with relatively neutral views, also seems to be a feature of contacting. Here, the strengths of the two outlooks are about the same (+15 and +16). Neither is, obviously, a major factor in explaining levels of contacting, but they do suggest that this arises both amongst citizens who are very wary about those who ultimately make the decisions and amongst individuals who see the authorities in a very beneficent light. Once more, however, if we just consider the highly efficacious, it seems that moderate levels of cynicism are the most conducive to contacting.

The one instance where the original hypothesis that positive, uncynical outlooks might facilitate participation is clearly supported lies in the area of voting. Here, as we can see in figure 8.4, the trusting citizens are the most regular voters and, as trust declines, so does turnout. Furthermore, given that in this instance high efficacy and low cynicism seem to reinforce each other, it is not surprising that we found turnout to be highest amongst those who do feel the most competent and also have the most trustful views of political authorities. Thus, electoral participation does seem to be an area where 'civic orientations' work in tandem (Verba and Nie 1972) and where even the 'semi-

mistrustful-efficacy' hypothesis is not quite on the mark, although it is much more accurate than the mistrust-efficacy combination.

The mobilisation efforts of the political parties during election campaigns are partially intended to reinforce the sense of political competence amongst the electorate. But it is also possible to detect here the expressive element in participation mentioned in chapter 1. The exercise of the ballot, treated by some instrumental schools as a 'cost' to be set by a rational actor against the putative benefits to the individual voter (Downs 1957), was something for which generations of people strove. The vast majority of our respondents not only exercised the right, but 86% regarded it as a 'duty to vote' in a general election. Apparently it expresses one's standing as a citizen.[22] Moreover, whatever the alleged logic of rational choice theories as to the instrumentality of voting, the majority of people (who have not attended lecture courses on the subject) do not accept it. Almost three-quarters rejected the view that 'your individual vote can make no difference in a General Election'. Similarly, 83% opposed the suggestion that it 'makes no difference which party forms the government'. Some complex combination of instrumental and expressive attitudes are at work in explaining voting behaviour in particular and possibly affecting other dimensions of participation (see Finkel, Muller and Opp 1989).

Conclusion

Clearly, there are some important connections between holding a cynical political outlook and participation in politics. But, as with political efficacy, the linkages are complex and at times even convoluted. The main general thrust runs against part of the original hypothesis in that cynicism is associated with action, not inaction. But there is support for the supposition that there could be a link between cynicism and unconventional rather than conventional forms of engagement. Overall, however, the patterns provide some backing for the revised suggestion that cynicism as well as trust can, in its different way, be 'healthy' for an active democracy. But even this seems to be contingent upon other aspects of the individual's view of the political world. Thus amongst the most competent, and therefore most active persons, extreme cynicism seems, for example, to moderate rather than enhance action. There are, moreover, significant differences between the modes of participation. All of this suggests a degree of caution in asserting a consistent and sustained association between political cynicism and participation. Moreover, it would seem that, by comparison, it is the sense of efficacy, of confidence in the capacity to act, which makes a greater impact than a person's broad attitude to the authorities who are targets of that action.

In general, political outlooks do make a difference to levels of participation. This is most true of voting which, perhaps because it is perceived as both a central right and for many also a duty, seems to be most consistently influenced by 'positive' political outlooks. Given that voting was also the mode of participation least affected by resources (figure 5.10), it would appear that turnout is as much, if not more, the product of outlook as of background. However, this is not typical of the other modes. For collective action, campaigning, contacting and direct action, these broad outlooks add relatively less to the equation, partly because in these cases resources are a more important explanatory force, but partly because of the varied impact of political cynicism.

At the same time, these very broad outlooks to politics constitute only part of the systems of values which might orient individuals towards participation. There are, in addition, outlooks more closely associated with the stuff of political debate – with the traditional standpoints of the political parties, with new cleavages in society or new perspectives on the role of government. Some of these are the subject matter of the next chapter.

9

PARTY AND VALUES

The previous chapter looked at very broad orientations towards the political system and the degree of confidence people had in their capacity to take effective action within it. Such action is very often prompted by quite specific issues and problems which people face. The context of issues within which people participated will be the subject of chapter 11. But, occupying an intermediate position between the broadest of perceptions of the political process and the recognition of immediate issues are a number of outlooks by means of which individuals place themselves in the political spectrum.

Amongst the most central of these outlooks in the modern political world tends to be the stance people take towards the political parties which play such a significant role in aggregating values. Closely linked to this sense of identification with political parties are the alignments of people on those issues which have traditionally distinguished the political left from the political right. Since the 1960s, however, new sets of issues have emerged with steadily increasing prominence which do not readily fit into the old dichotomy between left and right based, as it mainly is, on material issues. Amongst the issues of this 'new politics' are the environment, nuclear weapons and their potential threat to world peace and survival, and the status of women in a male-dominated society. The very emergence of these new issues carries with it some implication that old modes of participation have not handled them adequately. There is an accompanying possible inference that a different repertoire of actions will be required to get them fully onto the agenda.

All these values have some implications for present and future patterns of participation. They clearly come nowhere near exhausting the kinds of values which are of significance in British politics but, taken together, they do offer another way of investigating what is driving citizen activity.

Partisan commitments

As was seen in chapter 5, political parties play a very important role in facilitating and mobilising participation amongst that small group of citizens who are individual members. However, their relevance by no means ends there. For as parties have inserted themselves into the very centre of the political process in twentieth-century liberal democratic politics, so they have become important institutions which help to shape the

Table 9.1 *Strength and direction of party identification*

Direction	Very strong	Fairly strong	Not very strong	Leaners	Total	% Direction	N
Conservative	19·0	47·6	30·3	3·2	100·0	40·4	595
Labour	26·0	38·3	30·2	5·5	100·0	30·8	454
Liberal	5·3	32·2	57·2	5·3	100·0	10·3	152
Social Democrat	1·1	46·3	46·3	5·3	100·0	6·4	95
Scottish National	18·2	50·0	31·8	0·0	100·0	1·5	22
Other*	26·1	17·4	52·2	0·0	100·0	1·6	23
None**	—	—	—	—	—	9·0	133
Strength %	17·1	38·3	31·8	12·8	100·0	—	—
N	252	565	468	189	—	100·0	1,474

* Included Communist, Socialist Workers, Workers Revolutionary, Ecologist (Green), National Front and other responses.
** Before being pressed, 13·6% said 'none', and 4·9% 'didn't know'.

enduring outlooks of wide sections of the citizenry. Partisanship now forms a major part of the political culture (Almond and Verba 1965:ch. 4). It is, therefore, appropriate to enquire whether these feelings about parties also have an impact upon participation.

We have focused most of our attention on the personal self-images that citizens hold, how they see themselves in partisan terms. This idea of a 'party identification' has been a seminal concept in the study of electoral behaviour and has, in consequence, generated an enormous research literature concerned with its levels, characteristics, socio-economic associations and relevance for voting preferences. This is not the place to review this literature. It is sufficient to say that the concept has established itself in the study of political behaviour in Britain, if not without some criticism and debate (see Harrop and Miller 1987:139).[1]

We asked each of our respondents a version of the standard question concerning party identification, whether 'generally speaking, you think of yourself as Conservative, Labour, Liberal, Social Democrat or what?'.[2] As many as 81·3% immediately replied that they did have a partisan self-image and only 18·6% said they did not, or did not know (see Alt 1984; Crewe 1984). This is testament to how widespread partisan attachments have now become. Amongst the latter group we then asked whether 'you generally think of yourself as a little closer to one of the parties than the others?' – a question designed to elicit those who might have weaker, but nevertheless definite, partisan leanings. A further 7·8% then agreed that they did have such outlooks, reducing those without any party commitments to a mere 10·2%. For those 82% who had a clear party identification the first time round, we also asked them a supplementary about whether 'you [would] call yourself very strong [party], fairly strong, or not very strong?'. Here, just under a fifth (19·2%) of those asked thought of themselves as strongly committed, 43·3% as fairly committed and 37·5% as not very strong partisans. Again, therefore, it would appear that partisanship remains a very salient political identity for a substantial segment of the population.

From these various questions and responses it is possible to build up a map of partisan attachments covering both their aggregate direction and strength. This map is set out in table 9.1. It provides information about the proportions who are committed to each party (or to none) and the varying strengths of those commitments.

The largest partisan block is Conservative (40·4%), which is no doubt a reflection of the political and electoral ascendancy of that party in the 1980s. Within that grouping, nearly one-fifth (19·0%) are very committed partisans – just above the average for all parties (including leaners) of 17·1%. A further 47·6% are 'fairly strong' Conservative adherents – a figure well in excess of the national rate (38·3%). Conversely, only 30·3%, slightly fewer than average (31·8%), are weak partisans, with a tiny 3·2% who are leaners. The latter is a mere quarter of the figure for the population as a whole. The large band of Conservative Party sympathisers, is, in short, a relatively strongly committed group of people. Though relatively fewer are very strong in their self-images, the majority still seems to see itself as being committed rather than ambivalent partisans.

The same also applies to that 30·8% of the population who are Labour sympathisers. Again, around two-thirds continue to proclaim themselves to be strong supporters of their party, over a quarter (26·0%) emphatically so. Equally, it is only a minority who seem tepid in their commitments, including a very small 5·5% who attach themselves to the Labour cause only when pressed.

Between these two major parties, which account for nearly three-quarters of the adult citizenry, and the next largest grouping, the Liberals, there is a large numerical gulf.[3] The difference is not, however, a matter of mere numbers. The internal strength of that 10·3% Liberal commitment was not as great as for the major parties. Only 5·3% saw themselves as 'very strong' adherents – four to five times fewer than for the Conservative and Labour Parties. Conversely, well over half (57·2%) said they were 'not very strong' in their commitments, nearly double the rate for the 'big two'. This phenomenon, of relatively weak Liberal adherence, and hence relatively volatile voting support, has been noted over the years (see Butler and Stokes 1969: ch. 14; Himmelweit *et al.* 1981: ch. 10; Heath, Jowell and Curtice 1985: 113). Similar rather weak commitments also apply to the small number of Social Democrats (6·4%). Possibly in part because they were a new party, only a minority had very or fairly strong ties. That it is not smallness *per se* which is at work here is evidenced from the even tinier band of Scottish Nationalists (1·5%). Though there are very few Scottish Nationalists in our sample, the hints here are that the strengths of their attachments to their well-established party are commensurate with the Conservative Party and Labour Party.

The last set of partisans, the 1·6% 'others', are a very mixed group indeed. If anything, they have an extreme left character, but hidden amongst them is one National Front adherent and one 'Ecologist' – the only harbinger in our survey of partisan commitments of the surge in Green support that was to come in 1989. To the extent one can characterise their positions, they seem to contain one group with very ardent commitments – proportionately the equal of the Labour Party – but also another group who in size match the weaknesses of the Liberals and Social Democrats.

Finally, there is a group, some 9·0% of respondents (excluding 'don't knows'), who resist any partisan labels. They are the 'strong non-partisans', who perceive themselves as independent of any party leanings however slight.[4] That they are so few, however, is a measure of the continuing reach of parties within the British political culture.[5] Much

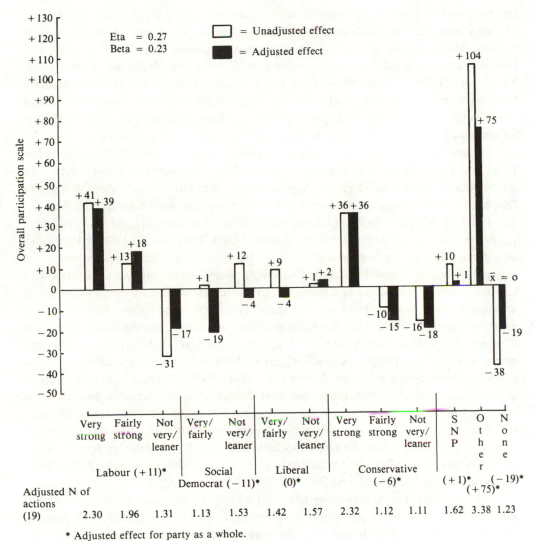

Figure 9.1 Levels of overall participation, by party identification, controlling for resources

has been written about 'partisan dealignment' – the gradual erosion of party-anchored outlooks and voting choices (see, for example, Särlvik and Crewe 1983:333–6). Certainly, compared with the 1960s, when upwards of 44% in surveys reported very strong partisan ties in Britain (Harrop and Miller 1987:143; see also Alt 1984:301), there has been considerable erosion.[6] Less than half that number retained equivalently strong attachments in 1985. Nevertheless, as table 9.1 suggests, there are still substantial numbers whose political outlooks are touched by party, and touched in ways they describe as very or fairly strong. The key question in the present context, however, is whether these sentiments affect political participation.

Initial evidence on this is provided in figure 9.1 which displays the relationship between different types of partisans and the overall participation scale. If we look first at the two major party groupings, Labour and Conservative, it can be seen that there is one constant and substantial pattern: those with very strong loyalties are much more likely to be active than those with weaker commitments. This is not, of course, a novel finding. Many studies in different countries have similarly found that citizens with intense party preferences participate more (see, for example, Butler and Stokes 1969; Verba and Nie 1972; Milbrath and Goel 1977). Indeed, if we separate partisan direction from partisan strength as distinct measures, the strength component is found to have a more substantial impact than party preference itself and this is true even after adjustment for resource differences (betas are 0·17 and 0·11 respectively).

There are, however, some interesting details and nuances beyond that basic similarity. First, at all levels of commitment, Labour Party sympathisers consistently out-participate Conservative adherents. Amongst core 'very strong' supporters, the gap in favour of Labour is only a slight one of +3, and amongst the least committed a thin +1. But amongst that large group of intermediate partisans (those with 'fairly strong' ties), the gap is a substantial 33 points (on an adjusted basis). The result is a Labour Party with an overall adjusted participation score of +11 compared with the Conservatives' −6 (see party figures below the graph). There is, it seems, some impulse associated with Labour loyalties that serves as a stimulant to participation whilst the equivalent effect amongst Conservatives is to de-activate them. This mirrors the pattern found amongst party members. Individual Labour Party members were also generally more active than Conservative activists (see figure 5.8).[7] It appears, therefore, that the ethos or ideology or value system currently operative within each of the two parties affects political participation in consistent ways. Within the Labour Party, members and sympathisers alike are more prone to participate than their Conservative counterparts. Just as Verba and Nie found an asymmetry in America that seemed to favour the party of the right so, by contrast, we find an asymmetry that favours the party of the left. It is interesting to note, however, that according to subsequent research, the American pattern changed. By 1972, five years after the Verba-Nie survey, the Republican impulse had entirely disappeared (see Nie, Verba and Petrocik 1979:208).

That there is a connection between left-oriented values (such as economic equality and job creation) and political participation will be more fully explored in the next section. But here we can at least demonstrate the connection by looking at what happens to participation levels within the two parties when such values are taken into account. The results are set out in figure 9.2 in which we repeat the basic (unadjusted) participation scores and the scores as adjusted for resource differentials from figure 9.1 and then add in levels adjusted also for values. As it turns out, there are substantial numbers of respondents who did not answer all the questions in our value scales and it is advisable to be more cautious in interpreting the results. However, introduction of values into the overall difference between the parties appears to eliminate the pro-Labour advantage. Whereas in figure 9.1 the gap was 17 points, in figure 9.2 it is precisely −1. The Labour score is, in fact, zero – exactly on the overall population average – while the Conservative is, in effect, the same – a paltry +1. These figures therefore suggest strongly that aggregate differences in participation between the two parties' sympathisers are mainly the product of their values (which of course help shape their party preferences) rather than the result of the mobilising impact of party loyalty.

At the same time, we can also see that there are some important details when we break

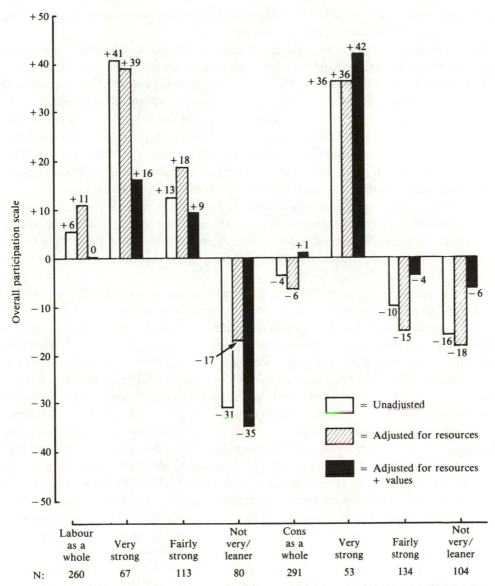

Figure 9.2 Overall participation within the Labour and Conservative parties, controlling for resources and political values

down those sympathisers into different levels of commitment. Amongst the very strong partisans, that slight Labour lead (of 3 points) is turned into a disadvantage of 26 points. Given that we have effectively equalised participatory impulses deriving from values, what we may be seeing here is the effect of party simply as a political organisation – its mobilisational capacity or its relevance as an institutional channel for participation. Here, the Conservatives might be expected to perform better – they were the party in power nationally and in a majority of local councils. Moreover, studies of the organisational effectiveness of the two parties seem consistently to favour the Conservatives (Ball 1981:205–21; Kavanagh 1985:127–9). Hence, it is perhaps less

surprising that, once the effect of values is taken into account, it is the strong
Conservative partisans who participate more.[8]

However, there is reason for a degree of caution. On the one hand, this account is
supported by what happens amongst the least committed partisans. The slim Labour
advantage (albeit a matter of being less under-participatory) before values are included
of 1 point (-17 to -18) is converted into a Conservative advantage of 29 points (-35
for Labour as against -6 for the Conservatives). On the other hand, in the middle
stratum, the Labour advantage remains in place. The initial gap of 23 points, which
widens to 33 when resources are included, remains a Labour advantage of 13 when
values are introduced. Although this is a very substantial reduction of the deficit, it is not
quite consistent with the view that these effects derive from the organisational capacities
of the two parties. It might be argued that the Conservative institutional advantage
exists amongst a certain inner circle of partisans and also amongst the most weakly
committed, but does not extend to those in between. However, why this should be the
case is unclear and the precise explanation of these patterns therefore remains something
of a puzzle.

Having explored the nexus between party commitments and overall participation
within the two main parties, we can now pick up on the remaining patterns in figure 9.1
– those associated with the minor partisan groupings. Amongst the Social Democrats,
there is a very unusual pattern in that the more strongly committed[9] appear to
participate less than those with only weak preferences. This inverse relationship is
somewhat amplified when resources are taken into account, and both categories fall into
the negative range. In view of the party's stress on participation, at least amongst its
national leadership (see, for example, Williams 1981), this is a somewhat surprising
result although, given the small numbers involved, it is dangerous to speculate as to the
reasons. Further adjustments for values leaves the stronger Social Democratic partisans
in an almost unchanged position (-21). If the impact of party on participation reflects
its organisational capacity, then it would appear that the Social Democrats were unable
to mobilise their sympathisers within our sample.

The Liberal pattern also shows an inverse pattern when adjustments are made for
resources. Again, this seems surprising given that party's programmatic stress on
participatory values (see chapter 2). Further adjustments for values do put both groups
back above the overall mean ($+13$ for stronger Liberals, $+8$ for weaker ones) which
may be some testament to the party as an institution. But this merely deepens the
problem about the effects of grass-roots values.

In the last three categories of figure 9.1 we find an extraordinary degree of variation,
but not amongst the Scottish Nationalists. They remain close to average throughout.
What little participation they have above the general average is largely due to resources,
and adjustments for values leaves them only slightly below (-6). The other two
groupings, on the other hand, produce the largest effects of all. The disparate collection
of 'other' partisans achieve extremely high levels of participation, levels that are only
mildly attenuated when resources are included ($+75$). In so far as values leave the score
almost unchanged ($+76$), we might infer that these tiny fringe parties manage to
mobilise very high levels of activity amongst those that are committed to them. As we
have seen, the analysis suggests that it is not so much values that drive the participation

Table 9.2 *Electoral participation by party, controlling for resources*

	Voting		Campaigning	
	Unadjusted	Adjusted	Unadjusted	Adjusted
Conservative	+13	+11	+6	+6
Labour	+5	+7	−3	−2
Liberal	+9	+8	−6	−7
Social Democrat	+24	+21	−22	−32
Scottish National	−18	−20	+48	+40
Other*	−37	−44	+81	+63
None	−96	−89	−19	−7

* As for table 9.1

of such adherents, as the fact of having some institutional preference, that probably entails a more active affiliation than would be true of the larger parties.

Non-partisans, finally, register consistently below-average rates of participation. In the absence of any party stimulus, it is not surprising that participation is strongly negative (−38). About half of this, however, is the product of an adverse resource position. In that sense, non-partisans suffer under a double disadvantage. When we take values into account, however, the extent of that disadvantage is made more pronounced. Non-partisans end up with a score of −58. There are hints here, in other words, that their values tend to raise participation levels. When the effects of these values are removed, it becomes clear how far the lack of a party political commitment has a negative effect on the propensity to become in any way politically active.

We can conclude this analysis of party by looking, relatively briefly, at the relationships within particular participatory modes. To simplify matters, we focus principally upon party effects in aggregate, rather than try to present detailed information about different levels of commitment. Equally, the evidence as presented in the tables makes adjustments only for resources. The effect of values will be commented upon in passing, but will be considered more fully in the following section.

We turn first to the two modes within the electoral domain – voting and campaigning. Relevant scores for each party are set out in table 9.2. As regards the two major parties, it can be seen that the Conservatives are indeed slightly but consistently more active. If values are at work here, they do not disadvantage the Tories at all. It is in other areas that their depressive effects operate. This appears to support the suggestion that the Conservatives are more effective as an electorally-oriented institution. This conclusion is partially confirmed if we take values into account. Equalising voting rates on this basis enhances the Conservative lead considerably (+17 to −1 for Labour) although the gap in campaigning remains little changed.[10]

Adherents to the two Alliance parties present a striking contrast between voting, where they are above average, and campaigning, where they are not. The latter may be a further testament to institutional effects (the pattern persisting when values are included). But why supporters should be so relatively unwilling to campaign, yet be as committed to voting as the two big parties, is unclear. The contrast in the case of the

Social Democrats is particularly vivid. It is possible that this reflects the problems of a party which originated from national-level politics and which, with media attention, could mobilise the vote but which lacked an effective grass-roots organisation that could generate campaign participation. However, more detailed analysis than we can give (with so relatively few Social Democrats in our sample) would clearly be required.

In the cases of the Scottish Nationalists and the 'other' partisans in our sample, the opposite is the case. They seem more than capable of generating committed partisans willing to undertake campaign work. Indeed, controlling for values merely accentuates this effect (+62 for the SNP, +94 for 'others'). But when it comes to mobilising votes they are very feeble. In the case of the very minor parties, which have little hope of winning elections, it may be more important to maintain the enthusiasm of their supporters through involvement in the party than in trying to win elections, although this would seem not to apply to the SNP, which has notable electoral victories to its name. Once again, the numbers in the sample indicate caution in their interpretation.

Not surprisingly, the non-partisans remain firmly at the non-participatory end of the two electoral ladders. Indeed, what is surprising is that they are not even less participatory than the scores suggest.[11] As things stand, non-partisans appear no less willing to campaign than Alliance supporters, which serves to emphasise the poor performance of the centre parties, at least amongst our respondents.

The scores for collective and direct action are set out in table 9.3. Here there is a major contrast between the two main parties, which indeed explains the overall participatory impulse within the Labour Party. This is a party where supporters (like its members, see table 5.9) are more ready to undertake direct action. To a lesser extent, this was true of collective action. Conservative adherents, on the other hand, are clearly averse to these types of engagement – and particularly to direct action, which is again what one would expect from the behaviour of the party members.[12] That values play a significant role in producing this outcome can be seen if we momentarily separate the effects due to partisan strength from those due to partisan direction. In the electoral domain (reported in table 9.2), strength of commitment generally counted for much more than which party was preferred. Here, the opposite is the case. In fact, for direct action, it is almost entirely a matter of direction rather than strength (betas of 0·18 and 0·03 respectively).

Further evidence as to the importance of values underlying partisan commitments can be adduced by adding a control for such outlooks. The result, in the case of collective action, is totally to explain and remove the disparity between the two parties (scores of −2 for each). In the case of direct action, on the other hand, a control for values reduces but does not eliminate the gap. When only resources are taken into account (as in table 9.3), that gap is 41 points. After values are included, this reduces to 24 points, which suggests that the association is partly a matter of values and partly a matter of institutional effects.

Amongst the remaining parties, the Liberals seem as inclined towards collective action as Labour sympathisers but not to be much concerned with direct action. Social Democrats, on the other hand, appear to have some leaning towards direct action. Neither connection disappears when values are taken into account. The Scottish National Party adherents, and the non-partisans, both have profiles broadly similar to that of the Conservatives in these respects. They have a general aversion to both modes.

Table 9.3 *Collective and direct action, by party, controlling for resources*

	Collective action		Direct action	
	Unadjusted	Adjusted	Unadjusted	Adjusted
Conservative	−8	−11	−20	−20
Labour	+2	+8	+20	+21
Liberal	+13	+9	+3	+1
Social Democrat	+17	0	+22	+12
Scottish National	+2	−7	−18	−23
Other*	+112	+85	+82	+69
None	−26	−8	−14	−7

* As for table 9.1

The 'others', by contrast, line up very much on the radical side of the fence, as befits their general composition. Their commitments to both types of activity are, in fact, the strongest of all. Once more, this is partly a product of values, but strong institutional effects remain even when value positions are taken into account. For them, it seems, collective action and direct action are akin to campaigning – a way in which adherents can be mobilised.

Contacting has been left to last because it merits the least attention of all in this respect. Party makes very little difference, all in all, to rates of contacting (beta = 0·06). Those most prone to contacting are the 'others' (+14) and Labour adherents (+8), but the linkages are obviously very modest. Equally, there are no instances of very negative scores, although non-partisans maintain their lower than average participation rates even here. However, it is much more a matter of their poor resource position than their non-partisanship that accounts for this particular outcome.

Linkages between partisan commitments and participation are generally quite important. In some areas, they make a lot of difference. Given that a substantial majority still claim some degree of party commitment, parties cannot be left out of the participatory equation. They are much more than resource elements. They provide political cues to action which can, at times, be highly significant for the level and style of citizen engagement. In the electoral arena, it was more a matter of strength of those commitments which affected the propensity to become active. But in other areas, and especially in the case of direct action, what appeared to be crucial was party preferences themselves. This points clearly to the relevance of the final set of outlooks to be examined in this chapter – the impact of political values themselves.

Political values

In the previous section it was seen that political parties functioned in part as the carriers of values. Those who identified with certain parties were liable to be influenced by the values those parties propagated. Now, it is appropriate to focus on those values directly and examine how they, too, shape the style and level of individual participation.

Certain connections between values and action have been well-established in previous research on participation. For example, Inglehart (1971, 1977, 1989) has demonstrated the existence of an association or affinity between post-material values and political protest in many countries. Indeed, he goes so far as to call it 'a new politics...throughout advanced industrial society' (1977:262) in which novel issues were brought to the fore and new patterns of political protest and collective action were established (see also Miller and Levitin 1976; Moran 1985; Offe 1985; Harding and Phillips with Fogarty 1986; Dalton 1988). He also found a linkage between post-materialism and conventional participation, although this was only pronounced in West Germany (Barnes, Kaase *et al.* 1979:ch. 12). But, even in Britain, the small number of post-materialists had a distinctly higher rate of activity in this area compared with materialists, as well as having a comparatively much stronger orientation to protest. It is these sorts of association between values and participation that will be investigated in this section of the study.

For these purposes, we have focused on four sets of value orientations in order to identify and map out the relevant empirical linkages. The first concerns the differences of value, or ideology, that lie behind the 'old materialist politics' of 'left' versus 'right'. In so far as a majority of the adult population, in Britain and elsewhere, probably still embrace the issues and conflicts of that politics (see Barnes, Kaase *et al.* 1979:331), its continuing relevance should not be underestimated. The left–right cleavage has also been shown to continue to distinguish the parties' manifestos from one another across many liberal democracies (Budge and Robertson 1987:392–8). At the same time, it is equally necessary to pay close attention to the way in which the issues and values of the 'new politics' have begun to insert themselves into the picture. To capture at least part of what is at stake here, we have devised values scales that relate to what might be called 'green/peace' issues and to the concerns of contemporary feminists. We have also included a measure that is explicitly oriented to participatory values. In part, this is because of the focus of the book, but also because a significant theme of the 'new politics' is indeed about participation. Together these constitute three directions in which the new patterns can be explored.

Left–right values

Measurement

The starting point must be with the more traditional values of left and right. To measure these outlooks, four issues were included. One was concerned with the long-standing issue of law and order. It entailed responses as to how much importance each individual in the survey thought that the British Government should place on 'Giving the police more power to deal with protestors and demonstrators'. The Conservative Party has been long associated with making this a priority – what they have in the past called 'backing the police' (Butler and Kavanagh 1984:257; see also earlier volumes in this series).[13] Furthermore, Mrs Thatcher's Governments have continued this emphasis, making it 'very much one of the big guns of the party's electoral platform and a key element in its programme for reform' (Savage 1987:230; and see also Norton 1984b).

In our survey, sentiments clearly favoured the position of the right. As many as 29·6% thought it very important that the Government should have more powers to control demonstrators and a further 28·8% thought this 'fairly important'. Those who opposed such moves were a much smaller group – 9·6% thinking it very important *not* to take these steps with 22·5% saying that it was fairly important. In the battle between police and protestors, which for many would have meant the miners, whose conflicts with the constabulary were reported almost nightly during the Miners' Strike of 1984–5, general sentiment seems to have favoured the forces of law and order.

The second item refers to the question of privatisation, again merely the latest stage in a long-term debate in British politics. The specific question related to how much emphasis the British Government should place on 'turning more nationalised industries into private businesses'. This programme has been the hallmark of Thatcherism in the 1980s, although it is perhaps fair to say that it was not something that was at the centre of the Conservative manifesto when Mrs Thatcher came to power (Kavanagh 1987:220–4; King 1987:123–6). However, the more general question of state intervention in, and control over, the economy, which the privatisation issue raises, certainly has been an issue between left and right over the decades (MacFarlane 1986:22–6; see also Butler and Stokes 1969:177).

The level of attention given to the issue gradually subsided in the 1960s and 1970s, until Mrs Thatcher seized upon privatisation as a way of dramatically highlighting her attempt to turn the British economy around and to expand the popular base of British capitalism. Throughout the period of our survey, fully one-third of state-owned industries were privatised, and the number of private shareholders doubled (Butler and Kavanagh 1988:20). Thus, measures of reactions to privatisation at the same time tap underlying and long-held differences of outlook between left and right. For this reason, similar items have been regularly used as markers of the position of voters along this political dimension (see Särlvik and Crewe 1983:183–96).

By the time of our survey, opinions were tipped significantly towards the privatisation option. To that extent, Mrs Thatcher's programme of 'rolling back the frontiers of the state, reversing the ratchet, and giving new life to capitalism' (Butler and Kavanagh 1988:21) was a popular one. In terms of our question, 15·9% thought it very important to continue privatisation schemes, while 32·4% thought this fairly important. Only a third thought that the process should be halted, 14·6% feeling this was a very important matter (see also Heath, Jowell and Curtice 1985:132). Thus, supporters for the value position of the right were not quite as numerous as in the case of the law and order item, but they were clearly stronger than those opposed.

Part of the *raison d'être* of Labour's commitment to state ownership through nationalisation was the idea of equality. This too, therefore, has long been an important value which has distinguished left from right (Ingle 1987; see also Alcock 1987:9–11). Indeed, this has been seen as a 'persistent and pervasive theme' of the left–right dimension (Inglehart and Klingemann 1976:257; see also Lipset *et al.* 1954:1,135). Accordingly, we included a third item aimed at discovering the emphasis respondents thought should be given to 'trying to get greater equality of wealth and income in Britain'. Whilst there has always been some ambiguity about how far the Labour Party seeks to go in achieving equality through redistributive policies, the whole issue of equality achieved greater prominence in the period of Mrs Thatcher's Government. In the belief that an excessively egalitarian tax regime discouraged wealth, the Government reduced taxes on high earners and pursued a range of economic and welfare policies which were alleged to have reversed any trends towards greater equality (Smail 1984; Jones 1987:3; Alcock 1987:126).

Not surprisingly, therefore, the whole question of equality has remained a central element in the left–right debate. The responses to the survey question overwhelmingly favoured the idea of a more equal society. As many as 37·2 % thought it very important to move in this direction, with another 44·6 % leaning that way. Only 6·7 % were against the enhancement of equality, a mere 1·3 % very strongly so. It would seem that, on the basis of the way the question was phrased at least, more economic equality rather than less is the preference of the majority of the British citizenry (but cf. Heath, Jowell and Curtice 1985:109–15).

One traditional way of alleviating the problems of poverty has been what amounts to government-sponsored job creation. Unemployment was for most of the post-World War II period a central focus of economic policy, and a particular concern of the Labour Party. Hence, the fourth and final indicator is a question asking whether 'more jobs should be created even if government spending and taxes rise'. The problem of unemployment which this addresses was even more salient than privatisation in the period of the survey.

At that time, it had reached historically high levels and became a major concern of the voters, as is reflected in our own study (see chapter 11). As a result, the Labour Party committed itself, if elected in 1983, to lowering what Michael Foot called 'this unemployment curse' to one million within five years (Butler and Kavanagh 1984:63, 115). By the 1987 Election, it had become a central focus of the party's platform (Butler and Kavanagh 1988:112, 219). The Conservatives under Mrs Thatcher's leadership, on the other hand, focused more on inflation as the key economic priority (Whiteley 1986; see also MacFarlane 1986:33–7). Furthermore, they argued that unemployment would only come down over the longer term, not by the tried-and-failed methods of governmental spending, but through creating conditions for an expanding and prosperous economy which, for them, meant a less regulated labour market.

The responses to the question posed on further economic equalisation were echoed in strong majority support for the idea that the government should do something about jobs, even at the cost of higher taxes. Well over two-thirds took that view, 17 % strongly, whereas only 27·2 % disagreed (3·3 % strongly). In this sphere, therefore, the positions of the respondents were more consistent with left orientations (cf. Heath, Jowell and Curtice 1985:109–15; Jowell and Witherspoon 1985:43).

However, the interest for analysing participation lies less in the detailed distribution of responses to individual items than in their formation into a left–right scale. Factor analysis of the four indicators suggested that they did form a single spectrum of opinion. The most central item (factor loading of 0·78) was the question about privatisation, followed by job creation (0·65), police power (0·62) and, lastly, equality of wealth (0·54).[14] One consequence of the top two items being distributed towards the left is that the most extreme left position (+231) is slightly closer to the average of zero than the individual with the most extreme right perspective (−276). But, overall, the scale is well-balanced.

Who are on the left and right?

The first step is, then, to see where the various categories of our respondents are located along the left–right dimension (for an alternative approach and a cross-national overview, see Harding and Phillips with Fogarty 1986:ch. 3). The results of such an analysis are set out in table 9.4. They show, not surprisingly, that party attachments have by far the strongest association. Indeed, the beta (0·62) is of an order not previously encountered in this study. This is satisfying testament to the extent to which the four items do form a coherent left–right value dimension.

What is perhaps of greater interest is the detail in the relationship. Despite the maximum left score being closer to the population average, the ardent Labour identifiers are somewhat more pronounced in their left-wing dispositions than are the Conservative equivalents in their right-wing outlooks.[15] This remains true even when wealth, class and all the other factors in the table are taken into account. Amongst the middle group of partisans, on the other hand, those 'fairly strongly' committed, the reverse is the case. Here, both sets of identifiers are, of course, much closer to the centre but the Conservative adherents are relatively the more 'extreme' (if we may use this term in an entirely non-pejorative sense). However, the gap between the two parties is halved (from 16 points to 7) and for the weakest partisans, there is no difference at all (−44 as against +45). It can be seen, therefore, that the partisan make-up of the two main parties forms a linear progression from left to right. The strong identifiers in both cases have very strong value orientations, most of all those attached to the Labour cause.

The minor parties also throw up some interesting patterns. The committed Liberals are almost exactly at the centre of the left–right spectrum (adjusted score of −1), a pattern also true of their weaker co-partisans (+2). Amongst Social Democrats, however, the weaker adherents are slightly on the right-wing side of the fence (−4) while the more committed have a much clearer leftist stance (unadjusted +21, adjusted +15), a product, possibly, of their political affiliations prior to the formation of the party.[16] Nevertheless, they are still closer to the centre (zero) than they are even to the weakest of the Labour partisans. So, although there is some discernible ideological daylight between the committed SDP supporters and their Alliance partners, in the broader context the SDP partisans are very much a centrist grouping.

Amongst remaining categories, the Scottish Nationalist partisans have a pronounced leftist orientation – more so indeed than the Social Democrats, a pattern which repeats the findings of an earlier study (see Inglehart and Klingemann 1976:255). However, in so far as these SNP supporters, too, lie between the Labour leaners and the centre on the left–right spectrum, they can fairly be described as essentially 'moderate' in these terms. This is less true of the 'others'. Although very much a mixed bag, the tendency is distinctly to the left, a position in fact adjacent to 'fairly strong' Labour sympathisers. Finally, the non-partisans are the only grouping, other than the Conservatives, to have a right-wing inclination. It is not strong, about the same (in the opposite direction) as the SDP, but clear enough. We are tempted to draw a parallel with a similar hidden conservative tendency detected amongst independent candidates (see Leonard 1968:51), but the latter are, in Weisberg's (1983) terms, 'positive' or committed independents whereas our non-partisans are seemingly largely 'negative independents'. Thus, their

Table 9.4 *Who holds left-wing and right-wing values?* ($N = 665$)

	Unadjusted Score*	Adjusted Score**	Beta
Party			0·62
Very strong Conservative	−113	−109	
Fairly strong Conservative	−64	−63	
Not very strong/leaners Conservative	−43	−44	
Very strong Labour	+127	+125	
Fairly strong Labour	+55	+56	
Not very strong/leaners Labour	+43	+45	
Very/fairly strong Liberal	−3	−1	
Not very strong/leaners Liberal	+1	+2	
Very/fairly strong Social Democrat	+21	+15	
Not very strong/leaners Social			
Democrat	+3	−4	
Scottish National	+38	+35	
Other***	+55	+58	
None	−11	−13	
Wealth			0·14
Poorest 5%	+29	+17	
Richest 5%	−69	−51	
Class			0·10
Working class	+17	−4	
Manual foremen	+17	+5	
Petty bourgeoisie	−45	−28	
Salariat	−15	+8	
Education			0·10
No qualifications	+8	−6	
College/further	+1	+25	
Degree	−11	+4	
Group ties			0·07
None	−4	−3	
5+	+32	+17	
Age			0·05
Young (15–29)	+4	−1	
Early middle (30–49)	−7	−1	
Late middle (50–64)	+7	+8	
Old (65+)	+4	−13	
Gender			0·00
Male	+2	0	
Female	−2	0	

* Negative scores indicate right-wing values.
** Scores adjusted for all other variables in the table.
*** As for table 9.1

mild conservatism may simply be part and parcel of their general apolitical stance (see also chapter 14).[17]

Compared with party affiliation, other factors have significantly weaker linkages with left–right values. Wealth proved the next important, but with only one quarter the partisan association (beta of 0·14). In table 9.4, the poorest and richest 5%s are identified. As can be seen, the poor do indeed have a left orientation and the wealthy a right-wing outlook. But the wealthy hold more extreme positions than the poor (adjusted gap of 24 points in absolute terms). Class has an even more limited impact, whether considered on an unadjusted basis or not. Here, the most right-wing are the petty bourgeoisie (see also Heath, Jowell and Curtice 1985:ch. 2). Their position suggests why they were the most conservative in their 1983 voting preferences. The salariat are also somewhat right-wing in inclination but, unlike the petty bourgeoisie, this is reversed if education and wealth are taken into account. Relative to their high earnings and levels of education, the salariat are actually somewhat pinkish in disposition. The opposite is true of the working class. They, along with the manual foremen, are on the left initially. But, unlike the foremen, relative to their income and educational make-up, they are slightly on the conservative side of the fence.

Co-equal with class in strength is education (beta = 0·10). Here, too, there are some interesting patterns. Those lacking any qualifications are, relatively to their wealth and class position, slightly right-wing, like the working class. At the other end of the scale, on the other hand, the opposite tendency is again found. Degree-holders, and still more those with college-level qualifications, have a distinct leftist tendency. Coupled with the profile of the salariat, we see here some evidence of values that might further explain earlier patterns which linked these groups with participation.

The last three factors in table 9.4 are the weakest of all. From a participatory point of view, it is noteworthy that the most highly resourced, in group terms, are somewhat to the left of the general population. Given that these resources are powerful stimuli to participation, there is here some further indication of that connection between leftist values and participation which was discerned in the discussion on parties. There is also some symmetry between lack of group ties, non-partisanship and a slightly rightist or conservative orientation. Age is surprisingly weakly related to values. Even on an unadjusted basis, the cohorts vary relatively little. The only noteworthy link is between old age and a right-wing outlook (which could be generational or life-cycle or both). If youth has distinctive values, they are not apparent in the traditional left-right domain. The same, finally, is even more true of gender. There are, of course, exceptions. Feminist group members, for example, have a very strong leftist inclination (+46 on an unadjusted basis). But the two genders taken overall vary not at all in outlooks. What slight conservative inclination women have is entirely a product of the other factors in table 9.4.

Left, right and participation

We are now in a position to consider the relationship between left–right values and political participation. To present this graphically, the scale was divided into six groups, two being the most extreme right-wing and left-wing 5%, two the next adjacent 20%, and two the middle quarters on either side of the overall average which are, therefore, the most centrist or moderate in left–right terms. The participatory profiles of these categories, with and without adjustments for other value orientations, party identifications and social backgrounds, are set out in figure 9.3.

Perhaps the first point to note is the strongly curvilinear pattern in the relationship. This means that those who hold strong or extreme value positions either on the left or on the right participate well above average. This is consistent with other research in the United States where intensely held positions on issues related to partisanship have generally been associated with heightened activity (Verba and Nie 1972:212–28; Beck and Jennings 1979:746; Levitin and Miller 1979:754; but see Leighley 1989). Centrists and moderates, by contrast, distinctly under-participate. As we have grouped them, the two centre categories are, of course, very numerous since each includes a quarter of all respondents. This makes it possible that some true centrist impulse has been swamped. However, focusing on the 5% on each side of the overall average, categories of the same size as the extreme right and left groups, there is no indication of a centrist impulse. It may be, therefore, that there is no centrist impulse to participate equivalent to those of the left and the right. But it may also be that those in the middle are not so much positive centrists as people who, across all four items making up the scale, have either inconsistent or not strongly held opinions. They may end up in the centre more by default than by choice. Thus, too much should not be read into the apparent negative effect on activism of 'moderation'.

What can be said with much greater confidence is that there is a distinct asymmetry about the relationship such that those with strong left-wing orientations are considerably more active than those on the right. This substantiates the earlier analyses of party adherents and party members. In contemporary Britain, the impulse to participate deriving from leftist values appears to be decidedly stronger than the equivalent impulse from the right. Whether this was always the case we cannot say. Furthermore, adjustments for party identification, other values (see later in this chapter) and social factors make relatively little difference. This also reinforces the analysis of party identification and its association with political values. The impact of party attachment on participation seems to derive mainly from its linkage with values. The Labour Party adherents, in other words, out-participate Conservatives in part because their relatively more extreme views give an impulse to their action, but more because those views *are* of the left which are more congenial to certain forms of action rather than of the right.

Further light on this general relationship can be shed by looking at the patterns formed between left and right views and the five individual modes. These are displayed in figure 9.4. They show a generally consistent pattern, in terms both of the overall U-shaped association, and of an asymmetry that favours the left. Holding extreme views, particularly of the left, is associated with activism in every participatory domain. For example, voting generally follows this pattern. The highest turnouts are registered amongst those with extreme views.[18] On an unadjusted basis these rates are identical, but relative to background factors, those with left-wing outlooks are more regular voters than those on the right.

Involvement in party campaign work is also associated with intense commitment, again particularly on the left when the figures are adjusted for other values, party adherence and social factors. The centrists, however, seem much less motivated by their

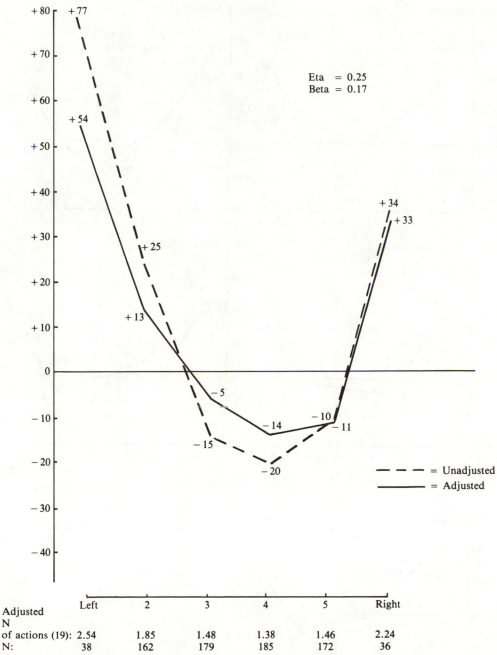

Figure 9.3 Overall participation by left–right values, controlling for other values and background factors

moderate values to get behind the parties in their part of the spectrum. Citizens on the left and on the right both punch their weight in the electoral arena whilst those in the ideological centre do not.

Contacting, too, is of a generally similar order to the overall pattern: intensely held views are associated with much higher levels of contacting. Furthermore, whether

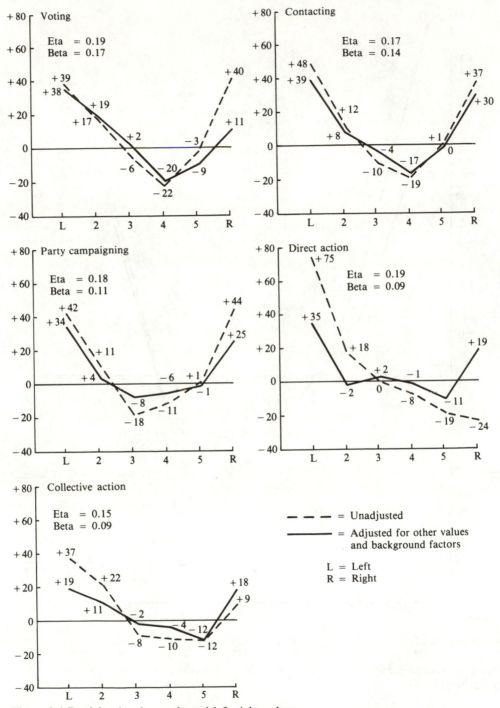

Figure 9.4 Participation by mode and left–right values

adjusted or not, strongly-held left-wing views produce the highest levels of contacting of all. Collective action also follows the by now familiar lines. The left are more active than the right, and both more than the centre. In this case, however, it is perhaps surprising that the left–right gap is so small once we control for other factors. It has been suggested earlier that values appear to play a particularly important role in motivating collective action. However, it seems that traditional left–right values do not now drive collective action.

Direct action, unlike the other modes, is largely a prerogative of the left – at least before other factors are considered (see also Harding and Phillips with Fogarty 1986:98). The key association appears to be with the concern over law and order and their opposition to a harder line against protestors and demonstrators (+48). When resources and other values are taken into account, the relationship reverts to the more 'normal' shape. That is, the leftists still exhibit a strong predilection for direct action, but those on the extreme right also appear relatively active (+19). It should be stressed, however, that this is only a relative matter. In absolute terms, those with views on the extreme right of the scale are the least inclined to direct action. Only relative to their resource position and other values do they appear better disposed.

Overall, therefore, left–right values add considerably to the account. There are relatively clear and consistent patterns linking extreme or at least strongly held views and a propensity to get involved. This is true above all for leftist opinions and holds up more or less consistently in all modes. What is left out is the middle – the moderate centre. In these terms, the nexus between values and participation accentuates rather than diminishes the left–right battle. Those with opinions in between seem not to have an equivalent commitment or zeal which leads them to get out into the gladiatorial arena. This in turn begins to tell us something important about how participation affects the character of the political battle. Political differences are clearly accentuated, and the left, through their own efforts both individually and organisationally, are consistently more prominent than others. However, when the chips are down, the Conservative sympathisers were, at this time, much more numerous. The battle between right and left is, though, only part of the story. In recent decades, new issues have come onto the political agenda, particularly on the left. Politics is no longer just about the more traditional debates of left versus right. Environmental and other issues have come on the scene, both electorally and in the world of pressure groups. It is, therefore, necessary to expand the analysis of the impact of values by bringing these newer concerns into focus.

Green/peace and feminist values

Prominent amongst the concerns of the 'new' politics in Britain are environmental issues (see Lowe and Goyder 1983; Offe 1985; Rudig and Lowe 1986; Frankland 1989:1). In this, the country has followed a path common to many advanced liberal democracies, although some, such as Germany, have gone further than others. A strong concern for the environment reflects values that are at odds with the traditional priorities of the two major parties. They have both been relatively slow to develop serious ecological policies that would emphasise qualitative ('green') rather than quantitative ('grey') economic and developmental criteria (Frankland 1989:13–17). Nevertheless, the history of 'green' politics suggests that it is a part of a wider radical agenda. The Socialist Environmental and Resources Association (founded in 1973) made a connection between environmentalism and the progressive left. And even though the Green Party has generally pursued a line of eschewing non-alignment on traditional partisan axes, its policies suggest a definite leftist orientation. Besides central ecological concerns like reducing industrial emissions, encouraging organic farming and curbing rural development, they also espouse withdrawal from NATO, equal treatment of homosexuals and heterosexuals, and unilateral nuclear disarmament. Not least, they are strong advocates of 'decentralized democracy based upon proportional representation and freedom of information' (Frankland 1989:9).

Measurement

The emphasis on participatory democracy will be examined in the next section of the chapter. Here, the focus will be on two central elements that can be used to identify a commitment to the green cause. These are questions we asked relating to nuclear power and to nuclear weapons – what jointly we will refer to as 'green/peace' values.

The first asked respondents how important it was for the Government to build, or not to build, 'more nuclear power stations'. This touches an issue that has been the subject of considerable public attention, in part because of disasters involving nuclear power stations in the USSR (Chernobyl) and in the USA (Three Mile Island). There have been repeated local objections in Britain and other countries to the expansion of domestic nuclear energy programmes which have given rise to discussions of the appropriate means whereby these developments can be made subject to democratic decision-making (Nelkin 1975). It has also achieved prominence through major domestic inquiries concerning the environmental impact of nuclear-generated power at Sizewell (O'Riordan, Kemp and Purdue 1988) and the storage of waste nuclear fuel at Windscale (Wynne 1980).

The climate of opinion in the survey was decidedly 'green'. Fully 25·3% thought it 'very important' for the Government *not* to proceed with further building and another 26·9% thought it 'fairly important'. Conversely, only 8·8% were strongly in favour of further nuclear power stations, although 28·4% were more mildly supportive (cf. Eurobarometre 1987:54–5). The second question used a similar format, but in this instance focused on whether or not the Government should 'remove nuclear weapons from Britain'. Here, however, those that supported the radical option were in the minority. Just over half thought Britain should retain nuclear weapons on its soil (23·2% strongly). The other view was taken by 41·4%, including a sizeable 26·3% who thought a non-nuclear Britain a 'very important' governmental objective. Not surprisingly, these two items are strongly associated (r = 0·50). And so, to identify those most committed to the 'green/peace agenda', we simply combined the two into one scale and focused attention upon that 16·6% of the total who strongly held the relevant positions on *both* issues.

Another important strand of the 'new' agenda has been the issue of female equality and liberation (Katzenstein and Muller 1987). Again, the main parties were somewhat slow to place the matter at the centre of their policy priorities. But it is fair to say that the 'feminist' cause has become a very salient element of contemporary radical politics. One strand of this has been the question of abortion, a matter that has retained its saliency as conservatives and religiously motivated individuals on both sides of the Atlantic have attempted to restrict the grounds on which an abortion could be legally granted. This, from the feminist perspective, involves a fundamental principle of the right of the woman to control the use of her own body. As Lovenduski puts it (1986:253),

Abortion…has been a watershed issue for women, its regulation illustrating many of the disadvantages for them of male-constructed political systems.

At the same time, abortion is an issue which does not fit clearly into the traditional left–right spectrum, as well as being one which divides people on religious grounds. Firm support for liberalisation of abortion, therefore, becomes one touchstone of feminist attitudes.

The survey question asked whether the respondent believed it important that government should make 'abortions easier to get for women who want them'. A plurality (48·4%) was in favour but only 13·4% thought this very important as against the 35% considering it only fairly important. Those opposed to it were divided equally into 18·2% for whom it was fairly important that government should *not* pursue this policy and 18% regarding it as very important. The remaining 15·4% felt that 'it did not matter either way'.

Alongside this social aspect of feminism was an issue intended to tap the fundamental economic objective of equality of opportunity in the job market. This is the arena in which, on the surface, progress had been made in Britain through legislation such as the Sex Discrimination Act of 1975 and the establishment of the Equal Opportunities Commission (Randall 1982). In practice, the consensus amongst supporters of the women's movement is that progress has been, to put it at its mildest, halting. The question in the survey asked whether respondents agreed with the proposition that 'Women at work should have the same opportunities as men for earnings and promotion'. Although the phrasing echoes that of the Equal Opportunities Commission, in retrospect it might have been wiser to have put forward a more radical proposal for consideration (involving, perhaps, a degree of positive discrimination). The idea, as it stood, was endorsed by 92·2% of the respondents – 40·4% agreed strongly. To some extent, this may reflect attitudes affected by the greater equalisation of participation as between men and women at the mass level (but not in elite positions) in Britain (see chapter 7). But it would seem that equality of opportunity is something which few are prepared to disavow, whatever the outcome may be in practice. This is also of a piece with broader attitudes to equality which formed part of the left–right scale.

The correlation between the social and economic measures of feminism was, understandably in view of the results, rather low (r = 0·15). But the interest here is, as in the case of Green/peace, to identify only those who both believed easier abortion to be a very important government policy *and* strongly agreed with equal opportunities for women at work. This combination would be likely to capture most of the more committed supporters of feminist causes. So although the total who could be regarded as pro-feminist (i.e. who agreed with equality and thought easier abortion was important) was 46·1% of the total, the strong feminists were a much smaller group of 8·3%.

Who are feminists and green/peace supporters?

The next stage is to compare the social composition of these strong believers in green/peace and in feminism. Do they share a common background? How much, indeed, do they share the same values? Existing research would lead us to expect that these two sets would exhibit the characteristics of the 'post-materialists'. They would be young, relatively well-off and would have received a more advanced education. And women would be well-represented. In our terms, they should be quite well-resourced individuals.

When looking at the following results, it should be noted that although, as will be apparent later, some of these social categories may be more inclined to support these new values, it might still be the case that their numbers are not sufficiently large greatly to affect the balance, given the overall population distribution. This is so in the case of the young. It will be shown below that those aged 18–29 are indeed radical but their contribution to the strongest green/peace advocates (22·6%) or feminists (22·1%) is actually slightly lower than their proportion in the sample as a whole (24·3%). Indeed, in both cases, the age profile broadly mirrors that of the population.

In chapter 7 we examined the suggestion that women might have become attracted into new causes which would lead them, in turn, to take up more radical forms of action. The evidence of our sample suggested, however, that whatever the truth of the claim about the new politics, in general women were not as involved in direct action as men, although the gap was very small indeed. We are now in a position to provide more information on the views women have about some of these new issues. Perhaps it was to be expected that women would be over-represented amongst the most ardent feminists. Nevertheless, the fact that women constituted 69·2% of this group (as against 56·6% of the sample) suggests both their relative degree of commitment and that men have some way to go before sharing women's evaluation of priorities. Women are also over-represented amongst the strong supporters of green/peace, but to nowhere like the same degree (59·9%). Thus, women in the sample constituted a majority of the vanguard of both these forms of new politics.

When it comes to the resource profiles of the two groups, the patterns diverge, and in some not entirely expected ways. The strong feminists fit the post-materialist image of being well-educated. Graduates form 11·3% against 6·5% in the population. They also include 11·7% drawn from the best-off 5% in the sample. The strong supporters of green/peace are, however, very different. The graduates (7·3%) correspond to the proportion in the population. The majority (55·6%) have no educational qualifications, which means that they are over-represented (45·7%). Furthermore, the pattern is repeated for those at the next highest level on the green/peace scale. The wealth profile reinforces this too, if to a less striking extent. The poorest 5% provide 7·6% as against 2·7% from the richest 5%. Confirmation is to be found in the class distributions. Of the feminists, a quarter are from the salariat and 29·6% from the working class. In the green/peace group, half are working class (38·3% in the population) and a fifth are salaried (24%).

It may be that the particular combination of peace and environmental attitudes has spread very widely amongst certain sectors of the population, including the working class. One reason might be the mobilising effect of the labour movement. Opposition to nuclear weapons was a controversial part of Labour Party policy in the period and was backed by many large trades unions. A large majority of the strong adherents of green/peace (62·9%) were Labour Party supporters. Indeed, over a fifth were very strong identifiers. Almost half the Labour supporters in the total sample (47·7%)

thought the removal of nuclear weapons very important, as had 30·4 % of current trades unionists. Just under a third (31·2 %) of the working class thought it similarly very important and a further 16·3 % fairly so. The position of the Labour Party on nuclear energy was more ambivalent but the Manifesto of 1983 put the emphasis on coal-fired power stations. Unions have tended to be divided but the miners have, no doubt from a mixture of interest and altruism, campaigned against nuclear energy. Again, 43·3 % of Labour supporters were strongly opposed to the building of nuclear power stations and 18 % fairly opposed. Trades unionists were not very different from the general population but the working class, with 29·9 % strongly opposed and 23·8 % fairly opposed, were the most hostile to nuclear power of all the classes.

It would appear, therefore, that there is a strong party effect on the composition of the leading green/peace advocates. Support has been activated beyond the confines of the middle-class nuclear disarmament and ecology lobbies for reasons which may contain a deal of environmentalism but also an admixture of economic interest. If this is so, the green/peace movement, as we have measured it, may be composed of two different groupings.

Since the strong green/peace supporters contain a mere 9 % of Conservatives, it is not surprising that three-quarters are to the left and, indeed, over half (54·1 %) are amongst the 25 % on the furthest end of the left–right scale. The feminists, whose backgrounds we have seen are quite different, are much more evenly spread. Labour supporters are the largest party grouping (36·7 %) and are over-represented, but 34·1 % are Conservatives which, even if they are under-represented, is a substantial contingent. Nevertheless, the feminists do include 14·4 % who are amongst the furthest 5 % on the left.

All in all, if the two sets of supporters of the new politics display elements in common – many are from the far left, a majority are women – there are also clear differences in the class and educational profiles in particular. The two sets are, moreover, not entirely divorced. Those who gain the highest scores on both the green/peace and the feminist scales constitute about 10 % of the total set – those with the strongest views on these issues. If the test is slightly relaxed and those with the next highest green/peace ranking are also included, the overlap with the high feminists increases to a little over a quarter of the combined set, who together form a core of 'eco-feminists' (Graham 1989).

It is thus possible still to think in terms of a new politics syndrome amongst a core of strong adherents, if not amongst the general public. It would also appear on the present evidence to be the case that the new politics is beginning to pull in other sympathisers who are far from all being the classic post-materialists. However, before going on to the crucial question of how much the top feminists and green/peace supporters participate, it is worth looking at the wider context of the whole sample. It is possible that, although their numbers are not enough to sway the balance of composition of the leading groups, nevertheless certain of the social strata who are normally predicted to hold these sorts of post-materialist positions do score highly.

To some extent, this is borne out, although the evidence also supports the mixture of patterns revealed by the earlier analysis. The two scales have been re-scored to run from zero, indicating strong opposition, to 10 which was the score of the topmost category on each scale which we have just been considering. The mean score for the population on green/peace was 5·30 and for feminism 5·67. Overall, men (4·93) were less supportive of green/peace than women (5·64) but, very surprisingly and despite the composition of the leading feminists, across the population there was almost no difference between the sexes on feminism. The young, perhaps significantly for the future, are the strongest supporters of both ideals amongst the age groups. Those aged 18–29 achieve 5·48 on green/peace and 6·10 on feminism. This persists in the face of the lack of educational resources. The young with no educational qualifications register one of the highest scores on the green/peace scale (6·50). However, they are just below average on feminism (5·58). This is the reverse of the pattern with the young graduates who are, disconcertingly, below average on green/peace issues (4·75), but amongst the stronger backers of the feminist cause (7·58). These younger degree-holders seem to be swimming against the stream of their generation on environment and peace. The explanation would appear to lie in the fact that half of them are Conservatives who would be opposed to nuclear disarmament. Certainly, the attitudes of our young graduates cause some extra hesitation in advancing a suggestion that there is a generational effect whereby the young as a whole, regardless of resources, have become swept along by a wind of change running in favour of environmentalism, fanned by media attention to ecology.

But not only the young. On green/peace it is the poor, rather than the materially well-off, who are most in favour. And it is those with no qualifications rather than the most educated. Thus, the poorest 5% score 5·91 and the next poorest 19% score 6·21. The richest 20% (4·49) and the very richest 5% (3·11) are at the bottom end of the scale. Those with no qualifications (5·74) outscore graduates, who are below the mean (5·14). This is the reverse of the post-materialist hypothesis.

However, things are somewhat different in the case of feminism. Here, the graduates as a whole head the list (7·07). Those without qualifications are, this time, at the bottom (5·33). The wealthiest quarter are also slightly more feminist than average, although they are again matched by the poorest 5%. The middle ranks are about average.

Combining education and wealth – the two individual resources – elicits a more intricate pattern. Graduates are, on average, sympathetic to feminism but the less well-off graduates are more so. Similarly, although degree-holders did not, as a whole, support green/peace their average was pulled down by the adverse stance of the richest amongst them. Those graduates who were in the middle to poorer ranges of wealth were in favour – even if the score of 5·60 still falls short of those with the lowest material and educational resources with 6·69.

There is some further evidence that these twin streams within the green/peace ranks, of the under-resourced and the better- (but not best-) resourced, may be affected by processes of mobilisation when the party and trade union patterns are examined. On the environmental and peace issues, the Labour Party score of 7·01 is the highest of all the categories considered. Trades unionists, both present (5·68) and past (5·35) are ahead of either staff association members or those who have never joined any such organisation. The tiny group of 'other' party supporters, who are also generally to the left, also score heavily (6·28). Another way of seeing this is that the green/peace score of those on the furthest left is 8·21. Clearly, these peace and environment issues cannot be divorced from the party battle. The low Conservative score of 3·64 could equally reflect counter-mobilisation by the party's propaganda. The positions of Liberals above the average and the Social Democrats below it equally match the relative stances of the two elements of the former Alliance on these issues, which indeed were to prove so troublesome to their survival as partners.

Similar mobilisational effects are not so apparent on the feminist issues. Despite the involvement of the Labour Party and the Trades Union Congress with abortion issues (Lovenduski 1986:81), the impact is not deeply registered in the attitudes of Labour supporters (5·78) or trades union members (6·08) which, whilst more feminist than the mean, are not as strongly so as the SDP and no different from Liberals (whose leader, David Steele, had initiated the reform in the abortion laws in 1967). The Conservatives are below the average (the first woman prime minister seldom being heralded by the feminist movement as its leading standard-bearer) but only fractionally so (5·62).

All in all, therefore, the feminist movement, by these measures, fits somewhat more closely with the expected pattern that radical causes will be associated with a certain level of affluence. But this evidence suggests that the environmentalists and nuclear disarmers would appear to contain two strands. There are those whose educational resources are high but whose material resources are at average to lower levels – the less well-off graduates. But there is also a strong phalanx of the generally low resourced – with few educational qualifications, poor and working class, as well also as the unemployed (6·00 on green/peace). The new politics also does not form an entirely new alignment to the old politics of left and right. The leftward leanings are common to both sets of adherents, though more evident in green/peace. It may be, however, that if the green strand comes increasingly to dominate over the peace issue (which is inextricably caught up in the party debate), the linkage with leftism will weaken. That is the ground the parties will be fighting over and the possibility of successful party mobilisation is suggested by the evidence of this survey. This general profile is strongly reminiscent of the alliance between the traditional left and the new social movements as analysed by Offe (see the discussion of the 'Alliance 3', 1985:858–68).

To some degree, but far from entirely so, the parties, in battling for the feminist vote and the green/peace vote, will be fighting for the support of people who have values in common. The highest green/peace supporters' score on feminism was 5·73. The feminists, whose politics are more mixed, score 5·83 on green/peace. In view of the highly publicised activities of certain small groups of women in peace demonstrations, such as the camp at Greenham Common air base, the scores are, overall, more modest than might be expected, but will contain small numbers who are very positive on both issues.

The question then remains as to how far these committed supporters of new politics express their ideas through political action.

Green/peace, feminism and participation

As table 9.5 shows, on these matters, strong values go with participation, although there is one particularly intriguing exception. On the overall participation scale, nevertheless, the impact of the values is not as considerable as might have been expected. The leading green/peace supporters have an unadjusted score of +25 which, whilst certainly positive, by no means matches that of certain other groups we have looked at (the farthest left gained $+77$). Moreover, when controls both for other values and for resources are introduced, the rate falls to $+12$. A very similar story is told by the figures for the most committed feminists who initially are at $+35$ but after adjustments drop to $+16$.

Neither group is involved in the most conventional forms of activity. Contacting levels are, after controls, only slightly positive. Voting presents a most disconcerting picture. The green/peace supporters are merely $+1$ but the feminists are -14. The reasons are not clear but seem to bear out, in more extreme fashion, the low voting rates of the otherwise highly active members of feminist organisations reported in chapter 7.

It is in collective action and direct action that these two highly motivated groups reveal their participatory characters. It is true that, after other factors are taken into account, the collective action scores fall to less remarkable levels, but the initial figures of $+17$ and $+27$ are some indication of the mixture of organised activities, informal groups, protest rallies and petitioning characteristic of many peace, environmentalist and feminist campaigns. A preference for solidaristic but less-structured types of collective action has been one of the contributions of these movements, and especially of feminism, to new forms of democracy (Bouchier 1983; Rowbotham 1986; Frankland 1989). It has also been argued that different participatory styles are to be found within feminism – a rights movement with a somewhat greater orientation to conventional forms and a women's liberation movement much more inclined to work outside the system (Lovenduski 1986:62–3). Both see themselves, however, as somewhat marginal to the system. It is possible that the findings are picking up traces of these orientations.

Direct action is, in some respects, an extension of these collectivist directions. The Campaign for Nuclear Disarmament made its impact through mass demonstrations (Parkin 1968). More radical campaigners have employed a variety of forms of demonstrations, boycotts, sit-ins, blocking traffic and civil disobedience in support of their causes. The organisation Greenpeace itself has employed some daring means to propagate its position (Hunter 1979).

Feminists have similarly organised large demonstrations over abortion and violence against women (Lovenduski 1986:79–82). In the case of the green/peace supporters, the adjusted rate for direct action is an unremarkable $+10$ but the initial figure of $+29$ is an indication of sympathy for this mode of participation. The feminists' involvement in direct action, however, is not only high ($+50$) but holds up well ($+37$) even when their other values and resources are taken into account. When it is recalled from chapter 7 that, generally, women themselves were slightly below the mean in direct action, we may here have a sign of the way in which the raising of consciousness amongst a particular group of people (here both men and women) can re-shape their attitudes towards unconventional modes of activity. This was already observed to be true of feminist groups.

Along with the earlier confirmation that the young are more inclined towards greater direct action and less concerned with conventional forms, there are here further signs that there could be some shift in the orientation of British citizens towards the various modes of participation. Such assessments are fraught with difficulties, some of which will be discussed in the final chapter. But there may be some growth in the number of groupings with intensive feelings about certain issues who are ready to add more

Table 9.5 *Participation of strongest supporters of green/peace and feminism*

	Green/peace		Feminism	
	Unadjusted	Adjusted*	Unadjusted	Adjusted*
Overall	+25	+12	+35	+16
Collective action	+17	+10	+27	+14
Voting	+9	+1	−1	−14
Party campaigning	+14	+9	+12	0
Direct action	+29	+10	+50	+37
Contacting	+7	+2	+15	+5
N of actions (19)*	2·16	1·97	2·27	1·87

* Adjusted for resources, personal factors and other political values.
** See note to table 7.1

conflictual modes of action to their political repertoire. To examine this further, the last section of this chapter will look at attitudes to the norm of participation itself.

Participation as a value

The final set of values are those surrounding participation itself. As chapter 1 showed, participation is at the centre of a debate about the very nature of democracy. For some democrats, the existing division of labour between professional politicians and fairly passive citizens is satisfactory, so long as the electoral system permits an adequate accountability. Others, however, call for a more participatory democracy in which the ordinary person will have greater opportunities to take an active part in politics, and will even be expected to do so.

How widespread are such participatory ideas in Britain and how far do those who hold them live up to their ideals by becoming politically active? The relevance of participatory norms is not confined to their direct impact on past levels of political involvement. It is also a significant question whether there is a more general sympathy towards the idea of participation within the population as a whole. The ideal of a 'civic culture' (Almond and Verba 1963) to which some theorists have aspired, is a mixture of a readiness to abide by democratically produced laws and also of a willingness to participate in their formulation. Participationists place the greater stress on cultivating the second aspect of that culture. An already existing normative orientation towards political involvement would increase their hopes for a transition towards the kind of participatory world they admire. At the same time, their expectations may not be high since they frequently insist that the prevailing patterns of politics in liberal democracies discourage citizen activity (Barber 1984).

Measurement

In order to test the extent of participatory values, we constructed a 'normative participation scale' out of three items which tapped different aspects of an orientation towards greater individual involvement. Two are overtly political but one asks about the extension of participation beyond that sphere. The first element is composed from responses to a question which asked:

Do you think that ordinary citizens should have more say in the decisions made by government or are these decisions best left to the elected representatives such as MPs or local councillors?

The question thus probes the attitudes of citizens to whether there should be a division of labour between citizens and politicians, with the representatives having the final say, or whether ordinary people should have a greater input.

The second question was concerned with open government which, for most believers in an extended democracy, must be a concomitant of greater participation. It is, of course, true that those other than the most ardent participationists may also support greater freedom of information. An Act to provide personal access to computer data files and protection against their dissemination was put on the statute book in 1984. Nevertheless, even if there are other believers in open government, strong participationists would be expected to regard it as essential. The question was whether or not respondents believed it was important to have a government policy of:

Giving the public more access to government documents even if it makes the government's job more difficult.

The third item in the scale concerns attitudes to extending participation in the workplace. A belief in industrial democracy has been characteristic of participatory democrats from the time of John Stuart Mill to the present (Pateman 1970). It has been seen both as a training ground for extending self-determination and as a logical consequence of the demand for a more genuine political democracy (Dahl 1985). On the other side, it has been resisted by those who believe that democracy is confined to the political realm and that within the economic sphere managers must be left to manage. The question asked whether the respondent agreed or disagreed with the statement that: 'Workers and employees should have more say in how the places where they work are run.'

The responses to the questions suggest that there is a broad background sympathy in Britain for more participation but that it is not without reservations. In answer to the question about more open government, a clear majority (58·3%) thought that it was fairly or very important that such a policy be pursued – a fifth thinking it very important. However, over a quarter were opposed (27·6%), leaving 14·1% indifferent on the matter. When it came to whether ordinary citizens should have more say in the decisions of government, the more participatory position was in a minority, even if a substantial one (47·6%). Thus, the majority view favoured the role of representatives. So far, therefore, the impression would be of a broad tendency towards a mildly reformist stance of opening up government rather than seeking radical change in a participatory direction. In the economic arena the participation response was more emphatic to the question on allowing workers and employees more say. The overwhelming majority (80·1%) were in favour. Again there was a significant block of 28·2% who were strong supporters of such a change.[19]

Overall, the correlations between the responses to the three questions were modest to weak but it is clear that there were bodies of people for whom a more participatory society was generally important. Thus, for example, of those favouring more say for ordinary citizens in government, 71% wanted more open government and 88·4% wanted more say for workers at their places of employment. Amongst those favouring open government, 73·8% also wanted more worker involvement.

In forming the scale of normative participation, all three items made a substantial contribution. However, the most central was that concerning open government.[20] The scale was divided into six tranches which ranged from the strongest believers in participation (9·2%) and the next strongest (16·3%) down to those most opposed (6·1%) and next most opposed (20·1%). The scores on the scale ranged from a lowest figure of −289 to a highest of +161. In so far as the average score was zero, this distribution suggests that there is a pronounced bias in the population as a whole towards positive evaluations of participation. Our major interest is in the topmost category of strongest participationists. Who are they and how much do they actually participate?

Who are the participationists?

One expectation concerning the make-up of the committed participationists would be that they would typically be well-educated and reasonably well-off, belonging, in short, to the post-materialist world. However, although, as will be seen, these groups do score well on the normative participation scale, they are not especially prominent amongst the high participationists compared with other social categories. The educational profile of the topmost participationists very much follows that of the population as a whole. Thus, 43·1% have no qualifications and, at the other extreme, 8·2% have degrees. The same is true of wealth, where the poorest and the wealthiest quarter are represented roughly in proportion. The salariat (16·7%) are actually under-represented and the working class (50·7%) over-represented. Only in the fact of a quarter of their numbers being affiliated to four or more organisations do the strong participationists appear particularly well-resourced.

Nor are they exceptionally youthful. Their average age is close to the mean for the population and the distribution in the age groups is broadly similar. The majority are male (54·5%). It is their party political positions rather than these background factors which may provide the first hint of what lies behind their participatory beliefs. Over half are Labour supporters. Indeed, almost a quarter (23·1%) identify very strongly with the party. Conservatives, who form the largest group of party identifiers, provide only 11·1% of the committed participationists – a mere 1·5% are very strong supporters. The Liberals (13·2%) outnumber Conservatives, and Social Democrats (8·9%) are not very far behind.

Nevertheless, although they may not make a major impact on the overall composition of the strong participationists, certain of the expected social categories do turn out to be more participation-minded but they are joined by others who might be thought less predictable. Degree level education appears to be an environment where the norm of activism is encouraged. Degree-holders score +25, whilst those with no qualifications score −3. This provides further concrete evidence as to the values which are associated with higher education alluded to in chapter 4. However, the story turns out to be more complex, and in some ways more surprising, than this. Education is not, in this instance, reinforced by the other individual resource of wealth. The richest 5% have a normative participation score of −7, scarcely bettered by the second richest 20% with −6. It is the very poorest who come out strongly in favour of participation. The poorest 5% score +26, followed by the next poorest 19% (+12) and the next poorest 18% (+5).

Examination of some of the combinations of education and wealth show how they pull in different directions. The small group of degree-holders who are in the richest 5% (admittedly only 8) have a score of +15 which hints that financial success, or a wealthy background, moderates the inclination towards valuing public participation. Graduates in the second richest 20% or, indeed, in the above average 33% both score better (+28 and +23 respectively). On the other hand, lack of educational qualifications does not affect the very positive scores of the poorest 5% since those with the combination of the lowest personal resources more than match the graduates by scoring +28.

This tendency for the less well-off to value participation (if not necessarily to undertake it) more than the better-off is reinforced by the pattern for the social classes and for trades unions. The salariat, who do actually participate more, are at zero on the normative scale. Here, it is the higher salariat who are unsympathetic (−8) whilst the lower grades are slightly favourable (+4). The working class who are less active than average are mildly positive about the idea (+11). So also are the white-collar routine non-manual class who are below managerial level (+11). The petty bourgeoisie, the self-employed and most atomised of social classes, are consistently both non-participatory and unsympathetic to it as an ideal. Although we have seen in chapter 4 that trades unionists are not now, as a whole, amongst the have-nots, there remains a powerful association with the working class. Present members of unions have a score of +24, but present members of staff associations (i.e. of salaried employees) are marginally below average (−3).

What may be partially at work here is a particularly positive reaction amongst workers to the question on greater involvement in the running of their places of work. This is not to 'explain away' their attitudes to participation. Rather, at a time when the European Community is seeking to expand and standardise workers' rights to industrial participation, it suggests that there is not inconsiderable feeling in its favour, particularly amongst the blue-collar and the white-collar workers who are both, in their different ways, subject to managerial direction. The working class and foremen and technicians were certainly even more ready than others to register strong agreement with the proposition – over a third in each case. Nevertheless, this is against a background of very wide support across the classes.

At various points in the book we have touched on the question as to whether there are signs of changing patterns to participation, and this question will again be addressed in the concluding chapter. One suggestion, about which the evidence has been ambiguous, is that there is a steady rise in the involvement of women. It was seen in chapter 7 that the gender gap had indeed narrowed very considerably. In some activities and amongst certain social categories, women out-participated men. Women also seem to value participation rather more, although here, too, the differences are very small. The participation score for women is +2 and for men is −2. However, the small number who were members of feminist groups registered +18.

The second major issue in estimating the possible long-run growth in participation is the attitude of the young. In chapter 7, the young were seen to be typically less participatory and a combination of life-cycle and generational factors were employed to explain this. But, in one respect they were more participatory. They were more likely to be involved in direct action and there was evidence to suggest that this represented a generational change in patterns of participation. Although, as was seen earlier in this chapter, the young are not over-represented amongst the high participationists, they are by far the most favourable of all the age groups towards participation as a value. They score +21. Some slight residual effect also lingers into early middle age (+5). Support for participation then drops to −6 in early middle age and down to −37 in old age. Coupling age and education emphasises the pattern. The young degree-holders (only 12 in number, however) are almost twice as supportive of active values (+47) as other graduates. The young with no qualifications also express a firm belief in the worth of participation (+31). Nor does poverty diminish the support of youth for participation as an ideal. The young who are in the poorest 5% (+32) and those in the next poorest 19% (+41) appear just as committed.

Thus although, with the exception of direct action, the young have yet to make a mark on actual participation, there may be, indeed, a generation for whom it represents a more positive value (Beer 1982). But the conversion of potential political energy into concrete action is to cross a very significant threshold. Nevertheless, it is worth considering whether those who do have a deep commitment to participation are also strong believers in certain values and causes. If this is so, and if they were then to translate their convictions into action, they might be able to colour future political debate to a degree incommensurate with their numbers.

A very strong belief in participation as a value does indeed turn out to form part of a radical syndrome. Those highest on the normative participation scale average 7·81 (out of the maximum score of 10) on the green/peace scale. (Conversely, the highest on green/peace are +55 on the normative scale.) By comparison, those who are least favourable to participation score 3·96 on green/peace. In the same vein, the participationists also adopt a radical position on feminism (6·98) just as the feminists are +60 on participatory values. Finally, the participationists reveal their traditional political credentials with a score of +99 on the left–right scale, which places them well over to the left. In return, the extreme left are the most ardent of believers in the idea of participation with a score of +103. The combination of participatory sentiments this represents is perhaps epitomised in the positions on citizen involvement, open government and worker participation advocated by such prominent Labour politicians as Tony Benn (Benn 1979) or David Blunkett (Blunkett and Jackson 1987).

Participationists and participation

Turning to participation itself, the strength of the relationship between the norm of political action and the overall participation scale is respectable (eta = 0·17) but reduces to a very modest level (beta = 0·07) when other values and resources are taken into account. The main interest, however, lies particularly with the most ardent participationists. Is it the case, as with so many of us, that we speak (or write!) a lot about it but we much less frequently *do* it? Or do the true believers act on their principles?

As can be seen in table 9.6, the overall participation measure suggests that they pay more than lip service. The unadjusted figure is a very solid +47 or 63 points on the scale above the most antiparticipationists who are at −16. However, when controls are introduced for other values, party affiliation and for resources, the participatory advantage, whilst remaining quite clear, becomes less dramatic. The surprise is that, given their credentials, the participationists are not more active than they appear to be. One reason is that a good part of the original level of activity is produced by the other associated values and party commitments which the participationists share. Taking these into account brings their score down to +18 (but, interestingly, depresses the most anti-participationists still further (−25)). When controls for resources are added, the very committed believers in participation drop a little more to +12 (whilst the strong opponents rise back to −18). Thus, a firm adherence to the worth of participation does appear to give some additional impetus to becoming active, even if it is relatively modest.

It could be the case, however, that strong participationists have a greater belief in the efficacy of certain types of action than others and that sharper patterns will be revealed by examining the different modes. There is some support for this possibility. In three instances, although the strong participationists do participate more than average, the effect appears to be due to factors other than the belief in participation as a value. In the case of voting, the strength of the overall relationship is, in any event, weak (eta = 0·08, beta = 0·05). Although, as table 9.6 shows, the committed participationists do have a positive score (+8), this is wiped out and even marginally reversed (−2) when values and resources are considered. The same applies, but more strongly, in the case of party campaigning. Again, the general relationship is weak (eta = 0·07, beta = 0·05). Before other factors are introduced, the strong participationists appear to be quite active (+18) but the effect of the controls is to leave them on the mean. The pattern is repeated for contacting. An initially respectable positive score (+13) declines, with controls, to a negative figure (−6).

However, the picture changes when we look at the two remaining modes – collective action and direct action. The strengths of the associations between normative values and action are somewhat greater and the committed participationists display levels of involvement which better survive the effects of controls. In the case of collective action, the strong supporters of participation achieve a score of +41. When controls for values and resources are brought in, the score drops to +14. It is direct action, however, which is the more striking. The association between holding participatory norms and protest is, initially, quite strong (eta = 0·21) although it reduces to a modest level with controls (beta = 0·10). The committed participationists are very involved in direct action with a score of +66, which is second only to that of the far left and is higher than that of the most ardent feminists and the strongest supporters of green/peace.

Part of the association between participatory ideals and direct action is due to the close connections between the value of action and these other political and partisan outlooks. Controlling for them reduces the association between strong normative participation and direct action to +35. This still leaves the high participationists on a par with the far left, the top feminists, and much higher than the strongest supporters of green/peace. Adding further controls for resources makes very little difference, merely reducing the direct action score to +33.

Table 9.6 *Participation of strongest supporters of normative participation*

	Unadjusted	Adjusted*
Overall	+47	+12
Collective action	+41	+14
Voting	+8	−2
Party campaigning	+18	0
Direct action	+66	+33
Contacting	+13	−6

* Controlling for resources, personal factors and other political values.

The picture that emerges, therefore, is that those who have a deep commitment to the ideal of participation do indeed participate above the mean. This is true overall and for every mode of participation. But part of the explanation lies in their sharing other values which give an impetus to action and, to a lesser degree, in their resources. What is distinctive about them is their orientation to collective action (which, it will be recalled, includes mild forms of protest) and above all to direct action. To the extent, therefore, that to place a very high value on participation leads people to be ready, in addition to the use of conventional tactics, to strike, demonstrate or block traffic in support of their political aims, then the spread of participatory norms may make for more conflictual politics. To be a strong believer in extending participation could be taken to run counter to many of the established practices of conventional, representative democracies which rest on an assumption of a political division of labour (see the contrasting views of Barber 1984 and Sartori 1987). We are very far from believing, as some writers have done, that increased participation is politically destabilising. A certain amount of conflict can be healthy. Nevertheless, it should not be assumed that a more participatory society will be also more consensual.

Conclusion

The values people hold constitute one of the major factors which shape their readiness to step into the public realm. Amongst these values certain ones stand out for the stimulus they provide to action. Participation is, on the whole, a value of the left. The further a person is to the left, the more likely he or she is to become politically involved (see figure 9.3). This is especially the case for collective and direct action. Commitment to the Labour Party is a reflection of this same pattern. The more strongly one identifies with the party, the more one is likely to be politically active.

There is, however, one significant countervailing factor to this leftward orientation towards participation. Those who identify very strongly with the Conservative Party actually out-participate the very strong Labour identifiers (figure 9.2). Those furthest to the right are similarly consistently active. Many of the social formations which have been seen as most likely to be active – the well-resourced – contain substantial bodies of Conservative supporters. It appears to be at the centre that participation is weakest. 'Consensus politics', unlike 'conviction politics' is not a strong rallying cry. The left may predominate amongst those whose values lead them to be particularly ready to take

highly publicised forms of collective or direct action. But this was a period of
Conservative Party hegemony and a large plurality (but not a majority) were voting to
maintain that party in office. Some, indeed, of the protest of the period, such as the
miners' strike, reflected the exclusion of the left from the political and economic
influence they had wielded in the past.

Commitments to party and a person's stance on the traditional, largely materialist-
based, left–right spectrum thus remain significant for participation. But a further
stimulus to participation is coming from the 'new politics' which surrounds such issues
as environmentalism, nuclear disarmament and feminism. Some of these values appear
to have been widely absorbed by various sectors of the population, and especially by the
young. The fact that they are often described as the 'new politics' contains a suggestion
that the 'old', conventional politics had failed to adapt itself to incorporate the new
issues and the alignments of social formations surrounding them. For this reason,
supporters of the new politics would be more ready to turn to less conventional modes
of participation in order to place their issues on the agenda. This is borne out by the
involvement of the strongest supporters of these values in collective and direct action
(see table 9.5).

The new politics and the old are not, however, at a complete disjuncture with one
another. Belief in environmentalism, nuclear disarmament and feminist causes is also, to
varying degrees, associated with the left. Moreover, the social formations surrounding
these issues are made up of an alliance of the moderately well-resourced (materially only
fairly advantaged, but educationally advantaged) and the poor and the working class
who were the one-time bastions of the Labour Party (see Offe 1985).

Many of the elements in these groupings are highly sympathetic to the value of
participation itself. Moreover, some of them, the highly educated for example, are
indeed active. In other instances, such as the young and the poor, participation is valued
as an ideal but they less often cross the threshold. It is not that they are badly lacking
in civic orientation. It would seem, rather, that their resources provide them with a less
firm basis for successful intervention. One of the factors which may determine the future
shape of British politics is the success or failure of the major parties in realigning
themselves around the new issues whilst holding on to, or in some cases recapturing,
their old constituencies – a task made more complicated by the tension between some
green values and the common orientation of left and right to economic growth.

Such a realignment would involve the incorporation into conventional politics of
groupings whose understanding of participatory norms includes in part the resort to less
conventional modes of action in the pursuit of their goals. British politics has been
viewed as elite-dominated, or as a subject-participant culture in which the subject
element prevails (Almond and Verba 1965; Beer 1982; see also Kavanagh 1980). To the
degree that the activists of the new politics also perceive the British system in that light,
and that these new values, especially environmentalism, become more widely diffused in
the wider population, we may see a slow but steady growth in more conflictual and direct
types of citizen action.

10

WHO ARE THE POLITICAL ACTIVISTS?

We can now draw together some of the materials presented in the previous chapters. So far, we have been examining the various modes of participation and have been showing how far these different ways of taking action have been pursued by people with differing patterns of resources, or from contrasting personal backgrounds, or who hold competing political attitudes. First, we shall try to consolidate these findings in an analysis that highlights their key elements. Secondly, we shall offer an alternative way of looking at the findings. This is to group individuals according to their greater or lesser propensity to pursue one kind of action rather than another. It is then possible to delineate the resource, personal and attitudinal profiles of each of these types of participant. In this way, the reader can gain an additional perspective on participation in Britain.

What makes for political activism?

As has been shown, the answer to what makes for political activism is not straightforward. Resources explain a lot, but more in some areas of participation than others (see figure 5.10). Equally, other important economic and personal factors we have considered add to the picture, but to varying degrees and sometimes only in combination with other attributes. The gender gap is one instance. It is also the case that, in many of the relationships reported, the effect varies from one part to another. The impact of age, for example, is of this sort – depressing participation amongst young and very old, raising it for those in between.

These qualities make it very difficult adequately to summarise all that has been uncovered within the compass of one causal model: something that might be taken to put meaningful numbers to the various elements in the overall model of participation presented in chapter 1 (chart 1.3). Nevertheless, it is important to try to bring together in some way all that has been said in order to provide an overview, even if some violence is done to particular findings and details.

To this end, we searched through all those major factors that have appeared in the previous chapters, deploying them simultaneously in order to identify the key ingredients that make for political activism. The aim is to look at their separate net effects on each mode of participation, ignoring more complex mutual contingencies and interactions.[1]

225

The results for the overall participation scale reaffirmed the conclusion of chapter 5 – that resources, and especially group-based resources, are indeed key ingredients for political activism. Even when all those other aspects of an individual's situation are brought into consideration (which were not, of course, included in figure 5.10), resources remain very important in distinguishing the active citizen from his or her passive compatriot. Indeed, ties to groups constitute the single-most critical element in this respect. Level of education also is highly significant, but as suggested in that earlier chapter, it is less than half as potent as the group-based component.

Three other factors also made a substantial contribution: in order, the direction and strength of party identification (second only to group resources); a sense of political efficacy; and left–right value outlooks. Hence, participation is not simply associated with resources. Other more directly political circumstances seem to retain a powerful and separate impetus. The general conclusion is, therefore, that high levels of overall participation, which substantively means taking part in collective action, contacting and party campaigning, are associated with well-developed links to formal networks, strong party commitments, feeling politically efficacious, espousing a consistent array of political values (especially of the left variety) and, not least, being well educated. Passivity, on the other hand, would go hand in hand with the mirror opposite of these traits – being disconnected from groups, lacking strong party and related political commitments, feeling ineffective and not possessing any formal educational qualifications.

Not surprisingly, analogous exercises carried out on the individual modes produced roughly comparable results, although there are, once more, significant variations from the overall pattern. This is particularly true in the case of voting. As noted in figure 5.10, resources are of relatively little account in predicting turnout. This is confirmed by the results of this more comprehensive analysis in which neither type of resources made a substantial impression. Rather, in addition to age, more overtly political factors are important – party attachments, political cynicism and efficacy and, again, left–right values. These additional elements do not raise the explanatory power of the whole model quite to the level recorded for overall participation (see also Verba, Nie and Kim 1971:57–9), but the gap is closed considerably.

In the other electoral mode, party campaigning, not surprisingly the most prominent ingredients are those of a partisan nature. Indeed, a substantial amount of the difference made by group resources across the sample as a whole can be accounted for by explicitly party linkages. Amongst these, party identification is the most salient, but left–right values also play a significant part. Again, however, campaigning is not just a matter of resources and party commitments. In this instance, having a sense of political efficacy is also an important part of the equation. But, as was seen in chapter 8, it is important to note that the lack of such political confidence is not a comparable handicap (see figure 8.2).

Participation in the form of collective action generates results the closest to those for the overall pattern. Once more resources, in the shape of group ties, are the single-most important ingredient although, given the nature of the activity, this is hardly surprising. Similarly, partisan factors, both attachments and values, continue to make a significant impression. Political efficacy, too, appears in the list. The one noteworthy difference is the addition of the normative attitudes towards participation discussed in chapter 9 (see table 9.6). For this form of activity especially, the varying evaluations people take about participation itself are of considerable account.

In the case of direct action, these general values also appear, although in this instance it seems that attitudes towards feminism generally made the stronger impact for all our respondents (see also table 9.5). A person's values are, indeed, a particularly distinctive element shaping this mode of participation. This is made all the more significant by the presence of education as a powerful explanatory influence. As suggested in the earlier analyses, values, acquired or reinforced through attending universities and polytechnics, seem to be the dominant motif associated with contemporary protest in Britain. It is important once again not to underplay other sources of protest rooted in material hardship which were uncovered in chapter 4 (see table 4.4 and figure 4.5). But our evidence is that the more important social and economic roots lie elsewhere. This summary analysis also indicates clearly that party attachments remain a major element associated with direct action. All in all, the analysis confirms that direct action is primarily a matter for the left. Nevertheless, even with this vastly expanded inventory of possible explanatory factors, direct action remains relatively the most poorly accounted for of all. It was already apparent from figure 5.10 that resources did not make a huge difference. Unlike voting, however, the gap in explanation is not made up to any appreciable extent when we widen our canvass. It is possible to offer predictions about direct action with the array of tools used so far but only to a relatively limited degree.

To a lesser extent, the same might also be said of contacting. This was explained substantially better than direct action but much less well than any of the other modes (see also Verba and Nie 1972:132). Within the framework of what can be predicted, however, resources, and especially once more those of a group-based nature, stand out. To this can also be added the familiar ingredients of partisan attachments and political efficacy.

It is, therefore, possible to highlight those elements which appear to make the largest contribution to political activity or passivity in Britain. Group-based resources are generally pre-eminent along with, and to a lesser degree, more individualistic endowments, especially education. Party seems to play an abiding role but also value outlooks, both of a left–right and a less directly partisan nature. Finally, amongst the broader cultural factors, the sense of political efficacy is a recurrent ingredient in participation.

As so often in the earlier analyses, there are sufficient common elements which influence participation in Britain that one can describe it as a distinct phenomenon; but there are also sufficient variations to demand that the student pays attention to the multiplicity of its dimensions. These features can be appreciated further if we now turn to our second way of summarising the findings in which we focus on *who* the activists are rather than on *what* makes them activists.

Types of participants

On the basis of finding that participation in Britain is multi-dimensional, it could be expected that the population group themselves according to their tendency to prefer certain modes of participation over others. There would be those who were quite inactive, beyond perhaps occasionally voting. There would be those who voted regularly but did little more. At the other extreme would be a small minority who were highly active and performed actions falling within most or all of the five modes of participation. In between, there could be people who, whilst not necessarily entirely eschewing other modes of action, were more attracted by one rather than another. Similar profiles have been identified in American research (Verba and Nie 1972; see also Barnes, Kaase *et al.* 1979:152–7).

In order to test this supposition, a form of 'cluster analysis' was employed in which individual respondents are grouped together into a small number of relatively homogeneous categories (see also Verba and Nie 1972: Appendix F).[2] These categories were created through this technique by using the five factors which were found to represent the essential empirical structure of political participation (see chapter 3). Thus, all individuals within any one group should exhibit roughly similar participatory profiles. The technique is intended to ensure that each individual is, on the whole, more like the others within his or her category than like the members of any other category. In 'distance' terms (which cluster analysis employs), all members are closer to the group's overall centre of gravity (centroid), as defined across the five dimensions of participation, than to the centroid of any other cluster. The size and character of the categories in this approach, therefore, arise largely from the data themselves. They are not constructed and imposed by the investigator.

The result of the cluster analysis can be seen in figure 10.1. The most striking feature is the difference in the size of the slices of the 'pie'. The largest by far, comprising just over half the population (51%), is composed of those who 'just vote' but do so very regularly. However, they are well below average in the other participatory areas. The other half (49%) breaks down into two almost equal, but very different components. First, there are the quarter (25·8%) who do not even vote regularly and who are, consequently, 'almost inactive'. The other quarter contains their mirror image. They are those who stand up and try quite hard to be counted. But in doing so, they appear to prefer certain modes of action over others. The largest category of these activists are those involved primarily in collective activity (8·7% of the total sample) followed by 7·7% who have mainly contacted representatives and officials. There is then a much smaller band of persons (3·1%) who are more prone to forms of direct action. They are slightly larger in numbers than those who have been more active in party campaigning (2·2%). This leaves the very smallest group – a mere 1·5% of the population – who are active more or less across the board and who might be called the 'complete activists' or the true 'gladiators' in the political games. This may seem a very small number, not least in comparison with the 11% recorded for the United States (Verba and Nie 1972:79). However, it should be recalled that the test for inclusion is the more demanding one of having been active across the spectrum of five modes of participation, including direct action.

Presenting the map of participation in this way can provoke contrasting reactions. From a participatory perspective, there may be dismay that the population is characterised more by passivity than activism. Setting aside those who 'just vote' and are almost inactive, less than a quarter of British citizens (23·2%) actively sustain the citizenry's role in political life. Translated into the population numbers these would

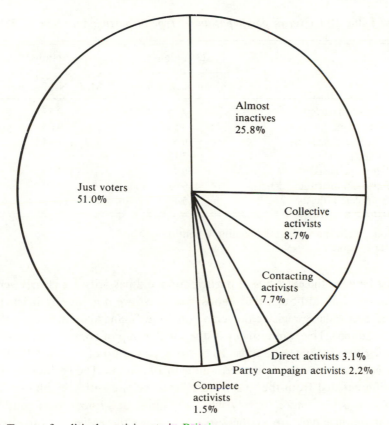

Almost
inactives
25.8%

Just voters
51.0%

Collective
activists
8.7%

Contacting
activists
7.7%

Direct activists 3.1%
Party campaign activists 2.2%

Complete
activists
1.5%

Figure 10.1 Types of political participants in Britain

represent, appearances may change. With an estimated adult population in 1985 of 41·6 millions, 23·2% would imply that 9·66 millions had been relatively participatory over the previous five year period. The core of 'complete activists' would represent around 625,000 individuals who had been regularly and widely active for the same time. The 'realist', non-participatory school of democracy would not, however, be disturbed. An active quarter is balanced by a generally passive half of the population which is, however, ready with its vote to hold the professionals to account at election time. This might be compared with a 'guesstimate' of around 50,000 for the size of the national and local elected and administrative political elite in Britain (for one approach to making such calculations, see Putnam 1976:10). Such an elite could fit comfortably into Wembley Stadium!

Before looking at who these various activists are, it is worth stating in summary terms what these forms of activism imply. This can be done in a relatively straightforward way by employing again the measure of numbers of actions performed. Here, as elsewhere in this chapter, we are not making the various adjustments for resources or other factors which were an essential part of the earlier analysis. Instead, we are reverting entirely to the raw, unadjusted figures which here seem more appropriate.

In table 10.1 the overall level of participation of the various categories is shown using both the full range of 23 actions and the 19-action measure which excludes the four 'easier' and most common actions of voting and signing petitions (see chapter 3). The

Table 10.1 *Overall participation by type of participant (N = 1,578)*

	23 Actions*	19 Actions**
	Mean N of actions	Mean N of actions
Almost inactives	2·05	0·57
Just voters	3·53	0·62
Contacting activists	6·54	3·44
Collective activists	7·13	3·66
Direct activists	6·96	3·70
Party campaign activists	10·03	7·68
Complete activists	15·75	11·71

* *All* actions, including voting and signing a petition.
** See note to table 7.1.

differences between the extremes of participation and passivity are clearly very marked. At the one extreme, although the 'almost inactives' are not entirely inert (not all will have failed ever to have registered even a vote), they manage on average only just over 2 of the 23 actions. The commitment of the small group of complete activists is readily seen by their performance of almost 16 of the activities on offer. Overall, they outstrip the party campaigners who are runners-up with 10 actions. The various activists are all sharply differentiated from the 'just voters' who 'belong with' the almost inactives.

The pattern is seen more sharply when the range of 19 actions is considered. The voters and the inactives are at the same level once the easier actions are removed. Discounting voting along with petitioning, the activities of the great majority, obviously deflates all the figures but again emphasises the gap between the active and the passive populations. It also leaves the complete activists and the party campaigners still firmly in the lead, with the other activists on a roughly similar level.

What distinguishes the activists from one another is the nature of their 'specialism'. It is not, of course, that they perform their specialist activities to the total exclusion of other types of action, but that they have a propensity for one more than others. Thus, the party campaigners have, on average, performed 3·50 out of the four types of campaign action on the list whereas the inactives have performed 0·04. The complete activists have done rather more than half (1·79) but the direct activists show a general disinclination to be involved with conventional party work (0·14). In similar fashion, the contactors have done 2·54 of the 4 contacting actions compared to the inactives with 0·27. Those inclined towards collective action have been involved in 3·20 of the six group activities, with the inactives again scoring a mere 0·67. The direct activists have performed 1·74 of the range of 4 protest actions on the list, whilst the inactives have on average done 0·10.

The breadth of the complete activists can be estimated by the fact that they have been concerned in more collective actions (4·73) than the collective activists, more contacting (3·54) than the contactors. In protesting they were second only (1·25) to the direct activists. They may also yield to the party campaigners on their home ground but here, too, they score a respectable 1·79. Needless to say, their voting record also ranks

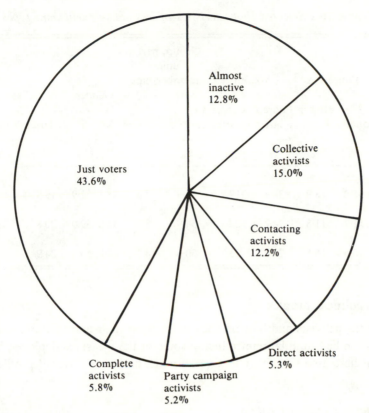

Figure 10.2 Total actions by participant type

amongst the highest. The complete activists may be few in number but they certainly get around.

This might be best appreciated if we look at the whole pool of participatory actions in the 23-item scale. The pool can be divided up according to the size of the contribution to it by each type of participant. The results are set out in figure 10.2, in which the shape of the 'participatory pie' is rather dramatically changed. Because the almost inactive 25% only undertake just over two actions each, their share of this pie is a mere 12·8%. Their participatory voice is half their proportionate size in the adult population. Conversely, the active quarter have a voice that is almost doubled in strength: their 23·2% share of the population generates a 43·4% share of the actions. Most dramatic of all are the complete activists who nearly quadruple their stake in the political arena. All in all, the figure provides a further vivid illustration of the way in which different sections of the chorus of citizens try to make themselves heard. The question remains, however, who it is that sings loudest and who stays silent. Once again, as has been seen in previous chapters, much evidence on this has already been provided but it is appropriate to review this central theme through the prism of analysis of participant types.

Table 10.2 *Selected characteristics of less active participant types*

	Education		Wealth		Group, party, union memberships		Gender		Class		
	No quals.	Higher educ.	Poorest quarter	Richest quarter	One or no ties	4+ ties	M	F	Salariat	Working	N
	%	%	%	%	%	%	%	%	%	%	N
Almost inactives	51·2	13·9	34·4	17·9	62·9	7·5	48·1	51·9	19·9	40·9	407
Just voters	51·7	11·5	24·2	22·3	54·9	8·8	41·0	59·0	20·8	38·4	804
Total sample	46·5	16·5	24·0	25·2	50·6	14·3	44·0	56·0	24·9	37·6	1,578

Social and political profiles

So who are the activists and how do they differ from their more passive compatriots? The answer can be found by reintroducing some of the measures deployed in previous chapters but here used selectively to give an indication of the overall profiles.

Almost inactives and just voters

The inactives and those who just vote present not dissimilar pictures (see table 10.2). In each case, they are heavily composed of people who are low on personal and collective resources. Over half in both groupings have no educational qualifications. The inactives also contain a disproportionate number (34·4%) of those in the poorest quarter of the population. Using for these purposes the single index of organisational ties which pulls together political party, trades union and voluntary group affiliation, the inactives and the voters are found to contain a large proportion of people who have at most a single membership. In the case of the inactives, this amounts to 62·9% of the total and 54·9% in the case of the voters.

Those at the other end of the resource scales are, conversely, under-represented to varying degrees. The wealthiest quarter provide 17·9% of inactives and 22% of those who just vote. Those with higher education are very slightly under-represented. Those with four or more organisational ties, who are 14·3% of the sample, constitute 7·5% of inactives and 8·8% of the voters.

The personal and economic characteristics of these two least participatory groupings are again fairly similar. In both cases, women are in the majority – 59% of the voters and 51·9% of the inactives. However, since women were 56% of the sample, they are somewhat under-represented in the inactive category. In its age profile, the inactives contain a rather large proportion (37%) from the youngest cohort (aged 18–29). This is not true of the voters, where they comprise only 17·6%. The class compositions are dominated by the working class – 40·9% in the case of the inactives and 38·4% for the voters – although these proportions largely reflect the pattern for the population as a whole. The salariat, by comparison, is under-represented in both categories.

Turning to political outlooks and values, those who are almost inactive include, as could be expected, a disproportionate number of the least politically efficacious. Over a third belong in the least efficacious quarter of the population. A similar proportion are also highly cynical. Such a combination of outlooks would certainly seem unpropitious for participation, although the inactives are at least as sympathetic to the values of participation as the population in general. It is just that they do very little of it. Throughout, the distribution of the voters along the various value dimensions is similar to that for the sample as a whole, which must in part reflect the fact that they do comprise half the total.

The contacting activists

The contactors are, as table 10.1 showed, the least active of the activists. As can be seen in the first line of table 10.3, amongst their number are a substantial group (35·5%) with no educational qualifications but these are balanced by 29% who have undertaken higher education. There is, however, a rather greater bias towards the wealthy in that almost 40% are amongst the richest quarter as against 14% from the poorest. The relatively, but not wholly, individualistic nature of this kind of activity is possibly reflected in the fact that (alone amongst the more active participant types) those who have no more than one organisational tie (44·6%) outweigh those with multiple connections of four or more (21·7%). Even so, the less well-connected are under-represented and the highly-integrated are over-represented compared with their membership of the population. But, taken as a whole, the contactors have, in this respect, a somewhat different profile to other types of activist.

The contactors also tend to be early middle aged (45%). A small majority are men (51·5%). In class terms, they are almost equally balanced between salariat (35·1%) and working class (31·3%). Thus, although this implies an over-representation of the more advantaged, and a corresponding under-representation of the less, it also means there are substantial numbers in both classes who have proven able to get in touch with those in authority to raise issues important to them.

The contactors are people ready to make their own path to the authorities to deal with problems. Although this might imply that they need some political knowledge, initiative and confidence which would bias such participants towards the well-resourced, it seems that this is only true to a moderate extent. No group in the population is shut out of the process and the contactors include respectable proportions of those who are lacking in individual and group resources.

The collective activists

The collective activists (see table 10.3) are those who have devoted much of their political time to working in support of an organised group or with informal groups. They may also have attended protest meetings and signed petitions, which are activities that imply group backing. It is, therefore, likely that such people would be well-integrated

Table 10.3 *Selected characteristics of activist participant types*

	Education		Wealth		Group, party, union memberships		Gender		Class		
	No quals.	Higher educ.	Poorest quarter	Richest quarter	One or no ties	4+ ties	M	F	Salariat	Working	
	%	%	%	%	%	%	%	%	%	%	N
Contacting activists	35·5	29·0	14·0	38·7	44·6	21·7	51·5	48·5	35·1	31·3	122
Collective activists	34·2	26·4	11·9	40·6	23·3	36·5	40·7	59·3	35·9	35·5	137
Direct activists	21·3	28·6	14·1	23·3	19·2	24·1	55·8	44·2	30·6	48·1	50
Party campaign activists	9·0	41·6	6·0	57·8	7·0	72·2	33·1	66·9	57·0	14·1	34
Complete activists	26·2	49·3	16·7	45·5	13·7	48·2	51·1	48·9	50·7	16·3	24
Total sample	46·5	16·5	24·0	25·2	50·6	14·3	44·0	56·0	24·9	37·6	1,578

into a network of group affiliations. This is not inevitable. Indeed, a small proportion (7·3%) had been involved in collective action without being a formal member of any group and a further 16% were members of only one. Nevertheless, over a third (36·5%) are members of four or more organisations, which is well above the figure for the general population (14·3%).

The interconnections between group and personal resources are reflected amongst the collective activists. A quarter (26·4%) have had higher education and 40·6% are in the richest 25% – although it is the second richest 20% rather than the wealthiest 5% who are the most prominent. But, as with the contactors, those with few resources are not excluded. In fact, a third have no educational qualifications and, although below the proportion in the general population, constitute the single largest educational category. Only 12%, however, are in the poorest quarter. These lower-resourced individuals are also reflected in the fact that working class collective activists (35·5%) are in proportion to the size of their class in the overall population. The petty bourgeoisie's individualist image is somewhat reinstated (compare chapter 6) by the fact that few are to be found amongst these specialised participants (5·7%). The salariat equally confirms its usual activism by constituting over a third of the group.

Collective participants more often display high senses of efficacy – nearly half are in the two topmost ranges on that scale. There is a very slight tendency for them to be also less cynical about politics. In their political values they do not hold positions markedly at variance with the rest of the population. This seems to be mirrored in their party identifications which are also generally close to the national distribution with a slight bias in favour of the Conservatives and the centre (especially the Social Democrats). Thus they are virtually on the mean on the left–right scale.

The collective activists are, like the contactors (but rather more so), slightly skewed towards the better resourced. The employment of more solidaristic forms of action by the working class and by the less advantaged as a whole, ensures that there is a significant representation of these groups in their ranks. Even so, it is not quite enough to balance the use of groups and of the milder forms of protest by the advantaged.

The direct activists

Those with a propensity to direct action are a special source of interest, partly because they have so frequently been seen as harbingers of a new, growing and possibly less comfortable style of political participation. Certainly, they do possess some features which distinguish them from other types of participant (see table 10.3). In the first instance, they are young – 40·7 % of them are aged between 18 and 29. This is the only participant type in which this age group is over-represented. Just as in chapter 7 it was suggested that there were signs of a generational change in favour of direct action, so the ethos of that generation seems to be the major factor in forming the direct activists. The gender gap, however, has not yet closed, since 55·8 % are men – their highest representation in the activist ranks.

In educational terms, these protesters are drawn disproportionately from the highly educated – 28·6 % have been to university or other further education institution (well above the 16·5 % in the population). If the better-off are represented only in proportion to their overall numbers, the direct activists are not typically from the ranks of the very poorest, who are under-represented. Nevertheless, the working class make a strong showing. Nearly half (48·1 %) of direct activists are drawn from it and this is the only category of participant in which this class is clearly over-represented. Yet, once more, the workers are partially counterbalanced by the 30 % from the salariat.

The protestors appear to possess a strong sense of efficacy – half of them are found in the top 35 % of that scale. At the same time, they are to be found towards the less cynical end of the spectrum, but only slightly more so than the general population. This may reflect the mixed relationship between cynicism and protest discussed in chapter 8. In terms of party, Labour identifiers are easily the largest group (38·5 %). It is, therefore, a little surprising that their score on the left–right scale is a mere + 16 – or a little left of centre. Their other value orientations are more towards those goals typically associated with the newer politics. These are, moreover, objectives which have sometimes been associated with the employment of direct action. They tend to favour feminist causes and just under a third are at the strongly supportive end of the green/peace scale.

Party campaign activists

Party campaigners form the first of the two small sets of very high participants. As can be seen in table 10.3, they again have a distinctive profile. They are, firstly, well-off. As many as 58 % come from the best-off quarter of the population. Secondly, they are well-educated. Over 40% have either a degree or a further education qualification. To add to these personal resources, they are very well-connected persons. Getting on for three-quarters (72·2%) are members of four or more groups. They are mainly in their early middle age. Well over half (57%) are from the salariat. And most of them are women (66·9%).

They possess the political confidence (and perhaps also the personal confidence too) to carry off the task of campaigning. Fully 80% are at the two most efficacious points on the scale. They generally combine this with low levels of cynicism – 60% being at the two least cynical points. All in all, a very positive attitude towards politics comes through.

The party campaigners being described are mainly Conservatives (55%). There are hints here that, whatever the complexion of other types of activist and however much it is the case that the voice of the Left makes itself heard through a variety of forms of participation (see chapter 9), the Conservatives can still rely on committed supporters to battle on its behalf and to weigh in with funds to gain electoral victory.

The complete activists

Finally, there are the gladiators themselves, who are devoted not only to party but expend their energies in many other directions as well. They appear, at first, to display some similar characteristics to the party campaigners (see table 10.3). As with that group, the well-educated are strongly represented, being half the total. However, a quarter have no qualifications. Somewhat under half were well-off (45·5%) with the second richest 20% being disproportionately active. They are strongly integrated into group networks, though rather less so than the campaigners with 48·2% belonging to four organisations or more. Most are, again, in early middle age – described before as the golden age of participation. But the very slight majority are men (51·1%) which means that women are marginally under-represented. Half are in salaried occupations.

To be so politically active would appear to require a strong sense of efficacy and almost three-quarters are at the two highest points on the scale. But unlike the case of the campaigners, cynicism is an example of the curvilinear pattern noted in chapter 8. Over a third (38·3%) are at the two most cynical points but another third (33·6%) are very low on cynicism. Some thus combine efficacy and beneficent views but there are others who preserve some scepticism about the system in which they are so active.

These outlooks offer, perhaps, a hint that the complete activists are rather different from the campaigners. The difference is confirmed when it is found that half of them (50·6%) are Labour supporters. Conservatives are very much under-represented (16·9%). The Tory campaigners get out the vote. The Labour complete activists pursue their goals across the participatory landscape. The values of the complete activists give some flavour of this. Their score of +93 on the left–right scale places them well over towards the far left. They are firm supporters of the feminist position, a quarter of them taking the strongest possible stance on these issues and a further 35% in the next strongest category. Similarly, a third express the most committed support for the green/peace stance. And, finally, over half affirm a clear belief in the value of participation itself which, in their case at least, is emphatically more than mere lip-service to a particular view of the democratic cause.

Thus, this small group of gladiators, who fight their causes with all the participatory weapons at their disposal, are certainly not a social or political microcosm of society. Their activism is one generated much more by the values of the left than the right. They make their voices heard but their numbers are probably not sufficient for them to set the whole tone of political debate. Even so, if participation has an impact, theirs should be much greater than their simple numbers would imply.

Conclusion

The existence of the different types of participants, each with a distinctive social profile, provides an alternative way of perceiving political participation in Britain. It also provides a means of confirming the basically multi-dimensional, or pluralist, picture of political activity. As the account starting with chapter 3 has been arguing, there is no neat pyramid of activity with a peak of activists and below it successive stages of people who perform fewer and fewer actions across the board.

There is, indeed, a select band of persons who are ready and able to pursue their goals by almost every means of political action available to them. It is also the case that there are many more people who are almost inactive. But they do not constitute the broad base of a single pyramid. There is a larger group in Britain who do use their voting rights extensively and, sometimes, to the full. Then, pursuing the analogy, there are four further pyramids of contacting, collective action, direct action and party campaigning. People have a predilection for certain of these modes of political participation over others (without necessarily being totally inactive outside their preferred mode).

These several dimensions to participation have appeared in sufficient other investigations to be taken as fundamental features of citizen activity in modern democracies. Those who would call for a more participatory form of political life might perhaps heed its pluralist character. It may be the case that there will never be more than a relatively small group of complete activists. But this is not to say that, in the right conditions, far more people might not find time and opportunity to contact their representatives to press an issue, or to campaign for a party, or join in a pressure group or, if necessary, take to the streets. These are all ways in which a variety of people with a range of abilities and a plurality of goals can keep the authorities on their toes. There is no single avenue for participation and a society of participatory 'specialists' can have much to commend it.

PART III

ISSUES AND ACTIONS

11

AGENDAS AND POLITICAL ACTION

So far we have looked at the levels of participation and the propensity of different sections of the population to participate irrespective of the specific context in which they act. Whilst we have been concerned with the extent to which the better educated, the wealthier, or those well-integrated into group networks are inclined to participate more, we have not so far looked at the immediate cause of the actions that they have taken.

Although such an analysis of the social background of participants tends to be the classic approach to the study of participation, it clearly leaves something important out of account. People take action in response to issues, needs and problems. Usually it is prompted by some sense of dissatisfaction with their circumstances. They may be threatened with a building development which could affect the value of their property or they may have a complaint about public transport or the location of health facilities which they require to use regularly. Others may be led to act about national issues such as unemployment or international problems which might, perhaps, include a concern with famine relief or nuclear defence. In this way, people come to have a range of different priorities or 'issue agendas'.

One way of looking at participation is, therefore, by examining the kinds of issues which give rise to action. A number of questions then present themselves which are of considerable relevance to understanding the patterns of political activity in a democracy. Is there a difference between the issue agendas of those persons who are active and those who are inactive? Are the inactive perhaps less conscious of issues or are they no less aware of problems but, for different reasons, disinclined to act upon them? If the categories of active people are broken down into those who display a greater propensity for group involvement than for protesting or for campaigning for political parties, do we find differences in the issues they raise? There is an interaction between a number of elements here. Some people may, as we have seen, be more inclined towards certain forms of activity than others, but issues themselves clearly play a part in determining what action is appropriate to a particular situation. For some problems and some persons, a quiet word with the local councillor may be what is required. For other issues, nothing less than an affirmation of solidarity with sympathisers in a protest march may be needed. Institutional structures will further shape the opportunities for activity. Attending the local MP's surgery can be an effective way of getting a response to a complaint about local council house repairs, even though this does not fall within the

MP's formal responsibilities. When defence decisions are, in effect, taken by NATO or in Washington, the most satisfactory form of action may be far from clear and this uncertainty may even deter attempts at involvement by ordinary citizens.

From what was in chapter 1 called an instrumental perspective particularly, but to a degree from the communitarian standpoint as well, a rational calculation of the chances of affecting an issue could be an important determinant of action. Many people may form a positive or a negative view of a particular mode of action as a whole – thinking, for example, that demonstrations are worthless. In many cases, however, the assessment may be of the appropriateness of the action to the issue. Demonstrations may pay off if directed against the closure of a local school but not if against the opening of a nuclear base. More generally, problems closer to home may be more amenable to action than great national issues about which the ordinary citizen may feel helpless. One plausible hypothesis, therefore, is that action may be a function of the immediacy of the issue or problem, and of the apparent ease or difficulty of finding satisfactory solutions. This would begin to suggest a typical issue agenda rather different from that where 'big issues' provoked 'big action'.

It is sometimes suggested that citizen participation is, by definition, voluntary activity. Certainly, there are conceptual problems in viewing the political rallies organised by some authoritarian regimes as genuine participation. However, this does not mean that citizens in liberal democracies are in total command of the situation, in control of their agenda or issues, and are intervening in the public arena in an entirely spontaneous manner. In some instances, people do make their own agenda. They perceive an issue or a need and seek to bring it to the attention of others. It may not even be a purely personal matter, although many are. Someone may become incensed about a moral issue and wage a campaign about it. Nevertheless, such spontaneous individual participation is one end of a continuum with 'mobilisation' at the other, where action is taken as a result of some initiative by another person or group calling for support. A core of persons may form to protest about an issue and mobilise others by taking a petition round for signing or by organising a well-publicised meeting to which the individual goes. We have already seen in chapter 5 that a substantial proportion of activity is mobilised in this way. In between spontaneity and mobilisation is 'reactive' participation. The individual's agenda is set by the action of others, usually an organisation, which affects his or her life. A local authority, for example, proposes a new ring road affecting property values and giving rise to local actions groups. In this way, the issue agenda is created by others and elicits reactions. Although to some degree individuals may select the issues to which they react, and although they may be what have been called 'sporadic interventionists' (Dowse and Hughes 1977), their agendas are rarely entirely self-determined. A good deal of such activity is, moreover, likely to be oppositional. Participants are frequently 'objectors' to proposals from the authorities which threaten their interests. If government is on one's side there may be less incentive to intervene oneself, unless it is felt that the policy requires public support to overcome vocal opposition.

Issues therefore provide, in part, a specific context in which participation takes place. The context may be national or local or even international. Thus, at the time, in the autumn and winter of 1984–5, the national news was dominated by the exceptionally lengthy miners' strike, accompanied as it was by bitter and often violent confrontations between police and pickets, brought home to viewers on their television screens. Unemployment stood throughout at over three million. One must expect that any study of issue-fed participation will reflect the events dominating the period. There is no 'close season' in politics when nothing significant happens.

However, as this chapter will indicate, there is another much less time-specific aspect to participation. Below the level of the great national issues is a sub-stratum of issues and problems of sometimes more pressing concern to ordinary citizens. They relate, among other matters, to housing, schooling for their children, planning applications, sports facilities. Each, while seemingly unique to the individual and contingent on circumstances, is associated with more limited patterns of action and reaction which do not change with any great rapidity. It is with these underlying patterns of activity that studies of participation must also concern themselves. The great national events will, of course, be registered in the findings, but the extent to which they affect the basic structure of behaviour remains to be examined.

The issues

In order to capture the range of matters which concerned them, respondents were not offered a fixed menu of issues on which to comment, but were asked to list the 'issues, needs or problems' which had been most important to them 'over the past five years or so'. The virtues and defects of this more open-ended approach can be debated (Verba and Nie 1972; Repass 1971). Though there are arguments about the appropriateness of both approaches, in the study of participation the advantages of open questions seemed to us paramount, in that they did not thereafter restrict the agenda which might be offered, nor, as might have happened, bias it towards national issues. In an election study where one is dealing more with an agenda set by the parties and the media, to which the electorate is reacting, perhaps a fixed menu of issues could be more appropriate.

In the event, it was found necessary to modify our open question in one significant respect. Respondents were asked to think in terms of issues, needs or problems which 'people might consider taking action on: actions such as contacting a local councillor or official, signing a petition, joining in a national protest or working in a group'. The aim was to draw attention to issues which might involve some kind of action in the 'public realm'. Without this precaution, respondents might have cited as their most pressing problems those concerned entirely with their domestic life. Whilst one could readily appreciate that, say, burst pipes in one's home will, more than anything else, preoccupy one's mind, these are unlikely to become a matter for public attention. However, even this kind of incident can take on broader dimensions if it occurs on a public housing estate and if the manner in which it is handled leads to complaints about the quality of repairs by the Housing Department. It should also be noted that, at this stage, respondents were not asked about 'political' issues. The term 'political' is a highly contested one. Hence, whilst as researchers we were legitimately only interested in activities with at least a minimal public content, whether respondents would call their activities 'political' was left to a later question.

When the respondents were asked to nominate the issues of concern to them, just over half (55·6%) were able to do so. The 55% provided, without further prompting on the interviewer's part, 1,610 discrete topics, or nearly two each, on average. However, there were a few (some 6%) who provided four, which was as many as we initially made provision for. Apart from these individuals, the remainder were then questioned again to see if they could think of any other personal, national or local matters that might concern them. This further prompt yielded another 672 issues raising the total to 2,282 and reduced to a third those who had no agenda of issues (35%). This, therefore, makes an important division within the population so far as linkages with the polity are concerned. That a third of adults could not offer any 'issue, need or problem' is, perhaps, remarkable, not least bearing in mind the political and economic climate in which the interviewing was carried out.

In order to treat everyone in a comparable fashion, we confine our attention in this chapter to the initial set of up to four issues raised before any further prompting on our part. From time to time we shall also be considering responses to some detailed questions which we asked concerning the 'prime issue' which was the one about which people said that they had taken most action or, if no action had been taken, which they said had been most important to them. These 1,610 issues constitute in total a substantial body of information which makes it possible to look at the way agendas and political action intersect. Furthermore, a number of these issues possessed more than one aspect. Most were single-faceted in that only one element was referred to – 'unemployment' or 'housing' for example. But about 10% touched on more than one topic and were 'multi-faceted', although only the main two in such circumstances were recorded. Thus, 'housing for elderly' and 'youth unemployment' are both issues with double reference points. Breaking such relatively complex issues down into their component elements in this way makes their analysis much more straightforward. If we then disaggregate such multi-faceted issues and treat them as two separate (though related) issues, the total number of unprompted issues is increased to 1,784.

The most immediately striking feature about these issues is their variety. Contrary to the impression given by opinion polls reported in the newspapers at the time, there was no one dominant concern, although all economic issues, including unemployment, taken together made up a quarter. For the rest, they spread themselves across a large number of categories such that, even with very crude schemes, the most numerous was never more than a relatively small proportion of the total. The agenda itself ranged from immigration matters to those affecting higher education, from housing repairs to hospital provision, from public transport to wages and inflation, from leisure facilities to defence and foreign affairs. Most opinion polls have concentrated on the great national issues and produced agendas in which pressing problems of the day, as reported in the media, have dominated over all other issues. Thus, in this period, the polls reported that the 'most urgent problem facing the country' was unemployment, followed by strikes and other economic issues, with defence coming next (Heald and Wynbrow 1986:94–5). But the more open-ended approach has indicated a different level of concern. This is a level which, as will be shown, has a clearer relevance to participatory behaviour than the great national agenda. For purposes of exposition, the original thirty-eight coded issue areas have been themselves re-grouped into a number of broader categories or families as in table 11.1. The table also gives a brief indication of the kinds of issue areas within each category.

Leaving aside the very disparate collection of matters included within the 'other'

Table 11.1 *The pattern of issues*

Issue category	% of all issues mentioned	% of population mentioning issue
Environment and planning (conservation; planning permission; community centres; refuse collection; litter)	15·3	14·3
Economic (not including unemployment) (taxes; wages; inflation; industrial relations; miners' strike; pensions; welfare benefits)	15·0	13·5
Unemployment (unemployment; redundancies; factory closures)	9·6	9·7
Transport (road traffic; car parking; public transport)	9·6	8·9
Education (pre-school; primary, secondary schools; higher education)	6·4	7·3
Housing (housing repairs; availability of council housing)	6·3	7·0
Defence and foreign affairs (nuclear weapons; disarmament; foreign affairs; aid)	6·2	7·0
Law and order (crime on streets; vandalism; riots; drunken driving)	6·0	5·8
Health (National Health Service; hospital closures)	4·9	5·3
Youth (provision of facilities)	4·1	4·0
Other (charity work; ethnic issues; local churches; media; elderly)	16·6	17·2
Total	100·0	100·0

Multi-faceted issues disaggregated, with each 'facet' counted separately.

category, it can be seen that material economic problems were most frequently mentioned. Unemployment and other economic issues together constituted a little under a quarter of all issues. Unemployment, with almost 10% of all issues, was a concern expressed by just under 10% of our respondents. In this instance, much of the interest in the issue and actions taken over it, such as going on a jobs march to London, were mobilised by unions. The broader economic category raised by nearly 13·5% of the sample and providing 15% of all issues, was made up of a diverse range of matters of roughly equal interest to people. Thus, the miners' strike, the most dramatic event of the decade in industrial relations, was mentioned by around 3% of respondents, including both people who organised donations to the miners and those who opposed local government backing for the strikers. Similarly, taxes and also wages and inflation were each mentioned by just over 3% of the population.

A less materialist picture of the population might initially be gained from the fact that environment and planning matters constituted the largest category of issues and was mentioned by just over 14% of our sample. A concern for the environment was one ingredient in Inglehart's measure of post-materialism (Inglehart 1977:39–53). However, our category includes not merely the more obviously 'green' environmental issue areas, but also problems of planning permission which can have more immediate personal and material sides to them. There were, for instance, many cases of objections to the building of local supermarkets and large stores. Of course, a concern for conservation of buildings and for the green belt can conceal what is, at bottom, protection of individual advantage, whilst a planning matter can involve altruistic considerations. Similarly, a concern for the provision of leisure and sports facilities (mentioned by just under 3% of people) could be interpreted in either direction. In any event, separation of responses into material and post-materialist categories did not prove possible. Most of the issues presented inextricably combined elements of both. Nevertheless, their prominence overall provides some further indication of the widespread concern with the environment noted in chapter 9.

Transport and traffic problems accounted for 9·6% of the issues and were mentioned by just under 9% of respondents. Most of these were concerned about traffic or road safety. Perhaps surprisingly, fewer than 2% mentioned problems with public transport. One of the recurrent themes of recent British politics has been law and order, with claim and counter-claim being advanced concerning the supposed rise in crime, and violent crime in particular. Just under 6% were troubled about law and order. Only a handful of these mentioned riots and civil disturbances. It was conventional crime which received the main attention. Housing, although widely believed to be the prime issue raised by constituents when meeting their MPs and councillors in regular 'surgeries', was mentioned by only 7% of our sample and constituted just over 6% of issues – figures almost exactly paralleled in the case of education. Clearly, these surgeries give a slightly misleading impression of the overall agenda, although they may reflect the concerns of particular sectors of the public – a possibility we look at later in the chapter. Foreign affairs, and particularly defence, are, according to much conventional wisdom, the dominant issues of our age. So they were for some of our respondents, but only for a modest number. Only some 5% of those interviewed raised the issue of defence, nuclear weapons and disarmament (4% of all issues). A variety of concerns over foreign aid, several involving action in support of famine relief campaigns, relations with the Commonwealth or with Europe, made up the balance of this category.

In most of the categories, there was a set of 'other' issues (i.e. 'other transport', 'other educational', etc.) which, because of the nature of the information provided, could not be placed with any certainty into a particular issue area. However, there is little reason to think that this could have any major effect on the ranking of issue areas within any category. Additionally, there remains the largest of all issue categories – the vast range of 'other issues' which include concern for charities, the problems of ethnic minorities, the needs of the elderly. Each, however important to our respondents, constituted only a very small number and percentage of all issues, needs or problems. In total, nevertheless, they add to that remarkable diversity of issues, needs and problems important to the population.

Action

The very diversity of issues is *prima facie* likely to give rise to some differences in the level and types of action taken. Where action is undertaken for instrumental rather than expressive reasons, one can hypothesise that the decision to act will be based very much on an estimate of the importance of the action and of the likelihood of success in comparison to the costs involved in terms of effort and resistance. The importance of an issue may, in fact, be in tension with the estimation of costs and benefits. Certain major issues may not appear susceptible to individual influence, whereas matters closer to home, but of less wide significance, may promise more chance of success. Though very broad and durable issues might be thought to involve a much wider range of people, the effect may be diffuse. For any given person, the matter may not be so salient (Cobb and Elder 1983:97). It may be the immediate and pressing problem which is what incites people to act.

In order to obtain a global picture of the amount of action taken over issues, respondents were asked, after they had nominated each issue, need or problem, whether they had taken any action about the matter. It will be recalled that 65 % had mentioned an issue. Those who reported taking any action constituted 42 % of the sample. These were asked to estimate whether they had taken 'a lot' of action, 'some' action or only 'a little' action and a mean score was computed on the basis of this information. In table 11.2, these scores are reported for each of the categories or families of issues.

As table 11.2 reveals, there was no category of issue which, on this subjective assessment, came near to engendering a 'lot' of action (a score of 3). Relatively, the most intense activity centred on housing (1·73), and within that category it was housing repairs that provoked the greatest attention. Environment and planning issues stimulated a fair degree of activity (1·48), with those matters involving planning permission most prominent. The least intense levels of reported activity occurred over national and international matters. Despite the importance of such problems as unemployment and redundancies, industrial relations and strikes (including the miners' strike), only 'a little' action was apparently generated. Similarly, defence, disarmament and foreign aid in general prompted lower levels of action.

This suggests that the instrumentalist hypothesis that people on the whole take action

Table 11.2 *Issues and action*

Category of issues	Mean action*
Housing	1·73
Environment	1·48
Transport	1·38
Education	1·30
Health	1·16
Law and Order	1·14
Youth	1·13
Economic (Other than Unemployment)	0·88
Defence and Foreign Affairs	0·67
Unemployment	0·60
Other	1·18
Overall mean	1·16

* No action = 0, 'A little' action = 1, 'Some' action = 2, 'A Lot' of action = 3.

Table 11.3 *Prime issues: self-assessed scope % (N = 1,025)*

Affected	Self and family	Friends and neighbours	District	Region	Britain
Very much	45·0	28·6	25·6	23·7	31·8
Quite a bit	29·8	36·7	39·4	32·0	24·3
Not much	14·1	18·0	14·7	15·0	9·4
Not at all	11·2	16·6	20·2	29·4	34·5
Total	100·0	100·0	100·0	100·0	100·0

on those problems close to home on which they can hope to exert some influence is valid. In order to test this hypothesis about the 'scope' of action, respondents were further asked, in the course of more detailed questions, about how far their 'prime issue' – the one on which they took most action or, only if they had not acted on it, which they stated to be most important to them – affected themselves or their family, their friends and neighbours, their district, their region and Britain as a whole. As table 11.3 shows, people tended to think that such issues 'very much' affected themselves, but that they affected the concentric circles of friends, district and region rather less. The proportion which saw the issues as very much affecting Britain as a whole then rose somewhat to a little under a third. At the same time, the more particularised aspect of these prime issues is emphasised by the 34·5% who were clear that these were matters with no wider national significance whatsoever.

The various categories of issues are viewed somewhat differently and tend to confirm the impression of the relationship between scope and action. Table 11.4 shows the mean scope computed for some categories of issue. The kinds of housing matters important to our respondents are very much to the personal end of the scale. They do not appear to be seen as problems common to the country as a whole. By contrast, unemployment

Table 11.4 *Scope of some categories of prime issues*

	Self and family	Friends and neighbours	District	Region	Britain
Housing	2·30	1·47	1·09	1·06	1·10
Education	2·33	2·00	2·08	1·75	1·65
Law and Order	2·14	1·92	1·86	1·87	2·12
Transport and traffic	2·03	1·99	1·89	1·08	0·57
Environment and planning	2·13	2·02	1·83	1·21	0·93
Unemployment	2·00	1·60	1·96	2·23	2·48
Defence and foreign affairs	2·11	1·74	1·79	1·82	2·03
Mean for all categories	2·09	1·78	1·71	1·50	1·54

How much does the problem affect...? Very much = 3; Quite a bit = 2; Not very much = 1; Not at all = 0.

is the issue which is regarded very much as affecting the country as a whole, as well as the region, whilst still being of real, but on average less immediate, significance to self and family or to friends and neighbours. The categories of law and order and of defence and foreign affairs display a somewhat different pattern. Respondents perceived these as affecting quite strongly both Britain as a whole and themselves and their families. The numbers mentioning these as their paramount issue are on the small side for interpretation, but it is possible that what is being detected is a flow of sympathy between nation and family whereby defence and disarmament are seen as national matters with potential effects on the individual and his or her children.

There is, therefore, an interconnection between action, issue and scope of issues such that more personal issues tended to be cited as important and for most action to be taken on these. One should not necessarily conclude that people are moved more by self-love than altruism. One element in the communitarian theory of participation – the disposition to act for the wider public good – might appear to be weak, though not entirely absent. However, this may be related more to the difficulty of influencing broader decisions than to any lack of concern. It is simpler to handle one's immediate troubles than to attempt to take on burdens which others share and which can only be alleviated by national or even international action.

The three categories of issues over which most action was taken were all ones where people, when asked who 'ought to be responsible for tackling it', thought that local government was the appropriate agency. Thus, 78·2% of people who cited housing as their prime issue said that local government ought to be responsible, against 16·8% referring to central government. In the case of environmental and planning matters, 65·8% looked to local government and 77·5% over transport and traffic problems. By contrast, the three areas where least action had been taken – unemployment, defence and foreign affairs and wider issues of the economy – were all instances where the central government was clearly seen as carrying the main responsibility. In the case of foreign affairs and defence, the reason is obvious. Just over half of those mentioning the economy as the prime issue (53·5%) placed the onus on central government to tackle it and 44·9% in the case of unemployment. Business and industry, trades unions and local government bore some responsibility but to a far lesser degree. Although during this period of Mrs Thatcher's political dominance there was much talk of the need to restore the values of individual responsibility and initiative, this appears to have met with little response from our sample of the population when it comes to problems to do with the economy and unemployment. A mere 7·6% of those mentioning wider economic issues saw the individual citizen himself or herself as being first amongst those who should seek to tackle these kinds of problems. In the case of unemployment, only 10·1% thought this way, in sharp contrast to the attitudes found amongst the American population where the individualist ethic still prevails (Schlozman and Verba 1979:199).

The evidence suggests, therefore, that when people do step out into the public realm, it is rather more with the defence of their personal and sectional interests in mind, than those of the wider community, or at the very least the two are intertwined. Some people may find this regrettable, if not entirely surprising. It might be felt that, without a concern for the commonwealth, national institutions could be in peril. However, it has been pointed out by some commentators that people to a very large extent find their happiness within the private domain and do not, necessarily, regard government or political decisions as impinging very strongly or directly on their lives (Rose 1984:242–8). Whether or not people are correct in thinking of the activity of government as remote, this capacity to insulate oneself from the major issues of the day which governments and opinion leaders confront, can give the political authorities a great deal of latitude for action. Moreover, it can, as Schumpeter (1943) insisted, make a great deal of sense to leave the big issues of the economy and unemployment to the professional politicians. That is why they have been elected.

The 'mix' of persons, issues and actions

Having reviewed agendas and levels of action in general, we turn now to the crucial question of how different types of political activists, or participants, look at issues and take action on them. Here the two approaches to understanding participation are brought together – the study of 'background' factors and the examination of the immediate context of the issues which led to action. Do some types of participants have longer agendas than others? Do they have different agendas? Above all, do some take more action about the problems of concern to them than others? It is in answering such questions that we begin to see how the various parts of the national agenda may come to receive different levels of attention. Ultimately this can have significant consequences for the functioning of democracy.

In order to examine these possibilities, we first of all utilised the classification of individuals, introduced in chapter 10, into complete activists, party campaign activists, collective activists, contacting activists, direct activists, just voters and the almost inactive. Using these categories, we looked first at the question of the length of their agendas, and, in order that all would be considered on the same basis, again considered only the unprompted responses which, it may be recalled, could be up to four.

Overall, and including the 44·3% who offered no unprompted issue, the respondents provided just over one issue each (1·20). This is, therefore, the baseline or norm against which can be set the different types of participants. The typology of activists generated very considerable variations. Thus, the 'complete activists', who only number 24, generated nearly two and a half issues each (2·44). This is some four times the average agenda of the 'almost inactives' at the other end of the scale (0·67 issues). The remaining categories are all located between these extremes. At the bottom (0·87) are the large number who just voted (805) but were otherwise relatively inactive. Indeed, the rank order of length of agenda generally matches that of overall participation levels. Thus, the second most active specialists (the party campaigners) have the third longest agenda (1·87), closely following the 'collective activists' (1·96) who are also quite active. The middle of the order, in both instances, is occupied by the 'direct activists' (1·66 issues on average) and the 'contacting activists' (1·50). In short, those individuals who are most involved in politics are simultaneously those who have the largest number of concerns. Conversely, the most inert are those with the lowest apparent problems or needs – that they can articulate to an interviewer at least. In fact, 57·5% of the inert group failed to suggest any issue. That there should be such a correspondence is, perhaps, not too surprising; after all, the two should be interlinked. At the same time, it begins to flesh out what being 'generally active' or 'inactive' means. It indicates that the inert are not those with long agendas who fail to find their voice but rather those, by and large, who have not, for a variety of possible reasons, a lot that, in political terms, they wish to say.

Overall, the amount of action taken – as assessed by the respondents – in pursuit of these agendas is, as has been seen, relatively small. The aggregate pattern can be seen in figure 11.1 which summarises the matter in a single scale which runs from zero (indicating no action at all) to 12 (which would imply a 'lot' of action on a full set of four issues). Two-thirds of the adult population are on the bottom rung of the ladder. Half of them have no issues on which to take action and the other half have issues, but declare that they did not press them in any way. In that sense, the 'visible' agenda, that which was acted upon even to the minimal extent of a 'little' on one issue, is the agenda of only one-third of the nation. As we can also see, however, even amongst the latter, the bulk did only take one small step, or perhaps two or three small steps, up the ladder of action. A mere handful, roughly 5% or less, by their own admission (and criteria) did bother to give substantial voice to their concerns. Not one of these, however, score a 'maximum' by doing 'a lot' on all four, though one was nearly in this position!

The average score was a mere 1·04 – just a single step. Our complete activists, however, managed some four times as much (4·41). Equally, the moderately active party campaigners score 2·63, collective activists 2·38, direct activists 2·04, and contacting activists 2·02. Once again, it is the relatively inert 'just voters' and 'almost inactives' who bring up the rear (0·69 and 0·51). In part, of course, such differences merely reflect the variation in the number of issues each person raises. With fewer issues, there is, naturally, a weaker basis for action than where one has many issues. However, this does not tell the full story. If one looks at the amount of action taken on each issue in turn, the differences persist. Thus, the 'complete activists' claim to have taken on average more action on each issue than do others. So not only do the more active types of participants pursue a wider range of issues, they also appear to follow up each of their interests with greater zeal.

As can be seen from figure 11.2, the quarter of the population which is most active is

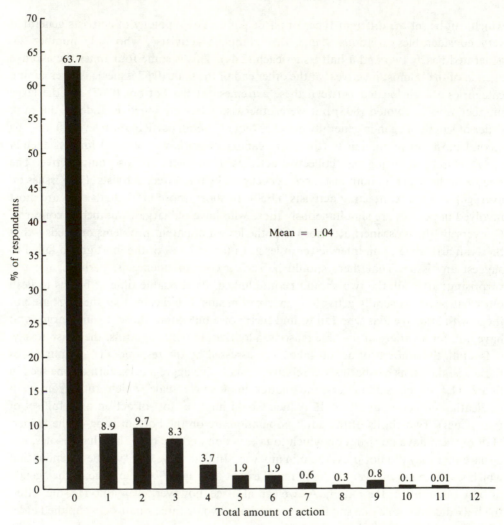

Figure 11.1 Overall amount of action taken on unprompted issue agenda

the source of 40 % of all the unprompted issues. In one sense, of course, the national issue agenda is dominated numerically by that large block of people who take virtually no further part in political life than to vote. They raised nearly 43 % of the unprompted issues, but they did make up 51 % of our sample. A more striking feature perhaps is that the 8·7 % of the collective activists (many of whom are also involved in petitioning and in attending protest meetings) mentioned as many issues as that quarter of the population which was inactive to the point of not even voting regularly.

In these ways, the more active segment of the population makes a much larger impact on the national issue agenda than their numbers would suggest. To the degree that elites form their own agendas by listening to the views of the population as to their issues, needs and problems, they will be hearing the voices disproportionately of the active minority. Since, as we shall see in chapter 12, over 70 % of those involved in the 'conventional' modes of participation said, in response to a further question, that they felt that they had 'got their message across', there is some reason to think that the active

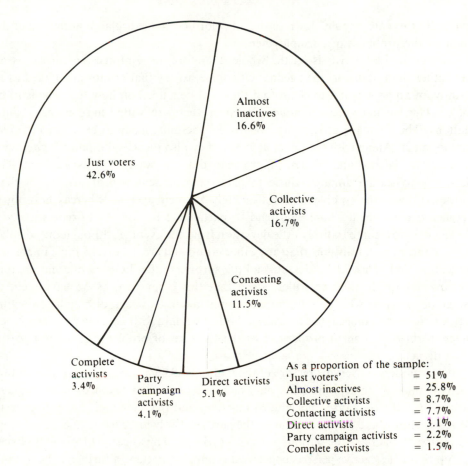

As a proportion of the sample:
'Just voters'	= 51%
Almost inactives	= 25.8%
Collective activists	= 8.7%
Contacting activists	= 7.7%
Direct activists	= 3.1%
Party campaign activists	= 2.2%
Complete activists	= 1.5%

Figure 11.2 Proportion of unprompted issues raised by types of participants

do have some effect on the overall agenda. However, as we have argued earlier, much participation is in reaction to issues raised by political leaders and groups. There is not, therefore, only a one-way process in which citizen action influences elite agendas, but also a process by which elites shape the agendas and actions of the citizen.

The priorities of the participants

As well as contributing disproportionately to the total agenda, it is also possible that the most active sector of the population might have a different set of priorities to that of the rest. The effect would be to push their concerns into the limelight, leaving the problems of the less active in relative shadow.

Table 11.5 shows the categories of issues raised by each of our clusters of participants. This suggests that there is a substantial consensus across the population as to the first two categories of issue. Leaving aside the residual 'other' category, in every case environmental and planning issues were either in first or second place in the frequency with which they were mentioned. The main challenger for the league leadership was the broad category of economic matters apart from unemployment. Only for the complete activists did this category slip down the list of priorities, to be displaced at the top of the agenda by the problems of unemployment.

The effect of the activists is on the whole, therefore, to reinforce the consensus on issues rather than to distort the agenda. Of course, to say that groups are agreed as to the status of an issue is not to claim that they will be agreed on how the issue is to be resolved. This has to be borne in mind. Moreover, there are, within the consensus, some variations. The complete activists are, relatively, the most likely to be concerned over unemployment. Along with the direct activists, they also displayed a much higher level of interest in defence and foreign affairs than did the population as a whole. The collective activists are amongst those to place environment well at the top of their priorities. Educational problems are also high on their agenda, whereas housing is infrequently mentioned. Those who tend to participate by contacting representatives and officials, show comparatively little deviation from the average, although they display a higher concern with transport than any other group and are, relatively, quite interested in education and in law and order. It is a little surprising that housing does not feature more prominently in their priorities, given that this is an area, as we have seen, of personal concern, on which rather more action is taken. However, although contacting local government is, indeed, the typical method of dealing with housing problems, such contacts form only a small proportion of the total set of problems of interest to the contacting activists.

A somewhat less consensual picture of the issue agenda emerges, however, if attention is focused on only that prime issue on which most action is taken or most concern expressed. Firstly, of course, the 'almost inactive' and the just voters have taken very little action. But where they have done so they are relatively more likely to act over more material issues than are the various ranks of activists. Thus nearly 14% of the issues taken up by the less active persons concerned economic matters, a further 10% were to do with unemployment and nearly 11% with housing. By comparison, amongst the issues taken up by the activists just under 10% were economic, and some 7% involved each of unemployment and housing. On the other side, the less immediately economic issues of environment and education were of greater concern to the activists than to the less active.

It would be wrong to over-emphasise the contrast. Nevertheless, if elites were to form their opinions of the national agenda on the basis of the active pressures placed upon them, they could be misled as to the prominence of the 'quality of life' issues which are dear to the hearts of the more affluent activists but which are of somewhat less concern to the almost silent majority (see further Parry and Moyser 1991).

Issue publics

In the previous section, we looked at the propensity of our various clusters of activists (as well as of the inactive) to mention certain issues rather than others. In this section, we turn our attention to what we term 'issue publics' – the extent to which certain issues tend to be mentioned by various social and economic groupings. We are seeking to discover how far, for example, an issue, such as housing, is raised more by manual workers than by salaried professional people or by women rather than by men. Looked

Table 11.5 *Categories of unprompted issues mentioned by types of participants* (%)

Categories	Almost inactives	Just voters	Collective activists	Contacting activists	Direct activists	Party Camp. activists	Complete activists	Total
Environment and planning	15·1	12·8	18·5	13·5	21·4	19·4	15·0	14·9
Economic (not including unemployment	15·8	16·1	11·0	12·5	14·2	22·3	10·0	14·7
Unemployment	9·6	10·0	6·8	6·0	3·6	7·5	18·3	8·8
Transport	8·2	9·5	6·2	13·5	9·5	6·0	11·6	9·1
Education	6·8	4·9	9·9	8·0	2·4	10·4	8·3	6·6
Housing	8·9	7·6	3·1	6·0	5·9	4·5	6·6	6·6
Defence and foreign affairs	9·6	5·3	7·2	5·5	11·9	3·0	11·6	6·8
Law and order	6·8	5·1	4·8	7·5	9·5	4·5	3·3	5·7
Health	3·1	6·0	7·2	4·0	3·6	1·5	1·6	5·0
Youth	3·4	4·3	4·1	3·5	3·6	1·5	—	3·7
Other	12·4	18·3	21·2	20·1	14·2	19·4	13·3	17·6
Total	100·0	100·0	100·0	100·0	100·0	100·0	100·0	100·0
N issues	291	749	292	199	84	67	60	1,742

at in purely instrumental terms, issues are not regarded as of equal importance by all sectors of the population. Some issues might, at the extreme, even turn out to be monopolised by particular minorities. Hence, the relative prominence of an issue on the agenda of the country as a whole may either be because it is of widespread concern to the generality of the public, or because of the intense interest shown by only a few groups of people, some of whom may be especially skilled at bringing the matter to the attention of the political authorities.

In order to establish whether the 'public' for a given issue was broadly or more narrowly based, we examined a range of social, political and demographic variables which appeared likely to influence the readiness to mention an issue. There are two ways of looking at the composition of these issue publics. One can ask what proportion of those who mention a particular family of issues is drawn from a given sector of the community. Thus, we shall refer to the percentage of housing matters which are raised by women or by supporters of the Labour Party. The alternative way of considering issue publics is to examine how far certain groups in the population are more likely than others to raise a type of problem. Hence, we ask how far the highly educated or the wealthy are more prone than other groups to mention education as an issue. Here our method was similar to that followed in the earlier chapters on participation, in that it aims to show how far a particular sector of society deviated from the mean for the population as a whole in its tendency to mention one category or family of problems. This is reinforced by a measure of 'over-' and 'under-representation' which indicates how far a particular category of the population is more or less present in the issue public compared with the proportion of that social category as a whole. Thus, if housing is mentioned by 8 % of the population but by only 6 % of males, then men are under-represented in the housing issue public by 25 %.[1]

Such deviations from the mean are seldom dramatic and probably could not be expected to be, at least in a society which is not so deeply divided socially, ethnically or religiously that whole sectors of society have totally divergent attitudes and priorities. It has already been seen from table 11.1 that a wide range of issues was mentioned by our respondents, with even the most frequently cited, environment and planning, providing only 15·3 % of the total issues, and raised by a similar proportion of the total population. Hence, housing, though a highly important concern in most people's lives and very much the routine case-load of the surgeries run by councillors and Members of Parliament, gained only some 6 % of mentions. Looking at it from the standpoint of the participants, around 7 % mentioned housing, which implies, of course, that 93 % did not. Statistically, this means that the social, economic and demographic variables here have rather poor predictive power. For this reason, the patterns have to be interpreted with a particular degree of caution. Nevertheless, making due allowances for these factors, certain features of the public for some of the issue families are well worth noting.

We have concentrated on four of the issue families – environment and planning as the largest and most widely cited category, unemployment, which was the leading single issue area in the economic field, and housing and education as tending to raise problems with local and national dimensions but which might, on the surface, be expected to affect rather different sets of people. Again we look at those issues, up to a maximum of four, which people mentioned first. Since we are interested in the likelihood of certain sectors of the population appearing in the issue publics, the baseline can be the total sample, regardless of the fact that many raised no issue whatsoever. The failure of some people to raise issues at all, clearly affects the composition of the issue public. The variables considered are age, gender, race, education, class, wealth, private and public sector of employment, public rather than private consumption patterns, whether people are employed or unemployed and political party leaning.

Environment and planning issues tended to be closer to the top of the agenda for more categories of people than any other matters. They were mentioned amongst the four leading issues by 14·3 % of respondents. Such issues, it will be recalled, cover a wide range of matters from pollution to complaints about town development. As a result, the 'issue public' for environment and planning appears to be a fairly broad reflection of the population. Relatively few groups appear to stand out as having any clearly stronger tendency to raise this type of issue and none of the associations are particularly strong. Such patterns as do emerge (see table 11.6) appear to suggest that environment and planning matters are more likely to be raised by the salaried professional and the petty bourgeoisie in class terms and also by those in the top quarter of the population measured by their wealth. Indeed, the salariat and the petty bourgeoisie are responsible between them for over half, and the wealthiest quarter for 40 %, of the references to this set of issues. The very richest 5 % with, no doubt, the most to conserve are especially prominent. Since 27·3 % mentioned environment or planning, this means that the very rich are 13 percentage points more likely than the average person to mention this type

Table 11.6 *Aspects of the composition of the environment and planning issue public*

(Proportion of population mentioning environment and planning = 14·3%)

	Unadjusted deviation	% Mentions	Adjusted deviation*	% Mentions	N
Class					
Salariat	+9	23·3	+5	19·3	247
Routine nonmanual	−2	16·3	−2	12·3	194
Petty bourgeoisie	+5	19·3	+6	20·3	96
Foreman and technicians	−7	7·3	−8	6·3	63
Working class	−5	9·3	−3	11·3	385
Eta/beta	0·16		0·11		
Wealth					
Poorest 24%	−11	3·3	−7	7·3	172
Next poorest 18%	−2	12·3	0	14·3	195
Above average 33%	−1	13·3	0	14·3	344
Second richest 20%	+8	22·3	+5	19·3	214
Richest 5%	+13	27·3	+9	23·3	57
Eta/beta	0·19		0·13		

* Controlling for other background factors.

of issue. This propensity of the wealthiest in the society to be concerned with environment and planning remains, if at a slightly reduced level (23·3% or 9 percentage points above the mean for the population in general) even when all the other factors are taken into account. Thus their over-representation in the issue public is 62·9%. The poorest quarter of the population are under-represented by 48·9% and are 7 percentage points less likely than average to mention these types of issue.

Another way of looking at such issue publics is to put together those who are most concerned about the issue and those apparently least likely to be interested. In the case of environment and planning (as can be seen from table 11.7 by way of illustration), the most prominent are the wealthiest 5%, the elderly and the petty bourgeoisie. Least prominent are the second poorest fifth of the population, the manual workers and the very young who, together, form almost a mirror image of the most interested parties. However, whilst some social groups are well represented amongst those concerned about environmental and planning problems, the general picture is that these are matters likely to impinge on a wide spectrum of the population. Indeed, it is certainly possible that much of the concern shown, and the participation which ensued, was reaction to planning proposals or environmental threats. The breadth of subjects covered by the family of issues is enough to ensure that there are few categories of people who will be totally unaffected by these kinds of developments. Moreover, such proposals and threats are often sufficiently close to the homes and livelihoods of people as to generate action almost, if not quite, regardless of their social, economic and political resources.

Unemployment, in contrast to environmental and planning issues, is a problem which is likely to strike certain sectors of the population more strongly and more frequently than others. This remains true even when, as at the time of the survey, unemployment

Table 11.7 *Most and least prominent members of environment and planning issue public*

(Mean level of concern = 14.3%)

	Adjusted %*
Most prominent	
Richest 5%	23·3
Elderly, aged 65 and over	21·3
Petty bourgeoisie	20·3
Least prominent	
Second poorest 19%	4·3
Manual workers	6·3
Aged 18–25	9·3

* Controlling for other background factors.

was at record post-war levels and was, in consequence, affecting a broader spectrum of people than is normal. However, unemployment affects many more people in an indirect way, whether because it touches on their own economic life-chances or because they feel a social concern for the problems of those out of work. At the time of the survey, unemployment was a dominant political issue and the subject of national debate. Attention was mobilised by opposition leaders and the political media. In the 1983 General Election, it had been the issue which had been most stressed in election addresses (Butler and Kavanagh 1984:259). Accordingly, the opinion polls tended to show it at the top of the nation's agenda.

It was mentioned as an issue by 9·7% of our sample. As such, it was a leading topic. The surprise may be that it was not more prominent. One would have anticipated that those most likely to feature in this issue public would be the working class and the least well off. Yet, as table 11.8 shows, this is only partly borne out and the effect of class, as measured by the eta and beta scores, is very weak. It is true that working class people are more prone to refer to unemployment (being the source of over 40% of all references to it) but a deviation of 3 percentage points is not marked. Their over-representation is of the order of 30%. The poorest sectors of the population are, however, actually less likely to raise the issue than the average (not shown in the table). The young and the black population are also disproportionately victims of unemployment yet, when the other background factors are taken into consideration, the 18–25 year old group does not differ from the average, and non-whites (a very small number in the sample) are less likely to raise the matter (these figures are not in the table).

Perhaps the most striking feature is the tendency of those with the highest educational qualifications to raise the unemployment issue. It has already been seen in chapter 4 that higher education tends to go with greater wealth and, presumably, for all the talk at the time of graduate unemployment, greater qualifications generally promote job opportunities. Thus, at least part of this concern must reflect some wider feelings about the predicament of the unemployed. Those with college and further education qualifications are four percentage points more likely than average to mention unemployment. In the case of graduates, the deviation is as much as fourteen points. When other background

Table 11.8 *Aspects of the composition of the unemployment issue public*

(Proportion of population mentioning unemployment = 9.7%)

	Unadjusted deviation	% mentions	Adjusted deviation*	% mentions	N
Class					
Salariat	0	9·7	−3	6·7	247
Routine nonmanual	0	9·7	0	9·7	194
Petty bourgeoisie	−4	5·7	−2	7·7	96
Foremen and technicians	−7	2·7	−3	6·7	63
Working class	+2	11·7	+3	12·7	385
Eta/beta	0·09		0·08		
Educational qualifications					
None	−2	7·7	−5	4·7	402
Less than O level	−2	7·7	−2	7·7	139
O level and equivalent	0	9·7	+1	10·7	193
A level and equivalent	−3	6·7	0	9·7	78
College and further education	+4	13·7	+8	17·7	107
Degree	+13	22·7	+20	29·7	66
Eta/beta	0·13		0·22		
Employment					
In paid work	0	9·7	−1	8·7	638
Unemployed	+17	26·7	+19	28·7	70
Not economically active	−5	4·7	−3	6·7	278
Eta/beta	0·17		0·17		
Political party identification					
Conservative	−4	5·7	−5	4·7	390
Labour	+6	15·7	+7	16·7	301
Liberal/SDP	−1	8·7	−1	8·7	181
Other	+3	12·7	+1	10·7	32
None	−4	5·7	−3	6·7	88
Eta/beta	0·15		0·17		

* Controlling for other background factors.

factors are considered, the effect actually increases in both cases, with almost 30% of graduates raising the issue. Their over-representation is by a massive 206%.

The graduates thus show themselves to be as concerned with unemployment as are the unemployed themselves and each group generates around 14% of the references to unemployment. The quite natural tendency of those without jobs to raise the issue can be recognised by the fact that getting on for 30% mention it, or 19 percentage points more than the mean for the general population when all other confounding factors are removed. They are over-represented in this issue public by 195·9%. Possibly the only surprise is that they are not more involved with the issue, since this figure does imply that as many as 70% of unemployed do *not* mention it, even when asked to list up to four problems facing them. It may possibly be that the perception of unemployment as a national issue beyond the capacity of the ordinary individual to affect in any direct way may have inhibited some persons from even placing the issue on their agenda, but this can only be speculation. Certainly, many of our sample of unemployed mentioned no issue whatsoever and hence placed themselves outside any issue public.

In political terms, the Labour Party confirms its claims to be the party with the unemployed closest to its heart. Not far short of half (46·3%) of references to unemployment were attributable to Labour supporters. Labour partisans identify themselves as alone amongst supporters of the main parties in being more inclined than average to list unemployment on their agenda. When the other background factors are removed, they are 7 percentage points more likely to refer to the problem of jobs. Compared with their membership of the population, they are over-represented by 72%. Conservative supporters comprise 40% of respondents but are the source of only a quarter of the unemployment issues. Thus, they display relatively less concern than the average with fewer than 5% mentioning it (and are under-represented by almost 62%), whilst the various shades of those at that time allied in the Liberal and Social Democratic Parties also appear fractionally below the mean. Overall, therefore, those most involved with unemployment are the unemployed themselves, those with university or polytechnic degrees or with some other form of higher educational qualification and Labour supporters. Least likely to mention jobs as an issue are Conservatives and those with no educational qualifications.

Housing issues are very much the 'bread and butter' of the surgeries run by councillors and Members of Parliament in their wards and constituencies (Munroe 1977; Barker and Rush 1970; Searing 1985). However, taken overall, housing was mentioned by only 7% of our respondents. Clearly, it is not as widespread a concern as environment and planning. Although everybody must be housed, only a certain proportion of people have housing problems which require attention by governmental authorities and which may respond to 'political' action in a broad sense of the term. The spread of private housing in Britain means that a broad sweep of housing matters, whether to do with the acquisition of housing or its upkeep, is handled by the market.

It is, therefore, to be expected that the issue would, in relative terms, attract the attention of the less well-off sectors of the community who tend to be more dependent on the public sector for housing provision. This turns out to be the case, although the patterns are not always very pronounced. The working class, comprising just over a third of the sample, provided a little over half (52·2%) of the housing issues. Moreover, the working class is the only class which is relatively more likely to raise the issue than the average, but the 3 point difference is not marked. Over-representation is close to 43%. The least concerned are the petty bourgeoisie, who would tend to be well-integrated into the private sector. The overall association with class is, however, not statistically very strong. Again, if we turn to wealth, it is, as table 11.9 shows, the poorer groups who mention housing more readily. The poorest quarter mention almost 40% of housing issues. Those above the average in wealth are correspondingly less likely to include housing on their list of issues. Half of the housing issues are raised by those who typically are consumers of public rather than private sector services, including being council tenants. The 11% of the sample who are the highest consumers of public services on the public-private consumption scale are, once other background factors are taken

Table 11.9 *Aspects of the composition of the housing issue public*

(Proportion of population mentioning housing = 7·0%)

	Unadjusted deviation	% mentions	Adjusted deviation*	% mentions	N
Wealth					
Poorest 24%	+2	9·0	+3	10·0	172
Next poorest 18%	+4	11·0	+6	13·0	195
Above average 33%	−4	3·0	−4	3·0	344
Second richest 20%	−2	5·0	−1	6·0	214
Richest 5%	−4	3·0	−3	4·0	57
Eta/beta	0·15		0·15		
Gender					
Male	−2	5·0	−2	5·0	488
Female	+2	9·0	+2	9·0	498
Eta/beta	0·06		0·08		

* Controlling for other background factors.

into account, twice as likely to raise housing issues than the average person. However, even though there is a moderate association between consumption patterns and raising housing issues (beta = 0·13), it is far from linear along the scale. Nevertheless, the fact that council tenants are, in particular, likely to put housing at the top of their agenda (as their prime issue) indicates that being in the public housing sphere propels the problems of accommodation to the forefront.

The other striking feature of the housing issue public is the relative interest shown by women. They were twice as likely as men to regard housing as their prime issue. Women, comprising 57·5% of those answering the relevant questions, were responsible for 65·2% of the references to housing issues. There is a temptation to read a great deal into this. One might, for example, advance the argument that for many women – though for fewer than at any earlier time – the horizons are set by home life and that such women are likely to be more conscious of the problems of the house and the need for action about them. The personal realm would thus become political. However, tempting as such thoughts may be, the difference, which remains unaffected when all other factors are taken into account, is slight (only 2 percentage points higher than the average) and the strength of the association with gender weak. It may be that women are more likely to concern themselves with housing than men, yet the findings still imply that 90% of women do *not* cite housing as a problem.

The general configuration of the housing issue public is, therefore, one in which the most prominent are the poor and the working class. By contrast, the petty bourgeoisie are virtually absent and the wealthy and better educated are less likely to become involved.

A somewhat similar gender pattern occurs in the case of education, which is mentioned by 7·3% of respondents and where there is a mild difference between the interests of women and men. Women are, as can be seen from table 11.10, more likely to refer to educational matters and, whilst the adjusted figure is not dramatic (3 percentage points above the mean), the association of gender with education is statistically significant, if very moderate in strength (beta = 0·10). Over twice as many women as men placed education at the very top of their agenda and they provide more than two-thirds of all educational issues. Their over-representation in the issue public is 41·1%. It would appear that women adopting, whether by choice or custom, a position of domestic responsibility, have developed a special concern with schooling which results in the prominence of their representation in the education issue public.

Educational matters were more likely to be mentioned by the better-off sectors of society and by those in the salaried and professional class. Approaching half of the references to education (46·7%) came from the salariat (28·2% of our respondents) and 42·4% arose from the richest quarter. However, once we take into account the range of background factors, any association between either wealth or class and education is wiped out. Moreover, the wealthier sectors now appear hardly more likely than any other group to raise an educational issue. The salaried class retain an edge over other classes but it is very slight. Given this general social pattern, it is perhaps not surprising that Conservative Party supporters generated 41% of the education issues but their involvement in the issue public is in line with their proportion in the sample.

The most striking feature of the education issue public is the concern of the better educated themselves. Whilst the strength of the association between educational qualifications and references to education is reduced when other background factors are removed, it remains at a moderately significant level (beta = 0·14). The basic pattern also persists whereby the higher the educational qualifications attained, the more prone one is to raise some aspect of education. Those with college or degree qualifications are twice as likely as the average member of the public to refer to the topic (15·3%). Whilst constituting 20·9% of respondents, those who had received higher education offered 42·3% of the education issues. Hence, although education affects in one way or another a very large sector of the population, the voice that authorities are especially likely to hear is that of the well-educated who have gained long experience of the system and can, presumably, reflect on the extent of such benefits as they may have received and may wish to pass on to others.

Conclusions

In this chapter, we have been examining participation within the context of the issues, needs and problems which give rise to action. This provides an alternative perspective both on what prompts participation and on the social and political patterns of participation.

To a very large extent, it would appear that participation occurs as a response to some event or action which has an immediate consequence for a person's own life. The kinds of issues which people mention as important to them and about which they are most ready to take action tend to be those which are closest to home. Accordingly, the kinds of issues which the investigation has revealed as of major concern to the average Briton do not necessarily correspond to the picture which is derived from the media. The press and television tend to focus on the issues of 'high politics' – the national and

Table 11.10 *Aspects of the composition of the education issue public*

(Proportion of population mentioning education = 7·3%)

	Unadjusted deviation	% mentions	Adjusted deviation*	% mentions	N
Gender					
Male	−3	4·3	−3	4·3	488
Female	+3	10·3	+3	10·3	498
Eta/beta	0·09		0·10		
Class					
Salariat	+6	13·3	+2	9·3	251
Routine nonmanual	+2	9·3	0	7·3	194
Petty bourgeoisie	−4	3·3	−2	5·3	96
Foremen and technicians	−6	1·3	−5	2·3	63
Working class	−3	4·3	0	7·3	385
Eta/beta	0·15		0·07		
Wealth					
Poorest 24%	−6	1·3	0	7·3	172
Next poorest 18%	−2	5·3	+1	8·3	198
Above average 33%	+1	8·3	0	7·3	347
Second richest 20%	+4	11·3	0	7·3	216
Richest 5%	+4	11·3	+1	8·3	57
Eta/beta	0·13		0·02		
Educational qualifications					
None	−3	4·3	−2	5·3	402
Less than O level	−3	4·3	−2	5·3	139
O level and equivalent	−2	5·3	−2	5·3	193
A level and equivalent	+1	8·3	+1	8·3	78
College and further education	+11	18·3	+8	15·3	107
Degree	+11	18·3	+8	15·3	66
Eta/beta	0·20		0·14		

* Controlling for other background factors.

international economy or foreign affairs and defence. But for the ordinary man or woman in the street, the predominantly local issues of the environment and planning head the list. Whilst problems of unemployment and the economy or foreign affairs do concern them, these do not generate high levels of action. Instead, it might appear that such matters are delegated to the professionals – the party politicians.

In terms of a calculation of the effectiveness of individual action, this may make a good deal of sense. People may well anticipate exerting more influence over more local matters and they can generate a greater sense of urgency where, for example, a planning matter threatens to affect their home or livelihood. In this way, the agenda of issues brought to light by the survey may be said to hint at the mundane, but nonetheless individually significant, patterns of problems which face the average British citizen away from the spotlight which surrounds the issues of 'high politics'. Thus, a very considerable proportion of the issues, needs and problems which face people across the nation are local in character and where they lead to action this is conducted within the confines of the local community. Where a governmental agency is involved in the matter, it is local rather than national government which very often carries the responsibility. For all past talk of the nationalisation of politics, or indeed the international interdependency of policies, it is important to recall how much of life is pursued at a local level and how comparatively rare it is for the individual citizen to cross the threshold of his or her local community in the course of political action.

A further aim of the chapter has been to examine how far the structure of the issue agenda reflects the broad range of concerns of the population or is, instead, shaped by the interests of certain sectors of society and, hence, 'distorted' or 'biased'. In the event, whilst it was the case that the most active persons in the community were also those who were responsible for raising a high proportion of the issues, the types of issue with which they were most concerned did not differ fundamentally from those of the less active part of the population. Although the intensity of participation varies across the different modes of participation, the overall pattern of what concerns people does not change markedly.

When we turned to look at the composition of issue publics – the profile of those who raised a particular issue – a less uniform picture emerged. In earlier chapters it was seen that, to varying degrees, those in the salariat class, those in the upper ranges of wealth and especially those with higher educational qualifications, tended to be amongst the most active participants. From this, one might have anticipated that these several sectors of the population could have dominated the range of issue publics. The issue agenda across the nation might have been the agenda of these advantaged groups.

The evidence does not entirely support this. Table 11.11 presents some of the patterns of over- and under-representation of various social categories within four out of the six major issue publics. These patterns, along with the evidence contained within previous tables, suggest a more pluralist picture of these publics. It is true that there are issues with which the better-resourced people in society – the wealthy, the salariat, the better educated – are concerned and other issues in which many of them show little interest. This would imply that there are types of issue which are likely to be pushed into the foreground by interested parties who possess considerable skill and influence. The most striking instance is environment and planning, which is, indeed, the top issue across the nation. This is a sphere in which the rich, the salariat and the petty bourgeoisie, along with the highly educated, are over-represented and where the poor are disproportionately absent. It is not that the poor are unaffected by the built environment or by planning developments. Very far from it. But many of these issues affect the interests of those with something to conserve. Private and public interest are highly intertwined. The well-educated, well-organised salariat may display genuine concern for the overall environment but it is a concern which can be especially acute when it is their particular environment which is under threat. 'Not In My Back Yard' is so much the underlying viewpoint of a great deal of single-issue reactive participation that it has even led to the journalistic invention of the term NIMBY to describe such a participant (*Sunday Times*, 8 January 1989:A10).

On the other side, housing is an issue relatively neglected by the wealthy and the petty

Table 11.11 *Over- and under-representation of selected social categories in issue publics* (%)

1. Environment and planning		2. Unemployment	
Over-represented		*Over-represented*	
Richest 5%	+62·9	Degree holders	+200·0
Salariat	+35·0	Unemployed	+195·9
Petty bourgeoisie and farmers	+42·0	Labour identifiers	+72·2
Degree holders	+27·9	Working class	+30·9
Under-represented		*Under-represented*	
Aged 18–25	−35·0	Conservative identifiers	−61·8
Poorest 24%	−48·9	Salariat	−30·9
3. Housing		4. Education	
Over-represented		*Over-represented*	
Poorest 24%	+42·8	Degree holders	+109·5
Working class	+42·8	Women	+41·1
High public consumption	+100·0	Salariat	+27·4
Women	+19·6		
Under-represented		*Under-represented*	
Richest 5%	−42·8	No qualifications	−27·4
Petty bourgeoisie	−85·7	Foremen and technicians	−68·5

bourgeoisie. It is the province of the poor, of those who are intensive consumers of public services and of the working class. Compared with environment and planning, there were only half the mentions of housing as an issue. This could be interpreted as the result of the individually better-resourced in society being able to press more effectively than the less-resourced to put their interests at the top of the agenda, whereas housing is half-way down. At the same time, housing is an issue on which more action is typically taken (see table 11.2 above) and of which local councillors are highly aware. It would not be correct, as will be shown in later chapters on local participation, to conclude that housing is neglected but it is an issue which lacks the participatory weight that might be given it by better-resourced individuals.

The composition of the unemployment issue public is different and in certain respects counter to what one might have anticipated. The over-representation of the unemployed and the working class would be readily predicted. But the poorest sector of the population, who are more usually victims of unemployment, are under-represented. On the other side, degree holders are heavily over-represented, even when potentially confounding factors are taken into account. Moreover, despite this not being a problem which individually and immediately engages the self-interest of the best-resourced and most participatory individuals, the condition of the jobless ranks third on the national agenda.

Finally, education is an issue which concerns one particular type of well-resourced individual – those who are already well-educated in the sense of having been through tertiary education. Although there is an association between such education and class and wealth, once all the contributing factors are controlled for, class and wealth count for almost nothing. The combination of forces that put environment at the head of the agenda is not the same as that which raised education to fifth place. If, however, one were tempted to seek one group in British society which did most, proportionately, to shape the agenda, it would be university and polytechnic graduates. In three out of four of the issue publics selected, they are over-represented. This is not to say, of course, that they out-number other groups. Notoriously, in Britain, graduates form only a small proportion of the population (7% of our sample). They do, however, out-participate many other elements in the population and constitute a significant part of the 'talking' classes who raise awareness of issues.

A plural interpretation of the mix of issues, people and participation appears appropriate. The bias to this pluralism (Connolly 1969) is not negligible but is also not consistent across all issues. An instrumentalist perspective suggests that people concentrate on those types of issues in which their personal interests are most at stake. Within each issue public it would seem that the most prominent group are indeed those with most at stake. In this restricted sense of the term, most participants appear to be 'rational actors'. Whether their involvement is also instrumentally effective is the topic of the next chapter.

12

DO PARTICIPANTS GET WHAT THEY WANT? THE COSTS AND BENEFITS OF PARTICIPATION

When people engage in some public activity such as writing to their Member of Parliament or going on a protest march, it might be presumed that they have some specific end in view. They want to get some policy changed or, more narrowly, persuade the relevant authority to attend to a problem they are facing. However, some action is less directive than this suggests. One reason people act in a public fashion may be to express in more general terms their standpoint on an issue, without any expectation that there will be any immediate and obvious benefit to themselves (see Hardin 1982:108–12). Sometimes gratification is a by-product of action which is intended to bring about a specific result (Elster 1983:97–100). As well as gaining the desired end (or even where the goal has not been achieved), a person may feel that there has been an educative effect whereby one has learned more about the political system, the aspirations of others and even about one's own priorities. There are other rewards derived from political participation which help give it a particular character, or 'charm' as Richard Crossman called it, even though they are not in themselves 'political'. For some participants in a group, a party or a demonstration, activity brings *camaraderie*, affection, a sense of service. Those who are able to occupy places of influence may also hope to gain power or even wealth from politics. The social rewards of politics are often quite significant (Chapman 1990) but we take the view that they occur within a context of participation undertaken for other more instrumental or communitarian reasons. Like the educative effect, they are a by-product rather than either a motive or a justification.

In this chapter we are concentrating on those actions which are instrumental in the sense of being described by those interviewed as directed at specific targets, whether institutions or individuals, in the hope of securing some benefit. Such 'directed' actions constitute over 80% of all those taken in connection with the issues which our respondents described as the ones in which they had been most involved.

Clearly, with such action, it is of some consequence to know whether it did achieve the results which the participants wanted. There would be little point to participation if it failed to produce benefits for those who engaged in it. Indeed, it is sometimes argued that the comparatively high levels of non-participation reflect a rational assessment by many people that participation is a waste of time. It is alleged that it is likely to fail to produce any benefits, or at the very least the costs, in terms of effort and sheer hassle involved, threaten to outweigh any possible advantage. The actual levels of satisfaction expressed by those who do participate is at least potentially relevant to future decisions about participation and to the viability of a more participatory democracy. But it is also important to find out *who* believe they benefit. Could it be that certain sectors of society not only participate more than others, as chapters 3 and 10 showed, but that amongst those who did there were groups who gained more from the process? It is also possible that certain modes of action are more likely to achieve results than others and that some types of authority tend, on the whole, to be more responsive than others. In considering the utility of a political act or evaluating the performance of the various parts of the British system of government, one consideration must be the track record of certain kinds of action and certain types of authority – local or central government, councillors or town hall administrators – in producing outcomes which people regard as, on the whole, satisfactory.

In order to examine the benefits and burdens of political action, we have made use of the full range of data on action available in the survey. Most of these actions are directed at a specific target or targets. In this respect, there was no significant difference between the various modes of participation. Actions on most types of issue were also seen in equally directed terms. In nearly every category of issue, well over 80% were directed at some known target. The only noticeable difference occurred over defence and foreign affairs, where with 74% of actions referring to some target, a quarter had raised the matter in more general and less directed terms. These included such activities as raising funds to alleviate famine in various parts of the world. In saying that their action was not directed at any specific target, such persons may well have been thinking of what they did as expressing a commitment that transcended any particular organisation and government. By and large, however, the actions were clearly focused on a person or institution believed to be in a position to tackle the problem.

The targets of action

It will already be apparent from chapter 11 that public participation is very much a localised matter. It is often a matter of contacting councillors and town halls. This is confirmed when we look at the persons or institutions at which action is directed. Table 12.1 shows that as many as 44% of all the targets of people's main action on their prime issues are to be found in local government, compared with only 15% in central government and a further 11% either in other government or quasi-governmental institutions such as health authorities or nationalised industries or where the level of government target was not entirely clear. Whatever may be said about the growing significance of the central government in people's lives, it remains the case that for the vast bulk of our respondents local government makes an apparently more immediate impact through its delivery of services which impinge on daily life. Housing, environment, transport and education are all largely local functions which together provided almost a third of all the issues cited. It is true that nearly all these are areas in which central government plays a highly significant part, such as in the determination of pay for teachers. Nevertheless, even if the population is aware of the ultimate role of central government, it is to the local authority that they turn for redress of grievances or to campaign for policy changes. From the standpoint of local government, this can sometimes seem the worst of both worlds in that it is seen as immediately responsible for

Table 12.1 *The targets of action**

	%	N
Central government (MPs, civil servants, government departments)	15·1	78
Local government (councillors, town hall, local officials)	44·2	228
Other governmental bodies (quangos, nationalised industries, other government bodies)	11·2	58
Non-governmental (business, trades unions, groups, individuals)	26·1	135
Other (including foreign governments)	3·4	18
Total	100·0	517

* Over the prime issue on which most action was taken.

the delivery of services the level of which is not fully within its financial control. On the other hand, it serves as a further reminder of the significance of local government and is, perhaps, a reflection of its traditional, if now somewhat limited, autonomy.

Some indication of people's attitudes to the proper spheres of government is provided by the fact that some of those who had directed their actions towards a particular target, nevertheless felt that responsibility for the matter ought, either wholly or in part, to belong with a different body. There were, clearly, significant questions in the minds of the respondents about the role of central government in particular. Central government was mentioned as the target of 78 of the actions on these prime issues. In just over half of these cases, it was also the body which was first mentioned as properly responsible. This implies that in just under half the cases, another institution or individual ought to be responsible – the main one being local government which was mentioned fourteen times (18%) as the alternative. In the case of local government targets, people were much clearer that they were dealing with the authority which ought properly to be tackling the issue. In only 10% of the 223 actions directed towards local government was there the feeling that the matter should fall within central government's responsibility. Generally, in those cases where they felt that their actual target was not the one ideally responsible for the issue, people were more likely to say that it should be within the local sphere, rather than be handled by central government. This belief appears still to be strong, perhaps reflecting a view that participation directed at such centres would prove to be more effective.

The effectiveness of participation

The success of participation can be estimated in several ways. Clearly, most people would, above all, hope that they would get precisely what they wanted, that their action would be effective in producing a helpful response from those at whom it was directed. A precondition for such success is that demands are actually communicated to the authorities who are to deal with them. Accordingly, the effectiveness of participation will be measured both in terms of the success with which participants felt that they had got their message across to those concerned and in terms of their estimation of the responsiveness of the authorities.

Generally, people were satisfied that, whatever the actual outcome of their actions, they had communicated their concerns effectively. Around three-quarters of those who had personally contacted representatives or officials or who were involved in group activities believed that they had succeeded in getting their message across. Protest actions were seen as slightly less effective means of communication but were generally still seen in a clearly positive light.[1] It proved about as easy to communicate with central as with local government representatives and officials and there was no sign that it was less easy to get one's message across over some issues rather than others. For those at least who had crossed that crucial threshold from inaction to action, it would seem that the problems they faced were not ones of communication.

With party campaigning, it is the candidate's message rather than the individual's which is being put across. Such activity is more incontestably political and other-directed. As has already been seen, few people engage in it. Of those who did, most simply claimed to have attempted to change the minds of family, friends or workmates about how to vote. This was apparently an enterprise which had mixed success in that only a minority (47%) of such actions were believed to have helped to put the candidate's message across 'a lot' or 'some'. The more passive aspects of campaigning, such as attending a meeting or raising funds for the party, were seen as ineffective in this respect since 60% (of a mere 69 actions in total) had not helped put a message across at all, even indirectly. The tiny numbers who cited the more active and dedicated roles of canvassing and clerical work (such as addressing envelopes) as their prime campaigning activity (a mere 49) were, by contrast, much more convinced of its success, with nearly 80% of such actions seen as having got a lot or some of the message across.

In order to examine the effectiveness of participation in producing actual outcomes, people were asked how far the targets at which action had been directed about their special issue had produced responses which were helpful, how much the targets had done and whether it was in direct response to the actions. There was also a general estimation of the success of the authority in dealing with the problem.

Setting aside the 11% of cases where the outcome was not yet apparent, just over half of those who had taken action on their major issue believed that the person or body responsible had produced a 'helpful' response. Very few had experienced an entirely unhelpful reaction but in 40% of cases it was found that the authorities had simply taken no action. Local government comes out of this assessment with rather better marks than other authorities in that 58% of actions had received 'helpful' reactions, with 36% eliciting no response that the individual interviewed could detect. The picture presented by the much smaller number of actions directed towards central government is rather less encouraging. A little over a third of these actions received 'helpful' responses whilst in over 60% of cases, the respondent felt that no attempt had been made to tackle the problem. Similarly, local government was thought to have done more about the problems than central government and it was rated by a higher proportion as dealing successfully with the problem.

It is arguable that to the extent that central government deals with problems of larger policy, fashioned by party considerations and by national and international factors, it is less surprising that individual complaints will receive fewer positive responses. The case of the student writing to the Secretary of State for Education about the inadequate level of grants would be a case in point. Another would be the person signing a petition about unemployment directed towards the Conservative Government. Moreover, where central government does act, it frequently does so in the form of general policy which can make a less immediate and visible impact than the action of a local authority repairing the pavement outside one's front door. In the long run, of course, the effect of central government may be much greater by affecting the structures within which citizens and organisations work but the operation of the effect is far more diffuse.

Many of the problems raised with local government were of a parochial nature. One individual had applied for advice about housing to the council surveyor and had, as a consequence, obtained a renovation grant; another had complained to the environmental health officer about pollution from a farm which had, as a result, been required to install equipment to control the problem; many had been in touch with their councils over litter in the streets. It was not in every case that the local authority had proved responsive without further prompting. In several cases, it appeared that it was the intervention of the local Member of Parliament which had brought a prolonged matter to a conclusion proving to one respondent that 'it is who you know that matters when you want things doing'.

The great diversity of non-governmental targets makes any assessment of their responsiveness to action difficult. Taken together, they appeared rather more prone than others to take action which was seen as positively 'unhelpful' (14%). In a little under 40% of the cases, they had been helpful and in over a third were seen to have done a great deal about the problem. In another 35% of these instances it was suggested that the persons or bodies involved had done nothing substantive about the matter. A formal noting of the complaint was not usually regarded by our respondents as an attempt to deal with the matter. Indeed, this was sometimes seen as adding insult to injury as in the case of the person who complained by letter to the director of a television programme about the use of four-letter words but who received merely an acknowledgement ignoring the contents but thanking the complainant for reading *TV Times* where he had obtained the address to which to write. Overall, the type of issue made little difference to the success of the action. One generally had rather more than an even chance of a helpful response regardless of the issue.

To assess the effectiveness of action, one must also establish if people believed that any response actually came as a result of the action, rather than because of some other factor. Where some steps had been taken by authorities, the vast majority believed that it was wholly or in part because of the respondent's own action. This was true for 90% of actions directed at local government and just over three-quarters of those dealt with by central government. One must not, however, jump to the conclusion that individual and group participation produces immediate responses. It has to be remembered that a large proportion of actions are concerned with the particular problems of individuals, such as the condition of housing or of local pavements, and that in these cases it is the individual who puts the matter on the agenda. Nevertheless it would appear that for those who did take action which produced some intervention by the targets, they could point to some return on their investment of effort.

Costs

Before the extent of this return on investment can be assessed, it is necessary to examine the extent of that investment, or the costs of participation. From the point of view of someone contemplating action, the prospect of success may be overshadowed by the expectation that it will be attended by so many drawbacks as to negate its value. People may possibly be deterred more by the costs of participation than enticed by its benefits. As a first step in considering this balance, we can look at the level of costs as experienced by those who undertook action.

There are various ways in which people might think about the costs of action. The first consideration would probably be the time and effort it involved. Some forms of action require the investment of a great deal of time whilst others, such as signing a petition about a matter on which one is in no way hesitant, occupy merely the moment needed to write one's signature. At the other extreme, forming a group to campaign about the closure of a school and taking the issue up to the highest level of government is something which, for the leaders, will clearly need a very significant commitment in terms of organisation which must be sustained over a long period. Whilst most of us know of people who appear to be able to make time for a myriad of activities, public as well as private, for many the lack of time is a deterrent to taking up issues which are clearly going to require much effort to see them through.

At the same time, it is true that there are occupations which enable people to spend time more readily on public participation. Many of the 'talking professions' such as teachers or self-employed lawyers have a certain flexibility in their hours of work which facilitates action. They may also possess intellectual and organisational resources which mean that for them the effort involved also appears less daunting.

Other actions may differ less through the combination of time and effort than because of the different kind of effort involved. Merely to sign a petition thrust in front of one on the street corner is often a reactive gesture which costs one little. To take a petition round to be signed involves initiative. The effort is not measured simply by the physical energy expended but also by the psychological resources employed in approaching others in order to enlist their support. One might thus be tempted *a priori* to divide actions into those which typically require a high degree of initiative and those which are more routine. One might speculate that for some actions more than others it is the first step across the threshold that takes the greatest effort.

More difficult to estimate are the opportunity costs involved in public participation. This is a matter of considering what people forego when they expend their time and effort in participatory activities. Complex issues are involved. It may be a case where participation in the pursuit of a matter of broad general concern conflicts with private interests. These cases generate one of the classic explanations of low rates of participation in collective endeavours. These rates arise from the certainty that the costs will fall upon the individual contrasted with the high degree of uncertainty that his or her intervention will make any perceptible difference to the general outcome (Hardin

1982). However, much participation is, as we have repeatedly seen, concerned with pursuing particular benefits (or avoiding particular evils). It is up to the individual to decide whether these are more pressing than the alternative sources of private benefit which are available. Sometimes participation is not what individuals would freely have chosen if they had not been impelled to react by the decisions of public authorities which affect them. But the calculus of costs, as of benefits, frequently has to be redrawn. For many people, no doubt, politics is 'a second-rate form of activity' (Oakeshott 1955:lxiv). However, these opportunity costs involve such problems of recollections and counter-factual suppositions as to escape the techniques of survey-based research, even if such costs should still be borne in mind when considering patterns of participation.

For many people, the possibility of conflicts with others represents a cost which they may anticipate as inevitable in public participation. Conflict is usually seen as basic to the definition of politics, but it is certainly plausible to suppose that some political activities are more conflictual than others. The readiness to be involved in conflict and argument with others in the pursuit of one's goals may reflect personal psychology. Those of an irenic disposition may be more ready to be involved in back-room work and leave to others the promotion of the cause in the 'front-line'. In party campaigning, those who address envelopes may differ from those who canvass the electors, including their political opponents, on the doorstep. In major issues, conflict could arise with established authorities overtly opposed to a policy or who try to keep the matter off the agenda.

In their study of participation in America, Verba and Nie noted these different dimensions to participation and particularly stressed the importance of conflict and of initiative (which they identified with time and effort) in helping to distinguish the various modes of participation, one from the other (Verba and Nie 1972:50–5). In doing so, they assumed that each mode had certain objective features. Thus, voting was described as a conflictual mode which set groups of citizens against one another. Group activity was thought to be on the whole non-conflictual as it typically involved the mobilisation of people in support of non-controversial demands rather than opposition between rival groups or hostility to established authorities. The activities of individuals in pursuit of more particular private benefits were also taken to involve little conflict since they did not entail competition with other citizens. There is, however, no mention of the conflict that might arise with the authorities themselves. Verba and Nie assume that these particularised contacts involve the highest level of personal initiative. The citizen, they suppose, chooses the agenda in these instances, although, as has been stressed, this is sometimes only because a problem has been created for him or her by others. At the other extreme, very little initiative or effort is considered to be required in voting. Campaigning is seen as a more difficult and effortful activity which requires some degree of individual initiative but is also supported and mobilised by parties themselves. Finally, Verba and Nie think of group activity as varying in the element of initiative, time and effort involved according to whether the individual was active in forming the group or merely joined an already existing body.

By isolating the different qualities likely to be required in the various modes of participation, Verba and Nie added strength to the argument that participation was a multidimensional activity (see also Parry 1972:5–10). Moreover, their distinctions seem plausible. They are, however, distinctions which are presumed by the researchers themselves and may not necessarily coincide with the subjective impressions of the participants. Perhaps obstacles which appear great to those outside are more easily surmounted in practice. It may even be the case that costs of participation are heavily discounted by the participants themselves. Accordingly, we have looked at the experiences of those who have acted and have concentrated on their impressions of the effort involved in participation and of the conflictual nature of the activity.

Effort

Political participation is something which requires effort. The majority of people described what they had done as having involved either 'a lot' or 'some effort' as opposed to 'very little' or 'none at all' (see table 12.2). As would be expected, the prime issue, need or problem which people had singled out as the one on which they had taken most action was, almost by definition, one which had needed a fair amount of effort. In total, 70% believed that they had put real effort into it, dividing equally between those thinking of it as 'a lot' and those describing it more modestly as 'some effort'.

When we turn to the broad range of other actions people had taken, we find that the various modes of participation display some variation, although not always that hypothesised by Verba and Nie. A fifth of contacting actions were described as having needed 'a lot' of effort and a further third need 'some'. There are no very dramatic contrasts in the experiences of those who had contacted different types of person or authority. It may be possible to detect a slight tendency for the effort to be greater when dealing with officials than with elected representatives. Thus, nearly 60% of contacts with town hall officials and 58% of those with civil servants in central government had required higher levels of effort compared with a little under 50% of such dealings with councillors and Members of Parliament. Even so, too much should not be made of what this implies about ease of access when one also notes that there is no difference when it comes to actions involving a lot of effort.

The process of contacting does not turn out to be distinguished for the large amount of effort entailed. It may be the case, as Verba and Nie supposed, that these activities require some initiative but this does not mean that they are necessarily marked by sustained effort. Satisfaction may come fairly readily if the council attends speedily to complaints about the litter in the streets or sorts out a person's housing problem promptly.

Group actions appear to need more effort than any other mode of participation. Moreover, contrary to expectations, no distinction can be made between those who got together with others to make up an informal group and those who became involved with an already organised group. Almost 70% of group actions needed at least some effort to be put into the group and very few people were prepared to describe themselves as virtual passengers who put in no effort at all. The support of other group members did not, therefore, appear to diminish the effort people felt they gave to the collective endeavour. We have seen that group membership is associated with higher than average rates of participation. It would also appear that activity within groups is more demanding. Involvement with others possibly places a moral onus on individuals to work harder for cooperative ends. There is little sign that people see themselves as

Table 12.2 *Effort involved in actions*

	A lot %	Some %	Very little/ none %	N actions
Actions over prime issue	34·8	35·2	30·0	650
Contacting actions	20·1	33·0	46·9	419
Contacted local councillors	21·1	27·2	51·7	147
Contacted town hall officials	23·4	36·3	40·3	124
Contacted MP	17·9	31·3	50·8	67
Contacted civil servant	21·1	36·6	42·3	52
Contacted media	3·5	48·3	48·2	29
Group actions	26·7	42·2	31·1	180
Supported/worked with organised group	26·3	41·0	32·7	95
Worked with others in informal group	27·0	43·6	29·4	85
Protest actions	16·1	29·9	54·0	335
Attended protest meeting	16·7	31·2	52·1	96
Taken petition round	23·7	42·4	33·9	59
Taken part in boycott	2·2	22·2	75·6	45
Gone on protest march	18·2	34·1	47·7	44
Taken part in 'political' strike	17·1	19·7	63·2	76
Blocked traffic in demonstration	13·3	33·3	53·3	15
Campaign actions	25·5	34·3	40·2	361
Canvassed	45·5	40·9	13·6	22
Attempted to change minds of others about how to vote	28·3	36·2	35·4	240
Attended party rally	4·6	18·6	76·7	43
Done clerical work for party	25·0	25·0	50·0	24
Raised funds for party	18·7	43·7	37·5	32

calculating, rational actors who can act as 'free riders' by allowing others in the group to take on the burden of pursuing collective aims (Olson 1971). But this is not to say that there were not also many non-participants who did not, as a result of such instrumental calculations, join any group action.

It is somewhat surprising to discover that protest actions do not, taken together, involve high levels of effort. One might anticipate that activities which fell somewhat outside the conventional pattern of life would involve a higher degree of initiative and a greater commitment of time and effort than those activities for which there were clearly established channels. When, however, we recall that protesting is a mode of participation which is composed of quite varied activities, it becomes apparent that these activities may require different qualities. Whilst protest meetings involve a good deal of organising by the leaders – ensuring publicity, booking a meeting place, arranging speakers – attendance may involve comparatively little effort beyond getting to the meeting and listening to the addresses. This appears to have been the case for many of our respondents since just over half of their attendances required little or no effort and less than a fifth needed a lot. Perhaps similar considerations apply to protest marches, although one would expect the initiative required to be rather greater. Boycotting goods is even more passive – an absence of action, in one way, if one disregards the effort involved in deciding to participate or in discovering whether the goods in question did indeed come from South Africa or whatever country of origin was the target. A strike, with political connotations, might also be a fairly passive affair for those not involved in picketing or in other prominent roles, and a majority of such actions were not seen as particularly demanding. Taking a petition round for others to sign is clearly a different matter. It is, for most individuals, a very positive action and distinctly more effortful than any other form of protest activity, although it may be regarded as, along with attending meetings, the most 'conventional'.

Circulating petitions clearly has something in common with canvassing at elections which is by far the most demanding of campaign actions. Indeed, it would appear to be the most difficult of all acts of participation with over 40% of experiences described as involving 'a lot' of effort. There were very few examples of canvassing amongst the actions reported (partly because opportunities are only episodic) and the commitment of time and of physical and mental effort involved no doubt explains the difficulties parties sometimes face in finding volunteers. Attending a party meeting is, on the other hand, a very passive form of action, though in the era of the televised party political broadcast there are even less strenuous ways of hearing the party message and this may be reflected in the relatively small proportions who had been to such a meeting. The only campaigning activity engaged in by any number is the attempt to change the minds of family, neighbours or workmates about their voting intention which, though carried out close to home, is in most cases seen as requiring some degree of effort to attempt.

Verba and Nie assume that voting requires little initiative and effort. The occasion is provided, and the agenda is set. In one sense the only effort is to get registered to go to the polls and to put a mark on a ballot paper. It is, in any event, a little strange that the vote, for the right to which people struggled for generations, should be treated by certain analysts of democracy as a cost. Nevertheless, it is something which requires more commitment than many British citizens are prepared to give, and even more so in the case of Americans. Rather than the act of voting, it may be better, therefore, to think of the effort involved in deciding which way to vote. There are, potentially, genuine costs. The ideal, but perhaps partly fictional, voter would seek the information on which to make a reasoned judgement on the issues and reach an assessment of the positions of the rival parties and candidates. On the other hand, much guidance as well as exhortation is provided by the parties and the media which reduce, in some ways at least, the information costs. And for many voters, even in an era of dealignment, when voting habits are broken, the decision is made well beforehand, with little effort required. In fact, for nearly 70%, very little or no effort was needed to come to a decision and only 12% experienced a lot of effort. A difference in this respect emerged between those who voted in the 1983 election and those who did not. A quarter of those who in the end did not vote reported that the decision as to which party to vote for in the General Election would require a lot of effort, whereas less than 10% of the voters saw the experience in these terms. The 'don't knows' and the 'uncertains' in our survey turned out often to be the 'didn't votes'. Despite all the blandishments of the parties and the heightened

Table 12.3 *Conflict involved in actions*

	% Yes	N Actions
Actions over prime issue	26·0	652
Contacting actions	21·6	425
Contacted local councillor	20·3	148
Contacted town hall official	25·2	115
Contacted MP	24·3	66
Contacted civil servant	23·9	67
Contacted media	3·5	29
Group actions	29·7	148
Supported/worked for organised group	28·8	73
Worked with others in informal group	30·7	75
Protest actions	32·6	337
Attended protest meeting	22·1	95
Taken petition round	43·2	60
Taken part in boycott	26·7	45
Gone on protest march	63·6	44
Taken part in 'political' strike	27·9	79
Blocked traffic in demonstration	[7·2]*	14
Campaign actions	44·3	350
Canvassed	61·9	21
Attempted to change minds of others about how to vote	61·4	228
Attended party rally	2·2	45
Done clerical work for party	4·2	25
Raised funds for party	0·0	31

* See note to table 5.10.

attention of the media, it appears that for some people the effort of voting remains a hurdle.

Conflict

Although politics is conventionally considered to be an activity involving diversity of opinion and requiring persuasion, bargaining and argument, the activities in which our respondents were engaged were not, for the most part, thought to have involved them personally in conflict with other people. Of course, as has been seen, many actions were not described as 'political' and one reason for this may, indeed, have been that so many were not general in scope and did not involve the clashes typical of high party politics. Nevertheless, most dealt with demands placed on the authorities, who might be resistant. Some required decisions which could, directly or indirectly, adversely affect the interests of other persons and groups and could lead to confrontations in public meetings or inquiries. Others could lead to difficult consequences for the complainant and some element of direct conflict might have been anticipated.

As table 12.3 shows, roughly a quarter of actions taken on people's prime issues were described as having involved conflict and this is also the experience with the generality of contacting and group activities which also involved conflict in 20% to 30% of cases. There is no sign that the target of the actions makes any difference to the likelihood of conflict.

Almost a third of protest actions were thought to have held an element of conflict. Here, the surprise is that the proportion is not higher for a mode of action described sometimes as 'aggressive political participation' (Muller 1979). However, as we have already seen, a distinction should perhaps be drawn between the relatively passive forms of protest and those which would as a rule bring a person more immediately face to face with a potential opponent. Thus, whilst it is the case that a strike involves an opposition of interests, what we are considering here is the personal experience of conflict. During the period of the study, the miners' strike was a spectacular instance of quite large numbers of workers in very direct conflict either with police or fellow miners and other examples will readily spring to mind. In many such disputes, however, it is only those most actively engaged in the front line of negotiation or picketing for whom the conflict takes on an immediate and personal quality. Certainly only a little over a quarter of those who had taken part in a strike which, for them, had a political element to it, had experienced personal conflict. More obviously oppositional was the protest march with getting on for two-thirds of demonstrators declaring that they found this conflictual. Here, too, it has to be remembered that many marches and demonstrations are orderly, peaceful occasions. Our question asked particularly about marches which had not been 'banned' and hence about those which are not to be considered as likely to give rise to extreme confrontations. Even when due allowance is made for the relatively small numbers of people giving details of such actions, the proportion who saw them in terms of conflict is significant.

Three other forms of action are thought of as typically conflictual and all involve highly personal relations. Taking a petition around for signing combines effort with the task of confronting those who are opposed to the campaign or of persuading the reluctant to sign. Circulating petitions is not always like preaching to the converted. As an activity, it has a great deal in common with some forms of party campaigning. Canvassing, as well as requiring much effort, can bring the individual into argument on the doorstep. The combination of costs entailed is, it appears, such as to deter all but the most politically committed and courageous. Similar considerations might apply to persuading others about the way they should vote in an election. It is sometimes suggested that the British tend to avoid talking about politics in social gatherings for fear of the conflict which it might engender. The controversial character of such attempts is clearly confirmed. At the same time, a relatively large minority claim, nevertheless, to have undertaken the attempt.

To say that relatively little conflict was perceived by participants is not, of course, to claim that most issues, or even many, are consensually resolved. There are winners and losers. It is to recount something different but nevertheless significant for the act of participation. For most people, the activity of taking part in some public matter or in a transaction involving the authorities would not appear to have been a personally stressful affair. This day-to-day political or quasi-political behaviour is thus at some distance from the picture presented by the idea of politics as essentially to do with conflict which can entail personal confrontations. Whether or not this traditional image and this prospect of conflict may deter potential participants, the experience of those who have actually participated should indicate that conflict is not in fact to be generally anticipated.

The distribution of costs

One reason that levels of participation differ across social groups could be that they perceive the costs and benefits of action differently. In order to assess this possibility, indices of costs and benefits were constructed from the relevant responses on the basis of which the mean levels of costs and benefits reported by various social categories could be compared.

The index of costs was constructed by putting effort and conflict into a single scale. Although, as we have seen, the various modes of activity give rise to differing perceptions of effort and conflict, there is an underlying cost dimension. Despite fewer people reporting conflict than the expenditure of effort, the two costs were related. Those who reported having put in a lot of effort were more inclined also to report conflict than those who had needed very little effort. It is not possible from the data to establish whether the effort arose precisely from the need to deal with the conflict engendered by opposition although there are hints in this direction. In the case of action taken over the prime issue, whereas 43·8 % of those who reported a lot of effort also encountered conflict, only 7·2 % of those expending very little or no effort had faced similar opposition. The pattern was comparable across the broad spectrum of contacting and group actions. Protesting differed somewhat in that almost a fifth of those activities which had taken only a little effort had also involved conflict.

The costs scale stretches from zero, implying no effort and no conflict to four which represents a lot of effort coupled with conflict. When put together, it appeared that people displayed some tendency to experience their various activities in a similar light. The levels of costs a person reported as resulting from different actions in one particular mode, such as contacting, tended to be related. Thus, where two contacting actions had been performed, the level of costs showed a significant degree of correlation. Moreover, there was a similarly strong correlation between costs involved in people's major contacting and protest actions.

A mean costs score was calculated on the basis of at least two actions, which resulted in 416 cases for analysis. The overall mean cost score was 1·39, implying fairly low costs as against a maximum score of four. Only 7% reported scores of over three, whilst around a third scored less than one. When we turn to comparing the level of costs experienced by various social categories of participants, the results are difficult to interpret. The problem partly arises from deciding what would be regarded as the most plausible hypothesis. It might be supposed that the better resourced participants would encounter fewer costs (and also be more likely to achieve benefits). The better educated and those with good organisational ties might be expected to know their way around politically and achieve their objectives with fewer difficulties. Their costs would be lower. Certainly, they participate more. However, the more one participates, the more effort in total one puts in, although whether the mean amount of effort would increase seems an open question.

In the event, the findings appear to run counter to the hypothesis that high resources should be related to lower costs. Amongst the major variables which are associated with high participation, only group membership behaves in the predicted manner. When the other major variables are controlled for, those who are members of two or more groups report lower than average costs (-0.13) whilst those who are members of one or none are higher than average ($+0.12$). The reverse is true for party members ($+0.38$) and for active trades unionists ($+0.25$). Organisational backing does not, therefore, reduce costs on the individual as one might have supposed. Similarly, educational skills apparently do not lead to greater participatory ease. Those with A level qualifications and above, who are the most participatory, report higher than average costs ($+0.12$) and the less active with fewer or no academic qualifications experience lower costs (-0.08).

The differences are not very great and the strength of the associations is not marked (e.g. for education, beta $= 0.13$). Nevertheless, the explanation of the direction of the association presents something of a puzzle. It is, admittedly, an assumption in constructing scales of costs and benefits that people view these uniformly. Any inter-personal comparisons of this type are questionable. Thus it might indeed by the case that those who participate most put, in their opinion, greater *relative* effort into their actions. Participation does not get any easier. People who do more do not, on this evidence, find that they require less effort. There is almost something masochistic about the regular participants who know that they will incur more costs whenever they enter the political arena. The question then arises whether they feel that they obtain more than average benefits, whether for themselves or the groups or localities for whom they are acting.

Benefits

The benefits of participation were measured by the extent to which respondents stated that they were 'satisfied with the results' of those actions which had produced some identifiable outcomes. In a substantial number of instances, no results had yet emerged – the picketing miner was still in the midst of the national strike, another person had written to an MP about famine in Ethiopia but it was too early to expect a reply with any positive results. But some of the respondents had been waiting an outcome for a considerable period and this would probably have affected perceptions of benefits.

'Satisfaction' represents a broad and perhaps impressionistic measure of benefit. Not every action that had produced a helpful response, and was in that sense effective, might necessarily give full satisfaction if it were felt that the response could have been still better. Equally, some people, perhaps not as demanding in character, might be satisfied with less than they had originally hoped for.

If an action had achieved some results, people were asked whether they were 'satisfied' with these results, 'dissatisfied', or whether they had 'mixed feelings'. The most striking feature of the findings is the high level of satisfaction people felt at the way that their various acts of public participation had turned out. It might be objected that for some people the mere fact that their problem had obtained any response at all would in itself contribute a satisfactory result. This would not necessarily be an overwhelming objection, however, since the very fact that people had obtained a reaction and an acknowledgement from those in authority could help to reinforce their faith in the system. In the event, the detail they provided about the circumstances surrounding their

Table 12.4 *Levels of satisfaction with results of actions*

	Satisfied %	Mixed feelings %	Dissatisfied %	Actions producing results N
Action over prime issue	61·5	28·8	9·7	361
Contacting actions	78·1	15·3	6·6	242
Contacted local councillor	78·4	14·8	6·8	88
Contacted town hall official	81·4	10·0	8·6	70
Contacted MP	72·4	17·2	10·4	29
Contacted civil servant	73·7	26·3	—	38
Contacted media	82·3	5·9	11·8	17
Group actions	74·8	21·2	4·0	99
Supported/worked with organised group	75·0	18·8	6·2	48
Worked with others in informal group	74·5	23·5	2·0	51
Protest actions	51·8	30·2	18·0	139
Attended public protest meeting	45·1	35·3	19·6	51
Taken petition round	59·1	36·4	4·5	22
Taken part in boycott	[23·1]*	[53·8]	[23·1]	[13]
Gone on protest march	62·5	18·7	18·7	16
Taken part in 'political' strike	59·4	15·6	25·0	32
Blocked traffic in demonstration	[80·0]	[20·0]	[0·0]	[5]

* See note to table 5.10.

actions indicates that in general people had more concrete results in mind – preventing a hospital closure, getting the pavement fixed, safeguarding a site for an archaeological dig, trying to get a change in the abortion law. When, for example, a complaint about railway services was met by a letter from the local British Rail manager merely explaining the situation, this was not satisfactory. Thus, satisfaction measures some real achievement in the minds of those who had taken action.

Both our qualitative data on action over people's prime issue and the less detailed and more quantitative data about the broader range of actions are consistent in showing that most people are satisfied with what they have managed to obtain. Indeed, in many instances, the levels of satisfaction are remarkably high. Table 12.4 shows the responses in connection with the whole range of participatory acts. Around three-quarters of contacts with a political representative or a public official, whether at local or central level, were described as having produced satisfactory results. At the other end, only in 6 % of cases do people say that they were dissatisfied with their experience of contacting such authorities, the remainder producing mixed feelings about the outcome. Such mixed feelings are sometimes the consequence of not entirely adequate action by the authorities or of action which solved the problem but only after delays. The satisfaction with dealings with local authorities is particularly high (see also Young 1986 and further discussion in chapter 18).

The experience of group actions both in support of organised bodies and in more informal work with friends and neighbours closely bears out the pattern for contacting.

Once again, very few express clear dissatisfaction. It is protest activity which appears to produce a rather different set of feelings. The satisfied still constitute a majority but it is by no means as large as for the more 'conventional' sphere of activity. Almost a fifth of actions produce dissatisfied reactions and a substantial proportion of people clearly feel doubtful about the outcome in reporting mixed feelings. In many respects, the differences between protests and other actions might have been expected. Protest is very often something to which people resort after they have failed to secure satisfaction through other channels of pressure. Accordingly, benefits are harder to obtain and the results will, in part, reflect the circumstances surrounding the action as well as being an assessment of the action itself.

The actions taken over the prime issue are of a varied sort and will include examples of all the broad modes of participation. The level of satisfaction reported might, therefore, stand as a general measure of the benefits to be gained from action with the rider that these are matters about which people displayed the greatest concern and where both satisfaction and disappointment were felt most keenly. In almost 40% of cases (N = 236) there was at the time of interview no firm result yet to report. In the remaining cases, over 60% of people were satisfied with how things had worked out and less than one in ten remained clearly discontented.

Who benefits?

Are there some sectors of the community which are, on average, more satisfied with the outcome of satisfaction than others? Clearly, it is of some consequence to a democracy if certain groups form a generally more favourable view of their participatory experience whilst others find the experience discouraging. Might it be the case that not only is the readiness to participate unequal, but the benefits which accrue from action as well – a pattern which could then become cyclical and self-reinforcing?

In this section, we look at the extent to which various groups in the population report different levels of satisfaction with their efforts at participation. Our method was to construct a 'benefits score' and then to see how far different people reported higher or lower benefits than the mean for the population at large. The benefits score was constructed out of the responses to the questions concerning satisfaction with the results of action. The scale was based on awarding zero for 'dissatisfaction', one point for 'mixed feelings' and two points for 'satisfaction'. As with the costs scale, a mean score was calculated on the basis of at least two of the range of actions on the prime issue and other contacting, group or protest activities.

The overall mean score was 1·5, reflecting the generally high level of satisfaction already discussed. It might be noted that these scores only apply where the respondents reported that there had been some outcome to at least two actions (N = 192). As has already been pointed out, a large number of actions had, at the time of asking, not yet produced any results. This could be because there had not been sufficient time or because there had been delays. If we were to take a harsh line and include all cases where there were no results (raising the number of respondents to 386), and if we awarded zero (equivalent to 'dissatisfied'), the mean score would fall to 0·93, which is a middling level of satisfaction.

When we look at those groups possessing the resources which might lead one to expect them to achieve favourable outcomes, we find a pattern rather similar to that reported for costs. The better resourced are, relatively, less satisfied. The differences are not great. Thus those with A level and above educational qualifications deviate very slightly below the mean level of satisfaction (-0.03) as, more markedly, do the most active trades union members (-0.12) and those who belong to more than two voluntary associations (-0.08). If we look more closely at the reactions to experiences over the prime issue, the differences do not arise because the highly resourced groups reported much greater levels of actual dissatisfaction but, rather, because they more frequently expressed mixed feelings about the outcome. Thus only 43.8% of degree holders displayed outright satisfaction compared with 66.5% of those without any formal qualifications. But 52.6% of graduates as against 21.8% of the unqualified said, with perhaps academic caution, that their feelings were mixed. Precisely the same pattern was found when members of more than two voluntary associations were compared with those who belonged to none and when active unionists were compared to non-members.

Conclusions

Overall, the levels of satisfaction reported in our interviews are significant and appear to imply a certain vote of confidence in the system which produced them. It must, however, be remembered that these respondents are in one sense a very special group and in certain respects a particularly fortunate one. First, they are part of that minority who have crossed the all-important threshold of action. They have emerged, however briefly, however cautiously, into the public realm and confronted authorities, even if it is only about a matter of very particular concern. It was, indeed, tempting to speculate whether those who had participated more frequently expressed a greater sense of effectiveness or satisfaction than those who had intervened only once. However, there was no consistent pattern to be found, either of disappointment or enhanced gratification. Secondly, these people are fortunate in that they have some outcome to report. For others, the result is still in the future.

The question then arises whether the perceptions of the costs and benefits of various actions might have been a deterrent to those who had never taken them. Accordingly, people were asked to suppose that they were to contact a councillor, work in a group, block traffic or canvass for a party. They were then asked whether they thought this would involve greater effort and conflict and whether the action would get results. Setting aside those who selected the option that 'it depends', there are some hints that those who do not act imagine greater effort and conflict than those who participated actually experience. Thus, 45.7% supposed that working with an organised group would involve a lot of effort and over half thought it would be conflictual. These proportions are much higher than the actual levels reported in tables 12.2 and 12.3. Nearly 70% imagined blocking traffic very effortful and nearly 80% saw it as a conflictual activity. The contrast with the view of those who had done this is great but the numbers are so few as to make analysis impossible. In the case of canvassing this was an activity which 45.5% of those who had gone knocking on doors found involved a lot of effort and 61.9% found conflictual. Those who had never done so were still more likely to expect high costs. It would seem, therefore, that the non-participants in these activities (some may have done other actions) perceive more potential costs. The actors themselves report lower costs or, perhaps, they are prepared to discount them more. The other side of the equation is the expected results. Table 12.4 showed actual satisfaction to be high. Those who attempted to suppose whether action might succeed were somewhat more cautious. About 60% thought contacting a councillor would get results, as against the 78% who were satisfied with their actual outcomes. But in the case of group action, the confidence it would succeed (70·7%) was not far short of the experiences of those engaged in it. The difference between perceptions of personal contacting and group action parallels the finding in chapter 8 about personal and collective senses of efficacy. Far fewer would expect results from blocking traffic but, again, comparisons with experience cannot be made.

There is, therefore, some suggestion that the active and the non-active view things differently and that the more active are ready to take the heat of political participation. Overall, the most significant aspect of this discussion of costs and benefits is that, as participants in the system, the majority are satisfied customers. But, before we can generalise from their satisfaction to an estimate of the quality of government in Britain, we must also recall yet again that a large part of the actions under consideration are to do with problems very close to home. They do not concern the state of national defence, the competitiveness of British industry or the distribution of resources in the welfare state. Instead, they are to do with the state of local roads or the availability of suitable schools for the children. Some concern the wider locality such as the person who sought, successfully, to involve local authorities in setting up a museum for inland waterways. The highest levels of satisfaction occurred over housing matters. As chapter 11 pointed out, it is these routine problems which sustain much of government in any country.

Certainly, this evidence suggests that government, both central and more especially local, is widely considered as reasonably capable of handling these day-to-day demands. Assistance over getting a council house, ensuring that a broken pavement is fixed, persuading the local authority to look into health hazards, are matters which, for example, local councillors or Members of Parliament can offer to deal with in the anticipation of a degree of success which will satisfy their constituents. These are means of showing themselves as good local representatives or hard-working constituency MPs.

This is not an aspect of good government to be lightly dismissed, dealing as it does with the vast bulk of personal and direct dealings between citizens and the authorities. Yet in the eyes of the media, the quality of government is assessed by its capacity to handle the big problems such as reducing unemployment, reviving industry or the defence of the realm. These are the issues on which, as chapter 11 showed, the average individual typically takes less action. Whilst there is no indication that these are areas in which people display a lower sense of effectiveness with their efforts, they are nevertheless matters of 'high politics' in which political leaders are less concerned with their responsiveness to individual participation and more with reacting to a multitude of national and international forces. The ensuing satisfaction from decisions within these areas demands a different kind of enquiry (for examples of such investigations in the case of the welfare state, see Le Grand 1982; Taylor-Gooby 1985; Le Grand and Goodin 1987). The more a matter falls within the category of a public rather than a private good, the less, perhaps, the satisfaction of the individual participant matters and the more one is concerned with measuring government by some more diffuse criterion of public confidence. It is, nevertheless, a moot question as to whether satisfaction over some of the routine matters or over the 'big national' issues is more important to the well-being of the nation.

13

LEARNING FROM POLITICAL PARTICIPATION

One of the great themes of participatory democracy has been the claim that citizen involvement in politics has an educative effect on the participant. The idea that participation forms part of a process of political and moral development in the individual citizen may be traced back to Aristotle, but its modern expression is usually taken to be found in Rousseau and John Stuart Mill (Pateman 1970; Parry 1972). According to Rousseau, in the civil state, man's faculties are stimulated and developed, his ideas extended, his feelings ennobled and his whole soul uplifted. He also acquires moral liberty, which 'alone makes him truly master of himself'. Liberty consists in following rules one prescribes to oneself and only by participating with others as a full citizen in the making of laws could a person achieve civil liberty (Rousseau 1973:195).

For Rousseau this implied a form of direct democracy on the model of classical Greece. John Stuart Mill sought more extended citizen involvement within a political framework of representative government. He saw such involvement as an aspect of a more general objective of the development of individual character (Halliday 1968). Such character was formed in the process of managing one's own manner of life. Social and political institutions should be so arranged as to maximise the individual's opportunities to determine the conditions under which he or she lived. For Mill this meant extending participatory opportunities in local, decentralised government and through industrial democracy as well as through national democratic forms. By participating in one's local and national affairs, one became more aware not only of one's own interests but of the aspirations and interests of others – to the benefit of society at large. Such broadening of perspective involved a moral education. The participant

is called upon ... to weigh interests not his own; to be guided ... by another rule than his private partialities ...
(Mill 1972:217)

This educative role for citizen involvement has been repeatedly stressed by contemporary participatory democrats (Pateman 1970; Benn 1979; Barber 1984; Marquand 1988). Carole Pateman puts the case forcefully:

The major function of participation in the theory of participatory democracy is ... an educative one, educative in the very widest sense, including both the psychological aspect and the gaining of practice in democratic skills and procedures.
(Pateman 1970:42)

In what is one of the most thorough-going statements of participatory theory, Benjamin Barber argues that

civic activity educates individuals how to think publicly as citizens...Politics becomes its own university, citizenship its own training ground, and participation its own tutor.

(Barber 1984:152)

So far in this book we have, like most other empirical students of participation, examined citizen activity from an instrumental perspective, viewing it as intended to defend or promote individual or group interests. We have looked at the costs and the benefits entirely from this perspective. The adoption of such an instrumental outlook is certainly defensible as a major strategy. A theme which unites most participatory democrats is that the existing structures of representative democracies are precisely not designed to offer opportunities for participation from which citizens may derive educative benefits. The researcher is unlikely to uncover much sign of an educative effect of participation in political societies which offer little encouragement for the practices which would give rise to such outcomes.

A second reason why the educative effects of participation have so seldom been in the forefront of survey research on citizen activity is that the educative experience is particularly difficult to capture with such techniques. This is because the learning process is said to occur within the act of participation. It usually implies an increase in awareness, a psychological development perceptible only gradually to the actor. It is arguable that such growth is best studied by more qualitative research techniques of in-depth interviewing or participant observation over an extended time period (for an outstanding example of such a study of participation, see Mansbridge 1980:354). By contrast, a standardised survey taken at one particular moment is less likely to capture what is essentially an experience which changes over time. At the very best, what appears to be required are repeated surveys of a panel of respondents, the development of whose ideas and knowledge can be tracked through several interviews (see Pedersen 1982; Finkel 1985, 1987).

These political and methodological caveats should, therefore, be borne in mind when considering the attempt which was nevertheless made to test whether citizen participation might have produced some form of educative effect. We have sought to isolate two different types of educative consequence – cognitive and affective. Cognitive effects would involve some increase in knowledge or understanding about how politics worked. This might be knowledge about how processes operated, about the ease or difficulty of political access, or about the helpfulness or otherwise of representation and officials. The affective aspects of the educative experience would include the extent to which people's evaluations of political processes and institutions changed as a result of participation.

Knowledge

The cognitive element in political education was tested by asking whether taking action on the prime issue or taking any other contacting, collective, protest or campaigning actions had increased 'your knowledge of how politics works'.[1] In this way respondents provided their own time perspective and self-assessment which effectively stands as a substitute for more objective measures of change that would only be possible through a panel study. In reporting the results, the various actions on the prime issue, such as contacting a councillor or forming a group, have been combined with other such contacting or group actions. Thus, for example, in table 13.1 we report the proportions of all contacting actions which were said to have increased the individual's knowledge about how politics works. For these purposes, voting has been treated separately.

It is probably not surprising, given the reservations already outlined, that most action was *not* seen to have increased political knowledge. There are two interesting exceptions – both forms of party campaining – in which a majority of actions were thought to have had an educative effect. Canvassing was seen in chapter 12 to be amongst the most demanding of activities in terms of the effort involved and the amount of personal conflict entailed. It now appears that it is also the type of action most likely to provide a new insight into politics. The other action with a similar effect is behind the scenes clerical work for a party. The numbers involved are, of course, rather low but it might seem that these activities entail intensive periods of involvement in, and heightened attention to, politics which are conducive to raising awareness. A sceptic might wonder whether those who intend that politics should achieve such consciousness-raising are committed to a politics which is perpetually sustained at the intensity of an election campaign. As one critic put it, politics 'can withstand a lot of apathy' (Crick 1962:147).

Although only a minority of respondents report increased knowledge of how politics works, in many instances these minorities are substantial. In more than half the types of action, at least a third of respondents report some educative effect. Any patterns in the responses are not easy to discern. Nevertheless, there are some signs that people acquire greater knowledge of politics, as the theory would imply, from their contacts with strictly 'political' representatives (Members of Parliament and councillors) rather than with the administration, whether central or local. It is possible that the higher educative effect of some party campaigning is produced by the very fact that they are themselves activities involving teaching (in the case of canvassing) or the distribution of information (clerical work) or learning (attending a campaign meeting). Furthermore, and partly for these reasons, it is such national politics which lie at the heart of most citizens' view of the 'political' arena. To this extent, it is perhaps understandable to find an increase in 'knowledge of how politics works' through an activity that is directly linked to such a conception (see Parry and Moyser 1988).

Beyond this, one may speculate cautiously that there is some association between increased knowledge and participation in more organised forms of activity. Apart from the higher levels in some forms of campaigning, it is rather higher in organised groups (43·8%) than in informal groups (33·7%). Attending a protest meeting is also relatively likely to be informative (40%). Whilst on many such occasions speakers are preaching to the converted, it also would appear that people frequently acquire information about the issue itself and the processes by which the matter is handled. By contrast, whether or not a protest march conveys information to the targets of the demonstration, it is not often perceived as providing new knowledge to the marchers themselves.

Table 13.1 *Cognitive educative effects of participation*

	Increased knowledge		
	% Yes	% No	N of responses
Contacting	32·0	68·0	429
Councillor	38·1	61·9	147
Local official	25·6	74·4	121
Member of Parliament	40·7	59·3	81
Civil servant	25·9	74·1	54
Media	14·3	85·7	28
Group activity	38·9	61·1	175
Organised group	43·8	56·2	89
Informal group	33·7	66·3	86
Protest activity	26·9	73·1	332
Protest meeting	40·0	60·0	80
Circulate petition	26·8	73·2	56
Sign petition	34·5	65·5	28
Boycott	11·8	88·2	34
Protest march	20·0	80·0	45
Political strike	17·6	82·4	74
Block traffic	[40·0]*	[60·0]*	15
Party campaign activity	38·0	62·0	358
Canvass	59·0	41·0	25
Change minds how to vote	35·2	64·8	234
Attend campaign meeting	38·9	61·1	42
Clerical work	60·2	39·8	26
Fund raising	21·1	78·9	31

* See note to table 5.10.

Affective impressions

The second measure of the educative effect of participation is intended to tap its affective dimension. The respondents were asked whether as a result of their various actions they had formed a more favourable or a less favourable impression of how politics worked or whether it had made no difference. In the vast majority of cases, as table 13.2 shows, the evaluation had *not* changed one way or the other. Changes of impression in either direction, therefore, apply to relatively few respondents.[2] Where people had revised their estimation of politics as a result of their own involvement, it was likely to be in a downward direction. This was especially true for such protest activities as the 'political' strike and signing a petition but was also the case for those taking part in informal groups. Only the small number of relatively committed party campaigners were inclined to take a rosier view of the political world as a result of canvassing and attending their party rallies. One may wonder whether participatory democrats should be concerned that action is likely to diminish one's view of political life or whether they would see participation as making people more realistic and less complacent (Kavanagh 1972b).

Table 13.2 *Affective educative effects of participation*

| | Impression of Politics | | | |
	More favourable %	Less favourable %	No difference %	N of responses
Contacting	10·0	20·0	70·0	429
Councillor	11·8	20·9	67·3	149
Local official	5·7	18·7	74·8	125
MP	12·5	22·5	65·0	69
Civil servant	12·1	22·4	65·5	56
Media	3·3	19·7	69·7	30
Group activity	7·4	25·7	66·9	163
Organised group	10·5	19·7	69·7	76
Informal group	4·5	30·7	64·8	87
Protest activity	5·4	21·7	72·8	322
Protest meeting	11·8	25·9	62·3	75
Circulate petition	1·7	18·3	80·0	56
Sign petition	4·5	29·4	61·7	28
Boycott	3·0	6·0	90·0	34
Political strike	2·7	32·4	64·7	75
Block traffic	[0·0]*	[40·0]	[60·0]	15
Party campaigning	8·2	6·0	85·3	369
Canvassed	17·6	8·8	73·6	25
Change minds how to vote	6·1	5·8	88·1	243
Attended rally	19·3	8·5	72·2	44
Clerical work	4·7	4·7	90·6	26
Fund raising	4·0	2·6	93·4	31

* See note to table 5.10.

Thus, although so many report satisfaction with the results of their actions (see chapter 12), political impressions are not on the whole improved. Perhaps there remains a healthy scepticism. Certainly, most people report themselves unmoved by the experience of their action. This is not to deny, however, that participation may have an affective impression in the longer term.

Who learns from politics?

It remains possible that some types of people tend to report a greater educative effect than others. How far, therefore, are these variations captured by the kind of factors which have been found to be strongly associated with participation?

In table 13.3 we again examine the set of variables which have proved to discriminate those who are politically involved from those for whom political engagement weighs lightly.[3] A 'cognitive education score' has been computed which is the percentage of political actions taken that 'increase knowledge of how politics works'. This score excludes voting, which is again treated separately for this purpose. Overall, the

Table 13.3 *Cognitive educative effects, resources and class*

	Cognitive Education Score*		
	Unadjusted %	Adjusted** %	N
Trade union membership			
Presently active	41·2	41·2	61
Other	30·5	30·5	601
Eta/beta	0·08	0·08	
Political party membership			
Member	46·2	45·2	71
Non-member	29·7	29·8	591
Eta/beta	0·12	0·12	
Voluntary group memberships			
More than two groups	45·8	44·7	128
Two groups or fewer	30·5	30·7	534
Eta/beta	0·05	0·04	
Educational qualifications			
Degree	42·9	41·4	65
College and further education	41·1	38·2	96
A level and lower	29·5	28·9	501
Eta/beta	0·09	0·11	
Wealth			
Poorest 25%	32·6	34·3	101
Middle 50%	29·9	29·9	340
Richest 25%	33·5	32·8	220
Eta/beta	0·09	0·10	

* Mean cognitive education score = 31·5.
** Controlling for other factors in the table and for class.

proportion of actions which increase respondents' knowledge is 31·5%. The table then shows the equivalent proportion for each category included. The analysis shows that the percentages do vary significantly from one category to another although, particularly in the case of voluntary group membership, the differences are very modest.

The results suggest that organisational resources – active union membership, party affiliation and, to a much more limited extent (beta = 0·04), membership of voluntary groups – are associated with markedly higher propensities to report that involvement had taught them something about politics. It would seem that participation with others in organisations reinforces and expands political experiences in the ways that the educative theory would suggest. The patterns provide confirmation of those in table 13.1 where group activity and party campaigning were more likely to increase knowledge than most forms of either contacting or protest. Thus 45·2% (adjusted figure) of members of political parties report an educative effect (or 13·7% above the overall percentage). In this case a strong impact is felt by a very small group of often intensively active people. Those who are presently active in unions were also more likely to say that their knowledge of politics increased. This did not extend to inactive members or past members. It appears that it is, once again, current involvement with others that is the key. Voluntary groups are, as has been noted previously, more remote from the political arena. It is, therefore, less surprising that such memberships have very little effect or that even those with more than two such ties are only slightly more likely than average to report some educative effect (34·7%). In terms of estimating the overall extent of educative experiences, however, one should perhaps set the relatively considerable degree to which a *few* intense activists in parties report it against the mild degree reported by the larger numbers in voluntary groups or unions.

In the case of personal resources, the main association is with higher education where, in particular, 41·4% of graduates report some increase of knowledge. Those with A level and lower qualifications are below average. The reason may be that further education provides some of the skills which enable one to extract more sense from the actions in which one is engaged. Wealth displays a faint curvilinear pattern whereby the rich and the poor report increased knowledge – both those who may have learned about how to defend their positions and those who may learn through collective action how better to promote theirs. The working class, indeed, although actually participating below the average, do report a somewhat higher educative score than average.[4]

Voting: a special case

Voting requires a brief separate treatment because it is an activity which occurs in a very different context of political information. At elections, the parties and the media are directing an uncommon level of political information at the electorate. The citizen is, first, being exhorted to participate. Voting is represented as being not merely a right but a duty. Secondly, even if few voters read the full party manifestos, virtually all receive an electoral address from the candidates along with other literature. If they ignore these, they can scarcely avoid entirely the media coverage and the posters. The ebb and flow of the issues seen as important by voters during election campaigns can also be related to the attention devoted to them by the media (see Miller *et al.* 1990). As a consequence, voting in general elections is by far the most widespread form of participation. For many, it is the only one. And, if fewer vote in local elections or in European elections, it still means that more do this than any act other than signing a petition.

Voting appears to have many of the hall-marks of an educative political experience. The reservation, and it is an important one, is that it is not a strenuous form of action which makes strong demands on a person's time and effort (see chapter 12). One learns from others – especially from the political professionals – rather than in the very course of activity, as the classic educative hypothesis would suggest.

As a consequence of the artificially heightened and concentrated attention to politics at elections, people appear to be more likely to report some learning experience.[5] In the case of increased knowledge, 44·2% thought that voting did have this effect – rather more believing this to be true of general than of local elections. An almost identical proportion (44·9%) agreed that voting gave a favourable impression of politics. And again slightly fewer thought this about local elections, but the differences are very slight.

No social group appears to diverge very much from the average on either measure of the educative effect of voting. More relevant to the electoral experience are party allegiances and political values. Those most consistently positive about elections on both dimensions were the very strong Conservative identifiers – they were, after all, on the winning side at the time. The very strong Labour supporters were more likely to consider that local elections both increased knowledge and gave a favourable impression. It will be recalled that Labour had retained major strengths at local level and, as chapter 2 pointed out, many on the left saw local government as a key to the political regeneration of the movement. Many Social Democrats, by contrast, thought that both levels of election made for an adverse image of politics. This would be consistent, of course, with their criticism of the unfairness of the first-past-the-post electoral system. Generally, those who identify with none of the parties also adopt negative views of voting.

Political values do not turn out to sustain a very consistent relationship with educative effects. Even the strong participationists are by no means always convinced that voting has this consequence. The most regular pattern is that those with the highest sense of efficacy are the most likely to report some learning process and that this is in a more favourable direction. Those with very low efficacy are the reverse. To this extent, it would seem that there might be at work the kind of reinforcement effect whereby political confidence breeds interest and greater knowledge of how the system operates.

Learning and acting

All in all, therefore, aside from the case of voting, it is those elements in the population with greater personal or collective resources and who have the greater propensity to participate who are also more likely on average to report that they find that participation is an educative experience. Is it then the case that the more *frequently* they take action, the more they say they learn?

A central tenet of educative theory is that it is only through exercising responsibility that people can acquire responsibility. As Carole Pateman succinctly puts it, we 'learn to participate by participating' (1970:105). If this is so, we should find that those who reported taking more actions should be more prone to report that they had learned from the experience.

In table 13.4 the various forms of action have been brought together under their broader headings. The table shows very strikingly that in each instance the more often persons report that they have taken action, the more they also say that it has increased their knowledge of politics. Thus, whereas slightly under 30% of one-off group actions had led to increased knowledge, over half of the actions of those who had often been involved in group action were reported to have done so. This means that the overall levels of educative effect in Table 13.1 above concealed the much higher effect on the small minority who had frequently taken the particular kinds of action. This is particularly well illustrated by protest activity. Although overall protest activities were regarded as having a low cognitive educative effect, those who had 'often' protested reported that 60% of their actions had raised their level of political knowledge. They were, however, only a small minority of the actions (6%) with a correspondingly limited impact on the general picture.

Table 13.4 *Increased political knowledge by frequency and type of action*

	Frequency of action				
	Often %	Now and then %	Only once %	N actions	N respondents
Contacting	50·0	32·3	29·5	412	295
Group activity	53·6	31·0	29·5	159	111
Protest activity	60·4	39·7	18·4	348	272
Party campaign activity	50·7	34·8	33·3	359	359

The percentages refer to the proportions of actions described by respondents as having 'increased knowledge of how politics works'.

Table 13.5 *Cognitive educative effect and political interest and discussion*

	% actions increased knowledge
Interest in politics and national affairs	
Very interested	36·6
Fairly interested	36·7
Slightly interested	20·6
Not at all interested	20·2
Talks about politics and national affairs	
Very often	42·5
Fairly often	36·3
Occasionally	30·0
Sometimes	17·7
Never	17·3

The most ardent educative theorist would not suppose every act of participation to expand political knowledge, particularly in a far from ideally participatory society. Therefore, the fact that substantial proportions did experience some enhancement of political understanding already offers some backing to the educative thesis. Moreover, this seems particularly true of those engaged with others in some form of organised activity. The fact, moreover, that the more people participate the more they report an increased knowledge of how politics works, provides still further significant support to the central tenet of participatory democrats such as Rousseau, Mill, Pateman or Barber that an active people is likely to be, as a consequence of its involvement, a more politically aware citizenry. As was acknowledged earlier, a survey taken at one point in time cannot expect fully to capture the dynamics of learning even when it asks its respondents to look back and sum up their experiences. There is accumulative interaction between political participation, political interest and political education. Nevertheless, something of this can be seen in table 13.5, which indicates that it is those who are most interested in politics and, above all, those who most frequently talk about it, who also learn most (and possibly, we may speculate, also teach others). Those who are locked out, or lock themselves out, of participation have fewer opportunities to learn.

If such political involvement does not necessarily give rise to a more favourable impression of the system, it must be acknowledged that learning can be an open process. A politically informed and active population may be a more critical one. But this does not deter many people from sticking at it. It is not simply that they are political masochists. Rather, it may be that they have learned to live with the disappointments which are entailed in political life.

PART IV

THE LOCAL PROCESS

14

THE LOCAL POLITICAL SCENE

Modern society is more mobile than at any time in the past. People move further and more frequently to find work and in the course of their employment. Many leave their home town to pursue further education. The wider ownership of private cars and the combination of greater relative prosperity and cheaper air travel have meant that more people take their vacations further afield and become aware of other lifestyles which would have been little known to older, static generations. At the same time, the interdependency of the world economy has meant that the lives and livelihoods of people in one country can be vitally affected by political and economic decisions taken in other countries many thousands of miles away. In response to these developments, central governmental power has steadily grown in order, in part, to counteract and regulate international forces. Still further, nations have recognised interdependency formally by entering into economic and partially political unions such as the European Community.

In the face of these trends, it may be thought that local society and politics have become of very little consequence. Yet this would be misleading. We nearly all have one home base and it is still true that for many people this area can remain more or less the same throughout their lives. People send their children to local schools, use the local shops, most live within a restricted radius of their work and have, perforce, to use the local transport facilities. They go to local hospitals and attend local churches. It may be the case in Britain that people are not, as a consequence, led to vote in high numbers in local elections. Yet, as the previous chapters have shown, the variety of other activities in which at least the participatory minority is engaged are, on the whole, concerned with local matters. They are to do with planning proposals in their neighbourhood, the availability of council housing, school closures, sports facilities for the area's young population. Many of these activities are directed at influencing those in positions of authority in their locality. The picture of activity across the nation which we have been describing is less one of national political participation than a kaleidoscope of local activities which, nevertheless, form coherent patterns.

It is then appropriate to ask whether there are some distinct local deviations from the general national patterns. It has been seen in studies of voting in British general elections, where national considerations might appear paramount, that regional differences have become more pronounced. Attitudes and behaviour have become affected by what have seemed disparities in economic well-being in the different regions of the country and to some extent in Wales and Scotland by nationalist sentiments.

Given that so much participation in the non-electoral arena is in response to local circumstances, it is reasonable to suppose that some variations in participatory levels and modes will be evident. To a considerable extent, these differences will be the result of the relative preponderance in a particular locality of those social factors which are associated with participation. Thus, on the basis of our earlier findings, an area with a larger than average proportion of people well-endowed with individual resources, such as wealth and education, should prove more generally participatory than a poorer, less integrated locality. Other factors which may conceivably influence the level of activity could be the presence of an active local council of a particular partisan leaning. Alternatively, a non-party council might inhibit the formation of political attitudes and perceptions amongst the local population.

It is the concatenation of these various factors which goes to make up a local political culture. But this culture may be rather more than the sum of its separate parts. The very presence of people with a generally greater propensity to participate might stimulate a greater involvement in political action amongst those groups who elsewhere show relatively less interest. Conversely, an inert local society may instil apathy amongst a wider circle. We are not talking of some vague process of osmosis but the sort of incentives to participation which may be created by the establishment in a given locality of a variety of groups, campaigning on an issue, or the frequent circulation of petitions and calling of meetings. In this way, a city, town or village may be rather more or less participatory than could be predicted even from its social and political make-up.

One additional factor which has historically been supposed to be an extra incentive to participation is a sense of community which entails a feeling of attachment to and identity with the locality, its population and its values. The communitarian theory (see chapter 1) has supposed that a high degree of commitment to the life of a particular locality will encourage action to support and defend its interests and values. The problematic nature of this theory arises very much from the ambivalence of the idea of 'community' which has both a descriptive and an evaluative component (Plant 1978; McCulloch 1984). When applied to a geographically defined area, a community tends to be thought of as somewhere which is distinct from its neighbours, perhaps with identifiable boundaries, somewhat akin to an island even if existing within a larger conurbation (Rossi 1972). However, what identifies a community may be less any physical characteristics than the prevalence of certain social attitudes amongst the population. Traditional villages have often been described as communities even when hierarchically ordered societies. In such cases, 'community' may induce deference to the leading notables rather than widespread participation. On the other side, it is sometimes supposed, generally by those with broadly socialist leanings, that a more egalitarian society with a tradition of mutual support will be what makes for genuine 'community' and that this should serve as the basis for relatively greater local commitment and participation.

The choice of the localities

There are many reasons, therefore, why local patterns of participation might diverge from the overall picture across Britain as a whole. For this reason, it becomes a complex matter to select a range of localities which could provide anything like an adequate test of the various hypotheses to explain local political sub-cultures. In an ideal world, one might have sought to study in depth a sample of all localities or communities in Britain. Actual possibilities are very different. It is, in any event, difficult to determine what would be the total 'universe' of British localities from which to sample – all settlements, villages, towns, local government authorities?

There are also major problems affecting the capacity to carry out any survey-based study. Resources are limited. The fundamental decision was whether to pursue a broad-based strategy of examining the activities and attitudes of a very small number of persons in a large number of localities or to concentrate on a more detailed contextual study of a restricted set of areas, allowing larger numbers of people to be interviewed. Each approach has its advantages and disadvantages (see Parry and Moyser 1984b). A broad-based approach can make a somewhat better claim to incorporate a representative sample of localities with a greater chance of isolating the specific types of local feature which differentiate localities from one another. The drawback is that it is possible to interview only a very small number of citizens and even fewer leaders in each locality and hence it is difficult to be confident that the study will have captured anything of the local political culture or the range of issues with which it has been concerned. The limited number strategy can explore such matters in relatively greater detail. In particular, it offers a greater hope of disentangling the complex of elements which go to make up a sense of local community and hence provide some test of the communitarian thesis. But it faces the danger of all restricted case studies in not being certain of being able to distinguish those features of a situation which are characteristic of a type of locality from those which are merely idiosyncratic.

Our ultimate decision was to concentrate the study on six localities (in contrast to the approach adopted for America by Verba and Nie 1972). The determining factors were the desire to explore the local context of issues in greater detail and the wish to put community theory to the test. Although there can be no sense in which six places could 'represent' all the localities of England, Wales and Scotland, it was necessary to ensure that each could plausibly illustrate the most significant interconnections between participation and type of locality and community. The selection sought to avoid arbitrariness but also to reflect judgements, based on past theorising, about the likelihood or not of any locality constituting a community of the sort which would be expected to enhance participatory levels.

Our starting point was the local government 'district' of which there are some 450 in England and Wales. Given that our concern was with 'political' participation, however broadly conceived, it was necessary to base the study in the first instance on local governmental units, even though by virtue of their average size and their often somewhat arbitrary boundaries created by the Local Government Act of 1972, few are likely candidates to be communities – a problem to which we shall return. The districts were sorted statistically into 'clusters' based on a large number of social and economic variables including age structure, prevailing types of occupation, housing ownership and conditions and ethnicity.

The analysis provided nine clusters or types of local government district in England from which we selected four as of particular potential interest to participation. These were a cluster of affluent towns mainly situated in or near the greenbelt area around

London; a set of inner London boroughs with large working class populations, many living in council housing; a group of older-established industrial towns mostly in the north of England; and a number of traditional market towns set in rural surroundings. Each of these clusters seemed promising subjects for enquiry. However, there were other kinds of situation which invited analysis, particularly from the standpoint of community theory. Mining villages are often perceived as the 'ideal-types' of working class communities, created by economic circumstances, shared experiences and the need for mutual support in work as well as in day-to-day life.

At the other extreme, it might be anticipated that very scattered, isolated rural settlements would lack the integration which would develop strong community sentiment and which would encourage common action. Additionally, we wished to take some account of the possibility that feelings of national identity could affect patterns of issues and action in Wales and Scotland, even in a period when devolutionary ardour had apparently somewhat diminished. Accordingly, we undertook further cluster analyses of Welsh and Scottish local government districts and identified groups of mining communities and rural areas, selecting a Welsh mining valley and a fairly remote Scottish country district for study.

This provided six types of area, each of which promised to illustrate the effect of locality on participation and also corresponded quite well with earlier studies of the range of British communities (Frankenberg 1966). In each case, we sought to choose a district which was close to the centre of the 'cluster' and was, hence, the most typical. At the same time, we were interested in obtaining districts which were run by councils of different political complexions. These considerations were generally compatible with one another and the districts chosen can, in some sense, 'stand for' their particular type.

The selection procedure was not yet at an end. To attempt a sample survey of six district authorities would have spread our resources too thinly. Still more problematic was the fact, alluded to earlier, that districts were seldom even potential 'communities', which are often thought to be quite small units, perhaps even a few streets (Hampton 1970). For this reason, we focused on a smaller area within each district, sometimes only two council wards. In the case of the greenbelt town and of the market town, selection of the area for special study was self-evident in that the town itself constituted the core of the local government district. In the other instances, the use of further cluster analyses of wards and of locally-gathered demographic data, along with local advice and consultation, led us to select an identifiable locality for study within the district. This locality was intended to be reasonably typical of the district as a whole in being close to the mean in its various social characteristics.

Finally, we wished our localities to provide tests for the theory that community identity stimulates participation. Hence the chosen localities had to be potential communities. Yet here a dilemma presents itself. To have selected localities possessing the expected basic characteristics of communities – identifiability, boundedness, continuity – might be to prejudge the issue. To then discover community feeling would merely be to confirm a self-fulfilling prophecy. Moreover, our selection of localities might reflect a particular notion of community which is itself an 'essentially contestable' concept, in that a person's idea of community is related to that person's ideological stance on other aspects of life, such as equality, liberty and fraternity.

The investigator has, in such cases, to break into the circle somewhere. We have, therefore, tried to examine the kinds of localities which have, from various standpoints in political theory, been regarded as 'communities' as well as those which have appeared less likely to generate community identity. The respondents were asked both about their perception of their locality as a community and about the values with which they associated community – a matter to be explored in chapter 15.

The final six localities (which are shown on map 14.1) which emerged from this process of selection were:

(i) Sevenoaks – the main town in the District of the same name in Kent
(ii) Penrhiwceiber – a mining village in the Cynon Valley in South Wales
(iii) Stockwell – an inner city area within the London Borough of Lambeth, South of the River Thames
(iv) Spotland – an area near the centre of Rochdale, an old-established industrial town near Manchester
(v) Oswestry – a market town in Shropshire near the border with Wales
(vi) The Machars – an area in South-West Scotland comprising small scattered settlements

Within each locality, between two hundred and twenty-five and nearly three hundred ordinary citizens were interviewed in a sample survey. The response rate ranged from about 78% in the Machars and 76% in Penrhiwceiber to 57% in Stockwell, with Spotland (73%), Oswestry (71%) and Sevenoaks (68%) falling in between. Many of the questions were common to our national survey, which was being conducted at around the same period, but most concentrated on participation at local level. In every case, a few questions were asked specifically about events in the particular area.

The localities

Sevenoaks

Sevenoaks is a medium-sized town in Kent with a population of around 17,000 within easy commuting distance of London and also near the orbital motorway around the metropolis. It is the principal town of the local government District to which it gives its name and contains the head offices of the local authority, although the county offices are centred elsewhere. Sevenoaks is surrounded by pleasant countryside. Much of the older architecture is distinguished and it is close to the great country house of Knole. In short, it enjoys the natural advantages and amenities which make it a very desirable residential area and one which attracts large numbers of people who work in London. As a result, many people in the area drew our attention to a distinction between those working in or near the town whose lives are most closely tied up with it and those for whom it is more in the way of a dormitory.

Sevenoaks is not exclusively a commuter town. It contains a few nationally-known firms involved in building materials, distribution, publishing and finance. The 1981 Census data show that employment in construction and in distribution is close to the national average. The service sector is well above the average and, in this, Sevenoaks is

Map 14.1 The six localities

representative of other urban areas in the South-east of England. Numbers in manufacturing industry are low and unemployment was less than half the national average which, at the time of the 1981 Census, stood at 11·6%. This was not, however, reflected in any greater evidence of residential mobility since average length of residence in Sevenoaks was, on the basis of our survey, not very different from the average for the six localities. The Census data for the town confirm the impression one readily derives from visits, that it is a very affluent town where the population is generally engaged in higher than average status occupations. The indicators for type of occupation, average levels of educational qualifications, private house-ownership and size of house and for car-ownership all point in the same direction.

These patterns are also represented in our own sample, which is drawn from the wards which compose the town itself and involve little spill-over into the neighbouring countryside. Very nearly half the sample (48·4%) was in the salariat class. The significance of this may be gauged by the fact that the next highest figure for the salariat was the 27·4% they made up of the Oswestry population. Indeed, a more refined class breakdown shows that just under 30% of the population were in the highest grade professional occupations. At the other end of the scale, the figure for the working class (19%) was less than half that for all the six localities taken together (44·3%). Our sample also suggested that Sevenoaks was not a town of the petty bourgeoisie since at 5·6% they, too, were around half the overall figure. Rather, we are concerned with the well-paid employee, since 83·6% are employed and the remaining 16·4% self-employed is below the average.

The sample also confirmed the affluence of Sevenoaks. It will be recalled that we have been employing a wealth index comprising ownership of car, home and shares alongside a high income. This index discriminates in a highly significant way between our localities. A remarkable 58·4% of our Sevenoaks respondents were on the two highest points of the index. No other local population came anywhere near this, the closest being the rural area in Scotland with 28% and in this case there is reason to think, as will be explained below, that our index may err slightly on the high side. A breakdown of the index brings home the degree of affluence. Income levels marked out Sevenoaks strongly from the other localities. With a quarter of its population in the highest household income bracket it provided 65% of those at this income level across the six localities. A little over 30% also owned shares in companies compared with an average of 14%, and contrasted sharply with Penrhiwceiber where a mere 1·5% (or four persons) held shares. (The survey occurred after the first mass privatisation scheme involving British Telecom shares, but before other major sales.)

As has already been shown in chapter 6, there is normally a close association between class, wealth and educational qualifications. Sevenoaks is no exception. Well over a quarter (29·3%) have received some form of higher education, and 17·9% have gained degrees – figures only approached by the inner London population of Stockwell. Although a third had no qualifications, this was well below the average of 55%.

On the basis of the material and skills resources of its population, Sevenoaks clearly has a high participation potential but it is possible that these might be counteracted by other local influences. Attitudes to the locality and its political affairs appear to suggest that, despite Sevenoaks being a pleasant place to live, residents wear their local loyalties relatively lightly. A fifth of the population feel a very strong attachment to the area – a rather lower figure than the average for our six localities. Just under 40 % regard its residents as displaying a sense of togetherness and fellowship, which is the second lowest figure. On the other hand, the strength of attachment to Britain as a whole is highest of all in Sevenoaks.

The town is politically Conservative and the party had an overwhelming majority on the District Council. Half of our sample reported that they had voted Conservative in the 1983 General Election. Sevenoaks itself is also represented by a town council (i.e. a parish level body) which has been quite active in the life of the town over a number of local issues. Three out of five respondents agree that the town hall is 'well provided for by the local council' and over a third here have a 'generally favourable impression of how local politics works', whilst two-thirds think that the local council 'understands local issues, needs and problems'. All these represent a middling proportion in comparison with the other localities. Possibly reflecting the relatively Conservative dispositions of the population, the favourable impression of 'how national politics works' was higher in Sevenoaks (46·3%) than elsewhere, as was the rating of the 'present Conservative Government' on a scoring system giving 'marks out of ten' – the score being 5·1. It is significant that Sevenoaks, along with Stockwell, stands out as an area where rather more people acknowledge that local voting is decided 'mainly on the basis of national matters' (40·8%).

The overall resultant impression is, perhaps, of a population reasonably well-satisfied with the amenities and services of their local area but displaying relatively more concern with national politics and, as a partial consequence, displaying less evidence of any strong sense of communal rootedness. Two possible inferences begin to suggest themselves. From a communitarian standpoint, these modest levels of community-mindedness could be expected to inhibit local participation. On the other side, the resources of the people of Sevenoaks point to its being amongst the most participatory of our localities.

Penrhiwceiber

There are probably not many greater contrasts in Britain between Sevenoaks and Penrhiwceiber. To visit them, as we did, in close succession is to begin to think in terms of 'two nations' – if there were not some argument for thinking that each of our six localities was a different 'nation'. Penrhiwceiber is a pit village which is adjacent to the town of Mountain Ash in the Cynon Valley of South Wales. The total population of the area covered by the survey is in the region of 8,000. The economy has been dominated by coal mining but at the time of our study the mine in the village itself was threatened by closure, which subsequently in fact occurred. The decline of mining had meant that as early as the 1981 Census, male unemployment was well above the national average and this proportion will have steadily increased since. During the period of our study, Penrhiwceiber was enmeshed in the national miners' strike. The area was one of many in Wales that stayed absolutely firm in its support of the National Union of Mineworkers.

The precarious economic conditions are evidenced in various other ways. Just over

17% of the sample described themselves as unemployed. If we confine our attention to those in the 'economically active' category, a staggering 33·5% were out of work – a figure well above even the next worst-off locality. Several of the shops in the area have closed. The housing, apart from a partially detached estate, consists of terraces strung out along the valley facing one another across narrow streets. Whilst their proximity and often neat appearance provides the basis for a strong sense of neighbourhood, the amenities of many of the houses are extremely poor. The 1981 Census had already shown that the proportion of houses in Cynon Valley as a whole lacking exclusive use of a bath or shower was, at 9%, three times the national average. But the extent of housing deprivation had only been fully revealed by a detailed survey carried out by the Borough Council just before the time of our study (Cynon Valley Borough Council 1984). This had received wide local and, indeed, some national publicity for establishing the existence of housing (privately owned) as poor as any in Britain.

Our own sample reflects these social characteristics. Penrhiwceiber is virtually a one-class locality. Three-quarters of the sample were in working class occupations, compared to an average for the localities of 44%. Conversely, 3·4% were in salaried, professional positions – by far the lowest proportion. The wealth index confirms this, although less dramatically and has to be unpacked a little into its components. Those on the bottom two points of the wealth scale represent 37·9% of the sample, which is clearly higher than the average of 28·2% but does not make Penrhiwceiber the poorest locality. Moreover, there are 13·8% in the wealthiest group which is on the average overall. Part of the explanation lies in the fact that, although housing in this valley is notoriously poor, it is largely privately owned (66·9%, which is not far short of the figure for Sevenoaks) for a number of historical reasons. As a consequence, this boosts the wealth index.

When it comes to household income, however, 68% of those in Penrhiwceiber fall within the bottom four brackets of the twelve-category income scale we used, compared with nearly 48% in the six areas as a whole. Not one was to be found in the top bracket. Half the sample had their own car, compared to 65% overall. Share ownership was next to non-existent. The profile of educational qualifications is also the mirror image of that for Sevenoaks. Only one person in our sample had a degree; almost 80% had no formal qualifications.

In Chapter 6 we discussed a social cleavage which has increasingly been considered significant between public and private consumption. The measures of consumption have some inevitable affinities to our scale of wealth but the point of the analysis is different and, again, the factor discriminates very sharply between localities. People can be separated into those who primarily consume services through the market and those who rely on public provision. The public consumption measure is composed of use of public transport, national health services and state education along with council tenancy; private consumption is the polar opposite. Over half of those in Penrhiwceiber are at the high public consumption end of the scale (20% at the extreme end). This is not the highest figure, largely because of the low level of council tenancy. But a mere 5% use private health treatment (compared with a third in Sevenoaks) and 10% are high private consumers over all. In Sevenoaks, 22·1% are at the public consumption end of the spectrum but 58·8% are at the private end.

All in all, the picture is of a deprived locality. Despite, or on some views because of, that, the population shows a considerable degree of attachment to the area – 38·4% (well above average) declaring a 'very strong' degree of attachment. There is a much higher proportion than usual of the population who have been resident in the locality for more than thirty years. Between 85% and 92% variously describe its population as displaying a sense of togetherness, as having similar needs and interests and the area as being 'a real community'. In other words, it overwhelmingly exhibits the solidarist sentiments traditionally expected of a mining village.

The Labour Party's domination of Cynon Valley Council and the Parliamentary elections is as complete as the Conservative's in Sevenoaks. Almost 70% of our sample had voted Labour in the 1983 General Election at a time when, nationally, 28·3% had voted for the party. Although regularly returning the same party to power, people in Penrhiwceiber were quite critical of aspects of local political life. Only a fifth thought the area well served by the local council – a lower figure than for any other locality. It also had the second smallest proportion with a generally favourable impression of how politics works. Yet a majority still believed that the council understood local needs and problems. Perhaps the voters were making a clear distinction between understanding needs and the capacity to act on problems which, however, have to be recognised as possibly even greater than those facing the other councils in our survey. A special difficulty consists in attracting new industry to an otherwise declining and deprived environment. Some perspectives on the evaluation may be gained by the fact that national governmental institutions were regularly given a still lower evaluation than local bodies. Most scathing was the rating on a scale of one to ten of the Conservative Government at 1·4, by comparison with which the score of 5·1 for the Borough Council, though lower than elsewhere, will seem respectable. Moreover, the average attachment to Britain as a whole was less than elsewhere – 13·2% wanting a separate government for Wales. However, only a tiny fraction, under 5%, supported Plaid Cymru.

A summary picture of Penrhiwceiber would be an area suffering very severe deprivation with a population which, whilst retaining feelings of attachment to the area, express a degree of scepticism about political institutions and processes. These institutions, however, themselves face extreme difficulties in rehabilitating the locality with limited local resources at their disposal. A converse image to that in Sevenoaks emerges. On the basis of individual resources, the prospects for participation look, on the surface, to be poor. It remains to be established whether this is the kind of place where collective and community resources can activate people who are otherwise at an economic, social and political disadvantage.

Stockwell

The inner London area of Stockwell is a less advantaged locality but of a type rather different to that found in Penrhiwceiber. It forms part of the London Borough of Lambeth and the population of the area covered by the survey (which extends beyond the Stockwell ward itself to include Larkhill ward and parts of three others) is around 32,000. The Borough itself encompasses areas very different in character, from desirable residential districts at the southern limits to the deprived area of Brixton, scene of the notorious riots in 1981 (Scarman 1982). Whilst Stockwell, to the northern end of the Borough, is at neither extreme in either affluence or deprivation, it is certainly towards the less advantaged end of the spectrum. It contains a very substantial core of council housing in estates and blocks built at various dates. There are also some privately-owned residences occupied by people from professional classes either working in Lambeth or, in some cases, possibly attracted by the area's proximity to central London. Stockwell, as well as Lambeth in general, has a substantial non-white population. In our sample, 22% was non-white made up of 16·5% who were Caribbean in descent and 3·2% who were of Asian background.

Our sample in this instance does not fully mirror the local population. As has been a common experience in other surveys in the inner city areas, a range of factors resulted in a disappointingly low response rate of 57% which means that all the findings for Stockwell have to be treated with a measure of caution. Moreover, the response was clearly lower in the areas of council housing, which meant that the most socially disadvantaged sector of the population was almost certainly distinctly under-represented. In our analysis we have, in this instance, sought to adjust for the discrepancy by 'weighting', so that the response rate from each polling district within the locality is, in effect, the same. Thus respondents from the central area with the lowest response rate have been made to count for more, and those from the periphery less. This reduces, but does not entirely remove, the bias due to difference in response rate. The results should be interpreted with this statistical adjustment in mind.

The working class constituted 39% of our sample which was, even with the built-in weighting, still somewhat lower than that for all six localities. A fifth of the sample were from the salariat which goes to emphasise how different this is from our mining village. This professional element results in a quarter of our Stockwell population having been in receipt of higher education and 16·4% being in possession of degrees – proportions second only to Sevenoaks.

In wealth terms, Stockwell's population is disproportionately to the lowest end of the ladder, with 42·9% on the two bottom rungs compared to an average of 28·2%. At the other end, 17·6% appear in the two richest categories. What marks Stockwell off in wealth terms is that fewer than elsewhere own their own homes. Over half (57%) are council tenants. Around half lack a private car. As a consequence, it is not surprising that nearly 62% of Stockwell residents are at the high public consumption end of the consumption scale (40% at the highest point). The dependence on public services is a factor which could potentially be significant in shaping political attitudes and in determining the kinds of issues which might be taken up in the area.

Stockwell differs very much in its pattern of life from the working class pit village. There is far more sign of mobility with only 9·1% of the sample having lived in the locality for thirty years or more and a further 11·6% for over twenty years – figures well below the average for the six areas. There is less of a sense of 'togetherness and fellowship' than anywhere else with only 28·7% detecting this, compared with 85·4% of Penrhiwceiber and 64·5% across the six localities. The 10·2% feeling very strong attachment to the area is also the lowest.

Politically, the London Borough of Lambeth was controlled at the time of the survey by a left-wing Labour Council. It was in the throes of a major dispute with the

Conservative Government concerning levels of services and rates, a dispute which was later to lead to the disqualification of several councillors for failing to set a legal budget. Members of the Council had also been prominent in the unsuccessful campaign to prevent the Government from abolishing the Greater London Council. Labour had received the votes of just over 40% of our sample in the 1983 General Election and nearly 86% had been opposed to the abolition of the Greater London Council. Despite this apparent sympathy with the Council's general orientation, the Stockwell population was the only one where a greater proportion (35·1%) had a 'generally unfavourable' as against a 'generally favourable impression' (21·8%) of how local politics works. The 67% who disagreed with the view that the area was well provided for by the local council was also higher than anywhere other than in Penrhiwceiber. There may be something in the view expressed to us by representatives of the Council that popular impressions were affected by adverse and allegedly biased media publicity surrounding the clash with Central Government and by what the Council saw as the financial obstacles placed in the way of providing fuller services.

Stockwell is rather less of a clearly defined locality than some others in our survey – though sufficiently identifiable to be recognised by its name. Unlike the pit village, its economy is not so precariously dependent on one industry but contains a number of large firms, especially in distribution. Possibly for this reason our sample included only 9·1% of unemployed (13·2% of the economically active labour force) – much lower than in the mining community – though this probably reflects sampling problems and actual levels in the area could have been well in excess of that figure.

Stockwell, as an inner city area, is the sort of locality usually considered to be fundamentally working class in character. However, it contrasts in significant ways with Penrhiwceiber, and not by any means entirely as a result of sampling problems. The social mix is greater in the London locality. The kind of deprivation in the two areas is not identical. Prevailing social sentiments differ. These point towards a potential for local variations in political concerns and in resulting patterns of participation.

Spotland

The Spotland area close to the centre of Rochdale represents a further social pattern. Rochdale itself is one of a number of industrial towns in the north-west which grew up with cotton and which, with the decline of that industry and the problems of the British economy in the 1970s, has faced severe problems of job losses. Spotland itself is a mixed area containing housing, shops, some industry, as well as Rochdale Football Club. The most striking feature of some of the residential area is the extensive rehabilitation programme in which local residents' organisations had become involved. As a result of this scheme, a good deal of old housing had been given a new lease of life. Spotland is one of the areas of Rochdale in which significant numbers of people of Asian descent have settled. Persons of Asian origin constituted 5% of our own sample which almost certainly under-represents the proportion living in the area.

Spotland is in many respects near the median of our six localities on a number of social characteristics. The 44·3% of our sample in the working class occupations is precisely on the average. It is marginally below average in the proportion in the salariat (18·3%). On the wealth scale, the population is very slightly poorer than the average with 33·7% in the two least wealthy categories and a little under a quarter in the two richest groupings. Correspondingly, the range of educational qualifications is fairly typical of the localities as a whole. Just over half have not gained any formal credentials; nearly 12% have been in higher education. Only in one respect does Spotland differ by much from the other areas. With higher than average council tenancy and a lower rate of private car ownership, Spotland shares some of the characteristics of large urban areas in consuming public rather than private services. Half the sample are placed at the strongly public end of the consumption scale compared with a fifth at the private end.

Spotland is not a locality which apparently arouses a strong sense of attachment – 13·5% feeling that way whilst 18·5% feel no attachment whatsoever. Only a small majority (53·8%) think that there exists a sense of togetherness and fellowship. Indeed, it is an area which lacks a very clear identity in that only half would say that its boundaries were clear and the survey covers rather more than the local government ward of Spotland. The total population of the locality within the survey would be in the region of 10,000.

At the parliamentary level, Rochdale has been Liberal, represented by the colourful and nationally famous figure of Sir Cyril Smith, M.P., very much a local man. Spotland itself had Liberal councillors and the majority on the Rochdale Council was, at the time of the study, held by an alliance of Conservatives and Liberals. Our own sample was equally divided, with a quarter each voting for Liberals and Labour in the 1983 General Election, but over half reported having voted Liberal in the last local election. The people of Spotland appear fairly well satisfied with the performance of the local authority, 63·4% thinking the area well provided for and the score of 5·8 out of ten for the council being exactly on the mean for all six localities. Although its long-standing liberal tradition implies some political individuality, Spotland is socially and economically typical of an important kind of older urban area in the north of England. At the same time, its closeness to the mean on many features also serves as a reminder that there is, amongst local differences, also a considerable degree of homogeneity in Britain likely to be reflected in participation patterns.

Oswestry

From the cluster analysis of English local government districts, Oswestry appeared to be the most typical of the set of country towns. One might qualify this by acknowledging that its situation in the county of Shropshire close to the border with Wales means that it does have a certain element of Welsh atmosphere, perhaps especially on market days. The study focuses on the wards which make up the town itself, with very little overspill into the countryside which surrounds it and gives it a well-bounded character recognised by 87% of our sample, making it subjectively the most sharply identified of our areas of study.

The town itself has a population of around 12,000. The 1981 Census shows that very few in the town are involved directly with agriculture. The town's status is indicated by the quarter of the population engaged in distribution. At one time, Oswestry had been a regional railway centre but, with the closure of the line, there had been serious job losses as well as the removal of one significant communication link. A major aim of the local authority has been to compensate for these closures by attracting light industry to industrial estates set up around the perimeter. The degree of success may be estimated by the 1981 Census figures which suggest that unemployment had been restricted to a figure close to the national average.

The class composition in Oswestry does not deviate far from the average pattern for the six areas. The working class are just under 43 % of the sample, the salariat a little over 27 %. In the scale of wealth, most people fall in the intermediate range – a lower than average proportion appear at both the poor and the rich ends. The distribution of educational achievement largely mirrors the pattern for the six localities taken together.

The sense of attachment to locality in Oswestry is higher than for any of the areas studied – 81 % feeling either strong or fairly strong positive sentiments. A higher proportion of the population than elsewhere (64·4 %) regard the locality as well-provided for by the council and similarly the 37·1 % who have a generally favourable impression of how local politics works is the highest amongst the six areas (21 % have a generally unfavourable view, the remainder having no views either way). The constituency in which Oswestry falls is a Conservative stronghold, the Member being Mr John Biffen who, at the time of the study, was in Mrs Thatcher's Cabinet. Amongst our own sample, 37 % reported having voted Conservative in 1983. The members of the Borough Council had mainly stood on a non-partisan basis even though some of these were recognised to be Conservative supporters. Of the 29 councillors, 18 were independents. In addition to the Borough Council, Oswestry itself had a Town Council with parish-level functions. This dual system of council responsibility was supported by 55 % of the sample yet as many as 65 % also found it confusing, presumably through lack of a clear understanding of their respective responsibilities.

Oswestry is likely to be quite representative of a style of local social and political life which was once much more widespread – somewhat isolated from the large urban centres which are more typical of England (it is, for example, about fifty miles from Birmingham), pursuing an 'apolitical', non-partisan mode of politics. But it is still far from alone and constitutes one, now relatively neglected, pattern of local politics (Grant 1977).

The Machars

The final locality is also rural but different in significant respects from Oswestry. Whereas Oswestry is a small, compact town with a rural hinterland, the Machars is an agricultural area with scattered settlements and farms and few villages of any size. The total population is around 6,000 and the largest centre contains a mere 1,000. As such, it would, on the surface, be rather less likely to have a strong common identity in the minds of its inhabitants, even though it has a name which nearly everyone in the area would recognise. The locality is very remote from large centres of population, situated in the South-west of Scotland. It forms part of the district of Wigtown within the Dumfries and Galloway Region. Its relative remoteness may be gauged by the fact that it lies some 30 miles from Stranraer which is the chief town of the District and the site of the council offices. Public transport presents a major problem.

The locality has been suffering from a degree of unemployment with relatively few opportunities for work outside agriculture, although efforts are being made to attract several businesses as well as tourism to an area with an attractive but unspoilt coastline. Amongst our sample, 9·5% were unemployed, or 17·8% of the economically active – a figure second to the pit village. As a consequence, the problem of unemployment loomed large in people's minds as an issue.

The class composition of the Machars displays some special features. It has the second highest proportion of persons in working class occupations, even if this only implies a figure (45·6%) a little above the overall average. This is, however, a rural working class, the largest two employers in the area both being creameries, processing locally-produced milk. Furthermore, 11·6% were agricultural workers directly employed in farming. This, as we shall see in chapter 15, has a very different organisational infrastructure to that in Penrhiwceiber or Stockwell, with different implications for participation. The salariat is relatively small (13·2%). The Machars is, of course, unique amongst our localities in including farmers (15·5%) – there was only one farmer in the Oswestry sample.

The area is around the average in the proportion who are at the highest levels of the wealth index. This may, however, be slightly misleading. In remote rural areas, car ownership becomes more of a necessity (76%) and this, coupled with average levels of home ownership, may raise some up our wealth scale. Only a handful place themselves in the highest income levels. On the other hand, nearly 54% are in the lowest four bands which implies that the Machars has a poverty problem not far short of that in Penrhiwceiber where the comparable figure reached 58%. Agriculture tends to demand fewer formal academic credentials than other sectors of employment and the 62·6% who have no qualifications is second only to Penrhiwceiber. At the higher education level, the proportion (13·5%) is near the norm.

The Scottish dimension of the area is reflected by the fact that in the recent past the area had been represented in Parliament by a Scottish Nationalist, although it was held by the Conservatives at the time of the study. The largest group in our sample had been Conservative voters in 1983 (44%) with 14·6% supporting the Scottish Nationalists. Scottish sentiment is considerable with 69·1% expressing very strong attachment to the country compared to 44·4% feeling the same way about Britain as a whole. Only 13·4%, however, would like to see a separate Scottish government, although a further 12·3% would like to see all important decisions taken there.

The District Council provides, like Oswestry, another example of independent non-partisan politics. The Machars is, as we shall see in the following chapter, not a very participatory locality – a fact which may partly be explained by the relative physical remoteness of the centres of local decision-making. However, the population is very supportive of the local governmental system. Only 13% had a 'generally unfavourable impression' of how local politics worked, which is the smallest proportion in the six localities. Over 60% saw the area as well provided for and the 'mark' of 6·8 out of ten for the District Council was the highest received. Consistent with this view was the finding that only in the Machars did a majority (55·7%) prefer to leave decisions to elected representatives rather than wish for more say for ordinary citizens – a deferential attitude perhaps, or simply satisfaction with the restricted range of functions which the local authority performs in such country areas.

The final aspect of life in the Machars is somewhat unexpected. A scattered rural population living and working in comparative isolation from one another might be expected to produce a rugged individualism. But the people of the Machars express strong communitarian sentiments – a higher sense of togetherness even than the Welsh mining village as well as a deep sense of attachment to the area.

The study of local leaders

As well as interviewing a sample of citizens in each locality, we also interviewed a number of local leaders. Our aim was to do something which we could not achieve at a national level. We wished to examine political participation as it was seen by those in various positions of authority and leadership who were very often those to whom citizen action was directed. We were interested to find out whether the various leaders felt that the processes of individual contacting or of group pressure were effective, or whether some sectors of the local population showed a greater capacity than others to put their views forward. The effectiveness of the process of political communication has to be seen from both ends – the originator and the target. At the same time, leaders are not necessarily the passive recipients of pressure but are in a position themselves to take the initiative. The elitist approach to politics (Putnam 1976; Nordlinger 1981) would indeed suggest that the key to understanding politics lies more with the leadership than with citizen participation.

To study the impact of participation on leaders, it is necessary to select the appropriate leaders. This is no simple task and the methodology has been the subject of considerable debate (Parry 1969; Moyser and Wagstaffe 1987). It is extremely difficult to claim that any sample of local leaders can be 'representative' since this supposes that there exists a well-defined, well-identified 'population' of leaders in any community. Our method was to combine the so-called 'positional' and 'reputational' approaches to the study of leaders or elites. Accordingly, in each locality, a certain number of people were selected for interview on the basis of their office or positions. Local research helped, in addition, to identify some persons who were 'reputed' to be influential in the area. We then approached all these persons for interviews and asked them in turn to suggest the names of others, whom they believed to possess local influence. Those who received multiple mentions were added to the list for interview and were also asked for further names.

This 'snowball' technique has the advantage of producing a form of consensus as to the set of local leaders. There is always a danger that a 'bias' could enter as leaders nominated others with whom they were most closely associated or in sympathy. This danger would be counter-acted to the extent that the initial set of positional and reputational leaders were drawn from diverse interests. Inevitably, there were judgements to be made about the number of multiple nominations required for inclusion in the leadership list, and about the 'cut-off' point when 'snowballing' had to be concluded.

The employment of such positional and reputational techniques to identify leaders has been heavily criticised in the extensive literature on the study of community power (see, e.g., Dahl 1961; Polsby 1963; Presthus 1964; Parry 1969). It is argued that neither the occupation of an official governmental position nor the possession of a reputation for power is any guarantee that the person in question actually exercises power. This, it is sometimes argued, can only be established by examining the process of decision-making itself (but see Bachrach and Baratz 1970; Lukes 1974; Morriss 1987). There is undoubted force in this criticism. However, it is not a criticism which negates this particular project. As will become apparent, our objective will be to examine the interaction between citizens and those in official positions or with a local reputation for influence. And, whilst the impact of participation on such leaders will be considered, it is not claimed that such elites are necessarily the effective decision-makers and that they shape local policy in the particular directions desired by the citizenry. It is true that we should have liked to have gone further in examining the decision-making process, in order to see which citizen demands were converted into political outputs and by whom. This would be a marriage of community power and participation studies in an ideal research world of almost unlimited funds and time. Meanwhile, we believe that, for the present purposes, our combination of positional and reputational methods will suffice.

The outcome of these methods was to identify around 50 leaders in each locality although in the area of the largest population – Stockwell – the numbers reached over seventy. In each area the 'positional' list included the councillors for the relevant wards, the chairs of council committees dealing with important local issues and the senior local government officers in charge of the relevant departments. They also included newspaper editors, church leaders, heads of educational institutions, the manager of the largest local business and the local leader of the largest trade union in the area. Our own research, coupled with snowball methods, generally identified the leaders of active associations and pressure groups. In some instances, the persons identified by their position in authority, such as the chairs of council committees, were not necessarily from the immediate area of study and when interviewed they often proposed less senior but more locally based representatives and officials for interview. As a result, the members of the leadership group vary in power and influence and they might, in total, be regarded as 'notables' rather than a 'power elite'. For this reason, we will later sometimes distinguish the strictly 'political stratum' of councillors and officials who are closest to the centre of political decisions from the remaining notables.

All the leaders were asked the same set of questions in a semi-structured interview which contained many questions closely corresponding to those asked of the ordinary citizens. As a separate exercise in each locality – the two principal investigators talked to the Member of Parliament, the leader of the Council and the Chief Executive of the local authority in a less formal manner to obtain a number of overall impressions about political life and issues as seen from, as it were, the peak of the local structure of political power.

Taken together, 'notables' and citizens combine to provide a variety of perspectives as to what makes local participation effective or ineffective – as well as distinctively 'local'.

15

LOCAL PARTICIPATION

The extent to which people are led to take political action over local matters has been made evident repeatedly in the preceding chapters. Here we wish to explore this further by examining how far patterns of participation vary across the six localities or whether there is a common process at work. The major social and economic characteristics of the localities were outlined in the previous chapter. The question now to be addressed is how far these social characteristics produce striking variations in the levels and modes of participation.

One school of thought in political science argues that politics is nowadays essentially nationalised, not to say internationalised. This would be particularly so in a relatively small country such as Britain. On this view, people are mobilised to political action on the basis of national issues identified by national parties and publicised in the nation-wide press, radio and television media. People have interests which arise primarily from their social location, whether as members of a social class or as workers in a particular production sector, or as persons with a particular profile of public or private consumption (see chapter 6 above). It would not, however, follow from this view that political behaviour was entirely uniform across the nation. Rather, differences in behaviour in different localities or regions would be explicable according to the variations in the preponderance of a particular social class or of a certain type of economic production in the area. Thus, to take the relatively straightforward example of voting, if it is the case that public sector manual workers tend to vote Labour, then a constituency in which there is a heavy concentration of public sector industry would be more likely to return a Labour Member of Parliament. The political geography would reflect economic geography but political behaviour would not, in this instance, be an effect of locality as such but would be prompted by a perception of interests which would tend to be shared by most other people in the same social location in other parts of the country (Dunleavy and Husbands 1985:20, 195). Differences between areas would merely reflect the differences in the social composition.

An alternative to this nationally-oriented view is offered by those who argue that the regional and local variation in political behaviour is greater than can be explained by the social and economic composition of an area and that there must, as a consequence, be some further, distinctively local, factor at work. We may illustrate this again by voting behaviour where this phenomenon has been increasingly widely studied (Miller 1977;

Curtice and Steed 1982; Harrop and Miller 1987:207–11; Johnston, Pattie and Allsopp 1988). Using our previous example, it may be found that, in localities with a heavy preponderance of public sector manual workers, such voters support Labour even more strongly than would be predicted on the basis of their social location. Similarly, middle-class people might be found to be still more likely to vote Conservative in middle class localities than in mainly working-class areas. There is, in fact, considerable evidence to support this suggestion that people who are in similar social situations behave differently according to where they live (Curtice and Steed 1982:263). There appears, therefore, to be some kind of 'locality effect' in voting participation at least – 'how people vote in Britain now depends more on *where they live* than on *what they do*' (Harrop and Miller 1987:207, emphasis in the original). The problem is, then, not merely to measure the extent and significance of such an effect but to explain the mechanism which produces it. It is clearly not enough to suppose some obscure process of osmosis whereby people take on the political characteristics of their environment.

Various hypotheses have been, or might be, advanced. The most frequent is an interactionist model according to which political attitudes are influenced by contacts with other people in their neighbourhood and workplace. In a weak form, it has been labelled a 'contagion' theory (Harrop and Miller 1987:209–11). People provide 'cues' to one another as to their political feeling through conversations and life-styles. Presumably, in a locality where one social class is dominant, people receive political cues which are of the same sort and are repeatedly reinforced, producing what has been called a band-wagon effect.

Contagion theory must, however, produce evidence of the frequency of political conversation and then demonstrate that it has an effect on political behaviour. Here, Dunleavy (1979:413) is rightly critical: 'We cannot assume that political alignment brushes off on people by rubbing shoulders in the street'. Nor does our own evidence about the mechanism of personal influence offer strong support. Only a third of respondents in the national sample reported that they talked with others about politics fairly frequently, although only 14% had never done so. But, perhaps more to the point is the rate at which individuals claimed to have 'attempted to change the minds of family, friends or workmates about how to vote'. Nationally, only 3·9% had done so 'often' with a further 12·4% 'now and then'. In the six localities, the overall figures were about the same – 5·2% and 11·9% – although in one (Spotland), they reached 8·1% and 15·0%. Taken by themselves, these do represent potentially significant processes, albeit processes initiated only by a small minority. But it has to be presumed that at least a fair proportion of these attempts at influence had no effect at all, a point on which we have no information. All in all, therefore, we cannot say that there is strong evidence of contagion effects, in this sense of the term, although it cannot be entirely discounted.

For this reason, a possibly more plausible form of interactionist explanation would look at the extent to which people are mobilised to act in a particular political direction by agencies and groups in the neighbourhood. An established Labour Party, reinforced by trades unions, tenants' associations and community groups, might publicise issues and mobilise participants in support in a homogeneous neighbourhood to a greater extent than in a more mixed environment. A converse pattern could be envisaged in a middle class area involving the local Conservative Party, the Chamber of Commerce and other associations. One of our own major findings has been the importance of organisation for participation in general (see chapter 5). Members of groups were more prone to participate than were those not attached, and in a substantial proportion of cases people were first prompted to take action by groups.

Another approach (not necessarily incompatible with other hypotheses) to identifying a local effect on participation is to concentrate on the local political culture. Alongside the existence of a multiplicity of local groups, one may find in certain localities a particular sense of sympathy for a variety of forms of participation. In other words, there may be a local normative climate which is more supportive of participation than is to be found elsewhere (the existence of which is discussed in chapter 18 below). Where other citizens and elites adopt encouraging attitudes towards participation, it should in principle prove more profitable to form or to join groups, hold meetings and contact leaders. By contrast, any impression gained of a less sympathetic local leadership, and of a more inert mass population inclined to accept things as they are, would act as a disincentive to action.

The longest-standing version of cultural theory is the 'community' model of participation. As was briefly outlined in chapter 1, this model can be dated back to Jean-Jacques Rousseau. It suggests that sentiments of identification with, or 'belonging to', a local area are likely to stimulate a concern with the needs and interests of the locality which would translate into community-orientated political participation. Not every locality will be a 'community'. Those which are 'communities' should, if this theory is to be persuasive, be more participatory than other localities. However, what makes for community is highly contestable (Plant 1978) and contains a mixture of descriptive and normative elements. For many, a 'community' possesses certain spatial character-istics – well-bounded and distinct from neighbouring areas and usually relatively small. Others would insist, either additionally or alternatively, on more cultural and 'subjective' qualities such as a sense of mutual support amongst the population, a degree of common interest and equality – qualities which may usefully be distinguished by the term 'communality'. We shall be endeavouring in this chapter to test whether any locality effect in participation patterns is to be explained by differences in the normative climate and, in particular, by the extent to which the population of any of the localities views itself in communitarian terms.

Local participation or nationwide patterns?

Before considering the possible explanation of any local effect on participation, it is, of course, necessary to establish the extent to which participation does vary across the localities (table 15.1). We can begin by looking at the basic frequencies of the various acts of participation and compare them with those reported for our national sample (see table 3.1 in chapter 3).

By the nature of the sampling process, the six localities cannot be regarded as equivalent to a statistical sample of the nation as a whole. Nevertheless, as the preceding chapter has explained, the localities have been selected so as to represent some of the major types of locality in England, Wales and Scotland. It is, therefore, striking that if we compare the column in table 15.1 for the average participation levels for the six localities with table 3.1 presenting the national figures, the results display considerable

Table 15.1 *How much participation is there in the localities? (% yes/at least once)**

	Spotland	Pen'ceiber	Sevenoaks	Machars	Stockwell	Oswestry	Six-locality average
Voting							
1 Vote Local	63·9	76·4	71·5	67·6	52·5	57·9	65·5
2 Vote General	74·3	78·6	85·0	73·4	69·6	76·2	76·3
Party campaigning							
3 Fund raising	6·1	1·3	6·8	9·5	3·1	2·7	5·0
4 Canvassed	6·7	2·2	5·8	5·1	3·5	0·6	4·0
5 Clerical work	4·8	1·3	4·5	2·3	4·3	2·2	3·2
6 Attended rally	9·9	9·6	10·2	13·3	10·5	3·6	9·5
Group activity							
7 Informal group	18·9	18·2	20·6	7·9	21·9	10·9	16·1
8 Organised group	13·6	10·2	17·4	7·6	19·6	9·6	12·7
9 Issue in group	4·0	2·4	5·3	2·0	6·2	1·5	3·5
Contacting							
10 MP	16·8	3·3	12·6	9·8	9·8	9·8	11·2
11 Civil servant	12·2	5·2	12·6	6·3	8·3	4·4	8·1
12 Councillor	27·3	37·3	23·2	19·5	23·6	14·8	24·4
13 Town hall	20·7	23·6	21·7	13·5	27·2	16·7	20·3
14 Media	5·3	3·7	7·6	2·5	6·2	2·7	4·6
Protesting							
15 Attended protest meeting	15·6	15·8	22·8	9·4	26·0	8·1	15·9
16 Organised petition	10·2	7·4	7·1	3·8	10·3	8·1	7·1
17 Signed petition	62·3	75·9	73·9	33·1	67·2	59·1	61·4
18 Blocked traffic	0·4	3·2	2·3	0·4	5·1	0·0	1·8
19 Protest march	10·0	10·6	2·7	1·5	18·8	2·5	7·4
20 Political strike	6·9	14·0	2·0	2·6	9·9	4·2	6·5
21 Political boycott	4·6	3·9	5·3	1·9	10·6	2·0	4·5
N	271	291	264	292	226	271	1,615

* For exact wording on each item see Chart 3.1.

similarities. As such, they provide some confirmation of the consistency of responses to our questionnaires.

Apart from the special case of voting, the most frequently performed activity across the nation and in the six localities was signing a petition (63·3% nationally and 61·4% in the localities). Next in frequency came local contacting activities. A fifth of our national sample and a quarter of the local sample had contacted a councillor and around a fifth a town hall official. The figures for joining an organised group to raise an issue were very consistent at between 11% and 13%, and those for working in an informal group were also relatively close. Similarly comparable sets of results are provided for the questions about the various forms of party campaigning and protest activities.

The initial reaction to these findings is that they lend support to the view that British political life is fundamentally homogeneous. Localities do not differ greatly in the frequency and regularity with which their citizens undertake the various modes of participation. However, a closer look suggests that the average figures for the six localities conceal some interesting variations. Although, for example, signing a petition is, across the nation and in most localities, the only form of political action apart from voting which a majority of people perform, in one of our localities only a third claim to have done it. This was the scattered rural settlements of the Machars, whereas in the mining village of Penrhiwceiber and the greenbelt town of Sevenoaks, around three-quarters have put their names to a petition.

Similarly, average figures for certain of the more 'extreme' protest activities also suggest that generally a very small proportion of the local populations has been prepared to take radical measures to pursue its objectives – which bears out the national sample returns. Nevertheless, whilst only 7·4% overall have gone on a protest march in the localities (5·2% nationally), in the inner London area of Stockwell not far short of a fifth (18·8%) had done so. The other more urban localities of Spotland and Penrhiwceiber also reported notably higher than average figures. Equally, in Penrhiwceiber, an area of solid support for the National Union of Mineworkers, the population who had taken part in a strike which they deemed in some way 'political' was over twice the average for the six localities and for the nation as a whole.

There are, therefore, more variations, and some of a potentially intriguing nature, than are revealed by a simple inspection of average figures. But it is difficult to discern a pattern to these variations by a straightforward perusal of the whole range of participatory items. The next step is, therefore, to examine local patterns of participation for their underlying structure, as was done for the national sample in chapter 3. Accordingly, a factor analysis was undertaken for each of the localities, comparable to that for the national data. The results in most respects confirm those for the nation as a whole and, hence, serve once more as a reminder of an important degree of homogeneity in political behaviour across Britain. But, at the same time, there is also further evidence of variation around this common core.

The factor analyses clearly upheld the multidimensionality of participation. Indeed, if anything, they tended to fragment the phenomenon of participation even further. Across the nation, five main factors, or dimensions, of participation were clearly uncovered in chapter 3 (setting aside a sixth factor in 'political violence'): voting; party campaigning; group, or collective, action; contacting; and direct action. These too remain the major dimensions in the localities and thus the local pattern carries the imprint of the national. However, apart from voting, in some localities the dimensions lose their clear character and as many as six or seven different factors are at times identified. Thus in Oswestry, for example, two dimensions of party campaigning appeared – the somewhat more public activities of canvassing and attending meetings as one factor and the behind-the-scenes activities of clerical work and fund-raising as another. Elsewhere, as in the nation as a whole, these forms of campaigning were not separate dimensions.

Here, however, it must be acknowledged that the numbers involved in these activities in any locality are small and, as a consequence, the factor analyses are almost certainly much more unstable. In these circumstances, therefore, it is the degree to which the national model distinctions are preserved which is most striking, along with the fact that the thrust is towards specialised and relatively independent spheres of action.

As with the national study, the next stage of this structural analysis is to see how far the modes of participation are associated with one another. As has been noted, in the national study the correlations between the modes were quite modest, with the collective action factor having the highest average correlation with the other dimensions, the most substantial being with contacting (see table 3.3). It is here that greater local variation is to be found.

Across all six localities, the broad distinction between the relative centrality to overall participation of collective action, contacting and party campaigning, and the relative marginality of direct action and voting, remains intact. In none of the research sites did voting make a significant contribution to a notional underlying and unidimensional scale. Nor, with one interesting and noteworthy exception, did direct action. On the other hand, the detailed definition of that common core did vary from place to place. Generally, contacting, if anything, featured more prominently, but only in Sevenoaks and Stockwell was this clearly the most central mode. Elsewhere, party campaigning held this position (in Spotland) or collective action (the Machars and Oswestry). The most deviant case, however, was Penrhiwceiber where direct action formed a major part of the local definition of participation, alongside collective action. But this may well merely reflect an important aspect of political participation in the mining village at that time. Politics was dominated by collective protest. Hence this is a satisfying confirmation of the extent to which our techniques do pick up local variations – where they exist. The message, however, is that variations in the structure or basic character of participation seem to be relatively minor in Britain. There is, in other words, a strong sense of the localities merely reflecting a wider national picture. But there are, plainly, exceptions to this: none repeats the national pattern exactly, and in at least one instance, that pattern is a very poor indicator of the local situation. In short, it is possible to speak of local variations around a national theme.

These variations in the structure of participation are certainly sufficient to reinforce the view that there are local participatory effects worth investigating. At the same time, although in certain localities different dimensions of participation appeared to be at the forefront, nowhere was the structure so different or idiosyncratic as to suggest that the analysis based on an overall participation scale and on the five distinct modes adopted throughout the national study was inappropriate to employ for the local investigation. This was something which required careful checking, such as we have done, but there was always good reason for expecting that a basic pattern would emerge, partly because of regularities in participation found in very differing societies (Verba, Nie and Kim 1978), partly because of the relative unity of British political practices and also partly because of the extent to which our national story was itself effectively constructed from a myriad of stories of participation in different locales.

It was therefore thought more appropriate to proceed by using the results of the national factor analysis to construct the participation scales in the six localities. For to produce these scales purely on the basis of information within each locality would be to risk perpetuating patterns made somewhat unstable by low case counts. As the evidence suggests that there is fundamentally one pattern, albeit nuanced in different ways, it is better to use the very stable national relationships (as set out in chapter 3) to recreate that pattern in each locale.

This does not, of course, mean that all local differences are eliminated. Rather, the structural differences are removed, but all other aspects of the local participatory patterns continue to vary. Indeed, this can be seen by looking first at the extent to which each locality deviates from the overall mean on the modes of action and in its overall rate of activity.

In figure 15.1, the means for the six localities taken together have been set at zero in order to show how each locality scores in terms of higher or lower rates of participation than the average. The unadjusted scores appear on the left-hand side of the figure. These scores may be compared with those for the national survey in figure 3.3. However, it should be borne in mind that the voting items in the national study differ from those in the local surveys in that the national study also incorporated an item on voting in the European elections omitted from the local study. Similarly, no attempt has been made to create a localised version of political violence with the 'physical force' item.

As figure 15.1 reports, there is, on this first impression, some variation in the overall level of participation across the six localities. Two are distinctly less participatory than the general mean; two are rather more participatory; the remaining two are close to the mean. The two non-participatory areas are the Machars (-22) and Oswestry (-29). Political participation is, relatively, more frequently to be encountered in Sevenoaks ($+19$) or in Stockwell ($+25$). It will be recalled from Chapter 14 that the Machars and Oswestry are both rural areas with a tradition of non-partisan local politics. Sevenoaks and Stockwell both possess party-political local councils and are both urban areas, albeit strikingly different in character.

These results may be compared with the initial findings for America by Verba and Nie (1972:231–7). They also found that isolated villages and rural areas, as well as isolated small towns, had low unadjusted participation rates. Large suburbs and 'small cities' in or near metropolitan areas (to which Sevenoaks might correspond, allowing for differences in terminology) had higher levels of participation. Verba and Nie considered a number of explanations for this contrast, some of which will be discussed in a later section of this chapter. One possible factor to be considered at this stage is the difference between 'centre' and 'periphery'. On this theory, those in 'central' urban areas were exposed more frequently to political stimulation as a result of interaction with the number and variety of political groups, exposure to more media of communication and closer contact with centres of political action, all of which tend to be more concentrated in urban environments. The converse would be true in 'peripheral' rural areas. A difficulty Verba and Nie found with this mobilisation hypothesis was that core cities would have been expected to show higher participation rates, whereas they proved to be close to the mean.

With our own concentrated studies of six localities, it is not possible to provide a sufficient test of such a broad-ranging theory. Our more limited data appear in some respects more consistent with the mobilisation model in that the core city area of Stockwell is also high on participation. Caution is, however, appropriate in that it might be suggested that the urban mobilisation thesis would have predicted rather higher rates of participation in Spotland, a part of an industrial town, and in the mining village of

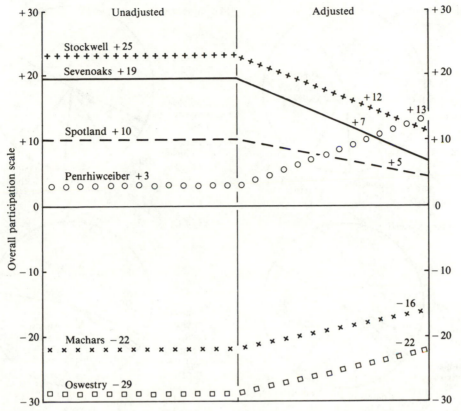

Figure 15.1 Overall participation by locality, controlling for individual and group resources and values

Penrhiwceiber, than the modest figures actually reported. As shall be seen below, several factors other than the urban-rural divide will need to be taken into account before one can begin to estimate the 'local effect' on participation.

Meanwhile, the overall rates of participation are somewhat differently composed in each locality. Comparing the two more participatory localities, in affluent Sevenoaks all modes of participation are higher than the mean, with the notable exception of direct action, whereas in Stockwell protest activity is exceptionally high, collective action similarly well-developed but the voting record is remarkably weak. Stockwell shares its protesting profile only with the Welsh pit community. The two rural localities are consistently below the mean in every mode of participation apart from the fractionally positive figure for party campaigning in the Machars which, in this locality, would be confined to national or Scottish regional levels, given the non-partisan nature of district politics. The rates in Spotland are on the low side but there are some positive figures for party campaigning and contacting in a locality where there is, indeed, an active three-party system and a Member of Parliament who is a local and a national celebrity – as table 15.1 showed, Spotland's MP had been contacted by the highest proportion of any of our samples.

As a final stage of the overview of local participation, we can also reintroduce the participant typology employed earlier in the national analysis (see chapter 10). Across

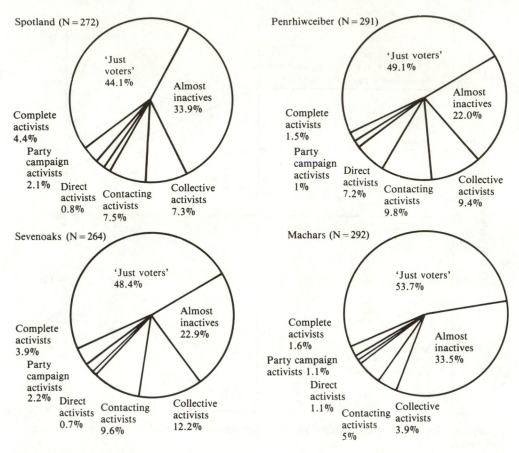

Figure 15.2 For legend see opposite page

the nation, half the country did little more than just vote and a quarter was inactive to the point of even voting less than average, leaving the burden of more active participation to fall on a quarter of the British population. A mere 1·5% was active across the various modes of activity. In figure 15.2 pie diagrams present the proportions of the participant types in each locality together with the combined distribution (cf. figure 10.1).

The first reaction might be to conclude that the composition of the participant population does not vary greatly across the nation. The localities appear to reinforce the national picture. Most strikingly, the rank ordering of the participant types is very similar in each locality to that in the nation as a whole. Thus, almost everywhere, those who 'just vote' form the largest component, followed by the 'almost inactive'. At the other end of the scale, the party campaign activists and the 'complete activitists' tend to be the rarest categories in the localities as they were in the national sample, with direct activists scarcely any thicker on the ground. All this again points to the nationalisation of political participation. It also means that, where appropriate, we can distinguish in broad terms between the activists and the remaining three-quarters of the population.

However, once more, a closer examination shows that there are, in fact, some significant local variations to be found. The low participation rates in the two rural localities are reflected in quite dramatic fashion by the fact that those who 'just vote' or

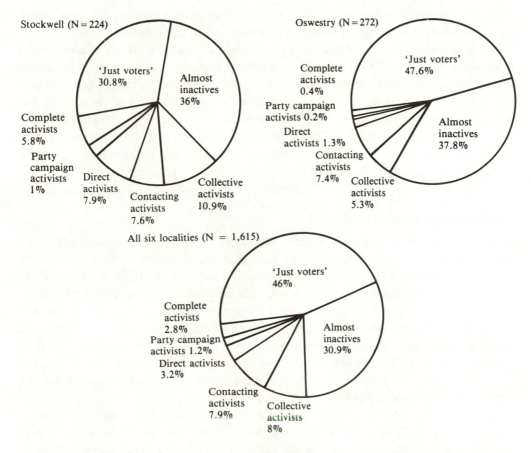

Figure 15.2 Types of political participants, by locality

are 'almost inactive' comprise 87·2% of the Machars sample and 85·4% in Oswestry. Putting it the other way round, here the bulk of the participatory activity is supported by less than 15% of the local population. By contrast, the inner London area of Stockwell has 66·8% in the two less active categories. Thus, hidden behind the national picture, in which just over three-quarters of the population form the least active of our participant types, are situations with 10% more and with 10% fewer in the less active groupings, which implies perceptible qualitative differences in local political life.

Such differences also appear at the other end of the participatory spectrum amongst the two most active clusters, the party campaign activists and the complete activists. In Stockwell, these two comprise some 6·8% of the total. This is still a small minority, but a minority that is nearly double the national proportion (3·7%) and several times the figures for the two least participatory areas (2·7% and 0·6%). Similar marked differences can be found within the intermediate participant types. Among those wedded to group action, for example (i.e. collective activists), Stockwell and Sevenoaks have proportions roughly three times those for the isolated Scottish villages. Perhaps even more striking are the variations recorded for direct activists. The proportions in the inner city area of Stockwell (with its problems of multiple deprivation and, around the time of the survey, political disputes with the government over funding and services) and for Penrhiwceiber (deeply involved in the miners' strike of 1984–5) were, not surprisingly, some ten times that for the prosperous, commuter town of Sevenoaks.

The various components of this overview of local participation taken together suggest that, while the national map does give a generally accurate picture of how participant populations in Britain are made up, there are sufficient variations for there also to be a need for local maps if we are to find our way to an understanding of the subject. But having shown that there are variations, we still need to return to the original theme to try to establish whether these variations reflect a genuine local effect of place or whether they simply mirror the social composition of the locality and are, hence, merely local instantiations of what is fundamentally a nation-wide behavioural pattern.

The sources of local variation

In chapters 4 to 9 we examined a very wide range of factors which might have been considered to have prompted political participation, either by way of constituting interests which might be advanced or defended by political involvement or by way of being resources which would facilitate action. These included what we termed 'resources' (such as wealth, education and organisational ties), social class, employment and consumption sector, party identification, outlooks and values. It was found that, whilst many of these background factors appeared initially and by themselves to have some associaton with participation, when we tried to pin down the particular effects of each one by controlling for the range of other background factors, only a limited number turned out to be crucial to the explanation.

Clearly, it is essential to follow the same procedure with the community data to establish whether the same factors are at work as with the national sample. It would have been somewhat burdensome to the reader to have been required to retrace in every detail the same paths of argument. In the event, this has not proved necessary since the patterns revealed by the analysis of overall participation in the six localities taken together proved remarkably similar across all the factors to those uncovered nation-wide. This provides substance for the view that the factors associated with participation are, at base, broadly similar across the country and that generalisations based on national data will not prove too wide of the mark. In presentational terms, it will also permit a concentration at appropriate points on the crucial nuances affecting participation in the localities without excessive repetition.

As will be seen in the case of Sevenoaks, a major part of the reason why its populace is so participatory is because it is highly resourced. For example, 48 % of the sample were members of the salariat. And, more generally, our evidence suggests that indeed part of the reason for variations in the levels of political activity across the country is to do with the different social compositions of the population, their attendant distributions of resources and the political values they hold.

But this does not seem to be the whole story. If it were the whole story, then by removing these compositional factors, the aggregate differences would tend to disappear. Thus, for example, the apparently high rate of participation of Sevenoaks would come down to the average rate for all the areas. As could be seen from the right-hand side scores in figure 15.1, however, this is not quite what happens. The adjusted side of the figure shows the result of equalising the localities on a number of factors which the earlier chapters showed to be associated with participation. These comprised education, group, union and party ties, age, political party identification and the most significant items on the efficacy, cynicism, left-right, green-peace and feminism scales.[2] Sevenoaks, after adjusting for these effects, remains somewhat above average (+7). Furthermore, although there is some general attenuation across all six localities, significant differences between them still remain. Stockwell retains a relatively high participatory profile (+12), whilst Oswestry and the Machars are still substantially below the overall mean (−22 and −16 respectively). Penrhiwceiber rises to be the league leader (+13).

Thus, there appears to be something beyond a compositional effect at work and possibly something which is owed in part to the peculiarities of the place. As figure 15.1 suggests, when differences in resources and values are discounted, the gaps in overall participation rates do not uniformly narrow. This would seem to imply that a variety of particular factors is at work shaping levels of activity and styles of participation. Thus, Sevenoaks is a town where one will encounter a fair degree of political partici-pation – and this is a 'reality' which must be borne in mind in the arguments which follow. But, it would seem, activity there is only a little more than one might have expected from the general status and composition of its residents. Conversely, in Penrhiwceiber, the participation rate is a lot higher than the norm, given the social position of its inhabitants, very few of whom, for example, have acquired the educational qualifications which have been shown earlier to have an important association with participation.

In removing, or making adjustments, for compositional effects across the six localities, we are seeking to give some empirical meaning to the notion of 'place'. More precisely, the method is intended, within the normal limitations of the data and statistical techniques, to isolate the apparent effect of living in place 'A' as against place 'B'. What has been seen in figure 15.1 is an estimate of those factors. The evidence suggests that, after deploying powerful variables to remove compositional differences, important place effects of this sort remain. They have, however, essentially a residual status. The place names stand for the extent to which residents of each area participate above or below the overall mean relative to their respective local resource and value profiles. But what do they mean?

It is possible that a small part is attributable to further unspecified compositional effects. But another part is, arguably, the summation of local experiences having to do with institutional arrangements and the 'nature of the times' in each area – a conjunction of time and place. In principle, the analysis of such macro-level contextual effects would proceed by insertion of theoretically well-specified and well-measured variables that would then test for the systematic effect of given institutional arrangements (for example) on individual behaviour. The result would be to decant out of 'place', explanations in terms of given properties (see Przeworski and Teune 1970:26–30). The effect of 'place' – as a set of real names (such as 'Penrhiwceiber' or 'Machars') – would then shrink until no further purchase on the explanatory power of the total model could be obtained. 'Place' would then indeed be a simple unspecified residual effect.

Unfortunately, our research design did not allow for the systematic investigation of these local macro-effects. That is the major cost of using the strategy of conducting intensive investigations but in only a limited number of research sites (see chapter 2; see also Parry and Moyser 1984). With only six observations at the macro level, we are not in a position to undertake the process of unpacking 'place' into more substantially precise component elements. All that is possible is to use a variety of indirect evidence to suggest how these place effects arise. This will be done through a series of case-studies of the more salient place effects identified in figure 15.1.

At the same time, however, it should be noted that the analysis makes one crucial assumption – namely that the process whereby individuals come to participate is the *same* in each locality. It assumes, in effect, that the role of 'place' is to raise or lower participation for given sets of local inhabitants over and above that common process. This would be, as it were, an 'add-on' effect of place. However, it is possible that place not only lowers or raises participation but also changes the nature of the politicisation process. It may be, for example, that local circumstances are such as to change, or even to reverse, particular national relationships. Where, generally, the well-educated participate more than the less well-educated, local circumstances may equalise their activity levels. Or, the less well-educated may participate more because of that local situation.

This type of 'place' effect is, obviously, more substantial and important. To the extent it exists, the notion of participation as resulting from an essentially uniform nationwide process would be undermined. The analysis in the first half of the book would not be a true representation, but merely an average of various significantly different local processes.

It is crucial, therefore, to examine this possibility. Fortunately, in this instance, our research design works in our favour. For there are sufficiently large samples of citizens in each locality to test the 'uniformity' proposition. This will be the subject of a later section of the chapter. Meanwhile, we turn to consider the first type of place effect – those which were highlighted in figure 15.1.

In an attempt to isolate the factors which lie behind these variations in patterns of participation, we shall treat certain of our localities as case studies in local and compositional effects. We shall then seek to draw some more systematic comparisons.

Case study 1: Sevenoaks and the effect of social composition

The first case is that of Sevenoaks which may be interpreted as primarily, but not entirely, an exemplar of the effect of social composition. Everything in Sevenoaks points to its being a town which will have a high rate of participation. In particular, its population is very well-endowed with individual resources. Almost half the residents fell within the top band of our scale of wealth (compared with 2% in Penrhiwceiber). Nearly 18% had gained a university or polytechnic degree. Almost three-quarters were members of one or more voluntary associations. All this is well-reflected in the local participation level of +19.

Yet this impression of a highly participatory environment largely dissolves once we control for resources. It seems, then, that Sevenoaks punches only about its participatory weight, or a little more (+7). Two-thirds of the initial participatory effect can be put down to the compositional effect of resources and values, of which resources play the

Table 15.2 *Participation in Sevenoaks, by mode and controlling for resources and values*

	Unadjusted	Adjusted
Voting	+19	+6
Party campaigning	+9	+1
Collective action	+21	+15
Contacting	+16	+1
Direct action	−12	−9

larger part. Before adjustment, as table 15.2 shows, the strengths of Sevenoaks were spread across every one of the modes of participation, bar direct action. Particularly strong were voting and collective action, but the process of equalising the factors leaves only collective action as exceptionally strong. This is despite ties to organisations forming an important part of the controls.

Table 15.1 showed that all forms of group activity in Sevenoaks were above average, as were attending protest meetings and signing petitions. These are, perhaps, the very types of mild, but firm, protest to be expected in such an environment. There had, in fact, been two issues in the town which had particularly aroused concern (see also chapter 16) – the closure of a hospital and the siting of a swimming pool. Both had led to well-attended meetings and associated protests. Clearly, environmental and planning issues of this kind can prompt the emergence of not only the members of formal groups but also wider informal networks of collective action.

These are not, perhaps, the types of issue which would lead to more radical forms of direct action (although other environmental threats have led to quite sharp outbreaks of sit-ins and blocking of traffic by middle class protesters). Certainly, these seem not to be the issues which would have incited involvement from the trades unions, leading to radical action. Thus, even when allowance is made for the population's Conservative political identity and associated leanings, direct action is at a very low level.

All in all, therefore, whilst there remains a small residual participatory impetus to be explained, the levels of activity to be found in Sevenoaks are almost entirely attributable to its social composition. Its population is well-provided with most of the appropriate personal and collective resources which have been seen to serve as the launching pad for political participation.

Case study 2: local mobilisation and Penrhiwceiber

The second case study is provided by Penrhiwceiber, in many respects the social polar opposite of Sevenoaks. Its unadjusted rate of participation is slightly above the average (+3). This in itself seems to invite an explanation since, in clear contrast to Sevenoaks, the population is far from well provided with the personal resources which make for participation. Only one person in our sample held a degree, a mere six held other educational qualifications above 'A'-level, whilst eight out of ten had no qualifications. Nor is there a particularly large network of groups to offer an alternative resource for participation. Half of the population belong to no voluntary group.

Penrhiwceiber residents do, however, possess one highly significant organisational resource which helps, in almost classical fashion, to counteract the lack of individual level resources associated with working class life (Goodin and Dryzek 1980). This resource is trades union membership. It has been seen to form one of the stronger associations with participation nationally, and in Penrhiwceiber the currently active unionists participate highly (+96) before controlling for other resources. Two-thirds of the population are, or have been, union members. This is a higher proportion than that registered in any of the other five areas. A measure of union involvement is that 38% of protest actions are described as having been initiated by them, a figure markedly higher than elsewhere. The union mobilises its members to march and demonstrate. In one form of direct action – strikes considered by the respondent to be 'political' – union mobilisation is a necessary condition. The 14% who had taken part in one is four times the figure reported anywhere else except Stockwell.

Hence, in these terms, Penrhiwceiber is not entirely under-resourced. Coupled with its solid union character is also the fact that, like Sevenoaks but at the other end of the political spectrum, this is a one-party 'local state'. Three-quarters of the sample identified with Labour and almost 70% of respondents voted that way in the 1983 General Election – a proportion vastly in excess of that for any party elsewhere. Such left-wing positions and associated values have also been seen to be associated with participation.

Thus, balancing the factors which would discourage participation, there are others which would encourage it and the resultant unadjusted figure seems to reflect this. When the effects of this range of resources, political commitments and values are removed, however, overall participation rises. Penrhiwceiber, indeed, comes to lead the participatory league table one point ahead of Stockwell and well in front of Sevenoaks. Moreover, the very modes of participation most mobilised by the unions – collective (+9) and direct action (+11) – remain strong or are even strengthened (see Table 15.3).

It would appear that there is a form of local 'contagion effect' whereby the union and the Labour Party mobilises the population, beyond the members themselves (since this factor is discounted). One element in this must, of course, be the special circumstance of the miners' strike. Support was solid in Penrhiwceiber. There was a range of actions in support of it by members of the village, other than mineworkers themselves, including notably on the part of women. The village was a supreme instance of a 'community under threat' in which mobilisation and participation are exceptionally heightened. Unemployment was high. The pit was known to be an early candidate for closure. And, in the absence of alternative industry, the whole future of the valley was in doubt. Some were so dispirited that, it was reported, they believed the solution would be to 'build a wall at the top and bottom of the valley and just have a dam here'. But for others, the national strike was not merely about the closure of collieries, 'We're talking about closing communities'. In these threatened circumstances, one might expect that people will indeed be tempted by some of the more direct modes of participation.

Controlling for resources, the residents of the pit village also contact to a high degree (+17) – although in absolute, unadjusted terms they are below the average of the localities. Certainly, in view of the compactness of the village itself, it should be relatively easy to contact councillors, even if the administrative centre of the Cynon Valley District

Table 15.3 *Participation in Penrhiwceiber, by mode and controlling for resources and values*

	Unadjusted	Adjusted
Voting	+17	+25
Party campaigning	−11	−5
Collective action	+5	+9
Contacting	−1	+17
Direct action	+20	+11

is a little further away. The area had, indeed, the highest level of contacting of councillors amongst the six areas. Although some of these contacts concerned the miners' strike, the largest number were over housing. As was mentioned in chapter 14, housing conditions in the area were very poor and overall this problem was second on the list of issues raised by residents (see chapter 16). Finally, voting is very high relative particularly to the resource patterns which would otherwise imply a low turn-out. The explanation cannot lie with a competitive party system activating even the marginal voter. Labour Party hegemony is such as to mean that the other parties are there merely to fly the flag. In such localities, voting takes on a particularly expressive aspect – a gesture of solidarity, perhaps, with a community where voting, and specifically for the Labour Party in General Elections, is 'natural', and is seen as registering a view about long-standing economic deprivation.

Penrhiwceiber thus appears to be an example of a locality where an under-resourced population is mobilised by political organisations deeply implanted in the area. Its intensity of participation in 1984–5 was certainly enhanced by the threat to its economic survival and, hence, to its very quality as a traditional, homogeneous community. But this was not a unique experience. Direct action was more of a way of political life. This is indicated by the 8·7% who had taken part more than once in a political strike (twice as many as even in Stockwell) and also by the high proportion of direct activists (see figure 15.1). The nature of participation is reinforced by what one might term an 'oppositional' political culture – a climate in which, as will be shown more fully in chapter 18, citizens and elites are in sympathy with 'unconventional' forms of action. Penrhiwceiber is also, as has been implied, a 'community' and it is possible that this perception of itself may contribute to its participatory quality. This aspect of its values will be discussed in a separate section of this chapter devoted to the communitarian aspects of participation.

Case study 3: local mobilisation and Stockwell

Stockwell provides the third case study. It is, like Penrhiwceiber, if not to the same degree, a study in mobilisation but of a different pattern. As figure 15.1 showed, Stockwell, in absolute terms, tops the participation league table. It is not obvious from the profile of resources why this should be so. Certainly, the population is not entirely lacking in them either personally or collectively. Whilst inner London areas are often thought of as predominantly working class and relatively deprived, Stockwell, as has been shown earlier, is more mixed. It has a good proportion of the salariat and the routine non-manual classes which implies the presence of more individual participatory resources than would exist in a uniformly working class environment, such as Penrhiwceiber. It comes, for example, just behind Sevenoaks in the proportion of the sample with degrees.

However, at the other end of the resource spectrum, Stockwell has a substantial black population. This means that the locality is not in this one respect fully comparable to the other areas. Although the numbers of black people in our sample is not large (51, representing 22·8% of the local sample), they provide what is probably a fair indication of the under-resourced condition of that minority. Unsurprisingly, black people in Stockwell are a lot poorer than whites.[3] In the six-band scale of wealth, whereas 37% of Stockwell whites are in the upper three bands, only 15% of non-whites are. Indeed, there is not one black person in the very top band, compared with 10% of whites. Educationally, the story is similar. Over a third of whites had 'A'-level qualifications and above, whilst just over a fifth of blacks had obtained them. In our sample, only one black graduate appeared. However, although individual resources display the disadvantaged position of black people, the group-based resources of whites and non-whites are virtually identical. Membership of voluntary groups is the same and blacks are slightly more unionised.

The combination of resources is such that it would be expected that black people would participate less than white. This is so. The average score for whites on the overall participation scale is +12, whilst for non-whites it is −46. As the unadjusted figures in table 15.4 show, the gap varies as between the modes of participation but is still quite marked. More intriguing, however, are the adjusted figures which indicate that when we discount resources alone, the participation gap between non-whites and whites, though reduced, remains quite substantial. Clearly, then, more than resources are at work. There is no opportunity here to examine the complex cultural and institutional forces which operate to inhibit black activism. And, without other cases to compare, it is not possible to consider how much of the difference between non-whites and whites is due to features common to the situation of black people in Britain and how much to the local conditions of Stockwell, where, however, much has been done officially and by groups to promote black political involvement. There is room for an intensification of research into the whole range of black participation beyond what has already been achieved within electoral studies (see, for example, the work of Welch and Studlar 1985; Anwar 1986; Fitzgerald 1987; Layton-Henry 1989).

Meanwhile, the general effect of this aspect of Stockwell's social composition, along with its working class component, would have been to reduce its average level of participation. On the other hand, there are aspects of the local situation in which the non-white and white populations share which would boost activity. Although Stockwell is in a more competitive party political system (at national and local level) than Penrhiwceiber, it is predominantly a Labour Party area. The position of the respondents on issues used to identify value systems was consistently towards the left, green/peace and feminism. All these have been seen to be linked with participation.

Table 15.4 *Participation rates of whites and non-whites in Stockwell, controlling for individual* and group-based resources*

	Unadjusted			Adjusted		
	Whites	Non-whites	Gap	Whites	Non-whites	Gap
Overall	+12	−46	58	+8	−31	39
Contacting	+11	−43	54	+8	−33	41
Voting	+10	−38	48	+7	−27	34
Collective action	+9	−36	45	+7	−36	43
Party campaigning	+5	−20	25	+1	−5	6
Direct action	+5	−20	25	+2	−8	10

* Including wealth.

Table 15.5 *Participation in Stockwell, by mode and controlling for resources and values*

	Unadjusted	Adjusted
Voting	−25	−28
Party campaigning	−3	−6
Collective action	+33	+19
Contacting	+18	+13
Direct action	+38	+23

The initial, unadjusted levels in table 15.5 may thus reflect a local society where quite highly resourced sectors are very involved, particularly in collective action and direct action. Their high rates would be dampened by other groups in the population who are very inactive – as registered by the low voting rates. This pattern was picked up earlier in the discussion of figure 15.2. Swinging the balance back towards participation would be the radical left orientation of many of the respondents.

By controlling for this variety of resource, party and value factors, the level of participation should be attenuated. This indeed occurs. The adjusted overall rate of activity is + 12 (see figure 15.1) indicating that about half the level of participation could be attributed to compositional effects. However, this leaves a further element to explain. As table 15.5 shows, the overall pattern is composed from a very strong adjusted input by direct action and collective action, counteracted by a remarkably weak rate of voting. The importance of collective action confirms the figures on levels of participation in table 15.1 where Stockwell comes out highest on all three group activities and in attendance at protest meetings which is part of the collective mode. Moreover, those who are members of voluntary groups generally participate at an adjusted rate well above the national norm. Thus, the larger number with only one such tie are far more active (+71) than the average across the country (see Figure 5.2). Stockwell has the second highest proportion of collective activists (see figure 15.2).

No single organisation dominates the political scene. To the degree that there is mobilisation in Stockwell, the sources are multifarious. Stockwell might well represent, in contrast to Penrhiwceiber, a modern, mobile, fragmented, heterogeneous, even atomised, local society. Such a society can well engender high levels of participation as individuals and groups interact and conflict in the pursuit of personal and sectional advantage.

The second major feature of Stockwell is its propensity to direct action (+23). This is the highest for all of the localities and the area has the largest proportion of direct activists (7·9%) (see figure 15.2) as well as complete activists (5·8%). Protest marches and political boycotts (table 15·1) are well above the average. The subjects of these actions are usually a mixture of economic issues, such as jobs, and foreign affairs, including nuclear disarmament. Despite controls, degree holders – who have a propensity to direct action – are very much more active overall than their counterparts nationally and are, as has been seen, well-represented. Another group which contributes to Stockwell's participation rate is public sector workers whose adjusted overall activity (+21) is well above the national level. Moreover, this is a group which, as was shown in chapter 6, has a record of higher involvement in direct action. One of the major public sector employers in the area was Lambeth Borough Council which had been engaged in a well-publicised struggle against the Conservative Government's expenditure restrictions. It was also heavily involved in the debate over the abolition of the Greater London Council. Issues concerning race discrimination (though not prominent – see chapter 17) had also been on the agenda. It would be unsurprising if some of these had not given rise at least to protest marches in addition to actions falling into the collective category and, certainly, one category of protest issues here was over local governmental matters.

Stockwell (along with, but in a different way, Sevenoaks) might be said to represent 'modernity', and may also provide support for the contention in the literature on participation, that 'central' rather than 'peripheral' localities will reveal higher levels of political involvement (Milbrath and Goel 1977:86–90; Verba and Nie 1972:229–30). The claim is that those who live in politically central locations – close to the metropolitan core – are more exposed to political communication, have a higher rate of social interaction and 'encounter more stimuli enticing them to participate' (Milbrath and Goel 1977:89). If centrality is measured by physical distance, Stockwell's situation, virtually within sight of the Houses of Parliament across the river, would count. More plausibly, centrality is usually understood in terms of a theory of communication. Certainly, at the time of the survey, the residents of Stockwell would have been receiving political messages from the centre with some frequency concerning the local Labour Council's well-publicised clashes with the Conservative Government over the running of local government. As a result, Lambeth Council and its political objectives were matters of direct media attention, as earlier had been the nearby Brixton riots. It is unlikely that, in the same period, the Machars received so much as a line in a national newspaper. Stockwell was not a community under threat but it was part of a locality under public scrutiny.

In these circumstances, it is perhaps significant that a distinctly high proportion of people in Stockwell reported that they discuss politics and national affairs with others very or fairly often – 37·3% as against 26·6% across the six localities as a whole. Interest in politics and national affairs was also higher, with 58·5% interested, compared with an average of 48·7%. More people (6·2%) had used a group to raise a political issue or problem than in any other area. More were members of groups in which social and political issues were discussed and more said that they themselves were involved in such discussions. In the case of the action taken on their prime issue, far more than elsewhere they described what they had done as 'political'. In these respects, Stockwell's closest counterpart was Sevenoaks, which would be regarded, indeed, as the other case of a 'central' locality. Talking about politics and displaying interest in it are not, in our terms, participation, but they may orient people towards it and provide a sympathetic climate for it. As chapter 17 will show, Stockwell does, in this respect, share with Penrhiwceiber a public opinion supportive of various forms of direct action. Coupled with a sense of local support for conventional participation, this means that the normative barriers against political involvement are low.

It appears, therefore, that if the effect of the level of resources and an array of values is discounted, which in Stockwell would in various ways boost and diminish participation, the high level of local activity is the product of a heterogeneous local society which offers a variety of stimuli to political interest. The major exception is voting. Here, we may be seeing the other side of inner city life – its mobility and atomisation which leaves many voters unregistered. In 1981, in inner London, 47% of young unemployed were not registered, along with a third of new Commonwealth immigrants (Harrop and Miller 1987:45). Amongst our Stockwell sample, 28% had not voted in the 1983 General Election (a figure markedly higher than elsewhere) and, of these, 37% said this was because they were not registered. Given the low rate of voting (and hence a body of 'almost inactives' only marginally smaller than that in peripheral Oswestry), Stockwell's overall level of participation is, in relative terms, all the more remarkable.

Case study 4: participation and de-mobilisation – the Machars

For the final case study[4] in local political effects, we turn to what is almost the archetypal peripheral area. The Machars is very remote from the capital of Britain and, indeed, quite remote from that of Scotland. It is at some distance from its own regional administrative town or even from any large centre of population. These are the very obverse of the conditions that make for effective political mobilisation. As table 15.1 shows, in nearly every form of activity, the people of the Machars are below the average. It also has the lowest proportion of activists (figure 15.2). From figure 15.1 it will be gathered that a relatively small part of the explanation for these low rates of participation appears to lie with the resource and value profile of the population. The initial score of -22 on the overall participation scale is modified only slightly to -16 when individual and group resources, party factors and values are taken into account.

There remain, therefore, some further local factors beyond composition which appear to demobilise the population in this rural area (as is also true of the other rural locality of Oswestry). There are, it should be insisted, small groups of very active people in the area involved, particularly, in some well-organised local community action programmes. Nevertheless, in every mode of participation except party campaigning, the Machars population as a whole is below average, despite equalising the levels of resources and the patterns of values (see table 15.6).

The prevailing mode of economic production in the area and its peripheral character appear to discourage participation. Although the working class constitute a large part of the population, there is the lowest level of past and current unionisation amongst the six localities (37%). The problems of union organisation amongst agricultural workers are of long standing and have, effectively, prevented the resort to forms of action (such as the 'political strike') available to industrial employees (see Danziger 1988:69–96). Much other union employment is also geared to the agricultural sector. Controlling for other factors finds the very active unionists under-participating in other directions. There is, thus, little impetus towards the kinds of collective or direct action which might be mobilised by unions.

If we couple these features of local economic life with the physical facts of the Machars – the scattered nature of its small settlements, its distance from administrative centres – the low levels of collective and direct action are readily explicable. Where people did act, fewer than elsewhere said that this was in response to any request from an organisation. Moreover, they reflect structural features of the political landscape of the Machars. As such, they are not counterbalanced by any powerful issue such as would engender a rapid upsurge of citizen activity. The issues which the people in the Machars raise are (as will be seen more fully in subsequent chapters) themselves long-term problems. They concern rural transport and the gradual decline of employment opportunities for the young in country areas.

The only positive participatory feature of the Machars is itself a little surprising. Party campaigning is strong. This is despite the fact that the area falls within a District Council which is one of the declining number whose politics is non-partisan. The parties thus do not play a role in mobilising for the most local level of elections. Against this there are the regional elections in Scotland as well as the General Elections which are quite intensely competitive. The Scottish National Party's presence is significant and the parliamentary seat had changed hands not many years previously.

All in all, after controlling for resources, the Machars remains an unpolitical area. Few people discuss politics. As chapter 18 will show, there is a widespread view that there is little sympathy for any form of less conventional participation. A general mood of acceptance of things would seem to offer little encouragement to would-be activists. This tends to compound the problems which isolation puts in the face of such basic participatory activities as contacting officials personally or getting signatures on a petition when there are no crowded town centres in which the support of the passer-by can be enlisted. In short, the Machars presents a picture of a demobilising local effect.

Community effects

Another explanation of local participation effects looks to less readily definable qualities of local life which, however elusive, have appealed to political theorists for generations. This is the communitarian theory. According to this view, participation is stimulated where there is a strong sense of commitment by local people to their 'community'. It is based upon two propositions which might appear to be distinct but which are closely, perhaps inextricably linked, namely, that the locality in question is a 'community' and that 'community' is a quality to be valued.[5] The former appears to be a descriptive statement whilst the latter is a normative proposition. In the event, such a distinction

Table 15.6 *Participation in the Machars, by mode and controlling for resources and values*

	Unadjusted	Adjusted
Voting	−2	−3
Party campaigning	+9	+9
Collective action	−32	−22
Contacting	−19	−19
Direct action	−19	−9

may prove impossible to sustain. 'Community' is almost a paradigm example of an 'essentially contestable concept' (Gallie 1955–6) where a person's very definition of the term is shaped by his or her ideological position on many other values such as, in this instance, liberty, equality or fraternity. As a result, there are fundamental disagreements as to what qualities of relationship would merit granting the title of 'community' to any given locality and its social life (Plant 1978). A traditional conservative could discover community in the ordered, hierarchical, deferential character of rural village life. A socialist would almost certainly hold that genuine community presupposes a more equal society or at least a society where people would provide one another with mutual support in shared conditions of adversity arising from disadvantages encountered in conditions of economic inequality (McCulloch 1984; McCulloch and Parry 1986).

For these reasons, an agreed, 'objective' meaning of community is difficult, perhaps impossible. As a result, any attempt to establish in some empirical manner that a sense of community exists and that it can be an impulse to participation must, to the degree that it is at all feasible, embody some normative assumptions. This is true of any attempt even to establish a 'minimal' definition of community. Nevertheless, in working with just such a minimal notion, we have to accept the criticism that some normative element is being introduced. This minimal measure is intended to capture something of the idea of *Gemeinschaft*, propounded in the classic work of Tönnies (1963), according to which, in order to warrant the term 'community', a locality has at least to attract a sense of identity and attachment. Accordingly, the minimal community index is composed of an affective and a cognitive element. In affective terms, people were asked how far they felt a sense of attachment to the area in which they lived. Cognitively they were asked whether they recognised the area to be a 'community', leaving them to use this term in their own ways. Heightened participation could be expected if it were the case that people's sense of attachment and the associated resonances of the term 'community' translated into a desire to defend and protect the conditions which gave rise to them.

That even this supposedly minimal view of community could contain an ideological element may be seen by testing the community index for its relationship to a more explicitly value-laden idea which we termed 'communality'. This embodies a particular conception of what community entails and is close to the socialist idea of solidarity. 'Communality' included the extent to which the respondent thinks that the people in the area share similar needs and interests; that they treat one another as equals; that they support each other; that there is a sense of 'togetherness' and 'fellowship' and that such

Table 15.7 *Scores on community index for six localities* (%)

	Spotland	Pen'ceiber	Sevenoaks	Machars	Stockwell	Oswestry	Total
High community	10·3	41·4	11·3	32·1	10·4	32·9	24·3
Intermediate	78·7	55·1	81·5	66·8	73·1	64·1	69·2
Low community	11·1	3·6	7·4	1·1	16·5	3·1	6·5
Total	100·0	100·0	100·0	100·0	100·0	100·0	100·0
N	226	278	251	279	195	252	1,481

a sense is important. The analysis showed that there was a significant correlation between the community index and the measures of communality. On the other hand, this was some way short of identity. Hence the minimal notion of community is not so normatively impregnated as to be only acceptable to a believer in socialist solidarity. Community, as it is measured here, can have a wider attraction and could, in principle, provide the impetus to uphold a variety of perceived communities.

As table 15·7 shows, the localities do differ in the intensity with which they are viewed as communities as measured on the scale. The index discriminates between the localities in a statistically highly significant manner. Across the six localities, a quarter of the population regard their areas in very communitarian terms. But far and away the most communitarian is the pit village of Penrhiwceiber, living up to the common image of the 'mining community' with 41·1 % scoring their area high on the index. It will be recalled that this is also one of the most participatory localities with a considerable capacity for mobilisation. However, before one jumps to any conclusions concerning the link between community and participation, it should be noticed that the next highest in the community league table are the two rural areas which consistently have the lowest rates of participation. Clearly, the internal mechanisms of relationships, if any, between community and participation need further investigation.

The first step is to see how far community feeling is associated, as one would predict, with positive rather than cynical attitudes towards local politics. This expectation was indeed confirmed. The measure of community was associated with a number of variables which tapped support for political institutions, persons and practices. In order to summarise this, we constructed an index[6] of political support or, looked at in reverse, of political cynicism. The index was composed of classic measures of trust and cynicism – trust in local councillors to do what is right; the view that most councillors are out for themselves rather than the public good; that most protesters and most community activists are similarly out for themselves. The only weak item on the index was that concerning protesters, the main factor being the cynical view of councillors. We also employed a further summary measure of supportive attitudes whereby the respondents gave their local district councils 'marks out of ten'.

As can be seen from figure 15.3, the high communitarians across the areas together did indeed score above the mean (+0·19), representing a positive attitude to their local political world. Conversely, those low in community-mindedness were on average below the mean (−0·63). The award of marks out of ten reinforced the pattern. Councils scored an average mark from all the respondents of 5·8 but the high communitarians

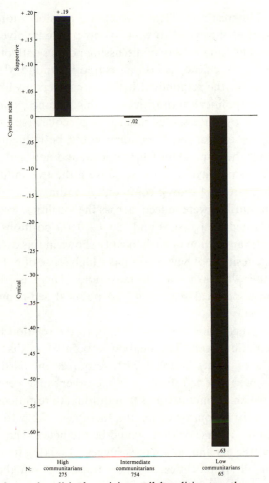

Figure 15.3 Community and political cynicism, all localities together

awarded 6·5 whilst those low on the community scale gave only 4·5. The pattern is repeated for nearly every locality. Low communitarians were everywhere more cynical and high communitarians, with the one exception of Stockwell where they are in any case thin on the ground, took a positive view of the local political process. In Sevenoaks, those high in community sentiment are also few in number but were very positive in attitude (+0·63). Penrhiwceiber has large numbers of communitarians. So, interestingly, has the Machars (where the high communitarians had a mean support rate of +0·40 and give their council 7·1 marks), even though the scattered nature of its residents might be thought to militate against the development of a sense of identity which would be expected in a similarly rural but more concentrated population such as Oswestry.

There is, therefore, ample evidence that basic community feeling is associated with positive attitudes towards the local polity. This might be regarded as the first building block in the community theory of participation whereby support for institutions and processes serves as a basis for becoming politically involved. There are, however, some indicators that this particular building may not be 'topped out'.

Although community is related to supportive sentiments, it is much less clearly related to feelings of political interest and efficacy which are possibly more crucial in shaping participation. Measures of the extent to which people were involved in political life by way of an interest in politics and by way of discussing politics with others had no relation to community. The sense of efficacy is also measured by an index[7] containing a classic component asking how far the respondent believes that persons like himself or herself can have influence over political authorities – in this instance, over local councillors. This was supplemented by an essential indicator of collective efficacy which asked whether a *group* of persons like the respondent could be influential. Finally, further questions asked how far the respondent felt that local and national politics were easy or difficult to follow. The main factors in the scale were the two influence items.

In this instance, as figure 15.4 shows, community sentiment had little relationship to efficacy. High communitarians were indeed, across the localities, less efficacious (-0.11) than those in the intermediate ($+0.05$) and low ($+0.01$) positions on the community scale. However, closer examination of each locality shows in this case little clear pattern, except that the average resident of Sevenoaks has a high sense of political self-confidence regardless of any other values he or she may hold. There is, therefore, no simple argument from positive political sentiments, to political self-confidence and, thence, possibly to participation.

This is, then, some preparation for now turning to the relation between community sentiment and participation itself. The method is parallel to that used in the earlier analysis of the effects of values coupled with resources on participation. Here, the community index has been inserted in place of the other value items. Thus, the results will show the impact which community makes additional to resources.[8] The results of the investigation are not very encouraging for the theory, as table 15.8 appears to show. Indeed, they are often the reverse of what would be predicted. The effect of community is in any case slight, as the eta and beta scores suggest. Looking first of all at the overall participation rate for all six localities together, those high on the community index participate slightly below the mean (-2). Removing the effects of the resource variables of organisational memberships and educational qualifications still leaves the high communitarians only virtually average participants ($+1$). By contrast, the low communitarians are more participatory than average ($+18$) or 20 points above those in the high category – a pattern upheld more strongly ($+24$) when controlling for resources. As table 15.8 also shows, this same pattern holds true for both contacting and collective activity.

In the case of direct action, the pattern is curvilinear with both high and low communitarians participating a little above average. It is not perhaps absolutely clear what the communitarian theory would predict in this instance. On the one side, one could hypothesise that where a community faced severe threats to its way of life, the high communitarians would be ready to employ strong measures in its defence. 'Community' was a rallying cry in the dispute over the national miners' strike and has similarly been a symbol around which have formed a variety of defenders of rural towns and villages whose traditional existence is confronted by outside pressures (see Cleaver 1989). Against such a hypothesis one could argue that direct action can be divisive. It may alienate others in a closely-knit society and the high communitarians would feel constrained about its use in a way that would be less true of the low communitarians.

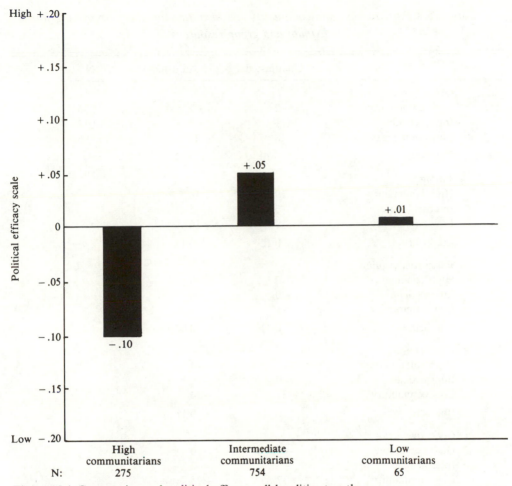

Figure 15.4 Community and political efficacy, all localities together

Much will depend on whether the action is internal to the locality or directed against outsiders. Certainly it is intriguing that in communitarian Penrhiwceiber, the high communitarians were indeed more prone than the intermediate or the very few low communitarians to take direct action, which consisted very considerably in striking against the 'outside' National Coal Board whose pit closure policy constituted a body-blow to the economic base of the valley's way of life.

The main glimmer of light so far for the communitarian theory is provided by voting, which is, paradoxically, one of the most nationally oriented activities. The high communitarians appear in this case to translate their positive commitments into political action, in clear contrast to those who share mild or low community sentiments.

It remains possible that by taking all the six localities together, some distinctive effects of community are being smothered. Already it has been seen that the intensity of community sentiments varies from area to area. Certainly, from table 15.9, which records the overall participation rates in each of the six localities, there appears rather more support for the community theory. But the record is uneven and far from easy to interpret except in a somewhat speculative manner. When the impact of resources is set

Table 15.8 *Participation and community: all localities together, controlling for individual and group resources*

	Unadjusted	Adjusted	N
Overall participation			
High community	−2	+1	356
Intermediate	−1	−2	1,012
Low community	+18	+24	96
Eta/beta	0·10	0·11	
Voting			
High community	+19	+16	
Intermediate	−5	−5	
Low community	−19	−16	
Eta/beta	0·12	0·12	
Party campaigning			
High community	−0	−0	
Intermediate	−0	−0	
Low community	+1	+1	
Eta/beta	0·03	0·04	
Contacting			
High community	−7	−4	
Intermediate	−0	−6	
Low community	+31	+34	
Eta/beta	0·11	0·11	
Collective action			
High community	−4	−0	
Intermediate	−0	−2	
Low community	+17	+25	
Eta/beta	0·11	0·11	
Direct action			
High community	+2	+3	
Intermediate	−1	−2	
Low community	+7	+6	
Eta/beta	0·09	0·09	

aside, the high communitarians do participate more than the average. The clear exception is Stockwell where they under-participate, possibly reflecting the low sense of spatial identity of the area which could stimulate commitment.

However, these enhanced levels of participation are frequently matched by those of the low communitarians. In the two most rural areas, the communitarian pattern is to be found. Both localities, as table 15.7 showed, have relatively high levels of community spirit and those people with the most intense sentiments are much more participatory than the handful who lack them. The Machars and Oswestry are rural societies in which the primacy of agricultural-related activity may induce cohesive social attitudes rather than a sense of class division. These localities contained the fewest who considered that

Table 15.9 *Community and overall participation in six localities*

	Spotland			Penrhiwceiber			Sevenoaks		
	Unadj.	Adj.*	(N)	Unadj.	Adj.*	(N)	Unadj.	Adj.*	(N)
High community	−18	+9	(21)	+14	+10	(114)	+41	+14	(28)
Intermediate	+3	−1	(174)	−12	−10	(152)	−8	−4	(201)
Low community	−5	+2	(25)	[+18]**	+35	(10)	+25	+16	(18)
Eta/beta	0·14	0·06		0·22	0·20		0·21	0·09	
	The Machars			Stockwell			Oswestry		
	Unadj.	Adj.*	(N)	Unadj.	Adj.*	(N)	Unadj.	Adj.*	(N)
High community	+6	+2	(89)	−29	−27	(20)	+2	+5	(83)
Intermediate	−2	−0	(184)	+2	−3	(141)	+2	−3	(160)
Low community	[−53]**	[−68]**	(3)	+12	+29	(32)	[−73]**	[−52]**	(8)
Eta/beta	0·08	0·10		0·12	0·15		0·21	0·16	

* Adjusted for individual and group resources.
** See note to table 5.10.

a good deal of class conflict is an inevitable feature of life (around 5%) and also a higher proportion who did not think of themselves in class terms. This combination of community sentiment and low class consciousness is often seen as a feature – even if a misleading one – of rural societies (Saunders *et al.* 1978). This is the arena of the last vestiges of non-party local politics where most, if not all, councillors stand as Independents (Grant 1977). The emphasis is on a form of consensual politics. Some might regard the overt local environment as apolitical. This may be considered to be an environment which communitarians find congenial and in which they are encouraged to translate their supportive attitudes into political action above what, it must nevertheless be remembered, is the generally low level for their areas.

Penrhiwceiber is homogeneous in a different way. It is a 'one-party local state' with a dominant social class. Over 40% are high communitarians; very few are lacking in community feeling. In many respects this would appear the ideal condition in which community sentiment can be rallied as people are aware that they are far from alone in their views. Lying behind the community sentiment are the mobilisatory group agencies of the pit village. Controlling for resources still leaves the communitarians participatory (+10) yet, curiously, not so much as the tiny group who do not share in the prevailing sentiments (+35).

Spotland, Sevenoaks and Stockwell contain few strong communitarians – in total only slightly more than half the number in Penrhiwceiber alone. Earlier it was suggested that Sevenoaks and Stockwell were central rather than peripheral localities, 'modern' rather than traditional (Spotland had a rather mixed status). Once resources are taken into account, the low communitarians are as active as the strong believers in Sevenoaks whilst in Stockwell they are 56 'points' higher on the participatory scale. In these environments, the non-communitarians, with their more sceptical view of political life, will not be deterred in the same way from participating in a more conflictual, *gesellschaftlich* rather than *gemeinschaftlich* politics. Nor are they deterred in Stockwell from acting in conflictual ways by direct action.

These, somewhat complex, results return at best a verdict of 'not proven' against the communitarian theory. A less accommodating view would say that it has failed to stand the test, as it has failed other earlier investigations (Putnam 1966; Alford and Scoble 1968). When all is said, the effect of adding community to resources as controls on levels of participation makes little difference to the end result. Nowhere does the overall adjusted participation rate change by more than three points on the scale. Taking away the effect of community sentiments in Penrhiwceiber does bring it three points closer to the mean and in Oswestry raises its rate by three points, implying some slight impact of such values on political action. The only effect on the adjusted participatory league table in figure 15.2 is that Penrhiwceiber drops again just below Stockwell. Yet the communitarian can discover some comfort. One response would be to say that modern society is not conducive to community life and, hence, it would be a surprise to find it surviving to any marked degree. For community to exist, society must be reconstructed and values must be transformed (Barber 1984). Thus, to the extent that almost a quarter of the sample expressed strong communitarian beliefs, this could be said to serve as some encouragement.

However, it is noticeable that community had relatively little meaning for those in the urban areas of Spotland and Stockwell or the commuters of Sevenoaks. Only, indeed, in the rural periphery and the traditional and economically declining pit village did community have a stronger resonance. There are those, indeed, who argue that such consensual perceptions reflect an unrealistic understanding of the fundamentally conflictual nature of modern, pluralistic, interest-based politics (Quantin 1989: 223–4). Certainly, those who would see community as the ground on which a more participatory Britain can be built (for example Marquand 1988) need first to convince the bulk of their fellow citizens of its relevance to modern life and then of its value as a stimulus to common action.

Community feelings may promote a benign view of political life without providing a consistent incentive to action. Individual and group activity is as much to do with promoting and defending personal or sectional advantage as with the attainment of some supposed community good. Those who regard participation as a good in itself almost, if never absolutely, independent of its substantive objectives, could expect to discover it more readily in a *Gesellschaft* than a *Gemeinschaft*. A conflict-ridden locality or a neighbourhood divided over some development proposal can, in reaction, engender the highest levels of participation from those individuals and groups contending over the allocation of benefits or to prevent the imposition of adverse effects. And in such conflict, the better resourced will tend to be to the forefront, whether in defence of their advantages or because their resources raise their reasonable hopes of success.

Structural place effects

Earlier it was argued that, as well as looking at compositional place effects, it was also essential to examine whether there were structural differences such that there was no consistent pattern to the process whereby people came to participate. In the event, the structure of participation, viewed in this way, proved remarkably similar across the six localities and, moreover, to the pattern of participation in the nation as a whole. The kinds of resources and the economic locations which proved good predictors of the propensity to participate across the country also turned out to be generally so in the six areas. The strengths of the associations (as measured by the beta scores) were also extremely consistent. On this evidence (and six examples is, of course, a somewhat uncertain basis), there are few fundamental structural differences in local participation such that the areas constitute radically different patterns.

Even so, there are a few deviations from the underlying patterns. Thus, in Penrhiwceiber, the working class participate, on the adjusted figures, at above the mean, in contrast to their performance nationally. They also compare well with their counterparts in Stockwell or in the Machars where their numbers are also substantial, albeit nowhere near those of the pit village. The same is true for those with no educational qualifications. Thus, the standard relationship between low individual resources and low participation does not hold in this traditional, homogeneous, strongly working class environment.

Another modest divergence from national patterns is to be found in Stockwell. Generally, it had been found that whether one was employed in the public sector or the private sector made no difference to overall participation once all other resource factors were considered (see figure 6.5). The association was virtually non-existent (beta = 0·03). In Stockwell, however, the association is stronger (beta = 0·11) than anywhere else. Moreover, the overall adjusted rate of participation of public sector workers is +21 as against −12 for private sector employees. Although there are suggestions in other localities that public sector workers are more participatory than the national figure, the rates are nowhere near as high as in Stockwell and the contrast with the private sector is not as great. There are more public sector workers in local government, health authorities and the civil service in Stockwell than the average of the six areas, but the proportion is not higher than, for example, Spotland. However, it is possible to speculate, as in the case study of Stockwell, that the deep involvement of the local authority in the area with national political controversies over the reorganisation of London government itself and over local expenditure levels would form part of the explanation. These would have heightened the 'political' rather than the 'administrative' character of the public sector vocation and impelled people to become more involved, even allowing for their resources, their political values and party identifications.

Although these two deviations from the fundamental patterns are intriguing evidence of the possibility of this second type of local effect, only one is a reversal of a national pattern. The basic impression is that the structure of participation is consistent across Britain and that the model generated by the national data works also for the local evidence.

Place and participation – some reflections

The interrelationship of place and politics is a very complex matter (see Agnew 1987 for a strong case in favour of its importance; also Cooke 1989). We are, accordingly, reluctant to entitle this section even as 'preliminary conclusions', for a number of reasons. Six localities provide an insufficiently broad basis to test all the hypotheses that might be generated. This is one of the drawbacks of the decision to pursue a small number of areas in depth rather than a strategy of studying many localities in a less detailed manner. In a study devoted to mapping political participation as a whole, there is, therefore, limited space to pursue some of the possibilities which political geography opens up. For example, a greater range of local cases would enable more examination of the fine-grain of the structural properties of participation in different localities which were briefly discussed earlier in the chapter.

Bearing these qualifications in mind, the method adopted was a version of the 'most different systems design' (Przeworski and Teune 1970:34–9). One of the main objectives in selecting localities which illustrated such contrasting types of area was, therefore, to test how far participants in Britain would display common characteristics even in the face of diverse social circumstances. In the event, despite this relatively robust, if limited, test it would appear that, in Britain, there is a fundamental pattern to participation which is found across the nation. The balance of activism and inactivism and the types of activism across the nation are broadly replicated in the different localities. There are, however, variations. Some of these variations are simply the effect of the social composition of the localities with the attendant impact on resources and values. It must be insisted that this compositional effect is important. The social composition of Sevenoaks, Stockwell or Penrhiwceiber, after all, makes them what they are as places to live in. And so, if one wishes to find the kind of place where there is, absolutely, a high level of participation, one should go to somewhere like Sevenoaks.

If, however, we discount those factors to seek out other distinctive elements, new variations are to be found. Some of these, admittedly, may also be 'compositional' in that controlling for resources and values does not, by any means, remove all national variation. Nevertheless, these variations are intriguing. Moreover, some of them are attributable to the factors which led to the original selection of the contrasting types of area – the reactions of a community under threat, the impact of party politicisation and party hegemony.

If an underlying pattern to these variations in the six localities can be discerned, we hypothesise that it may be explained in terms of distinctions between 'centre' and 'periphery' and between 'mobilising' and 'non-mobilising' localities. Along the centre–periphery dimension, Stockwell and Sevenoaks may be placed as 'central', whilst the Machars, Oswestry, Penrhiwceiber and, with some qualification, Spotland, may be seen as peripheral.

Centrality, it will be recalled, is usually defined by a combination of physical proximity to a metropolis and integration into urban patterns of communication. Stockwell is physically central and, in their work patterns, the Sevenoaks commuter population is undoubtedly part of the central core. Spotland is urban, part of a regional metropolis but, in the political, social and even physical geography of Britain, relatively remote from the south-east heartland. The Machars and Oswestry fit virtually every criterion for the peripheral. Penrhiwceiber satisfies the condition for physical distance. Although urban, its traditional way of life is also taking on a peripheral character in modern Britain, although there will be room for debate about this.

However, the centre-periphery distinction does not itself explain variations within

	Centre	Periphery
High mobilisation	Stockwell	Penrhiwceiber
		Spotland
Low mobilisation	Sevenoaks	The Machars
		Oswestry

Chart 15.1 Place and participation: a typology

central and peripheral localities (Agnew 1987:102). Part of the explanation of variations, it is suggested, lies in the capacity of certain organisations to mobilise people above what might have been expected on the basis of what is generally known of their normal participation rate. Accordingly, it is proposed that the localities might also be divided into those with high and low levels of mobilisation.

Taken together, this provides a four-fold typology as in chart 15.1. The two central localities, Stockwell and Sevenoaks, which in absolute terms are both participatory, are distinguishable once resources are taken into account by their levels of mobilisation. Multiple sources of activation boost participation, relative to resources in Stockwell, whilst in Sevenoaks, participation drops substantially towards the mean, implying that compositional factors counteract any mobilising factors. The peripheral localities also differ. Penrhiwceiber, as already noted, displays a distinct 'oppositional' process of activation. Spotland, which was not discussed in detail, reveals only slight mobilisational effects, possibly stemming from its very competitive three-party local political system. The Machars and Oswestry, however, are the exemplars of peripheral non-mobilised politics – low levels of political discussion, an environment which is only modestly affected by the major national issues and which has not generated any immediately pressing local problems. In neither have parties firmly entered local politics (Grant 1977). An apolitical, almost indeed an anti-political climate offers little incentive, and some disincentive, to involvement.

Clearly, such a typology must, on the evidence presented, be tentative in the extreme. Complexities abound and they would warrant further investigation. These complexities are, moreover, of interest to those with a normative concern for political participation. The mobilisational capacity of different areas varies markedly as, it will appear, does their underlying sympathy for certain modes of activism. The sense of community feeling, which has been so widely regarded as a basis for participation, also appears to have a variable and perhaps restricted potential outside peripheral and traditionalist areas. All in all, these variations suggest that, even in the global village, locality counts.

16

LOCAL ELITES, ACTIVISTS AND AGENDAS

Democratic theory is seldom entirely comfortable with either the idea or the fact of political leaders. The most participatory of groups sometimes endeavour to dispense with leaders altogether by such devices as rotation of office or consensual decision-making (Mansbridge 1980; Held and Pollitt 1986). Such groups are usually very small and it does not require a very great increase in the size of the political unit before the presence, and the problem, of leaders become apparent. Certainly, every democratic form of government, including the classical direct democracy of Athens, has had its leaders. Nevertheless, for some democrats, leaders should play as passive a role as possible in a system of 'government by the people'. They are the targets of action and exist to transform popular input into effective governmental output. Every effort should be made to limit their initiative and prevent the operation of the 'iron law of oligarchy' whereby, according to Michels, leaders escape the control of the mass of citizenry or of group members.

Others would, however, adopt a more positive attitude to the democratic role of political leaders. The job of rulers is not simply to mirror the preferences of the citizenry but to employ their experience and judgement in the promotion of some collective good. Elected leaders are granted the authority, as individuals or as representatives of a party, to weigh not only the demands of constituents but a variety of other national and local, political and administrative considerations in their selection of priorities and their policy-making (Sartori 1987). Leaders, at any level, may indeed be merely swept along by events. Particularly might this be so in local politics, where the pressures from centralised political and economic factors can be overwhelming (Dunleavy 1980). If the end result is that the agenda of the leaders does not fully match that of their constituents, this is not necessarily an adverse reflection on the operation of democracy. Rather, it may be a recognition of the different, and possibly even superior, vantage point of the leaders. For this type of democrat, the ultimate reckoning comes at the election when the voters decide whether or not to renew the mandate of the leadership in the light of its past, and expected future, performance.

In the hands of the 'revisionist' democrats, such as Schumpeter, the role of the citizen was largely relegated to that of intermittent voter and that of the leader was elevated to one of initiation (Schumpeter 1943). Indeed, some political scientists would go further and argue that to a very great extent leaders are 'autonomous' in that they can set priorities and carry through policies of their own choosing with little or no constraint from the citizens, whether acting as individual electors or through organised interest groups (Nordlinger 1981).

Whatever normative position one may adopt towards democratic leadership, in practice leaders play a variety of roles. Politicians are the targets of individual and group pressures as the persons able to solve problems or, at least, apparently responsible for producing solutions. They also perform an intermediary, brokerage function seeking, often by a process of compromise, to produce a set of priorities from amongst rival agendas. Finally, they initiate policy. Leaders are not merely reactive but proactive, and citizens may respond to leaders as much as the reverse. Elective political leaders are not, however, our only concern. Politicians are backed by appointed officials who, in Britain in particular, carry considerable weight not merely in providing guidance on policy implementation but also in policy formation. Alongside these are other leaders of intermediary bodies – business interests, voluntary associations, churches, trades unions, educational institutions – who are spokespersons of interests (and sometimes targets of pressure from their own 'constituencies') and people with potential influence on the political leadership stratum.

Our prime concern in this chapter will be with the interplay between these various types of local leaders and the citizenry. We shall be looking at the ways in which leaders are integrated into their local societies. We shall then compare the issue agendas of leaders and citizens, bearing in mind, as we have said, that many forces other than citizen participation help to shape the priorities of leaders. Attention will then turn to the extent to which agendas are indeed produced as a result of participation from 'below' or initiative from 'above'. In doing so, we shall be classifying our leaders in various ways, since it might be expected that their functional positions will greatly influence their perception of local issues. The leaders are accordingly grouped for certain purposes into eight elite types – elected local leaders (including councillors for the immediate area and Chairs of certain important council committees as well as a further group of about a dozen who were councillors cited as leaders because of their involvement in various local government bodies or as justices of the peace), local government officials, political party leaders, 'social' leaders (including ecclesiastical and educational figures), business leaders, trades union leaders, local group leaders and, finally, an 'other' category of, primarily, policemen and local media leaders.

For other purposes, there is a simple two-fold classification into a political or governmental stratum – composed of elected councillors and local government officers – and a non-political or non-governmental stratum, comprising the rest. This aims to distinguish those leaders with some formal responsibility for governmental outcomes, although we are not in a position in this context to refine this further to allow for the fact that, within this stratum, some councillors and officers will be more influential than others. Our concern, as was indicated in chapter 14, is less with analysing 'power elites' than with weighing the significance of political participation in the formation of issue agendas.

However, in comparing elites and their priorities with citizens, it is also necessary to distinguish between the degrees of activism amongst our citizens. Do the more active citizens genuinely make a distinctive impact? Are they a 'bridge' between the elites and the mass of the citizens? Accordingly, we shall draw a broad distinction between the active and less active citizenry. The activists are those in each locality who were in our categories of group, party campaigning, contacting or protesting 'specialists' or were 'generalists'; the inactive are the majority who either did little more than vote or were even infrequent voters.

Who are the leaders?

Leaders are by and large middle aged, middle class and male. There is, perhaps, little that is surprising in this pattern. It takes some years to attain leadership positions. Many such positions require the skills and education associated with the middle class. And the traditional obstacles to the rise of women need little rehearsal, especially if one recalls that 'top people' would generally have first entered their careers up to twenty years earlier when attitudes toward opportunities for women were still less favourable.

Across all the localities, rather under a half (44·4%) of the leaders were aged over fifty but a mere 4% were under thirty years of age. The localities varied little in this respect, although in Stockwell rather more leaders were in their thirties and fewer were over fifty.

Three quarters of all leaders were drawn from the salariat class. This is in part explained by the fact that all local government officials are, by definition, salaried professionals. However, virtually all the social leaders (97·6%) were also in salaried positions, as were 71·9% of those leading local groups. By contrast, only 11·1% of leaders were in working class occupations. Working class representation was somewhat higher amongst the elected politicians (13·4%) which reflected more accurately the class composition of some of the localities. Even so, over half of the politicians (56·7%) had been in salaried occupations. Clearly, the elite are at a social distance from the population at large. Only a fifth of citizens were from the salaried class whilst 44·3% were working class.

One would anticipate that the differing social complexions of the six localities would produce variations in the compositions of the elites. Whilst this is indeed the case, the differences are not dramatic except in two instances. In Sevenoaks, fully 90% of leaders were from the salariat – which is almost double the proportion in the local population – and not one was from the working class. Penrhiwceiber does not present a polar opposite since 59·5% of the leadership was salaried – reflecting the inclusion of officials and teachers. Nevertheless, here 38·1% of the leaders were working class, a figure not approached anywhere else. However, this is in a context where three quarters of the population is working class. In the Machars, farmers composed nearly a quarter of the leadership (23·5%) which, if added to the 66% from the salariat, would imply a middle class hegemony as considerable as that in Sevenoaks.

The middle class character of the elites is well reflected in their high educational qualifications compared to the mass of citizens. A fifth of the elite had not gone beyond secondary school; but this was true of 85% of citizens. Just over a third had been to university or a polytechnic. Still more (39·9%) had gained a further educational qualification. The various elite types differed in their educational backgrounds. Half the trades unionists had been only to secondary school but 45% had taken some form of further education. The most highly qualified were the social leaders, two-thirds of whom had been to university or polytechnic with nearly all the others having been to further education institutions. The elected politicians were, by comparison with most other elite groups, rather less well qualified educationally. A quarter had been to university or polytechnic and 36·1% had not gone beyond secondary school. These figures still mark the politicians off from those whom they represent when one considers that only 5·1% of the population of the six areas had degrees.

If we compare the localities, it is the Stockwell elite which overall contains the highest proportion of university or polytechnic educated persons (44·3%), followed by Sevenoaks (39·7%) and the Machars (38·3%). The lowest figure is, not surprisingly, in Penrhiwceiber (16·7%) but half had nevertheless obtained further education qualifications. Hence, the contrast with the generality of the local population in Penrhiwceiber, where fewer than 2% of the sample had any higher qualification, was in its way as marked as anywhere else.

Only a fifth of our leaders were women. There were only two female business leaders, two leading trades unionists and four local government officials. In relative terms, therefore, the fact that 29·2% of elected leaders were women means that the political elite could almost be described as open even if still far from offering equal opportunities. Low as this figure is, it actually surpasses the 19% reported for women councillors in a national survey of England and Wales (England 1986a:19). The only other elite type in which women were at all prominent was the local group leadership where they constituted a third.

These findings add up to a clear impression of social unrepresentativeness amongst the local elite. The significance of certain of these measures is often disputed in that it does not necessarily follow that the most effective spokespersons or policy-makers are those who are a precise social reflection of the forces that make up local society. Nevertheless, it is arguable that the ability of elites to appreciate the issues that concern the local population will be affected by the depth of their personal integration into that society.

The extent of this integration may be measurable by the length of time the leaders have been exposed to the conditions of local life and the degree to which they interact with the group life of the area. Half of the leaders lived in the immediate localities we were studying and a further 29% lived in the surrounding area. One characteristic of many members of our local elites is that they have lived in their area for a significant part of their lives. In particular, over a third of the political stratum who lived in the area had been there for over thirty years. This was especially true in Penrhiwceiber and the two rural areas. The exception was Stockwell where the relative youth of the elite meant shorter periods of residence and probably reflects a more mobile environment. Overall, the elites' average stay of 22 years in the same locality, whilst very slightly less than that of the citizenry, is certainly sufficient to provide a basis for an understanding of the needs and interests of the areas. In general, it might be remarked that, for all the talk of a more mobile society, it remains true that most people stay put in the same area for long periods of their life, further emphasising the continuing importance of locality in most of our lives. Several leaders stressed the desirability of both the politicians and the officials living in the localities they governed – not only for reasons of accessibility but to ensure that they experienced the conditions faced by the community. Few, however, would be able to say, as did one Oswestry leader, that 'we seem to be a family community – say thirty-odd thousand of us. And I'm probably related to one half and known to the other half!'.

Leaders tend to belong to a number of voluntary associations. In some cases, they are virtually *ex officio* members, as occurs when a councillor in effect represents the council on a local educational or charitable body. Accordingly, rather than ask for the total number of groups to which leaders belonged, we asked about the number of different *types* of group of which they were members. These types of group excluded political parties but included church-based organisations, charitable bodies, armed forces associations, community action groups and civic societies as well as sports and leisure organisations. The leaders belonged on average to between three and four different types of groups (3·48). Very few belonged to none, whilst over 10% were members of six or more. The elected political leaders were involved in an average of 3·41 types. They were surpassed by the local social leaders who were involved in 4·12 types of association. These social leaders in particular contained a few persons who were astonishingly 'clubbable', with one having connections with ten different types of group. By this measure, the elite of Sevenoaks was the most fully integrated into the local milieu. Sevenoaks leaders were members of, on average, 3·96 types of group, whereas in Penrhiwceiber they belonged, on average, to 2·86.

It must be acknowledged, however, that this is not a conclusive test of integration in that much turns on the nature of the milieu itself. Sevenoaks, as a middle-class environment, is a natural centre for social life organised on a group basis. There is a powerful group existence with which the elite can forge links and out of which the elite may itself emerge. Sevenoaks is a modern *Gesellschaft*. If Penrhiwceiber has elements of a traditional *Gemeinschaft* its small size and concentrated population may ensure that leaders have less need of the formality of group mechanisms to ensure their linkages with the local population. Nevertheless, even if group affiliation is not a decisive measure of integration, it says something about the Sevenoaks leadership structure that it should be more firmly linked into the local group world than other areas, whether urban, like Stockwell (3·70), or rural, such as the Machars (3·67).

The most frequent form of group membership is affiliation to a trade union or staff association. Half the elite were members. This was followed by membership of a church or a religious group (43%). The importance of civic societies in local politics (see Barker and Keating 1977) is underlined by the fact that 39% of the local elites held such memberships. The voluntary social groups, concerned with charitable and welfare action in the community, provided 35·3%. The picture, then, is of elites with quite broad-ranging connections into their local world which could, in principle, serve both as sources of information and pressure on the one side and avenues for elite mobilisation on the other.

The most overtly political of linkages is, of course, provided by party membership. A little under half (43·7%) of the elites were members of political parties – a figure which, not unexpectedly, is many times greater than that for the population as a whole or even for the most active participants. That the figure for elites is not even higher is explicable by two factors in particular. In general, in Britain, local government is party government. Since two of our areas, however, possess non-partisan councils, as many as 23·6% of even the elected political leaders were not formal party members, although some of these will have clear party leanings. Most senior local government officers are precluded by rules or custom from party affiliation. If we exclude the political stratum from consideration, party membership amongst the elite falls to 27·8% implying that the leadership as a whole is not intensively politicised to the extent of formal commitments.

Confining ourselves to the non-political stratum, our elites are most likely to be Labour Party members, reflecting their prominence amongst the trades union leadership (55%) and the local groups (30%) compared with the low level of any formal party membership amongst the business elite. Although businessmen may be Conservative sympathisers, only 22% of the business leaders in our sample were members of any party. The variations between the localities follow the lines one would anticipate. In the non-partisan climate of rural Machars and Oswestry, only 21·3% and 32·7% were party members, even including the political stratum. The highest levels of affiliation were found in Stockwell (57·1%). As many as four Labour members featured in the Sevenoaks leadership circles, but only one Conservative in Penrhiwceiber. In both Penrhiwceiber and Stockwell, over 40% of the elites were Labour Party members.

Who are the active citizens?

In previous chapters we outlined the extent to which participation in our six localities replicated the national pattern whereby the bulk of political activity was conducted by around a quarter of the population. We discovered that, whilst there were important local differences, the general picture was confirmed. Everywhere a large majority of people are content to do little more than vote or are not even committed to vote on a regular basis. Our interest in this chapter will turn increasingly to the active minority (23% across all six areas) in an attempt to establish their impact on issues and the special characteristics which dispose them to be particularly involved in their localities.

In very many respects, the activists appear to bridge the gap between leaders and the generality of the population. They share certain characteristics of the leaders but not to the same degree. In terms of the resource analysis we have been employing throughout, the typical activist is better resourced than his or her less involved neighbour but less so than most, but not all, elites.

Nearly a fifth (18·3%) of the activists had degree level education compared with 4·3% of the inactive – but this is also well short of the 34% for elites. The activists are also likely to be wealthier than the inactive, but in this case there are no comparable data for the elites. If we turn to collective resources in the form of group memberships, we find much the same story. Excluding membership of trades unions, the activists belonged on average to fewer than two types of group (1·79). This is twice the rate of the less active (0·87 types). Although trades union membership is one of the most widespread, almost 'routine', forms of group involvement, the gap between the inactive and the active is scarcely diminished. We have already seen that across the nation, as with other group memberships, trades unions serve as a participatory resource. Thus whilst just under a third of the less active were, or had been, trades unionists (32·5%), this is true of a little over half of the activist members (51·8%) – a figure close to that for the elites. Adding past and present unionists would raise the average group type membership of the inactive to 1·20 and of the active to 2·30.

Variations between the six localities confirm once again the basically active life of Sevenoaks (remembering that this is, as the previous chapter showed, largely an effect of its well-resourced population). The activists there belonged to 2·35 group types on average, apart from trades union affiliation. Indeed, the inactive population were more integrated into group life, with membership of on average 1·18 types of group, than the

Table 16.1 *Some social characteristics of elites, citizen activists and citizens in six localities*

	Elite	Activists	Other citizens
Salariat	74·3%	32·0%	18·3%
Working class	11·1%	33·0%	47·9%
Degree qualifications	34·0%	18·3%	4·3%
Political party membership	43·7%	14·3%	3·5%
Female	19·6%	48·5%	57·4%
Aged 50 and over	44·4%	34·4%	45·5%
N of types of group membership	3·47	2·30	1·20
N of years' residence in locality	22	21	24
N	322	1,245	372

activists in Penrhiwceiber, who were involved in only 1·08. As we surmised when looking at the elites, the pit village's sense of community is not sustained through a network of plural groups. What counts in Penrhiwceiber is membership of one type of group – the trade union. The high level of unionisation has already been suggested as a prime mobilising factor in the area and it is thus not unexpected that just under two thirds of the local activists (64·5%) were, or had been, trades unionists. Indeed, 41·5% of the inactive were also current or past members in comparison with 34·2% of Sevenoaks activists. The Machars provides a further contrast. The activist portion of the population was very small (a mere 12·7%) but these were people who were deeply involved with maintaining the area's associative life amongst its very scattered population. Their membership of 2·16 group types was not very much short of that in Sevenoaks.

Party membership has throughout this study been maintained as conceptually distinct from active participation but, equally, it has been shown to be a resource base for various forms of action. Hence it is to be expected that party members are well represented amongst the activist population. Party members formed only 6% of our local sample as a whole but over half (54·9%) of them were activists. As a result, party members constituted 14·3% of the activists. Again, it was in Sevenoaks that more party members were to be discovered.

The relationship between these individual and resource factors and social class further ensures that the social composition of the activists will also have some resemblance to that of the elites. The activists are disproportionately drawn from the professions. Whilst it remains the case that even amongst this class participation is a minority pursuit, the 36·5% of the salariat who are activists is a much higher proportion than for any other social class. At the other extreme, half that proportion of the working class (18·6%) appear in the activist stratum. As ever in these calculations, it should be recalled that the different numerical sizes of the social classes can mean that, as in this case, although the working class is less prone to active participation, it may still provide as many persons in absolute terms to the more participatory category as the salariat. Each in fact constitutes a third of the activist citizenry. But this also serves to emphasise the way that the elite is still more socially 'skewed' towards the upper class than the participant population, since the working class produce a mere 11·1% of the holders of leading positions against the 74·4% from the salariat. Sevenoaks, where 59% of activists were from the salariat and Penrhiwceiber, where the class structure ensures that the activists are 72% working class, offer the usual extreme contrasts.

Another striking instance of this pattern of increasing accentuation of social effects on participation as one moves up the scale of political involvement, is provided by gender. Women were in a majority in our local samples overall (55·3%). However, men were rather more inclined towards active participation (ignoring the social background controls discussed elsewhere) and 26·5% were activists as against 20·1% of women. As a result, women were by a small margin in a minority amongst the active population (48·5%). The mere 19·6% of women in elite positions, however, serves to emphasise the size of the threshold which they have to cross if they are to carry participation over into something which could be termed power. Finally, activists are by and large younger (or less middle-aged). Almost two-thirds (65·6%) are below 50 compared with around 55% for both the inactive population and the leaders.

If part of the task of political leaders is to listen to the views and appreciate the interests of the people in the areas in which they hold places of influence, then the evidence suggests that they have certain social and political advantages and disadvantages. Some of these are summarised in table 16.1. The leaders are generally far from being social mirrors of the citizen population. They are at some social distance which is reflected in their educational qualifications and economic class background. The extent to which this is a disadvantage is the subject of an old debate in which we have not space to enter here. Social distance may be a barrier to communication and may lead to a failure to understand needs and demands. But educational qualifications can imply capacities to act as advocates which the less advantaged may not possess. Nevertheless, social representativeness and the capacity for political representation must not be confused with one another. As against social distance, however, can be set indications of political proximity such as the relatively high level of integration of the leadership with the group life of their localities which can help smooth the input and output processes.

Intermediate between the local leaders and the generality of the citizenry is the participatory minority. We have been seeing throughout the book that around a quarter of the population actively sustain politics at citizen level. These activists occupy in most respects a status between elite and general public with respect to the resources which would allow them to 'represent' the body of the population (see table 16.1). They are similar enough to the citizenry for them to be expected to relay some of the priorities of the local population yet also at enough social distance for participatory democrats to fear that they might introduce a bias into the agenda of issues.

Our concern will therefore be to see how well the priorities of elites match those of the citizenry and how the active citizen contributes to the formation of local agendas. But first we need to look at the agendas themselves to assess their common features and their particularities.

The local agenda profiles

As can be seen from table 16.2, the frequency with which types of issue are raised exhibits some common features across our six areas and with the national patterns

Table 16.2 *Citizen agendas in six localities*

	Spotland		Pen'ceiber		Sevenoaks		The Machars		Stockwell		Oswestry		Overall	
	%	(Rank)	%	(Rank)	%	(Rank)	%	(Rank)	%	(Rank)	%	(Rank)	%	(Rank)
Environment & planning	17·8	(2)	29·6	(1)	44·2	(1)	17·3	(2)	13·6	(3)	27·8	(1)	26·7	(1)
Transport & traffic	11·5	(3)	9·3	(6)	17·7	(2)	20·8	(1)	5·9	(5)	21·4	(2)	14·5	(2)
Housing	24·3	(1)	13·5	(2)	3·2	(5)	5·1	(7)	25·6	(1)	6·6	(4 =)	12·3	(3)
Economic (excluding unemployment)	7·7	(5)	11·5	(4)	2·7	(7)	13·0	(3)	9·4	(4)	4·9	(8)	7·9	(4)
Health	3·4	(9 =)	3·9	(7)	16·0	(3)	9·3	(5)	1·3	(10)	6·6	(4 =)	7·4	(5)
Youth	5·8	(6)	13·0	(3)	5·3	(4)	7·3	(6)	3·8	(6 =)	8·8	(3)	7·2	(6)
Unemployment	4·8	(7)	10·0	(5)	0·6	(10)	12·8	(4)	3·8	(6 =)	6·4	(6)	6·0	(7)
Law & order	7·9	(4)	2·2	(9)	0·8	(9)	0·4	(10)	19·9	(2)	4·2	(9)	5·6	(8)
Education	4·1	(8)	1·1	(10)	2·9	(6)	2·9	(9)	1·9	(9)	6·1	(7)	3·0	(9)
Elderly	3·4	(9 =)	2·4	(8)	2·0	(8)	4·2	(8)	0·6	(11)	1·2	(10)	2·2	(10)
Race	3·1	(10)	0·2	(11)	0·4	(11)	0·0	(11)	2·3	(8)	0·2	(11)	1·0	(11)
Other	6·2	—	3·3	—	4·2	—	6·8	—	11·8	—	5·6	—	6·2	(—)
Total	100·0		100·0		100·0		100·0		100·0		100·0		100·0	
N issue aspects	416		460		662		452		476		407		2,873	

presented in chapter 11. This latter similarity is not unexpected since we have already seen that across the nation the preoccupations of most people are local. However, the table also makes clear that within the national profile are some distinctive types of local issue patterns as well as issues which are very particular to one area. The method of categorising issues is comparable to that in chapter 11. Where an issue mentioned by a respondent has two aspects to it – housing for the elderly, for example – both are coded, so that the total number of issues reflects this practice, although it does not affect the pattern to any extent. The main difference is that people were asked to mention, without any prompting as to topic, only local issues. Hence the category of defence and foreign affairs was scarcely raised and is here put into the 'other' category. On the other hand, problems affecting racial minorities – discrimination, harassment, family immigration problems – seemed at the outset to be ones which might make an appearance in two of the localities. Consequently, the 'race' category has been separated out.

In each locality, there appear to have been around three bigger sets of issues and then a variety of matters which attracted a small number of references and whose exact rank order is best treated with caution. The national survey showed that, across the country, environment and planning was the largest category of issues, although if general economic problems were combined with unemployment issues, they would constitute a larger block. Environment and planning is never out of the first three places in the 'league table' of issues in the local surveys. In Sevenoaks, it comprised 44·2% of all the issues, but it also headed the agenda in the very different world of Penrhiwceiber. Part of the reason is that it covers a very broad range of matters from permits for building to refuse collection, from the provision of leisure facilities to the preservation of old town centres. Because so many people cited a mixture of communal and private interests as activating their concerns in this area, it did not prove readily possible to split the issues into those which were more to do with planning rather than environment and ecology.

Nevertheless, one must recognise that environment and planning is not entirely the same matter in Sevenoaks as in Penrhiwceiber. In the pit village, half those mentioning this category wanted to see a sports and leisure facility created. Sevenoaks was also exercised over such facilities resulting, however, from a major local controversy about the site of a swimming pool. However, around 30% of this type of issue concerned the protection of the local environment and especially of the attractive town centre and the conservation of its character in the face of new commercial developments.

Economic issues, including both unemployment and other concerns such as wage levels and the broad outlook, do not occupy as salient a position as they did in the national sample. The explanation probably lies in the tendency to regard the economic sphere as a responsibility of national rather than local government – even though the local authorities themselves put the attraction of employment high on their priorities. Otherwise, it is difficult to understand why unemployment constituted only 10% of issues in the pit village – although this does represent nearly a quarter of all those persons who mentioned an issue. Indeed, it was the rural area of the Machars which placed most emphasis on unemployment in a remote part of Britain where it is difficult to find new sources of work. The prosperity of Sevenoaks is indirectly measurable by the place of unemployment in its rank order of local problems.

The three areas of dense urban population share in common a concern with housing problems. The main surprise is that this does not feature more prominently in

Penrhiwceiber where our survey coincided with an investigation by the local authority
into housing conditions which revealed quite remarkably low levels of amenity. In
Stockwell and Spotland, council house availability and repairs were major concerns –
as their representatives would probably testify. In Spotland, a programme to conserve
and restore some of the older terraces with council support also resulted in a significant
number of references.

The two areas in or near greater conurbations also shared a concern with law and
order – mainly burglary and street crime. In Stockwell, this was the second most
important item, representing a fifth of all issues. For all the alarmist talk of a nationwide
panic over crime and safety in the streets, when one deals with unprompted references
to problems, law and order comes everywhere else near the bottom of the agenda. So far,
it is a concentrated, but very genuine, problem of the cities.

The 'dog that did not bark' was the race issue. Spotland and Stockwell are areas with
concentrations of people with Asian and West Indian backgrounds respectively. In
neither locality was race an important issue. This may in part reflect the under-
representation of the ethnic minorities in the sample, leading to a failure to register
problems of discrimination. On the other hand, neither did the survey pick up any
significant negative attitudes on the part of the white population. No-one should
conclude from this that the conditions of the non-whites in British society are a 'non-
problem'. Nevertheless, the problems that were mentioned in our survey were not
presented by respondents in explicitly racial terms, but appeared to be shared concerns.
In Stockwell, for example, the issue priorities of whites and non-whites were very similar
– a finding which confirms several other differently conducted electoral studies
(Fitzgerald 1987:9–24; Welch and Studlar 1985; Studlar 1986).

The Machars and Sevenoaks each gave rise to an issue peculiar to itself which, despite
their particularity, illuminate the reactive character of so much participation. Transport
issues headed the agenda in the Machars. Unlike Oswestry and Sevenoaks, where the
issue had more to do with parking and traffic problems, in the Machars the problem was
a reflection of the area's remoteness from major centres of services. Although a main
through road had been improved to serve the general area, for those in particular
without ready access to private transport, travel to administrative offices or to the local
hospital is difficult and time-consuming. Many of the references to 'health' in the
Machars were, indeed, linked to the issue of transport to the hospital. A long-term
problem common to many rural areas – an aspect of a special form of deprivation – is
here surfacing in the agenda. In Sevenoaks, the prominence of 'health' – in third place
– was almost entirely the result of involvement in a vigorous local campaign about a
hospital closure. In this instance, the survey was picking up a 'one-off' issue capable of
inciting intense reactive participation. If the survey were to be repeated, the issue would
(unlike that of transport in the Machars) presumably disappear from the agenda.
Unique as it may be to a moment in the recent politics of Sevenoaks, in another sense
it is representative of a larger participatory theme. At any time, a sufficiently salient
matter is capable of stirring a previously relatively quiescent citizenry into involvement.
People otherwise disinclined to be politically engaged may become intensely, though
intermittently, active either through an almost spontaneous response to events or as a
result of the efforts of others to mobilise their support. This interrelationship of

Table 16.3 *Rank order of issues of activists and non-activists*

	Spotland		Pen'ceiber		Sevenoaks		The Machars		Stockwell		Oswestry		Overall	
	*A	N	A	N	A	N	A	N	A	N	A	N	A	N
Environment and planning	2	2	1	1	1	1	1 =	2	2	3	1	1	1	1
Transport	3	3	4 =	6	2	2 =	1 =	1	4 =	7	2	2	2	2
Housing	1	1	4 =	2	5 =	6	8	7	1	1	4 =	4 =	3	3
Economic (excluding unemployment)	4	5	6	4	8	5	3	4	4 =	4	3	9	4	6
Health	8 =	9 =	7 =	7	3	2 =	5 =	5	7 =	11	4 =	4 =	5	4 =
Youth	5 =	6	2	3	4	4	5 =	6	7 =	5	8	3	6	4 =
Unemployment	8 =	7	3	5	10	10	4	3	6	6	4 =	6	7	7
Law and order	5 =	4	9 =	8	11	9	10 =	10	3	2	9	8	8	8
Education	8 =	8	9 =	10	5 =	7	9	9	10	9	4 =	7	9	9
Elderly	11	9 =	7 =	9	7	8	5 =	8	11	10	10	10	10	10
Race	7	11	11	11	9	11	10 =	11	7 =	8	11	11	11	11

* A = Activist citizens; N = Non-activist citizens.

quiescence and mobilisatory capacity is something which needs to be taken into account in assessing the meaning of levels of participation – a matter to which we return in our concluding chapter.

As was found in the case of participatory activity itself, the national pattern of issues is generally confirmed in our local studies, which is an important reassurance as to the solidity of the findings, but with sufficient variation also to support the view that local political context and culture are important. Thus, the same associations between social background factors and propensity to mention particular kinds of issues is repeated (for example the interest that women show in housing or education relative to men; or the greater concern with housing of the less well-off). At the same time, local priorities do display differences partly explicable by social composition but also partly by special circumstances including mobilisation.

Agendas and participation

In chapter 11 on national agendas, we raised briefly the possibility that the priorities of activists might differ from those of the rest of the population, thus distorting the picture which the leadership may form of the preoccupations of the citizenry as a whole. It was found that, whilst there were differences, on the whole the activists reinforced the agenda of the general population. It is now possible to examine this further by relating the agendas of non-activists and activists to those of the elites themselves.

Table 16.3 presents the rank order of issues for the activists and the non-activists in the local polities omitting the miscellaneous 'other issues' category. As was the case in the national analysis, the priorities of the active quarter of the population do not deviate sharply from those of the non-active majority. Indeed, if we confine our attention to the top three issues in each locality, there is a remarkable degree of consensus as to the rank order. There is agreement in each locality as to the top issue. In four there is accord as to the second issue. Rather more dispute exists as to which issue sets obtain third place but, in most cases, the difference is not wide.

Nevertheless, behind these fairly simple rankings lie some differences of emphasis. Thus, although both sets of citizens in Stockwell place housing top of the agenda, it comprises 30% of the non-activists' issues as against 21% of the activist agenda. In the same locality, law and order is in second place on the non-active agenda with almost a quarter of issues (24·2%) but in third place for the activists with only 15·4% of their total issues. In the pit village, whereas environment comes first for both groups, it plays a larger part in the activists' agenda. Housing is clearly more significant (15·8% and second place) for the non-active than for their activist neighbours (10·3% and fourth). In Spotland, as in Stockwell, the non-activists show relatively more concern for law and order (9·2% as against 5·8%). These relatively small differences of emphasis have a cumulative effect which, as we hope to show shortly, are highly suggestive for the potential importance of participation.

The elite agenda

The picture of the local agenda can now be completed by delineating the agenda of the elites. As has already been emphasised, there are many forces which impinge on local elites, and particularly on politicians, apart from citizen participation. These forces, which may include national government stipulations or party policy can be entirely legitimate. Deviation of the elite agenda from that of the citizens is not necessarily to be regarded as sinister. At the same time, democrats may reasonably be concerned if there is very little consensus and if the elites appear to be going their own ways.

The profile of elite agendas, set out in table 16.4 can be compared with that of citizens in table 16.2. The rank order of elite concerns can similarly be compared with the ordering given by activist and non-activist citizenry displayed in table 16.3. The tables show strong evidence of consensus but also other instances of patterns of divergence.

In five out of six localities, there is entire consensus between elites, activists and non-activists as to the leading category of local problems. Only in the Machars do the three groups differ as to the major issue and even in this case the elite place second the problem of transport which the citizens put in top position. Moreover, in several cases, the relative weight of the issue amongst elites and citizens is remarkably similar. Thus, housing in Stockwell comprised 25·6% of citizen, and 25·9% of elite, issues, and a similar pattern is found in Spotland. In Penrhiwceiber, 31·8% of elite issues concerned environment which is extremely close to the 29·6% of citizen concerns. Agreement as to the second set of issues is less complete with only Spotland and Sevenoaks preserving a complete consensus, and Sevenoaks maintaining agreement down to the third issue. In Stockwell there is a near consensus on the second ranking of law and order but the active citizenry give this a slightly lower priority than do either elites or citizens.

Beyond the first two positions in the six league tables, the level of agreement on rankings declines somewhat, although at the lowest levels the precise ordering is not

Table 16.4 *Elite agendas in six localities*

	Spotland		Pen'ceiber		Sevenoaks		The Machars		Stockwell		Oswestry		Overall	
	%	(Rank)	%	(Rank)	%	(Rank)	%	(Rank)	%	(Rank)	%	(Rank)	%	(Rank)
Environment & planning	23·0	(2)	31·8	(1)	51·8	(1)	6·8	(5)	6·0	(5)	29·5	(1)	24·6	(1)
Transport	4·6	(6)	3·0	(8)	15·5	(2)	17·5	(2 =)	1·8	(9)	13·3	(3)	8·9	(5)
Housing	27·0	(1)	15·4	(3)	3·1	(5)	9·6	(4)	25·9	(1)	2·4	(9)	14·2	(2)
Economic (excluding unemployment)	5·2	(5)	14·4	(4)	2·2	(6)	17·5	(2 =)	11·7	(4)	11·9	(4)	10·4	(4)
Health	2·9	(10)	4·0	(6)	11·9	(3)	2·8	(8)	1·4	(10 =)	5·7	(6)	4·8	(8)
Youth	2·3	(11)	7·0	(5)	1·8	(7 =)	5·6	(7)	5·7	(6)	8·6	(5)	5·2	(7)
Unemployment	12·1	(3)	16·4	(2)	1·8	(7 =)	27·1	(1)	14·9	(3)	13·8	(2)	13·9	(3)
Law and order	3·4	(7 =)	2·5	(9)	0·0	(11)	0·0	(10 =)	17·0	(2)	4·3	(7)	5·3	(6)
Education	3·4	(7 =)	1·0	(10)	3·5	(4)	6·2	(6)	4·6	(7)	3·8	(8)	3·8	(9)
Elderly	3·4	(7 =)	3·5	(7)	1·8	(7 =)	1·1	(9)	1·4	(10 =)	0·5	(10)	1·9	(11)
Race	7·5	(4)	0·0	(11)	0·4	(10)	0·0	(10 =)	3·9	(8)	0·0	(11)	2·0	(10)
Other	5·2	(–)	1·0	(–)	6·2	(–)	5·6	(–)	5·7	(–)	6·2	(–)	5·0	(–)
Total	100·0		100·0		100·0		100·0		100·0		100·0		100·0	
N issue aspects	174		201		226		178		282		211		1,270	

necessarily to be treated as exact, given the low numbers of mentions of the relevant issues.

One significant pattern which emerges is the tendency of elites to give greater prominence to unemployment. Taking all the localities together, it was third on the elite agenda but only seventh on that of the citizenry. We surmised that citizens tended to see this as a national problem and responsibility. However, the detail of elite interviews showed that leaders, and especially elected politicians, considered themselves to have a major role to play in attracting new business and jobs to their area. They might well believe that the fundamental responsibility for the economic climate lay with national government but, within the overall limits set by the economy, they could, and should, be active in gaining what advantage they could for their own area. Conversely, youth problems tended to be higher on the citizen agenda. Yet these youth issues were in many ways related to the unemployment problem in that many people wanted to see recreation and training facilities for the jobless young.

There is some sign, therefore, that the elite were not picking up one aspect of a general problem with which, however, they had shown a clear concern. Finally, although numbers of mentions are low and not fully trustworthy, it would seem that elites in Spotland and Stockwell, who include some ethnic minority leaders, were more likely to raise race issues than the citizens. In Spotland, they formed twice as high a proportion of the elite agenda (7·5% of issues) and appeared a much higher priority than for the non-active citizens.

It might be argued that the most significant set of elite agendas would be those of the political leadership stratum. These are the leaders whom citizens, as well as other leaders, seek to persuade to take action on their problems. The broad set of political leaders would include both elected representatives and important local government officers who are at the very least policy advisers and also, to a significant degree, policy-makers. In table 16.5, the rank order of issues of this political leadership is compared with that of the 'non-political' elite. As with the other tables, this reveals elements of consensus and of disagreement. In five out of the six localities, the two sets of leaders were in accord as to the top category of problem and, in the remaining case, the two leading positions were simply reversed. If table 16.5 is then compared with table 16.3, an impressive level of consensus appears amongst types of elite, the politically active and the less active citizens as to what the topmost concern of each locality is. In some cases, as in Sevenoaks, one type of problem virtually dominates political life. There, environment and planning would appear to constitute half the agenda, no matter how involved or uninvolved a person may be.

There is, once more, rather less certainty between political and non-political elites in the particular localities as to the subsequent priorities. Thus in Penrhiwceiber, housing was in second place for the political elite as it is for the citizens. But, for both the non-political elite and for the activist citizens, housing was fourth in the frequency with which it came up as an issue. The political elite placed relatively more stress on housing than any other group in the community, since it comprised 22·5% of all their issues as against 13·5% of citizen problems. This may well reflect the then current preoccupation with the outcome of the Council's own study of poor housing conditions. At the other extreme, perhaps, is the concern over law and order in Spotland where it was fourth amongst

Table 16.5 *Rank ordering of issues of political and non-political elites*

	Spotland		Pen'ceiber		Sevenoaks		The Machars		Stockwell		Oswestry		Overall	
	Polit.	Non-polit.	Polit.	Non-polit.	Polit.	Non-polit.	Polit.	Non-polit.	Polit.	Non-polit.	Polit.	Non-polit.	Polit.	Non-polit.
Environment & planning	1	2	1	1	1	1	6 =	4	5 =	5	1	1	1	1
Transport	6 =	7	7 =	8	2	2	3	2	9	10 =	2 =	3	5	5
Housing	2	1	2	4	4	5 =	4	5 =	1	1	6 =	9	2	3
Economic (excluding unemployment)	6 =	5 =	3	3	5	7 =	2	3	4	4	4	4	4	4
Health	9	8 =	6	7	3	3	9	8	11	9	8	6	7 =	8
Youth	10	8 =	7 =	5	6 =	7 =	6 =	5 =	5 =	6	5	5	6	7
Unemployment	3	3	4	2	9 =	5 =	1	1	2 =	3	2 =	2	3	2
Law and order	11	5 =	10 =	6	11	10 =	10 =	9 =	3	2	9 =	7	10	6
Education	5	11	9	9 =	6 =	4	5	5 =	7 =	7	6 =	8	7 =	8
Elderly	6 =	8 =	5	9 =	6 =	7 =	8	9 =	10	10 =	9 =	10 =	9	11
Race	4	4	10 =	11	9 =	10 =	10 =	9 =	7 =	8	11	10 =	11	10

citizen concerns, fifth for the non-political elite but failed to receive a single mention from the political stratum. There are, therefore, signs that local politics works well in focusing on what is the most common concern of the area but that there may be rather more variation in the extent of agreement on other than the most major issues. This in turn may imply something about the success of participation in placing a matter firmly on the agenda, which is the subject of the next chapter.

17

PARTICIPATION AND THE MAKING OF THE LOCAL AGENDAS

In chapter 16 the agendas of citizens and elites were set side by side in order to provide an overall picture of the ways in which priorities varied both between localities and within them. However, such tables do not enable us very readily to compare the extent of local consensus. Nor, most crucially for the purposes of this volume, do they present the evidence in a way that helps the reader to appreciate the relationship between the agendas of the active, participatory citizens and of the elites which are the targets of their action.

In order to compare agendas in this way, a measure of 'concurrence' has been developed. As is so often the case in participation studies, concurrence owes its origins to the work of Verba and Nie (1972:299–341; 412–4). Concurrence 'measures the extent to which citizens and leaders in the community choose the same "agenda" of community priorities' (Verba and Nie 1972: 302). Each citizen is given a 'concurrence score' based on the frequency with which the problems he or she mentions also appear on the list of priorities of the elite as a whole. Similarly, each member of the elite has a concurrence score representing the match with the agenda of the citizens in the locality.

The method of constructing the concurrence score is an adaptation of that employed by Verba and Nie (for details see appendix B). Our measure combines two methods of assessing concurrence and the final 'score' is an average of the results of these two methods. The first method is to add together the number of issue categories which the citizen mentions which are also to be found on the agenda of the elite as a whole. If a person mentioned housing and transport as issues, that person would get a concurrence score which would be the sum of the issue aspects in these two categories of housing and transport mentioned by the leaders, divided by the total number of issue aspects mentioned by all leaders in that locality. An adjusted score was then calculated which represents the ratio of the level of agreement obtained on the basis of the issue categories *actually* mentioned by the individual to the set of issues which would have obtained the highest level of agreement – i.e. if the citizen had mentioned those categories which were at the top of the elite agenda. The second method of measuring concurrence is to give each individual 'credit' only for the highest issue on the elite agenda which he or she mentions, relative to the highest elite issue which he or she could have selected. Thus one might, for example, receive a score for selecting housing as an issue which lay second on

365

the local elite's agenda whereas the 'best' score would have been gained if one had mentioned environment, which was the elite's top issue category.

The first method gives credit for mentioning several issues which appear on the elite agenda. The second method focuses on the extent to which one was able to select at least one issue which came high on the elite priorities. By using a final concurrence score which is an average of the results of these two methods, we hope to give appropriate credit to a person to the extent that he or she was concerned with an issue high on the elite agenda and also to the individual who was sensitive to a wider range of local issues of which the elite might be expected to be aware. The highest feasible score would be 100, implying that the citizen selected the top issue on the elite agenda and that any other issues he or she mentioned were next in the rank order of importance given by the elite. One could fall short of the maximum score either by failing to mention the top elite issue or by citing issues lower down the list of the elite. The lowest score would be zero if the individual mentioned no issues or selected idiosyncratic issue categories which went unmentioned by any member of the elite. (Of course, one might have to acknowledge that such a person could be uniquely far-sighted in recognising issues which were still unperceived by the elite or, possibly, suppressed by it. Our measures cannot handle an entirely hidden agenda.)

This procedure applies *mutatis mutandis* to measuring the capacity of the elite to recognise the agenda of citizens. Elite concurrence scores in any locality will bear some relation to citizen scores. But they are not precisely the other side of the same coin. Only if the profiles of the elite and the citizen agendas were exactly similar would this be so – and this is unlikely even in the most consensual local milieux. Thus we have two measures – of the ordinary citizen's propensity to match the priorities of the local elite and of the individual leader's tendency to match the agenda of the local population as a whole.

Citizen concurrence – the localities compared

Given that there have been few studies of concurrence (despite the centrality of its basic aim to understanding political responsiveness in democracies) and that there is no commonly agreed method of measurement, it is difficult to say what a 'high' or a 'low' level of agreement would be – or what would be a 'good' or a 'bad' performance by an elite in matching the priorities of the local population. However, the relative scores in the six localities may provide some perspective on what can be achieved.

It will be clear from table 17.1 that the six localities do vary in the extent to which citizens cite a set of issues which matches that of the elite. Indeed, the citizen concurrence scores show some marked differences. Whether or not the score of 57·3 for the average Sevenoaks resident is to be regarded as a 'good' achievement in some absolute terms, it can be seen that it is almost twice as high as the score gained by the average inhabitant of the Machars. It is also a little under 20 % higher than the average score for all six areas together.

Another perspective on the rankings can be gained by noting that whilst a near 'perfect' score of 100 is not unattainable, in that one person obtained 99·3, only 5 % overall managed a mark of 90 and over. A fifth gained scores of over 80. As many as 44·9 % of those in Sevenoaks scored over 80 – a proportion twice as high as Stockwell

Table 17.1 *Citizen concurrence scores by locality*

Locality	Concurrence score	N
Sevenoaks	57·3	264
Stockwell	49·1	226
Penrhiwceiber	36·7	291
Spotland	36·5	272
Oswestry	34·9	272
The Machars	29·6	292
Average	40·2	1,618

which came second. At the other extreme, overall 32% scored zero, largely by failing to raise any issues. The Machars had the highest proportion in this category, thereby deflating their average score.

The question therefore arises as to what it is about the Sevenoaks situation which produces this result and whether any other common features can be found to explain the rank order. One element in Sevenoaks was the dominance of one category of issues but it is the common awareness of this fact which is to be explained. The first hypothesis might be that the shared consciousness of issues is the product of a shared social existence – that leaders and citizens agree because they come from a common social background. It is indeed the case that the leaders and citizens of Sevenoaks are the closest match in terms of social class. However, the other localities did not differ from one another very greatly in this respect. Moreover, the next highest levels of social 'matching' were found in Oswestry and the Machars which suggests that this is not a consistent explanation for high levels of concurrence.

An alternative societal explanation might be that awareness of issues is related to social background and this is confirmed to the extent that, everywhere, the salariats' concurrence score is above the local average. Sevenoaks, as the most middle class of the milieux, could be expected to produce a greater knowledge of local issues. The Sevenoaks salariat has the highest average concurrence score (63·6). However, once again, this does not provide us with a consistent explanation since Stockwell has a smaller salariat than either Oswestry or the Machars. A more promising relationship might be with educational qualifications since Sevenoaks and Stockwell contain the largest proportions of persons with higher qualifications, and these generally, but not uniformly, gain higher concurrence scores. Penrhiwceiber, however, which ranks third, has the lowest number of people with high qualifications.

An urban-rural distinction may also seem to provide a partial answer. Rural Machars is at the bottom end of the scale and a ready explanation might be found for the apparent disparity in their assessment of priorities in the physical remoteness of the citizens from some of the local elite. However, although Oswestry is both rural and second lowest in the list, it is, as we have seen, a small compact town in which a common recognition of issues might have been anticipated. The remaining areas are urban or suburban but it would be difficult to discriminate between them on this ground.

A basis of six localities is not, of course, sufficient to provide definitive proof of the inadequacy of these various societal accounts of concurrence levels. Nevertheless, it may suggest that there is justification for turning to the relationship which is at the core of our interest – between issue agreement and political participation.

Citizen concurrence and citizen participation

It is the relationship between the level of citizen participation and the extent of issue agreement with elites which provides some of the most encouraging news for participatory democrats which this research has uncovered. A close relationship between the priorities of elites and those of participating citizens is at least *prima facie* evidence that participation pays off. Although other factors would remain to be considered (and will be in later sections of the chapter), a match of this sort suggests that elites are responsive to those who make some effort to get heard. This is not to make any judgement that only the activists *should* be heard but, rather, to argue that any such correlation implies that it can be worth trying to make oneself heard.

We may commence with our simple dichotomy between the active and the inactive sectors of the population. As table 17.2 shows, in every locality the concurrence score of the activist sector is clearly above that for non-activists. The average gap is over 20 percentage points and is found to virtually the same extent in each locality.

As overall participation rises, so does the level of agreement between elites and citizens as to priorities. But there is no indication that the elite pay greater *relative* attention to activists than to inactivists in localities where participation is generally high as compared to those where it is low. In this respect, the findings do not appear to confirm those for the United States (Verba and Nie 1972:316–7). This means that compared with the overall concurrence rankings for the six areas in table 17.1, there is little substantial change. Sevenoaks and Stockwell still head the list and the Machars remains at the bottom for activists and non-active alike. The three remaining areas are so close that quite marginal differences could change the rankings.

This overall pattern of higher participation and high concurrence suggests that one should consider the further possibility that the different degrees of activism within the activist sector would also reveal a similar association. The results, shown in table 17.3, are dramatic. This table reverts to the sevenfold typology of participants employed earlier. Alongside the concurrence scores for each type of participant are placed the mean participation scores measured in terms of the average number of actions each reported having taken. The match is perfect.

The complete activists have on average performed nearly 14 of the 22 different actions about which we enquired in the interviews. Not far behind come the party campaigners with 11·4 actions. This gradation is paralleled in their respective concurrence scores of 62·3 and 60·3. And so on, down the ladder. Those designated 'just voters' and 'almost inactive' are clearly adrift from the rest in terms of numbers of actions and there exists a comparable gulf between their levels of concurrence and that of the various activists. The difference of almost 30 points in concurrence between the core of complete activists and the almost inactive gives strong grounds for thinking that it is the message as to priorities of the activists which is getting over to the elites rather than the preferences of

Table 17.2 *Citizen concurrence by dichotomised participant type and locality*

Locality	Non-activists	Rank	N	Activists	(Rank)	N
Sevenoaks	52·5	(1)	189	69·1	(1)	76
Stockwell	44·3	(2)	150	58·5	(2)	76
Oswestry	32·0	(3)	232	52·2	(5)	40
Spotland	31·7	(4)	212	53·9	(3)	60
Penrhiwceiber	30·3	(5)	207	52·3	(4)	84
The Machars	26·9	(6)	255	47·9	(6)	37
Average	35·2		1,245	56·8		372

* Maximum score = 22·0, the 'physical force' item having been included in this calculation.

Table 17.3 *Citizen concurrence by type of participant*

	Mean participation score*	(Rank)	Mean concurrence score	(Rank)	N
Complete activists	13·9	(1)	62·3	(1)	45
Party campaign activists	11·4	(2)	60·3	(2)	20
Collective activists	7·1	(3)	57·9	(3)	129
Direct activists	6·7	(4)	54·3	(4)	51
Contacting activists	6·6	(5)	53·8	(5)	128
Just voters	3·7	(6)	36·7	(6)	745
Almost inactives	2·1	(7)	33·0	(7)	500

the inactive. And even if, as has been seen, these priorities do not necessarily diverge sharply when it comes to the very topmost categories of issue, overall these findings suggest that participation makes the real difference that democratic theory would require. In particular, it raises issues in which the active minority are especially interested onto the elite agenda. It could also mean, however, that if activists were at some time or in certain respects to deviate more emphatically in their priorities, they could make an impact disproportionate to their numbers.

The relationship between participation and concurrence may be examined still further by looking at the extent to which participants not merely mentioned issues but actually became involved in taking action on them. Do those who positively take up the issues they consider important also have high levels of agreement on issues with leaders? If so, this would give support to the contention that the elite's awareness of priorities is formed as a result of these issues being raised in an active manner by citizens.

Respondents were asked whether they had taken any action on all of the issues they mentioned (up to four in number). This provided a scale of involvement from 0 (no action or no issues mentioned) to 4 (action on 4 issues). Such a scale would partly reflect the length of issue agenda and therefore a mean involvement measure was constructed by dividing the involvement figure by the number of issues so as to provide a scale ranging from 0 (no action) to 1·0 (action on all issues mentioned). The involvement scales in table 17.4 show that the Sevenoaks citizens take more issue-based action overall

Table 17.4 *Citizen issue involvement*

Locality	Involvement (Rank)	Mean Involvement (Rank)	N
Sevenoaks	0·95 (1)	0·39 (1)	264
Stockwell	0·85 (2)	0·37 (2)	226
Spotland	0·57 (3)	0·29 (3 =)	272
Penrhiwceiber	0·56 (4)	0·29 (3 =)	291
The Machars	0·36 (5)	0·16 (6)	292
Oswestry	0·34 (6)	0·19 (5)	272
Overall	0·59	0·28	1,618

Table 17.5 *Correlations† between issue involvement and concurrence, by locality*

Locality	Involvement*	Mean Involvement*	N
Sevenoaks	0·47	0·26	264
Stockwell	0·48	0·41	226
Penrhiwceiber	0·45	0·32	291
Oswestry	0·26	0·10**	272
Spotland	0·52	0·44	272
The Machars	0·34	0·24	292
Overall	0·45	0·33	1,618

† Pearson's r.
* sig. = 0·000 except as noted.
** sig. = 0·026.

(0·95) and also relative to agenda length (0·39) than residents of other localities. The people of Stockwell are not far behind, especially in their mean rate of involvement. At the bottom of the scales are, once again, the two least participatory localities of Oswestry and the Machars. Their involvement is roughly a third of that for Sevenoaks. Even when adjusted for the length of issue agendas, their average involvement in these issues is less than half that of the people of Sevenoaks.

The link between issue involvement and issue concurrence is shown in the form of correlations in table 17.5. In every locality, involvement and concurrence are quite strongly correlated. Moreover, even when correction is made for the length of the issue agenda in the mean involvement scale, the association between action and concurrence, with one possible exception, is highly significant. This adds to the accumulation of evidence in favour of the argument that a significant factor in the production of local agendas is, as democratic theory would hope, the participatory input of the citizens and the greater that input, the greater the impact.

However, before this conclusion can be drawn firmly, there remain several other considerations to be taken into account. It is necessary, first, to question further whether variations in concurrence can be the effect more of background resource factors than of participation. If this were the case, we might account in part for the persistent patterns of variation across the localities by the differences in resources which were seen to be

Table 17.6 *Participation and concurrence, controlling for individual and group resources, by locality*

	Unadjusted concurrence scores	Adjusted concurrence scores	N
Sevenoaks			
Non-activists	52·2	54·5	187
Activists	68·8	63·0	75
Eta/beta	0·20	0·10	
Stockwell			
Non-activists	44·2	44·6	150
Activists	58·0	57·1	74
Eta/beta	0·20	0·18	
Penrhiwceiber			
Non-activists	30·3	30·7	207
Activists	52·1	51·2	83
Eta/beta	0·29	0·28	
Oswestry			
Non-activists	32·3	33·1	229
Activists	52·0	47·7	40
Eta/beta	0·20	0·15	
Spotland			
Non-activists	32·3	32·9	203
Activists	53·9	52·1	60
Eta/beta	0·27	0·24	
The Machars			
Non-activists	27·0	27·7	254
Activists	49·2	44·5	36
Eta/beta	0·22	0·17	

factors in explaining participation itself. Hence, the capacity of people in Sevenoaks to identify, and agree upon, the major issues as also recognised by the local elite, could be the result of their being (as are the elite) well-resourced individuals with the skills and contacts to enable them to understand the main local issues whether or not they participate politically.

To test this possibility, we looked at the effect on concurrence levels, as between activists and non-activists, when controlling for the standard set of powerful individual and collective resources – educational attainment, membership of voluntary groups, involvement in trades unions and membership of a political party.

As can be seen in table 17.6, the gap in the concurrence scores between activists and non-activists is initially on average almost 20 percentage points and the strength of the relationship is reflected in the eta statistic that ranges between 0·29 in Penrhiwceiber and a still fairly substantial 0·20 in Sevenoaks, Stockwell and Oswestry. Controlling for resources reduces the gap between the activists and non-activists to some extent, as can be seen from the adjusted figures. The change is most marked in Sevenoaks where the gap is reduced from 16·6 to 8·5 percentage points, and the beta, measuring the strength of the adjusted relationship, to a relatively modest 0·10. To this extent, resource differentials in Sevenoaks are a part of the explanation, as they were for the level of participation itself. Indeed, that there is more to concurrence in Sevenoaks than can be fully explained by participation, is already foreshadowed by the fact that the non-activists in Sevenoaks have concurrence scores as high as the activists elsewhere.

On the other hand, Sevenoaks is exceptional. Across all six localities the gap narrows in every case but only on average by 3·9 percentage points which is less than half that recorded for Sevenoaks. Equally, the average beta remains a still very significant 0·19 – almost double that in Sevenoaks. Much more typical, therefore, is the situation in Spotland. Here, after controlling for resources, the adjusted concurrence score moves up from 32·3 to 32·9 whilst the better-resourced activists fall also very slightly from 53·9% to 52·1%. The discrepancy in concurrence levels between high and low participants of 19·2% is still very impressive and a potent refutation that it is in any way a spurious product of social background effects. The contention that citizen participation is effective in helping to shape the agenda which elites acknowledge and tackle retains its plausibility. However, we still need to consider the situation from the perspective of the leaders.

Elite concurrence

Just as citizen concurrence measured the extent to which each ordinary resident identified the issues which were also on the overall elite agenda, so elite concurrence records the degree to which the individual leader identified the item which appeared on the aggregate agenda of the citizens. Whilst one would anticipate some relationship between the two measures, they are not symmetrical. The leaders are chosen for their vantage points in the local polity and they should be expected to show greater sensitivity to the range of concerns in the area than the average resident, many of whom will have little interest in public affairs. Whereas the average citizen has relatively few issues in mind at any one time, the leaders tend to be able to mention a much longer list of problems. Many of the leaders are, after all, professionally concerned with the needs of the area.

If one compares table 17.7 presenting the elite concurrence scores with table 17.1, containing the corresponding citizen figures, it can be seen that the disparity is large – the average score is getting on for double that for the citizens. Indeed, it appears that the elite seldom failed to mention amongst their list of issues the category of problem which came top of the local citizen agenda. The gap between elite and the average activist is 18 points but relative to the complete activists it drops to 12 points.

In another respect, however, the two sets of scores are a close, but not quite perfect, match. The rank order of localities is, with one exception, the same for elites and citizens. The exception is the Machars where, in relative terms, the average leader is better able to identify the citizen agenda than vice versa. The Sevenoaks leaders head the table as before.

Table 17.7 *Elite concurrence scores by locality*

Locality	Concurrence Score	N
Sevenoaks	83·5	58
Stockwell	78·5	70
Penrhiwceiber	76·8	42
The Machars	71·7	48
Spotland	69·7	51
Oswestry	66·3	53
Average	74·8	322

In testing whether the common agenda of elite and citizens, to the extent that it exists, is significantly shaped by the impact of citizen participation, one might expect to find that there was higher concurrence amongst those leaders most exposed to citizen intervention. These would be councillors, who are subject to electoral pressures and contacts from their constituents, and voluntary group leaders who would be the channels through which many issues are raised. By contrast, other leaders might be expected to be somewhat more specialised and be relatively less aware of the full range of citizen problems. Some of these would, however, come into contact with the more participatory citizens within their own area of responsibility. This should be more true of local government officers.

To check this possibility, we looked at the concurrence scores of each of the eight types of leader distinguished in chapter 16. The figures presented in table 17.8 could be interpreted to support the participatory hypothesis in the sense that the elected leaders and the group leaders have joint highest scores. However, with two exceptions, the other leadership categories are in reality almost indistinguishable. The party leaders and the officials, who might be considered more insulated from the general public, have virtually identical scores. Only the business leaders (and the residual category including such figures as the police) are distinctly less likely to be in line with the citizens as to the local issues. This might present some mild, if indirect, backing for the centrality of participation since business and the residual positions are much the least likely sets of leaders to be the targets of citizen pressure and communication.

If the leaders are divided more simply into the political stratum (councillors, party figures and officials) and the rest, the picture is somewhat sharpened. In each locality, bar the Machars, the political stratum, who are those most frequently contacted about issues by the local residents, have the higher concurrence scores. As can be seen from table 17.9, the Sevenoaks political stratum heads the list – a score of 85·7 representing not too far off a perfect match with the citizens.

That the different categories of elite are likely to display different degrees of interaction with the local population is shown indirectly when examining the extent to which the different leaders took action on the issues they mentioned. The scales were constructed in analogous fashion to those for the citizenry. Thus, the leaders were asked whether they had become involved in each of the issues they mentioned. The two scores in table 17.10 represent the total level and the mean level of involvement. Comparison

Table 17.8 *Elite concurrence by type of leader*

Leader type	Concurrence	N
Elected	77·7	72
Group	77·7	69
Party	77·6	17
Official	77·3	43
Social	75·9	41
Trades union	70·5	20
Other	67·7	22
Business	64·7	38
Average	74·8	322

Table 17.9 *Concurrence of political leadership by locality*

Locality	Political stratum concurrence	N	Non-political elite concurrence	N
Sevenoaks	85·7	25	81·9	33
Stockwell	80·1	28	77·4	42
Penrhiwceiber	79·7	15	75·2	27
Oswestry	74·9	22	60·1	31
Spotland	72·7	20	67·8	31
The Machars	70·9	22	72·3	26
Average	77·6	132	72·8	190

Table 17.10 *Issue involvement by type of leader*

Leader type	Involvement	Mean involvement	N
Elected	2·44	0·78	72
Official	2·07	0·66	43
Group	2·06	0·67	69
Social	1·80	0·55	41
Trades union	1·65	0·62	20
Party	1·65	0·53	17
Other	1·59	0·52	22
Business	1·37	0·53	38
Average	1·95	0·64	322

with table 17.9 on citizen issue involvement emphasises the difference between leaders and ordinary citizens – overall the leaders are more than twice as involved with their issues than are citizens.

The elected leaders, as is to be expected from their more general political responsibility, are clearly the most involved in issues. They are followed by the group leaders and then by local government officials who would also be expected to be highly active but to be more restricted to their specialised functional spheres of responsibility. The business leaders are the least likely to be involved, just as they are also the ones most marginal to the participatory process. One could therefore make the altogether reasonable inference from this pattern that awareness of citizen priorities is likely to be higher amongst those leaders who are the direct targets of citizen action (elected councillors and officials) or are mediators of that action (group leaders). However, although some such association is detectable, the relationships between elite activity and concurrence do not possess the remarkable consistency and strength displayed by the evidence from the side of the citizens.

Concurrence: participation or mobilisation?

The close relationship between citizen priorities, participation and elite agendas is susceptible of an alternative explanation to that so far advanced. Rather than the elites responding to the impact of citizen activity, it could be the case that the elites set the agenda and that the citizens take their cue from the leaders. Thus, the more a person participates, the more he or she comes into contact with the views of the local elite. It may then be the case that the leaders 'mobilise' the citizens into displaying concern about a problem and into taking action on it.

As Verba and Nie, who tackled the same possibility in their study, point out (1972:331), this is a difficult hypothesis to refute on the basis of statistical data gathered at one point in time. For an adequate examination, it requires other kinds of evidence about the circumstances which induced people to raise issues and act upon them. Evidence of this nature is introduced later in the chapter.

This mobilisation hypothesis is, moreover, quite plausible in that political elites have a unique overview of local issues, are the centre of media attention and have a range of resources which would enable them to shape the issue agenda. There has been increased emphasis in political science on the need to appreciate the degree to which leaders, nationally and locally, possess autonomy of action (Field and Higley 1980; Nordlinger 1981; Gurr and King 1987). 'Societal' accounts of politics perceive elites as reacting to pressure from interest groups or from the general public and facing sanctions (such as loss of office) if they ignore such pressure. The alternative 'state-centred' – or neo-elitist – approach considers that many, if not most, leaders, particularly in the political stratum, are able to make their own policy preferences prevail even against powerful interests and, in doing so, escape serious sanctions.

Verba and Nie proposed one indirect statistical test of the mobilisation hypothesis which we have adopted in a slightly modified form. If citizen priorities are a response to elite activation, there should be a closer correlation between elite involvement in issues and elite concurrence than between citizen involvement and concurrence. This would register indirectly the extent to which elite action rather than citizen action on issues produced the commonly agreed local agenda. The results reported in table 17.11 show that the associations are much weaker than those for the citizens (table 17.5). Indeed, in only one locality is there a significantly positive correlation for the unadjusted scale (which records the absolute level of involvement), although this is true for the overall association. The strength of this overall association, however, is less than a third that of

Table 17.11 *Correlations† between elite issue involvement and concurrence, by locality*

Locality	Involvement	Mean involvement	N
Sevenoaks	0·13	−0·06	58
Stockwell	0·30*	0·10	70
Penrhiwceiber	0·16	0·01	42
Oswestry	−0·02	−0·22**	53
Spotland	0·10	−0·01	51
The Machars	0·18	0·11	48
Overall	0·13***	−0·03	322

† Pearson's r.
* sig. = 0·005.
** sig. = 0·056.
*** sig. = 0·008.

the citizens. In the case of the mean involvement scale, the overall correlation is not significant and in the only locality, Oswestry, where the correlation is significant, it is mildly negative.

This evidence would appear to reinforce the previous findings as to the importance of citizen participation. Those areas where there is a generally high rate of participation are also those where there is the greatest degree of concord between leaders and citizens as to the order of priorities. This is supported by the finding that the more intense minority who participate most frequently are still more likely to set an agenda on which the leadership will also agree. There is, therefore, good reason to think that citizen participation is a significant force helping to make leaders, and the political leadership in particular, so well attuned to the priorities of the average man and women in our local streets.

The formation of the local agenda

More light can be shed on the respective parts played by citizen participation and elite initiative in shaping local political issues by looking at their perceptions of how the agenda is produced. We asked citizens and leaders how they became involved in raising issues and dealing with them, whether they did so on their own initiative or as a result of the intervention of others. In this way, the still picture gained from a single survey at one moment in time can be supplemented by some understanding of the movements which led to political action.

In the following sections of the chapter we shall, therefore, look again, but from a different perspective, at three possible ways in which the local agenda might have been created. The first would be that it is created 'from below' by citizen action followed by elite reaction. As has been suggested, the evidence on issue concurrence gives much credence to this explanation which, from certain standpoints, would be the ideally 'democratic' situation. A second possibility is that the agenda is a result of elite initiative with little input from the citizens. A third hypothesis, related to the second, is that to the significant degree that the local population and their leaders agree on priorities, this is a result of the elite mobilising citizen concern and action.

There is a fourth explanation of agreement on issues, which is that both leaders and the general population are influenced by some common outside factor. This factor might be media publicity. Or it might be the effect of central government policy on the provision of local services which produces a common reaction by politicians and electorate. National policies regarding hospital provision or council house sales can put these matters on the apparently local agenda in different places across the nation. Similar general consequences can also flow from national policies by influential businesses or professions (Dunleavy 1980:98–133). These non-local influences on local politics are not properly captured by our locally-based survey approach. Consequently, one may give an impression of greater local autonomy than actually exists, and this must be borne in mind throughout. Certainly, many members of the 'political stratum' in our localities were at pains, regardless of party affiliation or of status as elected representative or appointed officer, to insist on the growing constraints on local autonomy as a result of government policies in the 1980s.

At the same time, it is striking that so many of the agenda items were indeed local. As was pointed out in chapter 11, people were not just responding to the 'big issues' which featured in the media – the economy or unemployment. Nor were they induced to give exceptional prominence to issues falling clearly within local jurisdiction, such as law and order, which sometimes acquire sudden media attention and provoke political leaders to take up positions on them (Balme 1987:168). To the degree that people are mobilised by these non-local pressures, perhaps this forms part of the constant, though also gradually changing, background.

Citizen action, elite reaction

The first step in looking at the dynamics of agenda formation is to establish the extent of interaction between elite and citizens. In one sense, this is measured by the overall levels of participation discussed in chapter 15. Here, however, we shall concentrate on specific contacts between citizens and leaders.

As with every other activity, apart from voting and signing petitions, those who have ever contacted a local councillor or a town hall official are a minority of the population – between a fifth and a quarter. What tables 17.12 and 17.13 bring home is the degree to which, when the local political elites are contacted by local residents, it is the views, complaints and demands of the activists that they are hearing. That there should be this gap follows from the fact that the activist segment includes the contacting activists (7·9% of the total). Even so, there is a sense in which the elites are meeting the same small number of people repeatedly.

Groups form the other main channels through which the local population can seek to influence the political elite. Although most people (58·8%) are members of some group or other (not counting trades unions), only 26·9% report that social or political issues are discussed at their meetings. This means that fewer than half of the group members belong to organisations in any way politically involved and only 17% say that they are members of more than one association in which there is such discussion. (Half of these persons are to be found in either Sevenoaks or Stockwell.) Those who are members of these more 'politicised' groups are themselves relatively more political. Two-thirds of

Table 17.12 *Citizen contacts with councillors by locality and participant type (%)*

	Spotland		Pen'ceiber		Sevenoaks		The Machars		Stockwell		Oswestry		Overall	
	*N	A	N	A	N	A	N	A	N	A	N	A	N	A
More than once	5·1	45·4	9·2	53·4	5·3	38·7	3·8	48·6	2·8	32·0	2·9	45·9	4·9	43·6
Only once	12·1	17·3	14·4	17·8	7·4	11·3	8·9	16·6	5·5	21·9	4·5	11·7	8·9	16·6
Never	82·8	37·3	76·4	28·8	87·3	50·0	87·3	34·8	91·7	46·1	92·6	42·4	86·2	39·8
Total	100·0	100·0	100·0	100·0	100·0	100·0	100·0	100·0	100·0	100·0	100·0	100·0	100·0	100·0
N	212	60	207	84	189	76	255	37	150	76	232	40	1,245	373

* N = Non-activists; A = Activists.

Table 17.13 Citizen contacts with town hall officials by locality and participant type (%)

	Spotland		Pen'ceiber		Sevenoaks		The Machars		Stockwell		Oswestry		Overall	
	*N	A	N	A	N	A	N	A	N	A	N	A	N	A
More than once	1·7	38·7	5·7	41·0	4·9	41·6	4·6	32·4	6·0	44·3	4·2	44·6	4·4	40·8
Only once	12·3	7·8	7·8	7·8	2·6	15·3	4·2	13·5	8·7	7·5	5·9	10·4	6·8	10·1
Never	86·0	55·5	86·5	51·2	92·5	43·1	91·2	54·1	85·3	48·2	89·9	45·0	88·8	49·1
Total	100·0	100·0	100·0	100·0	100·0	100·0	100·0	100·0	100·0	100·0	100·0	100·0	100·0	100·0
N	212	60	207	84	189	76	255	37	150	76	232	40	1,245	373

* N = Non-activists; A = Activists.

them say that they take part in the group's political discussions (three quarters in Sevenoaks and Stockwell). A much smaller proportion (15%) say that they actually made use of the group to raise a political issue. In Stockwell, about a quarter of these members claim to have done so.

But it is one thing for political discussion to take place within a group, another for that group to take political action to influence the local council. A mere 15% of the members of even these somewhat more 'politicised' groups report that their association took any such steps over a five-year period. Once again, small as the numbers are, it is notable that this was more likely to be the case in the same two localities.

It is clear that, for all the apparent power of pluralist accounts of politics as the interplay of group interests, very few people are members of, let alone actively involved in, groups which are themselves politically involved (see Finer 1972). The potential for group activity is very great. In reality, group pressure is conducted by a small set of activists. But, if the earlier concurrence analysis is correct, this is a set which is relatively more likely than others to highlight as important those issues on which the elite itself will focus its attention.

The leaders were asked in turn for their impressions of how much they were contacted by individuals and groups. Whilst such subjective perceptions are difficult to compare, they showed certain familiar patterns. The leaders in Sevenoaks and Stockwell presented a picture of high levels of individual and group contacting which corresponded to the high participation rates, in relative terms, of both areas. Across all six localities, 60% of the elites would say that they were contacted by individuals 'often' or 'very often'. In Sevenoaks and Stockwell, nearer 70% felt this way. More puzzlingly, it was not the two rural areas but Spotland (45·1%) and Penrhiwceiber (52·4%) which reported the lowest frequency of individual contacts, even though it was in the Machars and Oswestry that the fewest citizens reported having made such contacts.

The elected political leaders reported the highest levels of individual contacts, with 77·8% describing themselves as seeing constituents often or very often. They were followed by the group leaders (68·1%). The least frequent links were with the business elite and the police. This pattern corresponds closely to the patterns of elite concurrence, confirming again the importance of 'mass-elite linkages' (Putnam 1976:133–164) to agenda formation – though still not settling definitively the question of the direction of causality.

The elites were also asked to say whether they had been contacted by 'a lot' of groups, 'few', only on one occasion or never. A little over a third (32·9%) reported that they had been contacted by a lot of groups. Those in Stockwell (41·4%) were most likely to place the rate of group interaction at a high level. The Spotland and Penrhiwceiber leaders were again not so conscious of such pressures. As with individual contacting, the Machars and Oswestry leaders were as ready as elsewhere to report group interventions despite the citizens evidence of relatively low levels of group formation and involvement.

Group action does appear to differ from individual involvement in one interesting respect. A little under a third of all leaders (32·9%) report being faced by 'a lot' of groups but it is now the local government officials (51·2%) who meet with the interest groups rather than the elected representatives (37·5%). As at the national level of government, the groups appear to direct their attention more to the policy advisers and executants than to the politicians. It is probable, indeed, that the more senior local officials, with whom we are mainly dealing, are more accessible to groups than to individual residents who would be handled by persons somewhat lower in the hierarchy. If the official perception of the local agenda is influenced by the contacting process, then it would seem that they are somewhat more likely to hear the viewpoints of the interest groups than of the unaffiliated individual.

The most general impression the elite may obtain of citizen concern is through the overall level of activity on issues, whatever form it takes and at whatever target it is directed. The topics on which the citizens took action of any sort in each locality can be seen in table 17.14. This indicates that action was indeed most likely to be taken on those matters at the top of the overall agenda. Comparison with table 16.2 establishes that most action was in nearly every case taken over the two kinds of issues heading each local agenda. Thereafter, the numbers of issues on which action was taken become too few for deep significance to be attached to precise rankings. On the leading issues, therefore, action is shown again not to involve a serious distortion of priorities. As between the localities, Sevenoaks again heads the list as far as the number of issues on which action is taken, followed once more by Stockwell. However, when compared to the total number of issues mentioned, Stockwell and Spotland citizens took action on a higher proportion. The Machars and Oswestry populations acted upon the fewest issues and these were also the smallest proportions of their total issues, confirming the low propensity of these rural populations to participate in any way.

The elected politicians and local government officers can get information from citizens still more directly from personal contacts. These form between a quarter and 40% of actions on issues. The numbers of contacts with councillors and officials on some issues are too low for tables reporting proportions or rank orderings to be appropriate. The figures do, however, tell some interesting stories at the extremes. Environment and planning remain prominent subjects for contacts. As most councillors would affirm on the basis of their 'surgeries', housing is also a leading item, especially in the deprived urban areas. In Penrhiwceiber, it becomes the top item of contacting and is also the dominant contacting issue in Stockwell and Spotland. At the other end, it is striking that only two people across the six localities reported having contacted local politicians or officials about unemployment. In Stockwell, law and order was the second most important issue for the citizens, forming a fifth of the total. Yet not one person said that this had led him or her to get in touch with the local authority.

There are, therefore, certain problems, such as housing and planning, about which the local political and governmental elite is reminded very immediately by direct contact. There are other issues, such as was the case with law and order in Stockwell, where participation took other forms – petitions, meetings, group action – in order to put it on the agenda. And there is another set of issues, clearly no less important to the locality, which owes little or nothing to participatory inputs. Unemployment falls into this category. Relatively few citizens mention it is as a local problem. Even in Penrhiwceiber, it comes a little way down the list. It has already been suggested that it is perceived as a national rather than a local responsibility. Still fewer people take action about it. If they do, it may take the form of a demonstration. Virtually nobody raises it personally with the local authority. To the degree that the elite see jobs as an important issue (see tables

Table 17.14 *Issues on which citizens took action, by locality* (%)

	Spotland	Pen'ceiber	Sevenoaks	The Machars	Stockwell	Oswestry	Total
Environment & planning	16·4	23·4	47·1	21·0	13·3	25·7	26·2
Transport	10·6	10·3	16·8	17·4	7·6	11·5	12·5
Housing	27·5	20·1	4·1	9·4	30·7	12·4	17·3
Economic (excluding unemployment)	7·9	13·6	2·1	15·2	8·0	7·1	8·2
Health	4·2	5·4	21·6	7·8	2·2	12·4	9·7
Youth	2·6	9·2	1·4	5·1	3·6	6·2	4·2
Unemployment	2·1	9·8	0·0	5·1	1·3	1·8	3·0
Law & order	7·4	2·2	0·7	0·0	16·0	4·4	5·4
Education	4·2	1·1	2·4	4·3	1·3	10·6	3·3
Elderly	2·6	1·1	1·7	5·1	0·4	2·6	2·0
Race	4·8	0·0	0·7	0·0	3·6	0·9	1·7
Other	9·5	3·8	1·4	9·4	12·0	4·4	6·5
Total	100·0	100·0	100·0	100·0	100·0	100·0	100·0
N issue aspects	189	184	291	138	225	113	1,140

16.3 and 16.4), they reach that assessment on the basis of other evidence – whether group action, national attention or simply their own eyes.

This is supported by the testimony of the leaders themselves. When asked about the subjects on which they were most frequently contacted by individual members of the public, housing received the most frequent mention – a fifth of all issues. These accommodation issues – repairs and availability of council housing primarily – will seem instances of personal problems and 'particularised contacting'. Nevertheless, the overall view of the leadership was that, taking all the matters individuals raised together, they were overwhelmingly ones which affected the whole area and only a relatively small proportion were entirely private, family problems. As one political leader saw it, most of those coming to him with a housing difficulty were coming

with a multiple problem – a single parent family, say, with a health problem for a kid, on a fourth floor of a block of flats, with three kids under five, no lift, can't get the pram up, can't supervise the five-year old playing.

With surgeries where 'four out of five' cases could concern such housing problems, they were simply symptomatic of what were shared issues. The fact that most group contacts were also about either housing or about environment and planning, perhaps reinforces the extent to which such issues can have, simultaneously, both particular and general, community-wide implications.

Turning to the issues about which the leaders took some form of positive action, further interesting confirmation can be found of the patterns of relationship with citizen priorities and participation. The two issues on which the elites concentrated most were, as table 17.15 shows, first, environment and planning and, secondly, housing. These

Table 17.15 *Issues on which elites took action, by locality* (%)

	Spotland	Pen'ceiber	Sevenoaks	The Machars	Stockwell	Oswestry	Total
Environment & planning	25·0	33·8	54·2	4·1	6·8	31·2	25·1
Transport	5·2	3·3	15·3	20·5	1·8	6·5	7·0
Housing	25·0	15·9	2·5	12·3	27·1	2·9	15·8
Economic (excluding unemployment)	5·2	11·9	1·7	16·4	12·7	11·6	10·0
Health	1·7	4·0	11·9	1·4	1·3	6·5	4·3
Youth	1·7	6·0	0·8	6·8	6·3	10·1	5·5
Unemployment	12·1	16·5	1·7	28·8	11·8	14·5	12·4
Law & order	3·4	2·0	0·0	0·0	15·8	5·1	6·0
Education	2·6	1·3	4·2	0·0	5·0	2·2	2·9
Elderly	3·4	4·6	0·8	1·4	1·8	0·7	2·2
Race	8·6	0·0	0·0	0·0	4·5	0·0	2·4
Other	6·0	0·7	6·8	8·2	5·0	8·7	6·4
Total	100·0	100·0	100·0	100·0	100·0	100·0	100·0
N issue aspects	116	151	118	73	221	138	817

were the two spheres in which the citizens also participated most frequently. Comparison with table 17.14 shows that the emphasis given to these categories of issues was, across all six localities, virtually the same for leaders and the general public. Thus, environment and planning formed 26·2 % of the total issues on which the elite took action and 25·1 % of the problems on which citizens intervened. Within particular localities, moreover, there were other strong relationships. Leaders and public in Stockwell devoted precisely the same level of attention to law and order. In Sevenoaks, transport and traffic was equally the subject of citizen participation and elite problem-solving, as was also the case with transport problems of a different sort in the Machars.

There are, of course, also some differences of emphasis. The Sevenoaks public was concerned rather more with the health issue (threatened hospital closure) than were the leaders, but, even so, it was in third place in the frequency of elite action. The most important difference lies in the sphere which gave rise to little participation but which featured prominently on the elite's priorities. Unemployment received, overall, the third highest level of elite attention. By comparison, very few ordinary members of the public had taken any form of action on the matter. This had also been brought out in the national analysis. At a time when three million people were unemployed, this was perceived as a problem about which the man and the woman in the street could take little effective political action. Even by local leaders, it was often described as ultimately a national government responsibility but, nevertheless, also as a problem where action had to be taken to alleviate its effects on the immediate area. Very typical of the kinds of action involved would be those described by politicians and officials in Penrhiwceiber – deputations to government ministers to complain about changes in development status, liaison with the Welsh Development Agency over building new factory units, seeking assistance from the Welsh Office. All are instances of 'insider' politics, rather than activities in which the ordinary citizen would be able to contribute.

Once again, therefore, there appears a pattern where some issues and problems arouse the active involvement of citizens and elites but others belong to a level of 'high politics' in which only leadership action appears regularly possible. In the first sphere, the coincidence between participation and elite action is so striking as to encourage the democrat to conclude that we must be describing an effective process in which leaders are responsive to the activity of their public. These are matters where participation is instrumentally 'rational' – it pays off.

Elite initiative

The advocates of citizen participation, however, have not yet proved their case. The example of unemployment has already shown that there are very significant issues where action is a matter of elite initiative rather than of response to citizen pressure. It remains possible that the considerable coincidence in action on many issues between leaders and public is indeed just that – coincidence and not an example of responsiveness.

When the various leaders were asked how they had first become involved in the major issue on which they had actively worked, they stressed their autonomy of action much more than any influences which had been brought to bear on them. In the first instance, however, for many, and for the local government officials in particular, the matter had been simply part of their 'normal duties'. It had merely been one of the problems passing across their desks in the ordinary course of their work. This was true for 38·8 % of all the elite – and almost 70 % of officials. For the rest, a quarter said that they become involved on their own initiative. Only just under 11 % reported that they had been responding to some request for assistance by another individual or group, with a further 7·5 % saying that it had been the result of a mixture of personal initiative and outside impetus. The elected political leaders were more inclined than most to claim that their action was self-initiated (36·1 %).

This evidence, therefore, goes somewhat against the previously mounting support for the impact of citizen participation upon elite action. Instead, it provides backing for notions of elite autonomy (Nordlinger 1981; Gurr and King 1987). Leaders have a variety of sources of information on local needs and problems, apart from the impression gained by direct contacts with the public. Party programmes and internal policy formation processes (backed in the larger authorities by substantial statistical information and expertise) can increase the scope for independent action by the political elite.

There are, therefore, good reasons for attaching weight to the evidence of the leaders themselves that they can and do act in an independent fashion. However, certain qualifications should also be made. Unlike the earlier data on participation and elite action, these responses refer only to the single action in which the leader in question was most involved. It is not improbable that a person would identify as the prime action one in which he or she was able to exercise some initiative, and would be less prone to cite others in which the personal role was more reactive. In this respect, one might note that the leaders also did not, in this particular context, mention interventions which were undertaken in response to pressures imposed by central government, although in other respects the political elites in particular repeatedly emphasised the extent to which they were increasingly circumscribed by national decisions on the allocation of responsibilities and resources (Rhodes 1983; Newton and Karran 1985). This is not to say that the elite responses are in any way misleading but, and this is speculation, they may have highlighted one type of action at the expense of others that may have owed more to citizen pressure. Certainly, evidence for elite initiative has to be set against that for the effect of public participation but it is far from sufficient to constitute a refutation of the view that citizen involvement is a major factor shaping the agenda of local politics.

Elite mobilisation

A third possibility to be considered is that, to the degree that citizen activity is at all important, it is the product of elite 'mobilisation' (Nettl 1967). The line between action which is broadly self-engendered participation and that which is activated by outside pressure and organisation is fine. No action is entirely self-motivated and, at the other extreme, even in totalitarian systems, mass behaviour – in the form of political rallies and demonstrations – is unlikely to be completely coerced and involuntary. People respond with varying degrees of spontaneity or encouragement to situations.

The elites were asked how far, in their single most important action, they had involved other individuals or organisations. Nearly two-thirds (63·7%) had done so across all localities. There was no difference in this respect between the political and non-political elites, but there were certain variations within the localities. Almost 90% of the elite in Stockwell had sought to mobilise other actors behind their policies, as had three-quarters in Spotland. At the other extreme, in the Machars, less than a third of the elite (31·3%) and only 22·7% of the political stratum had gone out to get individuals and groups involved – which reflects in part, of course, the lower levels of participation there. Sevenoaks, however, conforms rather less with the already established patterns in that, whilst the political elite were around the average in their tendency to mobilise support, the non-political leaders were much less inclined to do so than the norm.

When we ask *whom* the elite mobilised, a rather less outgoing picture emerges. Much of the effort, as table 17.16 shows, goes into mobilising other members of the local elite. Overall, only 4·1% of those whose assistance was sought by the leaders could be described as ordinary members of the public. This compares with 17·1% who were councillors and 10% who were government officials at local or national level. Over half (51%) of those whose assistance was sought by the elected leaders were other councillors. A further 18·7% were political party figures.

It is true that the largest category to be mobilised were local voluntary groups. They constituted almost 40% of those whose involvement was requested by the elites as a whole. Even in this instance, however, one suspects that this implied the involvement as much of the leaderships of such organisations as of their general members. This may also be true of the economic groups, including in this both businesses and trades unions, who provided 11·6% of those contacted by the elites.

Two qualifications should be made to this impression of the prevalence of intra-elite mobilisation. The first is to repeat the point that the elites are here reporting only the one issue on which the particular leader himself or herself was most involved and, in his or

Table 17.16 *Individuals and groups mobilised by elites on major issues*

Categories mobilised	%
Citizens	4·1
Individual 'political' leaders	2·6
Councillors	17·1
Government officials	10·1
Party figures	7·0
Economic groups	11·6
Voluntary social groups	39·1
Informal groups	8·4
Total	100·0
N of persons/groups mobilised	345

her own view, tended to have taken the greatest initiative. It is perhaps less likely that such issues would have been taken out to public participation. Secondly, the elites are talking primarily about the decision-making and implementation stages of issues rather than the agenda setting stage. These are stages in which elites, rather than the general public, are much more likely to be involved. These qualifications having been made, however, clearly the evidence of the mobilisational activity points to local 'elite accommodation' (Lijphart 1976) and a certain degree of elite autonomy. It does not, however, suggest a process whereby the general public is being actively drawn into political life and their priorities shaped in a very positive manner so as to produce a common agenda.

It will, therefore, also be useful to look finally at the extent of mobilisation from the standpoint of the citizens. Table 17.17 presents the proportions of activities which citizens said were initiated by themselves as against those which were undertaken in response to some approach by another person or organisation. The actions are also divided into those on prime issues (those in which the person was most involved and which largely consisted of contacting or group activity), other contacting or group actions and, thirdly, protest actions. It will be seen that, except in the case of protest activities, by far the most action was self-initiated. The individual citizen had taken up the issue himself or herself. The proportion would be still greater if we considered action taken on the prompting of a personal relative, friend or neighbour as a form of self-starting. Otherwise, the only significant source of outside initiative was the various voluntary groups, which we have earlier seen to be a significant participatory resource. There is very little sign that action was undertaken in response to a stimulus from the political elite.

Protesting is quite different. This is essentially a mobilised form of activity, as well as being, with few exceptions, a collective enterprise. Only 14·5% of protest activities were taken on the initiative of the individual. Almost a third (31·5%) were prompted by a voluntary organisation. The most striking difference is that just under a further third of actions were taken in response to the urging of 'economic groups', which in this context were wholly composed of trades unions. Given the importance of union mobilisation in

Table 17.17 *Self-initiated and mobilised actions, six localities together*

	Action on prime issues		Contacting and group actions		Protest actions	
	%	(N)	%	(N)	%	(N)
Self-initiated	63·6	(376)	56·8	(415)	14·5	(53)
Mobilised						
Personal source	6·4	(38)	10·1	(74)	4·9	(18)
Economic source	4·1	(24)	4·8	(35)	31·2	(114)
Political source	4·6	(27)	3·8	(28)	1·9	(7)
Voluntary group source	15·7	(93)	13·4	(98)	31·5	(115)
Media source	—	—	5·6	(41)	12·6	(46)
Other source	5·6	(33)	5·5	(40)	3·3	(12)
Total	100·0	(591)	100·0	(731)	100·0	(365)

Penrhiwceiber, already noted in chapter 15, it is not surprising that a third of these examples of union initiative were reported in the pit village.

The only other noteworthy role in activating protest was the media (12·5%). A third of these were reported in Stockwell which, perhaps significantly for this instance, is the locality situated closest to the metropolitan centre. London issues rather than those of the periphery are likely to make national news. Political leaders, on the other hand, generally play a negligible role in stimulating protest. Clearly, certain elements amongst the established political elite will have no interest in encouraging even the most conventional forms of protest. However, their almost entire lack of involvement in promoting any form of protest is remarkable. The handful of examples are almost all provided by the Labour Party.

Conclusion

The issues on which ordinary people take action bear a generally close relationship to the issues about which they express most concern. If most of these actions are not seen by those taking them as mobilised by the elite, there is less reason to suppose that the issues themselves would have been regarded as created by the leaderships of the localities.

Neither the evidence of the concurrence analysis nor that drawn from the accounts given of the actions themselves suggests that, to the extent that a consensus exists between elites and citizens on issues, there is a major process whereby elites mobilise citizen feeling about local needs and problems. In particular, there is very little evidence of successful mobilisation by the political stratum. An exception may be over issues which led to protest, especially in the economic sphere. Here, the unions performed an important mobilisational role. In the case of economic problems, one can go still further and argue that the elite established unemployment as an issue quite independently of the actually expressed priorities of citizens or of the limited action taken by members of the public. This is a sphere of elite autonomy.

Outside the economic arena, where national factors possibly carry more weight than local ones, citizen participation gives every appearance of being a major influence in local politics. Participation may only be the work of a minority but, judged by the levels of concurrence on priorities, that minority can make itself count. It can make its weight felt on those issues, such as environment, planning and housing which can have an impact both on particular individuals and on the general public in the locality. There are, therefore, clear signs that elites do respond and that political action can produce results.

In the next chapter, we turn to enquire whether these signs are sufficient to produce a favourable view of the operation of politics in Britain. What overall impression do local leaders and the general public have of the operation of local democracy?

18

THE QUALITY OF LOCAL PARTICIPATION

Although local government was for long regarded as a foundation stone of British democracy, it has come under increasing criticism for its alleged inefficiency and profligacy. Defenders of local government would argue that its proximity to its constituents should ensure that it is more sensitive to their needs and problems. At the same time, this proximity to the local population makes citizen participation more feasible. People are more able to contact their local representatives and officials, or even to take a more direct part themselves as councillors, and in doing so they will bring to their participation a greater depth of knowledge than they could to the 'high politics' of parliament and national government (for discussions see Sharpe 1970; Newton 1982). Nevertheless, in the 1980s, there was a steady reduction in the autonomy of local government. The Conservative governments limited local government spending in an effort to restrain public expenditure and restructured local taxing powers. By such measures as encouraging the sale of council houses to tenants and permitting parents to elect to remove schools from local authority control, the governments also removed certain spheres of responsibility from local government.

Relations between central and local government have thus been transformed. Yet, as has been seen throughout this book, the bulk of political participation has, as theories of democracy have often supposed or indeed hoped, been conducted at the local level. In this chapter, we shall examine how those who were politically active, or who were merely resident in the six areas we have been studying, viewed the processes of local democracy. We shall look at the views of the elite, of the participatory citizens, and of the less active majority about the effectiveness of political participation. Who is regarded as capable of influencing decisions? Which processes of participation are believed to bring the best results? Finally, what impression do the people in the localities have of their politics?

The elite view of local participation

The elites have several viewpoints from which to regard the participatory process. As was argued in chapter 17, they are in certain respects the targets at which participation is directed, being contacted by significant numbers of individuals and local groups. They are also, in some spheres, those who set the agenda and seek to mobilise citizens and

groups to action. In these cases, they may view participation as a reaction to their own
initiatives, particularly those of the political stratum.

Although it is sometimes suggested that the average citizen is not well-informed about
politics, from these varied perspectives the clear view of the elites is that most
individuals are quite effective when they participate. Almost two-thirds (63·3%) thought
that individuals put their message across fairly or very well. Of course, the leaders were
describing that minority who had indeed taken some action which may give a misleading
conception of the political effectiveness of the average citizen. However, it is an
encouraging sign, from the standpoint of participatory democrats, of the potential for
activity in that leaders do not seem inclined to dismiss the capacity of individuals to
intervene politically.

A wide range of groups was identified as having contacted the elites. These groups
can be placed into four broad categories – social groups (such as sports, hobby and
recreational clubs), sectional or interest groups, community and welfare organisations
and political groups. Interest groups and community and welfare organisations were
about equally prominent amongst the groups contacting the elite (see figure 18.1).
Within the interest group category, the most frequently mentioned were civic societies
and residents' associations who, together, formed a fifth of all group contacts. Amongst
the community and welfare organisations, the elite had most dealings with voluntary
service groups which include such bodies as Meals on Wheels and other agencies serving
people in need or on welfare.

The localities differed somewhat in the kinds of groups which the elites saw as most
active. Given its housing structure, it was to be expected that in Stockwell the tenants'
associations were regarded as more active than the civic or residents' groups, which were
more prominent elsewhere. In the two rural areas of Oswestry and the Machars, the
elites reported most interaction with the community and welfare category of groups –
reflecting perhaps a tradition of voluntary service in such neighbourhoods. The two
localities situated in large conurbations (Spotland and Stockwell), by contrast were
those in which the majority of contacts were by sectional interest groups. Stockwell, it
may be recalled, was the least 'community-minded' of the six localities but, relatively,
one of the more participatory. Political activity appears here to take the form more of
the pursuit of individual and sectional interests, and may be all the greater for that.

The leaders were asked which groups were the most and the least effective in putting
their message across. Many leaders felt that the groups with which they had dealings
were equally good. Where they were prepared to mention a type of group as effective,
they were equally likely to pick a community or welfare organisation as an interest
group. Within these very broad categories, some distinctions were drawn. Across the six
localities, the political stratum considered civic groups and residents' associations
(37·9% of their nominations) to be clearly the most effective bodies. The other leaders,
who had received slightly fewer contacts from such groups, mentioned them less
frequently (18·5%) and considered the community groups the most effective. There is no
indication that elites consider that the best resourced groups, such as businesses, are
clearly more effective than others. They do not report a bias to local pluralism in this
respect.

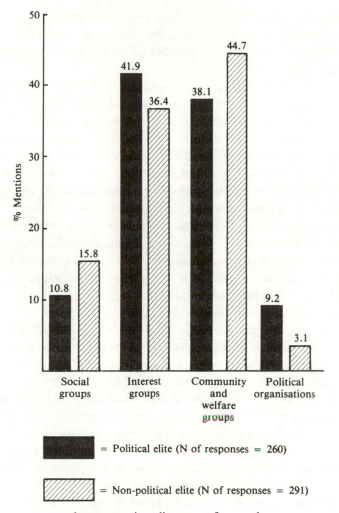

Figure 18.1 Groups reported as contacting elites most frequently

Fewer leaders were prepared to pick out groups which were less effective. Accordingly, numbers are low and conclusions are not entirely reliable. In the event, with one significant exception, no type of group was identified as having particular problems in putting its message across. The exception were ethnic groups. These existed only in Spotland and Stockwell. Whilst they were mentioned only sixteen times amongst the less effective groups, this means that they comprised over half of the elite's mentions (53·3 %) in Spotland and over a third in Stockwell (38·1 %). This is despite very clear informal evidence from our research that many of the leaders in these two localities have made particular efforts to encourage the activities of ethnic minorities. It would appear that, even in relatively open political environments, ethnic groups may be facing, at the very least, problems of communications. We shall see later that this impression is shared by some of the local citizens.

Nevertheless, one should not dwell on the problems facing groups. The general picture the elites portray is of individuals and groups who, when they do act, are reasonably effective in putting their case across. But the next issue is whether, even if most participants are roughly equal in their capacity to communicate, they are also seen as equally influential in local affairs.

The approach adopted towards assessing influence was primarily 'reputational' but crucially modified to take account of the pluralist possibility that individuals and groups can build up a reputation for influence over certain issues and not others (Parry 1969:106–18). The leaders in each locality were first asked to name persons or groups whom they believed to be influential on decisions about four specific types of issue known to be important in the area. They were then asked to name those who were influential in any other major field of local concern. Only then were they asked whether they also thought that 'across the whole range of decisions' affecting the locality, 'the same few people, groups or organisations' were influential or whether 'different ones were influential on different issues'. For our present purposes, we are concentrating on the answers to this last, more general, question about overall influence but it should be recalled that it was asked at the conclusion of a series of more 'pluralist' questions and not as an isolated item (see Dahl 1984:19–35).

Over half the members of the elites (56·4%) thought that the same few people were influential across the community, with 38% holding that different people were influential according to the issue. The remainder (5·6%) gave more qualified responses. There was not a marked difference between the perceptions of the political and the non-political leaderships. The most 'elitist' response came from Penrhiwceiber where fully 77·5% believed the same few wielded influence. The most 'pluralist' was Stockwell where 38·8% believed in some form of inner circle compared to 50·7% thinking that influence depended on the issue involved. This would appear to lend support to the evidence about the importance of a variety of interest groups in pursuing political contacts in Stockwell and in acting as vehicles of participation. This is certainly something which politicians and officials in the area were at pains to emphasise. Speaking of Lambeth as a whole, it was the belief of one of the elected leaders that it had

probably the highest number of various types of community groups and user groups coming together than ... any authority in the country.

An official, making the same point, added: 'I don't think we need to do much mobilisation!' A large number of these organisations in fact received financial assistance from the council.

When we enquire into who constitute the 'same few' people who influence the broad range of decisions, the answer is not so much elitist as a reaffirmation of orthodox representative democracy. As table 18.1 shows, councillors are regarded as the most influential figures in the localities. This perception is shared equally by the political and the non-political leaders. Overall, the political stratum is clearly seen as having the decisive voice. It is, however, intriguing to note that central government, which has intervened so significantly in the affairs of local authorities in the 1980s, received very few references. It was understood, perhaps, to be a structural background factor in the context of these questions on local influence.

Outside the political stratum, organised groups received around a third of mentions

Table 18.1 *Individuals and groups perceived by leaders as exercising influence across local issues: all localities together* (%)

	Political leaders	Non-political
Political stratum	67·3	52·1
Individuals	8·5	7·6
Councillors/the council	43·1	41·2
Local officials	3·0	3·3
Central government (elected representatives, departments and officials)	1·8	2·8
Political parties	10·9	7·6
Organised groups	31·5	37·5
Economic groups	7·9	7·1
Residents' groups	12·1	14·7
Other groups	11·5	12·4
Local population	1·2	3·3
Total	100·0	100·0
N of responses	165	211
N of respondents	132	190

with the various forms of resident, tenant and civic associations regarded as wielding wide influence. Whatever the ultimate authority of the electorate, very few members of the elite suggested that the population at large, or any broad categories (such as 'the wealthy') or any informal groups possessed a major voice in local affairs. Organisation is, on this evidence, a necessary condition for any influence.

The same basic pattern is upheld if, instead of considering general influence, we examine influence within each distinct local issue area. Councillors are still most frequently cited, the only significant difference is that the local officials who deal with the particular issue are now more frequently mentioned than they are when broader questions of influence are raised. This is, of course, entirely understandable in conventional liberal-democratic terms according to which the officials perform a specialised function. The elites do not seem inclined to see the officials as the *éminences grises* of local politics. Rather, the overall picture is one in which the elected politicians are perceived as having power and, presumably, responsibility.

The previous chapter assembled evidence to suggest that elites are responsive to citizen participation. At the same time, the elites appear to perceive themselves as occupying the political high ground. One can detect here something of the division of labour between politicians and the ordinary population which Schumpeter believed was essential to a properly functioning democracy (Schumpeter 1943; see chapter 2 above). Do local elites see this distance between themselves and the electorate as desirable in the way that Schumpeter did? Or would they wish to see a more active, participatory citizenry? Are there different local 'normative climates' which might favour or inhibit participation? (Muller 1979: 95–100).

In order to form some impression of how supportive leaders were of citizen participation, they were asked how far they approved of various forms of political action. They were then asked whether these types of action 'got results'. It would be quite consistent for someone to approve in principle of forms of activity which, however, they believed were ineffective. Conversely, one might disapprove of some types of behaviour yet admit, albeit with regret, that they obtained the outcomes the participants desired.

In the event, as figure 18.2 shows, the most conventional activity received the overwhelming approval of the leaders. Virtually everyone supported the idea of citizens being active in organised groups. There was rather less unanimity as to the effectiveness of such action. Exactly three quarters considered that group action got results but most of the remainder thought that it simply depended on the issue and the group. Only a very few (4·3%) thought that group activity was, in general, unproductive. Turning to 'unconventional' participation, somewhat more surprisingly perhaps, over 90% approved of public protest meetings. Resorting to public meetings was regarded as rather less likely to achieve its objectives. Again, many believed this depended on circumstances (28·7%) but 11·9% thought that it was not worthwhile, leaving 59·4% considering that, on the whole, it paid off. The political leaders were rather more likely to believe that protest meetings were effective than the non-political elites.

As one moves to other forms of protest, the overall levels of approval decline. Taking a petition around for signing would appear a fairly innocuous form of political action but it met the actual disapproval of a quarter of the leaders. The political leaders were indeed slightly more disapproving than others. The leadership in the Machars, where petitioning was least frequent, were the most opposed (46·7% disapproving). At the other extreme, 90% of Stockwell leaders supported petitioning as did 87·5% in Penrhiwceiber. There is, however, greater scepticism as to the effectiveness of petitions. Almost 30% of leaders said that they do not get results, a third thought that it depended on circumstances and the remainder thought that they did work. The most convinced as to the productiveness of petitions were the Penrhiwceiber leaders (61·9%); the greatest sceptics were to be found in the Machars where 43·5% considered that they are ineffective.

Moving further along the spectrum of participation from the mild to the less mild and common, the balance of approval changes again. Opposition to people taking part in a protest march reached 40·3%. Elite support for such demonstrations was again highest in the Labour Party strongholds of Penrhiwceiber (81%) and Stockwell (83·2%). In rural Oswestry, 57·1% of leaders disapproved of protest marches, in the Machars 58·7% and in Conservative-dominated Sevenoaks, fully 72·2% opposed such methods of seeking to influence outcomes. The proportion of leaders who consider marches and demonstrations to be ineffective now rises to almost half (49%). Only just over a quarter (26·3%) believed them to produce results with the remaining quarter saying that it depended on conditions. Only in Penrhiwceiber did a majority (54·8%) of the leaders believe that marches achieve their objectives. In Stockwell, widespread approval of the activity was accompanied by greater doubts as to its usefulness since only 29·4% were prepared to say that it gets results. Over 60% of leaders in Sevenoaks and the Machars shared the view that marches do not obtain the desired outcomes. Overall, there was no difference in attitudes to marches and demonstrations between political and non-

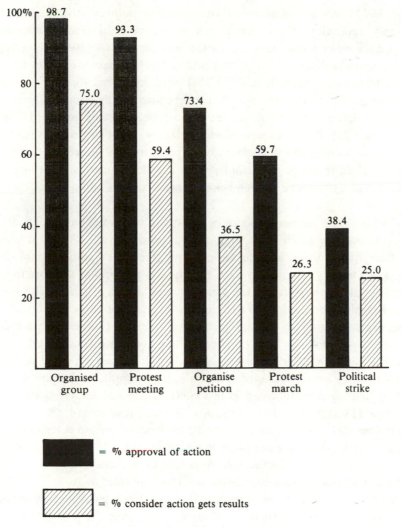

Figure 18.2 Elite perceptions of acts of participation

political leaders. The highest levels of approval and of confidence in the results of protest marches was found amongst the trades union leaders.

The most 'extreme' of the actions put to the elites for their assessment was 'taking part in a strike which they considered political'. As many as 61·6% disapproved of this form of participation. Overall, there was no difference between the political and the non-political leaders. The trades union leaders, however, were overwhelmingly in favour (75%). Clearly, they had few reservations about attaching a 'political' label to certain strikes despite the norm that striking should be described as an economic rather than a political act. The two centres of Labour Party power stand out from the other areas. In Penrhiwceiber, 68·3% of the leadership approved of such strike action (over a quarter approving strongly). It will be recalled that this was at the time of the national miners' strike. This would certainly explain union support but political strikes were also backed by 57·2% of political leaders. In Stockwell, where the council was in dispute with central government, 38·2% of the leaders approved strongly of political strikes with a further quarter simply approving. Over two thirds of the political leaders approved. In Sevenoaks, on the other hand, only one person was prepared to give strong approval.

Although over 60% disapproved of 'political strikes', leaders are rather less certain about their effectiveness. Around half (51·7%) were convinced that they did not get results but over a fifth (23·3%) thought that it depended on the circumstances. Thus, a quarter believed that political strikes were a successful form of action. The greatest confidence in the political effectiveness of such strikes was, not surprisingly, to be found in Stockwell (36·2%) and Penrhiwceiber (39%). This implies, however, that approval does not always lead to sanguine attitudes as to the likely outcome, just as elsewhere there are many who disapprove of such behaviour but ruefully admit that it can achieve its goals.

This analysis provides further evidence of the way in which the local political climate impinges on the level of participation, even if the direction of causality is not necessarily apparent. Everywhere there is elite support for the most conventional form of participation and usually for mild protest. But there is not similar support for, indeed in most localities there is hostility to, the more 'extreme' forms of action. This is not true everywhere. Penrhiwceiber and Stockwell provide instances of elites who do not merely tolerate, but are actually ready to back protest as a means of influencing decisions. In part they are, as we shall see below, reflecting local citizen attitudes. From another standpoint, the elites create an environment in which certain types of participation flourish whilst others are discouraged. Not only, for example, is the political strike a weapon of the mining community, it is one which their local leaders understand and which they regard as legitimate. Elsewhere, protest would tend to de-legitimise the group employing it. One may also wonder whether the tendency of certain elites to believe that some modes of participation are less likely to get results actually contributes to ensuring that they will indeed prove ineffective. Aversion to a certain manner of political behaviour may lead one to be less likely to want to surrender to it.

It has been seen throughout the study that Britain is not a participatory society even if there are variations between areas. To discover how active the population appeared to the elites, we asked the leaders whether in general people in the area 'accepted things as they were' or whether they tried to get things changed. They were also asked whether they believed that higher levels of participation would help the process of solving problems. Setting aside those (12%) who thought that the degree of popular involvement depended on circumstances, a significant majority (59·7%) across the localities thought that people simply accepted things as they were. Only in Stockwell did most leaders (61·4%) believe that theirs was a locality in which people generally tried to get things changed. It will be recalled that this was the locality with the highest proportions of general activists and of protest specialists. Despite the relatively high participation rate in Sevenoaks, most leaders were inclined to regard the population as inactive. In Oswestry, as many as 82·4% of the leaders had formed the view that the population was largely acquiescent, an opinion shared by the citizens themselves and confirmed partly by the low rates of participation (see chapter 15 above). When asked whether this acceptance resulted from a positive sense of satisfaction or from an attitude that 'nothing could be changed', virtually all the leaders (86·9% of those answering) interpreted the popular attitudes as being one of resignation.

There is certainly evidence to justify many of the leaders in their conviction as to the inactivity of three-quarters of their local residents. One source for the elite's attitudes might lie in their experience in obtaining active support for the organisations in which they themselves are involved. Accordingly, the party political leaders were asked how readily they could obtain help for such activities as canvassing at elections and for general clerical support between elections. Similarly, group leaders were asked about the ease with which they obtained voluntary help for their organisation or cause. The experience of the party leaders was not as adverse as might have been anticipated from the very low figures who are, in fact, involved in party work. As many (just over 40%) thought there was 'no trouble' in getting volunteers as believed that there was 'some trouble' and only 16·7% had faced 'a lot' of difficulty. In comparable vein, half the group leaders also reported no trouble in obtaining volunteers. Slightly greater difficulty was reported in the urban centres of Spotland and Stockwell; the fewest obstacles were faced in Sevenoaks. Hence, it would appear that the impression of popular acquiescence is a diffuse one which does not arise out of adverse experience in recruitment of support. One interpretation may be that the elite do not find the citizens to be spontaneously very active but that they are capable of being mobilised. It remains true, however, that even if there are sufficient volunteers, they may still add up to a tiny proportion of the citizenry as a whole.

Finally, the leaders gave their views as to how far an active populace was of positive assistance in the solution of problems. Those leaders who believed that the local population did try to get things changed were asked how much this activity did in fact help. The elite's response was clearly positive. Rather under a half (45·4%) assessed citizen involvement as helping a fair amount and just over a quarter (27·3%) as contributing a great deal, which still leaves a further 27·3% who found it of little or no assistance. The leaders who believed that people generally accepted things were asked to speculate whether more active citizen involvement would be a help in handling local issues. Here again, the local leaders implied that they would welcome participation in that almost half (47%) believed it would help a great deal and over a third more (35·1%) thought that it would help a fair amount. Under a fifth were sceptical (17·9%). There was little difference either between localities or between elites in these respects.

Sometimes leaders admit that they have, to differing degrees, revised their views about the contribution which can be made through citizen participation. One senior official began by saying:

I assume you want an honest answer. We never welcome the people stirring the pot or muddying the waters or whatever.

However, he then went on to relate an instance where a campaign by individuals and local groups against a council-backed development had led, in his opinion, to a better, albeit more expensive, solution. An officer in another authority similarly acknowledged that, in the early days of community involvement in housing redevelopment schemes, many of the officials were sceptical of its value but that the experience had 'changed us' and that the community participants 'were right; we were wrong'.

If we can sum up the view of citizen participation from the bridge, it is that it is limited in amount and, perhaps as a consequence, is not directly decisive on policy-making, even though, as the previous chapter suggested, there are good reasons for thinking that

Table 18.2 *Citizen satisfaction with results of contacting and group actions* (%)

	Spotland	Pen'ceiber	Sevenoaks	The Machars	Stockwell	Oswestry	Total
Satisfied	65·6	87·1	65·7	67·2	66·1	76·3	72·2
Mixed feelings	31·1	5·4	20·0	27·9	21·0	18·6	20·2
Dissatisfied	3·3	7·5	14·3	4·9	12·9	5·1	7·6
Total	100·0	100·0	100·0	100·0	100·0	100·0	100·0
N. of actions achieving a result	90	93	70	61	62	59	435

indirect influence through the formation of agendas is considerable. The absence of participation is something which leaders deplore. Or at least they would appear to regret the relatively low levels of conventional participation. There is generally less toleration, and still less encouragement, for resort to direct forms of political action. At the same time, there are parts of the country where such modes of participation are seen as legitimate. For the most part, however, elites regard themselves as working within fairly acquiescent populations.

The citizens' view of local participation

In chapter 15 we reviewed the levels of participation across the six localities. Here, we are concerned with the perception of the citizens as to the value of that participation. The first striking feature is that the minority of the population who were involved in local groups or who contacted local representatives and officials were overwhelmingly satisfied with the results. The figures in table 18.2 confirm those reported across the nation in chapter 12 above. Where an outcome had been reached, almost three quarters of participants were satisfied with what had been achieved. The proportion actually dissatisfied with the outcomes of their dealings with local authorities is remarkably low (7·6%) and is consistent across councils with quite different political complexions. These results accord very closely with the findings of a survey carried out on behalf of the Committee of Inquiry into the Conduct of Local Authority Business (the Widdicombe Report) in which similarly high levels of satisfaction with contacts with councillors and officials were recorded (Young 1986:40–7). Some comparable results were also obtained from a survey of local voting behaviour (Miller 1988:33).

The local studies also confirm the curious finding reported for the nation as a whole that satisfaction appears to decline with greater participation. Across the localities, 79·2% of the less active population were satisfied, whereas 67·9% of the activists felt the same way. Over a fifth of activists (22·4%) were dissatisfied against 16·7% of the rest. As was suggested earlier, we can only surmise that either the more active one is, the more critical one becomes of the outcomes or that a critical disposition stimulates action.

As can be seen from table 18.2, it is in the more active localities (Sevenoaks, Spotland and Penrhiwceiber) that the greatest relative dissatisfaction with conventional participation is reported, but even so the proportions are quite small. Protest actions, shown in table 18.3, engender less satisfaction than other modes of participation and across the six areas a quarter were discontented with the results. Nevertheless, as many as 60·8% were satisfied. (The low numbers should suggest caution in comparing the localities.) This may partly explain why some of the leaders who did not approve of the more 'extreme' forms of protest were prepared to acknowledge their effectiveness in certain circumstances.

Measured in these ways, local participation can once more be viewed as effective from the point of view of the minority who have been even occasionally active. Some further support for this conclusion may be found in the replies of those who had taken action on their prime issue as to whether they were led to infer that they could have more influence or less influence over how things were done in their locality. Nearly two thirds (63·8%) said that it had made no difference but 30% considered that the experience had encouraged them in the belief that they could have more influence. Thus, only 6·2% had drawn an adverse conclusion about their capacity to affect outcomes.

Experience may encourage a feeling of effectiveness. It may also be the case that a sense of efficacy gives a person confidence to take political action. This is, indeed, borne out by the standard test of 'political efficacy'. Respondents were asked if they thought that, individually, people like themselves could 'have no influence over local councillors'. As is shown is table 18·4, over half of the sample (56·7%) across all localities were, on this measure, lacking in political efficacy (i.e. agreed with the proposition). However, if the population is divided into the activist and non-activist segments, the activists are indeed found to be more efficacious than the non-activists (59·3% as against 38·3%).

The sense of personal political efficacy appears highest in Sevenoaks. Over half the population (52·3%) regards itself as efficacious, as do 77% of the activists. Given the composition of the Sevenoaks population, this is not surprising. Educational qualifications appear to be among the major determinants of an efficacious attitude. Nowhere else is a sense of efficacy felt by a majority of the population but everywhere at least half of the activists share it.

However, a personal sense of efficacy is not (or should not be) the only appropriate measure of the belief in the capacity of people to influence events. Political action can be collective as well as individual and a measure of 'collective efficacy' is therefore also required. When people are asked whether they assent to the view that a *group* of persons like themselves can have no influence over councils, the responses are very different. Over two-thirds (68·3%) possess a sense of group efficacy. Moreover, although Sevenoaks residents still show more efficacy (76·8%), the majority everywhere now takes a positive view of the potential of collective action. This is true of less active and active alike but the response of the activists is particularly strong, with 82% believing in the capacity of groups to influence the local council. This conviction may be lower amongst the least well-off, the unemployed and the less educated, yet even amongst these groups, a majority shares the attitude. Whether or not people actually engage in collective action, there is, therefore, a faith in the possibility of being able to mobilise effective group action if it should be needed. The actual propensity to take group action is, however, as has been seen, not so uniformly spread amongst the population as is this belief in its potential.

Table 18.3 *Citizen satisfaction with results of protest action* (%)

	Spotland	Pen'ceiber	Sevenoaks	The Machars	Stockwell	Oswestry	Total
Satisfied	60·0	62·5	52·4	73·3	61·0	[57·1]*	60·8
Mixed feelings	31·4	20·0	33·3	6·7	26·0	[14·3]*	24·0
Dissatisfied	8·6	17·5	14·3	20·0	13·0	[28·6]*	15·2
Total	100·0	100·0	100·0	100·0	100·0	100·0	100·0
N. of actions achieving a result	35	40	21	15	46	14	171

* Brackets indicate Ns. below 15.

Table 18.4 *Citizen perceptions of individual and collective efficacy* (%)

	Individual efficacy*	Collective efficacy**
Agree strongly	11·3	4·4
Agree	45·4	27·3
Disagree	38·8	57·6
Disagree strongly	4·5	10·7
Total	100·0	100·0
N	1,553	1,547

* 'People like myself can have no influence over local councillors.'
** 'A group of people like myself can have no influence over local councillors.'

A belief in the capacity to exercise influence, whether personally or collectively, does not mean that influence is actually perceived as being diffused amongst the different interests in local society. The citizens' perception of influence was examined in the same way as in the case of the leaders. Respondents were asked to list whom they believed to be influential over each of several different local issue areas. They were then asked whether they thought that 'the same few people' were influential across the whole range of decisions in the locality or whether, rather, different people were influential over different issues.

Well over a third (38·6%) said that they did not know whether the 'same few' were influential or not. This compared with only 5·6% of the leaders who confessed ignorance on this point. Omitting these 'don't knows', the population across all six areas divided equally between the 'elitists' and the 'pluralists' who thought that different people were influential on different issues. Most pluralists were in Sevenoaks and Spotland, followed by Stockwell (which contained the most pluralists amongst the leadership). In the remaining three localities, the balance of elitists and pluralists was much the same, with the former slightly outweighing the latter. Hence, the citizens of Penrhiwceiber did not view local influence as so narrowly based as did the leaders themselves.

The citizen population broadly shared with the leaders an 'orthodox liberal democratic' view of where influence in the local system mainly lay (see table 18.5).

Getting on for three quarters (71·8%) nominated individuals or groups in the political stratum. The majority (54·7%) thought that councillors – usually as a body – constituted the 'same few' who exercised influence across the range of issues. This represents about 10% above that for the leaders themselves (see table 17.2 above), although both groups place councillors in first place. Compared to the leadership, the ordinary person is less inclined to nominate organised groups as broadly influential. Around a third of leaders did so but fewer than a fifth (18·9%) of the local population referred to the ability of groups to wield general influence.

Although the citizens were some three times more likely (9·3%) than elites to accord some influence to informal groups and the population in general, the figures scarcely suggest that they consider themselves decisive. Rather, the citizenry acknowledges the actuality of the political division of labour between electors and representatives. Nor do they suppose that, behind the scenes, there lurks a hidden group who exercise the real say – a power elite or a ruling class. Whether they are correct in this belief would require a different form of investigation designed to uncover the actuality of the exercise of power in each locality. Here, we are concerned with the perception of political influence within which participants operate.

Across all the localities, therefore, the actual experience of participants is supportive of political action. Those taking it have been satisfied with outcomes, have often felt that their impression of the responsiveness of the system to influence has increased. Participants have generally retained a positive sense of their own individual political efficacy. And even if this is not shared by the less participatory, there is, nevertheless, confidence in the capacity of more collective forms of behaviour to obtain some results.

There remains the question whether people believe that the local climate is equally favourable to the various modes of participation. Elites, it has been seen, were generally sympathetic to conventional participation but, with the notable exception of two of the localities, this sympathy declined as more radical forms of action were considered. The citizen respondents were not asked, as were the leaders, whether they themselves approved of the various modes of participation but whether they believed that people in the area in general approved. The object was to ascertain the image the respondents had of the local political climate (see table 18.6).

Everywhere there was confidence that the local population would approve of the conventional modes of participation. Over 90% thought there would be support for working in an organised group, and over 80% believed there would be sympathy for party political canvassing. Turning to protest activities, the vast majority anticipated approval for attending meetings but people were evenly divided about whether their fellow residents would approve of taking part in a protest march. The activists were more inclined to expect acceptance of such action. Here the contrasts in the perceptions of the local political climate are striking. In Penrhiwceiber, there was almost, if not quite, total unanimity (89·5%) in the conviction that there would be approval for the tactic of protest marches. By contrast, in the Machars, 67·2% and in Oswestry, 70·1% believed that marches or demonstrations would meet with local disapprobation. Across all six areas, not far short of two thirds (62·6%) felt that political strikes were weapons that would not get local sympathy. The predictable exception is the mining community, where 85·8% believed there would be local support – a conviction presumably enhanced

Table 18.5 *Individuals and groups perceived by citizens as exercising influence across local issues: all localities together*

	%
Political stratum	71·8
Individuals	7·6
Councillors/the council	54·7
Local officials	3·2
Central government (elected representatives, departments and officials)	1·8
Political parties	4·5
Organised groups	18·9
Economic groups	4·6
Residents' groups	7·0
Other groups	7·3
Local population	9·3
Total	100·0
N. of responses	561
N. of respondents	1,518

Table 18.6 *Citizen perception of local approval of modes of participation* (%)

	Spotland	Pen'ceiber	Sevenoaks	The Machars	Stockwell	Oswestry	Total
Working in organised group	89·3	91·7	98·4	91·2	92·2	84·0	91·9
Canvassing	81·0	90·9	86·8	78·2	76·8	80·9	82·9
Attending protest meeting	83·6	95·9	94·5	85·8	85·6	75·5	86·6
Taking part in protest march	48·9	89·5	31·2	33·2	73·6	29·0	50·8
Taking part in a political strike	31·6	85·8	10·4	16·5	60·4	20·7	37·4

Do people in area approve or disapprove of activities? Combining 'approve' and 'strongly approve' responses.

by the then current experience of a national strike. The only other area where a majority (60·4%) considered there would be approval for such strike action was Stockwell. In Conservative Sevenoaks, not surprisingly, nine out of ten said that such conduct would meet with disapprobation and in the two rural areas 80% or more took the same view.

In chapter 15, variations in political participation were seen to be partly the product of the social composition of the locality and partly of a distinctive local effect. One element in that local effect is likely to be the perception of a local climate either of presumed support or of opposition to specific forms of action. This was already suggested when seeking to explain the ways in which certain communities, such as

Penrhiwceiber, activated particular types of protest participation. Almost certainly there is an interactive process at work. Social and economic resources, coupled with the prospect of individual and group benefit, incline people towards participation and towards certain forms of action, rather than others. It is, however, also likely that the knowledge that most people in the area are prone to consider certain types of action as appropriate and others as illegitimate will have some impact on how a person will proceed politically. Local leaders appear to reflect the attitudes of their fellow citizens quite closely in this respect. There is relatively little sign that the leaders are very markedly less inclined than the average person in the particular locality to regard any type of action as legitimate.

Prospective participants need to take into account not merely the merits of their case but also the perceptions of their methods. Whilst there is a national consensus on the 'easy' forms of conventional participation, there are considerable local differences as to how readily the more 'extreme' modes of action will find acceptance either with the mass of the citizenry or with the leaders whom they may be intended to influence. Hence, there will be parts of the country which are more likely than others to see the employment of certain forms of protest participation and in which, additionally, these actions are likely to make more headway or, at least, where they are less likely to be dismissed as illegitimate kinds of pressure and to undermine the case of the participants. Just as participation does not display an entirely uniform pattern across the country, so the potential for future participation, and especially for protest, will also vary.

The evaluation of local politics

The evidence of those – admittedly a minority – who have taken some form of action over local grievances would appear to provide grounds for satisfaction to those who believe in local government as a basic element in a democracy. Participants displayed remarkable degrees of contentment with the outcomes of their dealings with local authorities. Amongst the most active section of the population, the sense of individual efficacy was at a respectable level. These findings might appear to contradict the apparent belief of critics of local government that it is failing in its job and that it must be held more precisely to account whether to its local constituents or to an ever more regulatory and *dirigiste* central government.

It could, however, still be the case that these two sets of attitudes are not totally contradictory. There may be a level of day-to-day handling of issues – 'low politics' – where local government does well. At the same time, it is possible that there are wider responsibilities which local government handles less well and of which the ordinary citizen is more critical. Accordingly, in this final section, we look at the overall impressions leaders and citizens have gained of the processes of local politics.

The leaders were asked how well local government understood the issues, needs and problems of the particular area. Overall, the replies were favourable – 81·4% thought that the authorities understood them either 'very well' or 'fairly well', dividing equally between these two responses (see table 18.7 below). There were some variations between the localities in the strength of these evaluations. In Penrhiwceiber, 72·5% of leaders believed that local government understood the issues 'very well' which was a much stronger commendation than made anywhere else. But everywhere a large majority supported the local government. The most reservations were in Spotland where 31·9% of the leaders thought that the local authority understood issues 'not very' or 'not at all' well. Just over a fifth of Sevenoaks leaders also thought that the authority did not appreciate issues 'very well'. As was seen in chapter 17, this would not be borne out by the analysis of levels of issue concurrence, where the Sevenoaks leadership more closely matched the agenda of the citizens than did any of the other local elites.

It might have been anticipated that the political stratum of the elite would have claimed, on behalf of local government, a better understanding of needs than would other elites. Whilst it is true that the political elite were more inclined to say that local government understood conditions 'very well' (48% as against 34% for the non-political elites), when the 'very well' and 'fairly well' responses are taken together, there is little difference. Within the political stratum, the local officials displayed the greatest confidence with over 90% offering one of the two positive responses.

When the elites were asked to offer more general impressions of how local politics works, enthusiasm was moderated (see table 18.9 below). Just over half of the leaders (51·1%) had a 'generally favourable' impression. Of the remainder, a little over a quarter (26·4%) had formed a 'generally unfavourable' view, whilst 22·5% preferred to say that their view was 'neither one way nor the other'. The main reasons for holding a favourable impression were based on the proximity and accessibility of local government (13·7% of favourable opinions) and the associated view that it was accountable and democratic (15%). Almost a fifth (19·5%) praised the quality of the councillors themselves. Interestingly, amongst the unfavourable opinions it was the alleged lack of accessibility which was the chief complaint (21·7%). Clearly, accessibility is regarded ideally as the chief virtue of local government – a virtue which is intimately connected with political participation.

There was not a great deal of variation between the views of the local leaders. The exception was Spotland. There, 40% had formed an unfavourable impression of local politics, in contrast to the Machars, where only 17·1% felt this way. The criticism appeared to arise from the non-political elite, many of whom found local affairs 'too political' or too much concerned with party politics. It will be recalled that Spotland itself had a strong Liberal Party presence, and the Rochdale Borough Council was, at the time, finely balanced between Conservatives, Liberals and Labour. There is still a certain suspicion of 'politics' (see also Parry and Moyser 1988) which survives particularly at the local level where politicisation, in a party-political sense, arrived late in some areas. The political leadership in Spotland naturally did not share this apolitical, or even anti-political, stance and 68·4% of them had a favourable impression of local politics as against only 27·6% of the non-political elites. This was the largest discrepancy between the two categories of leaders, even though, as a general rule, the political elite was, not unexpectedly, the more positive about the performance of local politics.

Only in one of the localities, therefore, was there even a plurality of non-political leaders who had formed an unfavourable view of the local political process. Amongst the political stratum, the resentment against national government's limitations on resources was shared by politicians of all parties and by officials. There was a certain hankering after a system of single-tier all-purpose local authorities. And whilst there was a cautious

Table 18.7 *Elite and citizen perceptions of how well local government understands local needs and problems*

| | Spotland | | Penrhiwceiber | | Sevenoaks | | The Machars | | Stockwell | | Oswestry | | Total | |
	Elite	Citizens	Elite	Citizens	Elite	Citizens	Elite	Citizens	Elite	Citizens	Elite	Citizens	Elite	Citizens
Very well	14·9	12·6	72·5	17·7	31·6	6·5	34·9	14·9	47·6	12·9	44·2	8·2	40·6	12·3
Fairly well	53·2	58·9	10·0	41·6	45·6	59·8	46·5	56·6	39·7	42·0	46·2	63·8	41·0	53·9
Not very well	25·5	21·1	10·0	22·7	22·8	29·5	9·3	20·2	9·5	30·6	9·6	26·4	14·6	24·7
Not at all well	6·4	7·4	7·5	18·0	0·0	4·2	9·3	8·3	3·2	14·5	0·0	1·6	4·0	9·1
Total	100·0	100·0	100·0	100·0	100·0	100·0	100·0	100·0	100·0	100·0	100·0	100·0	100·0	100·0
N	47	248	40	285	57	246	43	275	63	200	52	253	302	1,506

welcome for the bottom tier of community or parish councils as organs for consultation, there was on the whole less enthusiasm for decentralising decision-making powers to such a 'grass-roots' governmental level. The survey did not, however, detect amongst the elites, the widespread disillusionment with local government which has sometimes been supposed to prevail in Britain.

The assessment of local politics by the citizenry is more mixed. Although participants were generally well-satisfied with the outcomes of specific acts of local participation, their more general assessments of local politics were distinctly more cautious. When asked whether local government in their area understood local issues, needs and problems, the responses, although favourable overall, were less positive than those of the elites (table 18.9). Two-thirds (66·2%), as against 81·4% of leaders, believed that problems were understood either 'fairly' or 'very well' but only 12·3% chose the stronger response. Nevertheless, everywhere a majority considered the authority did appreciate the problems. The rural areas were most positive, followed by Spotland. There is, therefore, no indication that smaller local authorities give rise to a better sense that problems are understood. Although Oswestry and the Machars have small populations, they are very different in their degree of concentration. Moreover, Spotland is part of a large conurbation.

When attention turned to whether the area had been, in their opinion, well-provided for by the local council, the citizens' reservations were more pronounced. The population divided almost equally, with those who agreed that the provision had been good constituting a small majority (52·3%). Understanding the problems of a locality is not the same as providing for their solution. The contrast may be seen in the case of Penrhiwceiber. Almost half the respondents (49·3%) considered that local government understood their needs and problems 'fairly' or 'very' well – a figure which contrasts sharply with the 82·5% of leaders, who believed that problems were well-understood. However, as many as 79% did not think that the locality was well-provided for by the local council. This is despite the fact that the Penrhiwceiber residents reported high levels of satisfaction with the results of their own contacting or group actions (see table 18.4 above). These positions are not necessarily inconsistent in that respondents may be reasonably content with how their own problems are handled, yet unhappy with the general situation. It would have to be said that by most standards the difficulties the Cynon Valley Borough Council faces in Penrhiwceiber exceed those encountered by the other local authorities. The severity of unemployment, the difficulties in attracting new jobs and the poor housing stock are problems which would daunt any governmental agency. Stockwell was the other locality in which a majority (57%) felt that the area had not received good provision. Again, this was an authority with particular problems of resources and also involved in political dispute with central government over expenditure. In every other area, 60% or more of the population stated that the area had been well provided for.

This general impression of local authority provision should not be allowed to disguise the fact that people do recognise that some sections of the population fare less well than others. Respondents were asked whether they thought that there were some groups in the area which tended to 'lose out most of the time'. Just over half (52·4%) thought that there were. Although there was a wide scatter of groups mentioned, each with a handful of nominations, some stand out as losers. As table 18.8 shows, the poor, the unemployed and the elderly are regularly perceived as the most disadvantaged, followed by the young. The concern for the opportunities for the young in Penrhiwceiber and in Oswestry and for the unemployed in the Machars reflect some of the priorities on the respective issues agendas (see table 17.2 above). One further group of 'losers' stands out. In Stockwell, it is the black minority which was singled out above all others – unemployed and poor included – as more disadvantaged. This is not paralleled in Spotland, which is the only other locality with a substantial ethnic minority. It does, however, mirror the earlier finding that some of the local leaders believed that the ethnic minority groups were not always effective in communicating their interests. The corresponding question as to whether there were sections of the population that 'came out on top' most of the time found a similar proportion (55·3%) believing that there were. Over half of these singled out one group – 'the rich'.

Only in Stockwell did most of our respondents (56·4%) conclude that local politics and society should undergo substantial change. Almost a fifth (17·8%) wanted 'drastic change' compared with only around 6% elsewhere. In Penrhiwceiber, just over 40% wanted considerable change. Across all the localities together, however, attitudes were conservative with 42·4% asking for 'a little' change and 28·1% wanting things to stay as they were. In the Machars, 41·4% wanted local politics and society to stay as it is – reinforcing the picture of acceptance of life which this rural community has consistently demonstrated. The activist minority is, taking all localities together, more reformist. At one end of the spectrum, 9·3% of activists as against 5·3% of the less active want 'drastic change'; at the other end, 19% of activists would like the local system to stay as it is whilst 31% of the less active want to preserve the *status quo*.

Two further broad-brush measures of the performance of local government remain. Citizens were asked to give 'marks out of ten' for the performance of various institutions in British politics and society. The overall average score for local councils was 5·8. Behind this average score is a distribution in which over a quarter (26·5%) gave marks of between eight and ten, whilst 11% marked the council at between zero and two. The highest average score was 'gained' by the Wigtown District Council in the Machars with 6·8 (15% gave the Council ten out of ten!). The lowest marks were awarded in Penrhiwceiber (5·1) and Stockwell (5·3) which is consistent with the opinions expressed concerning service provision. Lest these scores appear very low, some perspective may be gained from other ratings. The average score for 'the present Conservative Government' was 3·9, reaching as low as 1·4 in Penrhiwceiber. Everywhere, including in Conservative Sevenoaks, the Government scored lower than the local authority but it must be remembered that this will reflect the presence, and the ratings, of supporters of the opposition parties. A more apposite comparison might be with 'the overall system of parliamentary government'. Whilst designed to measure support for the system rather than for any particular government, there is reason to think that the two are linked in the minds of some respondents. Nevertheless, to the extent that this question does tap an aspect of regime support, the average score of 5·9 across the six areas suggests that respect for local government in Britain is little less than for other political institutions.

Like the elites, the citizens were asked to give an overall impression of how local politics worked. As can be seen from table 18.9, compared with the leaders, the balance

Table 18.8 *Sections of the population perceived as 'losing out'* (%)

	Spotland	Pen'ceiber	Sevenoaks	The Machars	Stockwell	Oswestry	Total
The unemployed	11·4	21·6	4·4	22·4	14·6	18·1	15·6
The poor	14·3	10·8	43·4	14·0	7·3	13·8	16·4
The young	2·8	18·5	14·0	14·0	5·2	15·7	11·8
The elderly	22·9	22·9	8·8	19·6	14·6	13·8	16·9
Ethnic minorities	7·6	0·0	1·5	0·0	18·7	0·0	5·0
Other	40·9	26·2	27·9	30·0	39·6	38·6	34·3
Total	100·0	100·0	100·0	100·0	100·0	100·0	100·0
N. of responses	105	157	136	143	192	166	899

was somewhat less favourable to the local process. Most ordinary citizens have no pronounced views one way or the other. Of the remainder, more (31·8%) are favourably impressed than not, but the proportion is lower than amongst the leaders. Indeed, it is almost half that for the political leaders. It is again the case that the activists are also the most critical. Everywhere, they are more likely than the less active to offer unfavourable responses. It remains the case, however, that only in Stockwell do more people have unfavourable than favourable impressions, although the proportions are also quite evenly balanced in Penrhiwceiber.

A modest level of support with some reservations seems to be the general assessment of local politics. But the more one participates, the greater it would appear, are one's reservations. It may, however, be the case that the more critical one is, the more one will participate. There remains, however, something of a disjunction between what many people (including the activists) report of their particular experiences with local government and how they perceive the performance of local politics as a whole.

The final measure of attitudes to local politics focuses on a view of the role of participation itself. In the opening chapter, a broad distinction was drawn between a participatory vision of democracy and one in which there was a division of labour between citizens and politicians and in which elected representatives have very broad authority to take decisions. Leaders and citizens were both asked whether they believed that ordinary citizens should have 'more say in the decisions made by local government' or that these decisions were 'best left to locally elected representatives'. Overall, the responses for leaders and of citizens are remarkably alike. Amongst the elites, 57·9% thought that citizens should have more say. The corresponding figure for the citizens was 58·9%. This represents a solid majority in favour of strengthening citizen participation. At the same time, there is a substantial minority favouring the Schumpeterian view of democracy that leaders are elected precisely to take policy decisions.

One official emphasised the drawbacks to citizen participation:

My view is that we over-consult. In doing that we raise expectations which we very frequently are unable to satisfy.

His concern was that it could not be a matter of merely asking people what they thought, without some explanation of the limits set by resources. There were certain matters

Table 18.9 *Elite and citizen impression of how local politics works across six localities* (%)

	Political leaders	Non-political leaders	All leaders	Active citizens	Non-active citizens	All citizens
Generally favourable	60·0	45·2	51·1	35·2	30·7	31·8
Generally unfavourable	24·8	27·4	26·4	33·2	19·7	22·9
Neither one nor other	15·2	27·4	22·5	31·6	49·6	45·3
Total	100·0	100·0	100·0	100·0	100·0	100·0
N	125	186	311	363	1,167	1,530

which were simply inappropriate to participation. However, an elected leader in the same community argued that the process of participation, particularly through groups, itself provided an education in political realism:

I think that people have become much more understanding of how the council machinery works. It is a matter of being able to use the machine for their own rightful interests and they probably know more about the machinery...than even councillors or chief officers know.

The overall results tend to iron out some sharp local differences in attitudes to the roles of 'ordinary citizens' and leaders. The divergences are such, indeed, that the aggregate figures can be misleading. In Stockwell, the ordinary citizens themselves and, still more, the leaders, exhibit a strong belief in extending the influence of the citizenry. Amongst the general population, 68·7% consider that citizens should have more say and fully 86·2% of the elite think the same way. The Lambeth Borough Council had been engaged in a policy of decentralising its services, especially housing, to improve access. However, Spotland is the only other area where a majority of the leaders (79·5%) would wish for such an extension of citizen influence. In the Machars, 69% of the leaders think that decisions are best left to the elected representatives. That this is not necessarily to be identified with a Conservative Party position may be perceived from the fact that in Penrhiwceiber, 60% of leaders also favour the same option. Amongst the citizens, there is a more consistent position in favour of increasing their say. The strongest support is in the two most consistently participatory localities, albeit ones with very different political complexions. In Sevenoaks, 67·7% and in Stockwell, 68·7% support such a line. The contrast, as might be anticipated, is with the two much less participatory rural areas of Oswestry and the Machars. Even so, a small majority in Oswestry (53·7%) favour a greater role for citizens. The Machars stands out as the only locality in which a majority (56·7%) believe that matters are best left to elected representatives – a view which is consistent with the high rating given to their council (as well as with the views of the overwhelming majority of the representatives themselves).

It may be tempting to interpret these results as reflecting the 'deference' of rural societies and politics. The theory of deference, however, is a temptress which should be resisted more frequently than it is (Kavanagh 1971). There may be good instrumental grounds for leaving decisions to the professionals – even if only to save the time for other things. Whatever the reason for preferring to leave matters to the representatives, it is notable that everywhere the active citizens are more likely (65%) than the less active 57·1%) to take the participatory option.

There would, therefore, appear to exist a general sympathy amongst the population for reforms of local government which would allow citizens more say in decision-making. This is a view which is shared by a substantial portion of the elite but which is by no means universal amongst them. Not only do certain areas of the country adopt a more traditional stance but the political stratum of the elite is more cautious than the non-political. The political elite is evenly divided whilst the non-political favours greater citizen involvement (63·2%). Moreover, only a minority of the elected leaders (46·9%) is favourably inclined to the citizen viewpoint (compared to 56·8% of local officials).

It is not possible to say what reaction either citizen or elite respondents would have had to some of the more radical proposals for extending political participation, such as will be discussed in our concluding chapter, but there is enough evidence to suggest that citizens are looking for more say in decision-making and that this is appreciated by many sections of the local leadership. Earlier, it was pointed out that its accessibility was the major object of praise for local government as well as the prime source of criticism. Even if most people do not participate, it may be the case that the availability of proximate channels of influence is itself regarded as desirable. Throughout the study it has been stressed that where people do participate, it is likely to be in the locality and about a local issue. There are, therefore, grounds for believing that schemes for extending participation would meet with a welcome, even if it would also be utopian to anticipate a consequent burgeoning of political activity.

The survey did not uncover widespread discontent with the operation of local politics and virtually no call that the powers and remit of local government be limited. At an individual level, satisfaction with the results of dealings with local government was found to be remarkably high. The sorts of personal contacts and group-based involvements with local leaderships are not a source of complaint. Yet when people are asked about their general view of local politics, or about the performance of their local council, they are more reserved in their praise. One possible interpretation of this finding is that there is a disjunction between immediate personal experiences and the broader assessment which is influenced by other factors, including critical public debate and media comment. However, the two stances are not necessarily inconsistent or effects of a form of 'false consciousness'. It may be the case that people recognise that local government can operate successfully at the level of personal contacting where the citizen is acting like a consumer of services. They may, nevertheless, be more sceptical about the capacity of the local political system to handle local public goods, such as the provision of transport services or major tasks such as the rehabilitation of the inner city. Even so, a small majority of the population considers the locality well provided for by local government, a larger majority that it understands local needs and problems and more people have a favourable than an unfavourable view of its operations. In these respects, it stands as high as, and sometimes higher than, national governmental institutions in the estimation of the citizens.

It would be going too far to say that for most people local politics is the foundation stone of democracy or is, as J. S. Mill believed it should be, a school of politics. People are not as yet sufficiently participatory-minded to talk very readily in such terms. However, to the degree that people look for a change in local arrangements, it is towards providing opportunities for more say in their own local affairs.

PART V

CONCLUSIONS

19

PARTICIPATION AND DEMOCRACY IN BRITAIN

Our first objective in this book was to draw the map of political participation in Britain. This map was intended to display the two fundamental dimensions of participation relevant to democracy. The first dimension would show the extent of citizen activity. The second dimension would show the social profile of participation – who participates. Following from these twin concerns, it would then be possible to try to trace the impact of participation.

The interest in citizen participation was prompted by a normative concern with the condition of modern democratic processes in general and with those in Britain in particular, since they have long been regarded as exemplars of one of the major types of liberal democracy. Chapter 1 drew attention to the centrality of the idea of participation to current debates about the nature of democracy and about its future. In chapter 2 it was shown that participation had also appeared, from time to time, as part of the rhetoric of British politics. However, despite contending views as to the value of participation, information about the actual level of citizen activity and about its impact in Britain was hitherto limited and scattered. Without such knowledge, the normative debate about the desirability and potential of enhanced citizen involvement in modern democratic politics, whilst not meaningless, lacks empirical grounding. The study of what 'is' the case and what 'ought' to be the case may be logically distinct. Nevertheless, much debate about democracy incorporates assertions and counter-assertions about actual and likely citizen behaviour. Some understanding of that behaviour and how it is perceived by the citizens involved may be regarded as capable of informing the discussions. As Jane Mansbridge has argued,

field studies of what happens to various ideals when people try to live by them could prove useful in clarifying a wide range of normative questions. (Mansbridge 1980:xii)

A first refinement that can be made to the participation debate arises by seeking to establish whether participation is a single phenomenon which may be inhibited or promoted or whether it is, instead, composed of a number of different kinds of activity. If participation is found to be the label given to different, if related, modes of behaviour, one inference, at least, for normative discussions could be that these modes have different consequences for democracy.

In chapter 3 it was established that, as in other countries, participation in Britain was multi-dimensional. It was not a case of people doing more or less of it across the board. Rather, people (to the degree that they participated at all) tended to have taken one type of action – contacted a councillor or gone on a protest march. Any policies designed to promote participation might then appropriately take this into account. As was suggested in chapter 18, certain local political cultures appear more sympathetic to some kinds of behaviour than others. Forms of participation, especially of protest, frowned on in one locality, can be well regarded, even by the political authorities, in others. The extent and direction of citizen activity is not simply the product of individual and group initiative. It is affected by structural opportunities and by the extent of the encouragement offered by the elites. The degree to which citizens will contact representatives and officials may have something to do with accessibility. The fact that levels of involvement are much higher on local than on national issues is some indication of this.

The second concern of the volume has been with the question of 'Who participates?'. Democracy is predicated on equality of citizen rights. But not all individuals avail themselves of these rights – whether to vote, to demonstrate or to write to their Member of Parliament. This failure on the part of its citizens to take up rights does not mean that a system ceases to be democratic. A free society implies a freedom not to participate. There have been justifiable qualms about forced participation such as compulsory voting (Morris-Jones 1954; Wertheimer 1975).

Nevertheless, it is plausible to argue that the quality of a democracy is adversely affected either when few participate or when those who are most active are highly unrepresentative of the population as a whole. If one of the advantages (though not the only or most decisive one) of democracy lies in its claim to achieve greater responsiveness by the political leaders to the people, then more equal and representative participation could help to ensure that the authorities hear the voices of as many sectors of the population as possible. If, however, certain groups or classes are consistently more active than others, the elites are in some danger of mistaking the pressures of these groupings for the views of the citizenry as a whole. A concern for equality of access clearly motivated the path-breaking work of Verba and Nie, as the titles of their books indicate (Verba and Nie 1972; Verba, Nie and Kim 1978). This same interest has been a thread running through the portions of the present work devoted to the profile of participants, the resources required for participation and the construction of political agendas.

There would, however, be little point to participation if it were not effective. Indeed, sceptics would claim that citizen participation in the modern world has little impact, is marginal to the political process and, consequently, is, when looked at from an instrumental standpoint, 'irrational'. The other strand of the investigation has, hence, been to examine the effectiveness of participation – both the costs it involves and the kinds of results it can bring.

The value of participation

How one will evaluate the implications for British democracy of these findings about citizen participation will depend on one's view of democracy. The Barnes, Kaase team, contemplating the low levels of participation in Britain and some other countries, commented that 'The "grass roots" of politics seem shrivelled and starved of the nourishment of participation by the citizens' (Barnes, Kaase *et al.* 1979:84). Such remarks imply a participatory democratic inclination or, at least, the view that participation is an essential foundation for parliamentary systems. The levels of involvement uncovered in the present study would probably not relieve the gloom for those with faith in participation (Marquand 1988:234).

As was seen in chapter 10, for about half the British population political activity is virtually confined to voting in periodic elections. Another quarter do not regularly take up the opportunities to vote. The question is, therefore, whether voting is enough for a liberal democracy. It was also seen, however, that, partially counter-balancing the less involved portion of the population, there is the body (just under a quarter) of activists. In total their numbers are far from insignificant, especially in comparison with the most generous estimates of the size of the British political elite. But their importance lies not just in their numbers but in the proportion of the citizen political activities they perform (see figure 10.2). They demonstrate what is possible even in the unfavourable conditions, as participatory democrats would perceive them, of contemporary liberal democracies.

A critic of participatory democracy would find nothing amiss in this balance between activism and passivity. Whilst some of the severest challenges to the participatory ideal have been in response to the more radical versions of direct democracy (Pennock 1979; Sartori 1987), there are powerful arguments which can be mounted against even moderate, reformist positions. Anti-participationist democratic theory tends to be an elaboration upon the arguments propounded by Schumpeter (1943). The complexities of a world of large bureaucratic organisations render hopes for forms of government which are predicated on active, informed involvement by ordinary citizens unrealistic (Sartori 1987:110-81). Modern politics requires the division of labour, whereby citizens elect professional politicians who will devote themselves to political issues, develop judgements and take decisions. Sartori would presumably side with the 38% of the local leaders and the 40% of local populations who took the view that decisions were best left to elected representatives.

In the face of the difficulties confronting citizens wishing to have a more direct influence on national affairs, it is often argued by supporters of participation that effective and informed involvement is more possible at the local level. It can be directed towards the solution of known personal and local needs and problems. This appears to be borne out by the kinds of citizen activity reported in the present study. Even so, the anti-participationists retain their doubts. Local action can be merely defensive and parochial. The catchphrase 'Not in My Back Yard' ('Nimby') has been mentioned previously. Implicit in such a phrase can be acceptance that the particular development which threatens oneself nevertheless serves a wider national purpose. Rejection of a nuclear waste site, a motorway, a rail link, by every neighbourhood which is mobilised to action, can result, in the manner of the prisoners' dilemma, in leaving all worse off (Pennock 1979:460).

Some centralists look therefore to the state as not merely an umpire but as the guardian of the equitable distribution of benefits and burdens. It has been a concern of one major school of socialists. Local political involvement, led by middle class activists, could be designed for the preservation of the interests of the better-off. Conversely, to the extent that the under-privileged were less effective political actors, they might, left to themselves, be incapable of securing the distribution of goods and services which they needed.

Verba and Nie in the concluding passages of their study expressed similar reservations about a policy of extended non-electoral participation. Their evidence suggested that such participation was, as they put it, 'a potent force: leaders respond to it' (Verba and Nie 1972:336) – a conclusion which our findings appear to confirm still more strongly. But if this is put together with other evidence that the better-off participate more than the poorer, the result could mean that policies would increasingly be skewed in favour of 'the particular participant groups and away from a more general "public interest"' (Verba and Nie 1972:342). In this, Verba and Nie are not propounding a social law of the 'bias of participation' but, rather, drawing attention to the fact which, however obvious, can be ignored by enthusiasts, that participation is a right that benefits those who use it – whoever they may be and for good or ill.

Political participation is not, therefore, an unalloyed democratic ideal. Nevertheless, for the participationist it is the key element in a genuinely democratic theory. Confining citizen activity almost entirely to periodical elections is to limit it to employing a very blunt instrument to communicate views to political leaders. Elections provide leaders with a broad authority to act. The detail of legislation is subject to little scrutiny – still less the quantity of delegated legislation. In Britain, considerable discretion is left to various levels of officialdom, central and local. In the face of this, the citizen's right to complain to representatives and officials, to form pressure groups, join protest marches, is an essential mechanism of self-protection. Looked at purely in instrumental terms, participation is, firstly, reactive and defensive. Secondly, it is promotional – employed to put an issue or need onto the political agenda.

In certain circumstances, the individual or group can set the agenda, particularly perhaps on local issues, which are, as have been seen, not matters of 'high politics'. One reason for the focus on local politics in theories of participation is that the citizen can, in principle, bring to it a greater knowledge of the needs and problems of the immediate neighbourhood. The effects of local developments are more immediately felt than national measures (even if they are not necessarily greater in the long term). In these conditions, the lack of political knowledge which the 'realist' school attributes to the citizen can be challenged. Information costs are lower, benefits are more immediate, and hence local involvement can appear more instrumentally 'rational'.

The more ardent participationists go further and question the 'limits of realism', ignoring in their turn, according to Sartori, the 'limits of idealism'. They look to a radical restructuring of political systems to transfer more power to the people. Typically, this would imply decentralisation of decision-making to the 'community' (see Barber 1984 for an elaborate treatment). David Marquand, as an academic political scientist politically active on the centre of British politics in the 1980s, may be taken to typify those who look to some form of communitarian, participatory alternative to contemporary democratic practice. He would prefer 'politics as mutual education', implying the presence of citizens who are members of a political community which is a partnership in a common enterprise (Marquand 1988:209–47).

Such communitarian ideas of citizenship have undergone a remarkable revival in philosophical circles in Britain and the United States (see, amongst many others, Plant

1978; Sandel 1982; Walzer 1983; Schwartz 1988; Black 1988; King and Waldron 1988; Cochran 1989). This was in marked contrast to the 'Nozickian Moment' of the 1970s which was dominated by individualist political theorising (Nozick 1974). There must, however, be some scepticism as to whether political participation is best rooted in a sense of 'community'. The symbolic use of the term is widespread in Britain. Nonetheless, the evidence from the localities in our survey did not, as chapter 15 reported, establish an unequivocally positive relationship between community orientations and participation – indeed, the reverse was sometimes the case. The notion of community had its strongest hold in the more tradition-minded and politically peripheral localities. In the 'modern' environments of the inner city or the affluent greenbelt, the idea of community had less meaning.

The communitarians, of course, recognise this and tend to attribute the loss of community to the operation of a competitive and adversarial economic and political system which requires reforming. Yet it may well be the case that such an adversarial society is more conducive to participation, whatever qualitative judgements may be formed about the objectives of the activities. If the relationship between community and participation is tenuous, that between pluralism and political involvement is clearer. Affiliation to groups has been shown to be one of the best predictors of a propensity to participation. The groups may be oriented towards community welfare but they may be equally, if not more frequently, pursuing sectional interests. The evidence suggests that, on the current political stage, higher levels of participation are as likely to be the by-product of a pluralistic, even conflictual, society as of a communitarian one.

But whether such participation is competitive or communitarian in spirit, in order for it to expand requires a political system which can provide opportunities for citizens to take effective action to influence decisions which concern the allocation of resources as well as those which very immediately touch upon their local interests. There are divergent pressures in modern society towards decision-making units which can handle the increasing range of cross-national issues and towards units which are closer to ordinary citizens (Ionescu 1975). Thus Marquand advocates a 'mosaic' of decision-making units from parish councils to regional assemblies in local government and from self-governing schools and hospitals to corporate national bodies, all providing for a multiplicity of avenues of representation over and above parliamentary elections. As Dahl and Tufte put it in one of the all too rare theoretical discussions of this matter:

If the giant units are needed for handling transnational matters of extraordinary moment, very small units seem to us necessary to provide a place where ordinary people can acquire the sense and the reality of moral responsibility and political effectiveness in a universe where remote galaxies of leaders spin on in courses mysterious and unfathomable to the ordinary citizen.

(Dahl and Tufte 1974:140)

For participationists, wider citizen involvement is a necessary condition if modern governments are to be grounded upon consent (Crouch 1979). In Britain in the 1980s, as Marquand sees it (1988:241), the established political institutions had lost their authority because 'the Schumpeterian assumption that democratic politics revolve around a competitive struggle for the people's vote...can no longer provide the basis for a legitimate political order'. We return, therefore, to the clash between rival theories of democracy with which this volume opened. It now appears, furthermore, that this rivalry between a market-oriented, competitive view of democracy in which the citizen plays a limited role, largely through the ballot box, and a more participatory vision, could increasingly become part of the ideological battle in British politics. If it is to become a part of political rhetoric in the future, what might be the prospects of actual citizen participation in Britain in the near future?

The prospects for participation

In seeking to assess the likely future patterns of participation, one has to make a number of assumptions about the persistence of existing social behaviour and institutional arrangements or about the direction of political policies.

It is safest to begin by assuming that the present, broadly Schumpeterian, forms of competitive party democracy will persist and that major upheavals in the direction of more participatory institutions which could release more activity, both nationally and locally, cannot be expected. But even without any such dramatic reforms of the political opportunity structure, some political analysts have detected signs of increasing participation and predicted that it will grow further. Because, Marquand argues, the established political system is in disarray 'some of the spectators in the stands have begun to descend on to the field' (Marquand 1988:237).

What evidence exists, however, in support of this widespread belief that citizen participation has been increasing? For the reasons given more fully in chapter 2, it is difficult to establish the existence of trends in citizen activity. In the case of violent forms of crowd action, for example, there is evidence that it has declined in Britain during this century (Dunning *et al.* 1987). Survey data for periods earlier than the 1970s are very scattered. Other data for the 1970s and 1980s have been collected on a variety of bases which are not entirely comparable with one another. Nevertheless, some pointers are available.

Some of the most significant studies in the 1970s were those conducted by Alan Marsh and reported in his own volume (Marsh 1977) and in his contributions to the cross-national study led by Barnes and Kaase (Barnes, Kaase *et al.* 1979). In both works, the concern was primarily with the bases of protest participation and, as a result, neither the range of activities covered nor the sample design employed can be precisely compared with the present study. Marsh concluded that there was likely to be a growth in protest as a younger generation, with more ideological and less deferential attitudes, entered the political arena. The Barnes, Kaase research suggested that the 'repertory' of political actions employed by citizens was widening. Conventional forms of electoral activity were being supplemented by certain varieties of protest action. Moreover, to the degree again that a more 'post-materialist' climate was developing in advanced countries, this would be accompanied by a greater tendency to employ less conventional and more direct types of action to influence events.

A comparison of the figures in table 19.1 drawn from Barnes, Kaase and from the present study would suggest that, making due allowances for the differences in the construction of the data, there has not been the dramatic upsurge of participation that some have predicted. Apart from the remarkable difference in numbers signing petitions, it would appear that the early 1980s did not see a major increase in protest in Britain.

Table 19.1 *Levels of political participation compared* (%)

	Barnes, Kaase* et al. 1979 Have done	British Political Participation Study** 1984–5 Have done in last five years
'Conventional'		
Contacted officials or politicians	24·2	35·9†
Attended political meetings	21·0	8·6
Campaigned for candidate	7·8	7·2††
'Unconventional'		
Petitions	23·1	63·3
Lawful demonstrations	5·8	5·2
Boycotts	5·7	4·3
Blocking traffic	1·3	1·1

* Adapted from tables TA.1 and TA.3, Barnes, Kaase *et al.* 1979: 541, 543; and from *Political Action*, 1979.
** Adapted from table 3.1 above.
† Contacting MPs, civil servants, local councillors.
†† Canvassing, raising funds and clerical work for a party.

The patterns of conventional participation also seem to have changed relatively slowly. Contacting would appear to have grown but party activity to have remained low or even declined. Research conducted for the Widdicombe Committee of Inquiry into the Conduct of Local Authority Business largely confirms this steady level of participation in the 1980s. A fifth of respondents had contacted a local councillor, although as many as 49% had been in contact with council officers (Young 1986:37). A national sample survey for the Audit Commission on Attitudes to Local Authorities and their Services, published in 1986, reported that within the past twelve months, 12% of respondents had contacted a councillor about a local matter and 7% had written to a Member of Parliament (MORI 1986:6). Comparison with the British Social Attitudes survey for the period most comparable to our own is difficult because this was concerned with whether people had taken action in response to 'an unjust or harmful' law. Since 69% of respondents had never considered a law unjust or harmful, one is dealing with what is perceived as an extreme situation, rather than the more routine actions examined in the present study. As a result, only 3% had taken action by contacting a Member of Parliament, 9% had signed a petition, 2% gone on a demonstration and 1% formed a group (Jowell and Airey 1984:21; later figures are higher, see Jowell, Witherspoon and Brook 1987; also Topf 1989).

The 'steady-state' of political participation should not, perhaps, be so surprising. Our contention is that the activities being described are, indeed, constant and routine. Unlike electoral politics, which are subject to intensive, periodic mobilisation by parties and the media, contacting an official or a representative, joining a group, signing a petition, are steps taken by people up and down the country every day of every year. Without some major institutional changes which open up the structure of opportunities for greater citizen involvement, it is unlikely that there will be a rapid increase in participation. Given the persistence of present institutional arrangements, changes in patterns of participation are more likely to reflect slow alterations in society and, in particular, changes in the distribution of resources.

A regular finding of this and of other work on participation has been the influence of education on the propensity to become politically involved. A more educated citizenry is likely to be more active. As the British population acquires more educational qualifications, the level of participation should rise. It might also involve more in the way of protest since the highly educated are rather more inclined to such forms of action. Changes in social composition bring not simply more participation but, given its multi-dimensional character, a different mix of action. But educational advance is a slow process. In the first half of the 1980s, around a fifth of school-leavers had A level qualifications or the equivalent, which represented a slight increase on a decade before. The numbers of people going to university and polytechnic have risen considerably in line with a growing population, but as a proportion of the age group, they remain only around 10%. Even allowing that there could be a developmental process whereby the educated encourage their peers to become more active, the increased contribution that a more highly qualified public will make to overall participation will be very gradual. Given the connection between the possession of other socio-economic resources and education, this development will take still longer to reduce the inequality of participation. The under-representation of women and, even more, of ethnic minorities in higher education is, on present evidence, going to take some years to repair.

The other major influence on citizen involvement in Britain is membership of groups. Indeed, chapter 5 demonstrated that groups are a more powerful factor than individual resources. If there is a single key to political participation in Britain, it must be group memberships. The proportion of the population belonging to a group is already high, even if most of the groups in question are rarely, if ever, concerned with politics. The importance of groups is in part that they can mobilise people to action in support of interests and causes. Indeed, as we saw in chapter 5, half the participation uncovered in the study was of a mobilised nature. But groups are also of importance as a conduit through which individual citizens can hope more effectively to raise issues and problems that concern them. British politics is firmly in the collectivist age and, so, organisation counts.

Some groups, such as trades unions, tend to mobilise their members for a restricted range of economic objectives. Unions also activate uniquely for such activities as strikes and are a particularly important mobiliser of other forms of protest such as marches. If union membership declines further or if unions become more representative of middle income earners – a pattern which we remarked upon in chapter 5 – there may be consequential changes for participation. For example, the strike weapon as a political instrument may have less appeal in some union quarters.

Single-issue groups to defend or promote interests and values may well become even more frequent. The effect could be to enhance participation. This need not imply a nation of regular activists, noisy and restless. Rather, such groups would suggest the existence of a highly mobilisable population of 'sporadic interventionists' (Dowse and Hughes

Table 19.2 *Present and potential participation compared* (%)

	Have done at least once in past five years	Would 'certainly' or 'probably' consider action in future	'Might consider'	Would 'never' consider
Contacting				
Local councillor	20·7	33·3	40·4	26·3
Town hall	17·4	28·4	41·1	30·5
MP	9·7	24·2	39·5	36·3
Civil servant	7·3	18·8	38·6	42·6
Media	3·8	11·0	30·7	58·3
Group activity				
Informal group	13·8	16·4	34·9	48·7
Organised group	11·2	14·4	31·3	54·3
Campaigning				
Fund-raising	5·2	6·2	14·8	79·0
Canvassed	3·5	5·0	13·1	81·9
Clerical work	3·5	4·0	14·3	81·7
Attended rally	8·6	8·8	23·9	67·3
Protesting				
Attended protest meeting	14·6	23·8	39·8	36·4
Circulated petition	8·0	14·0	36·4	49·6
Blocked traffic	1·1	2·4	9·2	88·4
Protest march	5·2	7·3	20·3	72·4
Political strike	6·5	8·0	15·8	76·2
Political boycott	4·3	9·5	25·8	64·7

1977). These are persons who, otherwise fairly quiescent, are capable of being roused to action on specific issues. Even if this is regarded as reactive participation, it is an important element in a civic culture. It reflects a significant form of political efficacy. We have drawn attention (see chapter 8) to the fact that, in addition to the sense people may have about their own personal capacities to influence their representatives, there is considerable confidence in the ability of groups to affect outcomes. This perception of collective political efficacy, coupled with the existence of a network of group allegiances (even if normally apolitical), suggests the presence of latent participation ready to emerge in episodic and reactive forms.

It has, indeed, been argued that such potential for participation is a more significant political fact than actual participation. Thus Barnes, Kaase *et al.* suggest that, since actual political behaviour is contingent on particular events, it is more important to study the readiness of people to be mobilised, which they take to be 'an abiding property of a wide sector of the whole community' (1979:58). Excessive concentration on current levels of action will, they suggest, blind the observer to the possibility that at any time a considerable body of persons may emerge out of their past quiescence.

The general tenor of the Barnes, Kaase study was to predict growing protest but their data for Britain suggest greater caution (see also Rootes 1981). A majority in Britain was only prepared even to consider three types of protest – petitions, lawful demonstrations and boycotts. One in ten said they 'would' take part in a rent strike and 7% in an unofficial strike and in blocking traffic. However, the overwhelming majority would 'never do' any of these (Barnes, Kaase *et al.* 1979:548). The British Social Attitudes study in 1984 also asked what people 'would do' in the more extreme event of a law being considered by Parliament which they considered unjust and harmful. A majority would sign a petition (54%) and a little under that proportion (46%) would contact a Member of Parliament. Only relatively small numbers would go on a demonstration (8%) or form a group with others (6%), suggesting once more that future participation would continue to follow conventional rather than the radical channels which some have hoped, or feared, might be taken (Jowell and Airey 1984:21). Subsequent Social Attitude surveys showed somewhat higher figures but not a striking change.

Our respondents were asked whether they would 'consider' taking each of the actions, regardless of whether they had ever done so. Amongst the range of 'conventional' actions, a majority of the sample was only even prepared to consider contacting local or national representatives or officials and working with an informal group (see table 19.2). Even in these instances, only around twenty to thirty per cent say that they would 'certainly' or 'probably' consider such action. There is also little reason to expect an upsurge in party campaigning. Over threequarters of respondents say that they would 'never' consider canvassing, clerical work or fund-raising for a party.

The prospects for protest action are similarly low. Attending a protest meeting and taking a petition round for signing were the only protest actions a majority would contemplate. The vast majority would 'never' consider going on a protest march (72·4%), or a political strike (76·2%), boycotting (64·7%) or blocking traffic (88·4%). There is little sign here of the 'populist revolt' which Samuel Beer believed marked the decline of the civic culture in Britain (Beer 1982; see chapter 2 above). Nor could the radical participationist take much heart except by expressing confidence that those who 'might' consider actions would indeed perform them. The sceptic, however, will allow for a certain slippage between intention or contemplation and action.

If, nevertheless, one compares, as in table 19.2, those who would 'certainly' or 'probably' consider various forms of action with those who had performed them, we do, however, find that those who are prepared seriously to contemplate each mode of participation are everywhere greater than those who have done them. It seems reasonable to infer that there is a significant pool of persons who are ready in certain circumstances to participate. The largest pool of potential participants is for the conventional actions of contacting and group action. By contrast, it would seem that the current level of party activism is about as much as the parties can expect. The story so far, as told by the protesting figures, is that there is no reason to expect that protest will be any less in the future than it was in the 1980s. Equally, the gap between the numbers who would consider the more 'extreme' acts and those who had performed them is not great. The largest potential is for those more 'moderate' acts – attending meetings and petitioning – which were closely associated with conventional group activity. A similar picture emerged when people were asked whether certain types of action were likely to be approved or disapproved in their neighbourhood (see chapter 18 above). The conventional activities were uniformly perceived as legitimate, whereas the more direct forms of action, such as protest marches or 'political' strikes, were regarded as likely to incur disapproval. Support for protest was, however, forthcoming in certain areas of traditional working-class strength – mining communities and the inner city – which some social commentators would argue are in secular decline.

The implication of these findings is that, whilst participation may increase in Britain, this is most likely to be a gradual process and it will continue, in the main, to adopt conventional forms. If much of this participation may be in response to events, rather than entirely self-moved, it does at least imply that authorities who introduce new programmes or developments can continue to anticipate participatory reactions from a substantial portion of the population. Even so, this will still be a minority since, with respect to many modes of participation, the majority does not even consider itself as ever likely to become involved.

It could, however, be argued that a factor sustaining participation at a higher level in future would be the emergence of a growing number of issues onto the political agenda which typically give rise to citizen action, often of a less conventional nature. The so-called 'post-materialist' issue of environmental protection would be at the forefront. It is around such issues that, according to many social scientists, there are coalescing 'social movements'. Such groupings adopt principled positions on single, but broad, issues such as care for the environment, peace, and women's rights (see chapter 9). The movements have typically attracted, it is argued, the highly educated, middle classes involved in public services and 'decommodified' groups who are outside the standard labour market, such as the unemployed, students, housewives. The movements do not correspond to the traditional class-based party alignments and they are tempted to employ a variety of forms of 'unconventional' participation to check and control the impact of political elites in their particular spheres of interest (Offe 1985). It has been proposed that such movements will widen the scope of participation.

There is some basis in our data for such expectations. In the first place, environmental issues were amongst those more likely to stimulate action (see chapter 11). There is every likelihood of continuing disputes over proposals by the state or by private developers to construct motorways, build in green-belt villages, dispose of noxious industrial waste. This might particularly be the case if the state relaxes central planning controls, giving rise to the possibility of more frequent clashes between private developers and local interests. Not only is this the stuff of reactive participation, its effects are localised. As has been seen, it is within the local arena that most participation takes place. There has been a learning process whereby people have come to know about the techniques of protest in such cases. Local populations are available to be mobilised. Whether this will make for a participatory society in the sense of a population of more regular activists to boost the numbers of our specialist participants is much less certain. Rather, one may again foresee a growing army of 'sporadic interventionists' – ready to act for a combination of materialist and non-materialist reasons when their backyards are threatened.

A second reason for giving credence to the theory of emergent new patterns of participation is that there are some signs of a greater readiness on the part of certain sections of the community to become more active in future. Far fewer of those aged between 18 and 29 say that they would 'never' consider the various forms of action.

However, if we confine our attention, as in table 19.3, to those who are rather more definite about their attitudes, it will be seen that the gap between the young and the older population is not wide. In conventional activity there is little difference, with the young showing, if anything, less interest in political parties. However, the young are more likely to contemplate protest, just as we saw in chapter 7 that they are presently more prone to direct action. Furthermore, the evidence also suggests that readiness to embrace direct action may evaporate as that generation advances into middle age. It is never easy to be confident about such matters however. Life-cycle effects can take their toll on youthful protestors, who are, in any event, a minority of their generation. They will become subject to unknowable future and contingent political events (Jennings 1987). The inter-war depression, the rise of Fascism, the spread of nuclear weapons, the war in Vietnam, all left some imprint on their respective generations. Both those putative generational effects and the figures reported in table 19.3 suggest that the rise in direct action, if it occurs, will not be very dramatic.

It is possible, however, that the 'green/peace' issues discussed in chapter 9 may come to constitute a dominant concern in politics for a new generation. Support for environmental and peace issues was seen to be drawn from a quite wide spectrum of society. If anything, the social and educational centre of gravity of the green-peace 'issue-public' was tipped towards the poorer and less well-educated sectors of Britain's young adults. Thus, the impact of such issues, and their association with direct action, is not confined to the relatively small ranks of Britain's graduates. Because of their skills, graduates may be very important as mobilisers, propagandists or 'movement entrepreneurs' (Schmitt 1989) but, from the point of view of mass participation, the resonance of the green agenda amongst the non-graduate population, noted in chapter 9, may well be of much greater political and, indeed, electoral import. What this may suggest is the latent possibility of a strategic alliance between this new type of social movement and the traditional forces of the left in the political arena. Such a strategic red–green coalition based, in part, on shared values, but also pooling somewhat divergent social constituencies, may prove to have a bearing on the future of British politics, as the German example may attest. This logic may then present fresh opportunities and challenges to those involved to re-shape the movement of mass political participation.

If the graduate elite are far from alone at the centre of the green/peace movement, they have certainly been shown to be quite participatory and to have an especial affinity to direct forms of action. Both their involvement in conventional forms of action and their readiness to protest are reflected in table 19.4. Just as those with higher level diplomas are currently more active so they are relatively more ready to contemplate participation in the future. Nevertheless, even this category of the population remains more willing to commit itself to the most conventional and mild forms of action than to radical and strenuous forms of protest. So, once again, the prospects appear to be for a gradual rather than an abrupt, increase across the whole range of activities.

The growing involvement of women in politics has been seen as a factor which might be expected to raise the levels of participation. We have seen in chapter 7 that, on our measures, women generally participate at a somewhat lower rate than men but that the differences are relatively slight. In part, this reflects a modest but persistent discrepancy

Table 19.3 *Potential participation by age* (%)

	Would 'certainly' or 'probably' consider action in future	
	Age 18–29	Age 30+
Contacting		
Local councillor	35·7	32·6
Town hall	27·1	29·1
MP	24·3	24·1
Civil servant	21·0	18·2
Media	14·2	9·9
Group activity		
Informal group	20·3	15·4
Organised group	17·2	13·4
Campaigning		
Fund-raising	4·9	6·4
Canvassed	5·0	4·9
Clerical work	2·2	4·4
Attended rally	9·2	8·6
Protesting		
Attended protest meeting	26·2	23·2
Circulated petition	14·9	13·7
Blocked traffic	4·6	1·6
Protest march	12·1	5·8
Political strike	15·1	5·9
Political boycott	13·4	8·2
N	*c.* 350	*c.* 1,150

in resources. The impact of this discrepancy also seems to register in the realm of potential participation. As table 19.5 indicates, female respondents also report a lower readiness to participate. However, the analysis in chapter 7 showed that if resources are equalised, the current participatory gap is closed and even reverses itself. To the extent that this gap has a generational ingredient (see also table 19.5) then time will effect a shift in favour of women's participation.

On the other hand, this should not obscure the challenge at the level of resources. It is in this area that some further potential for enhanced female political activity is to be found. Indeed, this achieves concrete expression in the profile of that small band of members of feminist groups. As already noted, they indicate that political consciousness surrounding feminist issues can be a powerful stimulus to citizen action, but the obstacles remain obviously far higher at more elite levels (see chapter 16). Furthermore, the logic that linked the 'green/peace' movement to the left may, in some respects, extend to the feminist cause. Amongst the general run of the respondents, sympathy for the rights of women is fairly evenly spread across the political spectrum. Nevertheless, amongst the strongest adherents to feminism there are those who are well to the left and there are also those 'eco-feminists' who combine their position on women's issues with

Table 19.4 *Potential participation by selected educational qualifications* (%)

	Would 'certainly' or 'probably' consider action in future	
	No qualifications	College, further education & degree
Contacting		
Local councillor	26·0	40·1
Town hall	22·3	36·6
MP	17·1	36·4
Civil servant	13·6	27·0
Media	7·1	19·1
Group activities		
Informal group	11·6	29·6
Organised group	8·8	23·7
Party canvassing		
Canvassed	2·2	8·9
Attended rally	4·2	15·6
Clerical work	2·1	8·6
Fund-raising	2·7	11·2
Protesting		
Attended protest meeting	15·8	34·0
Circulated petition	11·1	16·4
Blocked traffic	2·1	2·7
Protest march	4·8	10·3
Political strike	6·0	10·8
Political boycott	7·3	15·2
N	713	257

environmentalism. Like the leading green/peace supporters they lean rather more towards collective and direct action than voting and party campaigning. At the same time, the large, potential size of the female constituency, coupled with the broad support for feminist issues reflected amongst the respondents, suggests, once again, that there are political alliances ready to be made. All of this provides a background against which there can also be intense and influential activity by minorities of both men and women in new forms of democracy, as well as in those more private spheres which, on some definition of the 'political', should be drawn into the study of citizen participation (Rowbotham 1986).

It is always conceivable that major national issues may appear which would mobilise large-scale mass activity. This is not something which may readily be predicted. The Campaign for Nuclear Disarmament led large numbers to take part in marches and rallies (Parkin 1968), as have other major movements in the past. Nevertheless, our evidence suggests that individual involvement in national issues is much less frequent than in local matters. The major national problems of unemployment and the international issues of defence aroused the lowest levels of action (see chapter 11). Even though the survey coincided with the highest levels of unemployment since the war, the

Table 19.5 *Potential participation by gender and age* (%)

| | Would 'certainly' or 'probably' consider action in future | | | |
| | Age 18–29 | | Age 30+ | |
	Male	Female	Male	Female
Contacting				
Local councillor	36·5	35·1	36·9	29·3
Town hall	26·5	27·8	32·7	26·1
MP	30·2	19·3	25·6	22·9
Civil ser ...nt	20·7	21·4	20·7	16·1
Media	15·0	13·6	10·8	9·2
Group activity				
Informal group	20·5	20·1	16·7	14·3
Organised group	17·7	16·8	15·0	12·2
Party campaigning				
Canvassed	4·4	5·7	4·7	5·0
Attended rally	10·8	8·0	10·8	6·8
Clerical work	2·5	2·0	3·9	4·7
Fund-raising	4·8	5·0	5·2	7·3
Protesting				
Attended protest meeting	28·2	24·4	25·1	21·5
Circulated petition	11·4	17·9	13·1	14·0
Blocked traffic	6·3	3·1	2·1	1·3
Protest march	15·9	8·9	7·3	4·7
Political strike	17·2	13·4	6·3	5·7
Political boycott	14·8	12·2	10·6	6·4
N	*c.* 170	*c.* 190	*c.* 500	*c.* 650

amount of action reported to have been taken (by way of contacts or protests) was quite small. This is not to be interpreted as indifference but as a rational assessment of the effectiveness of individual or even group action in such matters. The opportunities for participation in policy-making at the highest level where decisions on resource allocation are made are few. For most people, these appear to fall within the framework of 'high politics'. One may vote and support a political party and thereby seek to influence policy. For most people, however, action beyond that is best taken nearer home. It is about the local environment, housing or transport.

It is, then, an important question whether these concerns represent the priorities of the population at large. The possibility arises that the active minority, who are not a microcosm of society, may be putting onto the agenda only those matters which are of prime concern to themselves. The evidence about 'issue publics' in chapter 11 and about local agendas in chapters 16 and 17 suggests that, whilst certain social groups are to the forefront in voicing priorities, currently these differ only to a limited extent from the priorities of the wider public. To the extent that the ranking of the issues does not differ markedly between the participants and the less active, the political agenda is not biased in favour of a socially unrepresentative activist stratum. Such findings do not, however, definitively dispose of the issue of bias. First, to agree on the priority of issues is not to agree on solutions. Secondly, the existing divergences could become more significant. Thirdly, the relative lack of citizen participation in national-level issues means that there is a significant arena where the ordinary person makes little direct impact. The allocative decisions which structure so much of politics remain in the hands of the political professionals and the route to influence for the citizen is still largely through the parties and through voting for the packages they offer to the electorate. Schumpeter's division of labour still holds true in this very important respect. Although there may be remarkable moments when mass participation through the ballot or by more direct action can reshape the political scene, these are very rare. And their very rarity could mean that citizen involvement in great issues is unpractised and all the less effective. There can be a hole in the centre of participation. This is not necessarily to accept the 'democratic deficit' of national politics as entirely inevitable. Creative institutional reforms to increase access even to central decision-making are feasible, even if some spheres are unlikely to become open to citizen influence in our complex, interdependent world (Ionescu 1989:420–3).

Nevertheless, it is important not to dismiss the value of the participation, primarily local, that does go on in Britain – the value being both to the participant and the political system. Possibly the most telling argument in favour of public participation which the advocate could construct on the basis of the present findings is that, for so many who have taken action, it has worked. Satisfaction with the results of participation is, as chapter 12 showed, remarkably high. The issues involved may not have been those of high politics. They may, moreover, be issues which only arise as a result of higher policy decisions in which the citizen has had little say. Admitting all this, it remains significant that such a high proportion of those who had taken action could report that they were reasonably happy either with their attempts to put a stop to neighbourhood pollutions, to keep a hospital ward open, to get the council to improve a building which was a local eyesore or, at a more individualistic level, to obtain the support of a councillor in getting a flat for an elderly, disabled relative.

A political system which is able to respond to these levels of needs may not seem inspiring but is worthy of some respect. There is a level at which government in Britain seems to deliver to its consumers. Such an impression, gained from the experiences of the participants, is reinforced by the extent to which, as chapter 17 showed, the priorities of the local political elites matched those of the citizens. In particular, their priorities were closest to those of the activists. It seems, therefore, that there is a genuine return on participation.

The positive experience afforded by political action might seem to constitute a reason in itself for a further steady growth in participation. An awareness of success should breed more action. It must be remembered, however, that the satisfaction reported with participation is, by definition, confined to those who have crossed the threshold into the public sphere. The vast majority have rarely or never done so and thus have had little or no opportunity to experience the costs and benefits of action. Substantial numbers, as has been seen, would not even consider such involvement. Moreover, it is still an open question whether new entrants into the political world would be as successful as those often highly resourced participants who are already there. For successful participation to stimulate greater participation, it is necessary for there to be a wide diffusion of information about citizen action. To a considerable extent, this is occurring. The local and national media regularly report at least the more dramatic confrontations between developers and objectors and the most controversial public inquiries. As a consequence, some information circulates concerning the tactics of participation and about the outcomes of inquiries. There is every sign that the kinds of environmental, planning and housing issues which give rise to public action will retain their prominence on the local agendas across the nation. They, and the groups campaigning on them, frequently capture more attention than local party politics. Some, particularly the 'green' issues, also appear to be climbing up the national and international agendas of the 1990s.

This combination of changing social patterns and changing agendas would imply that citizen participation in Britain will grow steadily. The present profile of participation is something that has built up slowly in the post-war period. It reflects in many ways the underlying structure of resources in society. As such, it will not change overnight but continue to bear the imprint of that structure which, whilst itself changing, is not subject to rapid transformation. Nevertheless, the direction of the changes points towards a more active citizenry.

A more participatory Britain?

The debate about the nature of democracy shows that it is too simplistic to say without qualification that the more participation there is, the more democracy there is. Political participation has many dimensions. One should not, therefore, think in terms of increasing participation *per se* but of the directions in which political activity might grow and of the possible consequences of its developing along certain dimensions rather than others.

Voting is the political activity that most British people perform. It is a right and also, for most, a duty. In that sense, voting is also the most egalitarian mode of participation. But, by comparison with the USA, the opportunities for Britons to vote are relatively infrequent. It could be argued, therefore, that one means of extending citizen participation, if that is the prime democratic goal, would be to increase the number and frequency of elections. Elected school boards, health authorities, residents' and neighbourhood councils might expand citizen involvement at the expense of appointed managements. Cautious experiments with the referendum have been made at local and even national levels. Perhaps the logical conclusion is the home voting machine made possible by modern communications technology (Barber 1984; McLean 1986; Arterton 1987; Budge 1989) which could, in principle, transform participation even in central decision-making. It is, of course, possible that, with greater frequency of ballotting, custom could stale and participation come to pay diminishing returns. In the USA, voting turnout has declined markedly (although the reasons are complex). In Britain, the decline is less pronounced but electoral participation, involving party campaigning, appears, on the present evidence, to have less appeal to the younger generation. Nevertheless, partly because of the intense mobilisation surrounding it, voting remains far more familiar to the person in the street than any other mode.

Although it was concluded that participation in other modes would probably rise, it should be recognised that such a development is not without its problems for democrats. There is little sign that in the near future participation will become any other than a minority taste, albeit a somewhat larger minority. It has been seen that resources provide the base for much of the participation that currently takes place. By and large, these resources tend to be cumulative rather than countervailing. Wealth, education and organisational affiliations go together more than they pull in opposed directions. The less individually advantaged might be expected to compensate for any political weakness by collective, solidaristic action. However, the evidence of the present survey suggests that some of the traditional working class organisations, such as unions, are no longer the preserve of the have-nots and that other groups in which the less well-off are likely to be members are politically not very active. Who will then mobilise the disadvantaged to participate in defence of their interests? It is, therefore, possible that the initial effect of rising levels of participation may be to amplify the already louder voice of the advantaged in British society – those with higher education and well-integrated into group networks. And, to the extent that participation is effective, not only will their voice be heard, but their demands may also be acted upon. So long as there is consensus upon objectives this may not matter, but where the interests of the better and the less-well resourced diverge, the participatory advantages of the socially advantaged may make themselves count.

Countervailing forces would not be entirely lacking, of course, in a more participatory society. If the better-resourced might be tempted to act to conserve their established positions, it is also the case that the strongest participatory sentiments are to be found on the left. Moreover, the far left, along with the strongest supporters of the new politics, are also more ready to adopt direct modes of participation. Since this is also true of the very highly educated, it may well be the case that a Britain in which there is more participation will also be one in which there is more frequent resort to various forms of protest. This is emphatically not to predict that there will be a rapid upsurge in direct action or that it will form anything but a secondary feature of participation. It is to suggest that more participation is likely to involve some alterations in its pattern.

If this is indeed the case, a more participatory Britain may be a less tranquil political society. It should not be assumed that an active society will be consensual and communitarian. Political action may be sectional, defensive, even divisive. Critics sometimes regard this kind of participatory society as the negative side of pluralism (Beer 1982) and as de-stabilising. It may indeed be that the self-interest of the individual or group is not the noblest sentiment to which the dedicated participationist would wish to appeal. But it is a very real motive for action, if not the only one. People may gain other benefits from their involvement, such as self-development or political education. It may even be the case that some sense of community or public good emerges out of the participatory experience rather than being the precondition for active citizenship. In the meantime, participation is at the very least an essential mechanism of self-defence, not merely against the abuse of power but against indifference and insensitivity. And, as John Stuart Mill put it, 'the rights and interests of every or any person are only secure from being disregarded when the person interested is himself able, and habitually disposed, to stand up for them' (1972 ed.:208).

Britain is a long way from being a participatory democracy. Most people find many other things to do with their time. They are not, in this sense, political animals. Participation, to adapt a remark made about socialism, takes up too many evenings. Nevertheless, in a complex, modern society such as Britain, the active involvement of citizens has to be an essential part of democratic life. If the price of liberty is eternal vigilance, the price of democracy is, to put it at its least demanding, a willingness to participate. There are in Britain very many who are so willing and there are also many, even if less numerous, who are not only willing but who do act, whether out of interest or altruism. John Stuart Mill (1972 ed.:217), when discussing the ideally best policy, concluded that

the only government which can fully satisfy all the exigencies of the social state is one in which the whole people participate; that any participation, even in the smallest public function, is useful; that the participation should everywhere be as great as the general degree of improvement of the country will allow; and that nothing less can be ultimately desirable than the admission of all to a share in the sovereign power of the state...

Britons do participate – more so than is sometimes imagined. But by these demanding standards there remains some way to go before there is full participation or full democracy in Britain.

Appendix A: Survey methods

This appendix outlines the main methodological approaches taken in the British Political Participation Study.

The study encompassed the following aspects:

(a) a national citizen survey study of 1,578 respondents;
(b) community citizen surveys totalling 1,641 respondents in six localities selected so as to cover a range of typical communities;
(c) a series of community elite studies comprising a total of 321 questionnaire interviews across the same six localities;
(d) a series of 'in-depth' semi-structured interviews with key members of the elite in each of the same six localities conducted by the two principal researchers.

National study

Sampling and weighting

The national citizen survey was based on a sample of residents of Britain, south of the Caledonian Canal in northern Scotland, who were eighteen years or older. A two-stage selection procedure was used to choose 20 electors from each of 120 polling districts (N = 2,400). 'Door-step' enumeration and selection by interviewers ensured that non-electors and recently arrived electors were also included in the base sample with the correct probability of selection.

The 120 parliamentary constituencies from England, Wales and Scotland were selected from a list stratified by the following variables: region, population density, proportion of 1979 General Election Labour vote and proportion of population with professional qualifications. The second stage in the selection process entailed choosing one polling district within each constituency. Finally, 20 electors were selected using a random start, fixed interval procedure from the electoral lists for each of these polling districts.

In order to permit separate analysis of the countries within Britain, Scotland and Wales were oversampled by a factor of two and three respectively.

Doorstep enumeration

The issued sample of 2,400 included only voters whose names appeared on the relevant electoral registers. In effect, the issued names were used to provide a set of addresses, each chosen with probability proportionate to the number of registered electors at the given address. A 'doorstep' enumeration procedure was then used to select an interviewee from all the residents at each address who fell within the scope of the study. The procedure is a variant of the Marchant-Blyth

434

technique which permits inclusion in the sample of individuals not in the original sampling frame; for example, non-electors and electors who have moved house too recently to be listed in the electoral register.

Weighting

Weighting of the data is required to offset the non-random aspects of sampling selection: over-representation of Scotland and Wales and aspects of doorstep enumeration. The calculation of these weights is described in a separate research paper (Day, Moyser and Parry 1985a).

Questionnaire design, testing and pilot

The development of the questionnaire was preceded by an extensive review of questions used in previous surveys of political participation. An underlying principle in the design of the questionnaire was to move from unprompted questions about issues and political actions towards closed questions asking about specific types of action. In this way, the dangers of prompting respondents were minimised. A further design principle was to establish a number of internal consistency checks to ensure accurate reporting of political acts by respondents. For instance, initial open questions about political activity were checked against closed questions later in the interview.

The questionnaire was extensively pre-tested in lengthy interviews conducted by the research team in which respondents were asked to elaborate and explain answers in an attempt to detect misunderstood items. In a pre-pilot, experienced interviewers tape-recorded two interviews and were extensively debriefed. This was followed by a full-scale pilot of a sample of 60, leading to 34 successfully completed interviews. The pilot replicated the data collection and processing activities to be followed in the main survey. Several changes were made to the questionnaire in consequence. A detailed account is contained in the technical report on the National Survey (Courtenay 1985).

Fieldwork and data processing

Fieldwork took place between October 1984 and January 1985. The data were edited manually, punched and verified and further edited by computer to check for range, filtering and routing. Verbatim listings of open-ended questions were made from 100 questionnaires and these were then used to develop coding frames by the research team at Manchester. A detailed account is also contained in the technical report on the National Survey (Courtenay 1985).

Community studies

Selection of localities

Three major difficulties stood in the way of selection of localities for study. First, an operating definition of a locality had to be developed; secondly, the definition had to be operationalised in terms of indicators that were appropriate for the definition and available; and, thirdly, a selection of six localities had to be made so as to maximise the range of types covered by the project. These matters are discussed in research papers from the project (Day, Moyser and Parry 1984; Day, Moyser and Parry 1985b) and also in chapter 14 above. After much experimentation, a procedure was adopted that combined statistical rigour with interpretative selection. Only a brief outline is provided here.

It was decided to select four localities in England and one each in Wales and Scotland. Local district councils were chosen as the initial unit of analysis, with attention focusing down to ward and polling district level later in the procedure.

The localities were selected principally through a cluster analysis of 1981 Census variables. Thirty-six variables were used to measure local authority characteristics on age structure, family structure, ethnic composition, housing, urban-rural and occupational structure. The cluster analysis (involving both hierarchical fusion and iterative relocation procedures) sorted all the local authorities into broad types. Three major solutions were then examined in detail but eventually we settled on four groupings of districts from the nine-cluster solution. These seemed to provide identifiable types of local authorities from which selections could be made: inner urban areas; northern towns; prestige commuter areas near large cities; and large market towns. The specific selections themselves were made by calculating which local authority was most typical of its cluster – the so-called 'centroidal' case.

Most of the clusters produced by the analyses conducted for Scotland and Wales could be identified with those derived from the analysis of English data. In Scotland, a separation of rural clusters at the six-cluster level produced a markedly agricultural cluster and it was from this that the Machars locality was drawn. In Wales, a cluster of mining districts provided a marked contrast and it was from this cluster that the locality of Penrhiwceiber was selected.

Having made an initial selection of local authority areas, it was necessary to determine the specific localities within them that would provide the basis for the local studies. This aspect of the selection combined several methods. In some areas, for example the inner London boroughs, a further cluster analysis was conducted at ward level to determine which areas shared characteristics which exemplified the district as a whole. Researchers made preliminary visits to all the sites eventually selected, plus several others which were under active consideration. Final selection also involved consideration of a number of political variables covering *per capita* local authority spending, partisan composition of the district level council and political continuity (re-districting).

The initial statistical analysis of all local districts meant that a full range of possible types of district had been considered. The selection of centroidal cases ensured that the most typical of these districts were used as the basis of the local studies. The selection of localities within districts ensured that the area finally chosen provided a feasible and substantially interesting venue for the examination of local place effects. The preliminary visits by researchers also permitted salient local issues to be identified for inclusion in the local questionnaires.

Community citizen surveys

Citizen surveys were conducted in each locality. Approximately 300 names were drawn from electoral registers covering the whole of each locality using a procedure identical to that described for the national study.

The weighting of the community data sets differs from that for the national data sets in two ways: first, there is no requirement to weight by region to offset the over-representation of Scotland and Wales. Secondly, because of the poor response rate achieved in Stockwell (despite extensive re-issuing) and because the response rate in the council housing estate area was much lower than that achieved elsewhere, it was decided to weight so that the distribution of respondents across polling districts should be identical to that known for the total population.

Questionnaire design and testing for the community studies

Much of the content of the community questionnaire was identical to that from the national study to enable each locality to be described relative to the country as a whole. Because of this, there was little need extensively to test or pilot the major part of the questionnaire. There was, however, a questionnaire insert for each separate locality that focused on the local issues identified as salient by researchers visiting the community. The selection and wording of these items was carefully checked during preliminary interviews with local government officials and group activists in each locality.

The Spotland locality in Rochdale was surveyed a few months in advance of the other communities and served as a type of pilot study, although no subsequent changes were required in the questionnaire or field procedures. The fieldwork for community studies was similar to that for the national study (for further details, see England 1986b).

Community elite studies

In each of the six localities, structured interviews were held with elite respondents. In all, 326 elite persons were selected for interview, the numbers ranging from 71 in Lambeth to 42 in Penrhiwceiber.

Identification of elite

Elite respondents were selected through a combination of positional and snowball methods. Initially, respondents were selected by virtue of occupying a relevant formal position, be it governmental, political, economic or social. For example, councillors for the wards represented in the research locality were included, as were locally most prominent business and trades union leaders. This elite was then asked for further names, if any, of those with an important standing within the public life of the research locality. Any person mentioned at least twice was added, 'snowball' fashion, to the interview list. They, too, were asked for further names until two snowball cycles were complete. As things turned out, few names would have been added in any locality by continuing the process further.

Because the selection of elite respondents is non-random, weighting of the data is not appropriate. Further discussion of the selection of elites may be found in chapter 14.

Elite questionnaire survey

The elite questionnaire included many items adapted from the community and national questionnaires for purposes of comparison. Because of this substantial overlap with the questionnaires already used in the field, extensive pre-testing was not required, although fieldwork in Rochdale, in advance of the main body of elite interviewing, was used as a 'live pilot' to check for possible difficulties.

The elite questionnaire included a higher number of open-ended questions. These were felt to be more appropriate for the respondents. The smaller numbers made processing of open replies more feasible. Fieldwork commenced in Rochdale in May 1984 and ended in Lambeth in May 1985 (England 1986b).

Interviews with key elite members

In addition to the survey of positional and snowball elites, semi-structured interviews were conducted with the MP representing the locality, and the leader and chief executive of the local district council. These were used to obtain further background material on the localities and a perspective on their overall character in the wider political context.

Response rates

Survey research in political fields has become more difficult in recent years leading to lower response rates, particularly in inner city areas. Although a higher rate would be desirable in the citizen surveys, the level of response is comparable to that achieved by other surveys in the 1970s and 1980s and adequate for the analysis. The response rate in the elite survey, on the other hand, was excellent. There were only two refusals, and the third missing response resulted from its loss during data processing and transmission.

Conclusion

The methods used in the British Political Participation Study provide a multi-faceted approach to the major questions about political participation. The various phases of the study interlock, permitting 'triangulation' of many aspects of the research. The design provokes many interesting comparisons. For example, it is possible to check many parameters from the separate community surveys against the national norms available from the national data set. Many comparisons between elite and citizenry are possible within communities.

Table A.1. *Study sample sizes and response rates*

	N issued	N in scope	N respondents	N non-respondents	%-Response rate
National survey	2,400	2,331	1,578	752	68·0
Community citizen survey					
Rochdale	400	374	272	102	72·7
Penrhiwceiber	400	383	291	92	76·0
Sevenoaks	400	390	264	126	67·7
The Machars	400	378	292	86	77·2
Lambeth	400	394	224	170	56·8
Oswestry	400	381	272	109	71·4
All communities	2,400	2,300	1,615	685	70·2
Elite survey					
Rochdale	51	51	51	0	100·0
Penrhiwceiber	42	42	42	0	100·0
Sevenoaks	58	58	58	0	100·0
The Machars	49	48	48	0	100·0
Lambeth	71	71	69	2	97·0
Oswestry	54	54	53	1	98·0
All communities	326	324	321	3	99·0

Appendix B: Measuring elite-citizen concurrence

The concurrence scales used in chapter 17 are intended to measure the extent of issue agreement between mass and elite respondents in each locality.

All these scales are based upon questions about the 'issues, needs or problems' in the local area as perceived by the leaders and citizenry. In each locality, therefore, there are two 'issue agendas' representing the aggregation of, respectively, elite and citizen responses within a common framework of 13 categories of issues. Up to 4 issues were coded at the elite and the citizen levels for each respondent. Where there were two aspects to an issue, such as 'youth unemployment', these were counted as two issues – 'youth' and 'unemployment'. This meant that a maximum of eight responses could be coded for each individual.

A score was derived that would measure the degree of similarity (and hence concurrence) between the two agendas in each locality. Each individual leader was assigned a similarity or concurrence score measuring the extent of the correspondence between that particular individual's personal issue agenda and the aggregate agenda of the citizenry in his or her locality. Equally, a score was given for each citizen, reflecting the amount of agreement between that individual's agenda and the aggregated leader agenda in the given locality. These two sets of concurrence scores are related because they derive from the same agendas in each locality. But they are not identical or symmetrical. Hence, citizen agreement with leaders is not, technically or substantively, the same as leaders agreeing with citizenry.

From the point of view of the citizen's score, we construed the aggregate elite agenda in the given locality as a 'target'. The individual would score as many points as there were elite responses in each of the corresponding categories of issues (up to eight) mentioned by the citizen. This was then divided by the total number of responses in the corresponding number of *most* frequently mentioned categories on the local elite agenda. Thus, if an individual citizen mentioned a full set of eight issue responses, these would be judged against the 'best' (most numerous) eight categories on the elite agenda. But if the individual only offered two issues, then his or her points total would be divided by only the total of the top *two* elite categories. The citizen's score was, then, a ratio measuring the extent to which that individual's personal issue agenda matched the highest priority issues on the corresponding aggregate elite agenda. The more the citizen nominated the top categories, the more that individual could be said to be in agreement or concurrence with those leaders about local priorities. Conversely, the more the citizen picked issues that few leaders also shared, the less the amount of agreement for that individual. If the ratio is then multiplied by 100, a 'perfect' score (of 100) would arise in those instances where the individual citizen picked the most frequent elite category and then as many more proceeding down the elite agenda as the individual citizen had issue mentions. Conversely, zero would arise if the individual's issue agenda related to categories containing no leader responses from his or her locality. Similarly, 50 would mean that the citizen did half as well as he or she might have done in picking the top elite issue categories and thus maximising agreement with the local leaders.

One possible problem with this approach is that it may give undue weight to those articulate citizens with long personal agendas. Thus, for example, an individual with eight issues would have eight 'shots' at picking the 'top' issue. The inarticulate individual with only one issue mention, on the other hand, would have just one chance at agreeing with most leaders. It is the case, of course, that the eight-issue citizen would be judged according to his or her ability to pick the top eight elite issues, whereas the one-issue respondent would be judged by how high up the agenda that one issue was located. This obviously handicaps the articulate individual *pro rata* to the inarticulate.

Nevertheless, in order to be more sure that the concurrence scores we ended up with did *not* give undue weight to the articulate (who would tend to be the better educated and more participatory), we devised a second score that simply counted the one 'best' issue amongst the citizen's issue set (if there were multiple responses) or the one issue if the citizen offered only one. To arrive at the final concurrence score, we then took the average between the full-issue score and the one-issue score. This seemed to represent a fair balance between recognising the scope for the more articulate to agree with more leaders, by virtue of having more issues to generate that agreement, and yet not 'rewarding' that greater scope too much. To discount longer agendas too much (Verba and Nie 1972:412–14) seems to ignore an important and relevant aspect of reality here. A longer agenda may not merely reflect articulacy but could also indicate the sensitivity of an individual to local needs and problems. But, at the same time, it is important to ensure that the 'reward' is not too great. In fact, however, the results reported in chapter 17 are very robust: they turn out virtually the same whichever of the three scoring systems is used.

For elite concurrence an analogous set of three measures was devised representing the capacity of individual leaders to pick the top issues as defined by aggregated citizen responses within the locality. The same considerations applied to elites as to citizens and, hence, the final elite concurrence score was an average of the score arising from a leader's full set of issues and that of the best one issue. The elite and citizen scores would not be the same unless the shape of the two 'targets' in each locality is the same – which is highly unlikely to be the case. In other words, the distribution of responses across the elite categories will not, normally, be the same as the distribution across the citizen categories. Hence, the end products of the two points-scoring mechanisms will not be the same either. For example, the points accrued by a citizen for hitting the number one elite category of issues will be very unlikely to be the same as the points accruing to a leader for doing the equivalent. They will differ according to the distribution of responses and, to some extent possibly, according to the total number of respondents involved. There were, on average, about five times as many citizens interviewed in each locality as leaders. This may, therefore, be a source of discrepancies between the two sets of targets, even when using proportions, as in effect we do, rather than the raw issue counts.

Appendix C: The national questionnaire

	Col./ Code	Skip to
BACKGROUND		

1 First, for how long have you been living in your   years: ☐☐
   town/borough/suburb/village/local area   OR
                                             months: ☐☐

CARD A

2 People often feel differently about various geographical areas. Could
you tell me which of the statements on this card best describes the
way *you* feel about each of the areas I mention.

READ OUT EACH ITEM	*Attached*:				Does not apply	DK
	Very strongly	Fairly strongly	Not very	Not at all		
a) ...your neighbourhood, that is, the streets in the immediate area round where you live?	1	2	3	4	5	8
b) ...this town/borough/ suburb/village?	1	2	3	4	5	8
c) the County in which you live (IN SCOTLAND: region)?	1	2	3	4	5	8
SCOTLAND/WALES ONLY						
d) And which of the statements best describes the way you feel about Scotland/Wales?	1	2	3	4	5	8
ALL						
e) ...Britain as a whole?	1	2	3	4	5	8
f) ...the particular place where you were born?	1	2	3	4	5	8
g) ...Europe as a whole?	1	2	3	4	5	8

h) Is there any other area to which you feel attached?	Yes	1	i)
	No	2	Q.3

IF YES AT h)

i) Which areas? WRITE IN :_____
   (IF MORE THAN ONE, RECORD ONE TO WHICH MOST ATTACHED)

j) Which of the statements on the card (CARD A) best describes how you feel about _____(AREA)?	very strongly attached	1
	fairly strongly attached	2
	not very attached	3
	not at all attached	4
	does not apply	5
	DK	8

| | | | | | | | Col./ Code | Skip to |

CARD B

3 Next, I want to ask how you feel about some groups of people. Using Card B, you could tell me which statement best describes the way you feel about each of the groups, or types of people that I mention.

| READ OUT EACH ITEM | Attached: | | | | Does not apply | DK |
	Very strongly	Fairly strongly	Not very	Not at all		
a) ...People who do the same sort of work as you do?...	1	2	3	4	5	8
b) ...people of the same ethnic origin or language group?	1	2	3	4	5	8
c) ...people of the same religious belief or background?	1	2	3	4	5	8
d) ...people who share your interests in hobbies, sports or leisure?	1	2	3	4	5	8
e) ...people of the same political views, or party?	1	2	3	4	5	8
f) ...people of the same social class?	1	2	3	4	5	8

ISSUES, NEEDS, PROBLEMS

4 Next I'd like to ask about the issues, needs and problems that people might consider taking action on: actions such as contacting a Local Councillor or official, signing a petition, joining in a national protest or working in a group.

a) *Whether or not* you have taken any action on them, what particular issues, needs or problems have been important to you over the past five years or so? EXPLAIN IF NECESSARY: Any sort of issue, need or problem that has been important to you.

RECORD UP TO 4 ISSUES/NEEDS/PROBLEMS UNDER (a) BELOW. DO NOT PROBE

ASK ABOUT EACH ISSUE/NEED/PROBLEM LISTED AT (a) – (IF NONE, GO TO c)

b) Would you say that _____ (READ OUT ISSUE/NEED/PROBLEM) is the sort of thing that people might take action about, for example, actions such as contacting an MP or Local Councillor?

RECORD UNDER (b) BELOW

IF *THREE OR FEWER* ISSUES/NEEDS/PROBLEMS CODED 1 AT (b) GO TO (c)
IF *FOUR* ARE CODED 1 AT (b) – GO TO (d)

IF THREE OR FEWER CODED 1 ('YES') AT (b)

c) What issues, needs or problems are there at a local level, or that affect you or your family, or that affect the country as a whole that people might take action about?

RECORD UNDER (c) BELOW IF NO ISSUES/NEEDS/PROBLEMS AT (b) OR (c) ⟶ 1 Q21

ASK ABOUT EACH ISSUE/NEED/PROBLEM CODED 1 AT (b) OR LISTED AT (c)

d) About how much action have you, yourself taken on _____ (READ OUT ISSUE/NEED/PROBLEM) – a lot, some, a little or none at all? RECORD UNDER (d)

(a)   (b)   (d)

prob. no.	(a)	(Col.)	(b)	A lot	Some	A little	None at all
1	_____		Yes 1 No 2	1	2	3	4
2	_____		Yes 1 No 2	1	2	3	4
3	_____		Yes 1 No 2	1	2	3	4
4	_____		Yes 1 No 2	1	2	3	4

(c)

	(c)						
5	_____		✕	1	2	3	4
6	_____			1	2	3	4
7	_____			1	2	3	4
8	_____			1	2	3	4

e) Which of the problems you have told me about did you take *most* action on?   WRITE IN PROBLEM NUMBER FROM GRID ☐   Q.5

No action taken on any problem (all code 4 at d)   0   f)

IF CODE 'O' AT d)

f) Which problem was most important to you?   ☐   Q.5
WRITE IN PROBLEM NUMBER FROM GRID

| SELECTED NEED/PROBLEM |

5　a)　WRITE IN SELECTED NEED/PROBLEM FROM Q.4 GRID: _____

CARD C

b)　I'd like to ask a bit more about_____(SELECTED NEED/PROBLEM). From the card, who has put *most effort* into tackling the problem, or has nobody tackled it?

RING CODE IN GRID UNDER b)

IF CODE 01–09 AT b) (OTHERS GO TO d)

c)　How successful would you say they have been in dealing with the problem: very successful, fairly, not very, or not at all successful?

　　RING CODE UNDER (c) AGAINST 'MOST EFFORT' GROUP

d)　Still from the card, who do you think *ought* to be responsible for tackling _____

　　(NAME PROBLEM)? CODE ALL THAT APPLY UNDER (d)

	(b) Most effort	(c) Very	Fairly	Not very	Not at all	Other	DK	(Col.)	(d) Ought to tackle
1　Central Government	01	1	2	3	4	5	8		1
2　Parts of Government responsible for Scotland and Wales	02	1	2	3	4	5	8		2
3　Local Government	03	1	2	3	4	5	8		3
									CARD 03
4　The individual citizen by himself or herself	04	1	2	3	4	5	8		4
5　Business and industry	05	1	2	3	4	5	8		5
6　Trade unions	06	1	2	3	4	5	8		6
7　Voluntary organisations etc	07	1	2	3	4	5	8		7
8　Political action group	08	1	2	3	4	5	8		8
9　Other (LIST BELOW)	09	1	2	3	4	5	8		1
10 Nobody/None of them	10 } d)								2
11 DK	98 }								3

_____ (WRITE IN): _____
_____
_____
_____

					Col./ Code	Skip to

CARD D

6 Still thinking about _____ (SELECTED PROBLEM) – how much does the problem affect...READ OUT...

a) ...you, or your immediate family? RECORD UNDER (a)

b) ...your friends or neighbours? RECORD UNDER (b)

c) ...people living in your district? RECORD UNDER (c)

d) ...and how much does it affect people living in this region? RECORD UNDER (d)

e) ...and how much does it affect Britain as a whole? RECORD UNDER (e)

	(a) You/ Family	(b) Friends/ Neighbours	(c) District	(d) Region	(e) Britain
Very much	1	1	1	1	1
Quite a bit	2	2	2	2	2
Not much	3	3	3	3	3
Not at all	4	4	4	4	4
DK	8	8	8	8	8

	Col./Code	Skip to
7 INTERVIEWER CHECK Q.4d) Respondent *took action on Selected Problem* (codes 1–3 ringed at Q.4d) against selected problem)	1	Q.8
Respondent *did not take action on selected problem* (Code 4 ringed at Q.4d) against problem)	2	Q.17
IF ACTION TAKEN ON SELECTED PROBLEM CODE 1 AT Q.7		

8 Now I'd like to ask about the actions you took in connection with _____ (SELECTED PROBLEM).

a) First, could you describe the main action that you took.

   EXPLAIN IF NECESSARY: I mean the action that took most effort.

   PROBE FULLY. RECORD VERBATIM

b) How did you first get the idea of taking this action?

   PROBE FULLY. RECORD VERBATIM

		Col./Code	Skip to
9 a) Do you think that your action had any results?	Yes No DK	1 2 8	b) Q.10
IF YES b) Were you satisfied or dissatisfied with the result of your action, or did you have mixed feelings?	Satisfied Dissatisfied Mixed feelings	1 2 3	
Other (SPECIFY): _____		4	
	DK/CR	8	
10 How much effort did your action take; a lot, some, very little or none at all?	A lot Some Very little None at all	1 1 3 4	
Other (SPECIFY) _____		5	

	Col./ Code	Skip to

11 Did taking the action involve you personally in a lot of argument or conflict with other people?

Yes — 1

No — 2

Other (SPECIFY): _____ — 3

---

12 a) Generally speaking would you describe this action as political in any way?

Yes — 1 — b)

No — 2 — Q.13

Depends/both yes and no — 3 — b)

DK — 8 — Q.13

IF CODE 1 OR 3 AT a) ASK b) AND c)

b) Did taking the action increase your knowledge of how politics works?

Yes — 1

No — 2

Other (SPECIFY): _____ — 3

DK — 8

c) And did it give you a *more* favourable or a *less* favourable impression of how politics works, or did it make no difference?

More favourable — 1

Less favourable — 2

No difference — 3

Other (SPECIFY) _____ — 4

DK — 8

---

13 a) Was the action that you took directed at a person or group or organisation?

IF YES: Was it directed at *one* person group or organisation or more than one?

Yes, at one — 1 — b)

Yes, at more than one — 2 — c)

No, action was *not* directed at any individual, group or organisation — 3

Other (SPECIFY): _____ — 4 — Q.16

DK — 8

IF CODE 1 AT a)

b) Who was the action directed at?

WRITE IN BOX BELOW

IF CODE 2 AT a)

c) Which was the *main* person, group or organisation that the action was directed at?

WRITE IN BOX BELOW

> WRITE IN NAME OF GROUP/ORGANISATION/OFFICE OF PERSON
>
> _____

	Col./ Code	Skip to

14 Would you say that your action got the message across... READ OUT...

...very well,	1	
fairly well,	2	
not very well.	3	
or, not at all well?	4	
DK	8	

15 a) Did the person, group or organisation at whom the action was directed attempt to do anything about the problem? IF YES: did they attempt to do something helpful or unhelpful

Yes – helpful	1 ⎫	b)
Yes – unhelpful	2 ⎬	
No, they did not attempt to do anything	3 ⎫	
Other (SPECIFY): _____	4 ⎬	Q.16
DK/CR	8 ⎭	

IF CODES 1 OR 2

b) Do you think that they did something about the problem *because of* the action you took? IF YES: Was it wholly or in part because of the action you had taken?

Yes, wholly	1	
Yes, in part	2	
No, not because of the action	3	
DK	8	

c) How *much* did they do about the problem ...READ OUT...

...a great deal,	1	
quite a lot,	2	
or, not very much?	3	
DK	8	

16 Briefly, what, if anything, happened as a result of your action?

WRITE IN BELOW. DO NOT PROBE

NOW GO TO Q.21

	Col./ Code	Skip to

IF NO ACTION TAKEN, CODE 2 AT Q.7

CARD E

17 This card lists some of the reasons why people might not take any action on a particular issue need or problem. For each reason listed could you tell me whether or not it applied to you in connection with the particular problem we have been talking about.

	Yes, applied	No, did not apply	DK
a) I did not have the time	1	2	8
b) I just accept these sorts of problems	1	2	8
c) These sorts of problems cannot be solved by an individual alone	1	2	8
d) These sorts of problems cannot be solved anyway	1	2	8
e) I would not know what to do about the problem	1	2	8
f) To have done anything would have made me look like a trouble maker	1	2	8

18 a) Was there any other reason why you didn't take action on the problem?

		Col./Code	Skip to
	Yes	1	b)
	No	2	Q.19

IF YES

b) What was the reason? PROBE FULLY. RECORD VERBATIM

19 a) Looking back over the problem we've been talking about, is there anything else you wish you had done?

		Col./Code	Skip to
	Yes	1	b)
	No	2	Q.20

IF YES

b) What do you wish you had done?

WRITE IN

20 a) And, looking ahead, if a similar problem arose again, would you take any action?   CARD 04

		Col./Code	Skip to
	Yes	1	b)
	No	2 }	Q.21
	DK	8 }	

IF YES

b) What sort of action might you take?

WRITE IN BELOW

ACTIVITIES

ASK ALL – CARD F (BLUE)

21 Now I want to ask about different forms of political activity that you might have been involved with over the past five years or so; or that you might get involved with in the future. For each activity I read out, I'd like you to tell me whether you have done it, using the items at the *top* of the card, and then whether you would consider doing it in the future, using the items at the *bottom* of the card.

ASK a) AND b) ABOUT EACH ITEM LISTED BELOW. RECORD ANSWERS IN GRID.

a) In the *past* have you, yourself, ever contacted a _____? RECORD UNDER (a)

b) And, in the future, how likely are you to consider doing so? RECORD UNDER (b)

READ OUT...	PAST				(Col.)	FUTURE				
	Often	Now & then	Only once	Never		Certainly	Consider: Probably	Might	Never	DK
1 ...Local Councillor?	1	2	3	4		1	2	3	4	8
2 ...Town Hall or County Hall official? (EXCLUDE ROUTINE CONTACTS)	1	2	3	4		1	2	3	4	8
3 ...Member of Parliament?	1	2	3	4		1	2	3	4	8
4 ...Department of Central Government, or a Civil Servant?	1	2	3	4		1	2	3	4	8
5 ...radio or television programme, or a newspaper, about a political issue?	1	2	3	4		1	2	3	4	8

CARD F (BLUE)

22 Next, I'd like to ask about working on political matters with other people...

a) In the *past* have you_____(READ OUT ITEM 1 BELOW) RECORD UNDER (a)

b) And, in the future, how likely are you to consider doing so? RECORD UNDER (b)

REPEAT (a) AND (b) READING OUT ITEM 2 IN GRID BELOW

	PAST				(Col.)	FUTURE				
	Often	Now & then	Only once	Never		Certainly	Consider: Probably	Might	Never	DK
1 ...Supported, or worked in, an *organised group* to raise an issue?	1	2	3	4		1	2	3	4	8
2 ...got together with other people to raise an issue?	1	2	3	4		1	2	3	4	8

	Col./ Code	Skip to

23 INTERVIEWER TO CHECK Q.21 & Q.22

In the *past* – Respondent has –

taken *no* political action (Code 4 only ringed at Q.21a)/Q.22a)	1	Q.28
taken *only one* political action (only one Code 1, 2 or 3 ringed at Q.21a/Q.22a)	2	Q.24
taken *more than one* political action (more than one Code 1, 2 or 3 ringed at Q.21a/Q.22a)	3	Q.25

---

24 IF ONLY ONE POLITICAL ACTION, CODE 2 AT Q.23

Have you already told me about the action when we were discussing issues, needs and problems?

	Yes	1	Q.28
	No	2	Q.27

IF MORE THAN ONE POLITICAL ACTION TAKEN (CODE 3 AT Q.23)

CARD G

25 a) This card lists the actions we've been talking about. Thinking *only* of the actions that *you* have taken, which one were you *most* involved with? EXPLAIN IF NECESSARY: Which took the most effort? RECORD UNDER (a)

b) And which one were you *next most* involved with? RING CODE UNDER (b)

(a)   (b)

	Most	Next most		
1 Local Councillor..	1	1 ⎫		
2 Town Hall or County Hall Official........................	2	2		
3 Member of Parliament.....................................	3	3		
4 Department of Central Government, or Civil Servant..	4	4 ⎬		Q26
5 Radio, television, newspaper	5	5		
6 Organised group..	6	6		
7 Getting together with other people	7	7 ⎭		

CARD G

26 a) Can I just check, have you already told me about either of these actions, when we were discussing issues, needs and problems?

	Yes	1	b)
	No	2	Q.27

IF YES

b) DELETE IN GRID AT Q.25 THE ACTION ALREADY DISCUSSED AND ASK 'Which action were you next most involved with?' RECORD AT Q.25 UNDER (a) OR (b) AS APPROPRIATE. THEN GO TO Q.27.

If not involved with any other action	1	Q.28

SELECTED ACTIONS

27 I'd like to ask a bit more about some of the things that you've just told me about.

> ASK (a)–(l) ABOUT THE ONLY, OR 'MOST IMPORTANT' ACTION.
> THEN REPEAT FOR 'NEXT MOST' IMPORTANT ACTION WHEN APPROPRIATE.

a) WRITE IN ACTION
    i) 'ONLY' OR 'MOST IMPORTANT': _____
    ii) NEXT MOST IMPORTANT: (IF APPROPRIATE) _____

b) I'd like to ask about _____ . What was it about? WRITE IN BELOW.
    (IF DONE MORE THAN ONCE, ASK ABOUT MOST RECENT OCCASION)

    'ONLY/MOST IMPORTANT'   'NEXT MOST' IMPORTANT

c) How did you first get the idea of taking this action? WRITE IN BELOW
    'ONLY/MOST IMPORTANT'   'NEXT MOST' IMPORTANT

	MOST	NEXT MOST	Skip to
d) Do you think your action had any results? Yes	1	1	e)
No	2 }	2 }	f)
DK	8	8	
IF YES AT d)			
e) Were you satisfied or dissatisfied with the result of your action, or did you have mixed feelings Satisfied	1	1	
Dissatisfied	2	2	
Mixed feelings	3	3	
Other (SPECIFY) _____	4	4	
DK/CR	8	8	
f) How much effort did it take…READ OUT… …a lot,	1	1	
some,	2	2	
very little,	3	3	
or, none at all?	4	4	
Other (SPECIFY) _____	5	5	
g) Did the action involve you personally in a lot of argument or conflict with other people? Yes	1	1	
No	2	2	
Other (SPECIFY) _____	3	3	
DK	8	8	
h) Did taking the action increase your knowledge of how politics works? Yes	1	1	
No	2	2	
Other (SPECIFY) _____	3	3	
DK	8	8	

		Col./ Code		Skip to
		MOST	NEXT MOST	

i) And did it give you a more favourable or a less favourable impression of how politics works, or did it make no difference?

		MOST	NEXT MOST	
	More favourable	1	1	
	Less favourable	2	2	
	No difference	3	3	
Other (SPECIFY)_____		4	4	
	DK	8	8	

j) Were you trying to put a message across to some person, group or organisation when you took the action?

		MOST	NEXT MOST	Skip to
	Yes	1	1	k)
	No	2	2	l)
Other (SPECIFY)_____		3	3	

IF YES AT j)

k) Would you say that you got the message across...READ OUT...

		MOST	NEXT MOST	
	...very well,	1	1	
	fairly well,	2	2	
	not very well,	3	3	
	or, not at all well?	4	4	
	DK	8	8	

l) If a similar situation arose again, would you take the same action, some other action, or would you do nothing?

		MOST	NEXT MOST	
	Same	1	1	
	Some other	2	2	
	Both same and some other	3	3	
	Do nothing	4	4	
Other (SPECIFY)_____		5	5	
	DK	8	8	

—REPEAT (a)–(l) FOR 'NEXT MOST' IMPORTANT ACTIVITY THEN GO TO Q.28

—IF THERE IS NO 'NEXT MOST' IMPORTANT, GO TO Q.28

	Col./ Code	Skip to

ASK ALL

28 a) INTERVIEWER TO CHECK:

Contacting a Local Councillor:		Col./ Code	Skip to
	– was asked about at Q.27	1	Q.29
	– was *not* asked about at Q.27	2 }	b)
	– Q.27 was not asked of this Respondent	3 }	

IF CODES 2–3

b) Supposing you were to contact a local councillor, how much effort would it take ... READ OUT ...

		Col./ Code	Skip to
	...a lot,	1	
	some,	2 }	c)
	very little,	3 }	
	or, none at all?	4 }	
(Respondent said would never contact a local councillor)		5	Q.29
	(Depends)	6 }	
Other (SPECIFY)_____		7 }	c)
	DK	8 }	

IF CODES 1–4 OR 6–8 AT b) ASK c)–e)

c) Do you think it would involve you personally in a lot of argument or conflict with other people?

		Col./ Code
	Yes	1
	No	2
Other (SPECIFY)_____		3
	DK	8

d) Would you expect it to increase your knowledge of how politics works?

		Col./ Code
	Yes	1
	No	2
	Depends	3
Other (SPECIFY)_____		4
	DK	8

e) If you were to contact a local councillor would you expect to get the result you wanted?

		Col./ Code
	Yes	1
	No	2
	Depends	3
Other (SPECIFY)_____		4
	DK	8

	Col./ Code	Skip to

ASK ALL

29 a) INTERVIEWER TO CHECK:

Working with an organised group: – was asked about at Q.27 — 1 — Q.30

– was *not* asked about at Q.27 — 2

Q.27 was not asked of this Respondent — 3 } b)

IF CODES 2–3

b) Supposing you were to work with a community or local
civic group to raise an issue or problem,
how much effort would it take... READ OUT... ...a lot, — 1

some, — 2

very little, — 3 } c)

or, none at all? — 4

(Respondent said would never work with an organised group) — 5 — Q.30

Depends — 6

Other (SPECIFY) _____ — 7 } c)

DK — 8

IF CODES 1–4 OR 6–8 AT b) ASK c)–e)

c) Do you think it would involve you personally in a lot of
argument or conflict with other people? Yes — 1

No — 2

Other (SPECIFY) _____ — 3

DK — 8

d) Would you expect it to increase your knowledge of how
politics works? Yes — 1

No — 2

Depends — 3

Other (SPECIFY) _____ — 4

DK — 8

e) And would you expect such a group to get the result you
wanted? Yes — 1

No — 2

Depends — 3

Other (SPECIFY) _____ — 4

DK — 8

| TRADE UNION/STAFF ASSOCIATION |

ASK ALL

30 a) Are you *currently* a member of a trade union or
staff association concerned with the terms and
conditions of employment? Yes, trade union — 1

Yes, staff association — 2 } Q.31

No, none of them — 3 — b)

IF CODE 3

b) Have you *ever* been a member of a trade union
or staff association concerned with the terms
and conditions of employment? Yes, trade union — 1

Yes, staff association — 2 } Q.31

No, none of them — 3 — Q.37

IF PAST OR PRESENT MEMBER, CODES 1–2 AT Q.30a) OR b)

31 What is the name of the trade union/staff association?
WRITE OUT IN FULL BELOW
(IF BELONGED TO MORE THAN ONE, ASK ABOUT MOST RECENT)

	Col./Code	Skip to
(ASK Q.32–Q.35 IN PAST TENSE IF REFERRING TO PAST MEMBERSHIP)		
32 Generally, how satisfied or dissatisfied are you with your trade union/staff association? PROBE BEFORE RECORDING ANSWER: Is that *very* satisfied/dissatisfied or just satisfied/dissatisfied?		
Very satisfied	1	
Satisfied	2	
Dissatisfied	3	
Very dissatisfied	4	
Other (SPECIFY) _____	5	
DK/CR	8	
33 Is there a closed shop agreement at the place where you work that covers membership of *your* union/staff association?	1	
Yes		
No	2	
DK	8	
Spare		
	CARD 05	
34 Would you say you are ...READ OUT... ...very active,	1	
fairly,	2	
not very,	3	
or, not at all active in the union/staff association?	4	
35 a) How much notice does the *local leadership* of the union/association take of the views of ordinary members...READ OUT... ...a lot,	1	
some,	2	
very little,	3	
or, none at all?	4	
DK	8	
b) And how much attention does the *national leadership* of the union/association pay to the views of local branches...READ OUT... ...a lot,	1	
some,	2	
very little,	3	
or, none at all?	4	
(No national leadership)	5	
DK	8	
36 a) Have you *ever* held any office, been on any committees, been a delegate, or held any other official position in the union/staff association? Yes	1	b)
No	2	
DK/CR	8	Q.37
IF YES AT a)		
b) Have you done so over the past five years? Yes	1	
No	2	
DK/CR	8	

		Col./Code	Skip to

GROUP MEMBERSHIP

CARD H

37 a) On this card are listed some different types of groups and organisations. For each one, could you tell me whether or not you are a member or regularly attend meetings or events of such a group.
CODE UNDER (a) IN GRID
FOR EACH GROUP RESPONDENT IS MEMBER OF/ATTENDS MEETING, i.e. EACH CODE 1, ASK b), c) & d)

b) How many different_____ clubs/groups are you involved with?
ENTER NUMBER UNDER (b) IN GRID

c) Would you say you take part in all, most, a few, or none of the club's/group's activities? RECORD UNDER (c)

d) How often are political and social issues discussed formally or informally in the club/group; often, sometimes or never?
RECORD UNDER (d)

IF MORE THAN ONE CLUB/GROUP AT (b) ASK (c) & (d) ABOUT THE ONE IN WHICH THE RESPONDENT IS MOST ACTIVE

		(a)	(b)	(c)				(d)		
		Member	Number of Clubs, Groups	All	Most	A few	None	Often	Some-times	Never
No.	Name	Yes No								
01	Social Club	1 2	☐	1	2	3	4	5	6	7
02	Hobby or Sports Club	1 2	☐	1	2	3	4	5	6	7
03	Armed Forces Association	1 2	☐	1	2	3	4	5	6	7
04	Evening class or study group	1 2	☐	1	2	3	4	5	6	7
05	Art, literary or cultural group	1 2	☐	1	2	3	4	5	6	7
06	Political club or organisation (exclude Party Membership)	1 2	☐	1	2	3	4	5	6	7
07	Church or religious organisation	1 2	☐	1	2	3	4	5	6	7
08	Professional Society	1 2	☐	1	2	3	4	5	6	7
09	Voluntary Service Group	1 2	☐	1	2	3	4	5	6	7
10	Community or local civic group	1 2	☐	1	2	3	4	5	6	7
11	Self help group	1 2	☐	1	2	3	4	5	6	7
12	Feminist group	1 2	☐	1	2	3	4	5	6	7
13	Other (SPECIFY BELOW)	1 2	☐	1	2	3	4	5	6	7
14	*None of them*	8 —————————————————————————————————→								Q.49

LIST OTHER GROUPS BELOW

	Col./ Code	Skip to

38 a) INTERVIEWER CHECK Q.37
    Respondent –

1 does not belong to any club/group at which social or political issues are discussed (Code 7's only ringed at Q.37d)	1	Q.49
2 belongs to *one club only at which political and social issues are discussed* (only one Code 5 or Code 6 at Q.37d).......................	2	Q.40
3 belongs to *more than one club/group at which political or social issues are discussed* (more than one code 5 and/or Code 6 at Q.37d).	3	Q.39

IF CODE 3 AT Q.38

CARD H

39 Thinking now of the clubs or groups on this list that you belong to and at which political and social issues are discussed; in which club or group are you, personally, *most* active?

  a) ENTER NUMBER OF CLUB/GROUP FROM Q.37:   [|]   Q.40

       | SELECTED CLUB/GROUP |

40 a) What is the *full* name of the club/group?

    WRITE IN (BUT OMIT ANY PLACE NAME): _____

    _____

  b) What were the main reasons that you first became involved with this club/group? PROBE FULLY. RECORD VERBATIM.

41 a) Over the past five years, has the club/group tried to influence political decisions of local or central government, or governments of other countries?

Yes	1	b)
No	2 ⎫	
DK	8 ⎭	Q.42

  IF YES

  b) Has it happened ... READ OUT ...

...often,	1	
occasionally,	2	
or, rarely?	3	
DK	8	

42 Do you personally get involved with discussions about political or social issues within this group
  ... READ OUT ...

...often,	1	
occasionally,	2	
rarely,	3	
or, never?	4	

43 a) Does the club/group have any formal or official leadership positions?

Yes	1	b)
No	2	Q.46

  IF YES

  b) Have you ever held any office, been on any committees, or held any other official position in the club/group?

Yes	1	c)
No	2 ⎫	
DK/CR	8 ⎭	Q.44

    IF YES AT b)

  c) Have you done so over the past five years?

Yes	1	
No	2	
DK/CR	8	

	Col./ Code	Skip to

44 a) How much notice does the leadership of this club/group
take of the views of ordinary members...
READ OUT...

...a lot,	1	
some,	2	
very little,	3	
or, none at all?	4	
DK	8	

b) Does the leadership listen equally to *all* ordinary members,
or are some listened to more than others?

All equally	1	
Some more than others	2	
Depends	3	
Other (SPECIFY) _____	4	
DK	8	

45 a) Are the leaders or office holders of the club/group
elected?

Yes	1	b)
No	2 }	
DK	8 }	Q.46

IF YES

b) Is there usually just one person standing in the election for a
particular post or are the elections usually contested,
with more than one person standing?

Usually one person	1	
Usually contested	2	
Varies/depends	3	
DK	8	

46 Thinking about the past five years or so, have you ever
been an unofficial or informal leader in this club/group?

Yes	1	
No	2	
DK	8	

CARD I

47 Still thinking of _____(SELECTED CLUB/GROUP) could you tell
me, from the card, how often over the past five years or so, you
personally have done each of the following...READ OUT...

	Often	Occas- ionally	Rarely	Never	Not Applic.
a) ...helped out with social functions for the club/group?	1	2	3	4	5
b) ...done some clerical or administrative work for the club/group?	1	2	3	4	5
c) ...used the club/group to raise a political need or issue?	1	2	3	4	5

48 Would you say that this club/group has been better than
you expected, about the same as you expected, or worse
than you expected when you first became associated with it?

Better	1	
Same	2	
Worse	3	
Better in some ways/worse in others	4	
DK	8	

	Col./ Code	Skip to

SPECIAL ACTIVITIES

ASK ALL

CARD J

49 a) Could you tell me, for each of the functions and organisations listed on this card, whether or not you would describe it as *political*. RECORD IN GRID UNDER (a)

b) Over the past five years or so have you, personally, had any of the functions listed, or been involved in the organisation or administration of any of them? RECORD IN GRID UNDER (b)

	(a)			(b)	
	Political:			*Involved*:	
	Yes	No	DK	Yes	No
1 Government Advisory Panels	1	2	8	1	2
2 Industrial Tribunals	1	2	8	1	2
3 Rent Tribunals	1	2	8	1	2
4 Territorial Army	1	2	8	1	2
5 Special Constables	1	2	8	1	2
6 Justices of the Peace	1	2	8	1	2
7 Magistrates	1	2	8	1	2
8 Voluntary Welfare Organisations, e.g. Meals on Wheels	1	2	8	1	2
9 School Governors	1	2	8	1	2

c) Over the past five years or so, have you been involved in the organisation or administration, of any *other* activities similar to those listed on the card?

Yes   1   d)

No   2   Q.50

IF YES AT c)

d) What activities or organisations have you been involved with?

LIST EACH ON A SEPARATE LINE BELOW

_____

_____

_____

_____

_____

PROTEST

CARD F (BLUE)

50 a) Now I would like to ask about signing petitions. In the same way as before, could you first tell me, from the *top* of the card how often over the past five years you have signed a petition?

Often   1

Now and then   2

Only once   3

Never   4

b) Now using the answers from the *bottom* of the card, could you say what you would do if, in the future, somebody asked you to sign a petition?

I would certainly consider it   1

I would probably consider it   2

I might consider it   3

I would never consider it   4

DK   8

ASK ALL

CARD F (BLUE)

| | Col./Code | Skip to |

51 Now I'd like to ask about the ways in which people raise objections or protest about political matters. In the same way as before, could you first tell me from the *top* of the card how often over the past five years or so, you have done each of the things I will read out. Then, from the *bottom* of the card, whether you would consider doing it in the future.

ASK (a) & (b) ABOUT EACH ITEM LISTED BELOW. RECORD THE ANSWERS IN GRID

a) In the *past*, have you yourself _____? RECORD UNDER (a)

b) In the future, how likely are you to consider doing so?
   RECORD UNDER (b)

	(a)				(b)				
	PAST: Now				FUTURE:				
READ OUT	Often	& then	Only once	Never	Certainly	Probably	Might	Never	DK
1 ...*attended a public meeting* to protest about an issue?	1	2	3	4	1	2	3	4	8
2 ...taken a *petition* round asking people to sign it?	1	2	3	4	1	2	3	4	8
3 ...taken part in a *boycott* about a political issue?	1	2	3	4	1	2	3	4	8
4 ...taken part in a *protest march* which had not been banned by the police?	1	2	3	4	1	2	3	4	8
5 ...taken part in a *strike* about an issue which you feel is political?	1	2	3	4	1	2	3	4	8
6 ...*blocked traffic* with a street demonstration?	1	2	3	4	1	2	3	4	8
7 ...used *physical force* against political opponents?	1	2	3	4	1	2	3	4	8

c) In the past five years or so, have you done any other sorts of political protesting or objecting?   Yes | 1 | d)
                                                                                       No | 2 | Q.52

IF YES

d) What have you done? PROBE FULLY. RECORD VERBATIM, LIST EACH SORT OF PROTESTING ON A SEPARATE LINE

_____

_____

_____

_____

		Col./ Code	Skip to
52 a) INTERVIEWER TO CHECK, Q.51a)			
In the *past*- Respondent has *not done any* protesting (Code 4 only ringed at Q.51a)		1	Q.54
Respondent has made *only one* protest (only one Code 1, 2, or 3 ringed at Q.51a)		2	c)
Respondent has made *more than one* protest (more than one Code 1, 2, or 3 ringed at Q.51a)		3	b)

IF CODE 3

b) SELECT THE *TWO* FORMS OF PROTEST THAT ARE CODED 1,
2 OR 3 *NEAREST THE BOTTOM OF THE GRID AT Q.51a*),
I.E., PROTEST ITEM 7 BEFORE 6; 6 BEFORE 5, ETC.
RECORD IN GRID AT (c) BELOW

c) SELECTED PROTEST ACTIONS (RING CODE (S))

(c)
ACTIONS

	First or only	Second
1 Attended a public meeting	1	1
2 Taken a petition round	2	2
3 Taken part in a boycott	3	3
4 Taken part in a protest march that had not been banned by the police	4	4
5 Taken part in a strike about an issue which you feel is political	5	5
6 Blocked traffic with a street demonstration	6	6
7 Used physical force against political opponents	7	7

		Col./Code	Skip to
d) Can I just check, have you already told me about this particular action earlier in the interview?	Yes	1	e)
	No	2	Q.53

IF YES

e) DELETE IN GRID ABOVE, THE ACTION ALREADY DISCUSSED AND
REPLACE WITH ACTION DONE NEXT CLOSEST TO BOTTOM
OF LIST. THEN GO TO Q.53   If not taken part in any other action | 1 | Q.54 |

	spare	
	CARD 07	

SELECTED PROTEST ACTIONS

53 I'd like to ask a bit more about some of the things you've told me about.

ASK (a)–(l) ABOUT ONLY OR FIRST ACTION
(FROM Q.52c) THEN REPEAT FOR SECOND ACTION

a) WRITE IN ACTION (FROM Q.52c)
   i) FIRST ACTION. (OR ONLY): _____
   ii) SECOND ACTION: _____

b) (First) I'd like to ask about   . What was it about? WRITE IN
   BELOW. (IF DONE MORE THAN ONCE, ASK ABOUT MOST RECENT TIME)
                FIRST ACTION   SECOND ACTION

c) How did you first get the idea of taking this action? WRITE IN
   BELOW
                FIRST ACTION   SECOND ACTION

		Skip to
First	Second	

d) Do you think your action had any results?

	First	Second	
Yes	1	1	e)
No	2⎱	2⎱	f)
DK	8⎰	8⎰	

IF YES AT d)

e) Were you satisfied or dissatisfied with the result
   of your action or did you have mixed feelings?

	First	Second
Satisfied	1	1
Dissatisfied	2	2
Mixed feelings	3	3
Other (SPECIFY) _____	4	4
DK	8	8

	Col./ Code		Skip to
	First	Second	

f) How much effort did it take... READ OUT ...

	First	Second
...a lot,	1	1
some,	2	2
very little,	3	3
or, none at all?	4	4
Other (SPECIFY) _____	5	5

g) Did the action involve you personally in a lot of argument or conflict with other people?

	First	Second
Yes	1	1
No	2	2
Other (SPECIFY) _____	3	3
DK	8	8

h) Did taking the action increase your knowledge of how politics works?

	First	Second
Yes	1	1
No	2	2
Other (SPECIFY) _____	3	3
DK	8	8

i) And did it give you a more favourable or a less favourable impression of how politics works, or did it make no difference?

	First	Second
More favourable	1	1
Less favourable	2	2
No difference	3	3
Other (SPECIFY) _____	4	4
DK	8	8

j) Were you trying to put a message across to some person, group or organisation when you took the action?

	First	Second	Skip to
Yes	1	1	k)
No	2⎱	2⎱	l)
Other (SPECIFY) _____	3⎰	3⎰	

IF YES AT j)

k) Would you say that you got the message across... READ OUT ...

	First	Second
...very well,	1	1
fairly well,	2	2
not very well,	3	3
or, not at all well?	4	4
DK	8	8

l) If a similar situation arose again, would you take the same action, some other action, or would you do nothing

	First	Second
Same	1	1
Some other	2	2
Both same and some other	3	3
Do nothing?	4	4
Other (SPECIFY) _____	5	5
DK	8	8

REPEAT (a)–(l) FOR 'SECOND' ACTION, THEN GO TO Q.54
IF NO 'SECOND ACTION', GO TO Q.54

	Col./ Code	Skip to

54 a) INTERVIEWER TO CHECK FROM Q.53

Blocking traffic with a street   – was asked about at Q.53   1   Q.55
demonstration: – was *not* asked about at Q.53   2 }
    – Q.53 was not asked of this Respondent   3 }   b)

IF CODES 2–3

b) Supposing you were to join in blocking traffic with
a street demonstration, how much effort would it
take … READ OUT …

      … a lot,   1 }
      some,   2 }
      very little,   3 }   c)
      or, none at all?   4 }

     (Respondent said would never block traffic)   5   Q.55
      Depends   6 }
Other (SPECIFY)_____   7 }   c)
      DK   8 }

IF CODES 1–4 OR 6–8 AT b) ASK c)–e)

c) Do you think it would involve you personally   Yes   1
in a lot of argument and conflict with other people?   No   2
Other (SPECIFY)_____   3
      DK   8

d) Would you expect it to increase your knowledge of
how politics works?   Yes   1
      No   2
      Depends   3
Other (SPECIFY)_____   4
      DK   8

e) If you were to block traffic with a street demonstration,
would you expect to get the result you wanted?   Yes   1
      No   2
      Depends   3
Other (SPECIFY)_____   4
      DK   8

PARTY ALLEGIANCE

ASK ALL

55 a) How interested are you in politics and national
affairs: are you … READ OUT …   … very interested,   1
      fairly,   2
      slightly,   3
      or, not at all interested?   4
Other (SPECIFY)_____   5

b) About how often do you talk about politics and
national affairs with others … READ OUT …   … very often,   1
      fairly often,   2
      occasionally,   3
      sometimes,   4
      or, never?   5
      DK   8

	Col./ Code	Skip to

56 a) Some people say they *understand* the way British
politics works. Others say that it is too
difficult for them to follow. Thinking about
yourself, would you say that you find British
politics … READ OUT …

	Col./Code	Skip to
…too difficult to follow,	1	
a bit difficult to follow,	2	
fairly easy to follow,	3	
or, very easy to follow?	4	
DK	8	

b) Talking to people, we find that some have a
favourable impression of how British politics
works while others have an *unfavourable*
impression. Is your own view of how British
politics works … READ OUT …

	Col./Code	Skip to
…generally favourable,	1	
generally unfavourable,	2	
or, neither one way nor the other?	3	
DK	8	

57 a) Generally speaking, do you think of yourself as Conservative,
Labour, Liberal, Social Democrat (SCOTLAND: Scottish
Nationalist/WALES: Plaid Cymru) or *what*?

IF 'ALLIANCE', PROBE: Liberal or Social Democrat?

ONE CODE UNDER (a)

IF 'NONE/DK', CODES 09 OR 98

b) Do you generally think of yourself as a
little closer to one of the Parties than the others
IF YES: Which Party?
IF 'ALLIANCE' PROBE: Liberal or
Social Democrat?
ONE CODE UNDER (b)
Other (SPECIFY): a) _____
b) _____

	(a)	(b)	
Conservative	01	01	
Labour	02	02	
Liberal	03	03	
Social Democrat	04	04	
Scottish Nationalist	05	05	
Plaid Cymru	06	06	c)
	07	07	
Alliance (AFTER PROBE)	08	08	
None/No	09	09	
DK	98	98	

05 }c) (under (a)), 09 98 }b) (under (a))

IF PARTY CODED AT a)

c) Would you call yourself very strong _____
(QUOTE PARTY AT a), fairly strong, or
not very strong

		Col./Code	Skip to
Very strong		1	
Fairly strong		2	Q.58
Not very strong		3	
DK		8	

58 a) Are you a member of a political Party?
IF YES: Which one? DO NOT PROMPT
INCLUDE PEOPLE WHO HAVE TEMPORARILY NOT PAID SUBS,
BUT INTEND TO THIS YEAR, AND MEMBERS OF
YOUTH WING OF PARTY
Other (SPECIFY) _____
IF 'LABOUR'

	Col./Code	Skip to
No	00	Q.60
Yes: – Conservative	01	Q.59
– Labour	02	b)
– Liberal	03	
– Social Democratic	04	
– Scottish National	05	Q.59
– Plaid Cymru	06	
	07	

b) Are you a member of the Labour Party through
a trade union, or did you join as an
individual member?

	Col./Code	Skip to
Trade Union	1	
Individual	2	Q.59
Both	3	

	Col./Code	Skip to

IF PARTY MEMBER

59 Do you ever attend Party meetings?

IF YES: About how many do you attend each year?

WRITE IN: ☐☐

Never attend	00
Varies	96
DK/CR	98

60 a) Was your *father* a member of a Political Party when you were in your early teens? RECORD UNDER (a)

b) And was your *mother* a member of a Political Party then? RECORD UNDER (b)

(a) (b)

	Father	Mother
Yes	1	1
No	2	2
DK	8	8

c) And at that time, when you were in your early teens, were either of your parents active in local community affairs?

Yes – Mother	1
Yes – Father	2
Yes – both	3
No	4
Not applicable	5
DK/CR	8

CAMPAIGNING

CARD F (BLUE)

61 Now I'd like to ask about campaigning for political parties and candidates. Please tell me from the top of the card, how often over the past five years or so you have done each of the activities I will read out. Then, from the bottom of the card, whether you would consider doing it in the future.

ASK (a) AND (b) FOR EACH ITEM LISTED. RECORD ANSWERS IN GRID

a) In the *past*, have you _____ (READ OUT ITEM)? RECORD UNDER (a)

b) In the future, how likely are you to consider doing so? RECORD UNDER (b)

(a) (b)

	PAST: Now & then	Only once	Never	FUTURE: Consider: Certainly	Probably	Might	Never	DK
	Often							
1 Canvassed or knocked on doors for a candidate or political party?	1	2	3	4	1	2	3	4	8
2 Attempted to change the minds of family, friends or workmates about how to vote?	1	2	3	4	1	2	3	4	8
Attended a campaign meeting or rally for a Party or candidate	1	2	3	4	1	2	3	4	8
4 Done clerical, or office work for a political party or candidate?	1	2	3	4	1	2	3	4	8
5 Been involved in fund-raising for a political Party or candidate?	1	2	3	4	1	2	3	4	8

	Col./ Code	Skip to
62 INTERVIEWER TO CHECK FROM Q.61		
– Respondent has *not done any* of the activities (Code 4 only ringed at Q.61a)	1	Q.67
– Respondent has done *only one* activity (only one Code 1, 2 or 3 at Q.61a)	2	Q.64
– Respondent has done *more than one* activity (more than one Code 1, 2 or 3 at Q.61a)	3	Q.63

IF CODE 3 AT Q.62

CARD K

63 Listed on this card are the activities we have been talking about.
Thinking only of the ones you have done, which *one* have you done *most often*? RECORD BELOW

(SELECTED ACTIVITY)		
Canvassing or doorknocking	1	
Attempting to change minds of family, friends, workmates	2	
Attending a campaign meeting or rally	3	
Doing clerical or office work for a political Party or Candidate	4	
Fund raising for a political Party or Candidate	5	

64 a) Can I just check, have you told me about (ACTIVITY) earlier in the interview?		
Yes	1	b)
No	2	Q.65

IF YES

b) DELETE ACTIVITY AT Q.63 AND ASK: 'Which activity have you done next most often?' RECORD ABOVE AT Q.63

If not done any other activity	1	Q.67

SELECTED CAMPAIGNING ACTIVITY

65 Now I'd like to ask a bit more about_____(SELECTED ACTIVITY AT Q.63 OR 'ONLY' ACTIVITY, CODE 2 Q.62

a) WRITE IN ACTIVITY:_____
(IF ACTIVITY DONE MORE THAN ONCE, ASK ABOUT MOST RECENT OCCASION)

b) How much effort did it take…READ OUT…		
…a lot,	1	
some,	2	
very little,	3	
or, none at all?	4	
Other (SPECIFY)_____	5	
DK/CR	8	

c) Did it involve you personally in a lot of argument or conflict with other people?		
Yes	1	
No	2	
Other (SPECIFY)_____	3	
DK/CR	8	

e) Did it increase your knowledge of how politics works?		
Yes	1	
No	2	
Other (SPECIFY)_____	3	
DK	8	

f) Did taking the action give you a more favourable or a less favourable impression of how politics works, or did it make no difference?		
More favourable	1	
Less favourable	2	
No difference	3	
Other (SPECIFY)_____	4	
DK	8	

	Col./ Code	Skip to

g) Would you say that what you did helped to get the Party's or Candidate's message across... READ OUT...

		Col./ Code	Skip to
	a lot,	1	
	some,	2	
	a little,	3	
	or, not at all?	4	
Other (SPECIFY)_____		5	
	DK	8	

66 INTERVIEWER CHECK:

		Col./ Code	Skip to
Respondent – *was* asked about canvassing/door knocking at Q.65		1	Q.68
– *was not* asked about canvassing/door knocking at Q.65		2	Q.67

IF CODE 1 AT Q.62 OR CODE 1 AT Q.64b) OR CODE 2 AT Q.66

67 Supposing you were to take part in canvassing or knocking on doors for a political Party or Candidate –
How much effort would it take... READ OUT...

		Col./ Code	Skip to
	...a lot,	1	
	some,	2	
	very little,	3	b)
	or, none at all?	4	
(Respondent said would never canvass etc)		5	Q.68
	Depends	6	
Other (SPECIFY)_____		7	b)
	DK	8	
	spare		
		CARD 08	

IF CODES 1–4 OR 6–8 AT a) ASK b)–d)

b) Do you think it would involve you personally in a lot of argument or conflict with other people?

		Col./ Code	Skip to
	Yes	1	
	No	2	
Other (SPECIFY)_____		3	
	DK	8	

c) Would you expect it to increase your knowledge of how politics works?

		Col./ Code	Skip to
	Yes	1	
	No	2	
	Depends	3	
Other (SPECIFY)_____		4	
	DK	8	

d) Do you think that canvassing or knocking on doors for a candidate or political Party would help to get the message across to the voters ... READ OUT...

		Col./ Code	Skip to
	...a lot,	1	
	some,	2	
	a little,	3	
	or, not at all?	4	
Other (SPECIFY)_____		5	
	DK	8	

	Col./ Code	Skip to

VOTING

ASK ALL

Now I'd like to ask about voting.

68 a) Could you think first of the election to the European Parliament which was held this June (1984). Talking to people about the European Parliament election we have found that a lot of them did not vote. How about you? Did you vote in that election?

	Col./Code	Skip to
Yes	1	b)
No	2	Q.69
Too young to vote	3	Q.71

IF YES

b) Which Party did you vote for in the European Parliament election?

	Col./Code
Conservative	01
Labour	02
Liberal	03
SDP/Social Democrat	04
SDP/Liberal Alliance	05
Scottish National	06
Plaid Cymru	07
Other (SPECIFY) _____	08
DK/CR	98
Refused	99

69 And now, thinking back to the General Election, in June 1983, when the party leaders included Michael Foot and Margaret Thatcher, which Party did you vote for in that election or perhaps you didn't vote in that election?

	Col./Code	Skip to
Conservative	01	
Labour	02	
Liberal	03	
SDP/Social Democrat	04	Q.71
SDP/Liberal Alliance	05	
Scottish National	06	
Plaid Cymru	07	
Other (SPECIFY) _____	08	
Did not vote	09	Q.70
Too young to vote	10	
DK/CR	98	Q.71
Refused	99	

	Col./ Code	Skip to

IF DID NOT VOTE IN GENERAL ELECTION, CODE 09 AT Q.69

70 a) I'm going to read out a number of reasons that people have given for why they did not vote in the last General Election. Could you tell me, for each reason I read out, whether or not it applied to you.

	Yes applied	No did not	
READ OUT...			
1 ...I could not vote because I was ill	1	2	
2 ...because I was away	1	2	
3 ...because I was too busy	1	2	
4 ...Elections are not important enough to make me bother to vote	1	2	
5 ...my name was not on the Electoral Register where I live	1	2	
6 ...I couldn't get enough information to make a decision about voting	1	2	

b) Were there any other reasons why you didn't vote in the last General Election?	Yes	1	c)
	No	2	Q.71

IF YES

c) What were the reasons? PROBE FULLY. RECORD VERBATIM.

_____

_____

_____

_____

_____

_____

71 a) How much effort does/would it take you to decide which Party to vote for in a General Election... READ OUT ...		
...a lot,	1	
some,	2	
very little,	3	
or, none at all?	4	
Other (SPECIFY) _____	5	
DK	8	

b) And does/would deciding which Party to vote for involve you, personally, in a lot of argument or conflict with other people?		
Yes	1	
No	2	
Other (SPECIFY) _____	3	
DK	8	

							Col./ Code	Skip to

CARD L (GREEN)

72 I'm going to read out some things people have said about General Elections, and I'd like you to tell me, from the card, which statement best describes your own view.

READ OUT EACH ITEM...	Agree strongly	Agree	Disagree	Disagree strongly	Depends	DK
a) Your individual vote can make no difference in a General Election	1	2	3	4	5	8
b) It makes no difference which Party forms the government	1	2	3	4	5	8
c) I feel I have a duty to vote in General Elections	1	2	3	4	5	8
d) General Elections increase voters' knowledge of how politics works	1	2	3	4	5	8
e) General Elections give voters a favourable impression of how politics works	1	2	3	4	5	8

CARD M

73 Now I'd like to ask about local elections. First, could you tell me which of the statements on this card applies to you?

I vote in *every* local election	1
I vote in *most* local elections	2
I vote in only *some* local elections	3
I *never* vote in local elections	4
I am *too young* to vote in local elections	5
DK	8

CARD L (GREEN)

74 And now, some things that people have said about local elections. Would you tell me, from the card, which statement best describes your own view.

READ OUT EACH ITEM...	Agree strongly	Agree	Disagree	Disagree strongly	Depends	DK
a) Your individual vote can make no difference in a Local Election	1	2	3	4	5	8
b) It makes no difference which Party controls the Council	1	2	3	4	5	8
c) I feel I have a duty to vote in Local Elections	1	2	3	4	5	8
d) Local Elections increase voters' knowledge of how politics works	1	2	3	4	5	8
e) Local elections give voters a favourable impression of how politics works	1	2	3	4	5	8

	Col./ Code	Skip to

ASK ALL

CARD N

75 I'm going to read out some things that some people believe a *British Government should do*. For each item can you say whether you feel it is
– very important that it *should be done,*
– fairly important that it *should be done,*
– it does not matter either way,
– fairly important that it *should not be done,*
– very important that it *should not be done.*
If you *don't know* about any of the matters just say so. Now, using one of the answers on the card, what is your view about...

READ OUT...	Very important– should be done	Fairly important– should be done	Does not matter either way	Fairly important– should *not* be done	Very important– should *not* be done
1 ...Building more nuclear power stations	1	2	3	4	5
2 ...Trying to get greater equality of wealth and income in Britain	1	2	3	4	5
3 ...Giving the police more power to deal with protesters and demonstrators	1	2	3	4	5
4 ...Turning more nationalised industries into private businesses	1	2	3	4	5
5 ...Making abortions easier to get for women who want them	1	2	3	4	5
6 ...Giving the public more access to government documents, even if it makes the government's job more difficult	1	2	3	4	5
7 ...Removing nuclear weapons from Britain	1	2	3	4	5
8 ...Making it harder for police and government officials to get hold of confidential information about private individuals	1	2	3	4	5

	Col./Code	Skip to

CARD L (GREEN)

76 Now I'm going to read out some things about work and employment. I'd like you to tell me which of the statements on the card best describes *your* view.

READ OUT...	Agree strongly	Agree	Disagree	Disagree strongly	Other	DK
1 Workers and employees should have more say in how the places where they work are run	1	2	3	4	5	8
2 Women at work should have the same opportunities as men for earnings and promotion	2	2	3	4	5	8
3 Minority racial groups should have favoured treatment in getting employment	1	2	3	4	5	8
4 More jobs should be created even if government spending and taxes rise	1	2	3	4	5	8
5 More workplace training opportunities should be created for young people even if fewer adults are taken on at work	1	2	3	4	5	8

77 Let's say you gave each of the following a mark out of ten according to how satisfied or dissatisfied you are with it. If you are very *dissatisfied* you would give nought out of ten and if you are very *satisfied* you would give ten out of ten. Or you could give any of the marks in between to indicate your view. What mark would you give...READ OUT...

a) the particular district (or borough) council where you live? WRITE IN:

b) the present Conservative government? WRITE IN:

c) the role of the trade union movement in the British economy? WRITE IN:

d) the way that big private businesses and industries are run? WRITE IN:

e) the way government-owned or nationalised industries are run? WRITE IN:

f) Britain's state-run system of health care, pensions and benefits? WRITE IN:

g) Britain's overall form of parliamentary government? WRITE IN:

h) your own standard of living today? WRITE IN:

78 And next could you give a mark out of ten according to how much you favour or oppose the following political parties. The nearer ten, the more you *favour* a party and the nearer nought, the more you *oppose* it. What mark would you give...READ OUT...

CARD 09

a) the National Front WRITE IN:

b) the Communist Party of Great Britain WRITE IN:

c) the Conservative Party WRITE IN:

d) the Labour Party WRITE IN:

e) the Social Democratic Party WRITE IN:

f) the Liberal Party WRITE IN:

g) WALES ONLY: Plaid Cymru/Welsh Nationalists WRITE IN:

h) SCOTLAND ONLY: the Scottish National Party WRITE IN:

				Col./ Code	Skip to

79 Using the statements on the card, how much do you agree or disagree with each of the following:

READ OUT...	Agree strongly	Agree	Disagree	Disagree strongly	Other	DK
a) Individually, people like you can have no influence over Members of Parliament	1	2	3	4	5	8
b) A group of people like you can have no influence over Members of Parliament	1	2	3	4	5	8
c) Most Members of Parliament are out for themselves rather than the public good	1	2	3	4	5	8
d) Most people who are active in local Community groups are out for themselves rather than the public good	1	2	3	4	5	8
e) Most protestors and demonstrators are out for themselves rather than the public good	1	2	3	4	5	8
f) Most local councillors are out for themselves rather than the public good	1	2	3	4	5	8
g) You can generally trust Members of Parliament to do what's right	1	2	3	4	5	8

	Col./ Code	Skip to
80 Do you think that ordinary citizens should have more say in the decisions made by government or are these decisions best left to the elected representatives such as MPs and Local Councillors?		
Ordinary citizens should have more say	1	
Best left to elected representatives	2	
Other (SPECIFY)_____	3	
DK	8	
81 a) You often hear talk about social classes. Do *you* ever think of yourself as belonging to any particular class? No	1	b)
IF YES: Which class is that? Middle class	2⎫	Q.82
Working class	3⎭	
Other (SPECIFY)_____	4⎫	b)
DK	8⎭	
IF CODE 1 OR 4 OR 8		
b) Most people say they belong either to the middle class, or to the working class. If *you* had to make a choice, would you call yourself middle class or working class? Middle	1	
Working	2	
Other (SPECIFY)_____	3	
DK	8	
82 On the whole, do you think there is bound to be conflict between the different social classes or do you think they can get along together without conflict? IF 'BOUND TO BE CONFLICT': a lot of conflict, or just some? A lot of conflict	1	
Just some conflict	2	
Can get along without conflict	3	
No classes/does not apply	4	
DK	8	

Qs. 83–98: Social classification questions.

The full citizen questionnaires and data sets are deposited at the ESRC Data Archive, University of Essex.

Notes

1 Participation and democracy

1. Attempts in the pilot survey to tap the expressive perspective through the questionnaire proved a failure, not meeting with comprehension from our respondents. Whether this is attributable entirely to our own failure or to the infrequency of such conduct amongst the population is hard to say. Clearly, this is an area which requires further investigation.

2 The study of participation and its political context

1. Between 1945 and 1979, references to democracy (including participation and citizen involvement) constituted 2·8% of the content of the manifestos of British political parties. Positive references to decentralisation were a further 2·6%. This compares with 5·1% for social services which was the major issue. (Private communication from Ian Budge.) In general, a concern for democracy, decentralisation and civil liberties is typical of Liberal parties (Budge, Robertson and Hearl 1987:411–2).
2. For a brief but accessible introduction to the theory of sampling whereby this is possible, see Stuart (1962).
3. The same also applies to census information. Though collected about every individual, in its published form it is aggregated, albeit at a relatively low level. But, again, the census is devoid of questions that directly relate to political participation. For an example of census data used for political analysis, see Crewe and Payne (1971).

3 Patterns of political participation

1. In addition to the items listed in chart 3.1, there was a 24th which asked whether the respondent had attempted to 'change the minds of family, friends or workmates about how to vote'. In the subsequent analysis of the structure of participation, this item proved to be unrelated to the remaining body of material and is, therefore, not included amongst those on which the major part of the study is based. However, it will be included as a distinct form of political involvement in certain tables later in the book.
2. A question no doubt arises as to whether every action we describe is to be construed as 'political'. The idea of 'the political' is a contestable matter. Whilst we have taken all such actions which are directed towards public authorities as political, this is not necessarily how such actions are viewed by the respondents themselves. After establishing the nature of actions taken, those interviewed were asked whether they considered such actions 'political'. Overall, only 18·2% actions were so described. Around 40% of contacts with national officials or representatives were seen as political. Working in organised groups (37·8%) and protest

(30·7%) were also relatively politicised but in no case, apart from protest marching, was a majority of actions viewed from a clearly political perspective. It seems that the viewpoints of political scientists and the public about the nature of politics diverge markedly. In what follows, we have taken public participation to be, in a wide sense, 'political'. For further discussion, see Parry and Moyser (1988).

3. The observant reader will note that, compared with the true turnout figures, our respondents appear to have over-reported voting by about 10%. This seems consistent with other surveys on elections in this country and elsewhere (see, for example, Sigelman 1982). However, Swaddle and Heath (1989) indicate that the extent of actual over-reporting in the comparable 1987 British Election Study was only 3%. The remaining discrepancy could be accounted for by other technical factors, such as the redundancy rate of the electoral register and a slight sample bias. Whether over-reporting applies to other forms of participation is difficult to say because equivalent population rates for many of the activities are unknown. However, inspection of results from other election surveys in Britain suggest that the campaign participation rates given in the table are entirely in line with those. Similarly, figures obtained for various forms of contacting and protest activities are broadly consistent with those reported in the British Social Attitudes surveys (Jowell and Airey 1984) and in research conducted into local government and politics (Young 1986; MORI 1986). Our own questionnaire, moreover, contained a number of internal checks on the accuracy of responses. In particular, a substantial number of the activities an individual mentioned were followed up by questions asking about the subject matter of the action, the outcome and the general experiences of the participant.

4. Unfortunately, in making these comparisons, we were unable to incorporate references here and elsewhere to the study of participation in West Germany, the Netherlands and the USA in the period 1979–81 reported in M. Kent Jennings, J. van Deth *et al.*, *Continuities in Political Action: A Longitudinal Study of Political Orientations in Three Western Democracies*, Walter de Gruyter, Berlin, 1989. This volume reached us as our volume was going to press and too late for incorporation of cross-references.

5. A rigorous cross-national analysis of participation rates would require merging of data files from the different countries involved and then looking at the total pooled information. This, in turn, would require that comparable (equivalent) questions and response categories be established for all variables included, something that cannot normally be done unless the data are gathered in the context of one explicitly cross-national research project which is not the case here.

6. At this point, we examined the possibility that the items of participation would not just group themselves into a number of sets, but that each set would form cumulative or hierarchical scales. If this were so, we could identify the 'easy' and 'hard' actions in each and therefore have additional information about the internal relationships of each 'mode'. Perhaps more importantly, we also looked specifically at the possibility that all or most of the items, would also form a single cumulative scale which would present a very different picture of the structure of participation from that derived from our factor analysis. Barnes, Kaase *et al.* (1979), for example, claim in their study to have found such scales, thus challenging the multi-factor model of the Verba and Nie team (1971; 1972; 1978). Notwithstanding the fact that Britain appeared amongst the countries studied by Barnes, Kaase *et al.*, our results failed to support the cumulative scale model. The 23 participatory acts did not come anywhere near fitting together in a meaningful single overall cumulative scale. Nor did any other overall scale which might, in procrustean fashion, have been formed by dropping one or two 'misfits' from the total set. Furthermore, even the specific groupings, revealed by the factor analysis to have especially strong empirical bonds between them, failed the test – with one exception noted below. Thus, if there are 'easy' and 'hard' political actions, then the judgements about which are easy and which hard seem clearly to vary considerably from person to person – far too

much for a single hierarchical pattern to be established and imposed on the data. The one exception, however, was voting – ironically the item excluded as a misfit by Barnes, Kaase *et al.* (1979:86). Our results show that most of our respondents implicitly agreed in their consistent turnout patterns that voting in the European election was 'hard' and voting in the 1983 General Election was 'easy'. Local voting was, therefore, in between. We do not regard this as a finding that adds much to our map. It would have been very different if the other modes, or the full set had come out as the three voting items did. For a brief further discussion of results, see Moyser, Parry and Day (1986:16–17).

7. Verba and Nie (1972) were able to account for a higher proportion of variance (61 %) with only four factors. In part, this indeed reflects a slightly higher degree of commonality between the participation items they included – as indicated by somewhat stronger inter-item correlations. On the other hand, this is itself arguably the product of the narrower scope of their coverage – for example, excluding anything to do with political protest.

8. This practice of standardising means to zero and standard deviations to 100 is also followed by Verba and Nie (1972:128, 1978:63). For a further discussion of how means, medians and standard deviations are calculated, see, for example, Palumbo (1969:32–54).

9. This can also be seen if we simply count up the number of vote actions in our inventory. The maximum of 3 was scored by 41·7 %; 35·0 % scored 2; 12·9 % scored 1 and 10·4 % scored 0.

10. In fact, the 'norm' in voting is to score a maximum of 3! See note 8 above.

11. Counts for the items in the campaigning scale, for example, showed the following pattern:

Score	% of respondents
0	87·7
1	7·8
2	1·9
3	0·9
4	1·6

4 Individual resources

1. It could even be suggested that a resource-based analysis of participation is as old as political science. It has been proposed that Aristotle's distinction between the *aporoi* and the *euporoi* should be translated as 'those without resources' and 'those with resources' (see Sinclair 1988:121–3).

2. In implying a chain of causality here that moves from resources to participation we do not wish to deny the possibility that participation affects resources. Indeed, as we have noted, if participation is about the defence or promotion of interests, we would expect, assuming participation is effective, that there is such a connection. But, in looking at the question of why people participate, it is appropriate here to focus on the first causal effect and to leave consideration of the reverse relation to our chapter on benefits (chapter 12).

3. In a national survey conducted at the time of the 1987 General Election, 17 % of respondents claimed to own shares or unit trusts (see Miller *et al.* 1990:chapter 2).

4. For figure 4.1 and similar figures and tables throughout the book, we have used a statistical technique known as Multiple Classification Analysis (MCA) (see Andrews *et al.* 1969; see also *SPSS-X User's Guide*, 2nd ed., 1986:461–2).

5. The eta statistic is the equivalent of a simple beta in a bivariate regression. However, because the independent variable (here education) is treated as a series of categories, eta does not assume there to be necessarily a linear relationship present. In other words, it allows for the possibility of more complex non-linear associations which, as the analysis progresses in this and subsequent chapters, is a crucially important requirement. There are, however, times when the effect does appear to approximate a simple linear relationship and here we also state the value of the linear correlation statistic r. This measure of association, unlike eta, can take

on both negative and positive values, ranging from $-1\cdot0$ to $+1\cdot0$, depending on whether the linear relationship it represents is itself negative or positive in character. Where eta and r are very similar in magnitude, the relationship can be taken to be virtually linear. Where they sharply diverge (r being substantially less than eta), then this can be taken as evidence of a significant relationship that is not strictly linear in form.

6. Here, and throughout the book, we confront a common problem in data analysis – the need to separate out the effect of one variable upon another (or simply their mutual association) from the possibly confounding effects of other factors. This is achieved through what is known as 'statistical controlling'. In effect, we isolate the relationship of interest by making adjustments to hold constant the effects of other variables. These other variables are thereby 'controlled' – their influence is systematically taken into account in order to ensure that they are not spuriously affecting the relationship of central concern. How this is done is beyond the scope of this footnote, but for a lucid discussion, see Weisberg and Bowen (1977:ch. 12) and Rosenberg (1968).

7. The beta statistic is the equivalent, within multiple classification analysis, of a standardised partial regression coefficient, otherwise referred to as a partial beta or, more simply, beta. Here, the magnitude of this beta, summarising the strength of the relationship (linear or non-linear) between education and participation after making allowance for other resources is $0\cdot15$. This is, as noted, only half the apparent strength of the simple bivariate relationship, when other resource effects were not taken into account, represented by the value of eta ($0\cdot29$).

8. For a different line of reasoning, see Cotgrove (1982).

9. It should be added, however, that the results from the survey of the British General Election of 1987 suggest that graduate turnout did not deviate in the manner found in the present study (private communication from Anthony Heath).

10. For a more extended discussion of the analysis of the relationship between unemployment and protest, see chapter 6.

5 Group resources

1. It should be noted that the level of political discussion in the group does not measure the individual respondent's participation in those discussions. Hence it is appropriate to construe it as part of the member's resource base rather than as political participation itself. See also the comments on political discussion in chapter 3.

2. An important question is what happens to the party ties when activity rates are equalised and there the answer is that relatively little changes. Equalisation seems to affect participation in two ways. First, Labour ties become the most potent cues for voting, exceeding those of the other two, whereas, without adjustment, Labour ties were the least potent. Secondly, the campaign rates of Conservative adherents move past those of Labour members, but remain behind the 'Other' category.

3. Verba and Nie obtain the same result (1972:131–2).

6 Economic location

1. In dichotomising our sample in this way, we do not wish to suggest that the line can necessarily be drawn so sharply. For example, some senior executives become unemployed for a time yet can sustain a fairly high standard of living through generous severance payments. Equally, there is an important difference more generally between short-term and long-term unemployment, and being in a household with at least one wage earner, or not. However, the survey is a rendition of circumstances at the time of interview and it would take a more specialised survey than ours to examine subtler nuances than the basic distinction which we utilise here. See, for example, K. Schlozman and S. Verba (1979).

2. It is possible that the seeming mildness of unemployment as a stimulus to political action may

in fact understate the true strength of the connection. For at least some of the unemployed, our five-year time scale regarding political action would include a period before the relevant individuals became unemployed. Similarly, some of those registered as employed would have been unemployed within that five-year time frame. These effects may have attenuated the connection we have discerned.

3. We are indebted to Jenny Chapman for pointing out to us the range of possible interactions between unemployment and participation. Some activists may even choose to remain unemployed or, alternatively, find re-employment difficult.

4. In our survey, only 6·2% of respondents, if pressed, would think of themselves in other than 'middle' or 'working' class terms. It should be added, however, that initially 62·3% refused to think of themselves as belonging to a class. Clearly, at this cultural level, class now has less saliency, even if the idea of two categories ultimately retains its grip.

5. There are also more refined seven-category and eleven-category versions available, also developed by Goldthorpe. The latter will be used in the present analysis particularly when a fine-grained distinction is required at the top and bottom end of the five-class measure. A rival three-class scheme has been advanced by Robertson (1984:107–25) and a four-class scheme by Dunleavy and Husbands (1985:121–4).

6. The skilled are distinguished from the semi- and unskilled in the eleven-category version. Agricultural workers are also separated out, but they are very few in number.

7. Again, in the eleven-fold version, those with and without employees, and farmers, can all be separated. This did not seem necessary in the analysis, especially bearing in mind the small numbers involved.

8. This may well arise because they would themselves have come mainly from working class homes when they were younger, and acquiring formal educational qualifications. Only in adult life would they then have been 'promoted' into the foremen class, and achieved wealth and position in organisations commensurate with their position within the broader ranks of the manual stratum.

9. Taylor-Gooby (1986) also provides a useful review of the theories of consumption cleavages and of the views of critics (e.g. Franklin and Page 1984).

10. The one underlying factor extracted explained 41·9% of the total variance of all four. Amongst them, however, the transport indicator was the most central (with a factor 'loading' of 0·77), followed by housing (0·70), health (0·60) and education (0·49).

11. This linkage between wealth and private consumption is reflected in the construction of the two scales. In both cases, two of the four items are in common: car ownership (or access) and housing. In the latter case, the two usages overlap in that those who own their own home outright, or on a mortgaged basis, count as having wealth as well as being in the private sector. They are counter-balanced by council tenants being public sector and not wealthy. The only difference concerns those who rent privately or from a housing association who line up with the council tenants for wealth purposes but with home owners, etc. for the sectoral indicator. However, these are only 5·8% of the total sample.

12. We have summed the squared betas which gives a measure of the additive effects of all four, net of resource influences.

7 Personal factors

1. Men's standard deviation is 5 ± 107; i.e. the range is -102 to $+112$; women's standard deviation is -4 ± 93; i.e. range -97 to $+89$.
2. Standard deviations for 19-item scale: men $\pm 2 \cdot 33$; women $\pm 2 \cdot 14$.
3. Excluding the widowed (male and female) as being largely outside the age bracket 23–49 which we are considering here.
4. 59·4% of single parents were female; 40·6% male.

5. Given that only one man was married and simultaneously looking after the home and having the rent or mortgage paid by his spouse, this is perhaps some indication of the difficulties and possible gender biases of using information on joint incomes to assess wealth.

6. The low activity of those under twenty would be even more pronounced if the three voting items were included because many of them would not have had an opportunity to cast a ballot as a consequence of being too young to exercise the franchise.

7. There appears to be distinctly greater stability of residence in Britain than in USA. According to Verba and Nie (1972:145, fn. 4), 45% of Americans under 26 had lived in the community less than 3 years, whereas in our study, only 35·4% of the under-26s had been residents for less than five years.

8. In Verba and Nie's study, the peak of political activity came somewhat later – in the period 41–50 for the unadjusted figures (1972:139). However, this shift of about five years is probably explained by their not having included direct action which peaks in Britain, both adjusted and unadjusted, at age 21–22. If America exhibits approximately the same pattern, which the evidence suggests it would (Barnes, Kaase *et al.* 1979:108), then the peak for an overall participation that included direct action, and therefore was comparable with ours, would shift forward, leaving both countries in a very similar position.

9. Of ten hours a week or more.

10. For campaigning, 50 to 54 is the high point; for voting there is no one peak; on an unadjusted basis, there is a tie between 50–54 and 60–64, for rates corrected for resources, 65–69. See the discussion in the following section on old age.

11. This score entailed positive responses to 16 out of our 23 item battery.

12. Verba and Nie (1972:44) seem to find that education does make a difference, although income, a more life-cycle sensitive element, makes more.

13. Exactly the same pattern also applied to collective action.

14. This also seems to be true in the USA. Verba and Nie (1972:144) find that, on their scales, the over-65s score −17 (overall) and +2 (voting). Once more, life-cycle (income) counts for more than education (generation).

8 Political outlooks

1. Some scholars wish to extend the concept to include behaviour itself. But this conceptual stretching is one of the ways in which it becomes too all-embracing, and hence too blunt an instrument. We prefer, therefore, to maintain a strict demarcation between attitudes and behaviour.

2. Such outlooks would, of course, also shape the character of the polity as a whole, giving rise to the idea that the presence of a 'civic culture' is an important requisite in sustaining a liberal democracy. Since the original work of Almond and Verba, an enormous literature has grown up on the subject, including a 'revisited' and updated review of that first study (Almond and Verba 1980; see also Topf 1989a and 1989b). Political outlooks, in short, have become part not only of the 'standard model' (Verba and Nie 1972) of participation, but of the workings of democracy itself (see also Inglehart 1988).

3. A fifth item concerned with ease of understanding national politics was included but contributed very little to the scale, although it was to be, in a different form, more significant in the local efficacy scale employed in chapter 14.

4. They also refer to this as a sense of civic competence, or as citizen competence; not to be confused with political competence, which is about *actual* influence or subject competence, which is about competency in the administrative realm as subject.

5. Muller reserves the term 'political efficacy' to apply to 'measures of the comprehensibility and responsiveness of government to citizens in general', as distinct from the citizen's estimate of his or her own capacities to get the government to respond (see also Milbrath and Goel 1977:58). Although his analysis suggests a difference between the two, we feel it would be

confusing and inappropriate not to use political efficacy in the way Almond and Verba intended. For a further analysis of the concept, see Balch (1974).

6. It might be noted, in this connection, that Conway defines internal political efficacy as 'the belief that one can understand politics and government and that political events can be influenced by the activities of individuals like oneself'. However, our analysis suggests that this conflates two relatively weakly related elements – understanding and subjective competence. The loading of an item that tapped the former element, the perceived ease or difficulty in understanding how British politics works, on the political efficacy scale was 0·43, considerably less than the four principal items.

7. For a discussion of this point – of citizens as 'controllers' rather than 'participants' – which may be part of the difference here, see Parry and Moyser (1984).

8. The results showed that they did indeed form a single scale, to which all contributed to an approximately equal degree; factor loadings were: individual influence (0·71), group influence (0·72), general election vote (0·70) and local election vote (0·70).

9. I.e. +287 is nearer the fulcrum of the ladder (zero) than −349. The reasons are analogous to those discussed in chapter 3.

10. In one respect, however, the relationship between voting and efficacy is very different and that is in the specification of which efficacy items are the most critical. Here, by far the most important is the sense of the effectiveness of one's vote in local elections (beta = 0·20) which is three times stronger than in any other mode. Interestingly enough, the sense of the effectiveness of one's vote in a General Election remains very modest (beta = 0·05).

11. Barnes, Kaase *et al.* (1979) only report betas ('slope coefficients') not the detailed relationships for each item in their scale. But we assume that these were consistently linear.

12. Some scholars see cynicism as ultimately a syndrome associated with political alienation and anomie, although that widens, and can consequently blur, the perspective. For a critical discussion, see Hart (1978:ch. 1); cf. Citrin *et al.* (1975), Parry (1976).

13. A judgement also true of local versus national government in general. See table 8.3 and chapter 17.

14. But, as Hart notes, the presence of significant levels of distrust in the British political culture may not be a very recent phenomenon (see Hart 1978:78–9).

15. But for the difficulties of doing so, see Hart (1978:ch. 2).

16. Factor loadings were: MPs out for themselves 0·83; local councillors out for themselves 0·81; community activists out for themselves 0·74; trust MPs (−)0·56; 55·2% of total item variance accounted for.

17. This theoretical merger tends, however, to blunt the power of two well-developed and well-defined concepts. See, for example, Gamson (1968) and Hart (1978:17).

18. The multiple r in table 8.4 is 0·272 compared with 0·421 in table 8·2.

19. It should be noted, however, that if graduates are distinguished according to their wealth, then the poorest amongst them, falling into the 'next poorest 19%' category, have an average cynicism score of −60. This is much lower than any other group of graduates higher up the wealth scale. Though very few in number (10), they may suggest one combination of circumstances that does lead to very negative outlooks. See also the discussion of graduate voting turnout in chapter 4. It should be noted, however, that the strongest effect for education by itself is +25 for those with 'O' level qualifications (not reported in the table).

20. Those with just one tie have an adjusted score of −12.

21. The significance of the middle cynicism category will be discussed further below.

22. This does not necessarily imply, however, that a recognition of a duty in this regard translates into action. Over 80% believed there was a duty to vote in local elections, which is well in excess of any actual turnout.

9 Party and values

1. For a general review, see Nie, Verba and Petrocik 1979; Weisberg 1983; Asher 1984; ch. 3; Niemi and Weisberg 1984; Harrop and Miller 1987. For applications to Britain and critical reviews, see Butler and Stokes 1974; Budge, Crewe and Fairlie 1976; Robertson 1976; Crewe, Särlvik and Alt 1977; Crewe 1982, 1984; Särlvik and Crewe 1983; Alt 1984.

2. In Scotland we added Scottish Nationalist, and in Wales, Plaid Cymru.

3. Of course, time and events have moved on within the Liberal Party since our survey, but we are dealing with the period when they were in an alliance with the Social Democratic Party.

4. Weisberg (1983) rightly notes, in the American context at least, the necessity to distinguish between 'negative' independents who are uninterested and uninvolved in politics and 'positive' independents who expressly engage in politics on a non-partisan basis. In Britain, however, there is no equivalent tradition of the American 'independent', at least at the level of the mass voter. The nearest is the notion of the 'floating voter' which does not conjure up a sense of positive involvement outside of party. Hence, British studies have not pursued the distinction. It may be important to note, however, that our non-partisans seem, in aggregate, to act very much as 'negative' rather than 'positive' independents. This would seem to support the view that the distinction is not a vital one in the British context.

5. As noted in table 9.1, the size of the non-partisans depends on definitions. If we include leaners and don't knows, the proportion doubles to around 18·5%. This matches, near enough, the figures cited by Crewe (1984) and Alt (1984), but at the expense of including individuals who do, when pressed, express some weak partisan loyalties. The 9% quoted in table 9.1 is, therefore, perhaps a measure of 'core non-partisans'.

6. The American pattern of partisan dealignment is different. There, both levels and strengths of attachment fell (see Beck 1984).

7. Figure 9.1 no doubt reflects in part the differences between members. But, in so far as few in any party were members relative to those with an identification, the result cannot simply be the product of differences at that level.

8. It is interesting to note that in Verba and Nie's study (1972:227) a similar reversal took place when values were included. The Republican Party lead of 18 points, in other words, was turned into a deficit of 6 points.

9. Small numbers required that we combined very and fairly strongly committed individuals into one category.

10. Very weak and very strong Conservative partisans also vote much more frequently, on an adjusted basis, compared with Labour supporters. Amongst very strong partisans, the gap in favour of Conservatives is 74 points on the campaign scale and 12 points on the voting scale.

11. Controlling for values does reduce the campaign score to -22, the voting rate remaining unchanged.

12. The contrast between the propensity to direct action on the part of very strong and very weak partisans is a striking 81 points. The score for Conservatives is -34 and for Labour $+47$. It is possible that the American finding that Republicans were overall more prone to participate than Democrats arises from the fact that the Verba and Nie (1972) analysis did not include direct action to which Republicans, like British Conservatives, would have been expected to be averse.

13. It should be noted, however, that in the 1987 Election, there was less difference between the parties in the rate at which candidates' addresses mentioned law and order (see Butler and Kavanagh 1988:221).

14. This principal components analysis resulted in 42·7% of total item variance being accounted for by the one dimension.

15. This seems also to be true of party members. Numbers are small, but the Conservative members scored -102 (N = 37) and Labour members $+114$ (N = 24), amongst whom the six Labour members through trades unions were as left-wing as the individual members ($+117$

to +112). It is also interesting to note, therefore, that in both parties, members are no more 'extreme', and possibly less, than those larger numbers that merely have a strong self-identity with each party. This seems not to be so in the United States, at least in the 1950s (see McClosky, Hoffman and O'Hara 1960).

16. A detailed study of hyper-activists within the SDP, the 421 members of its Council for Social Democracy, showed that about 58% had been Labour sympathisers. The party was not, therefore, simply a splinter from Labour because there were minorities from the Conservatives and from no party at all. Nevertheless, Labour was the dominant source of recruitment (see Döring 1983).

17. In America, a similar connection between non-partisanship and a mild rightist stance has been detected (see Levitin and Miller 1979:757; see also Flanigan and Zingale 1983:111).

18. It is notable that voting has the highest association with left–right outlooks (beta = 0·17), strengthening the suggestion made earlier that voting is more a matter of outlook than of resource background.

19. Some caution may be required in interpreting the precise strength of this result since the question did not, unlike the others, state or imply an alternative position or the costs that might be entailed.

20. The factor loadings were 0·77 for 'Giving the public more access to documentation...'; 0·71 for 'Workers and employees should have more say...'; 0·65 for '...ordinary citizens should have more say...'. Overall, the scale explained 50·1% of the variation across the three items.

10 Who are the political activists?

1. As in earlier chapters, the results are those derived from a series of multiple classification analyses, a multivariate technique which can accommodate categorical independent variables with varied linear and non-linear effects on participation. However, there are technical limitations which constrain the number of these predictor variables that can be included at any one time (ten plus a further ten covariates). Equally important in such large-scale analyses is the cumulative effect of missing data. Unless special provision is made, this can pose considerable problems. In the present case, the extent of the problem varied from one mode to another, dependent upon the range of significant variables thrown up and included in subsequent runs. This is because some variables, particularly scales combining a wide set of attitudinal items, have higher missing data rates than other single item variables where 'don't know' or 'it depends' is an uncommon response – like gender for example!

2. As cluster analysis results can vary according to the choice of particular computing algorithms, an extensive investigation was undertaken of this point. Two different cluster routines were utilised, CLUSTAN (see Wishart 1982) and a Census Classification Programme (Openshaw n.d.). Using the CLUSTAN package, results from both hierarchical fusion and iterative relocation techniques were produced and evaluated. Options allowing for different treatments of missing data and the handling of difficult to classify cases were explored. Similarly, varying measures of distance, on which the allocation of cases to particular clusters is decided, were also deployed. However, it turned out that these various combinations of options and approaches produced very stable and consistent results. Regardless of the precise method used, the same general pattern nearly always emerged, although specific individual cases might be located in varying clusters. The same applied to the more limited options contained in the Census Classification Programme. The attraction of the latter was that, at the time, it alone could handle the full set of 1,578 cases. In the end, therefore, we used this programme to produce the cluster results analysed in the chapter, results based upon sequential assignment of cases, followed by relocation, using a squared euclidean measure of distance. Again, however, both random and sequential allocation produced the same pattern, so either could have been used.

11 Agendas and political action

1. The formula for over- and under-representation is that employed by Verba and Nie (1972:96) to calculate proportions of persons within their categories of activists:

$$PR = \frac{Y_i - X_i}{X_i} \times 100$$

where PR = ratio of over- or under-representation

Y_i = % of issue mentions in category Y_1
X_i = % of issue mentions overall.

12 Do participants get what they want? The costs and benefits of participation

1. In this chapter and the next, protest actions are those listed under this category in chart 3.1 and table 3.1. Group actions are those similarly listed. Thus, protest actions and group actions are not precisely equivalent to direct action and collective action as examined in earlier chapters (see also chart 3.2).

13 Learning from political participation

1. This question was asked, in the case of the prime issue, only of those who had identified their action as 'political'. In the other cases, the actions concerned were described in the question as 'political'.
2. Voting is discussed separately.
3. In the analysis of variance, the standard set of participatory resource variables are included with the addition of the class variable. The analysis reported here was attempted with and without the inclusion of the class measure. The effect of high levels of education is increased in the model when the class measure is included. This suggests that when we allow for the higher class of the better educated, their propensity to learn from political participation is even greater.
4. Class is incorporated in the analysis as a control but the table itself reports the standard set of resource factors.
5. To some extent, the high figures may, however, result from a different question format. Respondents were asked whether they agreed strongly, agreed, disagreed or strongly disagreed with the proposition that general and local elections 'increase voters' knowledge...' and 'give voters a favourable impression...'. This format asks voters about their views of the system rather than their personal experience. Moreover, strong disagreement that there was a favourable impression may imply either that the voter thought it gave an unfavourable view or that it made no difference.

15 Local participation

1. The observant reader may note that the unadjusted score of + 19 recorded for Sevenoaks does not quite match that reported in a previous publication (see Moyser and Parry 1989:50–1). There is also a slight discrepancy in its reported ranking relative to other localities (first instead of, as here, second). The difference arises in the way missing data were treated in the two analyses. In the previous discussion, the unadjusted figure quoted was that after cases were dropped which had valid information on the participation scales (where missing data were in fact zero) but not on one or more of the eight explanatory variables that were used. Subsequently, a decision was taken to use the known 'true' unadjusted participation score, based on all the cases, rather than that only for those with valid scores across all the particular variables included in the given specific analysis. Thus, the 'true' unadjusted rate, based on all 264 cases in Sevenoaks, is indeed + 19, as reported in the figure. The adjusted rate is, of course, the rate only for that somewhat smaller number who had valid scores on the other

variables by which that rate has been adjusted. Both treatments of missing data have their merits but, for the present study, we have preferred to use the known constant rate for all cases rather than to quote unadjusted rates that perhaps fluctuate slightly according to the precise set of other variables that are included in any given analysis.

2. For technical reasons, all possible variables cannot be incorporated into a single multiple classification analysis without serious loss of data. Instead, we have sought to incorporate those factors most likely on past evidence to produce strong compositional effects. Thus, for this local analysis, resources do not include wealth except when discussing race in Stockwell.

3. We have re-introduced wealth into the analysis of the position of the black population because of the marked difference between whites and non-whites. Nevertheless, the relationship found earlier between wealth and overall participation is broadly repeated in that, whilst the effect of wealth is pronounced before controlling for other factors (eta = 0·27), once controls are introduced, it is very much reduced (beta = 0·09).

4. The participation levels for Spotland and Oswestry are:

	Spotland		Oswestry	
	Unadjusted	Adjusted	Unadjusted	Adjusted
Voting	+4	−3	−11	−6
Party campaigning	+13	+9	−17	−13
Collective action	+4	−2	−22	−15
Contacting	+14	+11	−20	−20
Direct action	−3	−5	−19	−8

5. It has been argued that in modern society, community may have ceased to be local and that, instead, non-spatial communities are arising surrounding work (e.g. an 'academic community'), shared religion, political values or leisure interests (see discussions by Plant 1978; Wellman and Leighton 1979). Such ideas require further exploration, but in response to the question whether people in a range of such groupings formed a 'real community', fewer in general gave positive replies than in respect to their own localities. However, a third thought this was true of people in the same line of work and 38 % of those sharing a leisure or hobby, which is comparable to the proportions of residents who perceived Stockwell and Sevenoaks as communities.

6. The local cynicism scale was constructed on the basis of a factor analysis of the four components mentioned. Overall, the scale explained 46·7 % of the variation across the four items. The factor loadings were: 'councillors out for themselves' 0·83; 'community activists out for themselves' 0·75; 'protesters out for themselves' 0·39; 'trust in councillors to do what is right' −0·68.

7. The local efficacy scale was constructed on the basis of a factor analysis of the four components. Overall, the scale explained 52·5 % of the variance across the four items. Each factor contributed almost equally. The factor loadings were: 'people...no influence' 0·72; 'groups...no influence' 0·71; 'national politics difficult to follow' 0·74; 'local politics difficult to follow' 0·72.

8. Ideally, community would have been added to the previous analysis of resources and values. However, the addition of still further variables in the analysis at this point increases levels of missing data considerably. Given the strong effect of resource controls generally, it was therefore decided that an adequate test of community was to examine it in relationship to these factors alone.

Bibliography

Abramson, P. R. and Aldrich, J. H., 1982. The Decline of Electoral Participation in America, *American Political Science Review*, 76, 3:502–21.

Agnew, J., 1987. *Place and Politics: The Geographical Mediation of State and Society,* Boston: Allen and Unwin.

Alcock, P., 1987. *Poverty and State Support*, London: Longman.

Alford, R. and Scoble, H., 1968. Sources of Local Political Involvement, *American Political Science Review*, 62:1,192–206.

Alford, R. and Friedland, R., 1985. *Powers of Theory: Capitalism, the State and Democracy,* Cambridge: Cambridge University Press.

Alker, H. R. Jr., 1965. *Mathematics and Politics*, New York: Macmillan.

Almond, G. A. and Verba, S., 1963. *The Civic Culture*, Princeton, N.J.: Princeton University Press.

Almond, G. A. and Verba, S., eds., 1980. *The Civic Culture Revisited*, Boston: Little, Brown and Co.

Alt, J., 1984. Dealignment and the Dynamics of Partisanship in Britain. In R. Dalton, S. Flanagan and P. Beck, eds., *Electoral Change in Advanced Industrial Democracies*, Princeton, N.J.: Princeton University Press, pp. 298–329.

Alt, J. E. and Turner, J., 1982. The Case of the Silk-Stocking Socialists and the Calculating Children of the Middle Class, *British Journal of Political Science*, 12:239–48.

Andrews, F., Morgan, J. and Sonquist, J., 1969. *Multiple Classification Analysis*, Ann Arbor: Institute for Social Research.

Anwar, M. 1986. *Race and Politics: Ethnic Minorities and the British Political System,* London: Tavistock Publications.

Arblaster, A., 1972. Participation: Context and Conflict. In G. Parry, ed., *Participation in Politics*, Manchester and Totowa, N.J.: Manchester University Press, and Rowman and Littlefield, pp. 41–58.

Aristotle, 1948. *Politics*, ed. E. Barker, Oxford: Oxford University Press.

Arterton, F., 1987. *Teledemocracy: Can Technology Protect Democracy?,* Newbury Park, Ca.: Sage.

Asher, H., 1980. *Presidential Elections and American Politics*, rev. edn., Homewood, Ill.: The Dorsey Press.

Bachrach, P., 1967. *The Theory of Democratic Elitism*, Boston and Toronto: Little, Brown and Co.

Bachrach, P. and Baratz, M., 1970. *Power and Poverty: Theory and Practice,* New York: Oxford University Press.

Balch, G. I., 1974. Multiple Indicators in Survey Research: The Concept 'Sense of Political Efficacy', *Political Methodology*, 1, 2:1–43.

Ball, A., 1981. *British Political Parties: The Emergence of a Modern Party System,* London: Macmillan.

Balme, R., 1987. L'action politique au quotidien: les conseillers municipaux dans deux communes Françaises. In A. Mabileau, G. Moyser, G. Parry and P. Quantin, eds., *Les citoyens et la politique locale: Comment participent les Britanniques et les Français,* Paris: Pedone, pp. 155–75.

Barber, B., 1984. *Strong Democracy: Participatory Politics for a New Age,* Berkeley, Ca.: University of California Press.

Barker, A. and Keating, M., 1977. Public Spirits: Amenity Societies and Others. In *British Political Sociology Yearbook*, Vol. 3: *Participation in Politics*, ed. C. Crouch, London: Croom Helm, pp. 143–63.

Barker, A. and Rush, M., 1970. *The Member of Parliament and his Information,* London: Allen and Unwin.

Barnes, S., Kaase, M. *et al.*, 1979. *Political Action: Mass Participation in Five Western Democracies,* Beverly Hills and London: Sage.

Barry, B., 1965. *Political Argument*, London: Routledge and Kegan Paul.
   1970. *Sociologists, Economists and Democracy*, London: Collier-Macmillan.

Barton, T. and Döring, H., 1986. The Social and Attitudinal Profile of Social Democratic Party Activists: Note on a Survey of the 1982 Council for Social Democracy, *Political Studies*, 34:296–305.

Beck, P., 1984. The Dealignment Era in America. In R. Dalton, S. Flanagan and P. Beck, *Electoral Change in Advanced Industrial Democracies*, Princeton, N.J.: Princeton University Press, pp. 240–66.

Beck, P. and Jennings, M. K., 1979. Political Periods and Political Participation, *American Political Science Review*, 73, 3:737–50.

Beer, S., 1982. *Britain Against Itself: The Political Contradictions of Collectivism,* London: Faber.

Benn, S., 1979. The Problematic Rationality of Political Participation. In P. Laslett and J. Fishkin, eds., *Philosophy, Politics and Society*, 5th series, Oxford: Blackwell, pp. 291–312.

Benn, T., 1979. *Arguments for Socialism*, ed. C. Mullin, London: Jonathan Cape.

Bennett, S. and Resnick, D., 1988. Political Participation Reconsidered: Old Ideas and New Data, Paper presented to the Annual Conference of the Midwest Political Science Association Chicago, Illinois, 14–17 April, 1988.

Berry, D., 1970. *The Sociology of Grass-Roots Politics: A Study of Party Membership,* London: Macmillan.

Black, A., 1988. *State, Community and Human Desire: A Group-Centred Account of Political Values,* Hemel Hempstead: Wheatsheaf and New York: St Martins Press.

Blunkett, D. and Jackson, K., 1987. *Democracy in Crisis: The Town Halls Respond,* London: Hogarth Press.

Boaden, N., Goldsmith, M., Hampton, W. and Stringer, P. 1982. *Public Participation in Local Services,* London: Longman.

Bonham, J., 1954. *The Middle Class Vote*, London: Faber.

Bouchier, D., 1983. *The Feminist Challenge: The Movement for Women's Liberation in Britain and the USA,* London: Macmillan.

Brody, R. and Sniderman, P., 1977. From Life Space to Polling Place: The Relevance of Personal Concerns for Voting Behaviour, *British Journal of Political Science*, 7: 337–60.

Bryan, F., 1974. *Yankee Politics in Rural Vermont*, Hanover, N.H.: University Press of New England.

Budge, I., 1971. Support for Nation and Government among English Children: A Comment, *British Journal of Political Science*, 1:389–92.

1989. L'impatto politico delle tecnologie informatiche: Partecipazione o autoritarismo? Nuove questioni per la teoria democratica, *Teoria Politica*, 5:64–84.

Budge, I., Crewe, I. and Fairlie, D., eds., 1976. *Party Identification and Beyond: Representations of Voting and Party Competition,* London: John Wiley.

Budge, I. and Robertson, D., 1987. Do Parties Differ, and How? Comparative Discriminant and Factor Analyses. In I. Budge, D. Robertson and D. Hearl, eds., *Ideology, Strategy and Party Change: Spatial Analyses of Post-War Election Programmes in 19 Democracies,* Cambridge: Cambridge University Press, pp. 387–416.

Budge, I., Robertson, D. and Hearl, D., eds. 1987. *Ideology, Strategy and Party Change: Spatial Analyses of Post-War Election Programmes in 19 Democracies,* Cambridge: Cambridge University Press.

Bullock, A., 1977. *Report of the Commission of Inquiry on Industrial Democracy*, Cmnd. 6706, London: HMSO.

Burch, M. and Moran, M., 1985. The Changing British Parliamentary Elite, *Parliamentary Affairs*, 38:1–15.

Burns, J., 1988. *Political Participation in Rural China*, Berkeley, Ca.: University of California Press.

Butler, D. and Stokes, D., 1969. *Political Change in Britain: Forces Shaping Electoral Choice,* New York: St Martin's Press.

1974. *Political Change in Britain*, 2nd edn, London: Macmillan.

Butler, D. and Kavanagh, D., 1984. *The British General Election of 1983*, London: Macmillan.

1988. *The British General Election of 1987*, London: Macmillan.

Byrne, P. and Lovenduski, J., 1983. Two New Protest Groups: The Peace and Women's Movements. In H. Drucker, P. Dunleavy, A. Gamble, G. Peele, eds., *Developments in British Politics*, Basingstoke: Macmillan, pp. 222–37.

Campbell, A., Gurin, G. and Miller, W., 1954. *The Voter Decides*, Evanston, Ill.: Row Peterson.

Campbell, B. A., 1979. *The American Electorate: Attitudes and Action,* New York: Rinehart and Winston.

Castells, M., 1977. *The Urban Question*, London: Arnold.

Chapman, J., 1990. Politics and Personal Rewards, or What Candidates Get Out of Campaigning. Paper presented to ESRC/European Science Foundation Conference on Political Participation in Europe, University of Manchester.

Christy, C. A., 1987. *Sex Differences in Political Participation: Processes of Change in Fourteen Nations,* New York: Praeger.

Citrin, J., McClosky, H., Merrill Shanks, J. and Sniderman, P., 1975. Personal and Political Sources of Political Alienation, *British Journal of Political Science*, 5:1–31.

Cleaver, D., 1989. Local Political Mobilisation: A Case Study of a Welsh Community. In A. Mabileau, G. Moyser, G. Parry and P. Quantin, eds., *Local Politics and Participation in Britain and France*, Cambridge: Cambridge University Press, pp. 109–34.

Cobb, R. and Elder, C., 1983. *Participation in American Politics: The Dynamics of Agenda Building,* 2nd edn, Baltimore: Johns Hopkins University Press.

Cochran, C., 1989. The Thin Theory of Community: The Communitarians and Their Critics, *Political Studies*, 37:422–35.

Cochrane, A., 1986. Community Politics and Democracy. In D. Held and C. Pollitt, eds., *New Forms of Democracy*, London: Sage, pp. 51–77.

Cohen, G., 1978. *Karl Marx's Interpretation of History: A Defence,* Oxford: Oxford University Press.

Connolly, W., 1974. *The Terms of Political Discourse*, Lexington, Manchester: Heath.

Connolly, W., ed., 1969. *The Bias of Pluralism*, Chicago: Atherton.

Converse, P. E., 1969. Of Time and Partisan Stability, *Comparative Political Studies*, 2:139–71.

1976. The Dynamics of Party Support: Cohort-Analyzing Party Identification, *Sage Liberty of Social Research*, Vol. 35, Beverly Hills, CA: Sage.

Conway, M., 1985. *Political Participation in the United States*, Washington D.C.: Congressional Quarterly Press.

Cooke, P., ed., 1989. *Localities: The Changing Face of Urban Britain*, London: Unwin Hyman.

Cotgrove, S., 1982. *Catastrophe or Cornucopia: The Environment, Politics and the Future*, New York: John Wiley.

Courtenay, G., 1985. *Political Participation in Britain: Technical Report on a National Survey*, London: Social and Community Planning Research.

Crewe, I., 1982. Is Britain's Two-Party System Really About to Crumble?, *Electoral Studies*, 1:275–313.

1984. The Electorate: Partisan Dealignment Ten Years On. In H. Berrington, ed., *Change in British Politics*, London: Frank Cass, pp. 183–215.

1986. On the Death and Resurrection of Class Voting: Some Comments on *How Britain Votes*, *Political Studies*, 34:620–38.

Crewe, I., Fox, T. and Alt, J., 1977. Non-Voting in British General Elections 1966–October 1974. In C. Crouch, ed., *British Political Sociology Yearbook, Vol. 3: Participation in Politics*, London: Croom Helm, pp. 38–109.

Crewe, I. and Payne, C., 1971. Analysing the Census Data. In D. Butler and M. Pinto-Duschinsky, eds., *The British General Election of 1970*, London: Macmillan, pp. 416–36.

Crewe, I., Särlvik, B. and Alt, J., 1977. Partisan De-alignment in Britain, 1964–1974, *British Journal of Political Science*, 7:129–90.

Crick, B., 1962. *In Defence of Politics*, London: Weidenfeld and Nicolson.

Crosland, A., 1975. *Socialism Now and Other Essays*, Leonard, D. ed. rev. edn, London: Jonathan Cape.

Crouch, C., 1979. The State, Capital and Liberal Democracy. In C. Crouch, ed., *State and Economy in Contemporary Capitalism*, London: Croom Helm, pp. 13–54.

Cynon Valley Borough Council, 1984. *House Conditions Survey*, Aberdare.

Dahl, R., 1961. *Who Governs?*, New Haven: Yale University Press.

1963. *Modern Political Analysis*, Englewood Cliffs, N.J.: Prentice-Hall.

1984. *Modern Political Analysis*, 4th edn, Englewood Cliffs, N.J.: Prentice-Hall.

1985. *A Preface to Economic Democracy*, Berkeley, Ca.: University of California Press.

Dahl, R. and Tufte, E., 1974. *Size and Democracy*, Stanford: Stanford University Press, and Oxford: Oxford University Press.

Dalton, R., 1977. Was There a Revolution? A Note on Generational Versus Life Cycle Expectations of Value Differences, *Comparative Political Studies*, 9, 4:459–74.

1988. *Citizen Politics in Western Democracies*, New Jersey: Chatham House.

Dalton, R., Flanagan, S. and Beck, P., 1984. *Electoral Change in Advanced Industrial Democracies*, Princeton, N.J.: Princeton University Press.

Danziger, R., 1988. *Political Powerlessness: Agricultural Workers in Post-war England*, Manchester: Manchester University Press.

Day, N., Moyser, G. and Parry, G., 1984, *Conceptual and Empirical Problems in the Operationalisation of the Concept of 'Community'*, Research Paper No. 4, British Political Participation Study, Department of Government, University of Manchester.

1985a. *Weighting of National Survey Data Set and Community Survey Data Set*, Research Paper No. 13, British Political Participation Study, Department of Government, University of Manchester.

1985b. *Selection of Communities for Study in the British Political Participation Study: A Cluster Analysis*, Research Paper No. 14, British Political Participation Study, Department of Government, University of Manchester.

Döring, H., 1983. Who are the Social Democrats?, *New Society*, September, 8:351–3.

Downs, A., 1957. *An Economic Theory of Democracy*, New York: Harper.

Dowse, R. and Hughes, J., 1977. Sporadic Interventionists, *Political Studies*, 25:84–92.

Duke, V. and Edgell, S., 1984. Public Expenditure Cuts in Britain and Consumption Sectoral Cleavages, *International Journal of Urban and Regional Research*, 8:177–201.

Dunleavy, P., 1979. The Urban Basis of Political Alignment: Social Class, Domestic Property Ownership, and State Intervention in Consumption Processes, *British Journal of Political Science*, 9:409–43.

1980. *Urban Political Analysis*, London: Macmillan.

1988. Group Identities and Individual Influence: Reconstructing the Theory of Interest Groups, *British Journal of Political Science*, 18:21–49.

Dunleavy, P. and Husbands, C. T., 1985. *British Democracy at the Crossroads: Voting and Party Competition in the 1980s*, London: George Allen and Unwin.

Dunning, E. *et al.*, 1987. Violent Disorders in Twentieth-Century Britain. In G. Gaskell and R. Benewick, eds., *The Crowd in Contemporary Britain*, London: Sage, pp. 19–75.

Easton, D., 1965. *A Systems Analysis of Political Life*, New York: Wiley.

Elster, J., 1983. *Sour Grapes: Studies in the Subversion of Rationality*, Cambridge: Cambridge University Press.

England, J., 1986a. The Characteristics and Attitudes of Councillors. In *The Local Government Councillor*, Research Volume 2 of *The Conduct of Local Authority Business*, Cmnd. 9799, HMSO, pp. 9–123.

1986b. *Political Participation in Britain: Technical Note on the Community and Local Leader Studies*, London: Social and Community Planning Research.

Eurobarometre, 1987. *Public Opinion in the European Community on Energy in 1986*, Brussels.

Field, F., 1982. *Poverty and Politics: The Inside Story of the Child Poverty Action Group's Campaigns in the 1970s*, London: Heinemann.

Field, G. L. and Higley, J., 1980. *Elitism*, London: Routledge and Kegan Paul.

Finer, S. E., 1972. Groups and Political Participation. In G. Parry, ed., *Participation in Politics*, Manchester: Manchester University Press, and Totowa, N.J.: Rowman and Littlefield, pp. 41–58.

Finkel, S., 1985. Reciprocal Effects of Participation and Political Efficacy: A Panel Analysis, *American Journal of Political Science*, 29:891–913.

1987. The Effects of Participation on Political Efficacy and Political Support: Evidence from a West German Panel, *Journal of Politics*, 49:441–64.

Finkel, S., Muller, E. and Opp, K.-D., 1989. Personal Influence, Collective Rationality, and Mass Political Action, *American Political Science Review*, 83:885–903.

Fitzgerald, M., 1987. *Black People and Party Politics in Britain*, London: Runnymede Trust.

Flanigan, W. and Zingale, N., 1983. *Political Behavior of the American Electorate*, 5th edn, Newton, Mass.: Allyn and Bacon.

Foote, G., 1988. *A Chronology of Post-War British Politics*, Beckenham: Croom Helm.

Frankenberg, R., 1966. *Communities in Britain: Social Life in Town and Country*, Harmondsworth: Penguin.

Frankland, E., Gene, 1989. Does Green Politics have a Future in Britain? Paper delivered at the Annual Meeting of the American Political Science Association, Atlanta, Ga.

Franklin, M., 1985. *The Decline of Class Voting in Britain: Changes in the Basis of Electoral Choice, 1964–1983*, Oxford: Clarendon Press.

Franklin, M. and Page, E., 1984. A Critique of the Consumption Cleavage Approach in British Voting Studies, *Political Studies*, 32:521–36.

Fraser, J., 1970. The Mistrustful-Efficacious Hypothesis and Political Participation, *Journal of Politics*, 32:444–9.

Fudge, C., 1984. Decentralisation: Socialism Goes Local? In M. Boddy and C. Fudge, eds.,

Local Socialism?: Labour Councils and New Left Alternatives, London: Macmillan, pp. 192–214.

Gallie, W., 1955–6. Essentially Contested Concepts, *Proceedings of the Aristotelian Society*, 55:167–98.

Gamble, A., 1979. The Conservative Party. In H. Drucker, ed., *Multi-Party Britain*, London: Macmillan, pp. 25–53.

Gamson, W., 1968. *Power and Discontent*, Homewood, Ill.: Dorsey Press.

Gilmour, I., 1977. *Inside Right: A Study of Conservatism*, London: Hutchinson.

Goldthorpe, J. H., 1980. *Social Mobility and Class Structure in Modern Britain*, Oxford: Clarendon Press.

Goldthorpe, J. H. and Hope, K., 1974. *The Social Grading of Occupations: A New Approach and Scale*, Oxford: Clarendon Press.

Goodin, R. and Dryzek, J., 1980. Rational Participation: The Politics of Relative Power, *British Journal of Political Science*, 10:273–92.

Graham, D., 1989. Class, Gender and Nature Conflicts: Democratic Left and Eco-Feminist Responses. Paper delivered at the Annual Meeting of the American Political Science Association, Atlanta, Ga.

Grant, W., 1977. *Independent Local Politics in England and Wales*, Farnborough: Saxon House.

Guest, D. and Knight, K., eds., 1979. *Putting Participation into Practice*, Farnborough: Gower.

Gurr, T. and King, D., 1987. *The State and the City*, London: Macmillan.

Gyford, J., 1985. *The Politics of Local Socialism*, London: Allen and Unwin.

Hailsham, Lord, 1959. *The Conservative Case*, Harmondsworth: Penguin.

Hain, P., 1975. *Radical Regeneration*, London: Quartet Books.

Halliday, J., 1968. *John Stuart Mill*, London: Allen and Unwin.

Hampton, W., 1970. *Democracy and Community: A Study of Politics in Sheffield*, London: Oxford University Press.

Hardin, R., 1982. *Collective Action*, Baltimore and London: Johns Hopkins University Press.

Harding, S. and Phillips, D. with Fogarty, M., 1986. *Contrasting Values in Western Europe: Unity, Diversity and Change*, London: Macmillan.

Harrop, M., 1980. The Urban Basis of Political Alignment: A Comment, *British Journal of Political Science*, 10:388–98.

Harrop, M. and Miller, W., 1987. *Elections and Voters: A Comparative Introduction*, Basingstoke: Macmillan.

Hart, V., 1978. *Distrust and Democracy: Political Distrust in Britain and America*, Cambridge: Cambridge University Press.

Hawkins, B. W., Marando, V. and Taylor, G., 1971. Efficacy, Mistrust and Political Participation, *Journal of Politics*, 33:1,130–6.

Heald, G. and Wynbrow, R., 1986. *The Gallup Survey of Britain, 1985*, London: Croom Helm.

Heath, A., Jowell, R. and Curtice, J., 1985. *How Britain Votes*, Oxford: Pergamon Press.

Heath, A., Jowell, R. and Curtice, J., 1987. Trendless Fluctuation: A Reply to Crewe, *Political Studies*, 35:256–77.

Held, D., 1987. *Models of Democracy*, Cambridge: Polity Press.

Held, D. and Pollitt, C., 1986. *New Forms of Democracy*, London: Sage.

Hills, J., 1981. Britain. In J. Lovenduski and J. Hills, eds., *The Politics of the Second Electorate: Women and Public Participation*, London: Routledge and Kegan Paul, pp. 8–32.

Himmelweit, H., Humphreys, P., Jaeger, M. and Katz, M., 1981. *How Voters Decide*, London: Academic Press.

Hirschman, A., 1970. *Exit, Voice and Loyalty: Responses to Decline in Firms, Organizations and States*, Cambridge, Mass.: Harvard University Press.

Hoggett, P. and Hambleton, R., eds., 1987. *Decentralisation and Democracy: Localising Public Services,* Occasional Paper 28, Bristol, School for Advanced Urban Studies.

Holme, R., 1985. Political Accountability and the Exercise of Power. In D. Steel, ed., *Partners in One Nation: A New Vision of Britain 2000,* London: Bodley Head, pp. 77–97.

Hunter, R., 1979. *Warriors of the Rainbow: The Chronicle of the Greenpeace Movement,* New York: Holt, Rinehart and Winston.

Ingle, S., 1987. *The British Party System,* Oxford: Blackwell.

Inglehart, R., 1971. The Silent Revolution in Europe: Intergenerational Change in Post-Industrial Societies, *American Political Science Review,* 65, 4:991–1,017.

  1977. *The Silent Revolution: Changing Values and Political Styles among Western Publics,* Princeton, N.J.: Princeton University Press.

  1981. Post-Materialism in an Environment of Insecurity, *American Political Science Review,* 75:880–900.

  1988. The Renaissance of Political Culture, *American Political Science Review,* 82, 4:1,203–30.

  1989. *Culture Shift in Advanced Society,* Princeton, N.J.: Princeton University Press.

Inglehart, R. and Klingemann, H., 1976. Party Identification, Ideological Preference and Left–Right Dimension among Western Mass Publics. In I. Budge, I. Crewe and D. Fairlie, eds., *Party Identification and Beyond: Representations of Voting and Party Competition,* London: Wiley.

Ionescu, G., 1975. *Centripetal Politics: Government and the New Centres of Power,* London: Hart-Davies, Macgibbon.

  1989. Political Undercomprehension, or The Overload of Political Cognition, *Government and Opposition,* 24:413–26.

Jennings, M. Kent, 1987. Residues of a Movement: The Aging of the American Protest Generation, *American Political Science Review,* 81:367–82.

Johnston, R., Pattie, C. and Allsopp, J., 1988. *A Nation Divided? The Electoral Map of Great Britain 1979–1987,* London: Longman.

Jones, B., 1987. The Thatcher Style. In B. Jones, ed., *Political Issues in Britain Today,* 2nd edn, Manchester: Manchester University Press.

Jowell, R. and Airey, C., 1984. *British Social Attitudes: The 1984 Report.* Social and Community Planning Research, Aldershot: Gower.

Jowell, R. and Witherspoon, S., 1985. *British Social Attitudes: The 1985 Report,* Aldershot: Gower.

Jowell, R., Witherspoon, S. and Brook, L., 1987. *British Social Attitudes: The 1987 Report,* Aldershot: Gower.

Kahan, M. J., Butler, D. E. and Stokes, D. E., 1966. On the Analytical Division of Social Class, *British Journal of Sociology,* 17:123–30.

Katzenstein, M. and Muller, C., eds., 1987. *The Women's Movements of the United States and Western Europe,* Philadelphia: Temple University Press.

Kavanagh, D., 1971. The Deferential English: A Comparative Critique, *Government and Opposition,* 6:333–60.

  1972a. Political Behaviour and Participation. In G. Parry, ed., *Participation in Politics,* Manchester: Manchester University Press, pp. 102–23.

  1972b. Allegiance Among English Children: A Dissent, *British Journal of Political Science,* 2:127–31.

  1972c. *Political Culture,* London: Macmillan.

  1980. Political Culture in Great Britain: The Decline of the Civic Culture. In G. Almond and S. Verba, *The Civic Culture Revisited,* pp. 124–76.

  1985. *British Politics: Continuities and Change,* Oxford: Oxford University Press.

  1987. *Thatcherism and British Politics: The End of Consensus?,* Oxford: Oxford University Press.

King, D., 1987. *The New Right: Politics, Markets and Citizenship*, London: Macmillan.

King, D. and Waldron, J., 1988. Citizenship, Social Citizenship and the Defence of Welfare Provision, *British Journal of Political Science*, 18:415–43.

Lafferty, W., 1978. Social Development and Political Participation: Class Organizations and Sex, *Scandinavian Political Studies*, new series, 1:233–54.

1979. Sex and Political Participation: An Exploratory Analysis of the 'Female Culture'. Unpublished paper, Institute of Political Science, University of Oslo.

Lasswell, H., 1936. *Politics: Who Gets What, When and How*, New York: McGraw-Hill.

Layton-Henry, Z., 1989. Black Electoral Participation: An Analysis of Recent Trends. In H. Gouldbourne, ed., *Black People and British Politics*, London: Hansib Press.

Le Grand, J., 1982. *The Strategy of Inequality*, London: Allen and Unwin.

Le Grand, J. and Goodin, R., 1987. *Not Only the Poor: The Middle Classes and the Welfare State*, London: Allen and Unwin.

Leighley, J., 1989. Political Attitudes and Participation: Does Intensity Breed Activity? Paper delivered at the Annual Meeting of the American Political Science Association, Atlanta, GA.

Leonard, R., 1968. *Elections in Britain*, London: Van Nostrand.

Levitin, T. and Miller, W., 1979. Ideological Interpretations of Presidential Elections, *American Political Science Review*, 73, 3:751–71.

Lijphart, A., 1978. *Democracy in Plural Societies*, New Haven: Yale University Press.

Lipset, S., Lazarsfeld, P., Barton, A. and Linz, J., 1954. The Psychology of Voting: An Analysis of Political Behavior. In G. Lindzey, ed., *Handbook of Social Psychology*, Vol. 2, Reading, Mass.: Addison-Wesley, pp. 1,124–75.

Lively, J., 1975. *Democracy*, Oxford: Blackwell.

Loney, M., 1983. *Community Against Government: The British Community Development Project, 1968–78 – A Study of Government Incompetence*, London: Heinemann.

Lovenduski, J., 1986. *Women and European Politics: Contemporary Feminism and Public Policy*, Brighton: Wheatsheaf; Amherst, Mass.: The University of Massachusetts Press.

Lowe, P. and Goyder, J., 1983. *Environmental Groups in Politics*, London: Allen and Unwin.

Lukes, S., 1974. *Power: A Radical View*, London: Macmillan.

Mabileau, A., Moyser, G., Parry, G. and Quantin, P., eds., 1989. *Local Politics and Participation in Britain and France*, Cambridge: Cambridge University Press.

McClosky, H., 1964. Consensus and Ideology in American Politics, *American Political Science Review*, 58:361–82.

McClosky, H., Hoffman, P. and O'Hara, R., 1960. Issue Conflict and Consensus among Party Leaders and Followers, *American Political Science Review*, 54:406–27.

McCulloch, C., 1984. The Problem of Fellowship in Communitarian Theory: William Morris and Peter Kropotkin, *Political Studies*, 32:437–50.

McCulloch, C. and Parry, G., 1986. Pluralism, Community and Human Nature. In J. Porter and R. Vernon, eds., *Unity, Plurality and Politics: Essays in Honour of F. M. Barnard*, London: Croom Helm, pp. 162–87.

McLean, I., 1986. Mechanisms for Democracy. In D. Held and C. Pollitt, eds., *New Forms of Democracy*, London: Sage, pp. 135–57.

MacFarlane, L., 1986. *Issues in British Politics Since 1945*, 3rd edn, London: Longman.

MacIntyre, A., 1981. *After Virtue: A Study in Moral Theory*, London: Duckworth.

1988. *Whose Justice? Which Rationality*, London: Duckworth.

Mansbridge, J., 1980. *Beyond Adversary Democracy*, New York: Basic Books.

Marquand, D., 1988. *The Unprincipled Society: New Demands and Old Politics*, London: Fontana.

Marsh, A., 1977. *Protest and Political Consciousness*, Beverly Hills and London: Sage.

Marsh, D. and King, J., 1987. The Unions under Thatcher. In L. Robbins, ed., *Political Institutions in Britain: Development and Change*, London: Longman, pp. 213–29.

Milbrath, L., 1965. *Political Participation: How and Why Do People Get Involved in Politics?*, Chicago: Rand McNally.

Milbrath, L. and Goel, M., 1977. *Political Participation: How and Why Do People Get Involved in Politics?*, 2nd edn, Chicago: Rand McNally.

Mill, J. S., 1972. *Representative Government*, Everyman Edition, London: Dent.

Miller, A. H., 1974. Political Issues and Trust in Government: 1964–70, *American Political Science Review*, 68:951–72, 989–1,001.

Miller, W., 1977. *Electoral Dynamics in Britain since 1918*, London: Macmillan.

1978. Social Class and Party Choice in England: A New Analysis, *British Journal of Political Science*, 8: 257–84.

1988. *Irrelevant Elections? The Quality of Local Democracy in Britain*, Oxford: Oxford University Press.

Miller, W. and Levitin, T., 1976. *Leadership and Change: Presidential Elections from 1952 to 1976*, Cambridge, Mass.: Winthrop Publishers.

Miller, W., Clarke, H., Harrop, M., Le Duc, L. and Whiteley, P., 1990, *How Voters Change*, Oxford: Oxford University Press.

Mole, S., 1983. Community Politics. In V. Bogdanor, ed., *Liberal Party Politics*, Oxford: Oxford University Press, pp. 260–77.

Moran, M., 1985. *Politics and Society in Britain: An Introduction*, Basingstoke: Macmillan.

MORI, 1986. *Attitudes to Local Authorities and Their Services*, London; MORI.

Morris-Jones, W., 1954. In Defence of Apathy: Some Doubts on the Duty to Vote, *Political Studies*, 2:25–37.

Morriss, P., 1987. *Power: A Philosophical Analysis*, Manchester: Manchester University Press.

Moyser, G. and Parry, G., 1989. Participation and Non-participation in an English Town. In A. Mabileau, G. Moyser, G. Parry and P. Quantin, eds., *Local Politics and Participation in Britain and France*, Cambridge: Cambridge University Press, pp. 39–61.

Moyser, G., Parry, G. and Day, N., 1986. Political Participation in Britain: National and Local Patterns. Paper delivered at the American Political Science Association Annual Meeting, Washington DC.

Moyser, G. and Wagstaffe, M., 1987. *Research Methods for Elite Studies*, London: Allen and Unwin.

Muller, E. N., 1970. Cross-National Dimensions of Political Competence, *American Political Science Review*, 64, 3:792–809.

1979. *Aggressive Political Participation*, Princeton, N.J.: Princeton University Press.

Munroe, R., 1977. The Member of Parliament as Representative: The View from the Constituency, *Political Studies*, 4:577–97.

Nelkin, D., 1975. The Political Impact of Technical Expertise, *Social Studies of Science*, 5:35–54.

Nettl, P., 1967. *Political Mobilization*, New York: Basic Books.

Newton, K., 1976. *Second City Politics: Democratic Processes and Decision-Making in Birmingham*, Oxford: Oxford University Press.

1982. Is Small Really so Beautiful?, *Political Studies*, 30:190–202.

Newton, K. and Karran, T., 1985. *The Politics of Local Expenditure*, London: Macmillan.

Nie, N. H., Verba, S. and Kim, J.-O., 1974. Political Participation and the Life Cycle, *Comparative Politics*, 6:319–340.

Nie, N., Verba, S. and Petrocik, J., 1979. *The Changing American Voter*, enlarged edn, Cambridge, Mass.: Harvard University Press.

Nie, N., Verba, S., Brady, H., Schlozman, K. and Lunn, J., 1988. Participation in America: Continuity and Change. Paper presented at the Annual Meeting of the Midwest Political Science Association, Chicago, Illinois.

Niemi, R. and Weisberg, H., eds., 1984. *Controversies in Voting Behaviour*, 2nd edn, Washington D.C.: CQ Press.

Nisbet, R., 1967. *The Sociological Tradition*, London: Heinemann.

Nordlinger, E., 1981. *On the Autonomy of the Democratic State*, Cambridge, Mass.: Harvard University Press.

Norton, P., 1984a. *The British Polity*, London: Longman.

Norton, P. ed., 1984b. *Law and Order and British Politics*, London: Gower.

Nozick, R., 1974. *Anarchy, State and Utopia*, Oxford: Blackwell.

Oakeshott, M., 1955. Introduction to Hobbes, *Leviathan*, Oxford: Blackwell.

 1962. *Rationalism in Politics*, London: Methuen.

Offe, C., 1985. New Social Movements: Challenging the Boundaries of Institutional Politics, *Social Research*, 52, 4:817–68.

Olson, M., 1971. *The Logic of Collective Action: Public Goods and the Theory of Groups,* Rev. edn, New York: Schocken Books.

Openshaw, S., n.d. *Cluster Analysis Programme: A Manual for Census Cluster Programme,* Newcastle-upon-Tyne, University of Newcastle, Department of Town and Country Planning.

O'Riordan, T., Kemp, R. and Purdue, M., 1988. *Sizewell B: An Anatomy of the Inquiry,* Basingstoke: Macmillan.

Owen, D., 1981. *Face the Future*, London: Jonathan Cape.

Palumbo, D., 1969. *Statistics in Political and Behavioural Science*, New York: Appleton-Century-Crofts.

Parkin, F., 1968. *Middle Class Radicalism*, Manchester: Manchester University Press.

Parry, G., 1969. *Political Elites*, London: Allen and Unwin.

 1972. The Idea of Political Participation. In G. Parry, ed., *Participation in Politics*, Manchester: Manchester University Press: Totowa, N.J.: Rowman and Littlefield, pp. 3–38.

 1974. Participation and Political Styles. In B. Chapman and A. Potter, eds., *W.J.M.M.: Political Questions. Essays in Honour of W. J. M. Mackenzie,* Manchester: Manchester University Press, pp. 190–204.

 1976. Trust, Distrust and Consensus, *British Journal of Political Science*, 6:129–42.

Parry, G. and Moyser, G., 1983. Political Participation and Community in Britain: Conceptual and Methodological Issues. Paper presented to the Annual Meeting of the American Political Science Association, Chicago.

 1984a. Participants and Controllers. In D. Kavanagh and G. Peele, eds., *Comparative Government and Politics: Essays in Honour of S. E. Finer,* London: Heinemann, pp. 169–94.

 1984b. Political Participation in Britain: A Research Agenda for a New Study, *Government and Opposition*, 19:68–92.

 1988. What is 'Politics'? A Comparative Study of Local Citizens and Leaders. In D. Sainsbury, ed., *Democracy, State and Justice: Critical Perspectives and New Interpretations, Essays in Honour of Elias Berg,* Stockholm: Almqvist and Wiksell International, pp. 33–54.

 1991. Voices and Signals: Active Citizens and the Market Place. In M. Moran and M. Wright, eds., *The Market and the State: Studies in Interdependence,* Basingstoke: Macmillan, pp. 81–99.

Parry, G., Moyser, G. and Wagstaffe, M., 1987. The Crowd and the Community: Context, Content and Aftermath. In G. Gaskell and R. Benewick, eds., *The Crowd in Contemporary Britain*, London: Sage, pp. 212–54.

Pateman, C., 1970. *Participation and Democratic Theory*, Cambridge: Cambridge University Press.

Pedersen, J., 1982. On the Educational Function of Political Participation: A Comparative Analysis of John Stuart Mill's Theory and Contemporary Survey Research Findings, *Political Studies*, 30:557–68.

Pennock, C., 1979. *Democratic Political Theory*, Princeton, N.J.: Princeton University Press.

Pizzorno, A., 1970. An Introduction to the Theory of Political Participation, *Social Science Information*, 9:29–61.

Plant, R., 1978. Community: Concept, Conception and Ideology, *Politics and Society*, 8:79–107.

Political Action, 1979. *Political Action: An Eight Nation Study 1973–1976*, Zentralarchiv Study No. 0765, Zentralarchiv für Empirische Sozialforschung, University of Cologne, Cologne.

Polsby, N., 1963. *Community Power and Political Theory*, New Haven: Yale University Press.

Potter, A., 1961. *Organised Groups in British Politics*, London: Faber.

Presthus, R., 1964. *Men at the Top*, New York: Oxford University Press.

Przeworksi, A. and Teune, H., 1970. *The Logic of Comparative Social Inquiry*, New York: Wiley.

Putnam, R., 1966. Political Attitudes and the Local Community, *American Political Science Review*, 60:640–54.

   1976. *The Comparative Study of Political Elites*, Englewood Cliffs, N.J.: Prentice-Hall.

Quantin, P., 1987. A la recherche de l'esprit communal dans une ville française. In A. Mabileau, G. Moyser, G. Parry, P. Quantin, *Les citoyens et la politique locale: Comment participent les Britanniques et les Français*, Paris: Pedone, pp. 241–260.

Randall, V., 1982. *Women and Politics*, London: Macmillan.

Repass, D., 1971. Issue Salience and Party Choice, *American Political Science Review*, 65:389–400.

Rhodes, R., 1983. *Control and Power in Central-Local Government Relations*, Aldershot: Gower.

Robertson, D., 1976. Surrogates for Party Identification in the Rational Choice Framework. In I. Budge, I. Crewe and D. Fairlie, eds., *Party Identification and Beyond*, London: Wiley, pp. 365–81.

   1984. *Class and the British Electorate*, Oxford: Basil Blackwell.

Rootes, C., 1981. On the Future of Protest Politics in Western Democracies – A Critique of Barnes, Kaase *et al.*, *Political Action*, *European Journal of Political Research*, 9:421–32.

Rose, R., 1984. *Understanding Big Government: The Programme Approach*, London and Beverly Hills: Sage.

Rose, R., ed., 1974. *Electoral Behaviour: A Comparative Handbook*, New York: Free Press.

Rose, R. and McAllister, I., 1986. *Voters Begin to Choose: From Closed-Class to Open Elections in Britain*, London: Sage.

Rosenbaum, W., 1975. *Political Culture*, London: Thomas Nelson.

Rosenberg, M., 1986. *The Logic of Survey Analysis*, New York: Basic Books.

Rossi, P., 1972. Community Social Indicators. In A. Campbell and P. Converse, eds., *The Human Measuring of Social Change*, New York: Sage, pp. 87–126.

Rousseau, J.-J., 1973. *The Social Contract*, Everyman Edition, London: Dent.

Rowbotham, S., 1986. Feminism and Democracy. In D. Held and C. Pollitt, eds., *New Forms of Democracy*, London: Sage, pp. 78–109.

The Royal Commission on the Constitution, 1973. Vol. 1, Report, Cmnd. 5460, London: HMSO.

Rudig, W. and Lowe, P., 1986. The Withered 'Greening' of British Politics: A Study of the Ecology Party, *Political Studies*, 34:262–84.

Sandel, M., 1982. *Liberalism and the Limits of Justice*, Cambridge: Cambridge University Press.

Särlvik, B. and Crewe, I., 1983. *Decade of Dealignment: The Conservative Victory of 1979 and Electoral Trends in the 1970s*, Cambridge: Cambridge University Press.

Sartori, G., 1962. *Democratic Theory*, Detroit: Wayne State University Press.

   1987. *The Theory of Democracy Revisited*, Chatham, N.J.: Chatham House Publishers.

Saunders, P., 1981. *Social Theory and the Urban Question*, London: Hutchinson.

1984. Beyond Housing Classes: The Sociological Significance of Private Property Rights and Means of Consumption, *International Journal of Urban and Regional Research*, 8:202–27.

Saunders, P., Newby, H., Bell, C. and Rose, D., 1979. Rural Community and Rural Community Power. In H. Newby, ed., *International Perspectives in Rural Sociology*, Chichester: Wiley, pp. 55–86.

Savage, S., 1987. Fighting the Enemy Within: Law and Order Under the Tories. In L. Robins, ed., *Political Institutions in Britain*, London: Longman, pp. 230–44.

Scarman, Lord, 1982. *The Scarman Report: The Brixton Disorders 10–12 April 1981*, Harmondsworth: Penguin.

Schlozman, K. and Verba, S., 1979. *Injury to Insult: Unemployment, Class and Political Response*, Cambridge, Mass.: Harvard University Press.

Schmitt, R., 1989. Organisational Interlocks between New Social Movements and Traditional Elites: The Case of the West German Peace Movement, *European Journal of Political Research*, 17:583–98.

Schumpeter, J., 1943. *Capitalism, Socialism and Democracy*, London: Allen and Unwin.

Schwartz, N., 1988. *The Blue Guitar: Political Representation and Community*, Chicago: Chicago University Press.

Searing, D., 1985. The Role of the Good Constituency Member and the Practice of Representation in Great Britain, *Journal of Politics*, 47:348–81.

Seeman, M., 1959. On the Meaning of Alienation, *American Sociological Review*, 24:783–791.

Sharpe, L. J., 1970. Theories and Values of Local Government, *Political Studies*, 18:153–74.

Shonfield, A., 1965. *Modern Capitalism*, London: Oxford University Press.

Sigelman, L., 1982. The Non-Voting and Voting Research, *American Journal of Political Science*, 26, 1:47–56.

Sinclair, R., 1988. *Democracy and Participation in Athens*, Cambridge: Cambridge University Press.

Skeffington, A., 1969. *People and Planning*, Report of the Committee on Public Participation in Planning, London: HMSO.

Smail, R., 1984. A Taxing Time for the Poor. In *Setting the Record on Taxes Straight*, London Low Pay Review Unit, No. 17.

Smith, B., 1985. *Decentralization: The Territorial Dimensions of the State*, London: Allen and Unwin.

Smith, G., Lees, R. and Topping, P., 1977. Participation and the Home Office Community Development Project. In C. Crouch, ed., *British Political Sociology Yearbook. Vol. 3: Participation in Politics*, London: Croom Helm, pp. 237–72.

Squire, P., Wolfinger, R. E. and Glass, D. P., 1985. Residential Mobility and Voter Turnout. Paper presented to the Annual Meeting of the American Political Science Association, New Orleans.

Steed, M., 1983. The Electoral Strategy of the Liberal Party. In V. Bogdanor, ed., *Liberal Party Politics*, Oxford: Oxford University Press, pp. 73–98.

Stuart, A., 1962. *Basic Ideas of Scientific Sampling*, Griffin's Statistical Monographs No. 4, London: Griffin.

Studlar, D., 1986. Non-White Policy Preferences, Political Participation and the Political Agenda in Britain. In Z. Layton-Henry and P. Rich, eds., *Race, Government and Politics in Britain*, London: Macmillan.

Swaddle, K. and Heath, A., 1989. Official and Reported Turnout in the British General Election of 1987, *British Journal of Political Science*, 19:537–51.

Taylor-Gooby, P., 1985. Pleasing Any of the People, Some of the Time: Perceptions of Redistribution and Attitudes to Welfare, *Government and Opposition*, 20:396–406.

1986. Consumption Cleavages and Welfare Politics, *Political Studies*, 34:592–606.

Tönnies, F., 1963. *Community and Association*, trans. C. P. Loomis, New York: Harper and Row.

Topf, R., 1989a. Political Culture and Political Participation in Great Britain and the Federal Republic of Germany 1959–1988, Paper presented to the Joint Sessions of Workshops, European Consortium for Political Research, Paris, April.

1989b. Political Change and Political Culture in Britain, 1959–87. In J. Gibbins, ed., *Contemporary Political Culture: Politics in a Postmodern Age*, London: Sage, pp. 52–80.

Tufte, E., 1970. Improving Data Analysis in Political Science. In E. Tufte, ed., *The Quantitative Analysis of Social Problems*, Reading, Mass.: Addison-Wesley, pp. 437–49.

Verba, S. and Nie, N., 1972. *Participation in America: Political Democracy and Social Equality*, New York: Harper and Row.

Verba, S., Nie, N. and Kim, J.-O., 1971. *The Modes of Democratic Participation: A Cross-National Comparison*, Beverly Hills, Ca.: Sage Comparative Politics Series No. 01–013.

1978. *Participation and Political Equality*, Cambridge: Cambridge University Press.

Waldegrave, W., 1978. *The Binding of Leviathan: Conservatism and the Future*, London: Hamish Hamilton.

Walzer, M., 1983. *Spheres of Justice: A Defence of Pluralism and Equality*, Oxford: Martin Robertson.

Wass, D., 1984. *Government and the Governed: BBC Reith Lectures 1983*, London: Routledge and Kegan Paul.

Weisberg, H., 1983. A Multidimensional Conceptualisation of Party Identification, *Political Behavior*, 2:33–60.

Weisberg, H. and Bowen, B., 1977. *An Introduction to Survey Research and Data Analysis*, San Francisco: Freeman.

Welch, S. and Studlar, D., 1985. The Impact of Race on Political Behaviour in Britain, *British Journal of Political Science*, 15:528–39.

Wellman, B. and Leighton, B., 1979. Networks, Neighbourhoods and Communities: Approaches to the Study of the Community Question, *Urban Affairs Quarterly*, 14:363–90.

Wertheimer, A., 1975. In Defence of Compulsory Voting. In C. Pennock and J. Chapman, eds., *Participation in Politics*, *NOMOS*, vol. 16, New York: Lieber-Atherton, pp. 276–96.

Whiteley, P., 1981. Who are the Labour Activists?, *Political Quarterly*, 52:160–70.

1986. *Political Control of the Macroeconomy*, Beverly Hills, Ca.: Sage.

Williams, R., 1976. *Keywords*, Harmondsworth: Penguin.

Williams, S., 1981. *Politics is for People*, Harmondsworth: Penguin.

Wishart, W., 1982. *CLUSTAN User Manual and Supplement*, 3rd edn, Edinburgh: University of Edinburgh Library Unit.

Wolin, S., 1961. *Politics and Vision*, London: Allen and Unwin.

Wynne, B., 1980. Windscale: A Case Study in the Political Art of Muddling Through. In T. O'Riordan and K. Turner, eds., *Progress in Resource Management and Environmental Planning*, vol. 3, Chichester: Wiley, pp. 165–204.

Young, K., 1986. Attitudes to Local Government. In *Report of the Committee of Inquiry into the Conduct of Local Authority Business* (Widdicombe Report), Research vol. 3, *The Local Government Elector*, Cmnd. 9800, London: HMSO.

Zukin, S., 1975. *Beyond Marx and Tito: Theory and Practice in Yugoslav Socialism*, Cambridge: Cambridge University Press.

Index